Frommer's®
Costa Rica

My Costa Rica

by Eliot Greenspan

COSTA RICA IS AT ONCE EXOTIC AND ALLURING. ITS BIOLOGICAL bounty is legendary; many travelers get their first taste of tropical nature here. Whether you come for adventure or rest and relaxation, this small Central American country offers a visual and sensory feast at almost every turn.

I have lived in Costa Rica for more than a decade, and the country continues to amaze me with its physical beauty—from the misty cloud forests of Monteverde to the imposing (and sometimes menacing) presence of Arenal Volcano. Its rainforests are a beguiling, dense patchwork of infinite shades of green. Hike the trails of a national park or visit one of the suspended bridge attractions to see for yourself.

Then there's the wildlife. I still get a giddy sense of awe every time I spot a troop of white-faced monkeys overhead. Or watch a newly hatched sea turtle take its first crucial dash to the sea. If you want adventure, sign up for a white-water rafting expedition. Learn to surf or ride a mountain bike along rural roads rutted by ox carts. Or strap on a harness and fly from treetop to treetop on a zip-line canopy tour. When you're tired and sore, take a soothing soak in the spectacular Tabacón hot springs.

The photos here capture some of my favorite Costa Rican images and experiences—I'm sure you'll have many more of your own.

WHITE-WATER RAFTING (right) Costa Rica's white water is wet and wild. I love taking 2-day trips on the Pacuare River, a class III–IV river that looks pretty much as pictured here for good stretches. More timid travelers can head out on gentler stretches of water, such as the Corobicí, Sarapiquí, or Reventazóon rivers.

TABACON RESORT (above) The setting at Tabacón Hot Springs Resort & Spa (www.tabacon.com), a hotel located at the foot of Arenal Volcano, is spectacular—and the waters are steamy and soothing. I like to walk the paths of the lush gardens here until I find a secluded and empty pool.

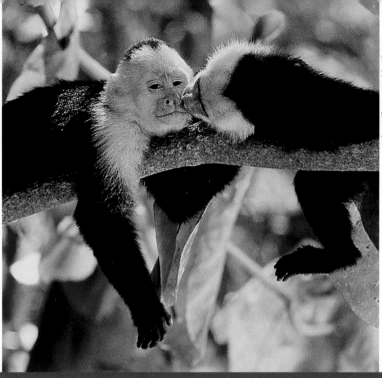

CAPUCHIN MONKEYS (above) Although these two are enjoying a quiet moment, white-faced, or capuchin, monkeys are some of the most active and acrobatic of the Costa Rican monkeys. Because they often travel in large troops, your best bet for spotting them is to listen carefully for movement in the canopy overhead.

MANUEL ANTONIO NATIONAL PARK (right) This is one of the most prized and most photographed views in Costa Rica. You don't have to stay at one of the fancier hotels in Manuel Antonio to enjoy it in person. Just head to the restaurant at La Mariposa (www.lamariposa.com) for a sunset cocktail.

NYMPAHLID BUTTERFLY (right) You'll certainly see plenty of butterflies flying free in the forests and parks of Costa Rica. But if you really want to get up close and personal with these winged beauties, be sure to visit one of the several "butterfly garden" type attractions around the country.

POAS VOLCANO NATIONAL PARK (below) Don't be fooled by the tranquil turquoise waters of the crater lake: You'll want to be upwind of the sulfuric gases rising out of the active Poás volcano. In addition to this beautiful view, there are several excellent trails through lush cloud forest here.

POISON DART FROG (above) The strawberry poison dart frog is also called the blue jean frog because its legs are the color of denim. Your best bet for seeing this guy is among tree roots and rainforest floor litter at La Selva Biological Station (www.ots.ac.cr) or in the Tortuguero area.

BASILISK LIZARD (right) Aside from looking really, really cool and somewhat prehistoric, this fellow can actually run across the surface of rivers and ponds. Hence, his more popular name: the "Jesus Christ lizard." Look for this guy along riverbeds and beside rainforest ponds across the country.

SEA TURTLE (right) You'll have to wake up very early, but you won't regret the lost sleep when you get to watch the amazing process of young hatchlings crawling toward the sea for the first time. If you're visiting Tortuguero or Playa Grande 2 to 3 months after the main nesting season, be sure to set an alarm.

CAHUITA BEACH (below) A 1991 earthquake raised the coral seabed around Cahuita by as much as 1m (3 ft.), eliminating a lot of beach but leaving a rugged and beautiful coastline. Grab a window seat at a beachside restaurant and enjoy the view.

HAND-PAINTED OX CART (above) Although Costa Rican commerce no longer relies on these ox-drawn carts, the carts remain a vibrant and popular symbol of the country's history and culture. You'll still see them used in rural areas, although they're usually more weathered and rugged than the version pictured here.

COFFEE WORKER (right) Coffee is Costa Rica's historic economic engine and primary export. Although tourism currently generates more income, coffee fields still cover most of the hillsides around the Central Valley. If you don't get to visit a plantation, at least be sure to pick up some fresh beans to bring home with you.

CAÑAS MOSAIC CHURCH If you're driving between San José and Guanacaste, make the tiny detour to visit the small city of Cañas. Hometown artist Otto Apuy is internationally known for his paintings and installations, but he returned to Cañas to make the local church perhaps the prettiest in the country. Apuy's cracked ceramic mosaics cover the entire exterior of the church, and run the gamut from abstract to representational.

ARENAL HANGING BRIDGE (above) Some 80% of a forest's biodiversity can be found in the canopy. In addition to sheltering birds, lizards, snakes, and monkeys, the canopy is home to an amazing array of epiphytic and parasitic bromeliads, orchids, vines, and lianas. Suspended bridges like this one are a great way to get a bird's-eye view of everything.

ARENAL VOLCANO (right) Folks flock to Arenal Volcano for the nighttime spectacle provided by its periodic eruptions, but the daytime views are just as impressive. Although you can't see the lava glow during the day, you can still hear earth-shaking deep rumblings and the high-pitched crackle of molten boulders crashing down its flanks.

MONTEVERDE CLOUD FOREST CANOPY TOUR Zip-line canopy tours are one of the most unique adventure options available in Costa Rica, although you're usually moving too fast to take in much scenery. The folks at The Original Canopy Tours (www.canopy tour.com) have operations at various destinations around the country.

Costa Rica

Golfo de Santa Elena

Lake Nicaragua

GUANACASTE RANGE

1

4

7

35

Murciélagos Islands

SANTA ROSA NATIONAL PARK **1**

2

Rincón de la Vieja

RINCON DE LA VIEJA NATIONAL PARK

3

6

Golfo de Papagayo

Río Tempisque

Interamerican Hwy.

Liberia

Guayabo

Lake Coter

Lake Arenal

Río Frío

4

La Fortuna

TILARAN RANGE

Arenal Volcano

GUANACASTE

Tilarán

142

8

Tamarindo

Santa Cruz

4

Monteverde **6**

LOS BAULAS MARINE NATIONAL PARK

21

5

18

Ostional Wildlife Refuge

160

Nosara

Nicoya

NICOYA PENINSULA

160

1

Puntarenas

Curú Wildlife Refuge

Golfo de Nicoya

Río

Pacific Ocean

Sámara

Tambor

9

34

Malpais

Montezuma

Playa de Jaco

Cabo Blanco Absolute Nature Reserve

COSTA RICA'S NATIONAL PARKS & BIORESERVES

Arenal National Park **8**
Barra Honda National Park **5**
Braulio Carrillo National Park **11**
Cahuita National Park **17**
Caño Negro National Wildlife Refuge **7**
Carara Biological Reserve **9**
Chirripó National Park **16**
Corcovado National Park **18**
Guanacaste National Park **2**
Guayabo National Monument **13**
Irazú Volcano National Park **14**
Manuel Antonio National Park **15**
Monteverde Biological Cloud
   Forest Reserve **6**
Palo Verde National Park **4**
Poás Volcano National Park **10**
Rincón de la Vieja National Park **3**
Santa Rosa National Park **1**
Tortuguero National Park **12**

0   25 miles

0   25 kilometers

Costa Rica

NICARAGUA

Río San Juan

Barra del Colorado
Wildlife Refuge

Río Colorado

NORTHERN ZONE

Caribbean Sea

35

4

140

141

Aguas Zarcas

Puerto Viejo de Sarapiquí

Río Sarapiquí

12

4 Guapiles

32

10

11

4

Naranjo

BRAULIO CARRILLO NATIONAL PARK

CENTRAL RANGE

Turrialba Volcano

Río Reventazón

Río Pacuare

135

1

Heredia

CARIBBEAN COAST

Limón

34

Río Grande/Virilla

Escazú

14

13

36

209

San Jose

Cartago

Cahuita

CENTRAL PACIFIC COAST

2

Cerro de la Muerte

CHIRRIPÓ NATIONAL PARK

16

Cerro Chirripó

Hitoy-Cerere Biological Reserve

Punta Uva

17

Río Telire

34

TALAMANCA RANGE

Quepos

15

San Isidro de el General

Interamerican Hwy.

PANAMA

MANUEL ANTONIO NATIONAL PARK

MARINO BALLENA NATIONAL PARK

34

Palmar Norte

SOUTHERN ZONE

Coronado Bay

Sierpe

Río Sierpe

2

San Vito

Wilson Botanical Park

Drake Bay

Golfito

OSA PENINSULA

Golfo Dulce

18

Puerto Jiménez

Zancudo

Pacific Ocean

Airport	✈
Ferry	- - -
Mountain	▲

To Heredia

To Limón

Calle Cipres

0   1/4 mile

0   0.25 kilometer

109

EL PUEBLO

Centro Comercial
El Pueblo
(Shopping Center)

108

TOURNON

Calle Central

Avenida 13

Avenida 11

OTOYA

Parque
Zoológica
Simón Bolivar

Avenida 15

Avenida 9

Avenida 7

Avenida 5

Calle 1

Calle 3

Calle 5

Calle 7

Calle 9

Calle 11

Calle 13

Calle 15

Calle 17

Avenida 13

Calle 4

Calle 2

Avenida 3

Avenida 1

Parque
Morazán

BARRIO
AMÓN

Calle 19

Calle 21

Calle 23

Calle 25

Calle 31

Calle 33

Calle 35

Calle 29

Calle 37

Plaza de
la Cultura

Parque
Nacional

Parque
Central

Catedrál
Metropolitana

Avenida 4

Avenida Central

Avenida 2

Paseo Ruben Darío

To San Pedro →

Avenida 6

SOLEDAD

Avenida 8

Calle 3

Calle 5

Calle 7

Calle 9

Calle 11

Calle 13

Calle 15

Calle 17

Calle 19

Calle 21

LOS YOSES

Calle 27

Calle 29

Calle 33

Calle 39

Avenida 10

Calle 2

Calle Central

Calle 1

Avenida 12

Paseo de los Estudiantes

Calle 35

Calle 37

Avenida 14

Avenida 16

Avenida 18

N

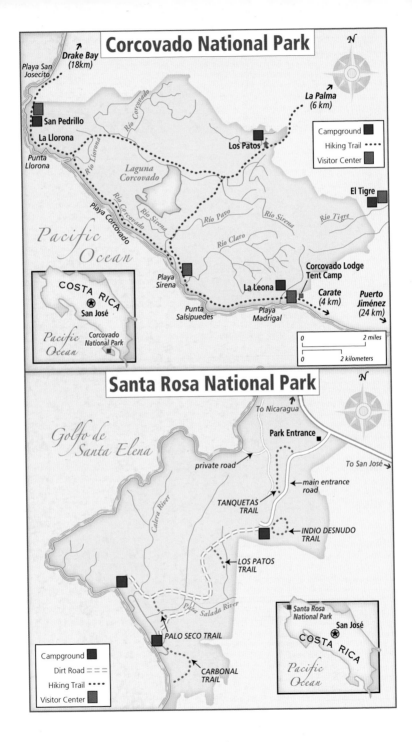

Corcovado National Park

Drake Bay (18km)

Playa San Josecito

San Pedrillo

La Llorona

Punta Llorona

La Palma (6 km)

Los Patos

El Tigre

Río Corcovado

Río Llorona

Laguna Corcovado

Río Corcovado

Río Sirena

Río Pavo

Río Sirena

Río Tigre

Río Claro

Playa Corcovado

Pacific Ocean

Campground	■
Hiking Trail	•••••••
Visitor Center	■

COSTA RICA

San José

Pacific Ocean

Corcovado National Park

Playa Sirena

La Leona

Corcovado Lodge Tent Camp

Carate (4 km)

Puerto Jiménez (24 km)

Punta Salsipuedes

Playa Madrigal

| 0 | 2 miles |
| 0 | 2 kilometers |

Santa Rosa National Park

To Nicaragua

Golfo de Santa Elena

Park Entrance

To San José

private road

main entrance road

TANQUETAS TRAIL

INDIO DESNUDO TRAIL

Calera River

LOS PATOS TRAIL

Playa Salada River

PALO SECO TRAIL

Santa Rosa National Park

San José

COSTA RICA

CARBONAL TRAIL

Pacific Ocean

Campground	■
Dirt Road	= = =
Hiking Trail	•••••••
Visitor Center	■

Frommer's®

Costa Rica

2008

by Eliot Greenspan

Here's what the critics say about Frommer's:

"Amazingly easy to use. Very portable, very complete."

—*Booklist*

"Detailed, accurate, and easy-to-read information for all price ranges."
—*Glamour Magazine*

"Hotel information is close to encyclopedic."

—*Des Moines Sunday Register*

"Frommer's Guides have a way of giving you a real feel for a place."
—*Knight Ridder Newspapers*

BICENTENNIAL
1807
WILEY
2007
BICENTENNIAL

Wiley Publishing, Inc.

About the Author

Eliot Greenspan is a poet, journalist, musician, and travel writer who took his backpack and typewriter the length of Mesoamerica before settling in Costa Rica in 1992. Since then, he has worked steadily as a travel writer, freelance journalist, and translator, and continued his travels in the region. He is the author of *Frommer's Belize, Costa Rica For Dummies, Frommer's Cuba, Frommer's Ecuador, Frommer's Guatemala,* and *The Tico Times Restaurant Guide to Costa Rica,* as well as the chapter on Venezuela in *Frommer's South America.*

Published by:

Wiley Publishing, Inc.

111 River St.
Hoboken, NJ 07030-5774

ISBN: 978-0-470-13831-1

Editors: Mike Kelly with Jennifer Reilly
Production Editor: Lindsay Conner
Cartographer: Tim Lohnes
Photo Editor: Richard Fox
Production by Wiley Indianapolis Composition Services

Anniversary Logo Design: Richard Pacifico
Front cover photo: Red-Eyed Tree Frog clinging to leaf
Back cover photo: Arenal Volcano: Tabacón Hot Springs in foreground

For information on our other products and services or to obtain technical support, please contact our Customer Care Department within the U.S. at 800/762-2974, outside the U.S. at 317/572-3993 or fax 317/572-4002.

Wiley also publishes its books in a variety of electronic formats. Some content that appears in print may not be available in electronic formats.

Manufactured in the United States of America

5 4 3 2

Contents

List of Maps

Acknowledgments

I say this every year, but I continue to be eternally grateful to Anne Becher and Joe Richey, who were instrumental in getting me this gig—*muchas gracias*. I'd also like to thank my parents, Marilyn and Warren Greenspan, who showed unwavering love, support, and encouragement (well, one out of three ain't bad) when I chose words and world-wandering over becoming a lawyer or a doctor. Jody and Ted Ejnes (my sister and brother-in-law) deserve a mention; they risked life and limb—literally—leading to two important tips that may help you save yours. (I now believe Ted, and he may have actually almost stepped on a crocodile). Mayling Charpentier did some excellent phone, fax, and fact-checking work on this edition. And a big tip of my hat to Jennifer Reilly for her editorial diligence and patience.

An Invitation to the Reader

In researching this book, we discovered many wonderful places—hotels, restaurants, shops, and more. We're sure you'll find others. Please tell us about them, so we can share the information with your fellow travelers in upcoming editions. If you were disappointed with a recommendation, we'd love to know that, too. Please write to:

Frommer's Costa Rica 2008
Wiley Publishing, Inc. • 111 River St. • Hoboken, NJ 07030-5774

An Additional Note

Please be advised that travel information is subject to change at any time—and this is especially true of prices. We therefore suggest that you write or call ahead for confirmation when making your travel plans. The authors, editors, and publisher cannot be held responsible for the experiences of readers while traveling. Your safety is important to us, however, so we encourage you to stay alert and be aware of your surroundings. Keep a close eye on cameras, purses, and wallets, all favorite targets of thieves and pickpockets.

Other Great Guides for Your Trip:

Costa Rica For Dummies

Frommer's Belize

Frommer's Cuba

Frommer's Guatemala

Frommer's South America

Frommer's Star Ratings, Icons & Abbreviations

Every hotel, restaurant, and attraction listing in this guide has been ranked for quality, value, service, amenities, and special features using a **star-rating system.** In country, state, and regional guides, we also rate towns and regions to help you narrow down your choices and budget your time accordingly. Hotels and restaurants are rated on a scale of zero (recommended) to three stars (exceptional). Attractions, shopping, nightlife, towns, and regions are rated according to the following scale: zero stars (recommended), one star (highly recommended), two stars (very highly recommended), and three stars (must-see).

In addition to the star-rating system, we also use **seven feature icons** that point you to the great deals, in-the-know advice, and unique experiences that separate travelers from tourists. Throughout the book, look for:

Finds	Special finds—those places only insiders know about
Fun Fact	Fun facts—details that make travelers more informed and their trips more fun
Kids	Best bets for kids, and advice for the whole family
Moments	Special moments—those experiences that memories are made of
Overrated	Places or experiences not worth your time or money
Tips	Insider tips—great ways to save time and money
Value	Great values—where to get the best deals

The following **abbreviations** are used for credit cards:

AE	American Express	DISC	Discover	V	Visa
DC	Diners Club	MC	MasterCard		

Frommers.com

Now that you have the guidebook to a great trip, visit our website at **www.frommers.com** for travel information on more than 3,600 destinations. With features updated regularly, we give you instant access to the most current trip-planning information available. At Frommers.com, you'll also find the best prices on airfares, accommodations, and car rentals—and you can even book travel online through our travel booking partners. At Frommers.com, you'll also find the following:

- Online updates to our most popular guidebooks
- Vacation sweepstakes and contest giveaways
- Newsletter highlighting the hottest travel trends
- Online travel message boards with featured travel discussions

What's New in Costa Rica

Costa Rica is no longer a buzzing, new hotspot. The tourism industry has definitely matured. Still, change and growth remain fairly constant. Here are some highlights related to new hotels and restaurants, and assorted other developments you'll find.

PLANNING YOUR TRIP

Work on the second phase of the expansion and remodeling of Costa Rica's **Juan Santamaría International Airport** is ongoing, but much delayed, and not expected to be finished until at least mid-2008.

As of April 2007, the **official exchange rate** was 518 colones to the U.S. dollar.

Check listings throughout the book, as more and more hotels and restaurants are adding Wi-Fi.

Budget carrier **Spirit Air** (© 800/772-7117; www.spiritair.com) has begun three weekly direct flights between Ft. Lauderdale and San José. Frontier Air (© 800/432-1359; www.frontierairlines. com) is scheduled to begin nonstop service between Denver and San Jose in November 2007.

Nature Air (© 800/235-9272 in the U.S. and Canada, or 299-6000; www. natureair.com) now offers daily direct flights to Limón.

See chapter 2 for detailed information on planning your trip to Costa Rica.

SAN JOSE

Hotel Grano de Oro (© 255-3322; www.hotelgranodeoro.com) has finished a major addition. Only four new rooms have been added, but their public areas and restaurant have been greatly expanded and updated.

Over on the west side of the city, the **Corteza Amarilla Art Lodge & Spa** (© 800/961-0419 in the U.S. and Canada, or 203-7503; www.corteza amarillalodge.com), is a delightful new boutique hotel, restaurant, and spa.

Close to the airport, the **El Rodeo Country Inn** (© 293-3909; www.elrodeo hotel.com) has completed a total remodel and expansion under new management.

Up in the coffee planted hills of Heredia, **Finca Rosa Blanca** (© 269-9392; www.fincarosablanca.com) is expected to finish its own expansion and remodeling by January 2008. The project will include several new rooms, a new spa, and a new, much larger restaurant.

Back to downtown San José, the **Museo de Jade Marco Fidel Tristán (Jade Museum;** © 287-6034) is now finally, and officially relocated and reopened on the first floor of the INS Building, having moved from its perch on the 11th floor of this same building.

The popular disco club **La Plaza** has changed its name to **Copacabana** (© 233-5516).

See chapter 5 for complete coverage of San José.

GUANACASTE & THE NICOYA PENINSULA

The plains and savannas of Guanacaste have an interesting new attraction in **Africa Mia** (My Africa; © 357-5555;

www.africamia.net), with safari-style open-jeep tours at its private reserve, which is populated with a wide range of non-native (mostly African) species.

On the flanks of the Rincón de la Vieja volcano, Hacienda Guachipelin has added a new spa. **Simbiosis Spa** ⬧ (☎ 666-8075; www.simbiosis-spa.com) offers a range of treatments to go along with local volcanic mud packs and soaks in their natural hot springs.

In Playa Hermosa, **Villa del Sueño Hotel** (☎ 800/378-8599 in the U.S., or 672-0026; www.villadelsueno.com) has added a lovely outdoor amphitheater that offers twice-monthly dinner-theater events featuring top acts from San José.

Playa del Coco is booming, and one of the best new developments here is the restaurant, bar, and beach club **Café de Playa** (☎ 670-1621).

The isolated little luxury resort **Hotel Punta Islita** (☎ 231-6122; www.hotelpuntaislita.com) has added a 9-hole executive golf course.

See chapter 6 for all the latest on this rapidly developing region.

THE NORTHERN ZONE

Hacienda Pozo Azul (☎ 761-1360; www.pozoazul.com) is a new one-stop shop for a variety of adventure tours in the Puerto Viejo de Sarapiquí area. These folks have an extensive zip-line canopy tour operation, and also offer white water rafting and kayaking, horseback riding, guided hikes, and mountain bike tours. They even run a tent camp and rustic lodge in the rainforest here.

A couple of new adventure tours are available around La Fortuna and the Arenal Volcano. **Arenal Bungee** (☎ 479-7440) offers a 40m (130-ft.) fall from a steel tower constructed on the outskirts of downtown La Fortuna. **Desafío Expeditions** ⬧⬧ (☎ 479-9464; www.desafiocostarica.com) runs a new canyoning tour in the rainforest just outside of town.

There are also a couple of restaurant developments in and around La Fortuna. **Lava Lounge** (☎ 479-7365) is an excellent new open-air place in downtown La Fortuna serving mostly light, healthy, and tasty international fare. The longstanding steakhouse **El Novillo** (☎ 849-1508) has had to move from its home near the Tabacón Hot Springs, to a new site on the other side of La Fortuna.

Speaking of Tabacón, they've changed their name to **Tabacón Grand Spa Thermal Resort** (☎ 877/277-8291 in the U.S. and Canada, or 460-2020 at the resort; www.tabacon.com). Coinciding with the name change are the addition of some new rooms and an overall upgrade in terms of service and facilities, at both the hotel and the hot springs.

Costa Rican artist Juan Carlos Ruiz runs **Casa Delagua** (☎ 692-2101; www.casadelaguacr.com), a studio, gallery, and coffee shop on the main road around Lake Arenal, about halfway between Nuevo Arenal and Tilarán.

In Monteverde—more precisely in Santa Elena—the **Orchid Garden** ⬧ (☎ 645-5308) has a new home, just across from the Pension El Tucano.

Also in Monteverde, **The Bat Jungle** (☎ 645-6566) is a new attraction that provides an in-depth look into the world, life and habits of these flying mammals.

Full details on the northern zone can be found in chapter 7.

CENTRAL PACIFIC COAST

The luxurious **Villa Caletas** (☎ 637-0505; www.hotelvillacaletas.com) has added the **Zephyr Palace,** seven all-suite units, each with its own pool, located on a hillside below the main hotel and villas.

Xandari By The Pacific (☎ 866/363-3212 in the U.S. and Canada, or 778-7070; www.xandari.com) is a new beachfront luxury hotel in Playa Esterillos, run by the folks at the successful Xandari

Resortin Alajuela. **Hotel Playa Bejuco** (℃/fax **778-8181;** www.mardeluz.com) is a new beachfront hotel in Playa Bejuco, run by the folks at the popular Mar de Luz hotel in Jacó.

Two excellent upscale resort hotels have opened in Manuel Antonio: **Arenas del Mar** (℃/fax **777-2777;** www.arenas delmar.com) and **Gaia Hotel & Reserve** (℃ **800/226-2515** in the U.S., or 777-9797; www.gaiahr.com).

The dining scene in Manuel Antonio has some welcome additions, including **Agua Azul** (℃ **777-5082**), with hearty upscale bar food and a spectacular panoramic view, and **La Hacienda** (℃ **777-3473**), with a lush setting and creative cuisine. **Tsunami Sushi** (℃ **777-2159**), of Jacó, has also opened up a restaurant in downtown Quepos.

Down in Dominical, **Coconut Spice** (℃ **787-0073**), the popular Thai and Indian restaurant, has a new home in the riverside Pueblo del Río shopping complex.

A little farther south, **Cuna del Angel** (℃/fax **787-8012;** www.cunadelangel. com) is a new luxurious boutique hotel just off the coastal highway. However, one of my favorite restaurants and small hotels in the Uvita region, **El Balcón de Uvita,** has shut down.

See chapter 8 for complete coverage of this region.

THE SOUTHERN ZONE

Bosque del Cabo Rainforest Lodge (℃/fax **735-5206;** www.bosquedelcabo. com) has nearly doubled the size of its swimming pool and added outdoor bathtubs to about half of its cabins.

After decades of success running one of the premiere fishing lodges in Costa Rica, Roy has sold his namesake lodge, and instead of being called Roy's Zancudo Lodge, the new owners have renamed the hotel **The Zancudo Lodge** (℃ **776-0008;** www.thezancudolodge.com). Most everything else has remained the same.

See chapter 9 for more information on this remote region.

THE CARIBBEAN COAST

In Cahuita, **Casa Creole** (℃ **755-0104**) has new owners. However, the ambience and cuisine remain similar, with more of a French and fusion focus being shown in the menu.

In Puerto Viejo, the owner and chef behind the superb **La Pecora Nera** has opened a nearby restaurant and bar **Gatta Ci Cova** (℃ **750-0490**), serving simpler, yet still stellar, fare.

See chapter 10 for complete coverage of this area.

The Best of Costa Rica

Costa Rica is consistently one of the hottest vacation and adventure-travel destinations in Latin America, with more than a million visitors each year. Despite the boom in vacationers, Costa Rica remains a place rich in natural wonders and biodiversity, where you can still feel far from the maddening crowds. The country boasts a wealth of unsullied beaches that stretch for miles, small lodgings that haven't attracted hordes of tourists, jungle rivers for rafting and kayaking, and spectacular cloud and rainforests with ample opportunities for bird-watching and hiking. In addition to the country's trademark eco- and adventure tourism offerings, a handful of large luxury resorts and golf courses have opened in recent years and more are on the way.

I've lived in Costa Rica for more than 16 years, and my "best of" experiences keep on coming. In this chapter I've selected the very best of what this unique country has to offer. Most of these places and experiences are covered in greater detail elsewhere in the book; this chapter is merely meant to give you an overview of the highlights so that you can start planning your own adventure.

1 The Best of Natural Costa Rica

- **Rincón de la Vieja National Park** (northeast of Liberia, in Guanacaste): This is an area of rugged beauty and high volcanic activity. The Rincón de la Vieja Volcano rises to 1,848m (6,061 ft.), but the thermal activity is spread out along its flanks, where numerous geysers, vents, and fumaroles let off its heat and steam. This is a great place to hire a guide and a horse for a day of rugged exploration. There are waterfalls and mud baths, hot springs, and cool jungle swimming holes. You'll pass through pastureland, scrub savanna, and moist secondary forest; the bird-watching is excellent. See p. 153.

- **The Río Sarapiquí Region** (north of San José between Guanacaste in the west and the Caribbean coast in the east): This region is a prime place for an ecolodge experience. Protected tropical forests climb from the Caribbean coastal lowlands up into the central mountains, affording you a glimpse of a plethora of life zones and ecosystems. **Braulio Carrillo National Park** borders several other private reserves here, and a variety of ecolodges will suit any budget. See "Puerto Viejo de Sarapiquí" in chapter 7.

- **Arenal Volcano/Tabacón Hot Springs** (near La Fortuna, northwest of San José): When the skies are clear and the lava is flowing, Arenal Volcano offers a thrilling light show accompanied by an earthshaking rumble that defies description. You can even see the show while soaking in a natural hot spring and having a drink at the swim-up bar at **Tabacón Grand Spa Thermal Resort** (© **519-1900;**

www.tabacon.com). If the rushing torrent of volcano-heated spring water isn't therapeutic enough, you can get an incredibly inexpensive massage here. See "Arenal Volcano & La Fortuna" in chapter 7.

- **Monteverde Biological Cloud Forest Reserve** (in the mountains northwest of San José): There's something both eerie and majestic about walking around in the early-morning mist surrounded by bird calls and towering trees hung heavy in broad bromeliads, flowering orchids, and hanging moss and vines. The reserve has a well-maintained network of trails, and the community is truly involved in conservation. Not only that, but in and around Monteverde and Santa Elena, you'll find a whole slew of related activities and attractions, including canopy tours that allow you to swing from treetop to treetop while hanging from a skinny cable. See p. 244.
- **Manuel Antonio** (near Quepos on the central Pacific coast): There's a reason this place is so popular and renowned: monkeys! The national park here is full of them, even the endangered squirrel monkeys. But you'll also find plenty to see and do outside the park. The road into Manuel Antonio has many lookouts that consistently offer postcard-perfect snapshots of steep jungle hills meeting the sea. Uninhabited islands lie just off the coast, and the beaches here are perfect crescents of soft,

white sand. See "Manuel Antonio National Park" in chapter 8.
- **Osa Peninsula** (in southern Costa Rica): This is Costa Rica's most remote and biologically rich region. **Corcovado National Park,** the largest remaining patch of virgin lowland tropical rainforest in Central America, takes up much of the Osa Peninsula. Jaguars, crocodiles, and scarlet macaws all call this place home. Whether you stay in a luxury nature lodge in **Drake Bay** or outside of **Puerto Jiménez,** or camp in the park itself, you will be surrounded by some of the most lush and most intense jungle this country has to offer. See chapter 9.
- **Tortuguero Village & Jungle Canals** (on the Caribbean coast, north of Limón): Tortuguero Village is a small collection of rustic wooden shacks on a narrow spit of land between the Caribbean Sea and a dense maze of jungle canals. It's been called Costa Rica's Venice, but it actually has more in common with the South American Amazon. As you explore the narrow canals here, you'll see a wide variety of herons and other water birds, three types of monkeys, three-toed sloths, and caiman. If you come between June and October, you might be treated to the awe-inspiring spectacle of a green turtle nesting—the small stretch of Tortuguero beach is the last remaining major nesting site of this endangered animal. See "Tortuguero National Park" in chapter 10.

2 The Best Beaches

With more than 1,200km (750 miles) of shoreline on its Pacific and Caribbean coasts, Costa Rica offers beachgoers an embarrassment of riches.

- **Santa Rosa National Park:** If you really want to get away from it all, the

beaches here in the northwest corner of Costa Rica are a good bet. You'll have to four-wheel-drive or hike 13km (8 miles) from the central ranger station to reach them. And once there, you'll find only the most

The Best of Costa Rica

THE BEST OF NATURAL COSTA RICA
Arenal Volcano/Tabacón Hot Springs **5**
Braulio Carrillo National Park **18**
Manuel Antonio National Park **25**
Monteverde Biological Cloud Forest Reserve **6**
Osa Peninsula & Corcovado National Park **26**
Rincón de la Vieja National Park **2**
The Río Sarapiquí Region **14**
Tortuguero Village & Jungle Canals **15**

THE BEST BEACHES
The Beaches around Playa Sámara **9**
Malpaís **11**
Manuel Antonio **25**
Playa Montezuma **12**
Punta Uva & Manzanillo **21**
Santa Rosa National Park **1**

THE BEST ADVENTURES
Battling a Billfish off the Pacific Coast **24**
Diving off Isla del Coco **10**
Hiking Mount Chirripó **22**
Kayaking Around Golfo Dulce **27**
Rafting the Upper Reventazón River **16**
Surfing & Four-Wheeling Guanacaste **8**
Surfing Pavones **28**
Windsurfing Lake Arenal **4**

THE BEST BIRD-WATCHING
Aviarios del Caribe/Cahuita National Park **20**
Caño Negro Wildlife Refuge **3**
Carara National Park **13**
Cerro de la Muerte **23**
La Selva Biological Station **17**
Parque del Este **19**
Río Tempisque Basin **7**
Wilson Botanical Gardens **29**

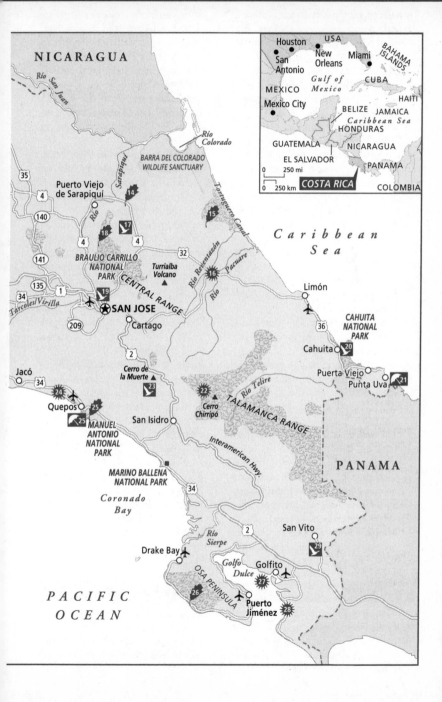

basic of camping facilities: outhouse latrines and cold-water showers. But you'll probably have the place almost to yourself. In fact, the only time it gets crowded is in October, when thousands of olive ridley sea turtles nest in one of their yearly *arribadas* (arrivals). See p. 158.

- **The Beaches around Playa Sámara:** Playa Sámara itself is nice enough, but if you venture just slightly farther afield, you'll find some of the nicest and least developed beaches along the entire Guanacaste coast. **Playa Carrillo** is a long, almost always deserted crescent of palm-backed white sand located just south of Sámara, while **Playa Barrigona** and **Playa Buena Vista** are two hidden gems tucked down a couple of dirt roads to the north. See "Playa Sámara" in chapter 6.

- **Playa Montezuma:** This tiny beach town at the southern tip of the Nicoya Peninsula has weathered fame and infamy, but retains a funky sense of individuality. European backpackers, vegetarian yoga enthusiasts, and UFO seekers choose Montezuma's beach over any other in Costa Rica. The waterfalls are what set it apart from the competition, but the beach stretches for miles, with plenty of isolated spots to plop down your towel or mat. Nearby are the **Cabo Blanco** and **Curú** wildlife preserves. See "Playa Montezuma" in chapter 6.

- **Malpaís:** While the secret is certainly out, there's still some time to visit Costa Rica's hot spot before the throngs arrive. With just a smattering of luxury lodges, surf camps, and simple *cabinas,* Malpaís is the place to come if you're looking for miles of deserted beaches and great surf. If you find Malpaís is too crowded, head farther on down the road to Santa Teresa, Playa Hermosa, and Manzanillo. See "Malpaís/Santa Teresa" in chapter 6.

- **Manuel Antonio:** The first beach destination to become popular in Costa Rica, Manuel Antonio retains its charms despite burgeoning crowds and mushrooming hotels. The beaches inside the national park are idyllic, and the views from the hills approaching the park are enchanting. This is one of the few remaining habitats for the endangered squirrel monkey. Rooms with views tend to be a bit expensive, but many a satisfied guest will tell you they're worth it. See "Manuel Antonio National Park" in chapter 8.

- **Punta Uva & Manzanillo:** Below Puerto Viejo, the beaches of Costa Rica's eastern coast take on true Caribbean splendor, with turquoise waters, coral reefs, and palm-lined stretches of nearly deserted white-sand beach. Punta Uva and Manzanillo are the two most sparkling gems of this coastline. Tall coconut palms line the shore, providing shady respite for those who like to spend a full day on the sand, and the water is usually quite calm and good for swimming. See "Puerto Viejo" in chapter 10.

3 The Best Adventures

- **Mountain-Biking the Back Roads of Costa Rica:** The lack of infrastructure and paved roads that most folks bemoan is a huge boon for mountain bikers. There are endless back roads and cattle paths to explore. Tours of differing lengths and all difficulty levels are available. Contact **Coast to Coast Adventures** (© **280-8054;** www. ctocadventures.com). See p. 68.

- **Swinging Through the Treetops on a Canopy Tour:** This unique adventure is becoming quite the rage. In most cases, after a strenuous climb using ascenders, you strap on a harness and zip from treetop to treetop while dangling from a cable. There are canopy tours all around Costa Rica. Check the various destination chapters to find a canopy tour operation near you.

- **Rafting the Upper Reventazón River** (near Turrialba): The Class V Guayabo section of this popular river is serious white water. Only experienced and gutsy river runners need apply. If you're not quite up to that, try a 2-day Pacuare River trip which passes through primary and secondary forests and a beautiful steep gorge. Plans to build a dam here have thankfully been rejected for now. **Ríos Tropicales** (© 233-6455; www.riostropicales.com) can arrange these tours. See p. 79.

- **Surfing and Four-Wheeling Guanacaste Province:** This northwestern province has dozens of respectable beach and reef breaks, from Witch's Rock at Playa Naranjo near the Nicaraguan border to Playa Nosara more than 100km (62 miles) away. In addition to these two prime spots, try a turn at Playa Grande, Punta Langosta, and playas Negra, Avellanas, and Junquillal. Or find your own secret spot. Rent a four-by-four with a roof rack, pile on the boards, and explore. See chapter 6.

- **Battling a Billfish off the Pacific Coast:** Billfish are plentiful all along Costa Rica's Pacific coast, and boats operate from Playa del Coco to Playa Zancudo. Costa Rican anglers hold world records for both blue marlin and Pacific sailfish. Go to Quepos (just outside Manuel Antonio) for the best *après*-fish scene, or head down to Drake Bay, the Osa Peninsula, or Golfo Dulce if you want some isolation. **Costa Rica Outdoors** (© 800/308-3394 or 282-6743; www.costarica outdoors.com) can help you find a good charter skipper or specialized fishing lodge. See chapters 6, 8, and 9.

- **Trying the New Adventure Sport of Canyoning:** While far from standardized, canyoning usually involves hiking along and through the rivers and creeks of steep mountain canyons, with periodic breaks to rappel down the face of a waterfall, jump off a rock into a jungle pool, or float down a small rapid. **Pure Trek Canyoning** (© 866/569-5723 or 461-2110; www.puretrekcostarica.com) in La Fortuna, and **Everyday Adventures** (© 353-8619; www.everydaycosta rica.com) near Puerto Jiménez, are two of the prime operators. See chapters 7 and 9.

- **Windsurfing Lake Arenal:** With steady gale-force winds and stunning scenery, the northern end of Lake Arenal has become a major international windsurfing hot spot.

- **Diving off the Shores of Isla del Coco** (off the Pacific coast): Legendary among treasure seekers, pirate buffs, and scuba divers, this small island is consistently rated one of the 10 best dive sites in the world. A protected national park, Isla del Coco is surrounded by clear Pacific waters, and its reefs are teeming with life (divers regularly encounter large schools of hammerhead sharks, curious manta rays, and docile whale sharks). Because the island is so remote and has no overnight facilities for visitors, the most popular way to visit is on 10-day excursions on a liveaboard boat, where guests live, eat, and sleep onboard—with nights anchored in the harbor. See p. 258.

- **Hiking Mount Chirripó** (near San Isidro de El General on the central Pacific coast): The highest mountain in Costa Rica, Mount Chirripó is one of the few places in the world where (on a clear day) you can see both the Caribbean Sea and the Pacific Ocean at the same time. Hiking to Chirripó's 3,724m (12,215-ft.) summit takes you through a number of distinct bioregions, ranging from lowland pastures and a cloud forest to a high-altitude *páramo,* a tundralike landscape with stunted trees and morning frosts. See "San Isidro de El General: A Base for Exploring Chirripó National Park" in chapter 8.

- **Kayaking around the Golfo Dulce:** Slipping through the waters of the Golfo Dulce by kayak gets you intimately in touch with the raw beauty of this underdeveloped region. Spend several days poking around in mangrove swamps, fishing in estuaries, and watching dolphins frolic in the bay. **Escondido Trex** (© 735-5210; www.escondidotrex.com) provides multiday custom kayaking trips out of Puerto Jiménez on the Osa Peninsula. See "Puerto Jiménez: Gateway to Corcovado National Park" in chapter 9.

- **Surfing Pavones** (on the southern Pacific coast): Just 13km (8 miles) from the Panamanian border at the southern reaches of Costa Rica's Pacific coast, Pavones is reputed to have one of the longest rideable waves in the world. When this left-point break is working, surfers enjoy rides of almost a mile in length. Much more can be said about this experience, but if you're a surfer, you've heard it all before. Contact **Casa Siempre Domingo** (© 820-4709; www.casa-domingo.com), the most comfortable hotel in town, for current wave reports and other local information. See "Playa Pavones: A Surfer's Mecca" in chapter 9.

4 The Best Day Hikes & Nature Walks

- **Lankester Gardens:** If you want a really pleasant but not overly challenging day hike, consider a walk among the hundreds of distinct species of flora on display here. Lankester Gardens (© **552-3247**) is just 27km (17 miles) from San José and makes a wonderful day's expedition. The trails meander from areas of well-tended open garden to shady natural forest. See p. 126.

- **Rincón de la Vieja National Park:** This park has a number of wonderful trails through a variety of ecosystems and natural wonders. My favorite hike is down to the Blue Lake and Cangrejo Falls. It's 5.1km (3¼ miles) each way, and you'll want to spend some time at the base of this amazing lake; plan on at least 5 hours for the outing, and bring along lunch and plenty of water. You can also hike up to two craters and a crater lake here, and the Las Pailas loop is ideal for those seeking a less strenuous hike. This remote volcanic national park is about an hour north of Liberia (it's only 25km/16 miles, but the road is quite rough), or about 5 hours from San José. See p. 153.

- **La Selva Biological Station:** This combination research facility and rustic nature lodge has an extensive and well-marked network of trails. You'll have to reserve in advance (© **766-6565**) and take the guided tour if you aren't a guest at the lodge. But the hikes are led by very informed naturalists, so you might not mind the company. The Biological Station is located north-northeast on the Caribbean slope of Costa Rica's central mountain range. It'll take you about 1½ hours to drive from San José via the Guápiles Highway. See p. 219.

- **Arenal National Park and Environs:** There's great hiking all around this area. The national park itself has several excellent trails that visit a variety of ecosystems, including rainforest, secondary forest, savanna, and, my favorite, old lava flows. Most of them are on the relatively flat flanks of the volcano, so there's not too much climbing involved. There's also great hiking on the trails at the Arenal Observatory Lodge, and the trail down to the base of the La Fortuna Waterfall is a fun scramble. It's about a 3½-hour drive from San José to La Fortuna and Arenal National Park. See "Arenal Volcano & La Fortuna" in chapter 7.

- **Monteverde Biological Cloud Forest Reserve:** In the morning rush of high season, when groups and tours line up to enter the reserve, you'd think the sign said CROWD FOREST. Still, the guides here are some of the most professional and knowledgeable in the country. Take a tour in the morning to familiarize yourself with the forest, and then spend the late morning or afternoon (your entrance ticket is good for the entire day) exploring the reserve. Off the main thoroughfares, Monteverde reveals its rich mysteries with stunning regularity. Walk through the gray mist and look up at the dense tangle of epiphytes and vines. The only noises are the rustlings of birds or monkeys and the occasional distant rumble of Arenal Volcano. The trails are well marked and regularly tended. It's about 3½ hours by bus or car to Monteverde from San José. See p. 244.

- **Corcovado National Park:** This large swath of dense lowland rainforest is home to Costa Rica's second-largest population of scarlet macaws. The park has a well-designed network of trails, ranger stations, and camping facilities. Most of the lodges in Drake Bay and Puerto Jiménez offer day hikes through the park, but if you really want to experience it, you should hike in and stay at one or more of the campgrounds. This is strenuous hiking, and you will have to pack in some gear and food, but the reward is some of Costa Rica's most spectacular and unspoiled scenery. Because strict limits are placed on the number of visitors allowed into the park, you'll always be far from the crowds. See "Puerto Jiménez: Gateway to Corcovado National Park" in chapter 9.

- **Cahuita National Park:** The trails here are flat, well-maintained paths through thick lowland forest. Most of the way they parallel the beach, which is usually no more than 90m (295 ft.) away, so you can hike out on the trail and back along the beach, or vice versa. White-faced and howler monkeys are common, as are brightly colored land crabs. See p. 350.

5 The Best Bird-Watching

- **Observing Oropendola and Blue-Crowned Motmot at Parque del Este:** A boon for city bird-watchers, this San José park rambles through a collection of lawns, planted gardens, and harvested forest, but it also includes second-growth scrub and dense woodland. Oropendola and blue-crowned motmot are common species here. Take the San

Ramón/Parque del Este bus from Calle 9 between Avenida Central and Avenida 2. See p. 127.

- **Spotting Hundreds of Marsh and Stream Birds along the Río Tempisque Basin:** Hike around the Palo Verde Biological Station, or take a boat trip down the Bebedero River with **Swiss Travel Services** (✆ **282-4898;** www.swisstravelcr.com) or **Safaris Corobicí** (✆ **669-6191;** www.nicoya.com). This area is an important breeding ground for gallinules, jacanas, and limpkins, and is a common habitat for numerous heron and kingfisher species. Palo Verde is about a 3½-hour drive from San José. See p. 154.

- **Looking for 300-plus Species of Birds in La Selva Biological Station:** With an excellent trail system through a variety of habitats, from dense primary rainforest to open pasturelands and cacao plantations, this is one of the finest places for bird-watching in Costa Rica. With such a variety of habitats, the number of species spotted runs to well over 300. See p. 219.

- **Sizing Up a Jabiru Stork at Caño Negro National Wildlife Refuge:** Caño Negro Lake and the Río Frío that feeds it are incredibly rich in wildlife and a major nesting and gathering site for aquatic bird species. These massive birds are getting less common in Costa Rica, but this is still one of the best places to spot one. **Caño Negro Natural Lodge** (✆ **265-3302;** www.canonegrolodge.com) sits right on the edge of the refuge and makes a great base for exploring this region. See p. 229.

- **Catching a Scarlet Macaw in Flight over Carara National Park:** Home to Costa Rica's largest population of scarlet macaws, Carara Biological Reserve is a special place for devoted bird-watchers and recent converts.

Macaws are noisy and colorful birds that spend their days in the park but choose to roost in the evenings near the coast. They arrive like clockwork every morning and then head for the coastal mangroves around dusk. These daily migrations give birders a great chance to see these magnificent birds in flight. The reserve is located about 2 hours from San José along the central Pacific coast. See p. 263.

- **Looking for a Resplendent Quetzal in the Cerro de la Muerte:** Don't let the name (Hill of Death) scare you away from the opportunity to see this spectacular bird, revered by the ancient Aztecs and Mayas. Serious bird-watchers won't want to leave Costa Rica without crossing this bird off their lists, and neophytes might be hooked for life after seeing one of these iridescent green wonders fly overhead, flashing its brilliant red breast and trailing 2-foot-long tail feathers. **Trogon Lodge** (✆ **293-8181;** www.grupomawamba.com) can almost guarantee a sighting. The Cerro de la Muerte is a high mountain pass along the way to San Isidro de El General about 1½ hours from San José. See "En Route to San José: Three Places to See Quetzals in the Wild" in chapter 8.

- **Spotting Hundreds of Species at Wilson Botanical Gardens:** With more than 7,000 species of tropical plants and flowers, the well-tended trails and grounds of this beautiful research facility are fabulous for birdwatching. Hummingbirds and tanagers are particularly plentiful, but the bounty doesn't end there—more than 330 different species of birds have been recorded here. Wilson Gardens is located about an hour outside the town of Golfito. See "Golfito: Gateway to the Golfo Dulce" in chapter 9.

- **Taking Advantage of the Caribbean's Best Birding at Aviarios del Caribe:** In just a few short years, Aviarios del Caribe (© **750-0775**) has established itself as the prime bird-watching resort on the Caribbean. If it flies along this coast, chances are good that you'll spot it here; more than 330 species of birds have been spotted so far. Located on the Caribbean coast, Aviarios del Caribe is about a 3-hour drive from San José. See p. 351.

6 The Best Destinations for Families

- **San José:** If you're spending any time in San José, you'll probably want to be outside the rough-and-tumble downtown area. The best place to experience Costa Rica's capital city (and still get a decent night's sleep) is the **Meliá Cariari** (© **888/956-3542** or 239-0022; www.solmelia.com). With facilities that include several large pools, gym, casino, shuttle service to a nearby spa and 18-hole golf course, and a game room (not to mention a babysitting service), there's something here for everyone. If you're traveling with teens, they'll feel right at home at the nearby Mall Cariari, which has a multiplex theater, an indoor skating rink, and, of course, a food court. Located just 15 minutes from downtown, it's well situated for exploring all of the city's sights and attractions. See p. 111.
- **La Paz Waterfall Gardens** (© **482-2720** or 225-0643; www.waterfall gardens.com): This multifaceted attraction features paths and suspended walkways alongside a series of impressive jungle waterfalls. Kids love the variety and vibrancy of the various attractions here, from the buzzing hummingbirds to the impressive power of the waterfalls. The rooms at the **Peace Lodge** here are some of the best in the country. See p. 111.
- **Playa Hermosa:** The protected waters of this Pacific beach make it a family favorite. However, just because the waters are calm doesn't mean it's boring here. Check in at **Aqua Sport** (© **672-0050**), where you can rent sea kayaks, sailboards, paddleboats, beach umbrellas, and bicycles. See "Playa Hermosa, Playa Panamá & Papagayo" in chapter 6.
- **Playa Tamarindo:** This lively surf town has a bit of something for everyone. This is a great spot for teens to learn how to surf or boogie-board, and there are a host of tours and activities to please the entire family. **Hotel Capitán Suizo** (© **653-0353;** www.hotelcapitansuizo.com; p. 183) has an excellent location on a calm section of beach, spacious rooms, and a great pool for kids and adults alike. See "Playa Tamarindo & Playa Grande" in chapter 6.
- **Monteverde:** Located about 160km (99 miles) northwest of San José, this area not only boasts the country's most famous cloud forest, but also sports a wide variety of related attractions and activities. After hiking through the reserve, you should be able to keep most kids happy and occupied riding horses; squirming at the local serpentarium; or visiting the butterfly farm, frog pond, and hummingbird gallery. More adventurous families can take a horseback ride or one of the local zip-line canopy tours. See "Monteverde" in chapter 7.
- **Playa de Jacó:** On the central Pacific coast, this is Costa Rica's liveliest and most developed beach town. The streets are lined with souvenir shops, ice-cream stands, and inexpensive eateries; there's even a miniature-golf

course. Older kids can rent a surf- or boogie-board, although everyone should be careful with the rough surf. The **Club del Mar Condominiums & Resort** (© **866/978-5669** or 643-3194; p. 266) is situated at the calm southern end of the beach. The hotel has a large free-form pool and some shady grounds, and is accommodating to families with small children. See "Playa de Jacó" in chapter 8.

• **Manuel Antonio:** Manuel Antonio has a little bit of everything: miles of gorgeous beaches, tons of wildlife (with almost guaranteed monkey sightings), and plenty of active-tour options. There's a load of lodging options, but **Hotel Sí Como No** (© **777-0777;** www.sicomono.com), with its large suites, two pools, water slide, and nightly movies, is probably your best bet. See "Manuel Antonio National Park" in chapter 8.

7 The Best Luxury Hotels & Resorts

• **Marriott Costa Rica Hotel** (San Antonio de Belén, San José area; © **888/236-2427** or 298-0844; www.marriott.com): Of all the contenders in the upscale urban market, the Marriott seems to be doing the best job. Maybe because it's the newest, but everything is in great shape, the service is bend-over-backward, the restaurants are excellent, and the hotel boasts all the facilities and amenities you could want. See p. 111.

• **Peace Lodge** (north of Varablanca; © **482-2720** or 225-0643; www.waterfallgardens.com): While the bathrooms of the deluxe units are the most luxurious and unique in the country, everything else is done in grand style as well. Each room comes with at least one custom-tiled Jacuzzi on a private balcony. The hotel adjoins the popular La Paz Waterfall Gardens. See p. 111.

• **Four Seasons Resort Costa Rica** (Papagayo Peninsula; © **800/819-5053** or 696-0000; www.fourseasons.com/costarica): This was the first major resort to really address the high-end luxury market in Costa Rica. Within its first month of operation Michael Jordan and Madonna were notable guests. A beautiful setting, wonderful installations, a world-class golf course, and stellar service continue to make this the current king of the hill in the upscale market. See p. 163.

• **Hotel Punta Islita** (on the Pacific coast in central Guanacaste; © **231-6122;** www.hotelpuntaislita.com): This great getaway is perched on a high, flat bluff overlooking the Pacific Ocean. It's popular with honeymooners, and rightly so. The rooms are large and comfortable, the food is excellent, and the setting is stunning. If you venture beyond your room and the hotel's inviting hillside pool, there's a long, almost always deserted beach for you to explore, as well as a wealth of activities for the more adventurous. See p. 200.

• **Flor Blanca Resort** (Playa Santa Teresa; © **640-0232;** www.florblanca.com): The individual villas at this intimate resort are some of the largest and most luxurious in the country. The service and food are outstanding, and the location is breathtaking, spread over a lushly planted hillside steps away from Playa Santa Teresa. See p. 212.

• **Villa Caletas** (north of Jacó; © **637-0505;** www.hotelvillacaletas.com): Spread out over a steep hillside high above the Pacific, these individual villas have a Mediterranean feel. The Greek Doric amphitheater follows the same motif. Carved into the hillside, the theater frequently features evening concerts of jazz or classical music. The "infinity pool" here was one of the first in Costa Rica and is still my favorite. Sitting in a lounge chair at the pool's edge, you'll swear that it joins the sea beyond. See p. 269.

- **Arenas del Mar** (Manuel Antonio; ℂ/fax **777-2777;** www.arenasdel mar.com): With large and ample rooms, excellent service and amenities, a beautiful little spa, and the best beach access and location in Manuel Antonio, this hotel has a lot to offer. See p. 283.
- **Hotel Sí Como No** (Manuel Antonio; ℂ **777-0777;** www.sicomono. com): Although there are fancier and more posh places in Costa Rica, the large modern suites and villas, spectacular views, attentive service, and first-rate facilities here earn this small resort a spot on this list. See p. 285.

8 The Best Moderately Priced Hotels

- **Hotel Grano de Oro** (San José; ℂ **255-3322;** www.hotelgranode oro.com): San José boasts dozens of old homes that have been converted into hotels, but few offer the luxurious accommodations or professional service found at the Grano de Oro. All the guest rooms have attractive hardwood furniture, including old-fashioned wardrobes in some rooms. When it's time to relax, you can soak in a hot tub or have a drink in the rooftop lounge while taking in San José's commanding view. See p. 106.
- **Hôtel Le Bergerac** (San José; ℂ **234-7850;** www.bergerachotel. com): This classy little hotel has been pleasing diplomats, dignitaries, and other discerning travelers for years. Ask for one of the garden rooms or get the old master bedroom with its small private balcony. See p. 107.
- **Villa del Sueño Hotel** (Playa Hermosa; ℂ **800/378-8599** or ℂ/fax 672-0026; www.villadelsueno.com): It's not right on the beach (you'll have to walk about 90m/295 ft.), but everything else here is right on the money: clean, comfortable rooms; a nice refreshing pool; and an excellent restaurant. You can't do better in Playa Hermosa. See p. 165.
- **Amor de Mar** (Montezuma; ℂ/fax **642-0262;** www.amordemar.com): Clean, spacious, and comfortable rooms set on a sloping lawn that leads down to a rocky coastline, with a natural pool carved into the rocks, all add up to my idea of a tropical paradise. See p. 208.
- **Hotel El Sapo Dorado** (Monteverde; ℂ **645-5010;** www.sapo dorado.com): Spacious wooden cabins with fireplaces and private porches are spread across an open hillside planted with fruit trees and tropical flowers. The hotel has an excellent restaurant and is a great place to enjoy some of the best sunsets in town. See p. 250.
- **Cariblue Bungalows** (Playa Cocles; ℂ **750-0035;** www.cariblue.com): Try to get one of the private wooden bungalows here. If you do, you might be so happy and comfortable that you won't want to leave. Just 90m (295 ft.) or so away, however, are the warm waves of the Caribbean Sea. If this place is full, the neighboring **Azania Bungalows** (ℂ **750-0540;** www. azania-costarica.com) is just about as good. See p. 363.

9 The Best Ecolodges & Wilderness Resorts

The term "ecotourism" is now ubiquitous within the travel industry, particularly in Costa Rica. Ecolodge options in Costa Rica range from tent camps with no electricity, cold-water showers, and communal buffet-style meals to some of the most luxurious accommodations in the country. Generally, outstanding ecolodges and wilderness resorts are set apart by an ongoing commitment (financial or otherwise) to minimizing their effect on surrounding ecosystems and to supporting both conservation efforts and the residents of local communities. They should also be able to provide naturalist guides and plentiful information. All of the following do.

- **La Selva Biological Station** (south of Puerto Viejo; ℂ **524-0628;** www.ots.ac.cr): Sure, this place is geared more toward researchers than tourists, but that (along with the surrounding rainforest and extensive trail system) is what makes this one of the best ecotourism spots in the country. See p. 219.

- **Arenal Observatory Lodge** (near La Fortuna; ℂ **290-7011;** www.arenal-observatory.co.cr): Originally a research facility, this lodge has upgraded over the years and features comfortable rooms with impressive views of Arenal Volcano. There are excellent trails to nearby lava flows and a nice waterfall. Toucans frequent the trees near the lodge, and howler monkeys provide the wake-up calls. See p. 227.

- **Monteverde Lodge** (Playa Carate; ℂ **257-0766;** www.monteverdelodge. com): One of the original ecolodges in Monteverde, this place has only improved over the years, with great guides, updated rooms, and lush

gardens. The operation is run by the very dependable and experienced Costa Rica Expeditions. See p. 251.

- **La Paloma Lodge** (Drake Bay; ℂ **293-7502;** www.lapalomalodge. com): If your idea of the perfect nature lodge is one where your front porch provides some prime-time viewing of flora and fauna, this place is for you. If you decide to leave the comfort of your porch, the Osa Peninsula's lowland rainforests are just outside your door. See p. 312.

- **Bosque del Cabo Rainforest Lodge** (Osa Peninsula; ℂ/fax **735-5206;** www.bosquedelcabo.com):   Large, comfortable private cabins perched on the edge of a cliff overlooking the Pacific Ocean and surrounded by lush rainforest make this one of my favorite spots in the country. There's plenty to do, and there are always great guides here. See p. 320.

- **Playa Nicuesa Rainforest Lodge** (Golfo Dulce; ℂ **866/504-8116** or 258-8250; www.nicuesalodge.com): This new lodge is by far the best option on the Golfo Dulce. Set in deep forest, the individual bungalows here are a perfect blend of rusticity and luxury. See p. 326.

- **Tortuga Lodge** (Tortuguero; ℂ **257-0766;** www.tortugalodge.com): The canals of Tortuguero snake through a maze of lowland primary rainforest. The beaches here are major sea-turtle nesting sites. This is not only the most comfortable option in the area, but also another of the excellent ecolodges run by Costa Rica Expeditions. See p. 344.

- **Selva Bananito Lodge** (in the Talamanca Mountains south of Limón; ℂ **253-8118;** www.selvabananito. com): This is one of the few lodges providing direct access to the southern Caribbean lowland rainforests. There's no electricity here, but that doesn't mean it's not plush. Hike along a riverbed, ride horses through the rainforest, climb 30m (100 ft.) up a ceiba tree, or rappel down a jungle waterfall. There's fabulous bird-watching here, and the Caribbean beaches are nearby. See p. 348.

10 The Best Bed & Breakfasts & Small Inns

- **Finca Rosa Blanca Country Inn** (Heredia; ✆ **269-9392;** www.finca rosablanca.com): If the cookie-cutter rooms of international resorts leave you cold, then perhaps the unique rooms of this unusual inn will be more your style. Square corners seem to have been prohibited here in favor of turrets and curving walls of glass, arched windows, and a semicircular built-in couch. It's set into the lush hillsides just 20 minutes from San José. See p. 110.
- **Vista del Valle Plantation Inn** (near Grecia; ✆ **450-0800;** www.vistadel valle.com): This is a great choice if you want something close to the air-port but have no need for San José. The separate cabins are influenced by traditional Japanese architecture, with lots of polished woodwork and plenty of light. The gardens are meticulously tended, and the chef is excellent. A nice tile pool and Jacuzzi overlook a deep river canyon. See p. 112.
- **Sueño del Mar** (Playa Tamarindo; ✆/fax **653-0284;** www.sueno-del-mar.com): You might think you're dreaming here. The rooms feature African dolls on the windowsills, Kokopeli candleholders, and open-air showers with sculpted angelfish, hand-painted tiles, and lush tropical plants. The fabrics are from Bali and Guatemala. Somehow all this works well together. Add in the requisite hammocks under shade trees right on the beach and a new small pool, and you really have something. The breakfasts here are earning local renown; yours is included in the price of your room. See p. 184.
- **Arco Iris Lodge** (Monteverde; ✆ **645-5067;** www.arcoirislodge. com): This small lodge is right in Santa Elena, and it's by far the best deal in the Monteverde area. The owners are extremely knowledgeable and helpful. See p. 251.
- **Cabinas Los Cocos** (Playa Zancudo; ✆/fax **776-0012;** www.loscocos. com): If you've ever dreamed about chucking it all and setting up shop in a simple house right on the beach, give it a trial run here first. See p. 330.
- **Cabinas Casa Verde** (Puerto Viejo; ✆ **750-0015;** www.cabinascasaverde. com): This is my favorite budget lodg-ing along the Caribbean coast. The rooms are clean and airy and have comfortable beds with mosquito nets. The owner is friendly and is always doing some work in the gardens or around the grounds. See p. 361.
- **Tree House Lodge** (Punta Uva; ✆ **750-0706;** www.costaricatree house.com): The collection of private houses at this small beachfront prop-erty are the most creative and luxuri-ous accommodations to be found on the Caribbean coast. I like the name-sake Tree House, although the Beach House Suite is quite spectacular as well. See p. 362.

11 The Best Restaurants

- **Tin Jo** (San José; ☎ 221-7605): In a city with hundreds of Chinese restaurants, this place stands head and shoulders above the competition. In addition to an extensive selection of Szechuan and Cantonese classics, there are Japanese, Thai, Indian, and Malaysian dishes on the menu. Tin Jo has the most adventurous Asian cuisine in Costa Rica. See p. 116.

- **Grano de Oro Restaurant** (San José; ☎ 255-3322): This elegant little hotel has an elegant restaurant serving delicious continental dishes and decadent desserts. The open-air seating in the lushly planted central courtyard is delightful, especially for lunch. See p. 118.

- **Bacchus** (Santa Ana; ☎ 282-5441): Set in a wonderfully restored and updated ancient adobe home, this restaurant serves up arguably the best Italian fare in the San José metropolitan area. See p. 121.

- **Ginger** (Playa Hermosa; ☎ 672-0041): Serving an eclectic mix of traditional and Pan Asian–influenced tapas, this sophisticated little joint is taking this part of Guanacaste by storm. They've got a list of creative cocktails to match the inventive dishes. See p. 165.

- **Mar y Sol** (Playa Flamingo; ☎ 654-4151): In a beautiful room on a high hilltop with great views, the Catalan chef here serves top-notch international fare. See p. 177.

- **Dragonfly Bar & Grill** (Tamarindo; ☎ 653-1506): Southwestern American and Pacific Rim fusion cuisines are the primary culinary influences at this popular restaurant. Portions are large, service excellent, and prices fair. See p. 187.

- **Nectar** (at Flor Blanca Resort, Santa Teresa; ☎ 640-0232): Guanacaste's best boutique resort also has one of its best restaurants. The menu changes nightly but always has a heavy Pan-Asian fusion flavor to it. The setting is romantic and subdued, in an open-air space just steps from the sand. See p. 214.

- **Playa de los Artistas** (Montezuma; ☎ 642-0920): This place is the perfect blend of refined cuisine and beachside funkiness. There are only a few tables, so make sure you get here early. Fresh, grilled seafood is served in oversize ceramic bowls and on large wooden slabs lined with banana leaves. See p. 210.

- **Sofia** (Monteverde; ☎ 645-7017): This restaurant serves excellent New Latin–fusion fare at a small space about halfway along the rough dirt road between Santa Elena and the Monteverde Cloud Forest Preserve. See p. 253.

- **Pacific Bistro** (Jacó; ☎ 643-3771): This place serves up a regularly changing menu of creative fusion fare with the freshest seafood and best beef available. Asian influences are prominent here. See p. 271.

- **El Patio Bistro Latino** (Quepos; ☎ 777-4982): This casually elegant little place has made a name for itself in the Manuel Antonio area. The chef's creative concoctions take full advantage of fresh local ingredients. Its intimate setting is a welcome little oasis in Quepos. See p. 290.

- **La Pecora Nera** (Puerto Viejo; ☎ 750-0490): I'm not sure that a tiny surfer town on the remote Caribbean coast deserves such fine Italian food, but it's got it. Your best bet here is to allow yourself to be taken on a culinary roller-coaster ride with a mixed feast of the chef's nightly specials and suggestions. See p. 367.

12 The Best Views

- **The Summit of Irazú Volcano** (near San José): On a very clear day, you can see both the Pacific Ocean and the Caribbean Sea from this vantage point. Even if visibility is low and this experience eludes you, you can view the volcano's spectacular landscape, the Meseta Central, and the Orosi Valley. See p. 144.

- **Iguanazul Hotel** (Playa Junquillal; © **658-8124;** www.iguanazul.com): Located on a high bluff above Playa Junquillal, this hotel has a wonderful view of the Pacific and the windswept coastline in either direction. It gets best around sunset and is better yet if you can commandeer one of the hammocks set in a little palapa on the hillside itself. See p. 190.

- **Tabacón Grand Spa Thermal Resort** (near Arenal Volcano; **877/277-8291** or 460-2020; www.tabacon.com): Arenal Volcano seems so close, you'll swear you can reach out and touch it. Unlike Irazú Volcano (see above), when *this* volcano rumbles and spews, you may feel the urge to seek cover. Most rooms have spectacular views

from sheltered private patios or balconies. See p. 226.

- **Villa Caletas** (Playa Hermosa de Jacó; © **637-0505**): You'll have a view over the Golfo de Nicoya and the Pacific Ocean beyond. Sunsets at the hotel's outdoor amphitheater are legendary, but it's beautiful here during the day as well. See p. 269.

- **Hotel La Mariposa** (Quepos; © **800/ 549-0157** or 777-0355; www.la mariposa.com): This place has arguably the best view in Manuel Antonio, and that's saying a lot. Come for breakfast or a sunset drink because, unfortunately, I've had bad luck with dinner here. See p. 284.

- **The Summit of Mount Chirripó** (near San Isidro): What more can one say? At 3,724m (12,215 ft.), this is the highest spot in Costa Rica. On a clear day, you can see both the Pacific Ocean and the Caribbean Sea from here. Even if it isn't clear, you can catch some pretty amazing views and scenery. See "San Isidro de El General: A Base for Exploring Chirripó National Park" in chapter 8.

13 The Best After-Dark Fun

- **Night Tours** (countrywide): Most Neotropical forest dwellers are nocturnal. Animal and insect calls fill the air, and the rustling on the ground all around takes on new meaning. Night tours are offered at most rain- and cloud-forest destinations throughout the country. Many use high-powered flashlights to catch glimpses of various animals. Some of the better spots for night tours are **Monteverde, Tortuguero,** and the **Osa Peninsula.** Volcano viewing in **Arenal** is another not-to-miss nighttime activity.

- **El Cuartel de la Boca del Monte** (San José; © **221-0327**): From Wednesday to Saturday, San José's young, restless, and beautiful pack it in here. Originally a gay and bohemian hangout, it is now decidedly mixed and leaning toward yuppie. There's frequently live music here. See p. 137.

- **San Pedro** (San José): This is San José's university district, and at night its streets are filled with students strolling among a variety of bars and cafes. If you'd like to join them, keep in mind that **La Villa** caters to artists and bohemians, **Mosaikos** is popular with young Tico rockers, **Omar Khayyam** is a great place to grab an outdoor table and watch the crowds walk by, and the **Jazz Café**, as its name indicates, is a hip live-music venue that often features local jazz and rock outfits. See "San José After Dark" in chapter 5.

- **San Clemente Bar & Grill** (Dominical; 🕾 **787-0055**): This is a quintessential surfers' joint, but whether you hang ten or not, this is where you'll want to hang out in Dominical at night. The fresh seafood and Tex-Mex specialties are hearty, tasty, and

inexpensive. And there are pool, Ping-Pong, and foosball tables, as well as televised sporting events and surf videos. See "Dominical" in chapter 8.

- **Puerto Viejo:** This small beach town on the southern end of Costa Rica's Caribbean coast is one of the most active after-dark scenes in the country. **Johnny's Place** and **Stanford's** take turns as the major dance-and-party spot, but there are several other happening spots, as well as a few after-hours beach bonfires and jam sessions, to be found. See "Puerto Viejo" in chapter 10.

14 The Best Websites about Costa Rica

- **The *Tico Times*** (www.ticotimes.net): The English-language *Tico Times* makes it easy for *norteamericanos* (and other English speakers) to see what's happening in Costa Rica. It features the top story from its weekly print edition, as well as a daily update of news briefs, a business article, regional news, a fishing column, and travel reviews. There's also a link to current currency-exchange rates.

- **Latin American Network Information Center** (http://lanic.utexas.edu/la/ca/cr): This site houses a vast collection of information about Costa Rica, and is hands-down the best one-stop shop for browsing, with helpful links to a diverse range of tourism and general information sites.

- **Maptak** (www.maptak.com): This is the best site I've found for online maps. The site is still expanding and improving, and there's a tiny bit of a learning curve here, but this is overall a very valuable resource.

- **The U.S. Embassy in Costa Rica** (www.usembassy.or.cr): The official

site of the U.S. Embassy in Costa Rica has a good base of information and regular updates of concern to U.S. citizens abroad, as well as about Costa Rica in general.

- **CostaRicaLiving** (http://groups. yahoo.com/group/CostaRicaLiving): This is the official home page of the best newsgroup dealing with Costa Rica. The active newsgroup deals with a wide range of issues, and its membership includes many long-time residents and bona fide experts. You have to join, but you'll find plenty of good information.

- ***La Nación* Digital** (www.nacion. com): If you can read Spanish, this is an excellent site to read regularly or simply browse. The entire content of the country's paper of record is placed online daily, and there's also an extensive searchable archive. It does maintain a small summary of major news items in English, although this section tends to run about a week behind the current events.

Planning Your Trip to Costa Rica

2

Costa Rica is beginning to be old hat. It seems like almost everybody's already been, or knows someone who's been. That said, most travelers will want to do some serious pretrip planning. When is the best time to go to Costa Rica? The cheapest time? Should you rent a car (or will you need 4WD), and what will it cost? Where should you go in Costa Rica? What are the hotels like? How much should you budget for your trip? These are just a few of the important questions that this chapter answers so that you can be prepared when you arrive in Costa Rica.

1 The Regions in Brief

Costa Rica rightfully should be called "Costas Ricas" because it has two coasts: one on the Pacific Ocean and one on the Caribbean Sea. These two coasts are as different from each other as are the Atlantic and Pacific coasts of North America.

Costa Rica's **Pacific coast** is characterized by a rugged (although mostly accessible) coastline where forested mountains often meet the sea. It can be divided into three distinct regions—Guanacaste and the Nicoya Peninsula, the Central Coast, and the Southern Coast. There are some spectacular stretches of coastline, and most of the country's top beaches are here. This coast varies from the dry, sunny climate of the northwest to the hot, humid rainforests of the south.

The **Caribbean coast** can be divided into two roughly equal stretches. The remote northeast coastline is a vast flat plain laced with rivers and covered with rainforest; it is accessible only by boat or small plane. Farther south, along the stretch of coast accessible by car, there are uncrowded beaches and even a bit of coral reef.

Bordered by Nicaragua in the north and Panama in the southeast, Costa Rica is only slightly larger than Vermont and New Hampshire combined. Much of the country is mountainous, with three major ranges running northwest to southeast. Among these mountains are several volcanic peaks, some of which are still active. Between the mountain ranges are fertile valleys, the largest and most populated of which is the Central Valley. With the exception of the dry Guanacaste region, much of Costa Rica's coastal area is hot and humid and covered with dense rainforests.

See the map on the inside back cover of this book for a visual of the regions detailed below.

SAN JOSE & THE CENTRAL VALLEY The Central Valley is characterized by rolling green hills that rise to heights between 900 and 1,200m (2,952–3,936 ft.) above sea level. The climate here is mild and springlike year-round. It's Costa Rica's primary agricultural region, with coffee farms making up the majority of landholdings. The rich volcanic soil of this region makes it ideal for farming. The country's earliest settlements were in this area, and today the Central Valley (which includes San José) is densely populated, crisscrossed by decent roads, and dotted with small towns. Surrounding the Central Valley are high mountains, among which are four volcanic peaks. Two of these, **Poás** and **Irazú,** are still active and have caused extensive damage during cycles of activity in the past 2 centuries. Many of the mountainous regions to the north and to the south of the capital of San José have been declared national parks (Tapantí, Juan Castro, and Braulio Carrillo) to protect their virgin rainforests against logging.

GUANACASTE & THE NICOYA PENINSULA The northwestern corner of the country near the Nicaraguan border is the site of many of Costa Rica's sunniest and most popular **beaches.** Because many Americans have chosen to build beach houses and retirement homes here, Guanacaste, in particular, is experiencing quite a bit of new development. Don't expect a glut of Cancún-style high-rise hotels, but condos, luxury resorts, and golf courses are springing up like mushrooms. That's not to say you'll be towel-to-towel with thousands of strangers. On the contrary, you can still find long stretches of deserted sands. That might not be true for long, however: Now that the new international airport in Liberia is up and running, travelers can get here on daily direct flights from North America.

With about 65 inches of rain a year, this region is by far the driest in the country and has been likened to west Texas. Guanacaste province sits at the border of Nicaragua and is named after the shady trees that still shelter the herds of cattle roaming the dusty savanna here. In addition to cattle ranches, Guanacaste boasts semiactive volcanoes, several lakes, and one of the last remnants of tropical dry forest left in Central America. (Dry forest once stretched all the way from Costa Rica up to the Mexican state of Chiapas.)

THE NORTHERN ZONE This region lies to the north of San José and includes rainforests, cloud forests, hot springs, the country's two most active volcanoes (**Arenal** and **Rincón de la Vieja**), **Braulio Carrillo National Park,** and numerous remote lodges. Because this is one of the few regions of Costa Rica without any beaches, it primarily attracts people interested in nature and active sports. **Lake Arenal** boasts some of the best windsurfing in the world, as well as several good mountain-biking trails along its shores. The **Monteverde Cloud Forest,** perhaps Costa Rica's most internationally recognized attraction, is another top draw in this region.

THE CENTRAL PACIFIC COAST Because it's the most easily accessible coastline in Costa Rica, the central Pacific coast boasts the greatest number of beach resorts and hotels. **Playa de Jacó** is the most popular destination here, a beach within a few hours' drive of San José that attracts many Canadian and German charter groups and plenty of Tico tourists on weekends. **Manuel Antonio,** a popular coastal national park as well as the resort area that surrounds it, caters to people seeking a bit more tranquillity and beauty. This region is also home to the highest peak in Costa Rica—**Mount Chirripó**—where frost is common.

THE SOUTHERN ZONE This hot, humid region is one of Costa Rica's most remote and undeveloped. It is characterized by dense rainforests and rugged coastlines. Much of the area is protected in **Corcovado** and **La Amistad** national parks. There is a wealth of wonderful nature lodges spread around the shores of the **Golfo Dulce** and along the **Osa Peninsula.** There's a lot of solitude to be found here, due in no small part to the fact that it's hard to get here and hard to get around. But if you like your eco-tourism challenging, you'll find the southern zone to your liking.

THE CARIBBEAN COAST   Most of the Caribbean coast is a wide, steamy lowland laced with rivers and blanketed with rainforests and banana plantations. The culture here is predominantly Afro-Caribbean, with many residents speaking an English or Caribbean patois. The northern section of this coast is accessible only by boat or small plane and is the site of **Tortuguero National Park,** which is known for its nesting sea turtles and riverboat trips. The towns of **Cahuita, Puerto Viejo,** and **Manzanillo,** on the southern half of the Caribbean coast, are increasingly popular destinations. The coastline here boasts many beautiful beaches and, as yet, few large hotels. However, this area can be rainy, especially between December and April.

2 Visitor Information & Maps

In the United States or Canada, you can get basic information on Costa Rica by contacting the **Costa Rican Tourist Board (ICT,** or Instituto Costarricense de Turismo) (*C* **866/COSTA RICA;** www.visitcostarica.com). Travelers from the United Kingdom, Australia, and New Zealand will have to rely primarily on this website because the ICT does not have toll-free access in these countries.

In addition to this official site, you'll be able to find a wealth of Web-based infor-mation on Costa Rica with a few clicks of your mouse. In fact you'll be better off surfing, as the ICT site is rather limited and clunky. See "The Best Websites about Costa Rica" in chapter 1 for some helpful suggestions about where to begin your online search.

You can pick up a map when you arrive at the ICT's information desk at the air-port, or at their downtown San José offices (although the map included with this book is generally better). Other sources in San José for detailed maps include **Seventh Street Books,** Calle 7 between avenidas Central and 1 (*C* **256-8251**); **Librería Lehmann,** Avenida Central between calles 1 and 3 (*C* **223-1212**); and **Librería Universal,** Avenida Central between calles Central and 1 (*C* **222-2222**).

Perhaps the best map to have is the waterproof country map of Costa Rica put out by **International Travel Maps** (www.itmb.com), which can be ordered direct from their website, or any major online bookseller, like Amazon.com.

3 Entry Requirements

PASSPORTS
For information on how to get a passport, go to "Passports" in the "Fast Facts" sec-tion of this chapter—the websites listed provide downloadable passport applica-tions as well as the current fees for pro-cessing passport applications. For an up-to-date, country-by-country listing of passport requirements around the world, go to the "Foreign Entry Requirements" Web page of the U.S. Department of State at **http://travel.state.gov**.

Citizens of the United States, Canada, Great Britain, and most European nations may visit Costa Rica for a maxi-mum of 90 days. No visa is necessary, but you must have a valid passport, which you should carry with you at all times while you're in Costa Rica. Citizens of Australia, Ireland, and New Zealand can enter the country without a visa and stay for 30 days, although once in the country, visitors can apply for an extension.

If you overstay your visa or entry stamp, you will have to pay around

US$45 (£23) for an exit visa. If you need to get an exit visa, a travel agent in San José can usually obtain one for a small fee and save you the hassle of dealing with Immigration. If you want to stay longer than the validity of your entry stamp or visa, the easiest thing to do is cross the border into Panama or Nicaragua for 72 hours and then reenter Costa Rica on a new entry stamp or visa. However, be careful: Periodically the Costa Rican government has cracked down on "perpetual tourists"; if it notices a continued pattern of exits and entries designed simply to support an extended stay, it might deny you re-entry.

If you need a visa or have other questions about Costa Rica, you can contact any of the following Costa Rican embassies or consulates: in the **United States,** 2114 S St. NW, Washington, DC 20008 (© 202/ 234-2945; www.costarica-embassy.org for consulate locations around the country); in **Canada,** 325 Dalhousie St., Suite 407, Ottawa, Ontario K1N 5TA (© 613/ 562-2855); and in **Great Britain,** 14 Lancaster Gate, London, England W2 3LH (© 020/7706-8844). There are no Costa Rican embassies in Australia or New Zealand, but you could try contacting the honorary consul in Sydney, Australia, at Level 11, De La Sala House, 30 Clarence St., Sydney NSW 2000 (© 02/9261-1177).

MEDICAL REQUIREMENTS

For medical requirements and recommendations, see "Health," p. 34.

CUSTOMS

For information on what you can bring into and take out of Costa Rica, go to **"Customs"** in the **"Fast Facts"** section of this chapter.

4 When to Go

Costa Rica's high season for tourism runs from late November to late April, which coincides almost perfectly with the chill of winter in the United States, Canada, and Great Britain. The high season is also the dry season. If you want some unadulterated time on a tropical beach and a little less rain during your rainforest experience, this is the time to come. During this period (and especially around the Christmas holiday), the tourism industry operates at full tilt—prices are higher, attractions are more crowded, and reservations need to be made in advance.

Local tourism operators often call the tropical rainy season (May through mid-Nov) the "green season." The adjective is appropriate. At this time of year, even brown and barren Guanacaste province becomes lush and verdant. I personally love traveling around Costa Rica during the rainy season (but then again, I'm not trying to flee winter in Chicago). It's easy to find or at least negotiate reduced rates, there are far fewer fellow travelers, and

the rain is often limited to a few hours each afternoon (although you can occasionally get socked in for a week at a time). *A drawback:* Some of the country's rugged roads become downright impassable without four-wheel-drive during the rainy season.

CLIMATE

Costa Rica is a tropical country and has distinct wet and dry seasons. However, some regions are rainy all year, and others are very dry and sunny for most of the year. Temperatures vary primarily with elevations, not with seasons: On the coasts it's hot all year; in the mountains it can be cool at night any time of year. Frost is common at the highest elevations (3,000–3,600m/9,840–11,808 ft.).

Generally, the **rainy season** (or "green season") is from May to mid-November. Costa Ricans call this wet time of year their winter. The **dry season,** considered summer by Costa Ricans, is from mid-November to April. In Guanacaste, the

Average Daytime Temperatures & Rainfall in San José

	Jan	Feb	Mar	Apr	May	June	July	Aug	Sept	Oct	Nov	Dec
Temp (°F)	73	75	77	78	78	78	77	77	76	77	75	73
Temp (°C)	23	24	25	26	26	26	25	25	24	25	24	23
Days of rain	1	0	1	4	17	20	18	19	20	22	14	4

dry northwestern province, the dry season lasts several weeks longer than in other places. Even in the rainy season, days often start sunny, with rain falling in the afternoon and evening. On the Caribbean coast, especially south of Limón, you can count on rain year-round, although this area gets less rain in September and October than the rest of the country.

In general, the best time of year to visit weather-wise is in December and January, when everything is still green from the rains, but the sky is clear.

HOLIDAYS

Because Costa Rica is a Roman Catholic country, most of its holidays are church-related. The biggies are Christmas, New Year's, and Easter, which are all celebrated for several days. Keep in mind that Holy Week (Easter week) is the biggest holiday time in Costa Rica, and many families head for the beach. (This is the last holiday before school starts.) Also, there is no public transportation on Holy Thursday or Good Friday. Government offices and banks are closed on official holidays, transportation services are reduced, and stores and markets might also close.

Official holidays in Costa Rica include **January 1** (New Year's Day), **March 19** (St. Joseph's Day), Thursday and Friday of Holy Week, **April 11** (Juan Santamaría's Day), **May 1** (Labor Day), **June 29** (St. Peter and St. Paul Day), **July 25** (annexation of the province of Guanacaste), **August 2** (Virgin of Los Angeles's Day), **August 15** (Mother's Day), **September 15** (Independence Day), **October 12** (Discovery of America/Día de la Raza), **December 8** (Immaculate

Conception of the Virgin Mary), **December 24** and **25** (Christmas), and **December 31** (New Year's Eve).

CALENDAR OF EVENTS

Some of the events listed here might be considered more of a *happening* than an event—there's not, for instance, a Virgin of Los Angeles PR Committee that readily dispenses information. If I haven't listed a contact number, your best bet is to call the **Costa Rican Tourist Board (ICT)** at ℭ **866/COSTA RICA** in the U.S. and Canada, or 223-1733 in Costa Rica, or visit **www.visitcostarica.com**.

For an exhaustive list of events beyond those listed here, check **http://events.frommers. com**, where you'll find a searchable, up-to-the-minute roster of what's happening in cities all over the world.

January

Copa del Café (Coffee Cup), San José. Matches for this international event on the junior tennis tour are held at the Costa Rica Country Club (ℭ **228-9333**). First week in January.

Fiesta of Palmares, Palmares. Perhaps the largest and best organized of the traditional *fiestas,* it includes bullfights, a horseback parade *(tope),* and many concerts, carnival rides, and food booths. First 2 weeks in January.

Fiesta of Santa Cruz, Santa Cruz, Guanacaste. This religious celebration honors the Black Christ of Esquipulas (a famous Guatemalan statue), featuring folk dancing, marimba music, and bullfights. Mid-January.

Fiesta of the Diablitos, Rey Curré village near San Isidro de El General. Boruca Indians wearing wooden devil and bull masks perform dances representative of the Spanish conquest of

Central America; there are fireworks displays and an Indian handicrafts market. Late January.

March

Día del Boyero (Oxcart Drivers' Day), San Antonio de Escazú. Colorfully painted oxcarts parade through this suburb of San José, and local priests bless the oxen. Second Sunday in March.

National Orchid Show, San José. Orchid growers throughout the world gather to show their wares, trade tales and secrets, and admire the hundreds of species on display. Contact the Costa Rican Tourist Board for location and dates in 2007. Mid-March.

April

Holy Week. Religious processions are held in cities and towns throughout the country. Week before Easter.

Juan Santamaría Day, Alajuela. Costa Rica's national hero is honored with parades, concerts, and dances. April 11.

May

Carrera de San Juan. The country's biggest marathon runs through the mountains, from the outskirts of Cartago to the outskirts of San José. May 17.

July

Fiesta of the Virgin of the Sea, Puntarenas. A regatta of colorfully decorated boats carrying a statue of Puntarenas's patron saint marks this festival. A similar event is held at Playa de Coco. Saturday closest to July 16.

Annexation of Guanacaste Day, Liberia. Tico-style bullfights, folk dancing, horseback parades, rodeos, concerts, and other events celebrate the day when this region became part of Costa Rica. July 25.

August

Fiesta of the Virgin of Los Angeles, Cartago. This is the annual pilgrimage day of the patron saint of Costa Rica.

Many people walk from San José 24km (15 miles) to the basilica in Cartago. August 2.

Día de San Ramón, San Ramón. More than two dozen statues of saints from various towns are brought to San Ramón, where they are paraded through the streets. August 31.

September

Costa Rica's Independence Day, celebrated all over the country. Most distinctive are the nighttime parades of children. September 15.

International Beach Clean-Up Day. This is a good excuse to chip in and help clean up the beleaguered shoreline of your favorite beach. Third Saturday in September.

October

Fiesta del Maíz, Upala. At this celebration of corn, local beauty queens wear outfits made from corn plants. October 12.

Limón Carnival/Día de la Raza, Limón. A smaller version of Mardi Gras, complete with floats and dancing in the streets, commemorates Columbus's discovery of Costa Rica. Week of October 12.

November

All Soul's Day/Día de los Muertos, celebrated countrywide. Although it is not as elaborate or ritualized as in Mexico, most Costa Ricans take some time this day to remember the dead with flowers and trips to the cemeteries. November 2.

December

Día de la Pólvora, San Antonio de Belén and Jesús María de San Mateo. Fireworks honor Our Lady of the Immaculate Conception. December 8.

Fiesta de los Negritos, Boruca. Boruca Indians celebrate the feast day of their patron saint, the Virgin of the

Immaculate Conception, with costumed dances and traditional music. December 8.

Fiesta de la Yeguita, Nicoya. A statue of the Virgin of Guadalupe is paraded through the streets, accompanied by traditional music and dancing. December 12.

Las Posadas. Countrywide, children and carolers go door to door seeking lodging in a reenactment of Joseph and Mary's search for a place to stay. Begins December 15.

El Tope and Carnival, San José. The streets of downtown belong to horses and their riders in a proud recognition of the country's important agricultural heritage. The next day, those same streets are taken over by carnival floats, marching bands, and street dancers. December 26 and 27.

Festejos Populares, San José. Bullfights and a pretty respectable bunch of carnival rides, games of chance, and fast-food stands are set up at the fairgrounds in Zapote. Last week of December.

5 Getting There

BY PLANE

It takes between 3 and 7 hours to fly to Costa Rica from most U.S. cities. Most international flights still land in San José's **Juan Santamaría International Airport** (airport code SJO). However, more and more direct international flights are touching down in Liberia's **Daniel Oduber International Airport** (airport code LIR). Delta, American, US Airways, America West, and Continental have regular nonstop commercial flights to Liberia from their hubs in Atlanta, Miami, Charlotte, Phoenix, and Houston, respectively. Liberia is the gateway to the beaches of the Guanacaste region and the Nicoya Peninsula, and a direct flight here eliminates the need for a separate commuter flight in a small aircraft or roughly 5 hours in a car or bus.

THE MAJOR AIRLINES

Numerous airlines fly into Costa Rica. Be warned that the smaller Latin American carriers tend to make several stops (sometimes unscheduled) en route to San José, thus increasing flying time.

The airlines listed here currently serve Costa Rica from the U.S. **American Airlines** (© 800/433-7300 in the U.S. and Canada or © 257-1266 in Costa Rica; www.aa.com) has flights from Los Angeles, Miami, and Dallas–Fort Worth to San José

and Liberia. **Continental** (© 800/231-0856 in the U.S. and Canada, or 0800/044-0005 in Costa Rica; www.continental.com) offers flights daily from Houston and Newark to San José, and a daily flight from Houston to Liberia. **Delta** (© 800/241-4141 in the U.S. and Canada, or 0800/056-2002 in Costa Rica; www.delta.com) offers two daily flights from Atlanta to San José and one daily flight from Atlanta to Liberia. Delta also has a once-weekly direct flight from Los Angeles to Liberia. **Frontier** (© 800/432-1359; www.frontierairlines.com) is scheduled to begin nonstop service between Denver and San Jose at the end of November 2007. **Mexicana** (© 800/531-7921 in the U.S. and Canada, or 441-9377 in Costa Rica; www.mexicana.com) flies from many North American cities, most connecting through Mexico City. **Spirit Air** (© 800/772-7117; www.spiritair.com) has three weekly direct flights between Ft. Lauderdale and San José. **US Airways** (© 800/622-1015 in the U.S. and Canada or 0800/011-0793 in Costa Rica; www.usairways.com) has direct flights from Charlotte to San José and Liberia. **Grupo Taca** (© 800/400-8222 in the U.S. and Canada, or 299-8222 in Costa Rica; www.grupotaca.com) is a group of Central American airlines, with direct flights or connections to and from Boston, Chicago, Los Angeles, San Francisco, Houston, New Orleans, New York, Miami, and Washington.

From Europe, you can take any major carrier to a hub city such as Miami or New York and then make connections to Costa Rica. Alternatively, **Air Canada** (www.aircanada.com) from Toronto, **Iberia** (www.iberia.com) from Spain, and **Martin Air** (www.martinairusa.com) from Holland have established routes to San José, some direct and others with one connection.

FLYING FOR LESS: TIPS FOR GETTING THE BEST AIRFARE

- Passengers who can book their tickets either **long in advance or at the last minute,** or who **fly midweek** or **at less-trafficked hours** may pay a fraction of the full fare. If your schedule is flexible, say so, and ask if you can secure a cheaper fare by changing your flight plans.
- Search **the Internet** for cheap fares. The most popular online travel agencies are **Travelocity.com** (www.travelocity.co.uk); **Expedia.com** (www.expedia.co.uk and www.expedia.ca); and **Orbitz.com**. In the U.K., go to **Travelsupermarket** (© 0845/345-5708; www.travelsupermarket.com), a flight search engine that offers flight comparisons for the budget airlines whose seats often end up in bucket-shop sales. Other websites for booking airline tickets online include **Cheapflights.com,   SmarterTravel.com, Priceline.com,** and **Opodo** (www.opodo.co.uk). Meta search sites (which find and then direct you to airline and hotel websites for booking) include **Sidestep.com** and **Kayak.com**—the latter includes fares for budget carriers like JetBlue and Spirit as well as the major airlines.

Site59.com is a great source for last-minute flights and getaways. In addition, most **airlines** offer online-only fares that even their phone agents know nothing about. British travelers should check **Flights International** (© 0800/0187050; www.flights-international.com) for deals on flights all over the world.

- Keep an eye on local newspapers for **promotional specials** or **fare wars,** when airlines lower prices on their most popular routes.
- Try to book a ticket **in its country of origin.** If you're planning a one-way flight from Johannesburg to New York, a South Africa–based travel agent will probably have the lowest fares. For foreign travelers on multi-leg trips, book in the country of the first leg; for example, book New York–Chicago–Montréal–New York in the U.S.
- **Consolidators,** also known as bucket shops, are wholesale brokers in the airline-ticket game. Consolidators buy deeply discounted tickets ("distressed" inventories of unsold seats) from airlines and sell them to online ticket agencies, travel agents, tour operators, corporations, and, to a lesser degree, the general public. Consolidators advertise in Sunday newspaper travel sections (often in small ads with tiny type), both in the U.S. and the U.K. They can be great sources for cheap international tickets. On the downside, bucket shop tickets are often rigged with restrictions, such as stiff cancellation penalties (as high as 50% to 75% of the ticket price). And keep in mind that most of what you see advertised is of limited availability. Several reliable consolidators are worldwide and available online. **STA Travel** (www.statravel.com) has been the world's

leading consolidator for students since purchasing Council Travel, but their fares are competitive for travelers of all ages. **Flights.com** (© **800/TRAV-800;** www.flights.com) has excellent fares worldwide, particularly to Europe. They also have "local" websites in 12 countries. **FlyCheap** (© **800/FLY-CHEAP;** www.1800fly cheap.com) has especially good fares to sunny destinations. **Air Tickets Direct** (© **800/778-3447;** www. airticketsdirect.com) is based in Montréal and leverages the Canadian dollar for lower fares; they also book trips to places that U.S. travel agents won't touch, such as Cuba.

- Join **frequent-flier clubs.** Frequent-flier membership doesn't cost a cent, but it does entitle you to free tickets or upgrades when you amass the airline's required number of frequent-flier points. You don't even have to fly to earn points; **frequent-flier credit cards** can earn you thousands of miles for doing your everyday shopping. But keep in mind that award seats are limited, seats on popular routes are hard to snag, and more and more major airlines are cutting their expiration periods for mileage points—so check your airline's frequent-flier program so you don't lose your miles before you use them. **Inside tip:** Award seats are offered almost a year in advance, but seats also open up at the last minute, so if your travel plans are flexible, you may strike gold. To play the frequent-flier game to your best advantage, consult the community bulletin boards on **FlyerTalk** (www.flyertalk.com) or go to Randy Petersen's **Inside Flyer** (www.insideflyer.com). Petersen and friends review all the programs in detail and post regular updates on changes in policies and trends.

LONG-HAUL FLIGHTS: HOW TO STAY COMFORTABLE

- Your choice of airline and airplane will definitely affect your legroom. Find more details about specific airlines at **www.seatguru.com**.
- Emergency exit seats and bulkhead seats typically have the most legroom. Emergency exit seats are usually left unassigned until the day of a flight (to ensure that someone able-bodied fills the seats); it's worth getting to the ticket counter early to snag one of these spots for a long flight. Many passengers find that bulkhead seating (the row facing the wall at the front of the cabin) offers more legroom, but keep in mind that bulkhead seats have no storage space on the floor in front of you.
- To have two seats for yourself in a three-seat row, try for an aisle seat in a center section toward the back of coach. If you're traveling with a companion, book an aisle and a window seat. Middle seats are usually booked last, so chances are good you'll end up with three seats to yourselves. And in the event that a third passenger is assigned the middle seat, he or she will probably be more than happy to trade for a window or an aisle.
- Ask about entertainment options. Many airlines offer seatback video systems where you get to choose your movies or play video games—but only on some of their planes. (Boeing 777s are your best bet.)
- To sleep, avoid the last row of any section or the row in front of an emergency exit, as these seats are the least likely to recline. Avoid seats near highly trafficked toilet areas. Avoid seats in the back of many jets—these can be narrower than those in the rest of coach. Or reserve a window seat so that you can rest your head and avoid being bumped in the aisle.

- Get up, walk around, and stretch every 60 to 90 minutes to keep your blood flowing and help avoid **deep vein thrombosis,** or "economy-class syndrome."
- Drink water before, during, and after your flight to combat the lack of humidity in airplane cabins. Avoid alcohol, which will dehydrate you.
- If you're flying with kids, don't forget to carry on toys, books, pacifiers, and snacks and chewing gum to help them relieve ear pressure buildup during ascent and descent.

BY CAR

It's possible to travel to Costa Rica by car, but it can be difficult, especially for U.S. citizens. After leaving Mexico, the Interamerican Highway (Carretera Interamericana, also known as the Pan-American Hwy.) passes through Guatemala, El Salvador, Honduras, and Nicaragua before reaching Costa Rica. All of these countries can be problematic for travelers for a variety of reasons, including internal violence, crime, corrupt border crossings, and visa formalities. If you do decide to undertake this adventure, take the **Gulf Coast route** from the border crossing at Brownsville, Texas, because it involves traveling the fewest miles through Mexico. Those planning to travel this route should purchase a copy of *You Can Drive to Costa Rica in 8 Days!,* by Dawn Rae Lessler (Harmony Gardens Publishing,

1998), which is available from the major online bookstores. You might also try to find a copy of *Driving the Pan-Am Highway to Mexico and Central America,* by Audrey and Raymond Pritchard (Costa Rica Books, 1997), which is harder to find. There is also a wealth of information online at **www.sanbornsinsurance.com** and **www.drivemeloco.com**.

CAR DOCUMENTS   You will need a current driver's license, as well as your vehicle's registration and the original title (no photocopies), to enter the country.

CENTRAL   AMERICAN   AUTO INSURANCE   Contact   **Sanborn's Insurance Company** (*C* **800/222-0158** or 956/686-0711; www.sanbornsinsurance.com), which has agents at various border towns in the United States. These folks have been servicing this niche for more than 50 years. They can supply you with trip insurance for Mexico and Central America (you won't be able to buy insurance after you've left the U.S.), driving tips, and an itinerary.

CAR SAFETY   Be sure your car is in excellent working order. It's advisable not to drive at night because of the danger of being robbed by bandits, especially in Mexico, Guatemala, El Salvador and Honduras. Also, drink only bottled beverages along the way to avoid any unpleasant microbes that might be lurking in the local tap water.

6 Money & Costs

It's always advisable to bring money in a variety of forms on a vacation: a mix of cash, credit cards, and traveler's checks. In many international destinations, ATMs offer the best exchange rates. Avoid exchanging money at commercial exchange bureaus and hotels, which often have the highest transaction fees.

CURRENCY

The unit of currency in Costa Rica is the **colón.** In May 2007, there were approximately 518 colones to the American dollar, but because the colón has typically been in a constant state of devaluation, you can expect this rate to change. Because of this devaluation and accompanying inflation, *this book lists prices in*

U.S. dollars only. To check the very latest exchange rates before you leave home, point your browser to **www.xe.com/ucc**.

The colón is divided into 100 **céntimos.** Currently, two types of coins are in circulation. The older and larger nickel-alloy coins come in denominations of 10, 25, and 50 céntimos and 1, 2, 5, 10, and 20 colones; however, because of their evaporating value, you will probably never see or have to handle céntimos, or anything lower than a 5-colón coin. In 1997 the government introduced gold-hued 5-, 10-, 25-, 50-, 100-, and 500-colón coins. They are smaller and heavier than the older coins, and while the plan was to have them eventually phase out the other currency, this hasn't happened yet.

There are paper notes in denominations of 1,000, 2,000, 5,000, and 10,000 colones. You might also encounter a special-issue 5-colón bill that is a popular gift and souvenir. It is valid currency, although it sells for much more than its face value. You might hear people refer to a *rojo* or *tucán,* which are slang terms for the 1,000- and 5,000-colón bills, respectively. One-hundred-colón denominations are called *tejas,* so *cinco tejas* is 500 colones. The 2,000 and 10,000 bills are relatively new, and I've yet to encounter a slang equivalent.

Forged bills are not entirely uncommon. When receiving change in colones, it's a good idea to check the larger-denomination bills, which should have protective bands or hidden images that appear when held up to the light.

If your ATM card doesn't work and you need cash in a hurry, **Western Union** (℗ **800/777-7777** in Costa Rica or 283-6336; www.westernunion.com) has numerous offices around San José and in several major towns and cities around the country. It offers a secure and rapid, although pricey, money-wire service. A $100 (£50) wire costs around $20 (£10),

and a $1,000 (£500) wire costs around $80 (£40).

You can change money at all banks in Costa Rica. However, be forewarned service at state banks can be slow and tedious. The principal state banks are Banco Nacional and Banco de Costa Rica. You're almost always better off finding a private bank. Luckily, there are hosts of private banks around San José, and in most major tourist destinations.

Since banks handle money exchanges, there are very, very few exchange houses in Costa Rica. One major exception to this is the **Global Exchange** office at the airport. However, be forewarned they exchange at more than 10% below the official exchange rate.

Hotels will often exchange money and cash traveler's checks as well; there usually isn't much of a line, but they might shave a few colones off the exchange rate. Be very careful about exchanging money on the streets; it's extremely risky. In addition to forged bills and short counts, street money-changers frequently work in teams that can leave you holding neither colones nor dollars. Also be very careful when leaving a bank. Criminals are often looking for foreigners who have just withdrawn or exchanged cash.

ATMs

The easiest and best way to get cash away from home is from an ATM (automated teller machine), sometimes referred to as a "cash machine," or a "cashpoint." The **Cirrus** (℗ 800/424-7787; www.mastercard.com) and **PLUS** (℗ 800/843-7587; www.visa.com) networks span the globe. Go to your bank card's website to find ATM locations at your destination. Be sure you know your daily withdrawal limit before you depart. *Note:* Many banks impose a fee every time you use a card at another bank's ATM, and that fee can be higher for international transactions (up to $5/£2.50 or more) than for

What Things Cost in Costa Rica	US$	UK£
Taxi from the airport to downtown San José	13	6.50
Double room, expensive	200	100
Double room, moderate	100	50
Double room, inexpensive	30	15
Three-course dinner for one without wine, moderate	12–25	6–13
Bottle of Imperial beer	1–1.50	.50–.75
Bottle of Coca-Cola	1	.50
Cup of coffee	1–1.50	.50–.75
Gallon of premium gas	4.17	2.08
Admission to most museums	2–5	1–2.50
Admission to most national parks	6	3

domestic ones (where they're rarely more than $2/£1). In addition, the bank from which you withdraw cash may charge its own fee. For international withdrawal fees, ask your bank.

Note: Banks that are members of the **Global ATM Alliance** charge no transaction fees for cash withdrawals at other Alliance member ATMs; these include Bank of America, Scotiabank (Canada, Caribbean, and Mexico), Barclays (U.K. and parts of Africa), Deutsche Bank (Germany, Poland, Spain, and Italy), and BNP Paribas (France). Scotiabank has branches in Costa Rica.

It's probably a good idea to change your PIN number to a 4-digit PIN number. While many ATM machines in Costa Rica will accept 5- and 6-digit PIN numbers, some will only accept 4-digit PIN numbers.

CREDIT CARDS

Credit cards are another safe way to carry money. They also provide a convenient record of all your expenses, and they generally offer relatively good exchange rates. You can withdraw cash advances from your credit cards at banks or ATMs but high fees make credit card cash advances a pricey way to get cash. Keep in mind that you'll pay interest from the moment of your withdrawal, even if you pay your monthly bills on time. Also, note that many banks now assess a 1% to 3% "transaction fee" on **all** charges you incur abroad (whether you're using the local currency or your native currency).

MasterCard and Visa are the most widely accepted credit cards in Costa Rica, followed by American Express. Most hotels and restaurants accept all of these, especially in tourist destination areas. Discover and Diner's Club are far less commonly accepted.

TRAVELER'S CHECKS

Given widespread acceptance of credit cards and growing prevalence of ATM machines, traveler's checks are becoming almost anachronistic. Still, they do provide a level of built-in insurance, and are accepted by most major tourist hotels and restaurants around Costa Rica. You can buy traveler's checks at most banks. They are offered in denominations of $20, $50, $100, $500, and sometimes $1,000. Generally, you'll pay a service charge ranging from 1% to 4%.

The most popular traveler's checks are offered by **American Express** (© 800/807-6233 or © 800/221-7282 for cardholders—this number accepts collect calls, offers service in several foreign languages, and exempts AmEx gold and platinum cardholders from the 1% fee.); **Visa** (© 800/732-1322)—AAA members can obtain Visa checks for a $9.95 fee (for checks up to $1,500) at most AAA offices or by calling ✆ 866/339-3378; and MasterCard (✆ 800/223-9920).

Be sure to keep a record of the traveler's checks serial numbers separate from your checks in the event that they are stolen or lost. You'll get a refund faster if you know the numbers.

American Express, Thomas Cook, Visa, and MasterCard offer foreign currency traveler's checks, useful if you're traveling to one country or to the Euro zone; they're accepted at locations where dollar checks may not be.

Another option is the new prepaid traveler's check cards, reloadable cards that work much like debit cards but aren't linked to your checking account. The American Express Travelers Cheque Card, for example, requires a minimum deposit, sets a maximum balance, and has a one-time issuance fee of $14.95. You can withdraw money from an ATM (for a fee of $2.50 per transaction, not including bank fees), and the funds can be purchased in dollars, euros, or pounds. If you lose the card, your available funds will be refunded within 24 hours.

7 Travel Insurance

The cost of travel insurance varies widely, depending on the destination, the cost and length of your trip, your age and health, and the type of trip you're taking, but expect to pay between 5% and 8% of the vacation itself. You can get estimates from various providers through Insure-MyTrip.com. Enter your trip cost and dates, your age, and other information, for prices from more than a dozen companies.

U.K. citizens and their families who make more than one trip abroad per year may find an annual travel insurance policy works out cheaper. Check www.money supermarket.com, which compares prices across a wide range of providers for single- and multitrip policies.

Most big travel agents offer their own insurance and will probably try to sell you their package when you book a holiday. Think before you sign. Britain's Consumers' Association recommends that you insist on seeing the policy and reading the fine print before buying travel insurance. The Association of British Insurers (✆ 020/7600-3333; www.abi.org.uk) gives advice by phone and publishes Holiday Insurance, a free guide to policy provisions and prices. You might also shop around for better deals: Try Columbus Direct (✆ 0870/033-9988; www.columbusdirect.net).

TRIP-CANCELLATION INSURANCE
Trip-cancellation insurance will help retrieve your money if you have to back out of a trip or depart early, or if your travel supplier goes bankrupt. Trip cancellation traditionally covers such events as sickness, natural disasters, and State Department advisories. The latest news in trip-cancellation insurance is the availability of expanded hurricane coverage and the "any-reason" cancellation coverage—which costs more but covers cancellations made for any reason. You won't get back 100% of your prepaid costs, but you'll be refunded a substantial portion. TravelSafe (✆ 888/885-7233; www.travelsafe.com) offers both types of coverage. Expedia also offers any-reason cancellation coverage for its air-hotel packages.

For details, contact one of the following recommended insurers: Access America (✆ 866/807-3982; www.accessamerica.com); Travel Guard International (✆ 800/826-4919; www.travelguard.com); Travel Insured International (✆ 800/243-3174; www.travelinsured.com); and Travelex Insurance Services (✆ 888/457-4602; www.travelex-insurance.com). For travel overseas, most U.S. health plans (including Medicare and Medicaid) do not provide coverage, and the ones that do often require you to pay for services up front and reimburse you only after you return home.

As a safety net, you may want to buy travel medical insurance, particularly if you're traveling to a remote or high-risk area where emergency evacuation might be necessary. If you require additional medical insurance, try **MEDEX Assistance** (② 410/453-6300; www.medexassist.com) or **Travel Assistance International** (② 800/821-2828; www.travelassistance.com; for general information on services, call the company's **Worldwide Assistance Services, Inc.,** at ② 800/777-8710).

Canadians should check with their provincial health plan offices or call **Health Canada** (② 866/225-0709; www.hc-sc.gc.ca) to find out the extent of their coverage and what documentation and receipts they must take home if they are treated overseas.

LOST-LUGGAGE INSURANCE

On international flights (including U.S. portions of international trips), baggage coverage is limited to approximately $9.07 per pound, up to approximately $635 per checked bag. If you plan to check items more valuable than what's covered by the standard liability, see if your homeowner's policy covers your valuables, get baggage insurance as part of your comprehensive travel-insurance package, or buy Travel Guard's "BagTrak" product.

If your luggage is lost, immediately file a lost-luggage claim at the airport, detailing the luggage contents. Most airlines require that you report delayed, damaged, or lost baggage within 4 hours of arrival. The airlines are required to deliver luggage, once found, directly to your house or destination free of charge.

8 Health

STAYING HEALTHY

Staying healthy on a trip to Costa Rica is predominantly a matter of being a little cautious about what you eat and drink, and using common sense. Know your physical limits, and don't overexert yourself in the ocean, on hikes, or in athletic activities. Respect the tropical sun and protect yourself from it. Limit your exposure to the sun, especially during the first few days of your trip and, thereafter, from 11am to 2pm. Use sunscreen with a high protection factor, and apply it liberally. Remember that children need more protection than adults. I recommend buying and drinking bottled water or soft drinks, but the water in San José and in most of the heavily visited spots is safe to drink. The sections below deal with specific health concerns in Costa Rica.

If you suffer from a chronic illness, consult your doctor before leaving. For conditions such as epilepsy, diabetes, or heart problems, wear a **MedicAlert identification tag** (② 800/825-3785; www.medicalert.org), which will immediately alert doctors to your condition and give them access to your records through MedicAlert's 24-hour hot line.

Pack **prescription medications** in your carry-on luggage, and carry prescription medications in their original containers. Also bring along copies of your prescriptions in case you lose your pills or run out, and carry the generic name of prescription medicines in case a local pharmacist is unfamiliar with the brand name. And don't forget an extra pair of contact lenses or prescription glasses.

Contact the **International Association for Medical Assistance to Travelers (IAMAT)** (② 716/754-4883 or, in Canada, 416/652-0137; www.iamat.org) for tips on travel and health concerns in the countries you're visiting, and for lists of local, English-speaking doctors. The

United States **Centers for Disease Control and Prevention** (© 800/311-3435; www.cdc.gov) provides up-to-date information on health hazards by region or country and offers tips on food safety. **Travel Health Online** (www.tripprep.com), sponsored by a consortium of travel medicine practitioners, may also offer helpful advice on traveling abroad. You can find listings of reliable medical clinics overseas at the **International Society of Travel Medicine** (www.istm.org).

GENERAL AVAILABILITY OF HEALTH CARE

Any local consulate in Costa Rica can provide a list of area doctors who speak English. The local English-language newspaper, the *Tico Times,* is another good resource. I've listed the best hospitals in San José in "Fast Facts: San José," in chapter 5; these have the most modern facilities in the country. Most state-run hospitals and walk-in clinics around the country have emergency rooms that can treat most conditions, although I highly recommend the private hospitals in San José, if your condition is not life-threatening and can wait for treatment until you reach one of them.

COMMON AILMENTS

TROPICAL DISEASES   Your chance of contracting any serious tropical disease in Costa Rica is slim, especially if you stick to the beaches or traditional spots for visitors. However, malaria, dengue fever, and leptospirosis all exist in Costa Rica, so it's a good idea to know what they are.

Malaria is found in the lowlands on both coasts and in the northern zone. Although it's rarely found in urban areas, it's still a problem in remote wooded regions and along the Caribbean coast. Malaria prophylaxes are available, but several have side effects, and others are of questionable effectiveness. Consult your doctor regarding what is currently

considered the best preventive treatment for malaria. Be sure to ask whether a recommended drug will cause you to be hypersensitive to the sun; it would be a shame to come down here for the beaches and then have to hide under an umbrella the whole time. Because malaria-carrying mosquitoes usually come out at night, you should do as much as possible to avoid being bitten after dark. If you are in a malaria-prone area, wear long pants and long sleeves, use insect repellent, and either sleep under a mosquito net or burn mosquito coils (similar to incense, but with a pesticide).

Of greater concern is **dengue fever,** which has had periodic outbreaks in Latin America since the mid-1990s. Dengue fever is similar to malaria and is spread by an aggressive daytime mosquito. This mosquito seems to be most common in lowland urban areas, and Puntarenas, Liberia, and Limón have been the worst-hit cities in Costa Rica. Dengue is also known as "bone-break fever" because it is usually accompanied by severe body aches. The first infection with dengue fever will make you very sick but should cause no serious damage. However, a second infection with a different strain of the dengue virus can lead to internal hemorrhaging and could be life threatening.

Many people are convinced that taking B-complex vitamins daily will help prevent mosquitoes from biting you. I don't think the American Medical Association has endorsed this idea yet, but I've run across it in enough places to think that there might be something to it.

One final tropical fever that I think you should know about (because I got it myself) is **leptospirosis.** There are more than 200 strains of leptospires, which are animal-borne bacteria transmitted to humans via contact with drinking, swimming, or bathing water. This bacterial infection is easily treated with antibiotics;

however, it can quickly cause very high fever and chills, and should be treated promptly.

If you develop a high fever accompanied by severe body aches, nausea, diarrhea, or vomiting during or shortly after a visit to Costa Rica, consult a physician as soon as possible.

Costa Rica has been relatively free of the cholera epidemic that has spread through much of Latin America in recent years. This is largely due to an extensive public-awareness campaign that has promoted good hygiene and increased sanitation. Your chances of contracting cholera while you're here are very slight.

AMOEBAS, PARASITES, DIARRHEA & OTHER INTESTINAL WOES

Even though the water in San José and most popular destinations in Costa Rica is generally safe, and even though you've been careful to buy bottled water, order *frescos en leche* (fruit shakes made with milk rather than water), and drink your soft drink warm (without ice cubes—which are made from water, after all), you still might encounter some intestinal difficulties. Most of this is just due to tender northern stomachs coming into contact with slightly more aggressive Latin American intestinal flora. In extreme cases of diarrhea or intestinal discomfort, it's worth taking a stool sample to a lab for analysis. The results will usually pinpoint the amoebic or parasitic culprit, which can then be readily treated with available over-the-counter medicines.

Except in the most established and hygienic of restaurants, it's also advisable to avoid ceviche, a raw seafood salad, especially if it has any shellfish in it. It could be home to any number of bacterial critters.

TROPICAL SUN   Limit your exposure to the sun, especially during the first few days of your trip and, thereafter, from 11am to 2pm. Use a sunscreen with a high protection factor, and apply it liberally.

Remember that children need more protection than adults.

RIPTIDES   Many of Costa Rica's beaches have riptides: strong currents that can drag swimmers out to sea. A riptide occurs when water that has been dumped on the shore by strong waves forms a channel back out to open water. These channels have strong currents. If you get caught in a riptide, you can't escape the current by swimming toward shore; it's like trying to swim upstream in a river. To break free of the current, swim parallel to shore and use the energy of the waves to help you get back to the beach.

BEES, SNAKES & BUGS   Although Costa Rica has Africanized bees (the notorious "killer bees" of fact and fable) and several species of venomous snakes, your chances of being bitten are minimal, especially if you refrain from sticking your hands into hives or under rocks in the forest. If you know that you're allergic to bee stings, consult your doctor before traveling.

Snake sightings, much less snakebites, are very rare. Moreover, the majority of snakes in Costa Rica are nonpoisonous. If you do encounter a snake, stay calm, don't make any sudden movements, and do not try to handle it. As recommended above, avoid sticking your hands under rocks, branches, and fallen trees.

Scorpions, black widow spiders, tarantulas, bullet ants, and biting insects of many types can all be found in Costa Rica. In general, they are not nearly the danger or nuisance most visitors fear. Watch where you stick your hands; in addition, you might want to shake out your clothes and shoes before putting them on to avoid any unpleasant and painful surprises.

WHAT TO DO IF YOU GET SICK AWAY FROM HOME

For travel abroad, you may have to pay all medical costs up front and be reimbursed later. Medicare and Medicaid do not provide coverage for medical costs outside the U.S. Before leaving home, find out what medical services your health insurance covers. To protect yourself, consider buying medical travel insurance (see "Medical Insurance," under "Travel Insurance," above).

Very few health insurance plans pay for medical evacuation back to the U.S. (which can cost $10,000 and up). A number of companies offer medical evacuation services anywhere in the world. If you're ever hospitalized more than 150 miles from home, **MedjetAssist** (© **800/527-7478;** www.medjetassistance.com) will pick you up and fly you to the hospital of your choice virtually anywhere in the world in a medically equipped and staffed aircraft 24 hours day, 7 days a week. Annual memberships are $225 individual, $350 family; you can also purchase short-term memberships.

U.K. nationals will need a **European Health Insurance Card (EHIC)** to receive free or reduced-costs health benefits during a visit to a European Economic Area (EEA) country (European Union countries plus Iceland, Liechtenstein and Norway) or Switzerland. The European Health Insurance Card replaces the E111 form, which is no longer valid. For advice, ask at your local post office or see www.dh.gov.uk/travellers.

9 Safety

Although most of Costa Rica is safe, petty crime and robberies committed against tourists are endemic. San José is known for its pickpockets, so never carry a wallet in your back pocket. A woman should keep a tight grip on her purse (keep it tucked under your arm). Thieves also target gold chains, cameras and video cameras, prominent jewelry, and nice sunglasses. Be sure not to leave valuables unsecured in your hotel room. Don't park a car on the street in Costa Rica, especially in San José; plenty of public parking lots are around the city.

Rental cars generally stick out and are easily spotted by thieves. Don't leave anything of value in a car parked on the street, not even for a moment. Be wary of solicitous strangers who stop to help you change a tire or take you to a service station. Although most are truly good Samaritans, there have been reports of thieves preying on roadside breakdowns. Public intercity buses are also frequent targets of stealthy thieves. Never check your bags into the hold of a bus. If this can't be avoided, keep your eye on what leaves the hold. If you put your bags in an overhead rack, be sure you can see the bags at all times. Try not to fall asleep.

10 Specialized Travel Resources

TRAVELERS WITH DISABILITIES
Most disabilities shouldn't stop anyone from traveling. There are more options and resources out there than ever before. Still, although Costa Rica does have a law mandating Equality of Opportunities for People with Disabilities, and facilities are beginning to be adapted, in general, there are relatively few handicapped-accessible buildings. In San José, sidewalks are crowded and uneven. Few hotels offer wheelchair-accessible accommodations, and there are no public buses thus equipped. In short, it can be difficult for a person with disabilities to get around San José and Costa Rica.

However, one local agency specializes in tours for travelers with disabilities and restricted ability. **Vaya Con Silla de Ruedas** (©/fax **454-2810;** www.gowith wheelchairs.com) has a ramp- and elevator-equipped van and knowledgeable, bilingual guides. It charges very reasonable prices and can provide anything from simple airport transfers to complete multiday tours.

Organizations that offer a vast range of resources and assistance to travelers with disabilities include **MossRehab** (© 800/ CALL-MOSS;   www.mossresourcenet. org); the **American Foundation for the Blind (AFB)** (© 800/232-5463; www. afb.org); and **SATH (Society for Accessible Travel & Hospitality)** (© 212/447-7284; www.sath.org). **AirAmbulance Card.com** is partnered with SATH and allows you to preselect top-notch hospitals in case of emergency.

Access-Able Travel Source (© 303/ 232-2979; www.access-able.com) has a comprehensive database of travel agents around the world with experience in accessible travel; destination-specific access information; and links to such resources as service animals, equipment rentals, and access guides.

Many travel agencies offer customized tours and itineraries for travelers with disabilities. Among them are **Flying Wheels Travel** (© 507/451-5005; www.flyingwheelstravel.com) and **Accessible Journeys** (© 800/846-4537 or 610/ 521-0339; www.disabilitytravel.com).

Flying with Disability (www.flying-with-disability.org) is a comprehensive information source on airplane travel. **Avis Rent a Car** (© 888/879-4273) has an "Avis Access" program that offers services for customers with special travel needs. These include specially outfitted vehicles with swivel seats, spinner knobs, and hand controls; mobility scooter rentals; and accessible bus service. Be sure to reserve well in advance.

Also check out the quarterly magazine *Emerging Horizons* (www.emerging horizons.com), available by subscription ($16.95 year in the U.S.; $21.95 outside U.S.).

The "Accessible Travel" link at **Mobility-Advisor.com** (www.mobility-advisor. com) offers a variety of travel resources to persons with disabilities.

British travelers should contact **Holiday Care** (© 0845-124-9971 in U.K. only; www.holidaycare.org.uk) to access a wide range of travel information and resources for the elderly and people with disabilities.

GAY & LESBIAN TRAVELERS

Costa Rica is a Catholic, conservative, macho country where public displays of same-sex affection are rare and considered somewhat shocking. Public figures, politicians, and religious leaders regularly denounce homosexuality. However, gay and lesbian tourism to Costa Rica is quite robust, and gay and lesbian travelers are generally treated with respect and should not experience any harassment.

For a general overview of the current situation, news of any special events or meetings, and up-to-date information, the website **www.gaycostarica.com** is your best bet, especially for gay men, and to a much lesser extent for lesbian women.

The International Gay and Lesbian Travel Association (IGLTA) (© 800/ 448-8550 or 954/776-2626; www.iglta. org) is the trade association for the gay and lesbian travel industry, and offers an online directory of gay- and lesbian-friendly travel businesses and tour operators.

Many agencies offer tours and travel itineraries specifically for gay and lesbian travelers. **Above and Beyond Tours** (© 800/397-2681; www.abovebeyond tours.com) are gay Australia tour specialists. San Francisco–based **Now, Voyager** (© 800/255-6951; www.nowvoyager. com) offers worldwide trips and cruises, and **Olivia** (© 800/631-6277; www. olivia.com) offers lesbian cruises and resort vacations.

Gay.com Travel (© 800/929-2268 or 415/644-8044; www.gay.com/travel or www.outandabout.com) is an excellent online successor to the popular *Out & About* print magazine. It provides regularly updated information about gay-owned, gay-oriented, and gay-friendly lodging, dining, sightseeing, nightlife, and shopping establishments in every important destination worldwide. British travelers should click on the "Travel" link at **www.uk.gay.com** for advice and gay-friendly trip ideas.

The Canadian website **GayTraveler** (**www.gaytraveler.ca**) offers ideas and advice for gay travel all over the world.

The following travel guides are available at many bookstores, or you can order them from any online bookseller: *Spartacus International Gay Guide, 35th Edition* (Bruno Gmünder Verlag; www.spartacusworld.com/gayguide); *Odysseus: The International Gay Travel Planner, 17th Edition* (www.odyusa.com); and the *Damron* guides (www.damron.com), with separate, annual books for gay men and lesbians.

SENIOR TRAVEL

Be sure to mention that you're a senior when you make your travel reservations. Although all major U.S. airlines except America West have cancelled their senior discount and coupon book programs, and it's not common policy in Costa Rica to offer senior discounts, don't be shy about asking for one anyway. You never know. Always carry some kind of identification, such as a driver's license, that shows your date of birth, especially if you've kept your youthful glow.

Members of **AARP** (formerly known as the American Association of Retired Persons), 601 E St. NW, Washington, DC 20049 (✆ **888/687-2277**; www.aarp.org), get discounts on hotels, airfares, and car rentals. AARP offers members a wide range of benefits, including *AARP: The Magazine* and a monthly newsletter. Anyone over 50 can join.

Many reliable agencies and organizations target the 50-plus market. **Elderhostel** (✆ **800/454-5768**; www.elderhostel.org) arranges worldwide study programs for those ages 55 and older. **ElderTreks** (✆ **800/741-7956** or 416/558-5000 outside North America; www.eldertreks.com) offers small-group tours to off-the-beaten-path or adventure-travel locations, restricted to travelers 50 and older.

Publications offering travel resources and discounts for seniors include the quarterly magazine *Travel 50 & Beyond* (www.travel50andbeyond.com) and the bestselling paperback *Unbelievably Good Deals and Great Adventures That You Absolutely Can't Get Unless You're Over 50* (McGraw-Hill), by Joan Rattner Heilman.

FAMILY TRAVEL

To locate accommodations, restaurants, and attractions that are particularly kid-friendly, refer to the "Kids" icon throughout this guide.

Hotels in Costa Rica often give discounts for children under 12, and children under 3 or 4 are usually allowed to stay for free. Discounts for children and the cutoff ages vary according to the hotel, but in general, don't assume that your kids can stay in your room for free.

Many hotels, villas, and cabinas come equipped with kitchenettes or full kitchen facilities. These can be a real money-saver for those traveling with children, and I've listed many of these accommodations in the destination chapters in this book.

Hotels offering regular, dependable babysitting service are few and far between. If you will need babysitting, make sure that your hotel offers it, and be sure to ask whether the babysitters are bilingual. In many cases they are not. This is usually not a problem with infants and toddlers, but it can cause problems with older children.

Recommended family travel websites include **Family Travel Forum** (www.familytravelforum.com), a comprehensive site with customized trip planning; **Family Travel Network** (www.familytravelnetwork.com), an online magazine providing travel tips; and **TravelWith YourKids.com** (www.travelwithyourkids.com), a site written by parents for parents offering comprehensive advice for long-distance and international travel with children.

WOMEN TRAVELERS

For lack of better phrasing, Costa Rica is a typically "macho" Latin American nation. Single women can expect a nearly constant stream of catcalls, hisses, whistles, and car horns, especially in San José. Women should be careful walking alone at night throughout the country.

Check out the award-winning website **Journeywoman** (www.journeywoman.com), a "real life" women's travel-information network where you can sign up for a free e-mail newsletter and get advice on everything from etiquette and dress to safety. The travel guide *Safety and Security for Women Who Travel* by Sheila Swan and Peter Laufer (Travelers' Tales Guides), offering common-sense tips on safe travel, was updated in 2004.

11 Sustainable Tourism/Ecotourism

Costa Rica is one of the planet's prime ecotourism destinations. Many of the isolated nature lodges and tour operators around the country are pioneers and dedicated professionals in the ecotourism and sustainable tourism field. Many other hotels, lodges, and tour operators are simply "green-washing," using the terms "eco" and "sustainable" in their promo materials, but doing little real good in their daily operations. The government-run tourism institute (ICT) provides a sustainability rating of a host of hotels, called the Certificate of Sustainable Tourism Program (CST). You can look up hotel ratings at the website **www.turismosostenible.co.cr**; however, the list is far from comprehensive, and die-hard ecologists find some of these listings somewhat suspect. Still, this list and rating system is a good start, and is evolving constantly.

Each time you take a flight or drive a car, CO_2 is released into the atmosphere. You can help neutralize this danger to our planet through "carbon offsetting"—paying someone to reduce your CO_2 emissions by the same amount you've added. In the U.S., you can purchase carbon offsets from companies such as **Carbonfund.org**

(www.carbonfund.org) and **TerraPass** (www.terrapass.org). In the U.K., check with **Climate Care** (www.climatecare.org).

Although one could argue that any vacation that includes an airplane flight can't be truly "green," you can go on holiday and still contribute positively to the environment. You can offset carbon emissions from your flight in other ways. Choose forward-looking companies that embrace responsible development practices, helping preserve destinations for the future by working alongside local people. An increasing number of sustainable tourism initiatives can help you plan a family trip and leave as small a "footprint" as possible on the places you visit.

Responsible Travel (www.responsibletravel.com) contains a great source of sustainable travel ideas run by a spokesperson for responsible tourism in the travel industry. **Sustainable Travel International** (www.sustainabletravelinternational.org) promotes responsible tourism practices and issues an annual Green Gear & Gift Guide.

You can find eco-friendly travel tips, statistics, and touring companies and associations—listed by destination under

Frommers.com: The Complete Travel Resource

It should go without saying, but we highly recommend **Frommers.com**, voted Best Travel Site by *PC Magazine*. We think you'll find our expert advice and tips; independent reviews of hotels, restaurants, attractions, and preferred shopping and nightlife venues; vacation giveaways; and an online booking tool indispensable before, during, and after your travels. We publish the complete contents of over 128 travel guides in our **Destinations** section covering nearly 3,800 places worldwide to help you plan your trip. Each weekday, we publish original articles reporting on **Deals and News** via our free **Frommers.com Newsletter** to help you save time and money and travel smarter. We're betting you'll find our new **Events** listings (http://events.frommers.com) an invaluable resource; it's an up-to-the-minute roster of what's happening in cities everywhere—including concerts, festivals, lectures and more. We've also added weekly **podcasts, interactive maps,** and hundreds of new images across the site. Check out our **Travel Talk** area featuring **Message Boards** where you can join in conversations with thousands of fellow Frommer's travelers and post your trip report once you return.

"Travel Choice"—at the TIES website, www.ecotourism.org. Also check out **Conservation International** (www.conservation.org)—which, with *National Geographic Traveler,* annually presents **World Legacy Awards** (www.wlaward.org) to those travel tour operators, businesses, organizations, and places that have made a significant contribution to sustainable tourism. **Ecotravel.com** is part online magazine and part ecodirectory that lets you search for touring companies in several categories (water-based, land-based, spiritually oriented, and so on).

In the U.K., **Tourism Concern** (www.tourismconcern.org.uk) works to reduce social and environmental problems connected to tourism and find ways of improving tourism so that local benefits are increased.

The **Association of British Travel Agents** (ABTA; www.abtamembers.org) acts as a focal point for the U.K. travel industry and is one of the leading groups spearheading sustainable tourism.

The **Association of Independent Tour Operators** (AITO; www.aito.co.uk) is a group of interesting specialist operators leading the field in making holidays sustainable.

For information about the ethics of swimming with dolphins and other outdoor activities, visit the **Whale and Dolphin Conservation Society** (www.wdcs.org) and **Tread Lightly** (www.treadlightly.org).

12 Staying Connected

TELEPHONES

Costa Rica has an excellent phone system, with a dial tone similar to that heard in the United States.

A phone call within Costa Rica costs around 10 colones (2¢/1p) per minute.

Pay phones take either a calling card or 5-, 10-, or 20-colón coins. Calling cards are much more practical, and coin-operated phones are getting harder to find. You can purchase calling cards in a host of gift shops and pharmacies. However, there are several competing calling-card companies, and certain cards work only with certain phones. **CHIP** calling cards work with a computer chip and just slide into specific phones, although these phones aren't widely available. Better bets are the **197** and **199** calling cards, which are sold in varying denominations. These have a scratch-off PIN and can be used from any phone in the country. Generally, the 197 cards are sold in smaller denominations and are used for local calling, while the 199 cards are deemed international and are easier to find in larger denominations. Either card can be used to make any call, however, provided that the card can cover the costs. Another perk of the 199 cards is the fact that you can get the instructions in English. For local calls, it is often easiest to call from your hotel, although you will likely be charged around 150 to 300 colones (30¢–60¢/15p–30p) per call.

To call Costa Rica:

1. Dial the international access code: 011 from the U.S.; 00 from the U.K., Ireland, or New Zealand; or 0011 from Australia.
2. Dial the country code 506.
3. Dial the number.

To make international calls: To make international calls from Costa Rica, first dial 00 and then the country code (U.S. or Canada 1, U.K. 44, Ireland 353, Australia 61, New Zealand 64). Next you dial the area code and number. For example, if you wanted to call the British Embassy in Washington, D.C., you would dial 00-1-202-588-7800.

For directory assistance: Dial 113 if you're looking for a number inside Costa Rica, and dial 124 for numbers to all other countries.

For operator assistance: If you need operator assistance in making a call, dial 116 if you're trying to make an international call and 0 if you want to call a number in Costa Rica.

Toll-free numbers: Numbers beginning with 0800 or 800 within Costa Rica are toll-free, but calling a 1-800 number in the States from Costa Rica is not toll-free. In fact, it costs the same as an overseas call.

CELLPHONES

The three letters that define much of the world's wireless capabilities are **GSM (Global System for Mobile Communications),** a big, seamless network that makes for easy cross-border cellphone use throughout Europe and dozens of other countries worldwide. In the U.S., T-Mobile, AT&T Wireless, and Cingular use this quasi-universal system; in Canada, Microcell and some Rogers customers are GSM, and all Europeans and most Australians use GSM. GSM phones function with a removable plastic SIM card, encoded with your phone number and account information. If your cellphone is on a GSM system, and you have a world-capable multiband phone such as many Sony Ericsson, Motorola, or Samsung models, you can make and receive calls across civilized areas around much of the globe. Just call your wireless operator and ask for "international roaming" to be activated on your account. Unfortunately, per-minute charges can be high—usually $1 to $1.50 (50p–75p) in Western Europe and up to $5 (£2.50) in places like Russia, Indonesia and Latin America.

Unfortunately, those with unlocked tri-band GSM phones cannot simply buy a local SIM card in Costa Rica.

For many, **renting** a phone is a good idea. However, renting a phone in Costa Rica is problematic. Due to a state monopoly on telecommunications, the entire cellphone rental industry exists in an area of legal limbo. Several local firms are renting cellphones to visiting tourists and businessmen, but this may be illegal, and the Costa Rican telecommunications institute could theoretically crack down on them at any time. However, to date, they've been able to go about their business, albeit discreetly. None of the rental companies has a booth or office at the airport, so you'll have to contact them either beforehand or from your hotel. Most will deliver the phone to your hotel. **Cell Service** (© **296-5553;** www.cellservicecr.com) and **GSM Rent A Cell** (© **231-5410;** www.gsmrentacell. com) both rent cellphones. Rates run around $5 (£2.50) per day or $35 (£18) per week for the rental, with charges of 70¢ to $1.50 (35p–75p) per minute for local calls and $2 to $3 (£1–£1.50) per minute for international calls.

VOICE-OVER INTERNET PROTOCOL (VOIP)

If you have Web access while traveling, you might consider a broadband-based telephone service (in technical terms, **Voice over Internet protocol,** or **VoIP**) such as Skype (www.skype.com) or Vonage (www.vonage.com), which allows you to make free or very inexpensive international calls over the Internet. If you have an account with either of these services, you can make calls from your own laptop, or from most cybercafes.

INTERNET/E-MAIL
WITHOUT YOUR OWN COMPUTER

To find cybercafes in your destination check **www.cybercaptive.com** and **www.cybercafe.com**. Cybercafes can be found all over Costa Rica, especially in the more popular tourist destinations.

Most major airports have **Internet kiosks** that provide basic Web access for a per-minute fee that's usually higher than cybercafe prices. Check out copy shops such as **Kinko's** (FedEx Kinko's), which offers computer stations with fully loaded software (as well as Wi-Fi).

WITH YOUR OWN COMPUTER

More and more hotels, resorts, airports, cafes, and retailers are going **Wi-Fi** (wireless fidelity), becoming "hotspots" that offer free high-speed Wi-Fi access or charge a small fee for usage. Most laptops sold today have built-in wireless capability. To find public Wi-Fi hotspots at your destination, go to **www.jiwire.com**; its Hotspot Finder holds the world's largest directory of public wireless hotspots.

For dial-up access, most business-class hotels throughout the world offer dataports for laptop modems, and a few thousand hotels in Europe now offer free high-speed Internet access.

Wherever you go, bring a **connection kit** of the right power and phone adapters, a spare phone cord, and a spare Ethernet network cable—or find out whether your hotel supplies them to guests.

Costa Rica uses standard U.S.-style two- and three-prong electric outlets with 110-volt AC current, and standard U.S.-style phone jacks. Wherever you go, bring a connection kit with power and phone adapters, a spare phone cord, and a spare Ethernet network cable—or find out whether your hotel supplies them to guests.

Package tours are simply a way to buy the airfare, accommodations, and other elements of your trip (such as car rentals, airport transfers, and sometimes even activities) at the same time and often at discounted prices.

One good source of package deals is the airlines themselves. Most major airlines

offer air/land packages, including **American Airlines Vacations** (© 800/321-2121; www.aavacations.com), **Delta Vacations** (© 800/654-6559; www.deltavacations. com), **Continental Airlines Vacations** (© 800/301-3800; www.covacations.com), and **United Vacations** (© 888/854-3899; www.unitedvacations.com). Several big

---

Tips **Ask Before You Go**

Before you invest in a package deal or an escorted tour:

- Always ask about the **cancellation policy.** Can you get your money back? Is there a deposit required?
- Ask about the **accommodations choices and prices** for each. Then look up the hotels' reviews in a Frommer's guide and check their rates online for your specific dates of travel. Also find out what types of rooms are offered.
- Request a complete **schedule.** (Escorted tours only)
- Ask about the **size** and demographics of the group. (Escorted tours only)
- Discuss what is included in the **price** (transportation, meals, tips, airport transfers, and the like). (Escorted tours only)
- Finally, look for **hidden expenses.** Ask whether airport departure fees and taxes, for example, are included in the total cost—they rarely are.

---

online travel agencies—Expedia, Travelocity, Orbitz, Site59, and Lastminute.com —also do a brisk business in packages.

Travel packages are also listed in the travel section of your local Sunday newspaper. Or check ads in national travel magazines such as *Arthur Frommer's Budget Travel Magazine, Travel + Leisure, National Geographic Traveler,* and *Condé Nast Traveler.*

14 Escorted General-Interest Tours

Escorted tours are structured group tours with a group leader. The price usually includes everything from airfare to hotels, meals, tours, admission costs, and local transportation.

Despite the fact that escorted tours require big deposits and predetermine hotels, restaurants, and itineraries, many people derive security and peace of mind from the structure they offer. Escorted tours—whether they're navigated by bus, motor coach, train, or boat—let travelers sit back and enjoy the trip without having to drive or worry about details. They take

you to the maximum number of sights in the minimum amount of time with the least amount of hassle. They're particularly convenient for people with limited mobility, and they can be a great way to make new friends.

On the downside, you'll have little opportunity for serendipitous interactions with locals. The tours can be jam-packed with activities, leaving little room for individual sightseeing, whim, or adventure—plus they often focus on the heavily touristed sites, so you miss out on many a lesser-known gem.

15 Getting Around Costa Rica

BY PLANE
Flying is one of the best ways to get around Costa Rica. Because the country is quite small, flights are short and not too expensive. The domestic airlines of Costa Rica are Sansa and Nature Air.

Sansa (© **290-4100**; www.flysansa. com) operates from a separate terminal at San José's **Juan Santamaría International Airport,** and offers a free shuttle bus from its downtown San José office to the airport.

Nature Air (© 800/235-9272 in the U.S. and Canada or 299-6000; www. natureair.com) operates from **Tobías Bolaños International Airport** in Pavas, 6.4km (4 miles) from San José. The ride from downtown to Pavas takes about 10 minutes, and a metered taxi fare should cost $7 to $10 (£3.50–£5). The ride from the airport to downtown is a different story: Most taxis refuse to use their meter, and the standard fee is set at double the metered rate, around $10 to $18 (£5–£9).

In the high season (late Nov–late Apr), be sure to book reservations well in advance. Both companies have online booking systems via their websites.

BY BUS

This is by far the most economical way to get around Costa Rica. Buses are inexpensive and relatively well maintained, and they go nearly everywhere. There are two types: **Local buses** are the cheapest and slowest; they stop frequently and are generally a bit dilapidated. **Express buses** run between San José and most beach towns and major cities; these tend to be newer units and more comfortable, although very few are so new or modern as to have bathroom facilities, and they sometimes operate only on weekends and holidays.

Two companies run regular, fixed-schedule departures in passenger vans and small buses to most of the major tourist destinations in the country. **Gray Line** (© 220-2126; www.graylinecostarica. com) is run by Fantasy Tours, and has about 10 departures leaving San José each morning and heading or connecting to Jacó, Manuel Antonio, Liberia, Playa Hermosa, La Fortuna, Tamarindo, and playas Conchal and Flamingo. There are return trips to San José every day from these destinations and a variety of interconnecting routes. A similar service, **Interbus** (© 283-5573; www.interbus online.com) has a slightly more extensive route map and more connections. Fares run between $19 and $39 (£9.50–£20) depending upon the destination. *Beware:* Both of these companies offer pickup and drop-off at a wide range of hotels. This means that if you are the first picked up or last dropped off, you might have to sit through a long period of subsequent stops before finally hitting the road or reaching your destination. Moreover, I've heard some horror stories about both lines, concerning missed or severely delayed connections and rude drivers. For details on how to get to various destinations from San José, see the "Getting There" sections in the chapters that follow.

BY CAR

Renting a car in Costa Rica is no idle proposition. The roads are riddled with potholes, most rural intersections are unmarked, and, for some reason, sitting behind the wheel of a car seems to turn peaceful Ticos into homicidal maniacs. But unless you want to see the country from the window of a bus (inconvenient) or pay exorbitant amounts for private transfers (expensive), renting a car is still your best option for independent exploring. Four-wheel-drives are particularly useful in the rainy season (May to mid-Nov) and for navigating the bumpy, poorly paved roads year-round.

Be forewarned, however: Although rental cars no longer bear special license plates, they are still readily identifiable to thieves and are frequently targeted. (Nothing is ever safe in a car in Costa Rica, although parking in guarded parking lots helps.) Transit police also seem to target tourists. Never pay money directly to a police officer who stops you for any traffic violation.

Before driving off with a rental car, be sure that you inspect the exterior and point out to the rental-company representative every tiny scratch, dent, tear, or any other damage. It's a common practice with many Costa Rican car-rental companies to claim that you owe payment for minor dings and dents that the company finds when you return the car. Also, if you get into an accident, be sure that the rental company doesn't try to bill you for a higher amount than the deductible on your rental contract.

These caveats aren't meant to scare you off from driving in Costa Rica. Thousands of tourists rent cars here every year, and the large majority of them encounter no problems. Just keep your wits about you.

Note: It's sometimes cheaper to reserve a car in your home country rather than book when you arrive in Costa Rica. If you know you'll be renting a car, it's always wise to reserve it well in advance for the high season because the rental fleet still can't match demand.

Among the agencies operating in Costa Rica are: **Alamo** (© 800/462-5266 in the U.S. or 242-7733; www.alamocostarica. com), **Avis** (© 800/331-1084 in the U.S. or 293-2222 in Costa Rica; www.avis. com), **Budget** (© 800/527-0700 in the U.S. or 255-4750; www.budget.co.cr), **Hertz** (© 800/654-3001 in the U.S. or 221-1818; www.hertz.com), **National** (© 800/227-7368 in the U.S. or 440-0085; www.natcar.com), **Payless** (© 800/582-7432 in the U.S. or 443-5286; www.paylesscr.com), and **Thrifty** (© 800/847-4389 or 258-5868; www.thrifty.com). For more listings of Costa Rican car-rental agencies, see "Getting Around" in chapter 5, as well as the "Getting Around" sections of other major tourist destinations.

GASOLINE   Gasoline is sold as "regular" and "super." Both are unleaded; super is just higher octane. Diesel is available at almost every gas station as well. Most rental cars run on super, but always ask your rental agent what type of gas your car takes. When going off to remote places, try to leave with a full tank of gas because gas stations can be hard to find.

If you need to gas up in a small town, you can sometimes get gasoline from enterprising families who sell it by the liter from their houses. Look for hand-lettered signs that say GASOLINA. At press time a liter of super cost 568 colones, or roughly $4.17 per gallon.

ROAD CONDITIONS   The awful road conditions in San José and throughout the country are legendary, and deservedly so. Despite constant promises to fix the problem, the hot sun, hard rain, and rampant corruption outpace any progress made toward improving the condition. Even paved roads are often badly potholed, so stay alert. Road conditions get especially tricky during the rainy season, when heavy rains and runoff can destroy a stretch of pavement in the blink of an eye.

Route numbers are rarely used on road signs in Costa Rica, although there are frequent signs listing the number of kilometers to various towns or cities. Your best bets for on-road directions are billboards and advertisements for hotels. It's always a good idea to know the names of a few hotels at your destination, just in case your specific hotel hasn't put up any billboards or signs.

RENTER'S INSURANCE   Even if you hold **your own car-insurance policy** at home, coverage doesn't always extend abroad. Be sure to find out whether you'll be covered in Costa Rica, whether your policy extends to all persons who will be driving the rental car, how much liability is covered in case an outside party is injured in an accident, and whether the *type* of vehicle you are renting is included under your contract.

Most **major credit cards** provide some degree of coverage as well—provided that they were used to pay for the rental. Again, terms vary widely, so be sure to call your credit card company directly before you rent. Usually, if you are **uninsured** or are **driving abroad,** your credit card provides primary coverage as long as you decline the rental agency's insurance. This means that the credit card will cover damage or theft of a rental car for the full cost of the vehicle. If you already have insurance, your credit card will provide secondary coverage, which basically covers your deductible. *Credit cards will not cover liability* or the cost of injury to an outside party and/or damage to an outside party's vehicle.

If you do not hold an insurance policy, you might seriously want to consider purchasing additional liability insurance from your rental company. Be sure to check the terms, however. Some rental agencies cover liability only if the renter is not at fault; even then, the rental company's obligation varies by location.

The basic insurance coverage offered by most car-rental companies, known as **Loss/Damage Waiver (LDW)** or **Collision Damage Waiver (CDW),** can cost as much as $20 (£10) per day. It usually covers the full value of the vehicle, with no deductible if an outside party causes an accident or other damage to the rental car. Liability coverage varies according to the company policy. If you are at fault in an accident, however, you will be covered for the full replacement value of the car, but not for liability. Most rental companies require a police report to process claims, but your private insurer will not be notified of the accident.

MAPS   Car-rental agencies and the ICT information centers (see "Visitor Information," earlier in this chapter) at the airport and in downtown San José have adequate road maps, although the map included with this book is generally better. Other sources in San José for detailed maps include **Seventh Street Books,** Calle 7, between avenidas Central and 1 (✆ 256-8251); **Librería Lehmann,** Avenida Central, between calles 1 and 3 (✆ 223-1212); and **Librería Universal,** Avenida Central, between calles Central and 1 (✆ 222-2222).

DRIVING RULES   A current foreign driver's license is valid for the first 3 months you are in Costa Rica. Seat belts are required for the driver and front-seat passengers. Motorcyclists must wear helmets. Highway police use radar, so keep to the speed limit (usually 60–90kmph/37–56 mph) if you don't want to get pulled over. Sometimes it seems that the police target rental cars. Never give the police any money. Speeding tickets can be charged to your credit card for up to a year after you leave the country if they are not paid before departure.

To reduce congestion and fuel consumption, a rotating ban on rush-hour traffic takes place in the central core of San José Monday through Friday from 7 to 8:30am and from 4 to 5:30pm. The ban affects cars with licenses ending in the digits 1 or 2 on Monday; 3 or 4 on Tuesday; 5 or 6 on Wednesday; 7 or 8 on Thursday; and 9 or 0 on Friday. If you are caught driving a car with the banned license plate during these hours on a specified day, you will be ticketed.

BREAKDOWNS   Be warned that emergency services, both vehicular and medical, are extremely limited outside San José, and their availability is directly related to the remoteness of your location at the time of breakdown. You'll find service stations spread over the entire length of the Interamerican Highway, and most of these have tow trucks and mechanics. The major towns of Puntarenas, Liberia, Quepos, San Isidro, Palmar, and Golfito all have hospitals, and most other moderately sized cities and tourist destinations have some sort of clinic or health-services provider.

If you're involved in an accident, you should contact the **National Insurance Institute (INS)** at ✆ **800/800-8000.** You should probably also call the **Transit Police** (✆ **222-9330** or 222-9245); if they have a unit close by, they'll send one. An official transit police report will greatly facilitate any insurance claim. If you can't get help from any of these, try to get written statements from any witnesses. Finally, you can also call © **911,** and they should be able to redirect your call to the appropriate agency.

If the police do show up, you've got a 50/50 chance of finding them helpful or downright antagonistic. Many officers are unsympathetic to the problems of what they perceive to be rich tourists running around in fancy cars with lots of expensive toys and trinkets. Success and happy endings run about equal with horror stories.

If you don't speak Spanish, expect added difficulty in any emergency or stressful situation. Don't expect that rural (or urban) police officers, hospital personnel, service-station personnel, or mechanics will speak English.

If your car breaks down and you're unable to get well off the road, check your trunk for reflecting triangles. If you find some, place them as a warning for approaching traffic, arranged in a wedge that starts at the shoulder about 30m (98 ft.) back and nudges gradually toward your car. If your car has no triangles, try to create a similar warning marker using a pile of leaves or branches. Finally, although not endemic, there have been reports of folks being robbed by seemingly friendly Ticos who stop to give assistance. To add insult to injury, there

have even been reports of organized gangs who puncture tires of rental cars at rest stops or busy intersections, only to follow them, offer assistance, and make off with belongings and valuables.

BY FERRY

Three different ferries operate across the Gulf of Nicoya. Two are car ferries: one from Puntarenas to Playa Naranjo, and one from Puntarenas to Paquera. The third is a passenger ferry that runs between Puntarenas and Paquera. There's also a once-daily passenger ferry between the southern cities of Golfito and Puerto Jiménez.

BY THUMB

Although buses serve most towns in Costa Rica, service can be infrequent in the remote regions, so local people often hitchhike to get to their destinations sooner. If you're driving a car, people will frequently ask you for a ride. In rural areas a hitchhiker carrying a machete is not necessarily a great danger, but use your judgment. Hitchhiking is not recommended on major roadways or in urban areas. In rural areas it's usually pretty safe. (However, women should be extremely cautious about hitchhiking anywhere in Costa Rica.) If you choose to hitchhike, keep in mind that if a bus doesn't go to your destination, there probably aren't too many cars going there, either. Good luck.

16 Tips on Accommodations

When the Costa Rican tourist boom began in the late 1980s, hotels popped up like mushrooms after a heavy rain. By the 1990s the country's first true megaresorts opened, more followed, and still more are under construction or in the planning phase. Except during the few busiest weeks of the year, there's a relative glut of rooms in Costa Rica. That said, most hotels are small- to midsize, and the best ones fill up fast most of the year. You'll generally have to reserve well in advance

if you want to land a room at any of the hotels on my "Best of" lists in chapter 1. Still, in broader terms, the glut of rooms is good news for travelers and bargain hunters. Less popular hotels that want to survive are being forced to reduce their rates and provide better service.

Throughout this book, I separate hotel listings into several broad categories: **Very Expensive,** $200 (£100) and up; **Expensive,** $126 to $200 (£63–£100); **Moderate,** $60 to $125 (£30–£63); and **Inexpensive,** under $60 (£30) for a double. *Rates given in this book do not include the 16.3% room taxes, unless otherwise specified.* These taxes will add considerably to the cost of your room. Also note that with rooms at the beach that cost under $25, you usually don't get hot water.

HOTEL OPTIONS

Upscale travelers are finally starting to get their due in Costa Rica. It has taken time, but spurred on by the example and standards of several international chains, service and amenities have been improving across the board, particularly in the upscale market. While the Four Seasons remains the only large resort guaranteed to please the exceedingly demanding luxury traveler, there are several wonderful high-end boutique hotels, both in San José and the Central Valley and around the country that are geared toward this niche.

The country's strong suit is its **moderately priced hotels.** In the $60 to $125 (£30–£63) price range, you'll find comfortable and sometimes outstanding accommodations almost anywhere in the country. However, room size and quality vary quite a bit within this price range, so don't expect the kind of uniformity that you may find at home.

If you're even more budget- or bohemian-minded, you can find quite a few good deals for less than $50 (£25) double. *But beware:* Budget-oriented lodgings often feature shared bathrooms and either cold-water showers or showers heated by electrical heat-coil units mounted at the showerhead, affectionately known as "suicide showers." If your hotel has one, do not adjust it while the water is running. Unless specifically noted, all rooms listed in this guide have a private bathroom.

Note: Air-conditioning is not necessarily a given in many midrange hotels and even some upscale joints. In general, this is not a problem. Cooler nights and a well-placed ceiling fan are often more

than enough to keep things pleasant, unless I mention otherwise in the hotel reviews.

Bed-and-breakfasts are now also abundant. Although the majority are in the San José area, you'll also find B&Bs (often gringo-owned and -operated) throughout the country. Another welcome hotel trend in the San José area is the renovation and conversion of old homes into **small hotels.** Most are in the Barrio Amón district of downtown San José, which means that you'll sometimes have to put up with noise and exhaust fumes, but these establishments have more character than any other hotels in the country. You'll find similar hotels in the Paseo Colón and Los Yoses districts.

Costa Rica is riding the ecotourism wave, and you'll find small nature-oriented **ecolodges** throughout the country. These lodges offer opportunities to see wildlife (including sloths, monkeys, and hundreds of species of birds) and learn about tropical forests. They range from spartan facilities catering primarily to scientific researchers, to luxury accommodations that are among the finest in the country. Keep in mind that although the nightly room rates at these lodges are often quite moderate, prices start to climb when you throw in transportation (often on chartered planes), guided excursions, and meals. Also, just because you can book a reservation at most of these lodges doesn't mean that they're not remote. Be sure to find out how you get to and from the ecolodge, and what tours and services are included in your stay. Then think long and hard about whether you really want to put up with hot, humid weather (cool and wet in the cloud forests); biting insects; rugged transportation; and strenuous hikes to see wildlife.

A couple of uniquely Costa Rican accommodation types that you might encounter are the *apartotel* and the *cabina.* An *apartotel* is just what it sounds like: an apartment hotel where you'll get a full kitchen and one or two bedrooms, along with daily maid service. *Cabinas* are Costa Rica's version of cheap vacation lodging. They're very inexpensive and very basic—often just cinder-block buildings divided into small rooms. Occasionally, you'll find a cabina in which the units are actually cabins, but these are a rarity. Cabinas often have clothes-washing sinks *(pilas)*, and some come with kitchenettes; they cater primarily to Tico families on vacation.

SURFING FOR HOTELS

In addition to the online travel booking sites **Travelocity, Expedia, Orbitz, Priceline,** and **Hotwire,** you can book hotels through **Hotels.com, Quikbook** (www.quikbook.com), and **Travelaxe** (www.travelaxe.net).

HotelChatter.com is a daily webzine offering smart coverage and critiques of hotels worldwide. Go to **TripAdvisor.com** or **HotelShark.com** for helpful independent consumer reviews of hotels and resort properties.

Your best bet in Costa Rica might be negotiating directly with the hotels themselves, especially the smaller hotels. Almost every hotel in Costa Rica has e-mail, if not its own website, and you'll find the contact information in this book. However, be aware that response times might be slower than you'd like, and many of the smaller hotels might have some trouble communicating back and forth in English.

It's a good idea to **get a confirmation number** and **make a printout** of any online booking transaction.

SAVING ON YOUR HOTEL ROOM

The **rack rate** is the maximum rate that a hotel charges for a room. Hardly anybody pays this price, however, except in high season or on holidays. To lower the cost of your room:

- **Ask about special rates or other discounts.** You may qualify for corporate, student, senior, frequent flier, or other discounts.
- **Dial direct.** When booking a room in a chain hotel, you'll often get a better deal by calling the individual hotel's reservation desk rather than the chain's main number.
- **Book online.** Many hotels offer Internet-only discounts, or supply rooms to Priceline, Hotwire, or Expedia at rates much lower than you can get through the hotel itself.
- **Remember the law of supply and demand.** You can save big on hotel rooms by traveling in a destination's off-season or shoulder seasons, when rates typically drop, even at luxury properties.
- **Look into group or long-stay discounts.** If you come as part of a large group, you should be able to negotiate a bargain rate. Likewise, if you're planning a long stay (at least 5 days), you might qualify for a discount. As a general rule, expect 1 night free after a 7-night stay.
- **Sidestep excess surcharges and hidden costs.** Many hotels have adopted the unpleasant practice of nickel-and-diming its guests with opaque surcharges. When you book a room, ask what is included in the room rate, and what is extra. Avoid dialing direct from hotel phones, which can have exorbitant rates. And don't be tempted by the room's minibar offerings: Most hotels charge through the nose for water, soda, and snacks. Finally, ask about local taxes and service charges, which can increase the cost of a room by 15% or more.
- Consider the pros and cons of **all-inclusive** resorts and hotels. The term "all-inclusive" means different things at different hotels. Many all-inclusive hotels include three meals

daily, sports equipment, spa entry, and other amenities; others may include most alcoholic drinks. In general, you'll save money going the "all-inclusive" way—as long as you use the facilities provided. The downside is that your choices are limited and you're stuck eating and playing in one place for the duration of your vacation.

- Carefully consider your hotel's meal plan. If you enjoy eating out and sampling the local cuisine, it makes sense to choose a **Continental Plan (CP),** which includes breakfast only, or a **European Plan (EP),** which doesn't include any meals and allows you maximum flexibility. If you're more interested in saving money, opt for a **Modified American Plan (MAP),** which includes breakfast and one other meal, or the **American Plan (AP),** which includes three meals. If you must choose a MAP, see if you can get a free lunch at your hotel if you decide to do dinner out.
- **Book an efficiency.** A room with a kitchenette allows you to shop for groceries and cook your own meals. This is a big money saver, especially for families on long stays.
- **Consider enrolling in hotel chains' "frequent-stay" programs,** which are upping the ante lately to win the loyalty of repeat customers. Frequent guests can now accumulate points or credits to earn free hotel nights, airline miles, in-room amenities, merchandise, tickets to concerts and events, discounts on sporting facilities—and even credit toward stock in the participating hotel, in the case of the Jameson Inn hotel group. Perks are awarded not only by many chain hotels and motels (Hilton HHonors, Marriott Rewards, Wyndham ByRequest, to name a few), but also individual inns and B&Bs.

Many chains partner with other hotel chains, car-rental firms, airlines, and credit card companies to give consumers additional incentive to do repeat business.

LANDING THE BEST ROOM

Somebody has to get the best room in the house. It might as well be you. You can start by joining the hotel's frequent-guest program, which may make you eligible for upgrades. A hotel-branded credit card usually gives its owner "silver" or "gold" status in frequent-guest programs for free. Always ask about a corner room. They're often larger and quieter, with more windows and light, and they often cost the same as standard rooms. When you make your reservation, ask if the hotel is renovating; if it is, request a room away from the construction. Ask about nonsmoking rooms and rooms with views. Be sure to request your choice of twin, queen-, or king-size beds. If you're a light sleeper, ask for a room away from vending or ice machines, elevators, restaurants, bars, and discos. Ask for a room that has been recently renovated or refurbished. If you aren't happy with your room when you arrive, ask for another one. Most lodgings will be willing to accommodate you.

In resort areas, particularly in warm climates, ask the following questions before you book a room:

- What's the view like? Cost-conscious travelers may be willing to pay less for a back room facing the parking lot, especially if they don't plan to spend much time in their room.
- Does the room have air-conditioning or ceiling fans? Do the windows open? If they do, and the nighttime entertainment takes place alfresco, you may want to find out when showtime is over.
- What's included in the price? Your room may be moderately priced, but

if you're charged for beach chairs, towels, sports equipment, and other amenities, you could end up spending more than you bargained for.

• How far is the room from the beach and other amenities? If it's far, is there transportation to and from the beach, and is it free?

17 Tips on Dining

Simply put, Costa Rican cuisine is less than memorable. San José remains the unquestioned gastronomic capital of the country, and here you can find the cuisines of the world served with formal service at moderate prices. However, the major beach destinations of Tamarindo, Manuel Antonio, and the Papagayo Peninsula are starting to catch up. At even the more expensive restaurants, it's hard to spend more than $50 (£25) per person unless you really splurge on drinks and wine. It gets even cheaper outside the city. You can find several excellent French, Italian and contemporary fusion restaurants around the San José area, as well as Peruvian, Japanese, Swiss, and Spanish establishments.

Costa Rica is a major producer and exporter of beef; consequently, San José has plenty of steakhouses. Unfortunately, quantity doesn't mean quality. Unless you go to one of the better restaurants or steakhouses, you will probably be served rather tough steaks, cut rather thin. Still, all is not lost. With the increase in international tourism and the need to please a more sophisticated palate, local chefs have begun to create a "nouvelle Costa Rican cuisine," updating timeworn recipes and using traditional ingredients in creative ways.

Outside the capital and major tourist destinations, your options get very limited very fast. In fact, many beach destinations are so remote that you have no choice but to eat in the hotel's dining room. Even on the more accessible beaches, the only choices aside from the hotel dining rooms are often cheap local places or overpriced tourist traps serving

indifferent meals. At remote jungle lodges, the food is usually served buffet-or family-style and can range from bland to inspired, depending on who's doing the cooking, and turnover is high.

If you're looking for cheap eats, you'll find them in little restaurants known as *sodas,* which are the equivalent of diners in the United States. At a *soda,* you'll have lots of choices: rice and beans with steak, rice and beans with fish, rice and beans with chicken, or, for vegetarians, rice and beans. You get the picture. Rice and beans are standard Tico fare and are served at all three daily meals. Also, although plenty of seafood is available throughout the country, at *sodas,* it's all too often served fried.

If you see a restaurant billing itself as a *mirador,* it means it has a view. If you are driving around the country, don't miss an opportunity to dine with a view at some little roadside restaurant. The food might not be fantastic, but the scenery will be.

I have separated restaurant listings throughout this book into three price categories, based on the average cost of a meal per person, including tax and service charge. The categories are **Expensive,** more than $25 (£13); **Moderate,** $10 to $25 (£5–£13); and **Inexpensive,** less than $10 (£5). (Note, however, that individual items in the listings—entrees, for instance—do not include the sales or service taxes.) Keep in mind that there is an additional 13% sales tax, as well as a 10% service charge. Ticos rarely tip, but that doesn't mean that you shouldn't. If the service was particularly good and attentive, you should probably leave a little extra.

FAST FACTS: Costa Rica

American Express American Express Travel Services is represented in Costa Rica by **ASV Olympia,** Oficentro La Sabana, Sabana Sur, in San José (✆ **242-8585),** which can issue traveler's checks and replacement cards and provide other standard services. To report lost or stolen Amex traveler's checks within Costa Rica, call the number above or ✆ **257-0155,** or call collect to 313/271-7887 in the United States.

Area Codes There are no area codes in Costa Rica. All local phone numbers are seven-digit numbers. However, toll-free numbers are inconsistent. Some begin with 800, others with 0800. Moreover, some actually have eight digits following the 800 or 0800.

ATM Networks See "Money & Costs," p. 30.

Business Hours Banks are usually open Monday through Friday from 9am to 4pm, although many have begun to offer extended hours. Offices are open Monday through Friday from 8am to 5pm (many close for 1 hr. at lunch). Stores are generally open Monday through Saturday from 9am to 6pm (many close for 1 hr. at lunch). Stores in modern malls generally stay open until 8 or 9pm and don't close for lunch. Most bars are open until 1 or 2am.

Car Rentals See "Getting Around Costa Rica," p. 44.

Cashpoints See "ATM Networks," above.

Currency See "Money & Costs," p. 30.

Customs **What You Can Bring Into Costa Rica** Visitors entering Costa Rica are officially entitled to bring in 500 grams of tobacco, 5 liters of liquor, and US$500 in merchandise. Cameras, computers, and electronic equipment for personal use are permitted duty-free. Customs officials in Costa Rica seldom check tourists' luggage.

What You Can Take Home from Costa Rica Every country has rules stating what its citizens are allowed to bring back. Be sure to understand your country's rules before beginning your trip to Costa Rica.

U.S. Citizens: For specifics on what you can bring back and the corresponding fees, download the invaluable free pamphlet *Know Before You Go* at **www.cbp.gov** (click on "Travel," and then click on "Know Before You Go! Online Brochure"). Or contact the **U.S. Customs & Border Protection (CBP),** 1300 Pennsylvania Ave., NW, Washington, DC 20229 (✆ **877/287-8667**) and request the pamphlet.

Canadian Citizens: For a clear summary of Canadian rules, write for the booklet *I Declare,* issued by the **Canada Border Services Agency** (✆ **800/ 461-9999** in Canada or 204/983-3500; **www.cbsa-asfc.gc.ca**).

U.K. Citizens: For information, contact **HM Customs & Excise** at ✆ **0845/ 010-9000** (from outside the U.K., 020/8929-0152), or consult their website at **www.hmce.gov.uk**.

Australian Citizens: A helpful brochure available from Australian consulates or Customs offices is *Know Before You Go.* For more information, call the **Australian Customs Service** at ✆ **1300/363-263,** or log on to **www.customs.gov.au**.

New Zealand Citizens: Most questions are answered in a free pamphlet available at New Zealand consulates and Customs offices: *New Zealand Customs Guide for Travellers, Notice no. 4.* For more information, contact **New Zealand Customs,** The Customhouse, 17–21 Whitmore St., Box 2218, Wellington (ⓒ **04/473-6099** or 0800/428-786; **www.customs.govt.nz**).

Driving Rules See "Getting Around Costa Rica," p. 44.

Drugstores Called *farmacias* in Spanish, drugstores are quite common throughout the country. Those at hospitals and major clinics are often open 24 hours a day.

Electricity The standard in Costa Rica is the same as in the United States: 110 volts AC (60 cycles). However, three-pronged outlets can be scarce, so it's helpful to bring along an adapter.

Embassies & Consulates The following are located in San José: **United States Embassy,** in front of Centro Commercial, on the road to Pavas (ⓒ **519-2000,** or 220-3127 after hours in case of emergency); **Canadian Consulate,** Oficentro Ejecutivo La Sabana, Edificio 5 (ⓒ **242-4400**); and **British Embassy,** Paseo Colón between calles 38 and 40 (ⓒ **258-2025**). There are no Australian or New Zealand embassies in San José.

Emergencies In case of any emergency, dial ⓒ **911** (which should have an English-speaking operator); for an ambulance, call ⓒ **128;** and to report a fire, call ⓒ **118.** If 911 doesn't work, you can contact the police at ⓒ **222-1365** or 221-5337, and hopefully they can find someone who speaks English.

Hospitals In San José try Clínica Bíblica (Avenida 14 between calles Central and 1), which offers emergency services to foreign visitors at reasonable prices (ⓒ **522-1000;** www.clinicabiblica.com), or the **Hospital CIMA** (ⓒ **208-1000;** www.hospitalsanjose.net), located in Escazú on the Próspero Fernández Highway, which connects San José and the western suburb of Santa Ana and has the most modern facilities in the country.

Language Spanish is the official language of Costa Rica. *Frommer's Spanish PhraseFinder & Dictionary* (John Wiley & Sons, 2006) is probably the best phrase book to bring with you. However, in most tourist areas, you'll be surprised by how well Costa Ricans speak English.

Laundromats Dry cleaners and laundromats—be they full-service or self-serve—are few and far between in Costa Rica. Hotel laundry services, which can sometimes be expensive, are far more common. For listings of laundromats, see individual city and town sections.

Legal Aid If you need legal help, your best bet is to first contact your local embassy or consulate. See "Embassies & Consulates" above for contact details. Alternatively, you can pick up a copy of *The Tico Times,* which usually carries advertisements from local English-speaking lawyers.

Liquor Laws Alcoholic beverages are sold every day of the week throughout the year, with the exception of the 2 days before Easter and the 2 days before and after a presidential election. The legal drinking age is 18, although it's almost never enforced. Liquor—everything from beer to hard spirits—is sold in specific liquor stores, as well as at most supermarkets and even convenience stores.

Lost & Found Be sure to tell your credit card companies the minute you discover your wallet has been lost or stolen, and file a report at the nearest police precinct. Your credit card company or insurer may require a police report number or record of the loss. Most credit card companies have an emergency toll-free number to call if your card is lost or stolen; they may be able to wire you a cash advance immediately or deliver an emergency credit card in a day or two. In Costa Rica, Visa's emergency number is © **0800/011-0030.** American Express cardholders and traveler's check holders should call © **0800/012-3211.** MasterCard holders should call © **0800/011-0184.** For other credit cards, or for a local representative of the above companies, call **Credomatic** © **295-9898.**

If you need emergency cash over the weekend when all banks and American Express offices are closed, you can have money wired to you via **Western Union** (© **800/777-7777** in Costa Rica; www.westernunion.com).

Mail The main post office *(correo)* is on Calle 2 between avenidas 1 and 3 in San José (© **800/900-2000** toll-free in Costa Rica, or 202-2900), and is open Monday through Friday from 8am to 5:30pm, and Saturday from 7:30am to noon. At press time, it cost 155 colones (30¢/15p) to mail a letter to the United States, and 180 colones (35¢/18p) to Europe. You can get stamps at a post office and at some gift shops in large hotels.

Given the Costa Rican postal service's track record, I recommend paying an extra 500 colones (96¢/48p) to have anything of any value certified. Better yet, use an international courier service or wait until you get home to post it. **DHL,** on Paseo Colón between calles 30 and 32 (© **209-0000;** www.dhl.com); **EMS Courier,** with desks at the principal metropolitan post offices (© **800/900-2000,** or 202-2900); **FedEx,** which is based in Heredia but will arrange pickup anywhere in the San José metropolitan area (© **800/463-3339;** www.fedex.com); and **United Parcel Service,** in Pavas (© **290-2828;** www.ups.com), all operate in Costa Rica. *Note:* Despite what you may be told, packages sent overnight to U.S. addresses tend to take 3 to 4 days.

If you're sending mail *to* Costa Rica, it generally takes between 10 and 14 days to reach San José, although it can take as much as a month to get to the more remote corners of the country. Plan ahead. Also note that many hotels and ecolodges have mailing addresses in the United States. Always use these addresses when writing from North America or Europe. Never send cash, checks, or valuables through the Costa Rican mail system.

Measurements Costa Rica uses the metric system. See the chart on the inside front cover of this book for details on converting metric measurements to non-metric equivalents.

Newspapers & Magazines There are six Spanish-language dailies in Costa Rica and one English-language weekly, the *Tico Times.* In addition, you can get *Time, Newsweek,* and several U.S. newspapers at some hotel gift shops and a few of the bookstores in San José. If you understand Spanish, *La Nación* is the paper you'll want. Its "Viva" and "Tiempo Libre" sections list what's going on in the world of music, theater, dance, and more.

Passports Allow plenty of time before your trip to apply for a passport; processing normally takes 3 weeks but can take longer during busy periods (especially spring). And keep in mind that if you need a passport in a hurry, you'll pay a higher processing fee.

For Residents of Australia: You can pick up an application from your local post office or any branch of Passports Australia, but you must schedule an interview at the passport office to present your application materials. Call the **Australian Passport Information Service** at © **131-232,** or visit the government website at **www.passports.gov.au**.

For Residents of Canada: Passport applications are available at travel agencies throughout Canada or from the central **Passport Office,** Department of Foreign Affairs and International Trade, Ottawa, ON K1A 0G3 (© **800/567-6868;** www.ppt.gc.ca).

For Residents of Ireland: You can apply for a 10-year passport at the **Passport Office,** Setanta Centre, Molesworth Street, Dublin 2 (© **01/671-1633;** www.irl gov.ie/iveagh). Those under age 18 and over 65 must apply for a 3-year passport. You can also apply at 1A South Mall, Cork (© **021/272-525)** or at most main post offices.

For Residents of New Zealand: You can pick up a passport application at any New Zealand Passports Office or download it from their website. Contact the **Passports Office** at © **0800/225-050** in New Zealand or 04/474-8100, or log on to **www.passports.govt.nz**.

For Residents of the United Kingdom: To pick up an application for a standard 10-year passport (5-yr. passport for children under 16), visit your nearest passport office, major post office, or travel agency or contact the **United Kingdom Passport Service** at © **0870/521-0410** or search its website at **www.ukpa.gov.uk**.

For Residents of the United States: Whether you're applying in person or by mail, you can download passport applications from the U.S. Department of State website at **http://travel.state.gov**. To find your regional passport office, check the U.S. Department of State website or call the **National Passport Information Center** toll-free number (© **877/487-2778)** for automated information.

Police In most cases, dial © **911** for the police, and you should be able to get someone who speaks English on the line. Other numbers for the **Judicial Police** are © **222-1365** and 221-5337. The numbers for the **Traffic Police (Policía de Tránsito)** are © **222-9330** and 222-9245.

Restrooms These are known as *sanitarios, servicios sanitarios,* or *baños.* They are marked *damas* (women) and *hombres* or *caballeros* (men). Public restrooms are hard to come by. You will almost never find a public restroom in a city park or downtown area. There are usually public restrooms at most national-park entrances, and much less frequently inside the national park. (There are usually plenty of trees and bushes.) In the towns and cities, it gets much trickier. One must count on the generosity of some hotel or restaurant. Same goes for most beaches. However, most restaurants, and, to a lesser degree, hotels, will let you use their facilities, especially if you buy a soft drink or something. Bus and gas stations often have restrooms, but many of these are pretty grim.

Smoking While not as bad as most of Europe, a large number of Costa Ricans smoke, and public smoking regulations and smoke-free zones have yet to take hold. Restaurants are required by law to have nonsmoking areas, but enforcement is often lax, air-circulation poor, and the separating almost nonexistent. Bars, as a whole, are often very smoke-filled in Costa Rica.

Taxes All hotels charge 16.3% tax. Restaurants charge 13% tax and also add on a 10% service charge, for a total of 23% more on your bill.

There is a $26 departure tax for all visitors leaving by air. This tax must be purchased prior to check-in. There are desks at the main terminal of all international airports where you can pay this tax (colones, dollars, and Visa credit cards are accepted). Some local travel agencies and hotels offer to purchase the departure tax in advance, as a convenience for tourists. You must give them authorization, as well as your passport number, and pay a small service fee.

Telephone Tips See "Staying Connected" on p. 41 for telephone tips for Costa Rica.

Time Zone Costa Rica is on Central Standard Time (same as Chicago and St. Louis), 6 hours behind Greenwich Mean Time. Costa Rica does not use daylight saving time, so the time difference is an additional hour April through October.

Tipping Tipping is not necessary in restaurants, where a 10% service charge is always added to your bill (along with a 13% tax). If service was particularly good, you can leave a little at your own discretion, but it's not mandatory. Porters and bellhops get around 75¢ per bag. You don't need to tip a taxi driver unless the service has been superior; a tip is not usually expected.

Useful Phone Numbers For directory assistance, call © 113; for international directory assistance, call © 124; and for the exact time (in Spanish), call © 112.

U.S. Department of State Travel Advisory: © 202/647-5225 (manned 24 hr.)
U.S. Passport Agency: © 202/647-0518
U.S. Centers for Disease Control International Traveler's Hot Line: © 404/332-4559

Water Although the water in San José is generally safe to drink, water quality varies outside the city. Because many travelers have tender digestive tracts, I recommend playing it safe and sticking to bottled drinks as much as possible. Also avoid ice.

3

Suggested Costa Rica Itineraries

Costa Rica is a rich and varied destination with numerous natural attractions and a broad selection of exciting sights, scenery, adventure activities, and ecosystems. On a trip to Costa Rica you can visit rainforests, cloud forests, and active volcanoes, and walk along miles of beautiful beaches on both the Pacific and Caribbean coasts. Adventure hounds will have their fill choosing from an exciting array of activities, and those looking for some rest and relaxation can grab a chaise longue and a good book. Costa Rica is also a relatively compact country, which makes visiting several destinations during a single vacation both easy and enjoyable.

The fastest and easiest way to get around the country is by small commuter aircraft. Most major destinations are serviced by reasonably priced regular commuter or charter airline companies. However, this does imply using San José as a periodic transfer hub. If your connections don't line up, you may end up having to tack on nights in San José in the middle

of your trip. Luckily, there are sufficient flights and internal connections to make this an infrequent inconvenience.

Driving around Costa Rica is another excellent option. Most major destinations are between 3 and 5 hours from San José by car, and many can be linked together in a well-planned and convenient loop. For example, one popular loop links Arenal Volcano, Monteverde, and Manuel Antonio. However, be forewarned that the roads here are often in terrible shape, many major roads and intersections are unmarked, and Tico drivers can be reckless and rude. See "By Car" under "Getting Around Costa Rica," in chapter 2 for more information on driving in Costa Rica.

The following itineraries are specific blueprints for fabulous vacations, and you can follow them to the letter. You might also decide to use one or more of them as an outline and then fill in some blanks with other destinations, activities, and attractions that strike your fancy from the rest of this book.

1 Costa Rica in 1 Week

The timing is tight, but this itinerary packs a lot into a weeklong vacation. This route takes you to a trifecta of Costa Rica's primary tourist attractions: Arenal Volcano, Monteverde, and Manuel Antonio. You can explore and enjoy tropical nature, take in some beach time, and experience a few high-adrenaline adventures to boot.

Day ❶: Arrive & Settle into San José

Arrive and get settled in **San José**. If your flight gets in early enough and you have

time, head downtown and tour the **Museo de Oro Banco Central (Gold Museum)** ✺✺ (p. 124).

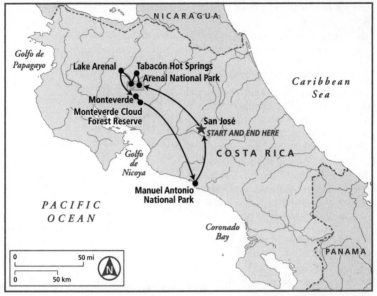

Head over to the **Teatro Nacional** (National Theater; p. 135). If anything is playing that night, buy tickets for the show. For an elegant and delicious dinner, I recommend **Grano de Oro Restaurant** ⊀⊀⊀ (p. 118), which is an elegant restaurant with seating in and around an open-air central courtyard in a beautiful downtown hotel.

Day ❷: Hot Rocks ⊀⊀

Rent a car and head to the Arenal National Park to see **Arenal Volcano** ⊀⊀. Settle into your hotel and spend the afternoon at the **Tabacón Grand Spa Thermal Resort** ⊀⊀⊀ (p. 232) working out

the kinks from the road. In the evening either sign up for a volcano-watching tour or take one on your own by driving the road to **Arenal National Park** and finding a quiet spot to pull over and wait for the sparks to fly.

Day ❸: Adventures around Arenal, Ending Up in Monteverde ⊀⊀

Spend the morning doing something adventurous around Arenal National Park. Your options range from white-water rafting to mountain biking to horseback riding and then hiking to the Río Fortuna Waterfall. My favorite is the **canyoning** adventure offered by **Pure Trek Canyoning** ⊀⊀ (p. 227). Allow at least 4 hours of daylight to drive around **Lake Arenal** to **Monteverde.** Stop for a break at **Toad Hall** ⊀⊀ (p. 237), on the road between Tabacón and Nuevo Arenal, where you can shop for gifts, artwork, and souvenirs. Once you get to Monteverde, settle into your hotel and head for a sunset drink and dinner at **El Sapo Dorado** ⊀⊀ (p. 252).

Day ❹: Monteverde Cloud Forest Reserve 🏵🏵🏵

Wake up early and take a guided tour of the **Monteverde Cloud Forest Reserve** 🏵🏵🏵 (p. 244). Be sure to stop in at the **Hummingbird Gallery** 🏵 (p. 248) next door to the entrance after your tour. There's great shopping, and the scores of brilliant hummingbirds buzzing around your head are always fascinating. Spend the afternoon visiting several of the area's attractions, which might include any combination of the following: the **Butterfly Garden** 🏵, **Orchid Garden** 🏵, **Monteverde Serpentarium, Frog Pond of Monteverde,** and the **World of Insects** (p. 247).

Day ❺: From the Treetops to the Coast 🏵🏵🏵

Use the morning to take one of the **zip-line canopy tours** here. I recommend the **Original Canopy Tour** 🏵🏵 (p. 246) in Monteverde for its unique ascent up the inside of a hollowed-out strangler fig. Be sure to schedule the tour early enough so that you can hit the road by noon for your drive to **Manuel Antonio National Park.** Settle into your hotel and head for a **sunset drink** at one of the several roadside restaurants with spectacular views over the rainforest to the sea. You can drop your car off at any point now and just rely on taxis and tours.

Day ❻: Manuel Antonio

In the morning take a boat tour of the **Damas Island estuary** (p. 281) with Jorge Cruz, and then reward yourself for all the hard touring so far with an afternoon lazing on one of the beautiful beaches inside **Manuel Antonio National Park** 🏵🏵 (p. 274). If you just can't lie still, be sure to hike the loop trail through the rainforest here and around **Cathedral Point** 🏵🏵. Make reservations at the **Sunspot Bar & Grill** 🏵🏵 (p. 290) for an elegant and intimate final dinner in Costa Rica.

Day ❼: Saying *Adiós*

Fly back to **San José** in time to connect with your departing flight home. If you have extra time, feel free to head back into Manuel Antonio National Park, do some souvenir shopping, or simply laze around your hotel pool. You've earned it.

2 Costa Rica in 2 Weeks

If you have 2 weeks, you'll be able to hit all the highlights mentioned above, as well as some others, and at a slightly more relaxed pace to boot. The first part of this itinerary is very similar to the 1-week itinerary laid out above. It's a real judgment call, but you might want to substitute a 2- to 3-day trip to Tortuguero for either the Guanacaste or the southern zone section listed below, or whittle down a day here or there along the way in order to squeeze in Tortuguero.

Days ❶ & ❷: San José

Spend as in **Days 1 and 2** in "Costa Rica in 1 Week," above. Another option for dinner on your second night is **Bakea** 🏵🏵 (p. 115), an elegant fusion restaurant in a wonderfully restored old colonial home in the heart of downtown.

Day ❸: Active in Arenal

Spend the morning doing something adventurous in **Arenal National Park,** as recommended in **Day 3** in "Costa Rica in 1 Week," above. If you're really active, you can schedule a second adventure for the afternoon or take time to visit the town of **La Fortuna.** In the evening return to the **Tabacón Grand Spa Thermal Resort.** If you were smart, you'll have already booked yourself a **spa treatment.**

Day ❹: Driving (& Shopping) Your Way around the Lake to Monteverde

Give yourself at least 4 hours of daylight to drive around **Lake Arenal** to **Monteverde.**

But you can take even longer. During your drive, be sure to stop at both **Toad Hall** ★★ (p. 237) and the **Lucky Bug Gallery** ★★ (p. 238), where you can shop for gifts, artwork, and souvenirs. Once you're in Monteverde, settle into your hotel and head for a sunset drink and dinner at **El Sapo Dorado** ★★ (p. 252).

Day ❺: Monteverde Cloud Forest Reserve

Spend **Day 5** as described for **Day 4** of "Costa Rica in 1 Week," above; however, head to **Sofia** ★★ (p. 253) for dinner and grab a window table fronting their well-lighted and lush gardens.

Day ❻: More Monteverde

There's just no way you can hit all the local **Monteverde** attractions in a day. Use today to visit a few that you missed. Also be sure to stop in at several of the local **art galleries** and **crafts shops.** Monteverde has one of the country's most vibrant arts scenes, and there are several worthwhile galleries, including **Casa de Arte and the Community Arts Center** (p. 248). In the evening, be sure to try **Sofia** ★★ (p. 253) for some top-draw Latin-fusion cuisine.

Day ❼: Monteverde to Manuel Antonio

Spend this day as in **Day 5** of "Costa Rica in 1 Week," above. However, after your sunset drink, head down into the town of Quepos for dinner at **El Patio Bistro Latino** ★★★ (p. 290), a cozy little spot serving some of the best food in the area.

Day ❽: Manuel Antonio ★★

Spend this day as in **Day 6** of "Costa Rica in 1 Week," above.

Days ❾, ❿ & ⓫: Southern Costa Rica

Fly from Quepos and Manuel Antonio to **Drake Bay** and settle into a remote **ecolodge,** such as **La Paloma Lodge** ★★★ (p. 312). You'll need 3 days to experience the many natural wonders of this southern zone. Aside from hiking in the rainforest, you'll be able to take scuba or snorkel outings, sportfishing trips, kayak adventures, and surfing lessons.

Days ⓬, ⓭ & ⓮: Guanacaste's Gold Coast

You've had enough nature and adventure; it's time to enjoy some pure R&R. From the southern zone, fly up to **Guanacaste** and spend your final days enjoying the pleasures of one of Costa Rica's **Gold Coast** beaches. If you can afford it and rooms are available, I recommend the **Four Seasons Resort** ⓇⓇⓇ (p. 163).

Alternatively, you might enjoy a smaller boutique hotel such as **Sueño del Mar** Ⓡ (p. 184).

If just lying on the beach or poolside is too mellow, there are scores of tour and activity options. If you're not feeling that active or adventurous, simply break out that novel you've been too busy to open and enjoy. On your last day, fly home from **Liberia.**

3 Costa Rica for Families

While Costa Rica is not a particularly kid-friendly destination, it isn't especially unfriendly either. So far, there are few attractions or activities geared for the very young and very few resorts with well-developed children's programs. However, youngsters and teens, especially those with strong adventurous and inquisitive traits, will do great here. The biggest challenges to families traveling with children are travel distances and the logistical challenges of moving around within the country, which is why I recommend flying in and out of Liberia and basing yourself in Guanacaste.

Day ❶: Arrive in Guanacaste

Fly directly into **Liberia.** From here it's a drive of 30 to 45 minutes to any of the area's many beach resorts, especially around the **Papagayo Peninsula.** I recommend either the **Four Seasons Resort** ⓇⓇⓇ (p. 163) or the **Allegro Papagayo Resort** ⓇⓇ (p. 162). Both have excellent children's programs and tons of activity and tour options.

Day ❷: Get Your Bearings & Enjoy Your Resort

Get to know and enjoy the facilities and activities offered up at your hotel or resort. Spend some time on the beach or at the pool. Enjoy the resort's on-hand watersports equipment and activities. Check out the **children's program** and any scheduled **activities** or **tours** that particularly appeal to anyone in the family. Feel free to adapt the following days' suggestions accordingly.

Day ❸: Rafting on the Corobicí River

The whole family will enjoy a **rafting tour** on the gentle Corobicí River. **Safaris Corobicí** (p. 154) offers leisurely trips that are appropriate for all ages, except

infants. In addition to the slow float and occasional mellow rapids, there'll be plenty of opportunities to watch birds and other wildlife along the way. If you're here between late September and late February, book a **turtle tour** (p. 182) at nearby **Playa Grande** for the evening. The whole family will be awestruck by the amazing spectacle of a giant leatherback turtle digging a nest and laying its eggs.

Day ❹: Parent's Day Off

Drop the kids off with the children's program for at least 1 full day and treat yourselves to a **sailboat cruise.** You'll spend some time cruising the coast, take a break or two to snorkel, and probably stop for lunch at a deserted beach. If you really want to pamper yourself, also schedule in some **spa services.**

Day ❺: Hacienda Guachipelín Ⓡ

It's time to head for the hills, which are mostly volcanoes in this neck of the woods. Book a full-day outing to **Hacienda Guachipelín** Ⓡ (p. 156), near

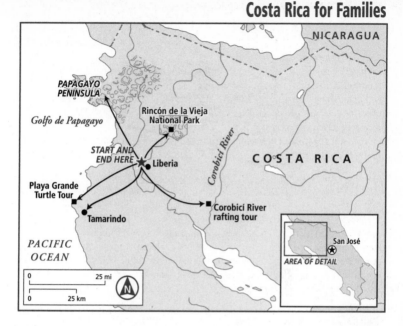

Costa Rica for Families

NICARAGUA

PAPAGAYO
PENINSULA

Golfo de Papagayo

Rincón de la Vieja
National Park

Corobicí River

COSTA RICA

START AND
END HERE · Liberia

Playa Grande
Turtle Tour

Corobicí River
rafting tour

Tamarindo

PACIFIC
OCEAN

San José

AREA OF DETAIL

0   25 mi

0   25 km

the Rincón de la Vieja National Park. Older and more adventurous children can sign up for a **horseback ride** or **canopy tour.** Younger children should get a kick out of visiting this working farm and cattle ranch.

Day ❻: Learn to Surf

Head to **Tamarindo** ❀❀ (p. 177) and arrange for the whole family to take **surf-** or **boogie-board lessons.** Hopefully you will have already booked a class with **Tamarindo Surf School** or **Witch's Rock Surf Camp** (p. 182). Be sure to rent your boards for a full day, so that you can practice after the lesson is over.

Day ❼: Leaving Liberia

Use any spare time you have before your flight out of **Liberia** to buy last-minute souvenirs and gifts, or just laze on the beach or by the pool.

4 A High-Octane Week of Adventures

Costa Rica is a major adventure-tourism destination. The following basic itinerary packs a lot of adventure into a single week; if you want to do more mountain biking or kayaking, just schedule that time in. If you're into windsurfing or kiteboarding, you'll definitely want to visit Lake Arenal between December and March.

Day ❶: Arrive & Settle into San José

Arrive and get settled in **San José.** If your flight gets in early enough and you have time, head downtown and tour the **Museo de Oro Banco Central** ❀❀ (p. 124) and the **Teatro Nacional** (p. 135). Take a break for an afternoon coffee at the **Cafeteria 1830** (p. 116). Be sure to grab an outdoor table and enjoy some people-watching. For a delicious dinner with a spectacular view, head to **La Cava Grill** ❀ (p. 121), which is located in the hills above Escazú.

A High-Octane Week of Adventures

Days ❷ & ❸: Get Wet & Wild

Take a 2-day white-water rafting expedition on the **Pacuare River** with **Exploradores Outdoors** 🎖 (p. 142). Camp out at their rustic tent camp on the river's edge. When you finish running the Pacuare, have them arrange for a transfer to **La Fortuna** at the end of your rafting trip. Settle into your hotel and head to the **Tabacón Grand Spa Thermal Resort** to have a soothing soak and to watch the volcano.

Day ❹: Waterfalls Two Ways

Go canyoning with **Pure Trek Canyoning** 🎖🎖 (p. 227) in the morning, and then hop on a horse or a mountain bike in the afternoon and be sure to stop at the **Río Fortuna Waterfall** 🎖. Take the short hike down to the base of the falls and take a dip in one of the pools there. In the evening check out the **Eco Termales** 🎖🎖 (p. 226) hot springs.

Day ❺: Getting There Is Part of the Fun & Adventure

Arrange a **taxi-to-boat-to-horse** transfer over to **Monteverde** with **Desafío**

Expeditions 🎖🎖 (p. 243). Settle in quickly at your hotel and take a zip-line **canopy tour** in the afternoon. I recommend the **Original Canopy Tour** 🎖 (p. 246) in Monteverde. Finally, if you've got the energy, take a **night tour** through the Monteverde Cloud Forest Reserve.

Day ❻: Monteverde Cloud Forest Reserve 🎖🎖🎖

Wake up early and head back to take a daytime guided tour of the **Monteverde Cloud Forest Reserve** 🎖🎖🎖. Be sure to bring a packed lunch. After the guided tour, spend the next few hours continuing to explore the trails through the cloud forest here. See if you can spot a **quetzal** (p. 244) on your own. Take a late-afternoon bus or transfer back to San José.

Day ❼: Squeeze in a Soccer Game before Splitting

Unfortunately, you'll most likely be on an early flight home from **San José.** If you have a few hours to kill, head for a **hike** or **jog** around Parque La Sabana or, better yet, try to join a **pick-up soccer game** here.

1 Plaza de la Cultura
2 Museo de Oro Banco Central
3 Museo Nacional de Costa Rica
4 Centro Nacional de Arte y Cultura
5 Plaza de la Democracia
○ Café Mundo

6 Teatro Nacional
7 Museo de Arte Costarricense
8 Parque La Sabana
9 Spirogyra Butterfly Garden
10 Mercado Central
○ La Cocina de Leña

5 San José in 3 Days

While most tourists seek to almost immediately get out of San José for greener pastures, there's still plenty to see and do in Costa Rica's vibrant capital. If you have even more days, take a white-water rafting trip on the Pacuare River, or head out to the Irazú Volcano, Orosi Valley, and Cartago area.

Day ❶: Getting to Know the City

Start your day on the **Plaza de la Cultura.** Visit the **Museo de Oro Banco Central** ✦✦ (p. 124), and see if you can get tickets for a performance that night at the Teatro Nacional. From the Plaza de la Cultura, stroll up Avenida Central to the **Museo Nacional de Costa Rica (National Museum)** ✦ (p. 124). After touring the museum, have lunch at one of the neighborhood restaurants. Then, head over to the neighboring **Centro Nacional de Arte**

y Cultura (National Center of Art and Culture) ✦✦ (p. 122). After you're finished taking in all this culture, some shopping at the open-air stalls at the **Plaza de la Democracia** (p. 131) is in order.

CAFÉ MUNDO ✦
Try dinner at the popular local hangout **Café Mundo,** at Calle 15 and Av. 9, 200m (656 ft.) and 100m (328 ft.) north of the INS building. See p. 115.

After dinner, head to the **Teatro Nacional** for the night's performance.

Day ❷: Enjoying Some Nearby Attractions

Get an early start for the **Poás Volcano** 𝒜𝒜 (p. 145), before the clouds sock the main crater in. After visiting the volcano, head to the **La Paz Waterfall Gardens** 𝒜𝒜 (p. 126). Take a walk on the waterfall trail, and also enjoy the immense butterfly garden and lively hummingbird garden. This is a good place to have lunch. On your way back to San José, you'll be making a loop through the hills of **Heredia,** with a stop at **INBio Park** 𝒜𝒜 (p. 126). In addition to being a fascinating natural-history museum, INBio Park also has a wonderful collection of intriguing animal sculptures by Costa Rican artist José Sancho.

Day ❸: More City Sights & Shopping

Spend your third day further exploring the capital. Start by heading out on Paseo Colón to the **Museo de Arte Costarricense (Museum of Costa Rican Art)** 𝒜 (p. 123) and **Parque La Sabana** (p. 94). Tour the museum and its growing sculpture garden, but also take a stroll around the beautiful and expansive downtown park. If you've brought kids along, you'll definitely want to visit the **Spirogyra Butterfly Garden** (p. 125). Intrepid travelers can also do some shopping at the **Mercado Central** (p. 130).

LA COCINA DE LEÑA

For a final taste of local culture, head to the El Pueblo entertainment center for dinner at **La Cocina de Leña**, Centro Comercial El Pueblo. See p. 116.

4

The Active Vacation Planner

It's not just fanciful marketing—Costa Rica really is an active and adventure tourism playground. While it's possible to come to Costa Rica and stay clean and dry, most visitors want to spend some time getting their hair wet, their feet muddy, and their adrenaline pumping. Opportunities for such action range from bird-watching to scuba diving to kiteboarding, and beyond.

There are myriad approaches to planning an active vacation in Costa Rica. This chapter lays out your options, from

tour operators who run multiactivity package tours that often include stays at ecolodges, to the best places in Costa Rica to pursue active endeavors (with listings of tour operators, guides, and outfitters that specialize in each), to an overview of the country's national parks and biore-serves. I also list some educational and volunteer travel options for those of you with a little more time on your hands and a desire to actively assist Costa Rica in the maintenance and preservation of its natural wonders.

1 Organized Adventure Trips

Because many travelers have limited time and resources, organized ecotourism or adventure-travel packages, arranged by tour operators in either Costa Rica or the United States, are a popular way of combining several activities. Bird-watching, horseback riding, rafting, and hiking can be teamed with, say, visits to Monteverde Biological Cloud Forest Reserve and Manuel Antonio National Park.

Traveling with a group has several advantages over traveling independently: Your accommodations and transportation are arranged, and most (if not all) of your meals are included in the cost of a package. If your tour operator has a reasonable amount of experience and a decent track record, you should proceed to each of your destinations quickly without the snags and long delays that those traveling on their own can occasionally face. You'll also have the opportunity to meet like-minded souls who are interested in nature and active sports. Of course, you'll pay more for the convenience of having all your arrangements handled in advance.

In the best cases, group size is kept small (10–20 people), and tours are escorted by knowledgeable guides who are either naturalists or biologists. Be sure to ask about difficulty levels when you're choosing a tour. Most companies offer "soft adventure" packages that those in moderately good, but not phenomenal, shape can handle; others focus on more hard-core activities geared toward only seasoned athletes or adventure travelers.

COSTA RICAN TOUR AGENCIES

Because many U.S.-based companies subcontract portions of their tours to established Costa Rican companies, some travelers like to cut out the middleman and set up their tours directly with these companies. That means that these packages are often less expensive than those offered by U.S. companies, but it doesn't mean they are cheap. You're still paying for the convenience of having your arrangements handled for you.

Scores of agencies in San José offer a plethora of adventure options. These agencies can arrange everything from white-water rafting to sightseeing at one of the nearby volcanoes or a visit to a butterfly farm. Although it's generally quite easy to arrange a day trip at the last minute, other tours are offered only on set dates or when enough people are interested. It pays to contact a few of the companies before you leave the United States and find out what they might be doing when you arrive. These local operators tend to be a fair share less expensive than their international counterparts, with 10-day tours generally costing in the neighborhood of $1,500 to $2,500 (£750–£1,250) per person, not including airfare to Costa Rica.

Coast to Coast Adventures *GG* (© 280-8054; www.ctocadventures.com) has a unique excursion involving no motor vehicles. The company's namesake 2-week trip spans the country, with participants traveling on horses and rafts, by mountain bike, and on foot. Custom-designed trips (with a minimum of motorized transport) of shorter duration are also available.

Costa Rica Expeditions *GG* (© 257-0766; www.costaricaexpeditions.com) offers everything from 10-day tours covering the entire country to 3-day/2-night and 2-day/1-night tours of Monteverde Biological Cloud Forest Reserve, Tortuguero National Park, and Corcovado National Park, where they run their own lodges. It also offers 1- to 2-day white-water rafting trips and other excursions. All excursions include transportation, meals, and lodging. Its tours are some of the most expensive in the country, but it is the most consistently reliable outfitter as well (and its customer service is excellent). If you want to go out on your own, Costa Rica Expeditions can supply you with just transportation from place to place.

Costa Rica Sun Tours *GG* (© 296-7757; www.crsuntours.com) offers a wide range of tours and adventures and specializes in multiday tours that include stays at small country lodges for travelers interested in experiencing nature.

Horizontes *GG* (© 222-2022; www.horizontes.com) is not a specifically adventure-oriented operator, but it offers a wide range of individual, group, and package tours. The company generally hires responsible and knowledgeable guides.

Serendipity Adventures *GG* (© 877/507-1358 in the U.S. and Canada, or 558-1030; www.serendipityadventures.com), an adventure-travel operator, offers everything from ballooning to mountain biking, and sea kayaking to canyoning, as well as most of the popular white-water rafting trips.

U.S.-BASED ADVENTURE TOUR OPERATORS

These agencies and operators specialize in well-organized and coordinated tours that cover your entire stay. Many travelers prefer to have everything arranged and confirmed before arriving in Costa Rica, and this is a good idea for first-timers and during the high season. *Be warned:* Most of these operators are not cheap, with 10-day tours generally costing in the neighborhood of $2,500 to $3,500 (£1,250–£1,750) per person, not including airfare to Costa Rica.

Abercrombie & Kent *G* (© 800/554-7016; www.abercrombiekent.com) is a luxury-tour company that offers upscale trips around the globe, and it has several tours of Costa Rica on its menu. It specializes in 9-day highlight tours hitting Monteverde, Arenal, and Tortuguero. Service is personalized and the guides are top-notch.

Costa Rica Experts 𝒜 (© 800/827-9046 or 773/935-1009; www.costaricaexperts. com) offers a large menu of a la carte and scheduled departures, as well as day trips and adventure packages.

Overseas Adventure Travel 𝒜𝒜 (© 800/493-6824; www.oattravel.com) offers good-value natural-history and "soft adventure" itineraries with optional add-on excursions. Tours are limited to 16 people and are guided by naturalists. All accommodations are in small hotels, lodges, or tent camps.

Tico Travel 𝒜 (© 800/493-8426; www.ticotravel.com) has offices in both the United States and Costa Rica. It specializes in surfing and sportfishing packages, but it can put together a wide range of tours.

In addition to these companies, many environmental organizations, including the **Sierra Club** (© 415/977-5522; www.sierraclub.org), the **Smithsonian Institute** (© 877/338-8687; www.smithsonianjourneys.org), and the **National Audubon Society** (© 800/967-7425 or 212/979-8947; www.audubon.org), periodically offer organized trips to Costa Rica.

2 Activities A to Z

Each listing in this section describes the best places to practice a particular sport or activity and lists tour operators and outfitters. If you want to focus on only one active sport during your Costa Rican stay, these companies are your best bets for quality equipment and knowledgeable service.

Adventure activities and tourism, by their very nature, carry certain risks and dangers. Over the years, there have been several deaths and dozens of minor injuries in activities ranging from mountain biking to white-water rafting to canopy tours. I try to list only the most reputable and safest of companies. However, if you ever have any doubt as to the safety of the guide, equipment, or activity, it's better to be safe than sorry. Moreover, know your limits and abilities, and don't try to exceed them.

See "A High-Octane Week of Adventures" in chapter 3 for additional tour ideas.

BIKING

There are several significant regional and international touring races in Costa Rica each year, but as a general rule the major roads are dangerous and inhospitable for cyclists. Roads are narrow, there's usually no shoulder, and most drivers show little care or consideration for those on two wheels. The options are much more appealing for mountain bikers and off-track riders. Nevertheless, fat-tire explorations are still relatively new to Costa Rica, but options are growing fast. If you plan to do a lot of biking and are very attached to your rig, bring your own. However, several companies in San José and elsewhere rent bikes, and the quality of the equipment is improving all the time. I've listed rental shops in each of the regional chapters that follow.

The area around **Lake Arenal** and **Arenal Volcano** wins my vote as the best place for mountain biking in Costa Rica. The scenery's great, with primary forests, waterfalls, and plenty of trails. And the hot springs at nearby Tabacón Grand Spa Thermal Resort is a perfect place for those with aching muscles to unwind at the end of the day. See chapter 7 for full details.

TOUR OPERATORS & OUTFITTERS

Bike Arenal 𝒜 (© 866/465-4114 in U.S. and Canada, or 479-9454; www.bikearenal. com) is based in La Fortuna and specializes in 1-day and multiday trips around the Arenal area.

Coast to Coast Adventures ✦ (© 280-8054; www.ctocadventures.com) offers mountain-biking itineraries among its many tour options.

Costa Rica Biking Adventures (© 235-4982; www.bikingincostarica.com) is a local outfit offering day trips and multiday excursions around the country using high-quality Trek and Cannondale bikes.

ExperiencePlus! Specialty Tours ✦✦ (© 800/685-4565 or 970/484-8489 in the U.S.; www.experienceplus.com) offers guided group and assisted individual bike tours around the country. This is the only company I know of that uses touring bikes. It also offers guided group hiking tours.

Lava Tours (© 888/862-2424 in the U.S. and Canada, or 278-2558; www.lava-tours.com) conducts a variety of fixed-date-departure and custom mountain-bike tours all over Costa Rica.

Serendipity Adventures ✦ (© 877/507-1358 in the U.S. and Canada, or 558-1030; www.serendipityadventures.com) offers several mountain-biking trips among its many other expeditions.

BIRD-WATCHING

With more than 850 species of resident and migrant birds identified throughout the country, Costa Rica abounds with great bird-watching sites. Lodges with the best bird-watching include **Savegre Lodge,** in Cerro de la Muerte, off the road to San Isidro de El General (quetzal sightings are almost guaranteed); **La Paloma Lodge** in Drake Bay, where you can sit on the porch of your cabin as the avian parade goes by; **Arenal Observatory Lodge,** on the flanks of Arenal Volcano; **La Selva Biological Station,** in Puerto Viejo de Sarapiquí; **Aviarios del Caribe** and **Selva Bananito Lodge,** both just north of Cahuita; **Lapa Ríos** and **Bosque del Cabo,** on the Osa Peninsula; **Playa Nicuesa Rainforest Lodge,** along the Golfo Dulce; **La Laguna del Lagarto Lodge,** up by the Nicaraguan border; and **Tiskita Lodge,** down by the Panamanian border.

Some of the best parks and preserves for serious birders are **Monteverde Biological Cloud Forest Reserve** (for resplendent quetzals and hummingbirds); **Corcovado National Park** (for scarlet macaws); **Caño Negro Wildlife Refuge** (for wading birds, including jabiru storks); **Wilson Botanical Gardens** and the **Las Cruces Biological Station,** near San Vito (the thousands of flowering plants here are bird magnets); **Guayabo, Negritos,** and **Pájaros Islands biological reserves** in the Gulf of Nicoya (for magnificent frigate birds and brown boobies); **Palo Verde National Park** (for ibises, jacanas, storks, and roseate spoonbills); **Tortuguero National Park** (for great green macaws); and **Rincón de la Vieja National Park** (for parakeets and curassows). Rafting trips down the Corobicí and Bebedero rivers near Liberia, boat trips to or at Tortuguero National Park, and hikes in any cloud forest also provide good bird-watching opportunities.

In San José your best bets are to head toward the lush grounds and gardens of the University of Costa Rica, or to Parque del Este, a little farther east in the foothills just outside of town.

COSTA RICAN TOUR AGENCIES

In addition to the agencies listed below, check in with the **Birding Club of Costa Rica** (costaricabirding@hotmail.com), which runs monthly outings and provides you with the opportunity to connect with local English-speaking birders.

Costa Rica Expeditions ✦✦ (© 257-0766; www.costaricaexpeditions.com) and Costa Rica Sun Tours ✦✦ (© 296-7757; www.crsuntours.com) are well-established

Where to See the Resplendent Quetzal

Revered by pre-Columbian cultures throughout Central America, the resplendent quetzal has been called the most beautiful bird on earth. Ancient Aztec and Maya Indians believed that the robin-size quetzal protected them in battle. The males of this species have brilliant red breasts; iridescent emerald green heads, backs, and wings; and white tail feathers complemented by a pair of iridescent green tail feathers that are more than .5m (1¾ ft.) long.

The belief that these endangered birds live only in the dense cloud forests cloaking the higher slopes of Central America's mountains was instrumental in bringing many areas of cloud forest under protection as quetzal habitats. (Since then, researchers have discovered that the birds do not, in fact, spend their entire lives here.) After nesting between March and July, resplendent quetzals migrate down to lower slopes in search of food. These lower slopes have not been preserved in most cases, and now conservationists are trying to salvage enough lower-elevation forests to help the quetzals survive.

Although for many years **Monteverde Biological Cloud Forest Reserve** was *the* place to see quetzals, throngs of people crowding the reserve's trails now make the pursuit more difficult. Other places where you can see quetzals are in the **Los Angeles Cloud Forest Reserve** near San Ramón, in **Tapantí National Wildlife Refuge,** and in **Chirripó National Park.** Perhaps the best place to spot a quetzal is at one of the specialized lodges located along the Cerro de la Muerte between San José and San Isidro de El General.

companies with very competent and experienced guides who offer a variety of tours to some of the better birding spots in Costa Rica.

U.S.-BASED TOUR OPERATORS
Field Guides (© 800/728-4953 or 512/263-7295; www.fieldguides.com) is a specialty bird-watching travel operator. Its 16-day tour of Costa Rica costs $4,275 (£2,138), not including airfare. Group size is limited to 14 participants.

Victor Emanuel Nature Tours (© 800/328-8368, or 512/328-5221 in the U.S.; www.ventbird.com) is a well-respected small-group tour operator specializing in bird-watching trips. Their 12-day "Best of Costa Rica" trip costs $3,850 (£1,925).

WINGS (© 888/293-6443 or 520/320-9868; www.wingsbirds.com) is a specialty bird-watching travel operator with 30 years of experience in the field. Its 14-day Costa Rica trip covers the major bird-watching zones in the country and costs around $4,590 (£2,295), not including airfare. Group size is usually between 6 and 14 people.

BUNGEE JUMPING
Tropical Bungee (© 248-2212; www.bungee.co.cr) will let you jump off an 80m (262-ft.) bridge over the Río Colorado for $65 (£33), including transportation from San José and a video of your jump. A second jump will cost you another $30 (£15). The jump site is located on a small bridge over the Río Colorado about 37km (23

miles) northwest of San José, just off the Pan-American Highway. There are obvious and well-placed signs on the highway. Someone should be there from 9am to 3pm every day. They prefer for you to have a reservation, but if you show up on your own, they'll probably let you jump, unless huge groups are booked ahead of you.

CAMPING

Heavy rains, difficult access, and limited facilities make camping a challenge in Costa Rica. Nevertheless, a backpack and tent will get you far from the crowds and into some of the most pristine and undeveloped nooks and crannies of the country. Those who relish sleeping out on a beach but wouldn't mind a bit more luxury (beds, someone to prepare meals for you, and running water) might want to consider staying at the **Corcovado Lodge Tent Camp** on the Osa Peninsula (p. 322) or at the **Almonds & Corals Tent Camp** down in Manzanillo (p. 362). Camping is forbidden in some national parks, so read the descriptions for each park carefully before you pack a tent.

If you'd like to participate in an organized camping trip, contact **Coast to Coast Adventures** (✆ **280-8054;** www.ctoadventures.com) or **Serendipity Adventures** (✆ **877/507-1358** in the U.S. and Canada, or 558-1030; www.serendipityadventures.com).

In my opinion, the best place to pop up a tent on the beach is in **Santa Rosa National Park** or at the Puerto Vargas campsite in **Cahuita National Park.** The best camping trek is, without a doubt, a hike through **Corcovado National Park** or a climb up **Mount Chirripó.**

CANOPY & CANYONING TOURS

Canopy tours are officially all the rage in Costa Rica, largely because they are such an exciting and unique way to experience tropical rainforests. It's estimated that some two-thirds of a typical rainforest's species live in the canopy (the uppermost, branching layer of the forest). From the relative luxury of Rain Forest Aerial Tram's high-tech funicular to the rope-and-climbing-gear rigs of more basic operations, a trip into the canopy will give you a bird's-eye view of a Neotropical forest. There are now canopy-tour operations in or close to nearly every major tourist destination in the country, including Monteverde, Manuel Antonio, La Fortuna, Tabacón, Montezuma, Punta Islita, Villablanca, and Rincón de la Vieja, as well as on Tortuga Island and around Guanacaste and the Osa Peninsula.

Most canopy tours involve strapping yourself into a climbing harness and being winched up to a platform some 30m (100 ft.) above the forest floor, or doing the work yourself. Many of these operations have a series of treetop platforms connected by taut cables. Once up on the first platform, you click your harness into a pulley and glide across the cable to the next (slightly lower) platform, using your hand (protected by a thick leather glove) as a brake. When you reach the last platform, you usually rappel down to the ground. (Don't worry—they'll teach even the most nervous neophyte.)

Although this can be a lot of fun, do be careful because these tours are popping up all over the place and there is precious little regulation of the activity. Some of the tours are set up by fly-by-night operators (obviously, I haven't listed any of those). Be especially sure that you feel comfortable and confident with the safety standards, guides, and equipment before embarking. One of the most reputable operators is **The Original Canopy Tours** ✦ (✆ **291-4465;** www.canopytour.com), which has sites in Monteverde, Drake Bay, and Mahogany Park, about an hour outside of San José, but there are other safe, well-run operations around the country. Perhaps my favorite canopy tour is the Original Canopy Tour's operation in **Monteverde,** which features an ascent up the hollow interior of a giant strangler fig tree. Before you sign on to any tour, ask whether you have to hoist yourself to the top under your own steam, and then make your decision accordingly. Another option is to try one of the tram or gondola tours through the canopy. The folks at Rain Forest Aerial Tram (see below) currently have two such operations, and there's a ski-lift-style gondola ride at **Turu BaRi Tropical Park** (© **428-6070;** www.turubari.com) outside of San José. See "Side Trips from San José" in chapter 5 for more information.

Canyoning tours are even more adventurous. Hardly standardized, most involve hiking down along a mountain stream, river, and/or canyon, with periodic breaks to rappel down the face of a waterfall, or swim in a jungle pool. The best canyoning operations in Costa Rica are **Pure Trek Canyoning** ★★ (© **866/569-5723** in the U.S. and Canada, or 461-2110; www.puretrekcostarica.com) and **Desafío Expeditions** ★★ (© **479-9464;** www.desafiocostarica.com), both in La Fortuna; and **Everyday Adventures** ★★ (© **353-8619;** www.psychotours.com), which operates outside of Puerto Jimenez.

Rain Forest Aerial Tram Caribbean ★ (© **257-5961;** www.rainforesttram.com) is located some 50 minutes from San José. For $55 (£28; transportation extra), this modern tram takes you on a 90-minute trip through the rainforest canopy in the comfort and safety of an enclosed cab. The entrance fee includes an additional guided hike and access to its trail system, butterfly garden, and other attractions. The best thing here isn't necessarily the tram ride, which I find somewhat disappointing, but the fact that this makes a good spot for a full-day excursion relatively close to San José. The outfit has a new sister project on the central Pacific coast just outside of Jacó. See "Side Trips from San José" in chapter 5 and "Playa de Jacó & Playa Herradura" in chapter 8 for more information.

CRUISING

Cruising options in Costa Rica range from transient cruisers setting up a quick charter business to converted fishing boats taking a few guests out to see the sunset.

The most popular cruise option is a day trip from San José (the boats actually leave from Puntarenas) to **Tortuga Island** in the Nicoya Gulf (see "Side Trips from San José" in chapter 5). Alternatively, you can book a cruise to Tortuga from Playa Montezuma at the tip of the Nicoya Peninsula (see chapter 8 for details). It's much cheaper from here (around $40–$50/£20–£25 per person), but the excursion doesn't include the gourmet lunch that's usually featured on cruises leaving from San José.

If diesel fumes and engine noise bother you, the best places to charter a sailboat are in Playa del Coco, Playa Hermosa, and Playa Flamingo in Guanacaste province (see chapter 6); Playa Herradura and Quepos along the central Pacific coast (see chapter 8); and Golfito along the southern Pacific coast (see chapter 9). You can get information about sailboat rides and charters at any one of the larger lodgings in these areas. My favorite place to charter a sailboat is **Golfito.** From here, it's a pleasant, peaceful day's sail around the Golfo Dulce (see chapter 9).

Tips Beach Blanket Bingo

If you plan to spend time at the beach, it's often a good idea to pack your own beach towel or mat. Many of the midrange and budget hotels in Costa Rica do not provide them.

DIVING & SNORKELING

Many islands, reefs, caves, and rocks lie off the coast of Costa Rica, providing excellent spots for underwater exploration. Visibility varies with season and location. Generally, heavy rainfall tends to swell the rivers and muddy the waters, even well offshore. Banana plantations and their runoff have destroyed most of the Caribbean reefs, although there's still good diving at **Isla Uvita,** just off the coast of Limón, and in **Manzanillo,** down near the Panamanian border. Most divers choose Pacific dive spots such as **Isla del Caño, Bat Island,** and the **Catalina Islands,** where you're likely to spot manta rays, moray eels, white-tipped sharks, and plenty of smaller fish and coral species. But the ultimate in Costa Rican dive experiences is 7 to 10 days on a chartered boat, diving off the coast of **Isla del Coco** (see "Diving Trips to Isla del Coco" on p. 258).

Snorkeling is not incredibly common or rewarding in Costa Rica. The rain, runoff, and wave conditions that drive scuba divers well offshore tend to make coastal and shallow-water conditions less than optimal. If the weather is calm and the water is clear, you might just get lucky. Ask at your hotel or check the different beach listings in this book to find snorkeling options and operators up and down Costa Rica's coasts. The best snorkeling experience to be had in Costa Rica is on the reefs off **Manzanillo Beach** in the southern Caribbean coast, particularly in the calm months of September and October.

DIVING OUTFITTERS & OPERATORS

In addition to the companies listed below, check the listings at specific beach and port destinations in the regional chapters.

Aggressor Fleet Limited &&& (© **800/348-2628** in the U.S., or 257-0191; www.aggressor.com) runs the 36m (118-ft.) *Okeanos Aggressor* on regular trips out to Isla del Coco.

Diving Mania (© **291-2936;** www.divingmania.net) is a San José–based outfit that offers equipment rental, certification classes, and tours.

Diving Safaris de Costa Rica && (© **672-1260;** www.costaricadiving.net) is perhaps the largest, most professional, and best-established dive operation in the country. Based out of the Sol Playa Hermosa Hotel in Playa Hermosa, this outfitter is also a local pioneer in nitrox diving.

Undersea Hunter && (© **800/203-2120** in the U.S., or 228-6613; www.underseahunter.com) offers the *Undersea Hunter* and its sister ship, the *Sea Hunter,* two pioneers of the live-aboard diving excursions to Isla del Coco.

FISHING

Anglers in Costa Rican waters have landed over 100 world-record catches, including blue marlin, Pacific sailfish, dolphin, wahoo, yellowfin tuna, guapote, and snook. Whether you want to head offshore looking for a big sail, wrestle a tarpon near a Caribbean river mouth, or choose a quiet spot on Arenal Lake to cast for guapote, you'll find it here. You can raise a marlin anywhere along the Pacific coast.

Many of the Pacific port and beach towns—Quepos, Puntarenas, Playa del Coco, Tamarindo, Flamingo, Golfito, Drake Bay, Zancudo—support large charter fleets and have hotels that cater to anglers; see chapters 6, 8, and 9 for recommended boats, captains, and lodges. Costs for fishing trips usually range between $400 and $1,600 (£200–£800) per day (depending on the size of the boat) for boat, captain, tackle, drinks, and lunch, so the cost per person depends on the size of the group.

Costa Rica Outdoors 🏅🏅 (© 800/308-3394 in the U.S. or 282-6743; www.costaricaoutdoors.com) is a well-established operation run by longtime resident, fisherman, and outdoor writer Jerry Ruhlow, specializing in booking fishing trips around the country.

FISHING LODGES

Aguila de Osa Inn 🏅 (© 866/924-8452 in the U.S. and Canada, or 296-2190; www.aguiladeosainn.com) is a luxury lodge in Drake Bay. See p. 311.

The **Río Colorado Lodge** (© 800/243-9777 in the U.S. and Canada, or 232-4063; www.riocoloradolodge.com) is located at the Barra del Colorado National Wildlife Refuge. See p. 337.

The **Zancudo Lodge** 🏅🏅 (© 877/529-6980 in the U.S., or 776-0008; www.thezancudolodge.com) is located in Playa Zancudo. See p. 330.

Silver King Lodge 🏅🏅 (© 800/847-3474 in the U.S., or 711-0708; www.silverkinglodge.net) is a luxury lodge at Barra del Colorado. See p. 337.

GOLF

Costa Rica is not one of the world's great golfing destinations—well, not yet, anyway. There are currently six regulation 18-hole courses open to the public and visitors, but several others are either under construction or in the planning stages, with a potential boom shaping up in Guanacaste.

Currently, the best option for golfers staying in and around San José is **Parque Valle del Sol** 🏅 (© 282-9222; www.vallesol.com), an 18-hole course in the western suburb of Santa Ana. Greens fees are $85 (£43), including a cart. The **Cariari Country Club** 🏅🏅 (© 293-3211), just outside of San José, is a private course and not open to the public. However, guests at the **Marriott Costa Rica** and neighboring hotels can play. If you can wrangle an invitation, or are staying at a hotel with an agreement with the club, greens fees are $60 (£30), including a mandatory caddy. You should expect to tip your caddy around $10 (£5), and pay an extra $25 (£13) for a cart.

The Meliá chain also runs the **Garra de León course** 🏅🏅 at the **Paradisus Playa Conchal** resort (© 654-4123; www.solmelia.com) up in Guanacaste. Greens fees here are $160 (£80), including a cart. With advance notice and depending on available tee times, this course is currently open to guests at other hotels in the region.

Another major resort course is at the **Los Sueños Marriott Ocean & Golf Resort** 🏅🏅 in Playa Herradura (© 800/228-9290 in the U.S., or 630-9028; www.marriott.com). Greens fees, including a cart, run around $125 (£63) for guests of the hotel and $155 (£77) for the general public.

Hacienda Pinilla 🏅 (© 680-7000; www.haciendapinilla.com) is an 18-hole links-style course located south of Tamarindo. This might just be the most challenging course in the country, and the facilities, though limited, are top-notch. Currently, the course is open to golfers staying at hotels around the area, with advance reservations. Greens fees run around $150 (£75) for 18 holes, including a cart.

The newest and most spectacular course in Costa Rica is at **Four Seasons Resort** 🏅🏅🏅 (© 212/688-2440 in the U.S., or 696-0871; www.fourseasons.com), but it is open only to hotel guests. Greens fees run around $185 (£93).

Golfers who want the most up-to-date information, or those who are interested in a package deal that includes play on a variety of courses, should contact **Costa Rica Golf Adventures** 🏅 (© 877/258-2688; www.golfcr.com).

HANG GLIDING, PARAGLIDING & BALLOONING

Paragliding with a pilot in a tandem rig is taking off (pardon the pun) in the cliff areas around Caldera, just south of Puntarenas, as well as other spots around Costa Rica. If you're looking to paraglide, check in with the folks at the **Costa Rican Association of Free Flying** (www.parapente-costa-rica.org).

Serendipity Adventures (© 877/507-1358 in the U.S. and Canada, or 558-1000; www.serendipityadventures.com) will take you up, up, and away in a hot-air balloon on a variety of single- or multiday tours, either in Turrialba, in Naranjo, or near Arenal Volcano. A basic flight costs around $570 (£285) for two people, or $990 (£495) for up to five people or 800 pounds.

Hang Glide Costa Rica (© 353-5514; www.hangglidecr.com) offers about a half-hour of gentle hang gliding in a tandem rig, which begins with a tow by an ultralight, for $99 to $150 (£50–£75) per person.

HORSEBACK RIDING

Costa Rica's rural roots are evident in the continued use of horses for real work and transportation throughout the country. Visitors will find that horses are easily available for riding, whether you want to take a sunset trot along the beach, ride through the cloud forest, or take a multiday trek through the northern zone.

Most travelers simply saddle up for a couple of hours, but those looking for a more specifically equestrian-based visit should check in with the following folks.

Coast to Coast Adventures (© 280-8054; www.ctoadventures.com) specializes in 2-week trips spanning the country via horseback, raft, or mountain bike, as well as on foot, with no motor vehicles involved. Other trips are also available.

Nature Lodge Finca Los Caballos ⚞ (©/fax 642-0124; www.naturelodge.net) has the healthiest horses in the Montezuma area.

Serendipity Adventures (© 877/507-1358 in the U.S. and Canada, or 558-1030; www.serendipityadventures.com) offers horseback treks and tours.

LANGUAGE IMMERSION

As more people travel to Costa Rica with the intention of learning Spanish, the number of options for Spanish immersion vacations increases. You can find courses of varying lengths and degrees of intensiveness, and many that include cultural activities and day excursions. Many of these schools have reciprocal relationships with U.S. universities, so, in some cases, you can even arrange for college credit. Most Spanish schools can arrange for home stays with a middle-class Tico family for a total-immersion experience. Classes are often small, or even one-on-one, and can last anywhere from 2 to 8 hours a day. Listed below are some of the larger and more established Spanish-language schools, with approximate costs. Most are located in San José, but there are also

---

⟮Tips⟯ Tai Chi in Paradise

For the past 18 years, tai chi master and two-time U.S. national champion Chris Luth has been leading weeklong retreats to Costa Rica, combining intensive classes in this ancient Chinese martial art with rainforest hikes, river rafting, and just enough beach time. For more information, contact **T'ai Chi in Paradise** (© 858/259-1396; www.taichiinparadise.com).

schools in Monteverde, Manuel Antonio, Playa Flamingo, Malpaís, Playa Nosara, and Tamarindo. (I'd certainly rather spend 2 weeks or a month in one of these spots than in San José.) Contact the schools for the most current price information.

Centro Lingüístico Conversa *ℛ* ((𝒞 **888/669-1664** in the U.S. and Canada, or 221-7649; www.conversa.net) has classes in both San José and Santa Ana (a suburb of the capital city). A 1-week course here with 4 hours of classes each day, including room and board with a Costa Rican family, costs between $500 and $715 (£250–£358) for one person, depending on which campus you choose.

Centro Panamericano de Idiomas (CPI) *ℛ* ((𝒞 **877/373-3116** in the U.S., or 265-6306; www.cpi-edu.com) has three campuses: one in the quiet suburban town of Heredia, another in Monteverde, and one at the beach in Playa Flamingo. A 1-week program, with 4 hours of class per day and a home stay with a Costa Rican family, costs $415 (£208).

Costa Rican Language Academy *ℛ* in San José ((𝒞 **866/230-6361** in the U.S., or 280-1685; www.spanishandmore.com) has intensive programs with classes held Monday to Thursday to give students a chance for longer weekend excursions. The academy also integrates Latin dance and Costa Rican cooking classes into the program. A 1-week class with 4 hours of class per day, plus a home stay, costs $312 (£156).

Costa Rica Spanish Institute (COSI) ((𝒞 **234-1001;** www.cosi.co.cr) offers small classes in the San Pedro neighborhood of San José, as well as a program at Manuel Antonio. The weekly cost of $425 (£213) includes a home stay.

Institute for Central American Development Studies (ICADS) *ℛℛ* near San Pedro ((𝒞 **225-0508;** www.icadscr.com) has one of the best and most extensive field-work and volunteer programs in Costa Rica, as well as quality Spanish-language immersion programs. A 4-week course with home stay costs $1,800 (£900).

Instituto Británico *ℛ* ((𝒞 **234-9054;** www.institutobritanico.co.cr) is a venerable institution with installations in the Los Yoses neighborhood of San José. A bit more attention seems to be paid to teacher training and selection here than at other institutions around town. A 2-week course with 4 hours of classes per day and a home stay costs around $615 (£308).

Escuela D'Amore *ℛ* ((𝒞/fax **262/367-8598** in the U.S., or 𝒞/fax 777-1143; www.escueladamore.com) is situated in the lush surroundings of Manuel Antonio National Park. A 2-week conversational Spanish course, including a home stay and two meals daily, costs $995 (£498). Fifteen percent of your tuition is donated to the World Wildlife Fund. This is a much nicer environment than San José for learning Spanish (for most everything else too, in fact).

Wayra Instituto de Español (𝒞/fax **653-0359;** www.spanish-wayra.co.cr) is located in the beach town of Tamarindo. A week of classes, 4 hours per day, will run you $250 (£125). Home stays and apartment rentals can be arranged.

MOTORCYCLES
Visiting bikers can either cruise the highways or try some off-road biking around Costa Rica. All the caveats about driving conditions and driving customs in Costa Rica apply equally for bikers. If you want to rent a Harley-Davidson for cruising around the country, **María Alexandra Tours** ((𝒞 **289-5552;** www.mariaalexandra.com) conducts guided bike tours, and rents well-equipped late-model Harleys by the day or the week. If your tastes run to off-road riding, **MotoAdventures** ((𝒞 **228-8494;** www.motoadventuring.com) runs guided multiday tours on Honda dirt bikes.

ROCK CLIMBING

Although this is a nascent sport in Costa Rica, the possibilities are promising. There are several challenging rock formations close to San José and along the Cerro de la Muerte, as well as great climbing opportunities on Mount Chirripó. The folks at **Tropical Bungee** (© 248-2212; www.bungee.co.cr) are the most dependable operators in this field, and they regularly organize climbing outings. Alternatively, you could visit **Mundo Aventura** (© 221-6934; www.maventura.com), an adventure- and climbing-gear store with an indoor climbing wall and in-house tour company.

SPAS & YOGA RETREATS

In addition to the places listed below, the bar just may be getting raised, as **Miraval Resorts** (© 800/232-3969 in the U.S. and Canada; www.miravalresort.com) is slated to open a destination spa in Guanacaste by late 2008.

Hotel Borinquen, Cañas Dulces (© 690-1900; www.borinquenresort.com; p. 156), on the flanks of the Rincón de la Vieja volcano, has the setting, natural hot springs, volcanic mud pots, and luxurious accommodations to be a world-class destination spa. But they've so far been unable to get the spa operation up to snuff.

The **Four Seasons Resort** ⁂ (© 800/819-5053 in the U.S., or 696-0098; www. fourseasons.com; p. 163) on the Papagayo Peninsula has ample facilities and treatment options, as well as scheduled classes in yoga, aerobics, and other disciplines.

Samasati ⁂, Puerto Viejo de Talamanca (© 800/563-9643 in the U.S., or 750-0315; www.samasati.com), is a lovely yoga retreat in some dense forest on a hillside above the Caribbean. Accommodations here range from budget to rustically luxurious. See "Puerto Viejo" in chapter 10.

Serenity Spa ⁂ (© 643-4094; serenityspa@racsa.co.cr) started out with a little storefront spa in Jacó but now contracts out the spa services at several large resorts up and down the Pacific coast. At last count, it was running the spas at the Los Sueños Marriott, Villas Caletas, Hotel Sí Como No, Hotel Club del Mar, Villablanca, and the San José Marriott, plus its original location in Jacó. See "Playa de Jacó" in chapter 8.

Sueño Azul Resort ⁂, Las Horquetas de Sarapiquí (© 764-1000; www.suenoazul resort.com; p. 221), is a nature lodge and retreat center with regular programs and retreats in a wonderful setting at the juncture of two rivers.

Tabacón Grand Spa Thermal Spa ⁂⁂⁂, Tabacón (© 877/277-8291 in the U.S. and Canada, or 519-1900; www.tabacon.com; p. 232), is a top-notch spa with spectacular hot springs, lush gardens, and a volcano view. A complete range of spa services and treatments is available at reasonable prices.

Xandari Resort & Spa ⁂⁂, Alajuela (© 866/363-3212 in the U.S., or 443-2020; www.xandari.com; p. 112), is a unique and distinctive little luxury hotel that has some top-notch spa facilities and services. This is a good choice if you're looking for a day or two of pampering, or for day treatments while staying in San José.

SURFING

When *Endless Summer II,* the sequel to the all-time surf classic, was filmed, the production crew brought its boards and cameras to Costa Rica. Point and beach breaks that work year-round are located all along Costa Rica's immense coastline. **Playas Hermosa, Jacó,** and **Dominical,** on the central Pacific coast, and **Tamarindo** and **Playa Guiones,** in Guanacaste, are becoming mini surf meccas. **Salsa Brava** in Puerto Viejo is a steep and fast wave that peels off both right and left over shallow coral. It has a habit of breaking boards, but the daredevils keep coming back for more. Beginners and folks looking to learn should stick to the mellower sections of **Jacó** and **Tamarindo**—surf lessons are offered at both beaches. Crowds are starting to gather at the more popular breaks, but you can still stumble onto secret spots on the **Osa** and **Nicoya peninsulas** and along the northern Guanacaste coast. Costa Rica's signature wave is still found at **Playa Pavones,** which is reputed to have one of the longest lefts in the world. The cognoscenti, however, also swear by places such as **Playa Grande, Playa Negra, Matapalo, Malpaís,** and **Witch's Rock.** An avid surfer's best bet is to rent a dependable four-wheel-drive vehicle with a rack and take a surfin' safari around the breaks of Guanacaste.

If you're looking for an organized surf vacation, contact **Tico Travel** (© **800/493-8426** in the U.S.; www.ticotravel.com), or check out **www.crsurf.com**. For swell reports, general surf information, live wave-cams, and great links pages, point your browser to **www.surfline.com**. Tico Travel also has a surf break map with at **www.tico travel.com/surfing**. Although killer sets are possible at any particular spot at any time of the year, depending upon swell direction, local winds, and distant storms, in broad terms, the northern coast of Guanacaste works best from December to April; the central and southern Pacific coasts work best from April to November; and the Caribbean coast's short big-wave season is December through March.

WHITE-WATER RAFTING, KAYAKING & CANOEING

Whether you're a first-time rafter or a world-class kayaker, Costa Rica's got some white water suited to your abilities. Rivers rise and fall with the rainfall, but you can get wet and wild here even in the dry season. The best white-water rafting ride is still the scenic **Pacuare River;** although there has been talk about damming it to build a hydroelectric plant, the project has thankfully failed to materialize. If you're just experimenting with river rafting, stick to Class II and III rivers, such as **Reventazón, Sarapiquí, Peñas Blancas,** and **Savegre.** If you already know which end of the paddle goes in the water, there are plenty of Class IV and V sections to run.

Die-hard river rats should get *Chasing Jaguars: The Complete Guide to Costa Rican Whitewater,* by Lee Eudy (Earthbound Sports Inc., 2003), a book loaded with photos, technical data, and route tips on almost every rideable river in the country.

Aventuras Naturales ⚡ (© **800/235-6150** in the U.S., or 225-3939; www.toenjoy nature.com) is a major rafting operator that runs daily trips on the most popular rivers in Costa Rica. Its Pacuare Jungle Lodge is a great place to spend the night on one of its 2-day rafting trips.

Canoe Costa Rica (©/fax **732/736-6586** in the U.S., or 282-3579; www.canoe costarica.com) is the only outfit I know of that specializes in canoe trips; it works primarily with custom-designed tours and itineraries, although it does have several set departure trips each year.

Exploradores Outdoors ⚡ (© **222-6262;** www.exploradoresoutdoors.com) is another good new company run by a longtime and well-respected river guide. They run the Pacuare, Reventazón, and Sarapiquí rivers, and even combine a 1-day river trip with onward transportation to or from the Caribbean coast.

If you're out on the Osa Peninsula, hook up with **Escondido Trex** ⚡ (©/fax **735-5210;** www.escondidotrex.com).

Ríos Tropicales ⚡ (© **233-6455;** www.riostropicales.com) is one of the major operators in Costa Rica, operating on most of the popular rivers. Lodgings include a very comfortable lodge on the banks of the Río Pacuare for the 2-day trips.

In Search of Turtles

Few places in the world have as many sea-turtle nesting sites as Costa Rica. Along both coasts, five species of these huge marine reptiles come ashore at specific times of the year to dig nests in the sand and lay their eggs. Sea turtles are endangered throughout the world due to over-hunting, accidental deaths in fishing nets, development on beaches that once served as nesting areas, and the collection and sale (often illegally) of their eggs. International trade in sea-turtle products is already prohibited by most countries (including the U.S.), but sea-turtle numbers continue to dwindle.

Among the species of sea turtles that nest on Costa Rica's beaches are the **olive ridley** (known for their mass egg-laying migrations, or *arribadas*), **leatherback, hawksbill, green,** and **Pacific green turtle.** Excursions to see nesting turtles have become common, and they are fascinating, but please make sure that you and/or your guide do not disturb the turtles. Any light source (other than red-tinted flashlights) can confuse female turtles and cause them to return to the sea without laying their eggs. In fact, as more development takes place on the Costa Rican coast, hotel lighting may cause the number of nesting turtles to drop. Luckily, many of the nesting beaches have been protected as national parks.

Here are the main places to see nesting sea turtles: **Santa Rosa National Park** (near Liberia), **Las Baulas National Marine Park** (near Tamarindo), **Ostional National Wildlife Refuge** (near Playa Nosara), and **Tortuguero National Park** (on the northern Caribbean coast).

See the regional chapters for descriptions of the resident turtles and their respective nesting seasons, as well as listings of local tour operators and companies that arrange trips to see sea turtles nesting.

WINDSURFING & KITEBOARDING

Windsurfing is not very popular on the high seas here, where winds are fickle and rental options are limited, even at beach hotels. However, **Lake Arenal** is considered one of the top spots in the world for high-wind boardsailing. During the winter months, many of the regulars from Washington's Columbia River Gorge take up residence around the nearby town of Tilarán. Small boards, water starts, and fancy gibes are the norm. The best time for windsurfing on Lake Arenal is between December and March. The same winds that buffet Lake Arenal make their way down to **Bahía Salinas** (also known as Bolaños Bay), near La Cruz, Guanacaste, where you can get in some good windsurfing. Both spots have also recently seen the opening of operations offering lessons and equipment rentals in the new high-action sport of kiteboarding. See "La Cruz" in chapter 6 and "Along the Shores of Lake Arenal" in chapter 7 for details.

3 Costa Rica's Top National Parks & Bioreserves

Costa Rica has 26 national parks, protecting more than 12% of the country. They range in size from the 212-hectare (524-acre) Guayabo National Monument to the 189,696-hectare (468,549-acre) La Amistad National Park. Many of these national parks are undeveloped tropical forests, with few services or facilities available for visitors. Others, however, offer easier access to their wealth of natural wonders.

Most of the national parks charge a $6 or $8 (£3 or £4) per-person per-day fee for any foreigner, although some have begun charging slightly more and a few slightly less. Costa Ricans and foreign residents continue to pay just $1 (50p). At parks where camping is allowed, there is usually an additional charge of around $2 (£1) per person per day.

This section is not a complete listing of all of Costa Rica's national parks and protected areas, but rather a selective list of those parks that are of greatest interest and accessibility. They're popular, but they're also among the best. You'll find detailed information about food and lodging options near some of the individual parks in the regional chapters that follow. As you'll see from the descriptions, Costa Rica's national parks vary greatly in terms of attractions, facilities, and accessibility. For a map of the country's parks, see the color insert at the front of this book.

If you're looking for a camping adventure or an extended stay in one of the national parks, I recommend **Santa Rosa, Rincón de la Vieja, Chirripó, Corcovado,** or **Cahuita.** Any of the others are better suited for day trips or guided hikes, or in combination with your travels around the country.

For more information, call the national parks information line at © **192,** or the main office at © **283-8004.** You can also stop by the **National Parks Foundation office** (© **257-2239**) in San José, located between Calle 23 and Avenida 15. Both offices are open Monday through Friday from 9am to 5pm.

SAN JOSE/CENTRAL VALLEY AREA

GUAYABO NATIONAL MONUMENT   This is the country's only significant pre-Columbian archaeological site. It's believed that Guayabo supported a population of about 10,000 people some 3,000 years ago. The park is set in a forested area rich in flora and fauna, although the ruins are quite small and limited when compared to sites in Mexico, Guatemala, and South America. **Location:** 19km (12 miles) northeast of Turrialba, which is 53km (33 miles) east of San José. See "Side Trips from San José" in chapter 5.

IRAZU VOLCANO NATIONAL PARK ⋪   Irazú Volcano is the highest (3,378m/ 11,080 ft.) of Costa Rica's four active volcanoes and a popular day trip from San José. A paved road leads right up to the crater, and the lookout also has a view of both the Pacific and the Caribbean on a clear day. The volcano last erupted in 1963 on the same day U.S. President John F. Kennedy visited the country. There are an information center, picnic tables, restrooms, and a parking area here. **Location:** 55km (34 miles) east of San José. See "Holy Smoke! Choosing the Volcano Trip That's Right for You" in chapter 5.

POAS VOLCANO NATIONAL PARK ⋪⋪   Poás is the other active volcano close to San José. The main crater is more than 1.6km (1 mile) wide, and it is constantly active with fumaroles and hot geysers. I slightly prefer Poás to Irazú because it is surrounded by dense cloud forests, and there are some nice gentle trails to hike here. Although the area around the volcano is lush, much of the growth is stunted due to the gases and acid rain. The park sometimes closes when the gases get too feisty. There are nature trails, picnic tables, restrooms, and an information center. **Location:** 37km (23 miles) northwest of San José. See "Holy Smoke!: Choosing the Volcano Trip That's Right for You" in chapter 5.

GUANACASTE & THE NICOYA PENINSULA

BARRA HONDA NATIONAL PARK   Costa Rica's only underground national park, Barra Honda features a series of limestone caves that were once part of a coral reef some 60 million years ago. Today the caves are home to millions of bats and impressive stalactite and stalagmite formations. Only Terciopelo Cave is open to the public. There are a camping area, restrooms, and an information center here, as well as trails through the surrounding tropical dry forest. **Location:** 335km (208 miles) northwest of San José. See "Playa Sámara" in chapter 6.

PALO VERDE NATIONAL PARK   A must for bird-watchers, Palo Verde National Park is one of Costa Rica's best-kept secrets. This part of the Tempisque River lowlands supports a population of more than 50,000 waterfowl and forest bird species. Various ecosystems here include mangroves, savanna brush lands, and evergreen forests. There are camping facilities, an information center, and some nice, fairly new accommodations at the Organization for Tropical Studies (OTS) research station here. **Location:** 200km (124 miles) northwest of San José. Be warned that the park entrance is 28km (17 miles) off the highway down a very rugged dirt road; it's another 9km (5½ miles) to the OTS station and campsites. For more information, call the OTS (© **240-6696;** reservas@cro.ots.ac.cr). See "Liberia" in chapter 6.

RINCON DE LA VIEJA NATIONAL PARK 🐾🐾   This large tract of parkland experiences high volcanic activity, with numerous fumaroles and geysers, as well as hot springs, cold pools, and mud pots. You'll find excellent hikes to the upper craters and to several waterfalls. You should hire a guide for any hot-spring or mud-bath expeditions as inexperienced visitors have been burned. Camping is permitted at two sites, each of which has an information center, a picnic area, and restrooms. **Location:** 266km (165 miles) northwest of San José. See "Liberia" in chapter 6.

SANTA ROSA NATIONAL PARK 🐾   Occupying a large section of Costa Rica's northwestern Guanacaste province, Santa Rosa has the country's largest area of tropical dry forest, important turtle-nesting sites, and the historically significant La Casona monument. There are also caves for exploring. The beaches are pristine and have basic camping facilities, and the waves make them quite popular with surfers. An information center, a picnic area, and restrooms are at the main campsite and entrance. **Location:** 258km (160 miles) northwest of San José. For more information, you can call the park office at © **666-5051.** See "La Cruz & Bahía Salinas" in chapter 6.

THE NORTHERN ZONE

ARENAL NATIONAL PARK 🐾🐾   This new park, created to protect the ecosystem that surrounds Arenal Volcano, has few services or attractions. Basically, the government has set up a tollbooth on the access road leading to an up-close view of the volcano's lava flows. Most travelers and tour operators choose to forgo the entrance fee and watch the volcano from spots along the dirt road leading to the Arenal Observatory Lodge, or from the road to Tabacón, where the view is just as good as it is inside the park. However, there are several excellent hiking trails inside the park that explore cooled-off lava flows and the neighboring rainforest. **Location:** 129km (80 miles) northwest of San José. See "Arenal Volcano & La Fortuna" in chapter 7.

BRAULIO CARRILLO NATIONAL PARK   This park, which occupies a large area of the nation's central mountain range, is the park you pass through on your way from San José to the Caribbean coast. A deep rainforest, Braulio Carrillo receives an average of 177 inches of rain per year. There are beautiful rivers, majestic waterfalls, and more than 6,500 species of plants and animals. The park has an information center, picnic tables, restrooms, and hiking trails. Camping is allowed but is not very common or recommended. Be careful here. Make sure you park your car in and base your explorations from the park's main entrance, not just anywhere along the highway. There have been several robberies and attacks against visitors reported at trails leading into the park from the highway. This park also seems to have the highest incidence of lost hikers. **Location:** 22km (14 miles) north of San José. See "Puerto Viejo de Sarapiquí" in chapter 7.

CAÑO NEGRO NATIONAL WILDLIFE REFUGE 🦅 A lowland swamp and drainage basin for several northern rivers, Caño Negro is excellent for bird-watching. There are a few basic cabinas and lodges in this area, but the most popular way to visit is on a combined van and boat trip from the La Fortuna/Arenal area. **Location:** 20km (12 miles) south of Los Chiles, near the Nicaraguan border. See "Arenal Volcano & La Fortuna" in chapter 7.

MONTEVERDE BIOLOGICAL CLOUD FOREST RESERVE 🦅🦅🦅 This private reserve might be the most famous patch of forest in Costa Rica. It covers some 26,000 acres of primary forest, mostly midelevation cloud forest, with a rich variety of flora and fauna. Epiphytes thrive in the cool, misty climate. The most famous resident is the spectacular resplendent quetzal. There is a well-maintained trail system, as well as some of the best-trained and most experienced guides in the country. Nearby you can visit both the Santa Elena and Sendero Tranquilo reserves. **Location:** 167km (104 miles) northwest of San José. See "Monteverde" in chapter 7.

CENTRAL PACIFIC COAST

CARARA NATIONAL PARK 🦅🦅 Located just off the highway near the Pacific coast, on the road to Jacó, this is one of the best places in Costa Rica to see scarlet macaws. There are several trails through the park, including one that is wheelchair accessible. The park is comprised of various ecosystems, ranging from rainforests to transitional forests to mangroves. **Location:** 102km (63 miles) west of San José. See "Playa de Jacó & Playa Herradura" in chapter 8.

CHIRRIPO NATIONAL PARK 🦅🦅 Home to Costa Rica's tallest peak, 3,761m (12,336-ft.) Mount Chirripó, Chirripó National Park is a hike, but on a clear day you can see both the Pacific Ocean and the Caribbean Sea from its summit. There are a number of interesting climbing trails here, and camping is allowed. **Location:** 151km (94 miles) southeast of San José. See "San Isidro de El General: A Base for Exploring Chirripó National Park" in chapter 8.

MANUEL ANTONIO NATIONAL PARK 🦅🦅 Though relatively small, Manuel Antonio is the most popular national park and supports the largest number of hotels and resorts. This lowland rainforest is home to a healthy monkey population, including the endangered squirrel monkey. The park is best known for its splendid beaches. **Location:** 129km (80 miles) south of San José. See "Manuel Antonio National Park" in chapter 8.

THE SOUTHERN ZONE

CORCOVADO NATIONAL PARK 🦅🦅🦅 The largest single block of virgin lowland rainforest in Central America, Corcovado National Park receives more than 200 inches of rain per year. It's increasingly popular but still very remote. (It has no roads; only dirt tracks lead into it.) Scarlet macaws live here, as do countless other Neotropical species, including two of the country's largest cats, the puma and the endangered

Monkey Business

No trip to Costa Rica would be complete without at least one monkey sighting. Home to four distinct species of primates, Costa Rica offers the opportunity for one of the world's most gratifying wildlife-viewing experiences. Just listen for the deep guttural call of a howler or the rustling of leaves overhead—telltale signs that monkeys are in your vicinity.

Costa Rica's most commonly spotted monkey is the white-faced or **capuchin monkey** (*mono cara blanca* in Spanish), which you might recognize as the infamous culprit from the film *Outbreak*. Contrary to that film's plot, however, capuchins are native to the New World tropics and do not exist in Africa. Capuchins are agile, medium-size monkeys that make good use of their long, prehensile tails. They inhabit a diverse collection of habitats, ranging from the high-altitude cloud forests of the central region to the lowland mangroves of the Osa Peninsula. It's almost impossible not to spot capuchins at Manuel Antonio (see chapter 8), where they have become a little too dependent on fruit and junk-food feedings by tourists. Please do not feed wild monkeys (and try to keep your food away from them—they're notorious thieves), and boycott establishments that try to attract both monkeys and tourists with daily feedings.

Howler monkeys (*mono congo* in Spanish) are named for their distinct and eerie call. Large and mostly black, these monkeys can seem ferocious because of their physical appearance and deep, resonant howls that can carry for more than a mile, even in dense rainforest. Biologists believe that

jaguar. There are camping facilities and trails throughout the park. **Location:** 335km (208 miles) south of San José, on the Osa Peninsula. See "Puerto Jiménez: Gateway to Corcovado National Park" in chapter 9.

THE CARIBBEAN COAST

CAHUITA NATIONAL PARK ✿   A combination land and marine park, Cahuita National Park protects one of the few remaining living coral reefs in the country. The topography here is lush lowland tropical rainforest. Monkeys and numerous bird species are common. Camping is permitted, and there are basic facilities at the Puerto Vargas entrance to the park. If you want to visit for only the day, however, enter from Cahuita village because the local community has taken over that entrance and is asking for only a voluntary donation, in lieu of the normal $6 (£3) fee. **Location:** On the Caribbean coast, 42km (26 miles) south of Limón. See "Cahuita" in chapter 10.

TORTUGUERO NATIONAL PARK ✿✿   Tortuguero National Park has been called the Venice of Costa Rica due to its maze of jungle canals that meander through a dense lowland rainforest. Small boats, launches, and canoes carry visitors through these waterways, where caimans, manatees, and numerous bird and mammal species are common. The extremely endangered great green macaw lives here. On the beaches green sea turtles nest here every year between June and October. The park has a small but helpful information office and some well-marked trails. **Location:** 258km (160 miles) northeast of San José. See "Tortuguero National Park" in chapter 10.

male howlers mark the bounds of their territories with these deep, guttural sounds. In the presence of humans, however, howlers are actually a little timid and tend to stay higher up in the canopy than their white-faced cousins. Howlers are fairly common and easy to spot in the dry tropical forests of coastal Guanacaste and the Nicoya Peninsula (see chapter 6).

Even more elusive are **spider monkeys** (*mono araña* in Spanish). These long, slender monkeys are dark brown to black and prefer the high canopies of primary rainforests. Spiders are very adept with their prehensile tails but actually travel through the canopy with a hand-over-hand motion frequently imitated by their less graceful human cousins on playground monkey bars around the world. I've had my best luck spotting spider monkeys along the edges of Tortuguero's jungle canals (see chapter 10), where howlers are also quite common.

The rarest and most endangered of Costa Rica's monkeys is the tiny **squirrel monkey** (*mono tití* in Spanish). These small, brown monkeys have dark eyes surrounded by large white rings, white ears, white chests, and very long tails. In Costa Rica, squirrel monkeys can be found only at Manuel Antonio (see chapter 8) and the Osa Peninsula (see chapter 9). These seemingly hyperactive monkeys are predominantly fruit eaters and often feed on bananas and other fruit trees near hotels in both of the above-mentioned regions. Squirrel monkeys usually travel in large bands, so if you do see them, you'll likely see quite a few.

4 Tips on Health, Safety & Etiquette in the Wilderness

Much of what is discussed here is common sense. For more detailed information, see "Health" in chapter 2. Although most tours and activities are safe, there are risks involved in any adventure activity. Know and respect your own physical limits before undertaking any strenuous activity. Be prepared for extremes in temperature and rainfall and for wide fluctuations in weather. A sunny morning hike can quickly become a cold and wet ordeal, so it's usually a good idea to carry along some form of rain gear when hiking in the rainforest, or to have a dry change of clothing waiting at the end of the trail. Be sure to bring along plenty of sunscreen when you're not going to be covered by the forest canopy.

If you do any backcountry packing or camping, remember that it really *is* a jungle out there. Don't go poking under rocks or fallen branches. Snakebites are very rare, but don't do anything to increase the odds. If you encounter a snake, stay calm, don't make any sudden movements, and *do not* try to handle it. Also avoid swimming in major rivers unless a guide or local operator can vouch for their safety. Although white-water sections and stretches in mountainous areas are generally safe, most mangrove canals and river mouths in Costa Rica support healthy crocodile and caiman populations.

Bugs and bug bites will probably be your greatest health concern in the Costa Rican wilderness, and even they aren't as big of a problem as you might expect. Mostly, bugs are an inconvenience, although mosquitoes can carry malaria or dengue (see "Health," in chapter 2, for more information). A strong repellent and proper clothing minimize both the danger and the inconvenience; you might also want to bring along some cortisone or Benadryl cream to soothe itching. At the beaches, you'll probably be bitten by *pirujas* (sand fleas). These nearly invisible insects leave an irritating welt. Try not to scratch because this can lead to open sores and infections. Pirujas are most active at sunrise and sunset, so you might want to cover up or avoid the beaches at these times.

And remember: Whenever you enter and enjoy nature, you should tread lightly and try not to disturb the natural environment. There's a popular slogan well known to most campers that certainly applies here: "Leave nothing but footprints; take nothing but memories." If you must take home a souvenir, take photos. Do not cut or uproot plants or flowers. Pack out everything you pack in, and *please* do not litter.

5 Ecologically Oriented Volunteer & Study Programs

Below are some institutions and organizations that are working on ecology and sustainable development projects.

APREFLOFAS (Association for the Preservation of the Wild Flora and Fauna) (© 240-6087; www.preserveplanet.org) is a pioneering local conservation organization that accepts volunteers and runs environmentally sound educational tours around the country.

Asociación de Voluntarios para el Servicio en las Areas Protegidas (ASVO) (©/fax 506/233-4989; www.asvocr.com) organizes volunteers to work in Costa Rican national parks. A 2-week minimum commitment is required, as is a basic ability to converse in Spanish. Housing is provided at a basic ranger station, and there is a $15 (£7.50) daily fee to cover food, which is basic Tico fare.

Costa Rica Rainforest Outward Bound School (© 800/676-2018 in the U.S., or 278-6058; www.crrobs.org) is the local branch of this well-respected international adventure-based outdoor-education organization. Courses range from 2 weeks to a full semester, and offerings include surfing, kayaking, tree climbing, and learning Spanish.

Earthwatch Institute (© 800/776-0188 in the U.S.; www.earthwatch.org) organizes volunteers to go on research trips to help scientists collect data and conduct field experiments in a number of scientific fields and a wide range of settings. Expeditions to Costa Rica range from studies of the nesting habits of leatherback sea turtles to research into sustainable coffee-growing methods. Fees for food and lodging average around $2,650 (£1,325) for a 2-week expedition, excluding airfare.

Eco Teach (© 800/626-8992 in the U.S.; www.ecoteach.com) works primarily in facilitating educational trips for high school and college student groups. Trips focus on Costa Rican ecology and culture. Costs run around $1,395 to $1,595 (£698–£798) per person for a 10-day trip, including lodging, meals, classes, and travel within the country. Airfare to Costa Rica is extra.

Global Volunteers (© 800/487-1074 in the U.S.; www.globalvolunteers.org) is a U.S.-based organization that offers a unique opportunity to travelers who've always wanted a Peace Corps–like experience but can't make a 2-year commitment. For 2 to 3 weeks, you can join one of its working vacations in Costa Rica. A certain set of skills, such as engineering or agricultural knowledge, is helpful but by no means necessary. Each trip is undertaken at a particular community's request, to complete a specific project. However, be warned: These "volunteer" experiences do not come cheap. You must pay for your transportation as well as a hefty program fee, around $2,295 (£1,148) for a 2-week program.

Habitat for Humanity International (© 296-3436; www.habitatcostarica.org) has several chapters in Costa Rica and sometimes runs organized Global Village programs here.

The **Institute for Central American Development Studies** ⚓ (© 225-0508; www.icads.org) offers internship and research opportunities in the areas of environment, agriculture, human rights, and women's studies. An intensive Spanish-language program can be combined with work-study or volunteer opportunities.

The **Monteverde Institute** (© 645-5053; www.mvinstitute.org) offers study programs in Monteverde and also has a volunteer center that helps in placement and training of volunteers.

The **Organization for Tropical Studies** ⚓ (© 524-0607; www.ots.ac.cr) represents several Costa Rican and U.S. universities. This organization's mission is to promote research, education, and the wise use of natural resources in the tropics. Research facilities include La Selva Biological Station near Braulio Carrillo National Park and Palo Verde, and the Wilson Botanical Gardens near San Vito. Housing is provided at one of the research facilities. There's a wide variety of programs, ranging from full-semester undergraduate programs to specific graduate courses (of varying duration), to its recently added tourist programs. (These are generally being sponsored/run by established operators such as Costa Rica Expeditions and Elderhostel.) These range in duration from 3 to 10 days, and costs vary greatly. Entrance requirements and competition for some of these courses can be demanding.

Vida (© 221-8367; www.vida.org) is a local nongovernmental organization working on sustainable development and conservation issues; it can often place volunteers.

San José

With the increasing number of direct flights into Liberia, San José is no longer the de facto transportation hub for all tourists coming to Costa Rica, but most do still fly in and out of the country's capital. For years, my stock advice to tourists in terms of San José has been to get in and out as quickly as possible. For most, this remains good council. But San José is the country's only major metropolitan city, with varied and active restaurant and nightlife scenes, several museums and galleries worth visiting, and a steady stream of theater, concerts, and other cultural events that you won't find elsewhere in the country.

At first blush, San José seems little more than a chaotic jumble of cars, buses, buildings, and people. The central downtown section of San José exists in a near-constant state of gridlock. Antiquated buses spewing diesel fumes and a lack of emission controls have created a brown cloud over the city's sky. Sidewalks are poorly maintained and claustrophobic, and street crime is a problem. Most visitors quickly seek the sanctuary of their hotel room and the first chance to escape the city.

Still, things have been improving in recent years. Mayor Johnny Araya has led ambitious and controversial campaigns to rid the narrow sidewalks of impromptu and illegal vendors, to reduce the clutter of billboards and overhead signs, and to bury a good share of the city's electrical and phone cables.

This chapter helps you plan whatever time you intend for the capital and ease your way through the pitfalls inherent in such a rough-and-tumble little city.

IT'S IN THE BEANS San José was built on the profits of the coffee-export business. Between the airport and downtown, you'll pass working coffee farms. Glance up from almost any street in the city and on the surrounding volcanic mountains you'll see a patchwork quilt of farm fields, most of which are planted with the *grano de oro* (golden bean), as it's known here. San José was a forgotten backwater of the Spanish empire until the first shipments of the local beans made their way to sleepy souls in Europe late in the 19th century. Soon San José was riding high. Coffee planters, newly rich and craving culture, imposed a tax on themselves to build the Teatro Nacional (National Theater), San José's most beautiful building. Coffee profits also built the city a university. Today you can wake up and smell the coffee roasting as you wander the streets near the Central Market (Mercado Central), and in any cafe or restaurant you can get a hot cup of sweet, milky *cafe con leche* to taste the bean that built San José.

Part of the reason the coffee grows so well is the climate. The Central Valley, in which the city sits, has what's often been described as a perfect climate. At 1,125m (3,690 ft.) above sea level, San José enjoys springlike temperatures year-round. The pleasant climate, along with the beautiful views of lush green mountainsides, makes San José a memorable city to visit. All you have to do is glance up at those mountains to know that this is one of the most beautifully situated capitals in Central America. And if a glance isn't enough for you, you'll find that it's extremely easy to get out into the countryside. Within an hour or two, you can climb a volcano, go white-water rafting, hike through a cloud forest, and stroll through a butterfly garden—among many other activities.

1 Orientation

ARRIVING
BY PLANE
Juan Santamaría International Airport (© 437-2626 for 24-hr. airport information; airport code SJO) is located near the city of Alajuela, about 20 minutes from downtown San José. A taxi into town costs between $12 and $16 (£6–£8), and a bus is only 60¢ (30p). The Alajuela–San José buses run frequently and will drop you off anywhere along Paseo Colón or at a station near the Parque de la Merced (downtown, between calles 12 and 14 and avs. 2 and 4). There are two separate lines: **Tuasa** buses are red; **Station Wagon** buses are beige/yellow. At the airport you'll find the bus stop directly in front of the main terminal, beyond the parking structure. Be sure to ask whether the bus is going to San José, or you'll end up in Alajuela. If you have a lot of luggage, you should probably take a cab.

Quite a few car-rental agencies have desks and offices at the airport, although if you're planning to spend a few days in San José itself, a car is a liability. (If you're heading off immediately to the beach, though, it's much easier to pick up your car here than at a downtown office.) Several car-rental agencies already have desks inside the new terminal, right where passengers exit Customs and Immigration; others are still awaiting completion of an airport remodeling (see below), so be sure to contact them first to confirm that they will have an agent or an office at the airport when you arrive.

At press time the airport was still in the midst of a major renovation and expansion. So far, the first phase of the new terminal has been completed, and all of the major airlines have moved their desks into the terminal. The baggage claim and Customs and Immigration areas, which are modern and spacious, are not necessarily fast and efficient. Moreover, despite the major remodeling, chaos and confusion continue to greet arriving passengers the second they step out of the terminal. You must abandon the luggage carts just before exiting the building and then face a gauntlet of aggressive taxi drivers and people offering to carry your bags. Fortunately, the official airport taxi service (see below) has a booth inside the terminal after you clear Customs. Most porters or skycaps wear a uniform identifying them as such, but sometimes "improvised" porters will try to earn a few dollars here. (Moreover, there's often really nowhere for them to have to carry your bags because the line of waiting taxis and shuttles is just steps away.) The entire airport renovation and expansion should be completed sometime in mid-2008. There is hope that things will improve some once the work is done and new facilities are opened.

In terms of taxis, you should stick with the official airport taxi service, **Taxis Unidos Aeropuerto** (© 221-6865), which operates a fleet of orange vans and sedans, charging fixed prices according to your destination. Head to its kiosk in the no-man's land just outside the exit door for arriving passengers. Here you can buy a prepaid voucher to the hotel or destination of your choice. Despite the fact that Taxis Unidos has an official monopoly at the airport, you will usually find a handful of regular cabs

"I Know There's Got to Be a Number Here Somewhere. . . .": The Arcane Art of Finding an Address in San José

This is one of the most confusing aspects of visiting Costa Rica in general, and San José in particular. Although there are often street addresses and building numbers for locations in downtown San José, they are almost never used. Addresses are given as a set of coordinates such as "Calle 3 between avenidas Central and 1." It's then up to you to locate the building within that block, keeping in mind that the building could be on either side of the street. Many addresses include additional information, such as the number of meters from a specified intersection or some other well-known landmark. (These "meter measurements" are not precise but are a good way to give directions to a taxi driver. In basic terms, 100m = 1 block, 200m = 2 blocks, and so on.) These landmarks are what become truly confusing for visitors to the city because they are often simply restaurants, bars, and shops that would be familiar only to locals.

Things get even more confusing when the landmark in question no longer exists. The classic example of this is "the Coca-Cola," one of the most common landmarks used in addresses in the blocks surrounding San José's main market. The trouble is, the Coca-Cola bottling plant that it refers to is no longer there; the edifice is long gone, and one of the principal downtown bus depots stands in its place. Old habits die hard, though, and the address description remains. You might also try to find someplace near the *antiguo higuerón* ("old fig tree") in San Pedro. This tree was felled years ago. In outlying neighborhoods, addresses can become long directions such as "50m (½ block) south of the old church, then 100m (1 block) east, then 20m (two buildings) south." Luckily for the visitor, most downtown addresses are more straightforward.

Oh, and if you're wondering how letter carriers manage, well, welcome to the club. Some folks actually get their mail delivered this way, but most people and businesses in San José use a post office box. This is called an *apartado* and is abbreviated "Apdo." or "A.P." in mailing addresses.

(in traditional red sedans) and "pirate" cabs, freelance drivers using their own vehicles. You could use either of these latter options, and they tend to charge a dollar or two less, but I recommend using the official service for safety and standardized prices. Keep a very watchful eye on your bags: Thieves have historically preyed on newly arrived passengers and their luggage. You should tip porters about 50¢ (25p) per bag.

You have several options for **exchanging money** when you arrive at the airport. There's an ATM in the baggage claim area, which is connected to both the PLUS and Cirrus networks. There's also a **Global Exchange** money exchange booth just as you clear Customs and Immigration. It's open whenever there are arriving flights; however, these folks exchange at more than 10% below the official rate. There's a branch of the **Banco de San José** inside the main terminal, on the second floor across from the airline check-in counters, as well as a couple more ATM machines up there. The taxi company and rental-car agencies accept U.S. dollars. See "Money & Costs," in chapter 2, for more details.

Tip: There's really no pressing need to exchange money the minute you arrive. Taxis Unidos accepts dollars. You can wait until after you settle into your hotel, and see if the hotel will give you a good rate of exchange, or use one of the many downtown banks or ATM machines.

If you arrive in San José via Nature Air, private aircraft, or another small commuter or charter airline, you might find yourself at the **Tobías Bolaños International Airport** in Pavas. This small airport is located on the western side of downtown San José, about 10 minutes by car from the center. There are no car-rental desks here, so unless you have a car or a driver waiting for you here, you will have to take a cab into town, which should cost between $10 and $18 (£5–£9).

BY BUS

If you're coming to San José by bus, where you disembark depends on where you're coming from. (The different bus companies have their offices, and thus their drop-off points, all over downtown San José. When you buy your ticket, ask where you'll be let off.) Buses arriving from Panama pass first through Cartago and San Pedro before letting passengers off in downtown San José; buses arriving from Nicaragua generally enter the city on the west end of town, on Paseo Colón. If you're staying here, you can ask to be let off before the final stop.

BY CAR

For those of you intrepid readers arriving by car, you'll enter San José via the Interamerican Highway. If you arrive **from Nicaragua and the north,** the highway brings you first past the airport and the city of Alajuela, to the western edge of downtown, right at the end of Paseo Colón, where it hits Parque La Sabana (La Sabana Park). The area is well marked with large road signs that direct you either to downtown (CENTRO) or to the western suburbs of Rohrmoser, Pavas, and Escazú. If you're heading toward downtown, follow the flow of traffic and turn left on Paseo Colón.

For those of you entering **from Panama and the south,** things get a little more complicated. The Interamerican Highway first passes through the city of Cartago and then through the San José suburbs of Curridabat and San Pedro before reaching downtown. This route is relatively well marked, and if you stick with the major flow of traffic, you should find San José without any problem.

VISITOR INFORMATION

There's an **Instituto Costarricense de Turismo (ICT)** (© 443-2883; www.visit costarica.com) desk at the Juan Santamaría International Airport, located in the baggage claims area, just before Customs. You can pick up maps and browse brochures, and they might even lend you a phone to make or confirm a reservation. It's open Monday through Friday from 9am to 5pm, which is more than a little bit pathetic because such a large number of flights arrive either on the weekends or after 5pm. If you're looking for the **main ICT visitor information center** in San José, it's located below the Plaza de la Cultura, at the entrance to the Gold Museum, on Calle 5 between avenidas Central and 2 (© 222-1090). The people here are helpful, although the information they have to offer is rather limited. This office is also open Monday through Friday from 9am to 5pm. There's also another ICT information desk at the **main Post Office** (© 258-8762; Calle 2 between avenidas 1 and 3), which is open Monday through Friday from 8am to 4pm.

San José

ACCOMMODATIONS ■

Aurola Holiday Inn **21**
Clarion Amón Plaza **18**
Gran Hotel Costa Rica **29**
Hotel 1492 Jade y Oro **43**
Hotel Aranjuez **40**
Hotel Britannia **19**
Hotel Cacts **9**
Hotel Del Rey **34**
Hotel Don Carlos **22**
Hotel Grano de Oro **6**
Hôtel Le Bergerac **42**

Hotel Parque del Lago **5**
Hotel Posada del Museo **39**
Hotel Presidente **33**
Hotel Rosa del Paseo **7**
Hotel Santo Tomás **20**
Pensión de la Cuesta **35**
Radisson Europa Hotel **12**
Raya Vida Villa **15**
Tryp Corobicí **2**

RESTAURANTS ◆

Bakea **17**
Café del Teatro Nacional **31**
Café Mundo **24**
Cafeteria 1830 **29**
Chelles **32**
Del Mar **34**
El Chicote **1**
Grano de Oro Restaurant **6**
Il Ritorno **41**
Jurgen's **45**
La Cocina de Leña **13**

Machu Picchu **8**
Olio **44**
Soda Tapia **4**
Tin Jo **36**
Vishnu **26, 27, 37**

ATTRACTIONS ●
Centro Nacional de Arte y Cultura **25**
Mercado Central **10**
Museo de Arte Costarricense **3**
Museo de Jade Marco Fidel Tristán **23**
Museo de Los Niños **11**
Museo Nacional de Costa Rica **38**
Museos del Banco Central de Costa Rica **28**
Parque Zoológico Simón Bolívar **16**
Spirogyra Butterfly Garden **14**
Teatro Melico Salazar **30**
Teatro Nacional **31**

CITY LAYOUT

Downtown San José is laid out on a grid. *Avenidas* (avenues) run east and west, while *calles* (streets) run north and south. The center of the city is at **Avenida Central** and **Calle Central.** To the north of Avenida Central, the avenidas have odd numbers beginning with Avenida 1; to the south, they have even numbers beginning with Avenida 2. Likewise, calles to the east of Calle Central have odd numbers, and those to the west have even numbers. The main downtown artery is **Avenida 2,** which merges with Avenida Central on either side of the downtown area. West of downtown, Avenida Central becomes **Paseo Colón,** which ends at Parque La Sabana and feeds into the highway to Alajuela, the airport, and the Pacific coast. East of downtown, Avenida Central leads to San Pedro and then to Cartago and the Interamerican Highway heading south. **Calle 3** takes you out of town to the north, onto the Guápiles Highway that leads to the Caribbean coast.

THE NEIGHBORHOODS IN BRIEF

San José is divided into dozens of neighborhoods known as *barrios*. Most of the listings in this chapter fall within the main downtown area, but there are a few outlying neighborhoods you'll need to know about.

Downtown In San José's busy downtown, you'll find most of the city's museums, as well as a handful of small urban parks and open-air plazas, and the city's main Cathedral. There are also many tour companies, restaurants, and hotels here. Unfortunately, traffic noise and exhaust fumes make this one of the least pleasant parts of the city. Streets and avenues are usually bustling and crowded with pedestrians and vehicular traffic, and street crime is most rampant here. Still, the section of Avenida Central between Calle Central and Calle 7 has been converted into a pedestrian mall, slightly improving things on this stretch.

Barrio Amón/Barrio Otoya These two picturesque neighborhoods, just north and east of downtown, are the site of the greatest concentration of historic buildings in San José. Some of these have been renovated and turned into boutique hotels and atmospheric restaurants. If you're looking for character and don't mind the noise and exhaust fumes from passing cars and buses, this neighborhood makes a good base for exploring the city.

La Sabana/Paseo Colón Paseo Colón, a wide boulevard west of downtown, is an extension of Avenida Central and ends at Parque La Sabana. It has several good, small hotels and numerous restaurants. This is also where many of the city's car-rental agencies have their in-town offices. The Parque La Sabana is the city's largest public park, with ample green areas, sport facilities, and the Costa Rican Art Museum.

San Pedro/Los Yoses Located east of downtown San José, Los Yoses is an upper-middle-class neighborhood that is home to many diplomatic missions and embassies. San Pedro is a little farther east and is the site of the University of Costa Rica. Numerous college-type bars and restaurants are all around the edge of the campus, and several good restaurants and small hotels are in both neighborhoods.

Escazú/Santa Ana Located in the hills west of San José, Escazú and Santa Ana are two fast-growing suburbs. Although the area is only 15 minutes from San José by taxi, it feels much farther away because of its relaxed atmosphere. This area has a large expatriate community with many bed-and-breakfast establishments and excellent restaurants.

Heredia/Alajuela/Airport Area Heredia and Alajuela are two colonial-era cities that lie closer to the airport than San José. Alajuela is closer to the airport; Heredia is about midway between Alajuela and the capital. For more information on Heredia, see "Side Trips from San José," later in this chapter. Several quite nice high-end boutique hotels are in this area, and several large hotels and one chain hotel are located on, or just off, the Interamerican Highway close to the airport.

2 Getting Around

BY BUS

Bus transportation around San José is cheap—the fare is usually somewhere around 10¢ to 30¢ (5p–15p)—although the Alajuela/San José buses that run in from the airport cost 60¢ (30p). The most important buses are those running east along Avenida 2 and west along Avenida 3. The **Sabana/Cementerio** bus runs from Parque La Sabana to downtown and is one of the most convenient buses to use. You'll find a bus stop for the outbound Sabana/Cementerio bus near the main post office on Avenida 3 near the corner of Calle 2, and another one on Calle 11 between avenidas Central and 1. This bus also has stops all along Avenida 2. **San Pedro** buses leave from Avenida Central between calles 9 and 11, in front of the Cine Capri, and take you out of downtown heading east. **Escazú-** and **Santa Ana**–bound buses leave from the Coca-Cola bus station, as well as from Avenida 1 between calles 24 and 28. Alternatively, you can pick up both the Escazú and Santa Ana buses from the busy bus stop on Calle 42, just north of Gimnasio Nacional.

Board buses from the front. The bus drivers can make change, although they don't like to receive large bills. Be especially mindful of your wallet, purse, or other valuables, because pickpockets often work the crowded buses.

BY TAXI

Although taxis in San José have meters *(marías),* the drivers sometimes refuse to use them, particularly with foreigners, so you'll occasionally have to negotiate the price. Always try to get them to use the meter first (say *"ponga la maría, por favor"*). The official rate at press time is around 80¢ (40p) for the first kilometer (½ mile) and around 60¢ (30p) for each additional kilometer. If you have a rough idea of how far it is to your destination, you can estimate how much it should cost from these figures. After 10pm taxis are legally allowed to add a 20% surcharge. Some of the meters are programmed to include the extra charge automatically, but be careful: Some drivers will use the evening setting during the daytime or (at night) to charge an extra 20% on top of the higher meter setting. **Tipping** taxi drivers is not expected. It's not uncommon for passengers to sit in the front seat with the driver.

Depending on your location, the time of day, and the weather (rain places taxis at a premium), it's relatively easy to hail a cab downtown. You'll always find taxis in front of the Teatro Nacional (albeit at high prices) and around the Parque Central at Avenida Central and Calle Central. Taxis in front of hotels and the El Pueblo tourist complex usually charge more than others, although this is technically illegal. Most hotels will gladly call you a cab, either for a downtown excursion or for a trip back out to the airport. You can also get a cab by calling **Coopetaxi** (✆ 235-9966), **Coopeirazu** (✆ 254-3211), or **Coopeguaria** (✆ 227-9300). **Cinco Estrellas Taxi** (✆ 228-3159) is another company that is based in Escazú but services the entire metropolitan area and airport, and claims to always have an English-speaking operator on call.

ON FOOT

Downtown San José is very compact. Nearly every place you might want to go is within a 15-by-4-block area. Because of traffic congestion, you'll often find it faster to walk than to take a bus or taxi. Be careful when walking the streets any time of day or night. Flashy jewelry, loosely held handbags or backpacks, and expensive camera equipment tend to attract thieves. **Avenida Central** is a pedestrian-only street for the blocks from Calle Central toward the Cultural Plaza and a little bit beyond. It has been redone with interesting paving stones and the occasional fountain in an attempt to create a comfortable pedestrian mall.

BY TRAIN

In mid-2005, urban commuter train service was reopened in downtown San José. A single-line connecting the western neighborhood of Pavas with the eastern suburb of San Pedro passes right through the downtown, with prominent stops at, or near, the U.S. Embassy, Parque La Sabana, the downtown court area, and the Universidad de Costa Rica (University of Costa Rica) and Universidad Latina (Latin University). The train runs in each direction roughly every 2 hours between 5am and 6pm. The fare ranges from 20¢ to 60¢ (10p–30p) depending on the length of your ride.

BY CAR

It will cost you between $35 and $110 (£18–£55) per day to rent a car in Costa Rica (the higher prices are for 4WD vehicles). Many car-rental agencies have offices at the airport. If not, they will usually either pick you up or deliver the car to any San José hotel. If you decide to pick up your rental car in downtown San José, be prepared for some very congested streets.

The following companies have desks at Juan Santamaría International Airport, as well as offices downtown: **Alamo** (✆ 800/462-5266 toll-free within Costa Rica, or 242-7733 for central reservations; www.alamocostarica.com), **Adobe Rent A Car** (✆ 442-2422 at the airport, or 258-4242 in downtown San José; www.adobecar.com), **Avis** (✆ 800/331-1084 in the U.S., or 293-2222 central reservation number in Costa Rica; www.avis.com), **Budget** (✆ 800/527-0700 in the U.S., 436-2000 at the airport, or 255-4750 in downtown San José; www.budget.co.cr), **Dollar** (✆ 443-2950 at the airport, or 257-0671 in downtown San José; www.dollarcostarica.com), **Hertz** (✆ 800/654-3001 in the U.S., 443-4645 at the airport, or 221-1818 in downtown

---

⟨Tips⟩ Car-Rental Advice

If you plan to rent a car, I recommend reserving it in advance from home. All the major international agencies and many local companies have toll-free numbers and websites. Sometimes you can even save a bit on the cost by reserving in advance. Costa Rica's car-rental fleet is not sufficient to meet demand during the high season when rental cars run at a premium. Sometimes this allows agencies here to gouge last-minute car-rental shoppers.

San José; www.hertz.com), **National Car Rental** (© **800/227-7368** toll-free within Costa Rica; 440-0085 at the airport, or 290-8787 in downtown San José; www.natcar.com), **Payless Rent A Car** (© **800/582-7432** in the U.S., 443-5286 at the airport, or 257-0026 in downtown San José; www.paylesscr.com), **Thrifty** (© **800/847-4389** in the U.S., 441-9366 at the airport, or 258-5868 in downtown San José; www.thrifty.com), and **Toyota Rent A Car** (© **441-1411** at the airport, or 258-5797 in downtown San José; www.toyotarent.com).

There are dozens of other car-rental agencies in San José, and most will arrange for airport or hotel pickup or delivery. One of the more dependable agencies is **Hola! Rent A Car,** across the street (west) of Denny's, La Uruca, San José (© **520-0100;** www.hola.net). For more advice on renting cars, see "Getting Around," in chapter 2.

FAST FACTS: San José

American Express American Express Travel Services is represented in Costa Rica by **ASV Olympia,** Oficentro La Sabana, Sabana Sur (© **242-8585**), which can issue traveler's checks and replacement cards and provide other standard services. To report lost or stolen Amex traveler's checks within Costa Rica, call the number above or call © **257-0155,** or call collect to 313/271-7887 in the United States.

Bookstores **Seventh Street Books,** Calle 7 between avenidas 1 and Central (© **256-8251**), has a wide range of new and used books in English, with an excellent selection of tropical biology, bird, and flora books; it's open daily from 9am to 7pm. For a wide selection of new books in English and Spanish, check out **Librería Internacional** (© **253-9553**; www.libreriainternacional.com), which has stores in the Multiplaza mall, as well as locations in downtown San José, Santa Ana, Zapote, Alajuela, Rohrmoser, Heredia, and Barrio Escalante.

Camera Repair **Dima,** Avenida Central between calles 3 and 5 (© **222-3969**), is your best bet for any equipment or repair needs.

Car Rentals See "Getting Around," above.

Currency Exchange It's easy to change money at banks in Costa Rica. In general private banks provide faster service than the state-run banks. Have someone direct you to a private bank or exchange house *(casa de cambio),* where you won't have to stand in line for hours. See "Money & Costs," in chapter 2, for more information.

Dentists Call your embassy, which will have a list of recommended dentists. Many bilingual dentists also advertise in the *Tico Times.* Because treatments are so inexpensive in Costa Rica, dental tourism has become a popular option for people needing extensive work.

Doctors Contact your embassy for information on doctors in San José, or see "Hospitals," below.

Drugstores There are countless pharmacies and drugstores in San José. Many of them deliver at little or no extra cost. The pharmacy at the **Hospital Clínica Bíblica,** Avenida 14 between calles Central and 1 (© **522-1000**), is open 24 hours every day. The pharmacy (© **208-1080**) at the **Hospital CIMA** in Escazú is also open 24 hours every day. **Farmacia Fischel** (© 295-7555; www.fischel.co.cr) has numerous branches around the metropolitan area.

Embassies & Consulates See "Fast Facts: Costa Rica," in chapter 2.

Emergencies In case of any emergency, dial © **911** (which should have an English-speaking operator); for an ambulance, call © **128**; and to report a fire, call © **118.**

Express Mail Services Many international courier and express-mail services have offices in San José, including **DHL,** on Paseo Colón between calles 30 and 32 (© **209-0000;** www.dhl.com); **EMS Courier,** with desks at the principal metropolitan post offices (© **800/900-2000** in Costa Rica; www.correos.go.cr); **FedEx,** which is based in Heredia but will arrange pickup anywhere in the metropolitan area (© **800/463-3339;** www.fedex.com); and **United Parcel Service,** in Pavas (© **290-2828;** www.ups.com). *Beware:* Despite what you might be told, packages sent overnight to U.S. addresses tend to take 3 to 4 days to reach their destination.

Eyeglasses Look for the word *óptica.* **Optica Vision** (© **255-2266**) is a widespread and dependable chain with stores all around San José and the rest of the country. They can do everything from eye exams to eyeglass repairs.

Hospitals **Clínica Bíblica,** Avenida 14 between calles Central and 1 (© **522-1000;** www.clinicabiblica.com), is conveniently located close to downtown and has several English-speaking doctors. The **Hospital CIMA** (© **208-1000;** www.hospitalsanjose.net), located in Escazú on the Próspero Fernández Highway, which connects San José and the western suburb of Santa Ana, has the most modern facilities in the country.

Internet Access Internet cafes are all over San José. Rates run between 50¢ and $2 per hour (25p–£1). Many hotels have their own Internet cafe or allow guests to send and receive e-mail. And many have added wireless access, either for free or a small charge. You can also try **Racsa,** Avenida 5 and Calle 1 (© **287-0087;** www.racsa.co.cr), the state Internet monopoly, which sells prepaid cards in 5-, 10-, and 15-hour denominations for connecting your laptop to the Web via a local phone call. Some knowledge of configuring your computer's dial-up connection is necessary, and you'll want to factor in the phone call charge if calling from a hotel.

Laundry & Dry Cleaning Self-service laundromats are uncommon in Costa Rica, and hotel services can be expensive. **Master** (© **226-9655**) and **Tyson** (© **225-7549**) are two dependable laundry and dry-cleaning chains with outlets all over town. The latter will even pick up and deliver your clothes free of charge.

Maps The Costa Rican Tourist Board (ICT; see "Visitor Information," earlier in this chapter) can usually provide you with decent maps of both Costa Rica and San José. Also try **Seventh Street Books,** Calle 7 between avenidas Central and 1 (© **256-8251**); **Librería Lehmann,** Avenida Central between calles 1 and 3 (© **223-1212**); and **Librería Universal,** Avenida Central and calles Central and 1 (© **222-2222**).

Newspapers & Magazines See "Fast Facts: Costa Rica" in chapter 2.

Photographic Needs Film is generally more expensive in Costa Rica, so bring from home what you need. You should also have your film processed at home, but if you must develop your prints here, try **Rapi Foto** (✆ **223-7640**) or **IFSA-Kodak** (✆ **223-1444**), both of which have several storefronts around downtown. For more serious photographic needs (equipment, repairs, and so on), try **Dima,** Avenida Central between calles 3 and 5 (✆ **222-3969**).

Police Dial ✆ **911** or ✆ **222-1365** for the police. They should have someone available who speaks English.

Post Office The main post office *(correo)* is on Calle 2 between avenidas 1 and 3 (✆ **800/900-2000** toll-free in Costa Rica, or 202-2900; www.correos.go.cr) and is open Monday through Friday from 8am to 5:30pm, and Saturday from 7:30am to noon. See "Mail" in "Fast Facts: Costa Rica" in chapter 2 for more information.

Restrooms These are known as *sanitarios* or *servicios sanitarios.* You might also hear them called *baños.* They are marked *damas* (women) and *hombres* or *caballeros* (men). Public restrooms are rare to nonexistent, but most big hotels and public restaurants will let you use their restrooms. Downtown, you can find public restrooms at the entrance to the Museo de Oro Banco Central (p. 124).

Safety Pickpockets and purse slashers are rife in San José, especially on public buses, in the markets, on crowded sidewalks, near hospitals, and lurking outside of bank offices and ATMs. Leave most of your money, and other valuables in your hotel safe, and carry only as much as you really need when you go out. If you do carry anything valuable with you, keep it in a money belt or special passport bag around your neck. Day packs are a prime target of brazen pickpockets throughout the city. One common scam involves someone dousing you or your pack with mustard or ice cream. Another scamster (or two) will then quickly come to your aid—they are usually much more interested in cleaning you out than cleaning you up.

Stay away from the red-light district northwest of the Central Market. Also be advised that the Parque Nacional is not a safe place for a late-night stroll. Other precautions include walking around corner vendors, not between the vendor and the building. The tight space between the vendor and the building is a favorite spot for pickpockets. Never park a car on the street, and never leave anything of value in a car, even if it's in a guarded parking lot. Don't even leave your car unattended by the curb in front of a hotel while you dash in to check on your reservation. With these precautions in mind, you should have a safe visit to San José. Also, see "Safety" in chapter 2.

Taxes All hotels charge 16.3% tax. Restaurants charge 13% tax and also add on a 10% service charge, for a total of 23% more on your bill. There is an airport departure tax of $26.

Taxis See "Getting Around," above.

Telegrams & Faxes With the spread of Internet communications, faxes and telegrams are becoming somewhat obsolete. Most hotels can send a fax for you. You can send telegrams and faxes from either the **ICE office** on Avenida 2 between calles 1 and 3 (www.grupoice.com; daily 7am–10pm), or **Racsa** (✆ **287-0087**; www.racsa.co.cr; Av. 5 and Calle 1; Mon–Fri 7:30am–5pm, Sat 9am–1pm), as well as from most **post office** branches (✆ **800/900-2000** toll-free in Costa Rica; www.correos.go.cr).

Telephones See "Staying Connected" in chapter 2. There are no city or area codes to dial from within Costa Rica; use the country code, 506, only when dialing a San José number from outside Costa Rica. (To call San José from the U.S., dial the international access code [011], then 506, and then the seven-digit number.)

Time Zone San José is on Central Standard Time (same as Chicago and St. Louis), 6 hours behind Greenwich Mean Time.

Useful Telephone Numbers For directory assistance, call © **113**; for international directory assistance, call © **124**; and for the exact time (in Spanish), call © **112**.

Water The water in San José is perfectly fine to drink. Nonetheless, some travelers experience stomach discomfort during their first few days in Costa Rica. If you want to be cautious, drink bottled water and *frescos* made with milk instead of water. *Sin hielo* means "no ice," and this is what you'll want to say if you're nervous about the water—just because it's frozen doesn't mean it's not water.

Weather The weather in San José (including the Central Valley) is usually temperate, never getting extremely hot or cold. May through November is the rainy season, although the rain usually falls only in the afternoon and evening.

3 Where to Stay

In San José, your hotel choices range from expensive luxury resorts to budget pensions charging only a few dollars a night. However, these two extremes are the exceptions, not the norm. The vast number of accommodations, and the best deals, are in the $80 to $150 (£40–£75) price range. Within this relatively moderate bracket, you'll find restored homes that have been turned into small hotels and bed-and-breakfasts, modern hotels with pools and exercise rooms, and older downtown business hotels.

While, in general, there are plenty of rooms to go around in San José, the small boutique hotels and better-run establishments (including those recommended here) are often booked well in advance during the high season.

CHOOSING WHERE TO STAY   **Downtown hotels,** many of which are in beautifully restored homes, are convenient to museums, restaurants, and shopping, but they can be noisy. Many people are also bothered by the exhaust fumes that permeate downtown streets. Moreover, because the streets of downtown are not especially safe, particularly at night, you should plan on taking taxis whether you stay downtown or in a nearby neighborhood or suburb. **Barrio Amón** is the downtown neighborhood with the most character and remnants of colonial architecture. If you want clean air and a peaceful night's sleep, consider staying out in the suburbs. **Escazú** and **Santa Ana** are both quiet yet modern suburbs, and many of the hotels there have great views. Heading east from downtown, **Los Yoses** is fairly close to the center of the action yet is still quiet. If you've rented a car, make sure your hotel provides secure parking or you'll have to find (and pay for) a nearby lot. If you plan to take some day tours, you can just as easily arrange these from a hotel situated outside the downtown area.

If you're heading out to Guanacaste, the central Pacific, or the northern zone, you might consider a hotel or bed-and-breakfast either near or beyond the airport. Sure, you give up proximity to downtown, but you can cut as much as an hour off your travel time to any of these destinations. Many car-rental companies will even deliver to or pick up cars from these establishments.

ALTERNATIVES TO HOTELS   If you plan to be in town for a while or are traveling with family or several friends, you might want to consider staying in an *aparto-tel,* a cross between an apartment complex and a hotel. You can rent by the day, week, or month, and you get a furnished apartment with a full kitchen, plus housekeeping and laundry service. Options include **Apartotel El Sesteo** ☆ ((© **877-623-3198** in the U.S. and Canada, or 296-1805; fax 296-1865; www.sesteo.com), **Apartotel La Sabana** ☆ (© **220-2422;** fax 231-7386; www.apartotel-lasabana.com), **Apartotel María Alexandra** (© **228-1507;** fax 289-5192; www.mariaalexandra.com), and **Apartotel Los Yoses** (© **225-0033;** fax 225-5595; www.apartotel.com).

Hint: You'll want to avoid motels in Costa Rica. To a fault, these are cut-rate affairs geared toward lovers consummating their affairs. Many rent out rooms by the hour. Some motels have private garages with roll-down doors outside each room, so that snoopy spouses or ex-lovers can't check for cars or license plates.

DOWNTOWN SAN JOSE/BARRIO AMON
EXPENSIVE
Aurola Holiday Inn *Overrated*   Situated directly across the street from the attractive downtown Parque Morazán, this is San José's only high-rise business-class hotel. The rooms are everything you might expect in this price range—but nothing more. Service can be somewhat hit-or-miss, and some of the rooms and furnishings are showing their age. Still, the location is great for exploring downtown on foot, and if you get one of the upper-floor rooms on the north side, you'll have one of the best views in the city.

Av. 5 and Calle 5 (A.P. 7802-1000), San José. © 800/465-4329 in the U.S. and Canada, or 222-2424. Fax 255-1171. www.holiday-inn.com. 200 units. $100–$130 (£50–£65) double; $160 (£80) junior suite; $220–$280 (£110–£140) suite; $750 (£375) presidential suite. AE, DC, MC, V. Free parking. **Amenities:** 2 restaurants; bar; poolside snack bar; indoor pool; exercise room; Jacuzzi; sauna; tour desk; car-rental desk; well-appointed business center; limited room service (6am–midnight); laundry service; nonsmoking rooms. *In room:* A/C, TV, dataport, minibar, coffeemaker, hair dryer, iron, safe.

Clarion Amón Plaza ☆   Located on the north edge of the historic Barrio Amón neighborhood, this hotel is larger and more luxurious than most of the area's smaller hotels. There's nothing particularly distinctive about the property or rooms here; however, in terms of service, location, and price, this hotel gets my nod over the nearby Holiday Inn. The rooms are all spacious, well kept, and come with plenty of amenities. And you are close to all the downtown action. While the food is merely average, the ambience of their little outdoor, sidewalk cafe, El Cafetal de la Luz, is delightful. There's also a fairly swank casino on site. You can usually do a bit better than the rack rates listed below if you book through www.choicehotels.com.

Av. 11 and Calle 3 bis (A.P. 4192-1000), San José. © 523-4600. Fax 523-4614. www.hotelamonplaza.com. 90 units. $120–$150 (£60–£75) double; $195–$225 (£98–£113) suite. AE, DC, MC, V. Free parking. **Amenities:** Restaurant; bar; lounge; casino; small exercise room; Jacuzzi; sauna; tour desk; modest business center; laundry service; babysitting; nonsmoking rooms. *In room:* A/C, TV, free Wi-Fi, coffeemaker, hair dryer, safe.

Radisson Europa Hotel ☆☆   This hotel is geared primarily to business travelers, but it's a good choice for anyone looking for a big, dependable luxury hotel near downtown San José. Wooden headboards, angular window nooks, and other small architectural details give these rooms an edge over those in the Aurola Holiday Inn and Clarion Amón Plaza, although it's not quite as convenient for walking around downtown. For a modest price increase, you can opt for an executive room, which is basically a standard room with a coffeemaker, a scale, terrycloth bathrobes, and an extra telephone in the bathroom. The junior suites come with all the above amenities, as well as a desk and chair, in-room fax machine, and small balcony. Both the executive rooms and suites have wireless Internet access. The hotel features a well-equipped gym that is part of the local Multispa chain. This hotel is particularly well-located if you are driving to or from the Caribbean coast, as it is set right off the main downtown entrance to the highway to Guapiles.

Calle Blancos, behind La República building (A.P. 538-2120), San José. ℂ 888/201-1718 in the U.S., or 257-3257. Fax 257-8221. www.radisson.com. 107 units. $85–$145 (£43–£73) double; $198 (£99) junior suite; $550 (£275) presidential suite. AE, DC, MC, V. Free parking. **Amenities:** 2 restaurants; bar; lounge; casino; pool; gym; tour desk; car-rental agency; full-service business center; small shopping arcade; limited room service; massage; laundry service; nonsmoking rooms. *In room:* A/C, TV, Wi-Fi, dataport, minibar, hair dryer, iron, safe.

MODERATE

In addition to the hotels listed below, the **Sleep Inn** (ℂ 222-0101; www.choice hotels.com; Avenida 3 between calles 9 and 11) is a modern, American-style chain hotel in the heart of downtown, while **Hotel Colonial** ℛ (ℂ 223-0109; www.hotel colonialcr.com; Calle 11 between avenidas 4 and 6) is a new boutique hotel in a restored Victorian-style home a couple of blocks south of the city center. **Hotel Doña Inés** (ℂ 222-7443; www.donaines.com) on Calle 11 between avenidas 2 and 6, and **Hotel Rincón de San José** (ℂ 221-9702; www.hotelrincondesanjose.com) on the corner of Avenida 9 and Calle 15, are also good options.

Gran Hotel Costa Rica   The Gran Hotel Costa Rica has arguably the best location of any downtown hotel (bordering the Teatro Nacional and the Plaza de la Cultura), and a major remodeling has finally brought the rooms and amenities almost up to snuff. Most of the rooms here are fairly large, and they sport fresh carpets, paint and furnishings. However, they still feel a bit spartan, and hot water seems to be on seriously short supply. Although it's set in a half block from busy Avenida 2, some find the street noise a problem here. The Cafeteria 1830, reviewed separately below, is perhaps the hotel's greatest attribute. It's memorable not so much for its food as for its atmosphere—it's an open-air patio that overlooks the National Theater, street musicians, and all the activity of the Plaza de la Cultura.

Av. 2, between calles 1 and 3, San José. ℂ 800/949-0592 in the U.S., or 221-4000. Fax 221-3501. www.gran hotelcr.com. 102 units. $87 (£44) double; $135–$179 (£68–£90) suite. Rates include breakfast buffet. AE, DC, MC, V. Free parking. **Amenities:** 2 restaurants; bar; small casino; small gym; tour desk; 24-hr. room service; laundry service. *In room:* TV, free Wi-Fi, minibar, safe.

Hotel Britannia ℛ   This is arguably the most luxurious of the many small hotels that have been created from restored old houses in downtown San José. Built in 1910, the large, low building, with its wraparound veranda, is certainly one of the most attractive in the neighborhood. However, the neighborhood has gone very downhill of late, and is pretty much now an annex to the city's red-light district. In the lobby, tile floors, large stained-glass picture windows, a brass chandelier, and reproduction Victorian decor all help set a tone of tropical luxury. Along with restoring the old home, the owners have built a four-story addition, which is separated from the original building by a narrow atrium. Rooms in the original home have hardwood floors and furniture; high ceilings and fans help keep them cool. In the deluxe rooms and junior suites, you get air-conditioning, one king or two queen-size beds, and a hair dryer in the bathroom. The standards come with either one king or two twin beds. Although the streetside rooms have double glass, light sleepers will still want to avoid them. The quietest rooms are those toward the back of the addition. In what was once the wine cellar, you'll find a casual restaurant. The buffet breakfast, along with afternoon tea and happy-hour drinks, is served in the adjacent sky-lit room.

Calle 3 and Av. 11 (A.P. 3742-1000), San José. (C) **800/263-2618** in the U.S. or 223-6667. Fax 223-6411. www.hotel britanniacostarica.com. 23 units. $89–$105 (£45–£53) double; $117 (£59) junior suite. AE, MC, V. Parking nearby. **Amenities:** Restaurant; bar; tour desk; Wi-Fi; limited room service; laundry service; nonsmoking rooms. *In room:* TV, safe, minibar.

Hotel Del Rey   You can't miss the Del Rey: It's a massive pink corner building with vaguely colonial styling. The lobby continues the facade's theme with pink-tile floors and stone columns. Inside, a carved hardwood door marks every guest room. The rooms vary in size and comfort: There are quiet interior rooms that have no windows, and larger rooms with windows (but also street noise). Try for a sixth-floor room with a balcony. The hotel's main restaurant is across the street in an old restored home, with plenty of stained glass. The hotel's 24-hour lobby bar and cafe serves respectable U.S.-style deli sandwiches, seafood, steaks, and pasta dishes. Much of the first floor is taken up with a bustling casino and the neighboring Blue Marlin Bar, which is very popular with tourists, expatriates, and prostitutes. The hotel's owners also manage the popular Key Largo Bar, just across the street.

Av. 1 and Calle 9 (A.P. 6241-1000), San José. (C) **866/255-8365** in the U.S. or 257-7800. Fax 221-0096. www.hoteldelrey.com. 104 units. $93–$110 (£47–£55) double; AE, MC, V. Parking nearby. **Amenities:** Restaurant; bar; tour desk; 24-hr. room service; laundry service. *In room:* A/C, TV, Wi-Fi, minibar, hair dryer, safe.

Hotel Don Carlos *(Finds)*   If you're looking for a small downtown hotel that is unmistakably Costa Rican and hints at the days of the planters and coffee barons, this is the place for you. Located in an old residential neighborhood, only blocks from the business district, the Don Carlos is popular with both vacationers and businesspeople. A large reproduction of a pre-Columbian carved-stone human figure stands outside the front door of this gray inn, which was a former president's mansion. Inside you'll find many more such reproductions, as well as orchids, ferns, palms, paintings, and parrots. After a day of exploring the capital, there's nothing like settling down in the lounge, the small courtyard, or the sunny deck, where the wicker furniture, bubbling fountain, and tropical breezes will make you think you're Hope or Crosby on the road to somewhere. The rooms are distinct and vary greatly in size, so be specific when you reserve, or ask if it's possible to see a few when you check in. Breakfast is served in an outdoor orchid garden and atrium. The gift shop here is one of the largest in the country, and guests get unlimited free local calls, one free international call, and free Internet access with the hotel's computer; if you brought your own laptop, you can use the hotel's Wi-Fi network.

779 Calle 9, between avs. 7 and 9, San José. (C) **221-6707**. Fax 258-1152. www.doncarloshotel.com. 33 units. $70–$90 (£35–£45) double. Rates include continental breakfast. AE, MC, V. Free parking. **Amenities:** Restaurant; bar; Jacuzzi; tour desk; limited room service (7am–9pm); laundry service. *In room:* TV, free Wi-Fi, hair dryer, iron, safe.

Hotel Presidente   This modern business-class hotel is an excellent midrange option in the heart of downtown. Although the hotel's eight stories practically qualify it for skyscraper status, very few of the rooms have any view to speak of; those with north-facing windows are your best bet. Rooms are all clean and well-kept and feature the basic amenities you'd expect. Most rooms come with one double and one single bed. If you want more space, opt for one of the junior suites. Rooms and suites with a "spa" designation come with a private Jacuzzi. The master suite is a massive two-bedroom affair, featuring a wide-screen TV in the living room and a private eight-person Jacuzzi. There's a very popular casual cafe-style restaurant just off the street.

Av. Central and Calle 7 (A.P. 2922-1000), San José. © 222-3022. Fax 221-1205. www.hotel-presidente.com. 100 units. $85 (£43) double; $125–$145 (£63–£73) junior or spa suite; $300 (£150) master suite. Rates include full breakfast buffet. AE, MC, V. Free parking. **Amenities:** Restaurant; bar; casino; small gym; rooftop Jacuzzi and sauna; tour desk; limited room service (6am–10pm); babysitting; laundry service. *In room:* A/C, TV, free Wi-Fi, minifridge, hair dryer, safe.

Hotel Santo Tomás *(Value* Even though it's on a busy downtown street, this converted mansion is a quiet oasis inside. Built more than 100 years ago by a coffee baron, the house has been lovingly restored and maintained by its owner, Thomas Douglas. Throughout the hotel you'll enjoy the deep, dark tones of well-aged and well-worked wood. The rooms vary in size, but most are fairly spacious and have a small table and chairs. All rooms are nonsmoking, although smoking is permitted in some of the common areas. Skylights in some bathrooms will brighten your morning, and firm beds provide a good night's sleep. There's also a small outdoor pool with a Jacuzzi above it; the two are solar heated and connected by a tiny waterslide. The staff and management are extremely helpful, and the restaurant here is excellent. This neighborhood is a little bit sketchy after dark, so you'd be advised to take a taxi to and from the hotel for any evening excursions.

Av. 7, between calles 3 and 5, San José. © 877/446-0658 in the U.S. or 255-0448. Fax 222-3950. www.hotelsanto tomas.com. 20 units. $70–$95 (£35–48) double. Rates include breakfast buffet. MC, V. Parking nearby. **Amenities:** Restaurant; bar; lounge; small pool; exercise room; Jacuzzi; tour desk; laundry service; nonsmoking rooms. *In room:* TV, free Wi-Fi.

Raya Vida Villa *(A* Located behind a big iron gate at the end of a narrow, dead-end lane, this little bed-and-breakfast is so secluded that it seems to be in a world all its own, yet it's in downtown San José. Behind the gate, in a shady old garden, is a miniature villa. The restored old stucco home is furnished with the owners' eclectic collection of crafts from around the world, and in the living room you'll find a grand piano and fireplace. Guest rooms are all different in style and decor. One features a four-poster bed with carved pineapples on the top of each post. The upstairs rooms have the largest bathrooms, and one even has a Jacuzzi tub. However, I like the downstairs room that opens onto a small open-air patio with a fountain.

Barrio Amón (A.P. 2209-2100), San José. © 223-4168. Fax 223-4157. www.rayavida.com. 4 units. $95 (£48) double. Rates include full breakfast and round-trip airport transfer. Rates lower in off season. MC, V. Free parking. *In room:* TV, no phone.

INEXPENSIVE

In addition to the places listed below, **Kap's Place** (© 221-1169; www.kapsplace.com), located across from the Hotel Aranjuez on Calle 19 between avenidas 11 and 13, is another good choice, while real budget hounds might want to try either **Tranquilo Backpackers** (© 222-2493; www.tranquilobackpackers.com), on Calle 7 between avenidas 9 and 11, or **Costa Rica Backpackers** (© 221-6191; www.costaricabackpackers.com), on Avenida 6 between calles 21 and 23.

Hotel Aranjuez *(Value* This is probably the best and deservedly most popular budget option close to downtown. Located on a quiet and safe street in the Barrio Amón neighborhood, this humble hotel is made up of five contiguous houses. All rooms are simple and clean, although some are a little dark. Rooms and bathrooms vary greatly in size, so ask when reserving, or try to see a few rooms when you arrive. The nicest features here, aside from the convivial hostel-like atmosphere, are the lush and shady gardens; the hanging orchids, bromeliads, and ferns decorating the hallways and nooks; and the numerous open lounge areas furnished with chairs, tables, and couches—great for lazing around and sharing travel tales with your fellow guests. The hotel has a couple of computers, as well as a free Wi-Fi network, and provides free local calling.

Calle 19, between avs. 11 and 13 (A.P. 457-2070), San José. © **877/898-8663** in the U.S. or 256-1825. Fax 223-3528. www.hotelaranjuez.com. 35 units, 6 w/shared bathroom. $25 (£13) double w/shared bathroom; $38–$42 (£19–£21) double w/private bathroom. Rates include breakfast buffet. V. Free parking. **Amenities:** Bar; several lounge areas; tour desk; laundry service. *In room:* TV, free Wi-Fi, safe.

Hotel Posada del Museo Located just across busy Avenida 2 from the Museo Nacional, this place offers up clean and cheerful rooms in the heart of downtown. The Victorian-style building dates to 1928 and has been immaculately restored. Rooms are spacious and feature either varnished wood or original ornate tile floors. The small restaurant here is set on a small pedestrian mall that leads to the Costa Rican Court complex, and features a few outdoor tables perfect for people-watching. The only downside here is the fact that Avenida 2 is one of the city's busiest and loudest, with a steady stream of bus, truck, and even train traffic struggling up the steep hill that crests right at this hotel. Even the rooms farthest from the street are susceptible to street noise.

Avenida 2 and Calle 17, San José. © **258-1027.** ©/fax 257-9414. www.hotelposadadelmuseo.com. 10 units. $50–$80 (£25–£40) double. Rates include full breakfast. Rates lower in off season. AE, DC, MC, V. Free parking. **Amenities:** Restaurant; lounge; tour desk; laundry service. *In room:* TV, free Wi-Fi.

Pensión de la Cuesta *(Value)* If you don't mind a clean communal bathroom down the hall from your room, this little bed-and-breakfast on the hill leading up to the Parque Nacional is a real bargain and definitely worth considering. It was once the home of Otto Apuy, a well-known Costa Rican artist, and original artwork abounds. The building itself is a classic example of a tropical wood-frame home and has been painted an eye-catching pink with blue and white trim. Some rooms are a bit dark and very simply furnished, but there's a sunny and cheery sunken lounge/courtyard area in the center of the house. Most rooms have one double and a set of bunk beds. Overall, the place feels a lot like a hostel. The owners give you free run of the kitchen and offer free use of their Internet connection. They also rent out a fully furnished apartment.

1332 Cuesta de Núñez, Av. 1 between calles 11 and 15, San José. © **256-7946** or ©/fax 255-2896. www.pension delacuesta.com. 15 units, none w/private bathroom. $28 (£14) double. Rates include continental breakfast and taxes. Children under 12 stay free in parent's room. AE, MC, V. Parking nearby. **Amenities:** Lounge w/cable TV; tour desk; laundry service. *In room:* Free Wi-Fi, no phone.

LA SABANA/PASEO COLON
VERY EXPENSIVE

Tryp Corobicí *(A)* Located just past the end of Paseo Colón and on the edge of Parque La Sabana, the Corobicí offers all the amenities you would expect at a large business-class hotel. The lobby is a vast expanse of marble floor faced by blank walls, although the Art Deco furnishings lend a bit of character. Guest rooms are modern and comfortable, with good beds and walls of glass through which, on most floors, you get good views of the valley and surrounding mountains. Joggers will enjoy the nearby Parque La Sabana. The Corobicí claims to have the largest health spa in

Central America; I don't think that this is still true, but you will find a well-equipped and modern gym featuring a large exercise room, on-staff trainers, and regular classes. The Fuji restaurant here is one of the better Japanese and sushi restaurants in San José. However, be sure to book directly via the hotel's website, as the rack rates they list below bear absolutely no relation to what you should and could be paying to stay here.

Autopista General Cañas, Sabana Norte (A.P. 2443-1000), San José. ✆ **888/95-MELIA** in the U.S. or 232-8122. Fax 231-5698. www.solmelia.com. 213 units. $255–$300 (£128–£150) double; $310–$500 (£155–£250) suite. AE, MC, V. Free parking. **Amenities:** 2 restaurants; bar; lounge; casino; midsize pool; health club and spa; Jacuzzi; sauna; tour desk; car-rental desk; business center; shopping arcade; salon; 24-hr. room service; in-room massage; babysitting; laundry service; nonsmoking rooms. *In room:* A/C, TV, free Wi-Fi, minibar, hair dryer, safe.

MODERATE

Hotel Grano de Oro ⟨Finds⟩   San José boasts dozens of old homes that have been converted into hotels, but none match luxurious accommodations and professional service found at the Grano de Oro. Located on a quiet side street off Paseo Colón, this hotel offers a variety of room types to fit a range of budgets and tastes. Personally, I prefer the patio rooms, which have French doors opening onto private patios. If you want a room with plenty of space, ask for one of the deluxe rooms, which have large, modern, tiled bathrooms with big tubs. All rooms are nonsmoking.

Throughout all the guest rooms, you'll find attractive hardwood furniture, including old-fashioned wardrobes in some rooms. For additional luxuries, you can stay in one of the suites, which have whirlpool tubs. The Vista de Oro suite is the hotel's crown jewel, with its own private staircase and wonderful views of the city and surrounding mountains. If you don't grab a suite, you still have access to the hotel's two rooftop Jacuzzis. The hotel's restaurant serves excellent international cuisine and some of the best desserts in the city. The owners of this hotel, Eldon and Lori Cooke, are the prime movers behind a noble shelter for young, unwed mothers, Casa Luz. Feel free to inquire as to how you can help.

Calle 30, no. 251, between avs. 2 and 4, 150m (1½ blocks) south of Paseo Colón, San José (mailing address: SJO 36, P.O. Box 025216, Miami, FL 33102). ✆ **255-3322.** Fax 221-2782. www.hotelgranodeoro.com. 40 units. $105–$160 (£53–£80) double; $190–$275 (£95–£138) suite. AE, MC, V. Free parking. **Amenities:** Restaurant; bar, lounge; 2 rooftop Jacuzzis; concierge; tour desk; limited room service (6am–10pm); laundry service; free Wi-Fi. *In room:* TV, dataport, minibar, safe.

Hotel Parque del Lago ⟨★⟩   This midsize business-class hotel is located on the western edge of busy Paseo Colón, right near the Costa Rican Art Museum and Parque La Sabana. Rooms are large and modern, but have a rather sober decor. The junior suites are especially spacious, with a comfortable couch, sitting area, wet bar, and microwave oven. The best room here is the rooftop penthouse, and it's not that much more expensive than the suites, and worth the slight splurge if available. There's wireless Internet throughout the hotel, and an elegant little restaurant and bar area just off the lobby. This hotel is convenient to both downtown and the western suburbs of Escazú and Santa, with easy access to the country's major highways.

Calle 40, between Avenida 2 and Paseo Colón, San José. ✆ **257-8787.** Fax 223-1617. www.parquedellago.com. 40 units. $114 (£57) double; $144 (£70) junior suite $194 (£97). Rates include full breakfast. AE, MC, V. Free parking. **Amenities:** Restaurant; bar; lounge; small gym; spa; Jacuzzi; sauna; tour desk; car-rental desk; business center; limited room service (11:30am–10pm); laundry service; nonsmoking rooms. *In room:* A/C, TV, free Wi-Fi, minibar, coffeemaker, hair dryer, safe.

Hotel Rosa del Paseo ⟨★⟩   This hotel is housed in one of San José's most beautiful old stucco homes, right on busy Paseo Colón. However, the rooms are all located away from the street and are pretty well insulated against the noise. Built more than 110 years ago, this old home has received regular upkeep and upgrading, yet is nevertheless richly appointed and surprisingly evocative of 19th-century Costa Rica. The rooms are all very comfortable. I'd definitely try to grab one of the rooms on the second floor, which feature wooden floors and front doors that open onto the open-air central courtyard. The master suite comes with its own balcony and Jacuzzi. There are beautiful details throughout the hotel: transoms, ornate stucco doorframes, and polished hardwood floors.

2862 Paseo Colón, between calles 28 and 30 (A.P. 287-1007, Centro Colón), San José. © 257-3225. Fax 223-2776. www.rosadelpaseo.com. 18 units. $75 (£38) double; $90–$120 (£45–£60) suite. Rates include continental breakfast. AE, DC, MC, V. Limited free parking. **Amenities:** Bar; lounge; tour desk; babysitting; laundry service; nonsmoking rooms. *In room:* TV, safe.

INEXPENSIVE
Hotel Cacts *(Finds)*   This is one of the more interesting and unusual budget hotels I've ever seen. It's housed in an attractive tropical contemporary home on a business and residential street. The current, and seemingly constantly expanding, complex is a maze of rooms and hallways on several levels. Rooms vary considerably in size, so it's always best to check out a few first if possible. The deluxe rooms here come with televisions and telephones, whereas the standard rooms lack both of these amenities. The newest additions here are a small pool and separate Jacuzzi, in a lush garden patio. The third-floor open terrace serves as the breakfast area. The staff here is very helpful, and the hotel will receive mail and faxes, change money, and store baggage for guests. All rooms are nonsmoking.

Av. 3 bis, no. 2845, between calles 28 and 30 (A.P. 379-1005), San José. © 221-2928 or 221-6546. Fax 221-8616. www.hotelcacts.com. 26 units. $45–$60 (£23–£30) double. Rates include breakfast buffet. AE, MC, V. Free parking. **Amenities:** Lounge; small outdoor pool; Jacuzzi; tour desk; laundry service; free Wi-Fi. *In room:* No phone in some rooms.

SAN PEDRO/LOS YOSES
MODERATE
In addition to the places listed below, the **Hotel Boutique Jade** (© 224-2455; www. hotelboutiquejade.com) is a modern business-class hotel with an excellent restaurant, while the **Hotel Don Fadrique** (© 225-8186; www.hoteldonfadrique.com) is another good option in a converted home.

Hotel 1492 Jade y Oro   Housed in a restored old home on a quiet street in the heart of the Barrio Escalante neighborhood just east of the city center, this little bed-and-breakfast makes a good base for exploring the city or this side of town. The rooms are simple and tastefully done with locally crafted wooden furniture, plenty of light, and a homey feel, but some are pretty small. All rooms have showers only. Breakfast is served in an open-air rancho overlooking a lovely little garden. The hotel is run by a Costa Rican family, and you really get the feel that you are staying in a local joint here.

Av. 1, no. 2985, between calles 31 and 33, Barrio Escalante. © 256-5913. Fax 280-6206. www.hotel1492.com. 10 units. $70–$80 (£35–£40) double. Rates include full breakfast. AE, MC, V. Free parking. **Amenities:** Laundry service; nonsmoking rooms; free Wi-Fi. *In room:* TV, hair dryer.

Hôtel Le Bergerac *★★ (Finds)*   With all the sophistication and charm of a small French inn, the Hotel Le Bergerac has ingratiated itself over the years with business travelers and members of various diplomatic missions. These visitors have found a tranquil environment in a quiet suburban neighborhood, spacious and comfortable accommodations, personal service, and gourmet meals. Still, you don't have to be a diplomat or business traveler to enjoy this hotel's charms. Le Bergerac is composed of three houses with courtyard gardens in between. Almost all the rooms are fairly large, and each is a little different. My favorite rooms are those with private patio gardens. Some rooms have king-size beds and refrigerators, and in the old master bedroom you'll find a little balcony.

In the evenings candlelight and classical music set a relaxing and romantic mood. The hotel's long-standing L'Ile de France restaurant serves gourmet French and continental dinners for guests and the public by reservation only.

Calle 35 no. 50 (A.P. 1107-1002), San José. ℂ **234-7850.** Fax 225-9103. www.bergerachotel.com. 26 units. $83–$130 (£42–£65) double. Rates include full breakfast. AE, DC, MC, V. Free parking. **Amenities:** Restaurant; lounge; concierge; tour desk; business and secretarial services; laundry service. *In room:* TV, hair dryer, safe.

Hotel Milvia ✿ *Finds* Art lovers should definitely look into this off-beat little hotel. This old converted home is chock full of paintings and sculpture by a wide range of contemporary Costa Rican artists. One of the owners, Florencia Urbina, happens to be one of these artists. Other artists represented include Mario Maffioli and Fabio Herrera. My favorite pieces are the large-scale sculptures by Leda Astorga, including two functional and funny chairs. The rooms are bright and airy, and most are plenty spacious. The hotel has a mix of courtyards and gardens that seem to beckon one to linger with a book or sketchpad in hand.

1 block north and 2 blocks east of the Muñoz y Nanne Supermarket, San Pedro. ℂ **225-4543.** Fax 225-7801. www.hotelmilvia.com. 9 units. $69 (£35) double. Rates include continental breakfast. AE, MC, V. **Amenities:** Restaurant; lounge; tour desk; laundry service. *In room:* TV, free Wi-Fi.

ESCAZÚ & SANTA ANA

Located about 15 minutes west of San José and about the same distance from the international airport, these affluent suburbs have experienced rapid growth in recent years, as the metropolitan area continues its urban sprawl. Both Escazú and Santa Ana are popular with the Costa Rican professional class and North American retirees and expatriates, and quite a few hotels have sprung up to cater to their needs. It's relatively easy to commute between Escazú or Santa Ana and downtown via bus or taxi. Taxi fare should run around $8 to $12 (£4–£6), each way. A bus costs around 30¢ (15p).

VERY EXPENSIVE

Real InterContinental San José ✿ This is a modern and luxurious large-scale business-class hotel. Three five-story wings radiate off a central hub. The large, open lobby has a beautiful flagstone-and-mosaic floor. The rooms are all well appointed, with either one king-size or two double beds, a working desk, a sitting chair and ottoman, and a large armoire housing a 25-inch television. For a little extra, you can stay on the Club InterContinental floor and enjoy personalized concierge and butler services, a separate check-in area, an on-floor buffet breakfast, and an assortment of refreshments, sweets, hors d'oeuvres, and drinks throughout the day. This floor is where most of the junior and master suites are located.

The hotel is just across from a large, modern shopping-mall complex, which is nice if you want access to shopping, restaurants, and a six-plex movie theater. Overall, the Inter-Continental offers many of the same features and amenities as the Marriott (p. 111), although the latter gets my nod in terms of service, restaurants, and ambience.

Autopista Próspero Fernández, across from the Multiplaza mall, Escazú. ℂ **208-2100.** Fax 208-2101. www.grupo real.com. 261 units. $275–$325 (£138–£163) double; $500–$1,000 (£250–£500) suite. AE, MC, V. Free parking.

Amenities: 3 restaurants; 2 bars; lounge; large free-form pool; tennis court; modest health club and spa; Jacuzzi; concierge; tour desk; car-rental desk; well-appointed business center; small shopping arcade; salon; 24-hr. room service; in-room massage; laundry service; nonsmoking rooms. *In room:* A/C, TV, Wi-Fi, minibar, coffeemaker, hair dryer, safe.

EXPENSIVE

Alta Hotel 🏨🏨   This small boutique hotel is infused with old-world charm. Curves and high arches abound. My favorite touch is the winding interior alleyway that snakes down from the reception through the hotel. Most of the rooms here have wonderful views of the Central Valley from private balconies; the others have pleasant garden patios. The rooms are all up to modern resort standards, although some have slightly cramped bathrooms. The suites are considerably larger, each with a separate sitting room with its own television, as well as large Jacuzzi-style tubs (no jets, though) in spacious bathrooms; they're definitely worth the slight splurge. If you opt to rent the entire upper floor, the penthouse becomes a three-bedroom, full-floor extravaganza, with a massive living room and open-air rooftop patio. The hotel's La Luz restaurant (p. 121) is one of the more elegant and creative dining spots in the Central Valley.

Alto de las Palomas, old road to Santa Ana. ⓒ **888/388-2582** in the U.S. and Canada or 282-4160. Fax 282-4162. www.thealtahotel.com. 23 units. $172 (£86) double; $202 (£101) junior suite; $402 (£201) master suite; $746 (£373) penthouse. Rates include continental breakfast. Rates lower in off season. AE, DC, MC, V. Free parking. **Amenities:** Restaurant; bar; midsize pool; exercise room; Jacuzzi; sauna; concierge; tour desk; secretarial services; limited room service (7am–10pm); in-room massage; laundry service. *In room:* A/C, TV, dataport, free Wi-Fi, minibar, coffeemaker, hair dryer, iron, safe.

Corteza Amarilla Art Lodge & Spa 🏨 *Finds*   Artistic touches abound in this whimsical hotel. Most of the rooms are classified as junior suites, although they really are just good sized rooms, with no separate sitting area, or other distinguishing factor that I usually associate with a junior. These are found in a series of individual and duplex buildings spread around the hotel's lush grounds. All come with wood floors, stone showers and artsy tile work on the bathroom sinks and counters. I prefer no. 4 through no. 7, which have higher ceilings. The two master suites are in the main building, and are larger, and come with massive flat screen television sets and a good-sized private patio garden. A variety of treatments and therapies are offered at the small spa here, and the in-house restaurant is excellent. This hotel is located, just outside of Santa Ana, on the main road to Ciudad Colón.

Prospero Fernández Highway, just outside of Santa Ana. ⓒ **800/961-0419** in the U.S. and Canada, or 203-7503 in Costa Rica. Fax 282-6641. www.cortezaamarillalodge.com. 13 units. $132 (£66) double junior suite; $158 (£79) master suite. Rates include full breakfast. AE, MC, V. **Amenities:** Restaurant; bar; small spa; Jacuzzi; tour desk; laundry service. *In room:* A/C, TV, minibar, coffeemaker, hair dryer.

MODERATE

In addition to the hotels listed below, the **Courtyard San José** (ⓒ **888/236-2427** in the U.S. and Canada, or 208-3000; www.marriott.com) and **Quality Hotel Santa Ana** (ⓒ **877/424-6423** in the U.S. and Canada, or 204-6700; www.choicehotels.com) are both modern business-class hotels a few miles of each other, right on the western Próspero Fernández Highway connecting Santa Ana and Escazú with San José.

Casa de las Tías *Finds*   This old Victorian-style home is comfortable and brimming with local character. The rooms are homey and simply decorated in a sort of Costa Rican country motif. The hotel has a wonderful covered veranda for sitting and admiring the well-tended gardens, as well as a TV room and common areas inside the house. The owners live on-site and are extremely helpful and friendly. Located on a quiet side street, Casa de las Tías is nonetheless just a block away from a busy section of Escazú, where you'll find scores of restaurants and shops. The hotel is located 100m (1 block) south and 150m (1½ blocks) east of El Cruce de San Rafael de Escazú.

San Rafael de Escazú. © **289-5517.** Fax 289-7353. www.hotels.co.cr/casatias.html. 5 units. $69–$79 (£35–£40) double. Rates include full breakfast. AE, MC, V. **Amenities:** Tour desk; laundry service, free Wi-Fi.

Hotel Casa Alegre *(Finds*   Housed in a converted home on a residential side street just a couple of blocks from Santa Ana's central square and church, this hotel offers spacious, comfortable rooms. The decor leans heavily on Southwest American artwork and design touches, combined with Guatemalan textiles and locally made heavy wooden furniture. My favorite rooms are the upstairs units. Rooms 3 and 4 even have skylights in their bathrooms. A midsize outdoor pool, that's good for lap swimming, takes up much of the backyard, but there's also a shady lounge area out back as well.

Santa Ana. ©/fax **203-7467.** www.hotelcasaalegre.com. 8 units. $65–$79 (£33–£40) double. Rates include full breakfast. AE, MC, V. **Amenities:** Tour desk; laundry service. *In room:* TV, free Wi-Fi.

HEREDIA & ALAJUELA (AIRPORT AREA)

Alajuela and Heredia, two colonial-era cities that lie much closer to the airport than San José, are two great places to find small, distinct, and charming hotels. To learn more about Heredia, see "Side Trips from San José," later in this chapter. If you plan to get yourself to a remote beach or rainforest lodge as quickly as possible and to use San José and the Central Valley purely as a transportation hub, or if you just detest urban clutter, noise, and pollution, you might do well to choose one of the hotels listed below.

VERY EXPENSIVE

Finca Rosa Blanca Country Inn *(Finds*   Finca Rosa Blanca is an eclectic architectural confection set amid the lush, green hillsides of a coffee plantation. Square corners seem to have been prohibited in the design of this beautiful home. There are turrets and curving walls of glass, arched windows, and a semicircular built-in couch. Everywhere the glow of polished hardwood blends with blindingly white stucco walls and brightly painted murals.

Inside, original artwork is everywhere, and each room is decidedly unique. The black and white room has a patio and bed made from coffee-tree wood. Another room has a bed built into a corner and a handmade tub with windows on two sides. The view is fabulous. If breathtaking bathrooms are your idea of the ultimate luxury, consider splurging on the master suite, which has a stone waterfall that cascades into a tub in front of a huge picture window. This suite also has a spiral staircase that leads to the top of the turret. The two separate villas have the same sense of eclectic luxury, with small kitchenettes and quite a bit of space and privacy. All rooms are nonsmoking.

A four-course gourmet dinner will run you $35 (£18) per person. Be sure to reserve early because there's limited seating. In a tiny space off the living room, there's an honor bar tucked into a reproduction of a typical Costa Rican oxcart. In 2007, the hotel was partially closed for a major renovation and expansion. Scheduled for completion by January 2008 are a new spa, a new reception, several new rooms, and a larger restaurant with both indoor and outdoor seating and an excellent view.

Santa Bárbara de Heredia (mailing address: SJO 3475, P.O. Box 25369, Miami, FL 33102). © **269-9392.** Fax 269-9555. www.fincarosablanca.com. 13 units. $215–$320 (£108–£160) double. Extra person $30. Rates include breakfast. AE, MC, V. Free parking. **Amenities:** Restaurant; small honor bar; lounge; small free-form pool set in the hillside; small exercise room; Jacuzzi; concierge; tour desk; limited room service; in-room massage; babysitting; laundry service; nonsmoking rooms. *In room:* Free Wi-Fi, minibar, safe.

Marriott Costa Rica Hotel ✹✹✹ For my money, the Marriott is the best large luxury resort hotel in the San José area. Amenities are plentiful, and service here reaches a level of attention to detail uncommon in Costa Rica. The hotel is designed in a mixed colonial style, with hand-painted Mexican tiles, antique red-clay roof tiles, weathered columns, and heavy wooden doors, lintels, and trim. The centerpiece is a large open-air interior patio that somewhat replicates Old Havana's Plaza de Armas. All rooms are comfortable and well appointed, with either a king-size or two double beds, two telephones, a working desk, an elegant wooden armoire holding a large television, plenty of closet space, a comfortable sitting chair and ottoman, and a small "Juliet" balcony. The bathrooms are up to par but seem slightly small for this price. The casual Villa Hermosa restaurant serves well-prepared "nouvelle Costa Rican" and international dishes, and there's a more upscale Spanish restaurant and tapas bar in a faux wine cellar. The large lobby-level bar features daily piano music and weekend jazz nights, with both indoor and patio seating. This hotel has a regular and free airport shuttle.

San Antonio de Belén (A.P. 502-4005). ℂ **888/236-2427** in the U.S. and Canada or 298-0844. Fax 298-0033. www.marriott.com. 299 units. $249 (£125) double; $299 (£150) executive level; $550 (£275) master suite; $1,000 (£500) presidential suite. Rates lower in off season. AE, DC, MC, V. Free valet parking. **Amenities:** 3 restaurants; bar; lounge; 2 pools; golf driving range; 3 tennis courts; small but well-appointed health club; Jacuzzi; sauna; concierge; tour desk; car-rental desk; free airport shuttle; business center and secretarial services; Wi-Fi; small shopping arcade; salon; 24-hr. room service; in-room massage; babysitting; laundry service; nonsmoking rooms. *In room:* A/C, TV, dataport, minibar, coffeemaker, hair dryer, iron, safe.

Meliá Cariari ✹✹ *(Kids)* With its use of stone walls, an open-air lobby, and lush garden plantings, the Cariari has a warm tropical feel. The rooms, which are done in dark and subdued tones, have either one king-size bed or two double beds, although I find most of the bathrooms a bit small. The suites are more spacious and similarly appointed. The Royal Service rooms come with extra perks and personalized service. The hotel offers shuttle service to Spa Centre at the Tryp Corobicí hotel (p. 105), which has a well-equipped and modern gym with large exercise room, on-staff trainers, and regular classes. The hotel shuttles guests to the nearby Parque Valle del Sol, and it has a sister course at its Paradisus Playa Conchal resort, which is also part of the Sol Melia chain, so this is still a good choice for golfers looking for a package tour. Families can also take advantage of the dependable babysitting, game room, and easy access to the modern mall nearby.

Autopista General Cañas, Ciudad Cariari (A.P. 737-1007, Centro Colón), San José. ℂ **888/956-3542** in the U.S. and Canada or 239-0022. Fax 239-2803. www.solmelia.com. 222 units. $300–$355 (£159–£178) double; $375–$550 (£178–£275) suite. Rates include airport and downtown shuttle. AE, DC, MC, V. Free valet parking. **Amenities:** 2 restaurants; 2 bars; lounge; casino; large pool w/swim-up bar; small exercise room and spa; game room; concierge; tour desk; car-rental desk; business center; Wi-Fi; salon; 24-hr. room service; in-room massage; babysitting; laundry service; nonsmoking rooms. *In room:* A/C, TV, dataport, minibar, coffeemaker, hair dryer, iron, safe.

Peace Lodge ✹✹ *(Finds)* The rooms at this outgrowth of the popular La Paz Waterfall Gardens just might be some of the most impressive in the country—and the bathrooms in the deluxe units easily earn that distinction. The rooms are quite large and feature sparkling wood floors and trim, handcrafted four-poster beds, beautiful stone fireplaces, intricately sculpted steel light fixtures, and a host of other creative touches and details. Every room has a private balcony fitted with a mosaic-tiled Jacuzzi. The aforementioned deluxe bathrooms come with a second oversize Jacuzzi set under a skylight in the middle of an immense room that features a full interior wall planted with ferns, orchids, and bromeliads and fed by a functioning waterfall system. Guests here have full access to all the tours and attractions of the La Paz Waterfall Gardens (p. 126) during normal operating hours and beyond. The lodge is located about 45 minutes from the airport and makes a good first stop if your itinerary takes you next to La Fortuna and Arenal Volcano, or to the Puerto Viejo de Sarapiquí region.

6km (3¾ miles) north of Varablanca on the road to San Miguel. © 482-2720 or 225-0643. www.waterfallgardens.com. 17 units. $235–$295 (£118–£148) double; $385 (£193) villa. Rates include breakfast and entrance to La Paz Waterfall Gardens. Rates lower in off season; higher during peak weeks. AE, MC, V. **Amenities:** Restaurant; bar; 2 outdoor swimming pools; Jacuzzi; tour desk; laundry service; free Wi-Fi. *In room:* A/C, TV, minibar, coffeemaker, safe.

Xandari Resort & Spa ★★ *(Finds* Xandari is yet another architecturally stunning small hotel not far from the airport. Set on a high hilltop above the city of Alajuela, Xandari commands wonderful views of the surrounding coffee farms and the Central Valley below. The villas are huge private affairs with high-curved ceilings, stained-glass windows, and handmade fine furniture. All come with both an outdoor patio with a view and a private covered palapa, as well as a smaller interior terrace with chaise longues. Most have king-size beds; the rest have two queens. There are spacious living rooms with rattan sofas and chairs, as well as small kitchenettes. The owners are artists, and their original works and innovative design touches abound. The hotel grounds contain several miles of trails that pass by at least five jungle waterfalls, as well as lush gardens and fruit orchards. The adjacent "spa village" features a series of private thatch-roofed treatment rooms, many with their own Jacuzzi, and most with stunning views. A wide range of spa and beauty treatments is offered, in addition to yoga and other fitness classes.

Alajuela (A.P. 1485-4050). © **866/363-3212** in the U.S. or 443-2020. Fax 442-4847. www.xandari.com. 22 villas. $215–$295 (£108–£148) villa for 2. Rates include continental breakfast and airport shuttle. $25 for extra person; children under 3 stay free in parent's room. Rates lower in off season. AE, DC, MC, V. **Amenities:** Restaurant; bar; lounge; 2 lap pools; spa; several Jacuzzis; in-room massage; laundry service. *In room:* Kitchenette, minibar, safe.

EXPENSIVE

Vista del Valle Plantation Inn ★★ *(Finds* If you have little need for San José and would like a comfortable base for exploring the rest of Costa Rica, consider this fine little country inn. It began as a converted private home, and the owners have been adding elegant little cottages around their grounds, which command an impressive view over the Río Grande and its steep-walled canyon. The architecture here has a strong Japanese influence. The rooms are all either independent or duplex villas. The villas are open and airy, with lots of windows letting in lots of light. You'll also find plenty of varnished woodwork, small kitchenettes (in some), and comfortable wraparound decks. My favorites are the Mona Lisa and Ylang-Ylang suites, which are octagonal affairs set on the edge of the bluff with great views and featuring private outdoor showers.

The grounds are wonderfully landscaped, with several inviting seating areas among a wealth of flowering tropical plants. There are stunning views from the restaurant, which features a regularly changing menu of fine international cuisine prepared with fresh local ingredients. The hotel is located 20 minutes north of the Juan Santamaría Airport, and staying here can cut as much as an hour off your travel time to the Pacific coast beaches, Arenal Volcano, and the Monteverde Cloud Forest.

A.P. 185-4003, Alajuela (mailing address: SJO 1994, P.O. Box 025216, Miami, FL 33102). © **450-0800** or ©/fax 451-1165. www.vistadelvalle.com. 11 units. $150–$170 (£75–£85) villa. Rates include full breakfast. Rates lower in off season. AE, MC, V. **Amenities:** Restaurant; midsize tile pool w/interesting little fountain/waterfall; tennis court; Jacuzzi; horseback riding; limited room service (6:30am–10pm); laundry service; free Wi-Fi. *In room:* Minibar, no phone.

MODERATE

El Rodeo Country Inn ⋆ Located around the "backside" of the airport, in San Antonio de Belén, this longstanding hotel has been entirely updated, expanded and redone. All of the rooms are spacious and feature new furnishings and decor, including sturdy beds with artistic wood and metal headboards adorned with sculpted cala lilies. Most have wood floors and large bathrooms. I'd ask for one either in the new section, or on the second floor of the older building. The suites have a Jacuzzi tub and sitting area. There are several lounge areas spread around the rambling structure, as well as a pool table on a large open second-floor veranda. The namesake El Rodeo steakhouse restaurant here is excellent.

San Antonio de Belén. ℂ 293-3909. Fax 293-3464. www.elrodeohotel.com. 29 units. $105 (£53) double; $160 (£80) suite. Rates include buffet breakfast. AE, DC, MC, V. Free parking. **Amenities:** 2 restaurants; bar; midsize pool; 1 unlit outdoor tennis court; Jacuzzi; tour desk; limited room service (noon–10pm); laundry service. *In room:* A/C, TV, free Wi-Fi, minibar, coffeemaker, hair dryer, safe.

Hampton Inn & Suites If familiarity, basic comfort, and proximity to the airport are important to you, then the Hampton Inn is your best bet. The rooms are what you'd expect from a well-known chain, and because the hotel is relatively new, they don't show much wear and tear. The hotel has both standard rooms and suites. Aside from being more spacious, the suites come with a minifridge and microwave oven. Breakfast is served, but no other dining options are on site; a Denny's and a separate Costa Rican fast-food chicken joint are just across the parking lot. There's a large swank casino, with a popular bar, just steps away as well. This is a good choice if your plane arrives very late or leaves very early and you don't plan to spend any time in San José. Free local calls, high-speed Internet access in all rooms, and Wi-Fi in public areas are all perks that will appeal to business travelers and vacationers alike. In fact, those staying in the suites get free international calls, over the hotel's VoIP network.

Autopista General Cañas, by the airport (A.P. 195-4003), San José. ℂ 800/426-7866 in the U.S. or 436-0000. Fax 442-2781. www.hamptoninn.com. 100 units. $123 (£62) double; $144 (£72) suite. Rates include buffet breakfast and airport shuttle. AE, DC, MC, V. Free parking. **Amenities:** Bar; small pool; small exercise room; tour desk; business center; free Wi-Fi; babysitting; laundry service; nonsmoking rooms. *In room:* A/C, TV, dataport, minifridge, coffeemaker, hair dryer, iron.

Hotel Bougainvillea ⋆ (Value) The Hotel Bougainvillea is an excellent choice—a great value if you're looking for a hotel in a quiet residential neighborhood not far from downtown. It offers most of the amenities of the more expensive resort hotels around the Central Valley, but it charges considerably less. The views across the valley from this hillside location are wonderful, and the gardens are beautifully designed and well tended. In fact, the bird-watching is pretty good in the hotel's relatively expansive gardens. Rooms are carpeted and have small triangular balconies oriented to the views. These folks offer free wireless Internet connections throughout most of the hotel. A complimentary hourly downtown shuttle bus will take you in and out of town.

In Santo Tomás de Santo Domingo de Heredia, 100m (1 block) west of the Escuela de Santo Tomás (A.P. 69-2120), San José. ℂ 244-1414. Fax 244-1313. www.hb.co.cr. 81 units. $95–$110 (£48–£55) double; $115–$130 (£58–£65) suite. Rates include hourly downtown shuttle bus. AE, DC, MC, V. Free parking. **Amenities:** Restaurant; bar; midsize pool in attractive garden; 2 lighted tennis courts; Jacuzzi; sauna; tour desk; business center; free Wi-Fi; limited room service; babysitting; laundry service; nonsmoking rooms. *In room:* TV, free Wi-Fi, coffeemaker, hair dryer.

Orquídeas Inn This little boutique inn is just 10 minutes from the airport on the road heading out of Alajuela to Grecia and the Poás Volcano. The rooms are all spacious and comfortable, with tile floors, private bathrooms, and colorful Guatemalan bedspreads. Most have televisions. The deluxe rooms are in a separate building up on a hill, and most of these offer wonderful views, particularly those with balconies facing one of the nearby volcanoes. There are a few larger minisuites located around the small pool, as well as a separate geodesic dome with a king-size bed in a loft reached by a spiral staircase, a large sunken tub in the bathroom, and a full kitchen and living-room area. The entire grounds are lush and tropical. The Marilyn Monroe bar serves up good drinks, *bocas* (appetizers), and some seriously spicy buffalo wings. The hotel provides free local calls and Internet access to guests.

A.P. 394, Alajuela. © 433-9346. Fax 433-9740. www.orquideasinn.com. 27 units. $69–$99 (£35–£50) double; $99–$150 (£50–£75) suite. Rates include breakfast buffet. AE, MC, V. Free parking. **Amenities:** Restaurant; bar; pool; Jacuzzi; concierge; tour desk; laundry service. *In room:* A/C, no phone.

4 Where to Dine

In broad terms, Costa Rican cuisine is easily disparaged and dismissed. Rice and beans are served at nearly every meal, the selection of other dishes is minimal, and Ticos generally don't go for spicy food. In recent years, though, some contemporary and creative chefs have been trying to educate and enlighten the Costa Rican palate, particularly in San José, and the results are promising. Still, most visitors to the capital city quickly tire of Tico fare, even in its more chichi incarnations, and start seeking out the many local restaurants serving international cuisines. They are richly rewarded.

San José has a rather amazing variety of restaurants serving cuisines from all over the world. Most restaurants fall into the moderate price range, although prices have crept up in recent years, and unless you stick to simple local joints, you probably won't find many true bargains. Service can be indifferent at many restaurants because the gratuity is already tacked on to the check, and tipping is not common among locals.

LOCAL CUISINE If you'd really like to sample the local flavor, head to a *soda*, the equivalent of a diner in the United States, where you can get good, cheap, filling Tico food. Rice and beans are the staples and show up at breakfast, lunch, and dinner (when mixed together, they're called *gallo pinto*). For breakfast, they're garnished with everything from fried eggs to steak. At lunch and dinner, rice and beans are the main components of a *casado* (which means "married"), the Costa Rican equivalent of a "blue-plate special." A *casado* generally is served with a salad of cabbage and tomatoes; fried plantains; and steak, chicken, or fish. A plate of *gallo pinto* might cost $2 (£1), and a *casado* might cost $2.50 to $4 (£1.25–£2), usually with a *fresco* (a fresh-fruit drink) thrown into the bargain.

While in Costa Rica, be sure to taste a few *frescos*. They're a bit like a fresh-fruit milkshake without the ice cream, and when made with mangoes, papayas, bananas, or any of the other delicious tropical fruits of Costa Rica, they're pure ambrosia. *Frescos* can be made with water *(con agua)* or with milk *(con leche),* and preferences vary. Certain fruits such as carambola (star fruit), *maracuyá* (a type of passion fruit), and *cas* (you'll just have to try it) are used only with water. But remember, although the water in Costa Rica is generally very safe to drink, those with tender stomachs or intestinal tracts should stick to *frescos* made with milk because it's pasteurized.

FRUIT VENDORS There's a fruit vendor on almost every street corner in downtown San José. If you're lucky enough to be in town between April and June, you can sample more varieties of mangoes than you ever knew existed. I like buying them already cut up in a little bag; they cost a little more this way, but you don't get nearly as messy. Be sure to try a green mango with salt and chile peppers—guaranteed to wake up your taste buds. Another common street food that you might be wondering

---

Tips **Shameless Plug**

If you want a more comprehensive guide to the restaurant scene in San José and around the country, pick up a copy of my *Tico Times Restaurant Guide to Costa Rica,* which is now in its third edition and features reviews of nearly 400 restaurants around Costa Rica, indexed by location, cuisine type, and overall quality. The guide is available in local bookstores, supermarkets, and gift shops, as well as online at **www.ticotimes.net**.

---

about is called *pejibaye,* a bright orange palm nut about the size of a plum. They're boiled in big pots on carts, you eat them in much the same way you eat an avocado, and they taste a bit like squash.

LATE-NIGHT BITES   San José has quite a few **all-night restaurants.** The best of these is **Cafeteria 1830,** which is described below. Another popular place, which is definitely a bit seedier, is **Chelles,** on Avenida Central and Calle 9 (see "San José After Dark," later in this chapter, for more information). The **Del Mar,** which belongs to and is across from the Hotel Del Rey (p. 103), is also open 24 hours. Finally, there's a **Denny's** (© 231-3500), located at the Best Western Irazú, on the highway out to the airport, and another beside the Hampton Inn at the airport.

DOWNTOWN SAN JOSE
MODERATE

Bakea 🅐🅐 *Finds* INTERNATIONAL   This restaurant is eclectic across the board, from its architecture to its cuisine. Housed in an old historic downtown home, it has one room with a Plexiglas floor and underfoot lighting revealing the original joists and foundations. There's also a separate intimate dining room, a courtyard patio done in a postmodern industrial chic style, and a main dining room that is both casual and elegant. The owner-chef, Camille Pérez-Ratton, is trained in classical French cooking, which she has updated with a host of modern and local flourishes. I particularly like the curried scallops served over a saffron risotto. The signature *cahuita y caramelo* dessert is a standout chocolate-banana tart with a molten chocolate center and macadamia pieces thrown in for good measure.

Calle 7 and Ave. 11, Casa 956. © **221-1051.** Reservations recommended. Main courses $10–$25 (£5–£13). AE, MC, V. Tues–Sat noon–midnight; Mon noon–3pm.

Café Mundo 🅐 *Finds* INTERNATIONAL   This popular place mixes creative cuisine with an ambience of casual elegance. Wood tables and Art Deco wrought-iron chairs are spread spaciously around several rooms in this former colonial mansion. There's additional seating on the open-air veranda and in the small gardens both front and back. The appetizers include vegetable tempura, crab cakes, and chicken satay alongside more traditional Tico standards such as *patacones* (fried plantain chips) and fried yuca. There's a long list of pastas and pizzas, as well as more substantial main courses. There are nightly specials and delicious desserts. One room here boasts colorful wall murals by Costa Rican artist Miguel Cassafont. This place is almost always filled with a broad mix of San José's gay, bohemian, theater, arts, and university crowds.

Calle 15 and Av. 9, 200m (2 blocks) east and 100m (1 block) north of the INS building. © **222-6190.** Reservations recommended. Main courses $5–$17 (£2.50–£8.50). AE, MC, V. Mon–Thurs 11am–11pm; Fri 11am–midnight; Sat 5pm–midnight.

Cafeteria 1830 *(Finds)* INTERNATIONAL   With veranda and patio seating directly fronting the Plaza de la Cultura, this is one of the most atmospheric spots for a casual bite and some good people-watching. A wrought-iron railing, white columns, and arches create an old-world atmosphere; on the plaza in front of the cafe, a marimba band performs and vendors sell handicrafts. Stop by for the breakfast and watch the plaza vendors set up their booths, or peruse the *Tico Times* over coffee while you have your shoes polished. The menu is basic and the food is unspectacular, but there isn't a better place downtown to bask in the tropical sunshine while you sip a beer or have a light lunch, and it's a great place to come before or after a show at the Teatro Nacional.

Av. 2, between calles 1 and 3, San José. © 221-4011. Sandwiches $6–$7.50 (£3–£3.75); main courses $6.50–$35 (£3.25–£18). AE, DC, MC, V. Daily 24 hr.

La Cocina de Leña COSTA RICAN   Located in the El Pueblo shopping, dining, and entertainment center, La Cocina de Leña ("The Wood Stove") is designed to invoke the ambience and vibe of a rustic rural Costa Rican home. There are stacks of firewood on shelves above the booths, long stalks of bananas hanging from pillars, tables suspended from the ceiling by heavy ropes, and, most unusual of all, menus printed on paper bags. If you're adventurous, you could try some of the more unusual dishes—perhaps oxtail stew served with yuca and *plátano* might appeal to you. If not, there are plenty of steaks and seafood dishes on the menu. *Chilasuilas* are delicious tortillas filled with fried meat. Black-bean soup with egg is a Costa Rican standard and is mighty fine here; the corn soup with pork is equally satisfying. For dessert, there's *tres leches* cake as well as the more unusual sweetened *chiverre,* which is a type of squash that looks remarkably like a watermelon.

Centro Comercial El Pueblo. © **255-1360** or 223-3704. Reservations recommended. Main courses $6–$24 (£3–£12). AE, MC, V. Daily 11:30am–11pm.

Tin Jo *(★★ (Finds)* CHINESE/PAN-ASIAN   San José has hundreds of Chinese restaurants, but most simply serve up tired takes on chop suey, chow mein, and fried rice. In contrast, Tin Jo has a wide and varied menu, with an assortment of Cantonese and Szechuan staples, as well as a range of Thai, Japanese, and Malaysian dishes, and even some Indian food. This is a true Pan-Asian restaurant. It's also a restaurant that pays attention to the details. Some of the dishes are served in edible rice-noodle bowls, and the pineapple shrimp in coconut-milk curry is served in the hollowed-out half of a fresh pineapple. Other dishes not to miss include the salt-and-pepper shrimp, beef teriyaki, and Thai curries. For dessert, try the sticky rice with mango, or banana tempura. The waiters here are some of the most attentive in Costa Rica. The decor features artwork and textiles from across Asia, and you'll have real tablecloths and cloth napkins. Tin Jo is also a great option for vegetarians, and even vegans.

Calle 11, between avs. 6 and 8. © **221-7605** or 257-3622. Main courses $8–$20 (£4–£10). AE, MC, V. Mon–Sat 11:30am–3pm and 5:30–10pm (Fri–Sat kitchen open till 11pm); Sun 11:30am–10pm.

INEXPENSIVE

In addition to the places listed below, the **Q'Café** (© **221-0707**) is a delightful little European-style cafe with a pretty perch above the busy corner of Avenida Central and Calle 2. Try to grab a view seat overlooking the action on the street below.

Café del Teatro Nacional *★* CONTINENTAL/COFFEEHOUSE   Even if there's no show on during your visit, you can enjoy a light meal, sandwich, dessert, or a cup of coffee here, while soaking up the neoclassical atmosphere. The theater was built in

Moments **Only in the Central Valley: Dining under the Stars on a Mountain's Edge**

Although there are myriad unique experiences to be had in Costa Rica, one of my favorites is dining on the side of a volcano with the lights of San José shimmering below. These hanging restaurants, called *miradores,* are a resourceful response to the city's topography. Because San José is set in a broad valley surrounded on all sides by volcanic mountains, people who live in these mountainous areas have no place to go but up—so they do, building roadside cafes vertically up the sides of the volcanoes.

The food at most of these establishments is not spectacular, but the views often are, particularly at night, when the wide valley sparkles in a wash of lights. The town of **Aserri,** 10km (6¼ miles) south of downtown San José, is the king of miradores, and **Mirador Ram Luna** (© 230-3060) is the king of Aserri. Grab a window seat and, if you've got the fortitude, order a plate of *chicharrones* (fried pork rinds). There's often live music. You can hire a cab for around $10 (£5) or take the Aserri bus at Avenida 6 between calles Central and 2. Just ask the driver where to get off.

There are also miradores in the hills above Escazú and in San Ramón de Tres Ríos and Heredia. The most popular is **Le Monestère** (© 289-4404; closed Sun), an elegant converted church serving somewhat overrated French and Belgian cuisine in a spectacular setting above the hills of Escazú. I recommend coming here just for the less formal **La Cava Grill** ®, which often features live music, mostly folk-pop but sometimes jazz. I also like **Mirador Tiquicia** (© 289-5839), which occupies several rooms in a sprawling old Costa Rican home and has live folkloric dance shows on Thursday.

the 1890s from the designs of European architects, and the Art Nouveau chandeliers, ceiling murals, and marble floors and tables are pure Parisian. There are also plenty of desserts and a wide range of coffee drinks. The ambience is French-cafe chic, but the marimba music drifting in from outside the open window and the changing art exhibits by local artists will remind you that you're still in Costa Rica. On sunny days, there's outdoor seating at wrought-iron tables on the side of the theater. In addition to the regular hours of operation listed below, the cafe is open until 8pm any evening that there is a performance in the theater.

In the Teatro Nacional, Av. 2 between calles 3 and 5. © 221-1329. Sandwiches $3–$6 (£1.50–£3); main courses $5–$11 (£2.50–£5.50). AE, MC, V. Mon–Sat 9am–4pm.

Vishnu VEGETARIAN   Vegetarians will likely find their way to this Vishnu restaurant or one of its many sister restaurants around the city. The vibe's a little too plastic, too loud, and too brightly lit for my tastes in a vegetarian joint. However, most people just come for the filling *plato del día* that includes soup, salad, veggies, an entree, and dessert for around $3.50 (£1.75). There are also bean burgers and cheese sandwiches on whole-wheat bread. At the cashier's counter you can buy natural cosmetics, honey, and bags of granola.

Av. 1, between calles 1 and 3. © 256-6063. Main courses $3.50–$10 (£1.75–£5). MC, V. Daily 7am–9:30pm.

LA SABANA/PASEO COLON

EXPENSIVE

In addition to the excellent restaurant at the Grano de Oro, you might try the new **Park Café** ☆ (✆ **290-6324**), which is housed inside the interior courtyard of an antique and imported furniture store, and is run by Richard Neat, who had a couple of successful and acclaimed restaurants in London and Marrakesh.

Grano de Oro Restaurant ☆☆☆ *Finds* INTERNATIONAL   Even after a reloca-tion, remodeling, and expansion, this elegant restaurant is set around a lovely interior courtyard of the wonderful Hotel Grano de Oro (p. 106). The atmosphere here remains intimate, relaxed, and refined, all at the same time. The menu features a wide range of meat and fish dishes. The *lomito piemontes* is two medallions of filet mignon stuffed with Gorgonzola cheese in a sherry sauce, while the *pernil de conejo* is a rabbit thigh stuffed with a mushroom pâté and served with a Dijon mustard sauce. If you opt for fish, I recommend the macadamia-encrusted corvina, which is served with a light and tangy orange sauce. Be sure to save room for the "Grano de Oro pie," a deca-dent dessert with various layers of chocolate and coffee mousses and creams. This place has a good wine list, including a range of options by the glass. When the weather's nice, grab a table around the fountain in the courtyard, a particularly nice option for lunch.

Calle 30, no. 251, between avs. 2 and 4, 150m (1½ blocks) south of Paseo Colón. ✆ **255-3322**. Reservations recom-mended. Main courses $8.50–$28 (£4.25–£14). AE, MC, V. Daily 6am–10pm.

MODERATE

El Chicote ☆ COSTA RICAN/STEAKHOUSE   This is one of San José's most popular steakhouses. The large room is divided by half-walls planted with tropical flora and a bevy of hanging ferns. There are heavy wooden beams and plenty of var-nished-wood accents all around. True meat aficionados should order the imported rib-eye or pound-and-a-half T-bone. There's an extensive selection of fish and poultry dishes as well. Everything comes with a choice of baked or mashed potatoes, black beans, and fresh tortillas. The wine list features a broad range of Italian, Spanish, French, and Californian wines. Waiters wear black jackets, white shirts, and black bow ties—typical of the unusually formal (for Costa Rica) service.

Av. Las Américas, 400m (4 blocks) west of the ICE building, Sabana Norte. ✆ **232-0936** or 232-3777. Reservations recommended. Main courses $8–$21 (£4–£11). AE, MC, V. Mon–Fri 11am–3pm and 6–11pm; Sat–Sun 11am–11pm.

Machu Picchu ☆ PERUVIAN/CONTINENTAL   Machu Picchu is an unpreten-tious little restaurant that is perennially one of the most popular places in San José. The menu is classic Peruvian. One of my favorite entrees is the *causa limeña,* lemon-flavored mashed potatoes stuffed with shrimp. The ceviche here is excellent, as is the *ají de gallina,* a dish of shredded chicken in a fragrant cream sauce, and octopus with garlic butter. For main dishes, I recommend *corvina a lo macho,* sea bass in a slightly spicy tomato-based seafood sauce. Be sure to ask for a pisco sour, a classic Peruvian drink made from pisco, a grape liquor. These folks have a sister restaurant over in San Pedro (✆ **283-3679**), and another in Santa Ana (✆ **203-7657**), set on a hillside with a great view over the valley below.

Calle 32, between avs. 1 and 3, 150m (1½ blocks) north of the KFC on Paseo Colón. ✆ **222-7384**. Reservations rec-ommended. Main courses $4–$16 (£2–£8). AE, DC, MC, V. Mon–Sat 11am–3pm and 6–10pm.

INEXPENSIVE

Soda Tapia COSTA RICAN   The food is unspectacular, dependable, and quite inexpensive at this very popular local diner. There's seating inside the brightly lit dining room, as well as on the sidewalk-style patio fronting the parking area. Dour but efficient waitstaff take the order you mark down on your combination menu/bill. This is a great place for late-night eats or for before or after a visit to Parque La Sabana or Museo de Arte Costarricense. These folks also have another site in a small strip mall in Santa Ana (☎ **203-7174**).

Calle 42 and Av. 2, across from the Museo de Arte Costarricense. ☎ **222-6734**. Sandwiches $2–$3.50 (£1–£1.75); main dishes $4–$7.50 (£2–£3.75). MC, V. Sun–Thurs 6am–2am; Fri–Sat 24 hr.

SAN PEDRO/LOS YOSES

In addition to the restaurants listed below, local and visiting vegetarians swear by the little **Comida Para Sentir Restaurante Vegetariano San Pedro** (☎ **224-1163**), located 125m (1¼ blocks) north of the San Pedro Church. Despite the massive size and popularity of the nearby **Il Pomodoro**, I prefer **Pane E Vino** (☎ **280-2869**), an excellent pasta-and-pizza joint on the eastern edge of San Pedro.

For Peruvian cuisine try **Bohemia** (☎ **253-6348**) in Barrio Escalante, or the branch of **Machu Picchu** (☎ **283-3679**; see above for review) in San Pedro. Finally, if you're hankering for sushi, try **Ichiban** ☞ (☎ **253-8012**) in San Pedro, or **Matsuri** ☞ (☎ **280-5522**), a little farther east in Curridabat.

MODERATE

Donde Carlos ☞☞ ARGENTINE/STEAKHOUSE   Bold architectural touches abound in this stylish restaurant, yet the food is built primarily around simple, perfectly grilled meats and fresh fish. You pass the wood-burning Argentine-style wood-fired grill as you enter. I like the outdoor tables on the second-floor balcony when the weather permits. Most folks stick to the hearty steak options, but you can also order a wide range of sausages and offal meats, as well as fresh tuna. All portions are huge, and this place has a good and reasonably priced wine list to boot.

100 block, north of the Fatima Church in Los Yoses. ☎ **225-0819**. Main courses $7–$20 (£3.50–£10). AE, MC, V. Mon–Fri noon–3pm; Mon–Thurs 6:30–10:30pm; Fri 6:30–11pm; Sun noon–7pm.

Il Ritorno ☞ ITALIAN   The name of this restaurant translates as "The Return," and it's the not-very-humble, yet arguably deserved, announcement of chef and owner Tony D'Alaimo's comeback after leaving the long-standing and popular Il Ponte Vecchio and Costa Rica for several years. The menu features a wide selection of antipasti, pastas, main dishes, and thin-crust wood-oven baked pizzas. I like the *vitello il ritorno*, delicate cuts of veal in a cognac-based sauce. Service is semiformal and attentive. There are a few specials each evening, and Tony's mother's recipe for fresh ravioli in a cream sauce flavored with nutmeg is usually available.

Barrio California, 200m (2 blocks) south of KFC. ☎ **225-0543**. Main courses $6–$18 (£3–£9). AE, MC, V. Mon–Sat noon–2:30pm and 6–10:30pm.

Jurgen's ☞☞ INTERNATIONAL   Housed in a boutique business-class hotel, this elegant little restaurant serves excellent European-style continental fare in a refined atmosphere. The lighting is low and service extremely professional. You'll find poached salmon with a dill sauce, and grilled tilapia with a Dijon mustard sauce. The steaks are top cuts of beef perfectly prepared. This place has one of the more extensive wine lists in town. The owner, Jurgen Mormel, also has several gourmet specialty food shops around San José and in Playa Herradura.

2½ blocks north of the Subaru dealership, Los Yoses. © **283-2239.** Main courses $8–$22 (£4–£11). AE, MC, V. Mon–Fri noon–2:30pm and 6–10pm; Sat 6–10:30pm.

Olio ⊕ (Value MEDITERRANEAN   The exposed brick walls, dark wood wainscoting, and stained-glass lamps imbue this place with character and romance. Couples might want to grab a table in a quiet nook, while groups tend to dominate the large main room or crowd the bar. There are even a few outdoor tables on a narrow sidewalk beside some train tracks. The extensive tapas menu features traditional Spanish fare, as well as bruschetta, antipasti, and a Greek *mezza* plate. For a main dish, I recommend the chicken Vesuvio, which is marinated first in a balsamic vinegar reduction and finished with a creamy herb sauce; or the *arrollado siciliano*, which is a thin filet of steak rolled around spinach, sun-dried tomatoes, and mozzarella cheese and topped with a pomodoro sauce. The midsize wine list features very reasonably priced wines from Italy, France, Spain, Germany, Chile, Greece, and even Bulgaria.

Barrio California, 200m (2 blocks) north of Bagelman's. © **281-0541.** Main courses $5–$12 (£2.50–£6). AE, DC, MC, V. Mon–Fri 11:30am–1am; Sat 4pm–midnight.

INEXPENSIVE

Whappin' ⊕ (Finds COSTA RICAN/CARIBBEAN   You don't have to go to Limón or Cahuita to get good home-cooked Caribbean food. In addition to *rondon,* a coconut milk–based stew or soup (see "That Rundown Feeling" on p. 365), you can also get the classic rice and beans cooked in coconut milk, as well as a range of fish and chicken dishes from the coastal region. I like the whole red snapper covered in a spicy sauce of sautéed onions. There's a small bar at the entrance and some simple tables spread around the restaurant, with an alcove here and there. Everything is very simple, and prices are quite reasonable. After a dinner of fresh fish, with rice, beans, and *patacones,* the only letdown is that the beach is some 4 hours away.

Barrio Escalante, 200m (2 blocks) east of El Farolito. © **283-1480.** Main courses $8–$11 (£4–£5.50). AE, MC, V. Mon–Sat 11:30am–2:30pm and 6–10pm.

ESCAZU & SANTA ANA

These two suburbs on the western side of town have the most vibrant restaurant scene in San José. Although there's high turnover and sudden closings, this remains a good area to check out for a variety of dining experiences. In addition to the places mentioned below, **Il Panino** ⊕ (© **228-3126**) is an upscale sandwich shop and cafe, located in the Centro Comercial El Paco. **Santa Ana Tex Mex** (© **282-6342**) is one of the most popular places on this side of town. Located a half-block north of the main church in Santa Ana, it serves up Tex-Mex cuisine in a lively atmosphere. Located just outside of Santa Ana, **Essentia** ⊕ (© **203-7503**) is another excellent fusion restaurant, located inside the hotel **Corteza Amarilla** (p. 109).

Finally, a good one-stop option to consider is the Plaza Itskatzu shopping center located just off the highway and sharing a parking lot with the Courtyard San José. Here you'll find a wide variety of moderately priced restaurant options, including **Tutti Li** (© 289-8768), a good Italian restaurant and pizzeria; **Icarus** (© 288-5021), an upscale Continental restaurant (and a bit more expensive than the others); **Chancay** (© 289-6964), which serves Peruvian and Peruvian/Chinese cuisine; **La Guagua**

(© 288-5112), serving up tasty Cuban food; **Las Tapas de Manuel** ⚘ (© 288-5700), a Spanish-style tapas restaurant; and franchise outlets of both **Hooters** (© 289-3498) and **Outback Steakhouse** (© 288-0511).

EXPENSIVE

Bacchus ⚘⚘⚘ *Finds* ITALIAN   Easily my favorite Italian restaurant in San José, this place is housed in a historic home that is over a century old. You'd never know it following the massive restoration and remodel. Nevertheless, this place somehow seamlessly blends the old with the new in an elegant atmosphere. The best tables are on the covered back patio, where you can watch the open kitchen and wood-burning pizza oven in action. The menu features a range of antipasti, pastas, pizzas, and main dishes. Everything is perfectly prepared and beautifully presented. The desserts are also excellent, and the wine list is extensive and fairly priced.

Downtown Santa Ana. © 282-5441. Reservations required. Main courses $8–$22 (£4–£11). AE, MC, V. Tues–Sat noon–3pm and 6–11pm; Sun noon–9pm.

Barbecue Los Anonos ⚘ COSTA RICAN/STEAKHOUSE   Good steaks and well-prepared Costa Rican cuisine have made this simple restaurant something of an institution. Most of the seating is at rustic wooden tables covered with red-and-white checkered tablecloths, and long and rustic booths set under the shelter of low interior red-tile roofs. Aged Angus beef is served, and this is *the* place to come if you're craving a 16-ounce T-bone. There are also a host of chicken, pork, and fish options; I recommend the mixed-grill plate for two, which comes with a little bit of everything.

600m (6 blocks) west of the Los Anonos bridge in San Rafael de Escazú, next to the Sarretto Market. © 228-0180. Reservations recommended. Main courses $11–$25 (£5.50–£13). AE, MC, V. Tues–Sat noon–3pm; Tues–Thurs 6–10pm; Fri–Sat 6–11pm; Sun 11:30–9pm.

La Luz ⚘⚘ CALIFORNIAN/FUSION   La Luz serves up some of the more adventurous food in Costa Rica, mixing fresh local ingredients with the best of a whole host of international ethnic cuisines. The fiery garlic prawns are sautéed in ancho-chile oil and sage and served over a roasted-garlic potato mash. Then the whole thing is served with a garnish of fried leeks and a tequila-lime butter and cilantro-oil sauce. I also enjoy the beef tenderloin in a strawberry-balsamic reduction, served over a champagne-infused risotto. On top of all this, there are nightly specials and a wide selection of inventive appetizers and desserts. The glass-walled dining room is one of the most elegant in town, with a view of the city lights. The waitstaff is attentive and knowledgeable. La Luz is also open for breakfast and lunch.

In the Alta Hotel (p. 109), on the old road to Santa Ana. © 282-4160. Reservations recommended. Main courses $11–$26 (£5.50–£13). AE, DC, MC, V. Daily 6:30am–10pm.

MODERATE

La Cava Grill ⚘ *Finds* COSTA RICAN/STEAKHOUSE   This place is a cozy and warm spot built underneath the popular yet overpriced and overrated Le Monestère restaurant. While the decor is much less ornate, the service much less formal, and the menu much less French, the view is just as spectacular. Grab a window seat on a clear night and enjoy the sparkle of the lights below. The menu features a range of simply prepared meat, poultry, and fish. More adventurous diners can try the *tepezquintle* (a large rodent, also called a *paca*), which is actually quite tasty. There's live music and a festive party most weekend nights in the attached bar. My big complaint here is that the wine list is borrowed from the upstairs restaurant, and is pretentious and expensive.

1.5km (1 mile) south of Centro Comercial Paco; follow the signs to Le Monestère. © **289-4404.** Reservations recommended. Main courses $6–$18 (£3–£9). AE, MC, V. Mon–Sat 6pm–1:30am.

Taj Mahal ⚘ *Finds* INDIAN   The only true and dedicated Indian restaurant in the country, this place does a good job. The menu is quite extensive and covers most of the traditional bases with biryanis, vindaloos, tikka masalas and a variety of curries. They have an authentic tandoor oven, and the tandoori meats are excellently prepared. The restaurant is spread out through several rooms in a converted home. The decorations and furniture are mostly imported from India. I like the few outdoor tables in the backyard, especially for lunch. As at Tin Jo, this is a great choice for vegetarians.

On the old road to Santa Ana, 1km (½ mile) west of Centro Comercial Paco. © **228-0980.** Reservations recommended. Main courses $7–$14 (£3.50–£7). AE, MC, V. Tues–Sun noon–11pm.

5 What to See & Do

Most visitors to Costa Rica try to get out of the city as fast as possible so they can spend more time on the beach or off in the rainforests. But there are a few attractions in San José to keep you busy. Some of the best and most modern museums in Central America are here, with a wealth of fascinating pre-Columbian artifacts. Standouts include the remodeled Museo de Jade Marco Fidel Tristán (Jade Museum) and the centrally located Centro Nacional de Arte y Cultura (National Center of Arts and Culture), featuring yet another museum and several performing-arts spaces.

There are also several great things to see and do just outside San José in the Central Valley. If you start doing day trips out of the city, you can spend quite a few days in this region. See "San José in 3 Days" in chapter 3 for additional touring ideas.

ORGANIZED TOURS   There really isn't much reason to take a tour of San José. It's so compact that you can easily visit all the major sights on your own, as described below. However, if you want to take a city tour, which will run you between $15 and $40 (£7.50–£20), here are some companies you can use: **Horizontes Travel** ⚘, Calle 32 between avenidas 3 and 5 (© **222-2022;** www.horizontes.com); **Gray Line Tours,** Avenida 7 between calles 6 and 8, with additional offices at the Hampton Inn and Best Western Irazú (© **220-2126;** www.graylinecostarica.com); and **Swiss Travel Service** (© **282-4898;** www.swisstravelcr.com). These same companies also offer a complete range of day trips out of San José (see "Side Trips from San José," later in this chapter). Almost all of the major hotels have tour desks, and most of the smaller hotels will also help arrange tours and day trips.

THE TOP ATTRACTIONS

In addition to the attractions listed below, you might consider a quick stop at San José's main **cathedral**. The church and its interior are largely unspectacular. However, you'll see a pretty garden, as well as a massive marble statue of Pope Juan Pablo II, with a woman and child, carved by celebrated Costa Rican sculptor Jorge Jiménez Deredia. Deredia also has a work at the Vatican. The cathedral is located at the corner of Avenida 2 and Calle central.

Centro Nacional de Arte y Cultura (National Center of Art and Culture) ⚘⚘
Finds   Occupying a full city block, this was once the National Liquor Factory (FANAL). Now it houses the offices of the Cultural Ministry, several performing-arts

centers, and the Museum of Contemporary Art and Design. The latter has done an excellent job of promoting cutting-edge Costa Rican and Central American artists, while also featuring impressive traveling international exhibits, including large retrospectives by Mexican painter José Cuevas and Ecuadorian painter Oswaldo Guayasamín. If you're looking for modern dance, experimental theater, or a lecture on Costa Rican video, this a good place to check out. Allow around 2 hours to take in all the exhibits here.

Calle 13 between avs. 3 and 5. ⓒ **257-7202** or 257-9370. www.madc.ac.cr. Admission $2 (£1), 80¢ (40p) for students w/valid ID, free for seniors and children under 12, free for everyone on Mon. Museum Mon–Sat 11am–6pm.

Museo de Arte Costarricense (Costa Rican Art Museum) ✮

This small museum at the end of Paseo Colón in Parque La Sabana was formerly an airport terminal. Today it houses a collection of works in all media by Costa Rica's most celebrated artists. On display are some exceptionally beautiful pieces in a wide range of styles, demonstrating how Costa Rican artists have interpreted and imitated the major European movements over the years. In addition to the permanent collection of sculptures, paintings, and prints, there are regular temporary exhibits. If the second floor is open during your visit, have a look at the conference room's bas-relief walls, which chronicle the history of Costa Rica from pre-Columbian times to the present with evocative images of its people. So far, the collection is small, but it does include at least one representative work each by José Sancho, Jorge Jiménez Deredia, Max Jiménez, and Francisco Zuñiga. Moreover, the outdoor setting is lovely. One of the best features here is the sculpture garden out back. You can easily spend an hour or two at this museum—more if you take a stroll through the neighboring park.

Calle 42 and Paseo Colón, Parque La Sabana Este. ⓒ **222-7155.** Admission $5 (£2.50) adults, $3 (£1.50) for students w/valid ID, free for children and seniors, free for everyone Sun. Tues–Fri 9am–5pm; Sat–Sun 10am–4pm.

Museo de Jade Marco Fidel Tristán (Jade Museum) ✮

Jade was the most valuable commodity among the pre-Columbian cultures of Mexico and Central America, worth more than gold. Located on the first floor of the INS (National Insurance Company) building, this popular museum houses a huge collection of jade artifacts dating from 500 B.C. to A.D. 800. Most are large pendants that were parts of necklaces and are primarily human and animal figures. A fascinating display illustrates how the primitive peoples of this region carved this extremely hard stone.

The museum also possesses an extensive collection of pre-Columbian polychrome terra-cotta vases, bowls, and figurines. Some of these pieces are amazingly modern in design and exhibit a surprisingly advanced technique. Particularly fascinating is a vase that incorporates real human teeth, and a display that shows how jade was embedded in human teeth merely for decorative reasons. All of the explanations are in English and Spanish. Allot at least an hour to tour this museum.

Av. 7 between calles 9 and 9B, INS Building. ⓒ **287-6034.** Admission $2 (£1) adults, free for children under 12. Mon–Fri 8:30am–3:30pm; Sat 9am–1pm.

Museo de Los Niños (Children's Museum) *Kids*

A former barracks and then a prison, this museum houses an extensive collection of exhibits designed to edify and entertain children of all ages. Experience a simulated earthquake or make music by dancing across the floor. Many exhibits encourage hands-on play. If you're traveling with children, you'll definitely want to come here, and you might want to visit even if you aren't. The museum sometimes features limited shows of "serious" art and is also the home of the National Auditorium. You can spend anywhere from 1 to 4 hours here, depending on how long your children linger at each exhibit. Be careful, though: The museum is large and spread out; it's easy to lose track of a family member or friend.

This museum is located a few blocks north of downtown, on Calle 4. It's within easy walking distance, but you might want to take a cab because you'll have to walk right through the worst part of the red-light district.

Calle 4 and Av. 9. ⓒ 258-4929. www.museocr.com. Admission $2 (£1) adults, $1.20 (60p) students and children under 18. Tues–Fri 8am–4:30pm; Sat–Sun 10am–5pm.

Museos del Banco Central de Costa Rica (Gold Museum) 🕰🕰 Located directly
beneath the Plaza de la Cultura, this unusual underground museum houses one of the largest collections of pre-Columbian gold in the Americas. On display are more than 20,000 troy ounces of gold in more than 2,000 objects. The sheer number of small pieces can be overwhelming and seem redundant, but the unusual display cases and complex lighting systems show off every piece to its utmost. This complex also includes a gallery for temporary art exhibits, separate numismatic and philatelic museums (coins and stamps, for us regular folks), a modest gift shop, and a branch of the Costa Rican Tourist Institute's information center. Plan to spend an hour or two here.

Calle 5, between avs. Central and 2, underneath the Plaza de la Cultura. ⓒ 243-4202. www.museosdelbanco central.org. Admission $6 (£3) adults, $4 (£2) students, 80¢ (40p) children under 12. Daily 9:30am–5pm.

Museo Nacional de Costa Rica (National Museum) 🕰 Costa Rica's most
important historical museum is housed in a former army barracks that was the scene of fighting during the civil war of 1948. As you approach the building, or walk around it, you can still see hundreds of bullet holes on the turrets at its corners. Inside this traditional Spanish-style courtyard building, you will find displays on Costa Rican history and culture from pre-Columbian times to the present. In the pre-Columbian rooms, you'll see a 2,500-year-old jade carving that is shaped like a seashell and etched with an image of a hand holding a small animal.

Among the most fascinating objects unearthed at Costa Rica's numerous archaeological sites are many *metates,* or grinding stones. This type of grinding stone is still in use today throughout Central America; however, the ones on display here are more ornately decorated than those that you will see anywhere else. Some of the *metates* are the size of a small bed and are believed to have been part of funeral rites. A separate vault houses the museum's collection of pre-Columbian gold jewelry and figurines. In the courtyard you'll be treated to a wonderful view of the city and see some of Costa Rica's mysterious stone spheres. It takes about 2 hours to take in the lion's share of the collection here.

Calle 17, between avs. Central and 2, on the Plaza de la Democracia. ⓒ 257-1433. www.museocostarica.go.cr. Admission $4 (£2) adults, $2 (£1) students and children under 12. Tues–Sat 8:30am–4:30pm; Sun 9am–4:30pm. Closed Dec 25 and 31.

Parque Zoológico Simón Bolívar (Kids This zoo no longer suffers from the over-
whelming sense of neglect and despair that once plagued it, though it's still pretty lackluster and depressing. Why spend time here when you could head out into the forests and jungles? You won't see the great concentrations of wildlife available in one stop here at the zoo, but you'll see the animals in their natural habitats, not yours. The zoo is really geared toward locals and school groups, with a collection that includes

Asian, African, and Costa Rican animals. There's a children's discovery area, a snake-and-reptile house, and a gift shop. You can easily spend a couple of hours here.

Av. 11 and Calle 7, in Barrio Amón. © 256-0012. Admission $2 (£1) adults, $1 (50p) children, free for children under 3. Mon–Fri 8am–4pm; Sat–Sun 9am–4:30pm.

Spirogyra Butterfly Garden   This butterfly garden is smaller and less elaborate than the Butterfly Farm (see below), but it provides a good introduction to the lifecycle of butterflies. It's also a calm and quiet oasis in a noisy and crowded city, quite close to downtown. Plan on a half-hour to several hours here, depending on whether they have lunch or refreshments at the small coffee shop and gallery. You'll be given a self-guided-tour booklet when you arrive, and an 18-minute video show runs continuously throughout the day. You'll find Spirogyra near El Pueblo, a short taxi ride from the center of San José. This is a convenient place to visit in combination with some shopping and a meal at El Pueblo.

100m (1 block) east and 150m (1½ blocks) south of El Pueblo Shopping Center. ©/fax 222-2937. www.infocosta rica.com/butterfly. Admission $6 (£3). Daily 8am–4pm (cafe till 7:30pm).

OUTSIDE SAN JOSE

The **Museo Historico Cultural Juan Santamaría,** Avenida 3 between calles Central and 2 (© 441-4775; www.mhcjs.go.cr), isn't worth a trip of its own, but if you're planning an afternoon in Alajuela, you may want to stop here before or after Zoo Ave. (p. 127). The museum commemorates Costa Rica's national hero, Juan Santamaría, who gave his life defending the country against a small army led by William Walker, a U.S. citizen who invaded Costa Rica in 1856, attempting to set up a slave state. The museum is open Tuesday through Sunday from 10am to 6pm; admission is free.

To locate the attractions below, see "The Central Valley" map on p. 141.

Butterfly Farm   At any given time, you might see around 30 of the 80 species of butterflies raised at this butterfly farm south of Alajuela. The butterflies live in a large enclosed garden similar to an aviary and flutter about the heads of visitors during tours of the gardens. You should be certain to spot glittering blue morphos and a large butterfly that mimics the eyes of an owl. Admission includes a 2-hour guided tour. In the demonstration room you'll see butterfly eggs, caterpillars, and pupae. There are cocoons trimmed in a shimmering gold color and cocoons that mimic a snake's head to frighten away predators. The last guided tour of the day begins at 3pm.

If you reserve in advance, the Butterfly Farm has three daily bus tours that run from many major San José hotels. The cost, including round-trip transportation and admission to the garden, is $30 (£15) for adults, $25 (£13) for students, and $15 (£7.50) for children under 12. Buses pick up passengers at more than 20 different hotels in the San José area.

In front of Los Reyes Country Club, La Guácima de Alajuela. © 438-0400. www.butterflyfarm.co.cr. Admission $15 (£7.50) adults, $10 (£5) students, $7.50 (£3.75) children 5–12, free for children under 3. Daily 8:30am–5pm.

Café Britt Farm   Although bananas are the main export of Costa Rica, most people are far more interested in the country's second-most-important export crop: coffee. Café Britt is one of the leading brands here, and the company has put together an interesting tour and stage production at its farm, which is 20 minutes outside of San José. Here, you'll see how coffee is grown. You'll also visit the roasting and processing plant to learn how a coffee "cherry" is turned into a delicious roasted bean. Tasting sessions are offered for visitors to experience the different qualities of coffee. There is also a restaurant and a store where you can buy coffee and coffee-related gift items. The entire tour, including transportation, takes about 3 to 4 hours. Allow some extra time and an extra $10 for a visit to their nearby working plantation and mill. You can even strap on a basket and go out coffee picking during harvest time. The folks here offer several full-day options that combine a visit to the Britt Farm with a stop at Poás Volcano, the Butterfly Farm (see above), or the Rain Forest Aerial Tram Caribbean. They've also begun offering mountain bike tours in the Heredia hills above their farm, ending with lunch or refreshments at their restaurant.

North of Heredia on the road to Barva. ℭ **277-1600**. www.coffeetour.com. Admission $19 (£9.50) adults, $14 (£7) children 6–11, $27 (£14) adults and $23 (£12) children, including transportation from downtown San José and a coffee drink; add $10 (£5) for full buffet lunch. 3 tours daily: 9 and 11am, and 3pm during the high season; reduced schedule in the off season. Store and restaurant daily 8:30am–5pm year-round.

INBio Park ⭑⭑ *Kids*   Run by the National Biodiversity Institute (Instituto Nacional de Biodiversidad, or INBio), this place is part museum, part educational center, and part nature park. In addition to watching a 15-minute informational video, visitors can tour two large pavilions explaining Costa Rica's biodiversity and natural wonders, and hike on trails that re-create the ecosystems of a tropical rainforest, dry forest, and premontane forest. A 2-hour guided hike is included in the entrance fee, and self-guided-tour booklets are also available. There's a good-size butterfly garden, as well as a Plexiglas viewing window into the small lagoon. One of my favorite attractions here is the series of wonderful animal sculptures donated by one of Costa Rica's premiere artists, José Sancho. There's a simple cafeteria-style restaurant here for lunch, as well as a coffee shop and gift shop. You can easily spend 2 to 3 hours here.

400m (4 blocks) north and 250m (2½ blocks) west of the Shell station in Santo Domingo de Heredia. ℭ **507-8107**. www.inbio.ac.cr. Admission $20 (£10) adults, $8 (£4) children under 13. Daily 8am–6pm (admission closes at 4pm). INBio Park can arrange round-trip transportation from downtown for $12 (£6) per person.

Lankester Gardens ⭑⭑   Costa Rica has more than 1,400 varieties of orchids, and no fewer than 800 species are on display at this botanical garden in Cartago province. Created in the 1940s by English naturalist Charles Lankester, the gardens are now administered by the University of Costa Rica. The primary goal is to preserve the local flora, with an emphasis on orchids and bromeliads. Paved trails meander from open, sunny gardens into shady forests. In each environment different species of orchids are in bloom. There's an information center and a gift shop, and the trails are well tended and well marked. Plan to spend between 1 and 3 hours here if you're interested in flowers and gardening; you could run through it more quickly if you're not. You can easily combine a visit here with an enjoyable tour at Cartago and/or the Orosi Valley and Irazú Volcano. See "Side Trips from San José," later in this chapter.

Paraíso de Cartago. ℭ **552-3247**. Admission $5 (£2.50) adults, $3.50 (£1.75) children 6–16. Daily 8:30am–4:30pm. Closed all national holidays. Take the Cartago bus from San José, and then the Paraíso bus from a stop 1 block south and ¾ block west of the Catholic church ruins in Cartago (ride takes 30–40 min.).

La Paz Waterfall Gardens ⭑⭑ *Kids*   The main attraction here consists of a series of trails through primary and secondary forests alongside the La Paz River, with lookouts over a series of powerful falls, including the namesake La Paz Fall. In addition to an orchid garden and a hummingbird garden, you can see a huge butterfly garden that, in fact, they claim is the largest in the world. A small serpentarium, featuring a mix of venomous and non-venomous native snakes, and several terrariums containing various frogs and lizards, are also parts of the attraction. The newest addition is a man-made trout pond where you can cast for trout. While the admission fee is a little steep, everything is wonderfully done and the trails and waterfalls are beautiful. A buffet lunch at the large cafeteria-style restaurant costs an extra $12 (£6). This is a good stop after a morning visit to the Poás Volcano. Plan to spend 2 to 4 hours here. The hotel rooms (Peace Lodge; p. 111) are some of the nicest in the country.

6km (3¾ miles) north of Varablanca on the road to San Miguel. © 482-2720 or 225-0643. www. waterfallgardens.com. Admission $29 (£15) adults, $18 (£9) children and students w/valid ID. Daily 8:30am–5:30pm. Take a Puerto Viejo de Sarapiquí bus from Calle 12 and Av. 9 (make sure it passes through Varablanca and La Virgen), and ask to be let off at the entrance. Buses are infrequent, and coordinating your return can be difficult, so it's best to come in a rental car or arrange transport.

Zoo Ave. 𝒢   Dozens of scarlet macaws, reclusive owls, majestic raptors, several different species of toucans, and a host of brilliantly colored birds from Costa Rica and around the world make this one exciting place to visit. Bird-watching enthusiasts will be able to get a closer look at birds they might have seen in the wild. There are also large iguana, deer, tapir, puma, and monkey exhibits—and look out for the 3.6m (12-ft.) crocodile. Zoo Ave. houses only injured, donated, or confiscated animals. It takes about 2 hours to walk the paths and visit all the exhibits here.

La Garita, Alajuela. © 433-8989. www.zooave.org. Admission $15 (£7.50), $13 (£6.50) students w/valid ID. Daily 9am–5pm. Catch a bus to Alajuela on Av. 2 between calles 12 and 14. In Alajuela, transfer to a bus to Atenas and get off at Zoo Ave. before you get to La Garita. Fare is 55¢ (30p).

6 Outdoor Activities & Spectator Sports

Due to the chaos and pollution, you'll probably want to get out of the city before undertaking anything too strenuous. But if you want to brave the elements, there are a few outdoor activities in and around San José.

Parque La Sabana (at the western end of Paseo Colón), formerly San José's international airport, is the city's center for active sports and recreation. Here you'll find everything from jogging trails, soccer fields, and a few public tennis courts to the National Stadium. All the facilities are free and open to the public. Families gather for picnics, people fly kites, and there's even an outdoor sculpture garden. If you really want to experience the local culture, try getting into a pickup soccer game here. However, be careful in this park, especially at dusk or after dark, when it becomes a favorite haunt for youth gangs and muggers.

For information on horseback riding, hiking, and white-water rafting trips from San José, see "Side Trips from San José," later in this chapter.

BIRD-WATCHING   Serious birders will certainly want to head out of San José, but it is still possible to see quite a few species in the metropolitan area. Two of the best spots for urban bird-watching are the campus at the **University of Costa Rica,** in the eastern suburb of San Pedro, and **Parque del Este** 𝒢, located a little farther east on the road to San Ramón de Tres Ríos. You'll see a mix of urban species, and if you're lucky, you might spy a couple of hummingbirds or even a blue-crowned motmot. To get to the university campus, take any San Pedro bus from Avenida Central between calles 9 and 11. To get to Parque del Este, take the San Ramón/Parque del Este bus from Calle 9 between avenidas Central and 1. To hook up with fellow birders, e-mail the **Birding Club of Costa Rica** 𝒢𝒢 (costaricabirding@hotmail.com), which frequently organizes expeditions around the Central Valley and beyond.

BULLFIGHTING   Although I hesitate to call it a sport, **Las Corridas a la Tica (Costa Rican bullfighting)** is a popular and frequently comic stadium event. Instead of the blood-and-gore/life-and-death confrontation of traditional bullfighting, Ticos just like to tease the bull. In a typical *corrida,* anywhere from 50 to 150 *toreadores improvisados* (literally, "improvised bullfighters") stand in the ring waiting for the bull. What follows is a slapstick scramble to safety whenever the bull heads toward a crowd of bullfighters. The braver bullfighters try to slap the bull's backside as the beast chases down one of his buddies.

You can see a bullfight during the various Festejos Populares (City Fairs) around the country. The country's largest Festejos Populares are typically held in Zapote, a suburb east of San José during Christmas week and the first week in January. Admission is $2 to $5 (£1–£2.50). However, due to zoning and health and safety issues, the traditional Festejos Populares in Zapote were cancelled in 2006 and 2007. It's not clear if they will return in 2008 or not. In 2007, they were shifted to the nearby town of Guacimo. This is a purely seasonal activity and occurs in San José only during the Festejos. However, there are yearly *festejos* in nearly every little town around the country. These are spread out throughout the year. Ask at your hotel; if your timing's right, you might be able to take in one of these.

GOLF & TENNIS   If you want to play tennis or golf in San José, your options are limited. If you're looking for a real local experience on some rough concrete courts, you can take a racket and some balls down to **Parque La Sabana.** However, the best facilities for visiting golfers and tennis players are found at **Parque Valle del Sol** (© **282-9222;** www.vallesol.com), in the western suburb of Santa Ana. The 18-hole course here is open to the general public. Greens fees are $85 (£43) per golfer per day, including the cart and unlimited playing both on the course and driving range. The tennis courts here cost around $6 (£3) per hour. Reservations are essential. The golf course at the Cariari Country Club is not open to the general public.

HOTEL SPAS & WORKOUT FACILITIES   Most of the higher-end hotels have some sort of pool and exercise facilities. You'll find the best of these at the Marriott Costa Rica Hotel (p. 111) and Tryp Corobicí (p. 105). If you're looking for a good, serious workout, I recommend the **Multispa** (© **231-5542**), located in the Tryp Corobicí. Even if you're not a guest at the hotel, you can use the facilities here and join in any class for $15 (£7.50) per day. Multispa has five other locations around the Central Valley.

JOGGING   Try **Parque La Sabana,** mentioned above, or head to **Parque del Este,** which is east of town in the foothills above San Pedro. Take the San Ramón/Parque del Este bus from Calle 9 between avenidas Central and 1. It's never a good idea to jog at night, on busy streets, or alone. Women should be particularly careful about jogging alone. And remember, Tico drivers are not accustomed to sport joggers on residential streets, so don't expect drivers to give you much berth.

SOCCER *(FUTBOL)*   Ticos take their *fútbol* seriously. Costa Rican professional soccer is some of the best in Central America, and the national team, or *Sele (selección nacional),* qualified for the World Cup in 2002 and 2006, although they made early exits both times. The soccer season runs from September to June, with the finals spread out over several weeks in late June and early July.

You don't need to buy tickets in advance. Tickets generally run between $2 and $15 (£1–£7.50). It's worth paying a little extra for *sombra numerado* (reserved seats in the shade). This will protect you from both the sun and the more rowdy aficionados. Costa Rican soccer fans take the sport seriously, and several violent incidents, both inside and outside the stadiums, have marred the sport in recent years, so be careful. Other options include *sombra* (general admission in the shade), *palco* and *palco numerado* (general admission and reserved mezzanine), and *sol general* (general admission in full sun).

The main San José team is Saprissa (affectionately called El Monstruo, or "The Monster"). **Saprissa's stadium** is in Tibás (take any Tibás bus from Calle 2 and Av. 5). Games are often held on Sunday at 11am, but occasionally they are scheduled for Saturday afternoon or Wednesday evening. Check the local newspapers for game times and locations.

SWIMMING If you aren't going to get to the beach anytime soon and your hotel doesn't have a pool, you can use the pool at the Multispa facility at the hotel **Tryp Corobicí** (© **231-5542**) for $15 (£7.50). Alternatively, for a real Tico experience, head to **Ojo de Agua** (© **441-2808**), on the road between the airport and San Antonio de Belén. The spring-fed waters are cool and refreshing, and even if it seems a bit chilly in San José, it's always several degrees warmer out here. This place is very popular with Ticos and can get quite crowded on weekends. Unfortunately, you have to keep an eye on your valuables here, and the place is perenially run-down. Admission is $2 (£1). Buses leave almost hourly for Ojo de Agua from Avenida 2 and Calle 12.

7 Shopping

Serious shoppers will be disappointed in Costa Rica. Aside from coffee and oxcarts, there isn't much that's distinctly Costa Rican. To compensate for its own relative lack of goods, Costa Rica does a brisk business in selling crafts and clothes imported from Guatemala, Panama, and Ecuador.

THE SHOPPING SCENE San José's central shopping corridor is bounded by avenidas 1 and 2, from about Calle 14 in the west to Calle 13 in the east. For several blocks west of the Plaza de la Cultura, **Avenida Central** is a pedestrian-only street mall where you'll find store after store of inexpensive clothes for men, women, and children. Depending on the mood of the police that day, you might find a lot of street vendors as well. Most shops in the downtown district are open Monday through Saturday from about 8am to 6pm. Some shops close for lunch, while others remain open (it's just the luck of the draw for shoppers). You'll be happy to find that the sales and import taxes have already been figured into the display price.

International laws prohibit trade in endangered wildlife, so don't buy any plants or animals, even if they're readily for sale. Do not buy any kind of sea-turtle products (including jewelry); wild birds; lizard, snake, or cat skins; corals; or orchids (except those grown commercially). No matter how unique, beautiful, insignificant, or inexpensive it might seem, your purchase will directly contribute to the further hunting of endangered species.

It's especially hard to capture the subtle shades and colors of the rainforests and cloud forests, and many a traveler has gone home thinking that his or her undeveloped film contained the full beauty of the jungle, only to return from the photo developer with 36 bright-green blurs. To avoid this heartache, you might want to pick up some postcards of the sights you want to remember forever and send them to yourself.

Tips Joe to Go

Two words of advice: Buy coffee. Lots of it.

Coffee is the best shopping deal in all of Costa Rica. Although the best Costa Rican coffee is allegedly shipped off to North American and European markets, it's hard to beat the coffee that's roasted right in front of you here. Best of all is the price: One pound of coffee sells for around $3 to $6 (£1.50–£3). It makes a great gift and truly is a local product.

Café Britt is the big name in Costa Rican coffee. These folks have the largest export business in the country, and, although high-priced, its blends are very dependable. My favorites, however, are the coffees roasted and packaged in Manuel Antonio and Monteverde, by **Café Milagro** and **Café Monteverde,** respectively. If you visit either of these places, definitely pick up their beans.

In general, the best place to buy coffee is in any supermarket. Why pay more at a gift or specialty shop? You can also try **Café Trébol,** on Calle 8 between avenidas Central and 1 (on the western side of the Central Market; © 221-8363). It's open Monday through Saturday from 7am to 6:30pm and Sunday from 8:30am to 12:30pm.

Be sure to ask for whole beans; Costa Rican grinds are often too fine for standard coffee filters. The store will pack beans for you in whatever size bag you want. If you buy prepackaged coffee in a supermarket in Costa Rica, the whole beans will be marked either *grano* (grain) or *grano entero* (whole bean). If you opt for ground varieties *(molido),* be sure the package is marked *puro;* otherwise, it will likely be mixed with a good amount of sugar, the way Ticos like it.

One good coffee-related gift to bring home is a coffee sock and stand. This is the most common mechanism for brewing coffee beans in Costa Rica. It consists of a simple circular stand, made out of wood or wire, which holds a sock. Put the ground beans in the sock, place a pot or cup below it, and pour boiling water through. You can find the socks and stands at most supermarkets and in the Mercado Central. In fancier crafts shops you'll find them made out of ceramic. Depending on its construction, a stand will cost you between $1.50 and $15 (75p–£7.50); socks run around 30¢ (15p), so buy a few spares.

MARKETS   There are several markets near downtown, but by far the largest is the **Mercado Central,** located between avenidas Central and 1 and calles 6 and 8. Although this dark maze of stalls is primarily a food market, inside you'll find all manner of vendors, including a few selling Costa Rican souvenirs, crude leather goods, and musical instruments. Be especially careful about your wallet or purse and any prominent jewelry because very skilled pickpockets frequent this area. All the streets surrounding the Mercado Central are jammed with produce vendors selling from small carts or loading and unloading trucks. It's always a hive of activity, with crowds of people jostling for space on the streets. Your best bet is to visit on Sunday or on weekdays;

Saturday is particularly busy. In the hot days of the dry season, the aromas can get quite heady. If you have a delicate constitution, don't eat any fruit that you don't peel yourself (oranges, bananas, mangoes, and so on).

There is also a daily street market on the west side of the **Plaza de la Democracia.** Here you'll find two long rows of outdoor stalls selling T-shirts, Guatemalan and Ecuadorian handicrafts and clothing, small ceramic *ocarinas* (a small musical wind instrument), and handmade jewelry. The atmosphere here is much more open than at the Mercado Central, which I find just a bit too claustrophobic. You might be able to bargain prices down a little bit, but bargaining is not a traditional part of the vendor culture here, so you'll have to work hard to save a few dollars.

Finally, two other similar options downtown include **La Casona,** Calle Central between avenidas Central and 1 (© 222-7999), a three-story warren of crafts and souvenir shops; and **El Pueblo,** a tourism complex built in the style of a mock colonial-era village, with a wide range of restaurants, gift shops, art galleries, bars, and discos.

MODERN MALLS   With globalization and modernization taking hold in Costa Rica, much of the local shopping scene has shifted to large megamalls. Modern multilevel affairs with cineplexes, food courts, and international brand-name stores are becoming more ubiquitous. The biggest and most modern of these malls include the **Mall San Pedro, Multiplaza, Terra Mall,** and **Mall Real Cariari.** Although they lack the charm of small shops found around San José, they are a reasonable option for one-stop shopping; most contain at least one or two local galleries and crafts shops, along with a large supermarket, which is always the best place to stock up on local coffee, hot sauces, liquors, and other non-perishable foodstuffs.

SHOPPING A TO Z
ART GALLERIES

Art lovers should check out Molly Keeler's one-day **Art Tour** ⭐ (© **359-5571** or 288-0896; www.costaricaarttour.com), which includes scheduled visits to the studios and personal shops of prominent local artists working in a wide range of media.

Arte Latino   This gallery carries original artwork in a variety of media, featuring predominantly Central American themes. Some of it is pretty gaudy, but this is a good place to find Nicaraguan and Costa Rican "primitive" paintings. The gallery also has storefronts in the Multiplaza Mall in Escazú and at the Mall Cariari, which is located on the Interamerican Highway, about halfway between the airport and downtown, across the street from the Hotel Herradura. Calle 5 and Av. 1. © **258-3306.**

Galería Amón ⭐   Located in a stylish old house in the historic Barrio Amón district, this gallery features contemporary artists from Central and South America. The spaces are ample and well-lit, giving this place almost a museum-like feel. No. 937 Calle 7 between Av. 7 and 9. © **223-9725.**

Galería Andrómeda ⭐   This small, personal gallery features contemporary national artists of good quality. There are usually prints and paintings by several artists on display, and prices are very reasonable. Calle 9 at Av. 9. © **223-3529.**

Galería 11–12 ⭐⭐   This outstanding gallery deals mainly in high-end Costa Rican art, from neoclassical painters such as Teodorico Quirós to modern masters such as Francisco Amighetti and Paco Zuñiga, to current stars such as Rafa Fernández, Rodolfo Stanley, Fernando Carballo, and Fabio Herrera. Plaza Itzkatzu, off the Prospero Fernández Highway, Escazú. © **288-1975.** www.galeria11-12.com.

Galería Jacobo Karpio   This excellent gallery handles some of the more adventurous modern art to be found in Costa Rica. Karpio has a steady stable of prominent Mexican, Cuban, and Argentine artists, as well as some local talent. Av. 1, casa no. 1352, between calles 11 and 13. ℂ 257-7963.

Galería Kandinsky   Owned by the daughter of one of Costa Rica's most prominent modern painters, Rafa Fernández, this small gallery usually has a good selection of high-end contemporary Costa Rican paintings, be it the house collection or a specific temporary exhibit. Centro Comercial Calle Real, San Pedro. ℂ 234-0478.

TEORetica ⭐⭐   This small downtown gallery is run by one of the more adventurous and internationally respected collectors and curators in Costa Rica, Virginia Pérez-Ratton. You'll often find very interesting and cutting-edge exhibitions here. Calle 7 between Av. 9 and 11. ℂ 233-4881. www.teoretica.org.

BOOKS

For English-language novels, field guides and general guide books, and natural history books, head to either **Seventh Street Books** (ℂ 256-8251; Calle 7 between avenidas 1 and Central), or **Librería Internacional** (ℂ 253-9553; www.libreriainternacional.com). Librería Internacional has several outlets around San José, including storefronts in most of the major modern malls.

HANDICRAFTS

The quality of Costa Rican handicrafts is generally very low, and the offerings are limited. The most typical items you'll find are hand-painted wooden **oxcarts.** These come in a variety of sizes, and you can ship the big ones to your home for a very reasonable price. If you want to stick to downtown San José, try the outdoor market on the **Plaza de la Democracia,** although prices here tend to be high and bargaining can be difficult. If you prefer to do your crafts shopping in a flea-market atmosphere, head over to **La Casona** on Calle Central between avenidas Central and 1.

Notable exceptions to the generally meager crafts offerings include the fine wooden creations of **Barry Biesanz** ⭐⭐ (ℂ 289-4337; www.biesanz.com). His work is sold in many of the finer gift shops around and at his own shop (see below), but beware: Biesanz's work is often imitated, so make sure that what you buy is the real deal (he generally burns his signature into the bottom of the piece). **Lil Mena** is a local artist who specializes in working with and painting on handmade papers and rough fibers. You'll find her work in a number of shops around San José.

You might also run across **carved masks** made by the indigenous Boruca people of southern Costa Rica. These full-size balsa-wood masks come in a variety of styles, both painted and unpainted, and run anywhere from $10 to $80 (£5–£40), depending on the quality of workmanship. **Cecilia "Pefi" Figueres** ⭐⭐ makes practical ceramic wares that are lively and fun. Look for her brightly colored abstract and figurative bowls, pitchers, coffee mugs, and more at some of the better gift shops around the city.

Scores of shops around San José sell a wide variety of crafts, from the truly tacky to the divinely inspired. Here are some that sell more of the latter and fewer of the former.

Biesanz Woodworks ⭐ _Finds_   Biesanz makes a wide range of high-quality items, including bowls, jewelry boxes, humidors, and some wonderful sets of wooden chopsticks. Biesanz Woodworks is actively involved in local reforestation. Bello Horizonte, Escazú. ℂ 289-4337. www.biesanz.com. Call for directions and off-hour appointments.

Boutique Annemarie ✦   Occupying two floors at the Hotel Don Carlos, this shop has an amazing array of wood products, leather goods, papier-mâché figurines, paintings, books, cards, posters, and jewelry. You'll see most of this stuff at the other shops, but not in such quantities or in such a relaxed and pressure-free environment. At the Hotel Don Carlos, Calle 9, between avs. 7 and 9. ✆ **221-6063.**

Galería Namu   This shop has some very high-quality arts and crafts, including excellent Boruca and Huetar carved masks and "primitive" paintings, many painted by rural women. It also carries a good selection of the ceramic work of Cecilia "Pefi" Figueres. This place organizes tours to visit various indigenous tribes and artisans as well. Av. 7 between calles 5 and 7. ✆ **256-3412.** www.galerianamu.com.

Green Turtle   This large shop has a vast selection of handicrafts and souvenirs. Most of it is of very standard to poor quality, but this does make a particularly convenient stop for some last-minute shopping on your way to the airport. 4 blocks north of Denny's, near the airport. ✆ **430-0211.**

Orinoco Arts & Crafts Gallery   With a stellar and varied collection from Costa Rica and around Latin America, particularly Venezuela, this shop has some of the best high-quality arts and craft pieces you'll find in the country. The selection ranges from paintings and sculptures, to baskets, wood carvings, and ceramic works. Plaza Itzkatzu, off the Prospero Fernández Highway, Escazú. ✆ **288-2949.** www.orinocoarts.com.

Suraska   Among the selections here are ceramics, mobiles, and jewelry. This store tends to carry higher-quality items than most gift shops downtown. However, be warned that prices are accordingly more expensive. Calle 5 and Av. 3. ✆ **222-0129.**

JEWELRY

Studio Metallo   The outgrowth of a jewelry-making school and studio, this shop has some excellent handcrafted jewelry made in a range of styles, using everything from 18-karat white and yellow gold and pure silver, to some less exotic and expensive alloys. Some works integrate gem stones, while many others focus on the metal work. 6½ blocks east of the Iglesia Santa Teresita, Barrio Escalante. ✆ **281-3207.** www.studio metallo.com.

Plaza Esmeralda   Part working jewelry factory, part shopping center, part tourist trap, this is still a good place to come to buy replicas of pre-Columbian jewelry. The several shops here carry a wide range of typical tourist souvenirs and locally produced arts and craftworks at fair prices. Visitors are treated to a 15-minute guided tour where you can see some of the jewelry being manufactured. Sabana Norte. 800m (8 blocks) north of Jack's in Pavas. ✆ **296-0312.**

LEATHER GOODS

In general, Costa Rican leather products are not of the highest grade or quality, and prices are not particularly low. In addition to the shop listed below, **Del Río** (✆ **262-1415**) is a local leather goods manufacturer, with stores in most of the city's modern malls. It also offers free hotel pickup and transfer to its factory outlet in Heredia.

Malety   At this outlet in San José, you can shop for locally produced leather bags, briefcases, purses, wallets, and other such items. A second store is located on Calle 1 between avenidas Central and 2. Av. 1 between calles 1 and 3. ✆ **221-1670.**

LIQUOR

The national drink is *guaro,* a rough, clear liquor made from sugar cane. The most popular brand is **Cacique,** available at every liquor store and most supermarkets. Costa Ricans drink their *guaro* straight or mixed with club soda or Fresca. When drinking it straight, it's customary to follow a shot with a bite into a fresh lime covered in salt.

Costa Ricans also drink a lot of rum. The premier Costa Rican rum is **Centenario,** but I recommend that you opt for the Nicaraguan **Flor de Caña** or Cuban **Havana Club,** both of which are far superior rums. *Note:* Because of the trade embargo, it is illegal to bring Havana Club into the United States.

Several brands and styles of coffee-based liqueurs are also produced in Costa Rica. **Café Rica** is similar to Kahlúa, and you can also find several types of coffee cream liqueurs. The folks at **Café Britt** produce their own line of coffee liqueurs which are quite good and available in most supermarkets, liquor stores, and tourist shops; the best prices I've seen are at the supermarket chain **Más × Menos.** There is a Más × Menos store on Paseo Colón and another on Avenida Central at the east end of town, just below the Museo Nacional de Costa Rica.

MUSIC

A CD of Costa Rican music makes a great souvenir. Many gift shops around the country carry a small selection of Costa Rican music. **Editus** is an inventive trio (guitar, violin, and percussion) that has several albums out. They've won two Grammy Awards for their collaborations with Rubén Blades on the albums *Tiempos* and *Mundo.* You should also see discs by **Cantoamérica,** which plays upbeat dance music ranging from salsa to calypso to meringue. Jazz pianist **Manuel Obregón** has several excellent albums out, including *Simbiosis,* on which he improvises along with the sounds of Costa Rica's wildlife, waterfalls, and weather; as well as his work with the *Papaya Orchestra,* a collaboration and gathering of musicians from around Central America. **Papaya Music** (www.papayamusic.com) is a Costa Rican label that produces and distributes an excellent range of local music, including everyone from Obregón to **Malpaís,** a local pop-rock band, to a broad selection of traditional folk music, including one of my favorite local discs, *Dr. Bombodee,* by the Costa Rican–born calypsonian Walter "Gavitt" Ferguson.

8 San José After Dark

Catering to a mix of tourists, college students, and just generally party-loving Ticos, San José has a host of options to meet the nocturnal needs of visitors and residents alike. You'll find plenty of interesting clubs and bars, a wide range of theaters, and some very lively discos and dance salons.

To find out what's going on in San José while you're in town, pick up a copy of the *Tico Times* (English) or *La Nación* (Spanish). The former is a good place to find out where local expatriates are hanging out; the latter's "Viva" and "Tiempo Libre" sections have extensive listings of discos, movie theaters, and live music.

THE PERFORMING ARTS

Theater is very popular in Costa Rica, and downtown San José is studded with small theaters. However, tastes tend toward the burlesque, and the crowd pleasers are almost always simplistic sexual comedies. The **National Theater Company** is an exception, tackling works from Lope de Vega to Lorca to Mamet. Similarly, the small independent group **Abya Yala** also puts on several cutting-edge avant-garde shows each year. Almost all of the theater offerings are in Spanish, although the **Little Theater Group** is a long-standing amateur group that periodically stages works in English. Check the *Tico Times* to see if anything is running during your stay.

Costa Rica has a strong modern-dance scene. Both the **University of Costa Rica** and the **National University** have modern-dance companies that perform regularly in various venues in San José. In addition to the university-sponsored companies, there's a host of smaller independent companies worth catching.

The **National Symphony Orchestra** is respectable by regional standards, although its repertoire tends to be rather conservative. Symphony season runs March through November, with concerts roughly every other weekend at the **Teatro Nacional,** Avenida 2 between calles 3 and 5 (© 221-3756; www.teatronacional.go.cr), and the **Auditorio Nacional** (© 256-5876) at the Museo de Los Niños (p. 123). Tickets cost between $3 and $20 (£1.50–£10) and can be purchased at the box office.

Visiting artists stop in Costa Rica from time to time. Recent concerts have featured pop phenom The Black Eyed Peas, rock star Sting, reggaeton giant Daddy Yankee, and Mexican singing sensation Ricky Martin. Many of these performances take place in San José's two historic theaters, the **Teatro Nacional** (see above) and the **Teatro Melico Salazar,** Avenida 2 between calles Central and 2 (© 221-4952), as well as at the **Auditorio Nacional** (see above). Really large shows are usually held at soccer stadiums or large, natural amphitheaters.

Costa Rica's cultural panorama changes drastically every November when the country hosts large arts festivals. In odd-numbered years, **El Festival Nacional de las Artes** reigns supreme, featuring purely local talent. In even-numbered years, the month-long fete is **El Festival Internacional de las Artes,** with a nightly smorgasbord of dance, theater, music, and monologue from around the world. Most nights of the festival offer between 4 and 10 shows. Many are free, and the most expensive ticket is usually around $5 (£2.50). For exact dates and details, you can contact the Ministry of Youth, Culture, and Sports (© 255-3188; www.mcjdcr.go.cr), although you might have trouble getting any information if you don't speak Spanish.

THE CLUB, MUSIC & DANCE SCENE

You'll find plenty of places to hit the dance floor in San José. Salsa and merengue are the main beats that move people here, and many of the dance clubs, discos, and salons feature live music on the weekends. You'll find a pretty limited selection, though, if you're looking to catch some small-club jazz, rock, or blues.

The daily "Viva" and Friday's "Tiempo Libre" sections of *La Nación* newspaper have weekly performance schedules. Some dance bands to watch for are Cantoamérica, Kalua, Chocolate, and Los Brillanticos. While Ghandi, Evolución, and Malpaís are popular local rock groups, Marfil is a good cover band, and both Harmony Roads and the Blind Pig Blues Band are outfits that play American-style rock, blues and folk music. If you're looking for jazz, check out Editus, El Sexteto de Jazz Latino, guitarist Federico Miranda or pianist Manuel Obregón. For a taste of something eclectic, look for Santos y Zurdo; Peregrino Gris; or Amarillo, Cyan y Magenta.

A good place to sample a range of San José's nightlife is in **El Pueblo,** a shopping, dining, and entertainment complex done up like an old Spanish village. It's just across the river to the north of town. The best way to get there is by taxi; all the drivers know

El Pueblo well. Within the alleyways that wind through El Pueblo are a dozen or more bars, clubs, and discos—there's even an indoor soccer playing field. **Fiesta Latina** (📞 222-1003), **Twister** (📞 222-5746) and **Friends** (📞 233-1559) are happening party spots. Across the street, **Copacabana** (📞 233-5516) is one of my favorite dance spots. For a mellower option, inside El Pueblo, try **Café Art Boruca** (📞 221-3615).

Most of the places listed below charge a nominal cover charge; sometimes it includes a drink or two.

Castro's 🔆 *(Finds)* This is a classic Costa Rican dance club. The music varies throughout the night, from salsa and meringue to reggaeton and occasionally electronic trance. There are several rooms and various types of environments, including some intimate and quiet corners, spread over a couple of floors. Avenida 13 and Calle 22, Barrio Mexico. 📞 256-8789.

Copacabana 🔆 This large, open, upscale disco seems to be the favored dance venue for the young and beautiful of San José. The interior is designed to resemble a colonial plaza. Tunes come in sets that can range from salsa to merengue to reggae to electronic. This place pulls a younger crowd than many of the other spots around town; the party here is Wednesday through Saturday nights till around 4am. Admission is around $3 (£1.50). Across from the El Pueblo shopping center. 📞 233-5516.

El Tobogán 🔆🔆 *(Finds)* The dance floor in this place is about the size of a football field, yet it still fills up. This is a place where Ticos come with their loved ones and dance partners. The music is a mix of classic Latin dance rhythms—salsa, cumbia, and merengue. It's open only on the weekends (till about 2am), but there's always a live band here, and sometimes it's very good. 200m (2 blocks) north and 100m (1 block) east of the La República main office, off the Guápiles Hwy. 📞 223-8920.

Salsa 54 This is the place to go to watch expert salsa dancers and to try some yourself. You can take formal Latin dance classes here, or you might learn something just by watching. This place is popular with Ticos, and tourists are a rare commodity here—tourists who can really dance salsa, even more so. It's open daily till 4am. Calle 3 between avs. 1 and 3. 📞 233-3814.

Vértigo Tucked inside a nondescript office building and commercial center on Paseo Colón, this new club has quickly become one of the more popular places for rave-style late-night dancing and partying. The dance floor is huge and the ceilings are high, and electronic music rules the roost. It's open daily till 4am. Edificio Colón, Paseo Colón. 📞 257-8424.

THE BAR SCENE

There seems to be something for every taste here. Lounge lizards will be happy in most hotel bars in the downtown area, while students and the young at heart will have no problem mixing in at the livelier spots around town. Sports fans can find plenty of places to catch the most important games of the day, and there are even a couple of brewpubs that are drastically improving the quality and selection of the local suds.

The best part of the varied bar scene in San José is something called a *boca,* the equivalent of a tapa in Spain: a little dish of snacks that arrives at your table when you order a drink. Although this is a somewhat dying tradition, especially in the younger, hipper bars, you will still find *bocas* alive and well in the older, more traditional Costa Rican drinking establishments. In most, the *bocas* are free, but in some, where the dishes are more sophisticated, you'll have to pay for the treats. You'll find drinks reasonably priced, with beer costing around $2 (£1) a bottle, and mixed drinks costing $2 to $4 (£1–£2).

Café Expresivo ✦   Laid back and funky, this cafe, restaurant and gallery features occasional live performances, which can range from open-mike sessions, to storytelling marathons, to folk and jazz concerts featuring some of the country's top talent. When there's no act, this is a mellow place to have a drink and good conversation. It's open Tuesday through Friday from noon to midnight, and Saturday and Sunday from 5pm to midnight. 4 blocks East of the Santa Teresita Church, Barrio Escalante. ℂ 224-1202.

Chelles *(Finds)*   This classic downtown bar and restaurant makes up for its lack of ambience with plenty of tradition and a diverse and colorful clientele. The lights are bright, the chairs surround simple Formica-topped card tables, and mirrors adorn most of the walls. Simple sandwiches and meals are served, and pretty good *bocas* come with the drinks. It's open daily, 'round the clock. Av. Central and Calle 9. ℂ 221-1369.

El Cuartel de la Boca del Monte ✦✦   This popular bar, one of San José's best, began life as an artist-and-bohemian hangout, and has evolved into the leading meat market for the young and well heeled. However, artists still come, as do foreign exchange students, visitors, and, a broad cross section of San José's youth, so there's always a diverse mix. There's usually live music here on Monday, Wednesday, and Friday nights, and when there is, the place is packed shoulder to shoulder. From Monday to Friday it's open for lunch and again in the evenings; on weekends it opens at 4pm. On most nights it's open till about 1am, although the revelry might continue till about 3am on Friday or Saturday. One corner has been separated into a more bohemian style bar or pub called La Esquina, or "the corner." Av. 1 between calles 21 and 23 (50m/½ block west of the Cine Magaly). ℂ 221-0327.

El Observatorio ✦✦ *(Finds)*   It's easy to miss the narrow entrance to this hot spot across from the Cine Magaly. Owned by a local filmmaker, the decor includes a heavy dose of cinema motifs. The space is large, with high ceilings, and one of the best (perhaps only) smoke extraction systems of any popular bar, making the place bearable, even though most of the clientele are chain smoking. There's occasional live music and movie screenings and a decent menu of appetizers and main dishes drawn from various world cuisines. Calle 23 between avs. Central and 1. ℂ 223-0725.

Key Largo ✦ *(Finds)*   Following a meticulous restoration in 2004, San José's most popular prostitute pickup bar is looking better than ever. Housed in a beautiful old building just off Parque Morazán in the heart of downtown, Key Largo is worth a visit if only to take in the scene and admire the dark-stained carved wood ceilings. There are a couple of pool tables, there's usually a live band, and there are always working women—however, this is still an acceptable place for visiting couples and those not actively shopping the wares. Calle 7 between avs. 1 and 3. ℂ 221-0277.

Shakespeare Bar   Located next to the Sala Garbo movie theater, this quiet little spot is a good place to meet after a movie or a show at the Sala Garbo or Laurence Olivier Theater next door. Intimate and reserved, it's open daily till midnight. Av. 2 and Calle 28. ℂ 258-6787.

HANGING OUT IN SAN PEDRO

The funky 2-block stretch of **San Pedro** ✦✦ just south of the University of Costa Rica has been dubbed La Calle de Amargura, or the "Street of Bitterness," and it's the heart and soul of this eastern suburb and college town. Bars and cafes are mixed in with bookstores and copy shops. After dark the streets are packed with teens, punks, students, and professors barhopping and just hanging around. You can walk the strip until someplace strikes your fancy—you don't need a travel guide to find **La Villa** (① 281-1571), **Omar Khayyam** (① 253-8455), **Marrakech Pool & Pizza** (① 253-2049), **Tavarua Surf & Skate Bar** (① 225-7249), or **Caccio's** (① 224-3261), which lie at the heart of this district—or you can try one of the places listed below. *Note*: La Calle de Amargura attracts a certain unsavory element. Use caution here. Try to visit with a group, and try not to carry large amounts of cash or wear flashy jewelry.

Hard rockers, metal freaks, ravers, and rowdy young crowds tend to congregate at the **Sand Bar** (① 225-9229), in the Centro Comercial Cocorí, and **El Yos** (① 283-0095), located 75m (¾ block) west of the Automercado in Los Yoses. The latter club often has live music or DJs.

You can get here by heading out (east) on Avenida 2, and following the flow of traffic. You will first pass through the neighborhood of Los Yoses before you reach a large traffic circle with a big fountain in the center (La Fuente de la Hispanidad). The Mall San Pedro is located on this traffic circle. Heading straight through the circle (well, going around it and continuing on what would have been a straight path), you'll come to the Church of San Pedro, about 4 blocks east of the circle. The church is the major landmark in San Pedro. You can also take a bus here from downtown.

Jazz Café ⟨ᵣ⟩   Run by a former owner of the popular but now defunct La Maga, the Jazz Café is consistently one of the more happening spots in San Pedro and one of my favorites, although low ceilings and poor air circulation make it almost unbearably smoky most nights. Wrought-iron chairs, sculpted busts of famous jazz artists, and creative lighting give the place ambience. There's live music here most nights. It's open daily till about 2am. Next to the Banco Popular on Av. Central. ① 253-8933.

Mosaikos   The entrance to this popular nightspot is a long, narrow corridor/bar that is generally packed solid. A larger room in the back has another bar, some tables, and some funky art. The crowd here is young and can get quite rowdy. They often have live DJs playing a mix of house, techno, and trance-style dance music, although you're also just as likely to hear reggae, ska, or hip-hop tunes blasting. It's open Monday through Saturday from 11am to 2am, Sunday from 5pm to 2am. 200m (2 blocks) east and 150m (1½ blocks) north of the Church in San Pedro. ① 280-9541.

THE GAY & LESBIAN SCENE

Because Costa Rica is such a conservative Catholic country, the gay and lesbian communities here are rather discreet. Homosexuality is not generally under attack, but many gay and lesbian organizations guard their privacy, and the club scene is changeable and not well publicized. For a general overview of the current situation, news of any special events or meetings, and up-to-date information, gay and lesbian travelers should check in at **Uno@Diez**, on Calle 3 and Avenida 7 (① 258-4561; www.1en10. com), a downtown coffeehouse, gallery, and Internet cafe.

The most established and happening gay and lesbian bar and dance club in San José is **La Avispa,** Calle 1 between avs. 8 and 10 (① 223-5343; www.laavispa.co.cr). It is popular with both men and women, although it sometimes sets aside certain nights of the week or month for specific persuasions. There's also **Buenas Vibraciones** (① 223-4573), out on Paseo de los Estudiantes; **Club Oh** (① 248-1500), on Calle 2 between avs. 14 and 16; **Pucho's Bar** (① 256-1147), on Calle 11 and Avenida 8;

El Bochinche (© 221-0500), on Calle 11 between avs. 10 and 12; and **Punto G** (© 280-3726) in San Pedro, half a block southwest of the Higuerón.

CASINOS

Gambling is legal in Costa Rica, with casinos at virtually every major hotel. However, as with Tico bullfighting, there are some idiosyncrasies involved in gambling *a la Tica*.

If blackjack is your game, you'll want to play "rummy." The rules are almost identical, except that the house doesn't pay 1½ times on blackjack—instead, it pays double on any three of a kind or three-card straight flush.

If you're looking for roulette, what you'll find here is a bingolike spinning cage of numbered balls. The betting is the same, but some of the glamour is lost.

You'll also find a version of five-card-draw poker, but the rule differences are so complex that I advise you to sit down and watch for a while and then ask questions before joining in. That's about all you'll find. There are no craps tables or baccarat.

There's some controversy over slot machines—one-armed bandits are currently outlawed—but you will be able to play electronic slots and poker games. Most casinos here are casual and small by international standards. You may have to dress up slightly at some of the fancier hotels, but most are accustomed to tropical vacation attire.

9 Side Trips from San José

San José makes an excellent base for exploring the beautiful Central Valley and the surrounding mountains. For first-time visitors, the best way to make the most of these excursions is usually to take a guided tour, but if you rent a car, you'll have greater independence. Some day trips also can be done by public bus.

GUIDED TOURS & ADVENTURES

A number of companies offer a wide variety of primarily nature-related day tours out of San José. The most reputable include **Costa Rica Expeditions** ☆☆ (© 257-0766; www.costaricaexpeditions.com), **Costa Rica Sun Tours** ☆ (© 296-7757; www.crsun tours.com), **Horizontes Tours** ☆☆ (© 222-2022; www.horizontes.com), and **Swiss Travel Service** (© 282-4898; www.swisstravelcr.com).

Before signing on for a tour of any sort, find out how many fellow travelers will be accompanying you, how much time will be spent in transit and eating lunch, and how much time will actually be spent doing the primary activity. I've had complaints about tours that were rushed, that spent too much time in a bus or on secondary activities, or that had a cattle-car, assembly-line feel to them. The tours below are arranged by type of activity. In addition to these, you'll find many other tours that combine two or three different activities or destinations.

BUNGEE JUMPING   There's nothing unique about bungee jumping in Costa Rica, but the site here is quite beautiful. If you've always had the bug, **Tropical Bungee** (© 248-2212; www.bungee.co.cr) will let you jump off an 80m (262-ft.) bridge for $65 (£33); two jumps cost $95 (£48). Transportation is provided free from San José twice daily. These folks also offer paragliding tours.

CANOPY TOURS & AERIAL TRAMS   Getting off the ground and up into the treetops is the latest fad in Costa Rican tourism, and there are scores of such tours around the country. You have several options relatively close to San José. The folks at the **Original Canopy Tours** ☆ (© 291-4465; www.canopytour.com) have their

Mahogany Park operation, located about 1 hour outside of San José. The tour here features 10 platforms, and at the end you have the choice of taking a cable to a ground station or doing an 18m (60-ft.) rappel down to finish off. The tour takes about 2 hours and costs $45 (£23).

Another option is the **Rain Forest Aerial Tram Caribbean** $☆$ ($©$ 257-5961; www.rainforesttram.com), built on a private reserve bordering Braulio Carrillo National Park. This pioneering tramway is the brainchild of rainforest researcher Dr. Donald Perry, whose cable-car system through the forest canopy at Rara Avis helped establish him as an early expert on rainforest canopies. The tramway takes visitors on a 90-minute ride through the treetops, where they have the chance to glimpse the complex web of life that makes these forests unique. These folks recently added several attractions, including a butterfly garden, serpentarium, and frog collection. They also have their own zip-line canopy tour. There are also well-groomed trails through the rainforest and a restaurant on-site, so a trip here can easily take up a full day. In fact, if you want to spend the night, there are 10 simple but clean and comfortable bungalows here, which cost $109 (£55) per person per day (double occupancy), including three meals, three guided tours, taxes, two tram rides, and unlimited use of the rest of the facilities.

The cost for tours, including transportation from San José and either breakfast or lunch, is $85 (£43). Alternatively, you can drive or take one of the frequent Guápiles buses—they leave every half-hour throughout the day and cost $2 (£1)—from the new Caribbean bus terminal (Gran Terminal del Caribe) on Calle Central, 1 block north of Avenida 11. Ask the driver to let you off in front of the *teleférico.* If you're driving, head out on the Guápiles Highway as if driving to the Caribbean coast. Watch for the tram's roadside welcome center—it's hard to miss. For walk-ins, the entrance fee is $55 (£28); students and anyone under 18 pay $28 (£14). Because this is a popular tour for groups, I highly recommend that you get an advance reservation in the high season and, if possible, a ticket; otherwise you could wait a long time for your tram ride or even be shut out. The tram handles only about 80 passengers per hour, so scheduling is tight; the folks here try to schedule as much as possible in advance.

Finally, **Turu BaRi Tropical Park** ($©$ 250-0705 or 428-6070; www.turubari.com) is another similar attraction that aims to cover as many bases as possible. Located about 90 minutes outside of San José, this park features a series of gardens, trails, and exhibits set in a deep valley that you can reach by means of a gondola-style ski lift, by cable and zip-line canopy tour, or on horseback. Down in the valley, you can wander around the botanical gardens, orchid gardens, and butterfly gardens, or grab a bite at the typical Costa Rican restaurant. The gondola ride here actually features enclosed cabin cars (with windows that open) and doesn't provide nearly the sense of intimacy or contact with the forest that the Aerial Tram does. Admission is $45 (£23) for adults, $40 (£20) for students, and $35 (£18) for children; all the various adventure tour options cost extra.

DAY CRUISES   Several companies offer cruises to lovely Tortuga Island in the Gulf of Nicoya. These full-day tours generally entail an early departure for the 2½-hour chartered bus ride to Puntarenas, where you board your vessel for a 1½-hour cruise to Tortuga Island. Then you get several hours on the uninhabited island, where you can swim, lie on the beach, play volleyball, or try a canopy tour, followed by the return journey.

The Central Valley

Butterfly Farm **2**
Café Britt Farm **6**
INBio Park **7**
Lankester Gardens **8**
La Paz Waterfall Gardens **4**
Rain Forest Aerial Tram
   Caribbean **5**
Termales del Bosque **9**
Turu BaRi Tropical Park **1**
Zoo Ave. **3**

*Map labels:*

To Limón →

Guapiles

Puerto Viejo de Sarapiquí

La Virgen

San Miguel

Aguas Zarcas

Ciudad Quesada

JUAN CASTRO BLANCO NATIONAL PARK

Los Angeles Cloud Forest Reserve

Zarcero

Naranjo

Sarchí

Grecia

Palmares

San Ramón

Interamerican Highway

To Guanacaste

To Puntarenas

Esparza

CORDILLERA DE TILARAN

Costanera Su

To Jacó

Nicoya Gulf

Orotiná

Atenas

La Garita

San Pedro de Poás

Poasito

POAS VOLCANO NATIONAL PARK

Vara Blanca

Volcán Barva

BRAULIO CARRILLO NATIONAL PARK

CORDILLERA CENTRAL

Sta. Bárbara

Barva

HEREDIA

Santo Domingo

Guadalupe

San Pedro

Curridabat

Tres Ríos

San José

Desamparados

Aserrí

Alajuelita

Escazú

El Rodeo Forest Reserve

Santa Ana

Ciudad Colón

Alajuela

Tapantí National Park →

Turrialba

Pacayas

Cartago

Paraíso

Guayabo National Monument

IRAZU VOLCANO NATIONAL PARK

Airport

141

The original and most dependable company running these trips is **Calypso Tours** ⚓ (✆ 256-2727; www.calypsotours.com). The tour costs $99 (£50) per person and includes round-trip transportation from San José, a basic continental breakfast during the bus ride to the boat, all drinks on the cruise, and an excellent buffet lunch on the beach at the island. The Calypso Tours main vessel is a massive motor-powered catamaran. A second runs a separate tour to a private nature reserve at **Punta Coral** ⚓. The beach is much nicer at Tortuga Island, but the tour to Punta Coral is much more intimate, and the restaurant, hiking, and kayaking are all superior here.

EXPLORING PRE-COLUMBIAN RUINS   Although Costa Rica lacks the kind of massive pre-Columbian archaeological sites found in Mexico, Guatemala, or Honduras, it does have **Guayabo National Monument** ⚓, a small excavated town that today is just a small collection of building foundations, cobbled streets, aqueducts, and a small plaza. **Costa Rica Sun Tours** (✆ 296-7757; www.crsuntours.com) offers a day trip here for around $125 (£63) per person. If you have a car or are an intrepid bus hound, you can do this tour on your own. Admission to the park is $6 (£3), and you can usually find a guide at the entrance for around $5 (£2.50). See the section on Turrialba, below for more information on Guayabo.

HIKING   Most of the tour agencies listed above offer 1-day guided hikes to a variety of destinations. In general, I recommend taking guided hikes to really see and learn about the local flora and fauna.

HORSEBACK RIDING   Options are nearly endless outside of San José, but it's more difficult to find a place to saddle up in the metropolitan area. The **La Caraña Riding Academy** (✆ 282-6106; www.lacarana.com) and **Centro Ecuestre Valle Yos Oy** (✆ 282-6934) are both located in Santa Ana, and offer riding classes as well as some guided trail rides.

MOUNTAIN BIKING   The best bicycle riding is well outside of San José—on dirt roads where you're not likely to be run off the highway by a semi, or run head-on into someone coming around a blind curve in the wrong lane. Several companies run a variety of 1-day and multiday tours out of San José. The 1-day tours usually involve a round-trip bus or van ride out of downtown to the primary destination, such as the towns of Sarchí and Turrialba, and the Irazú and Poás volcanoes. Several of these tours are entirely or primarily descents. **Costa Rica Biking Adventure** (✆ 225-6591; www.bikingincostarica.com) offers a variety of mountain-biking tours using high-end bikes and gear. A 1-day trip costs between $80 and $150 (£40–£75) per person.

Another company offering mountain-biking trips is **Coast to Coast Adventures** (✆ 280-8054; www.ctocadventures.com), which, in addition to its 2-week namesake adventure, also designs customized mountain-biking trips of shorter durations.

RAFTING, KAYAKING & RIVER TRIPS   Cascading down Costa Rica's mountain ranges are dozens of tumultuous rivers, several of which are very popular for white-water rafting and kayaking. If I had to choose just one day trip out of San José, it would be a white-water rafting trip. For between $75 and $100 (£38–£50), you can spend a day rafting through lush tropical forests; multiday trips are also available. Some of the most reliable rafting companies are **Aventuras Naturales** ⚓ (✆ 800/ 514-0411 in the U.S., or 225-3939), **Exploradores Outdoors** ⚓ (✆ 222-6262), and **Ríos Tropicales** ⚓ (✆ 233-6455). These companies all ply a number of rivers of varying difficulties, including the popular Pacuare and Reventazón rivers. For details, see "White-Water Rafting, Kayaking & Canoeing," in chapter 4.

The Sarapiquí River is also a popular waterway for day trips out of San José. **Ecoscapes Highlights Tour** (℃ **297-0664;** www.ecoscapetours.com) runs a jam-packed trip here that combines a stop at the La Paz waterfall, a visit to a banana plantation, a rainforest hike, and a boat ride on the river for $79 (£40) per person, including round-trip transportation, breakfast, and lunch.

Perhaps the best-known river tours are those that go up to **Tortuguero National Park** 𝒢𝒢. It's possible to do this tour as a day trip out of San José, but it's a long, tiring, and expensive day. You're much better off doing it as a 1- or 2-night trip. See chapter 10 for details.

CARTAGO & THE OROSI VALLEY

These two regions southeast of San José can easily be combined into a day trip. You might also squeeze in a visit to the Irazú Volcano (see box above, for details).

CARTAGO

Located about 24km (15 miles) southeast of San José, **Cartago** 𝒢 is the former capital of Costa Rica. Founded in 1563, it was Costa Rica's first city—and was, in fact, its *only* city for almost 150 years. Irazú Volcano rises up from the edge of town, and although it's quiet these days, it has not always been so peaceful. Earthquakes have damaged Cartago repeatedly over the years, so today few of the old colonial buildings are left standing. In the center of the city, a public park winds through the ruins of a large church that was destroyed in 1910 before it could be finished. Construction was abandoned after the quake, and today the ruins sit at the heart of a neatly manicured park, with quiet paths and plenty of benches. The ruins themselves are closed off, but the park itself is lovely.

Cartago's most famous building is the **Basílica de Nuestra Señora de los Angeles (Basilica of Our Lady of the Angels)** 𝒢, which is dedicated to the patron saint of Costa Rica and stands on the east side of town. Within the walls of this Byzantine-style church is a shrine containing the tiny figure of **La Negrita,** the Black Virgin, which is nearly lost amid its ornate altar. Legend has it that La Negrita first revealed herself on this site to a peasant girl in 1635. Miraculous healing powers have been attributed to La Negrita, and, over the years, thousands of pilgrims have come to the shrine seeking cures for their illnesses and difficulties. The walls of the shrine are covered with a fascinating array of tiny silver images left as thanks for cures affected by La Negrita. Amid the plethora of diminutive silver arms and legs, there are also hands, feet, hearts, lungs, kidneys, eyes, torsos, breasts, and—peculiarly—guns, trucks, beds, and planes. There are even dozens of sports trophies that I assume were left as thanks for helping teams win big games. Outside the church, vendors sell a wide selection of these trinkets, as well as little candle replicas of La Negrita. August 2 is the day dedicated to La Negrita; on this day, tens of thousands of people walk to Cartago from San José and elsewhere in the country in devotion to this powerful statue.

More than 1km (½ mile) east of Cartago, on the road to Paraíso, you'll find **Lankester Gardens** 𝒢𝒢 (℃ **552-3247;** p. 126), a botanical garden known for its orchid collection.

GETTING THERE   **Lumaca** buses (℃ **537-2320**) for Cartago leave San José every 3 to 5 minutes between 5am and 9pm, with slightly less frequent service until midnight, from Calle 3 and Avenida 2. You can also pick up one en route at any of the little covered bus stops along Avenida Central in Los Yoses and San Pedro. The length of the trip is 45 minutes; the fare is about 50¢ (25p).

Holy Smoke! Choosing the Volcano Trip That's Right for You

Poás, Irazú, and Arenal volcanoes are three of Costa Rica's most popular destinations, and the first two are easy day trips from San José (see below). Although numerous companies offer day trips to Arenal, I don't recommend them because there's at least 3½ hours of travel time in each direction. You usually arrive when the volcano is hidden by clouds and leave before the night's darkness shows off its glowing eruptions. For more information on Arenal Volcano, see chapter 7.

Tour companies offering trips to Poás and Irazú include **Costa Rica Expeditions** ✵✵ (✆ 257-0766), **Costa Rica Sun Tours** ✵✵ (✆ 296-7757), **Horizontes** ✵✵ (✆ 222-2022), and **Swiss Travel Service** (✆ 282-4898). Prices range from $30 to $45 (£15–£23) for a half-day trip, and from $50 to $100 (£25–£50) for a full-day trip.

The 3,378m (11,080-ft.) **Irazú Volcano** ✵ (✆ 551-9398) is historically one of Costa Rica's more active volcanoes, although it's relatively quiet these days. It last erupted on March 19, 1963, the day that President John F. Kennedy arrived in Costa Rica. There's a good paved road right to the rim of the crater, where a desolate expanse of gray sand nurtures few plants and the air smells of sulfur. The landscape here is often compared to that of the moon. There are magnificent views of the fertile Meseta Central and Orosi Valley as you drive up from Cartago, and if you're very lucky, you might be able to see both the Pacific Ocean and the Caribbean Sea. Clouds usually descend by noon, so get here as early in the day as possible.

The visitor center up here has information on the volcano and natural history. A short trail leads to the rim of the volcano's two craters, their walls a maze of eroded gullies feeding onto the flat floor far below. This is a national park, with an admission fee of $7 (£3.50) charged at the gate. Dress in layers; this might be the tropics, but it can be cold up at the top if the sun's not out. The park restaurant, at an elevation of 3,022m (9,912 ft.), with walls of windows looking out over the valley far below, claims to be the highest restaurant in Central America.

If you don't want an organized tour, buses leave for Irazú Volcano daily at 8am from Avenida 2 between calles 1 and 3 (across the street from the

OROSI VALLEY

The Orosi Valley, southeast of Cartago and visible from the top of Irazú on a clear day, is generally considered one of the most beautiful valleys in Costa Rica. The Reventazón River meanders through this steep-sided valley until it collects in the lake formed by the Cachí Dam. There are scenic overlooks near the town of Orosi, which is at the head of the valley, and in Ujarrás, which is on the banks of the lake. Near **Ujarrás** are the ruins of Costa Rica's oldest church (built in 1693), whose tranquil gardens are a great place to sit and gaze at the surrounding mountains. In the town of Orosi itself, there is yet another colonial church and convent, built in 1743. A small museum here displays religious artifacts. Near the town of Cachí, you'll find **La Casa** entrance to the Gran Hotel Costa Rica). The fare is $6 (£3) round-trip, with the bus leaving the volcano at 12:30pm. This company is particularly fickle; to make sure that the buses are running, call ℂ 530-1064, although that might not help much, since they often don't answer their phone, and only speak Spanish. If you're driving, head northeast out of Cartago toward San Rafael, and then continue driving uphill toward the volcano, passing the turnoffs for Cot and Tierra Blanca en route.

Poás Volcano ⟨★★⟩ (ℂ 482-2424) is 37km (23 miles) from San José on narrow roads that wind through a landscape of fertile farms and dark forests. As at Irazú, there's a paved road right to the top, although you'll have to hike in about 1km (½ mile) to reach the crater. The volcano stands 2,640m (8,659 ft.) tall and is located within a national park, which preserves not only the volcano but also dense stands of virgin forest. Poás's crater, said to be the second-largest in the world, is more than a mile across. Geysers in the crater sometimes spew steam and muddy water 180m (590 ft.) into the air, making this the largest geyser in the world. There's an information center where you can see a slide show about the volcano, and there are well-groomed and marked hiking trails through the cloud forest that rings the crater. About 15 minutes from the parking area, along a forest trail, is an overlook onto beautiful Botos Lake, which has formed in one of the volcano's extinct craters.

Be prepared when you come to Poás: This volcano is often enveloped in dense clouds. If you want to see the crater, it's best to come early and during the dry season. Moreover, it can get cool up here, especially when the sun isn't shining, so dress appropriately. Admission to the national park is $7 (£3.50).

In case you don't want to go on a tour, there's a daily bus ((ℂ 442-6900 or 222-5325) from Avenida 2 between calles 12 and 14 that leaves at 8am and returns at 2pm. The fare is $4.50 (£2.25) round-trip. The bus is often crowded, so arrive early. If you're driving, head for Alajuela and continue on the main road through town and follow signs for Fraijanes. Just beyond Fraijanes you will connect with the road between San Pedro de Poás and Poasito; turn right toward Poasito and continue to the rim of the volcano.

del Soñador (**The House of the Dreamer;** ℂ 577-1983), the home and gallery of the late sculptor Macedonio Quesada and his sons, who carry on the family tradition.

From the Orosi Valley, it's a quick shot to the entrance to the **Tapantí National Park** ⟨★⟩ (ℂ 552-4823), where you'll find some gentle and beautiful hiking trails, as well as riverside picnic areas. The park is open daily from 8am to 4pm; admission is $6 (£3).

If you're interested in staying out here, check out the charming little **Orosi Lodge** (ℂ 533-3578; www.orosilodge.com), which is located right next to some simple hot spring pools.

GETTING THERE   If you're driving, take the road to Paraíso from Cartago, head toward Ujarrás, continue around the lake, and then pass through Cachí and on to

Orosi. From Orosi, the road leads back to Paraíso. It is difficult to explore this whole area by public bus because this is not a densely populated region and connections are often infrequent or unreliable. However, there are regular buses from Cartago to the town of Orosi. These buses run roughly every half-hour and leave the main bus terminal in Cartago. The trip takes 30 minutes, and the fare is 60¢ (30p). There are also guided day tours of this area from San José (call any of the companies listed under "Guided Tours & Adventures," earlier in this section).

TURRIALBA

This attractive little town 53km (33 miles) east of San José is best known as the starting point and home base for many popular white-water rafting trips. However, it's also worth a visit if you have an interest in pre-Columbian history or tropical botany.

Guayabo National Monument ⚔ (✆ **559-1220**) is one of Costa Rica's only pre-Columbian sites that has been excavated and is open to the public. It's located 19km (12 miles) northeast of Turrialba and preserves a town site that dates from between 1000 B.C. and A.D. 1400. Archaeologists believe that Guayabo might have supported a population of as many as 10,000 people, but there is no clue yet to why the city was eventually abandoned only shortly before the Spanish arrived in the New World. Excavated ruins at Guayabo consist of paved roads, aqueducts, stone bridges, and house and temple foundations. There are also gravesites and petroglyphs. The monument is open daily from 8am to 4pm. This is a national park, and admission is $6 (£3) at the gate. For information about other parks in this area, see "Costa Rica's Top National Parks & Bioreserves," in chapter 4.

Botanists and gardeners will want to pay a visit to the **Center for Agronomy Research and Development** (CATIE; www.catie.ac.cr), which is located 5km (3 miles) southeast of Turrialba on the road to Siquirres. This center is one of the world's foremost facilities for research into tropical agriculture. Among the plants on CATIE's 2,000 acres are hundreds of varieties of cacao and thousands of varieties of coffee. The plants here have been collected from all over the world. In addition to trees used for food and other purposes, there are plants grown strictly for ornamental purposes. CATIE is open Monday through Friday from 7am to 4pm. Guided tours are available with advance notice for $10 to $15 (£5–£7.50) per person, depending upon the size of your group. Call ✆ **556-2700** for reservations.

While you're in Turrialba, you might want to spend a little time at **Turrialtico** (✆ **538-1111;** www.turrialtico.com), a rustic yet beautiful open-air restaurant and small hotel high on a hill overlooking the Turrialba Valley. The view from here is one of the finest in the country, with lush greenery far below and volcanoes in the distance. Meals are quite inexpensive; a double room will cost you around $62 (£31) including breakfast and taxes. This place is popular with rafting companies that bring groups here for meals and for overnights before, during, and after multiday rafting trips. You'll find Turrialtico about 10km (6¼ miles) out of Turrialba on the road to Siquirres.

If you're looking for more luxury in this area, check out **Casa Turire** ⚔⚔ (✆ **531-1111;** www.hotelcasaturire.com), where well-appointed rooms and suites in an elegant country mansion run between $135 and $290 (£68–£145). The hotel is set on the banks of the lake formed by the Angostura dam project, and you can take a kayak or paddleboat out on the lake here.

GETTING THERE   Buses (✆ **222-4464**) leave San José hourly for Turrialba between 5am and 10pm from Calle 13 between avenidas 6 and 8. The fare is $1.60 (80p). If you're driving, take the road from Cartago to Paraíso, then through Juan

Viñas, and on to Turrialba. It's pretty well marked. (Alternatively you can head toward the small town of Cot, on the road to Irazú Volcano, and then through the town of Pacayas on to Turrialba, another well-marked route.)

Turrialba itself is a bit of a jumble, and you will probably have to ask directions to get to locations out of town. Guayabo is about 20km (12 miles) beyond Turrialba on a road that is paved the entire way except for the last 3km (1¾ miles). There are also around three buses daily to Guayabo from the main bus terminal in Turrialba.

HEREDIA, GRECIA, SARCHÍ & ZARCERO

All of these cities and towns are northwest of San José and can be combined into a long day trip (if you have a car), perhaps in conjunction with a visit to Poás Volcano and/or the Waterfall Gardens. The scenery here is rich and verdant, and the small towns and scattered farming communities are truly representative of Costa Rica's agricultural heartland and *campesino* tradition. This is a great area to explore on your own in a rental car, if you don't mind getting lost a bit (roads are narrow, winding, and poorly marked). If you're relying on buses, you'll be able to visit any of the towns listed below, but probably just one or two per day.

The road to Heredia turns north off the highway from San José to the airport. If you're going to Sarchí, take the highway west toward Puntarenas. Turn north to Grecia and then west to Sarchí. There'll be plenty of signs.

HEREDIA

Set on the flanks of the impressive Barva Volcano, this city was founded in 1706. Heredia is affectionately known as "The City of Flowers." A colonial church inaugurated in 1763 stands in the central park. The stone facade leaves no questions as to the age of the church, but the altar inside is decorated with neon stars and a crescent moon surrounding a statue of the Virgin Mary. In the middle of the palm-shaded park is a music temple, and across the street, beside several tile-roofed municipal buildings, is the tower of an old Spanish fort. Of all the cities in the Meseta Central, Heredia has the most colonial feel to it—you'll still see adobe buildings with Spanish tile roofs along narrow streets. Heredia is also the site of the **National Autonomous University,** so you'll find some nice coffee shops and bookstores near the school.

Surrounding Heredia is an intricate maze of picturesque villages and towns, including Santa Bárbara, Santo Domingo, Barva, and San Joaquín de Flores. San Isidro de Heredia has a lovely, large church with an ornate façade. However, the biggest attraction up here is the **INBio Park** 🍃🍃 (ⓒ **507-8107;** p. 126). Located on 5 hectares (12 acres) in Santo Domingo de Heredia, this place is part museum, part educational center, and part nature park. This is also where you'll find the **Café Britt Farm** 🍃 (ⓒ **277-1600;** p. 125). On the road to Barva, you'll find the small **Museo de Cultura Popular** (ⓒ **260-1619**), which is open Monday through Friday from 8am to 4pm and Saturday and Sunday from 10am to 5pm; admission is $2 (£1). Anyone with an interest in medicinal herbs should plan a visit to **The Ark Herb Farm** 🍃 (ⓒ **846-2694** or 239-2111; www.arkherbfarm.com). These folks offer guided tours of their gardens, which feature more than 300 types of medicinal plants. The tour costs $12 (£6) per person, and includes a light snack and refreshments. Reservations are required.

If you make your way to San Pedro de Barva de Heredia, stop in at **La Lluna de Valencia** 🍃🍃 (ⓒ **269-6665**), a delightful rustic Spanish restaurant with amazing paella, delicious sangria, and a very amiable host.

Buses leave for Heredia every 5 minutes between 5am and 11pm from Calle 1 between avenidas 7 and 9, or from Avenida 4 between calles 12 and 14. Bus fare is 40¢ (20p).

GRECIA

The picturesque little town of Grecia is noteworthy for its unusual metal church, which is painted a deep red and has white gingerbread trim. Just off the central park, next to the Palacio Municipal, you'll find the humble **Grecia Regional Museum** (© 494-6767), which has some simple exhibits and information about the town's history. About 1km (½ mile) outside of Grecia, on the old road to Alajuela, you will find the **World of Snakes** (© 494-3700). Open daily from 8am to 4pm, this serpentarium has more than 150 snakes representing more than 50 species. Admission, which includes a guided tour, is $11 (£5.50) for adults, and $6 (£3) for children 7-14.

Buses leave San José every half-hour for Grecia from Calle 18 between avenidas 5 and 7 (on the east side of the Abonos Agros building). The road to Sarchí is to the left as you face the church in Grecia, but due to all the one-way streets, you'll have to drive around it.

SARCHI ✦

Sarchí is Costa Rica's main artisan town. The colorfully painted miniature **oxcarts** that you see all over the country are made here. Oxcarts such as these were once used to haul coffee beans to market. Today, although you might occasionally see oxcarts in use, most are purely decorative. However, they remain a well-known symbol of Costa Rica. In addition to miniature oxcarts, many carved wooden souvenirs are made here with rare hardwoods from the nation's forests. There are dozens of shops in town, and all have similar prices. Perhaps your best one-stop shop in Sarchí is the large and long-standing **Chaverri Oxcart Factory** ✦ (© 454-4411), which is right in the center of things, but it never hurts to shop around and visit several of the stores.

Aside from handicrafts, there are other reasons to visit Sarchí. Built between 1950 and 1958, the town's main **church** ✦ is painted pink with aquamarine trim and looks strangely like a child's birthday cake. There's also a new botanical gardens here. Located about 8 blocks north of the town's main soccer stadium, the **Else Kientzler Botanical Garden** ✦ (© 454-2070; www.elsekientzlergarden.com) features an extensive collection of several thousand types of plants, flowers and trees. The entire spread is beautifully landscaped, with gentle paths and a host of comfortable chairs, benches, and seating nooks. The garden is open daily from 8am to 4pm. Admission is $12 (£6) for adults, and $6 (£3) for students and children ages 5 to 12.

About five buses (© **258-2004**) leave San José for Sarchí from Calle 18 between avenidas 5 and 7. The fare is $1.20 (60p). Alternatively, you can take any Grecia bus from this same station. In Grecia they connect with the Alajuela-Sarchí buses, leaving every 30 minutes from Calle 8 between avenidas Central and 1 in Alajuela.

ZARCERO

Beyond Sarchí, on picturesque roads lined with cedar trees, you'll find the town of Zarcero. In a small park in the middle of town is a **menagerie of sculpted shrubs** that includes a monkey on a motorcycle, people and animals dancing, an ox pulling a cart, a man wearing a top hat, and a large elephant. Behind all the topiary is a wonderful rural **church.** It's not really worth the drive just to see this park, but it's a good idea to take in Zarcero as a quick stop on the way to La Fortuna and Arenal Volcano.

Buses (© **255-4300**) for Zarcero leave from San José hourly from the Atlántico del Norte bus station at Avenida 9 and Calle 12. This is actually the Ciudad Quesada–San Carlos bus. Just tell the driver that you want to get off in Zarcero, and keep an eye out for the topiary. The ride takes around 1½ hours, and the fare is around $1.50 (75p).

Guanacaste & the Nicoya Peninsula: The Gold Coast

Guanacaste is known as Costa Rica's "Gold Coast." More and more visitors to Costa Rica are choosing Guanacaste as their first—and sometimes only—stop. Beautiful beaches abound along this coastline. Some are still pristine and deserted, some are packed with a mix of hotels and resorts, and others are backed by small fishing villages. Choices range from long, broad stretches of sand to tiny pocket coves bordered by rocky headlands.

This is Costa Rica's most coveted vacation destination and the site of its greatest tourism development. Change here is dramatic and ongoing. Large resorts have sprung up, and more are in the works. The international airport in Liberia receives daily direct flights from major U.S. and Canadian hub cities, allowing tourists to visit some of Costa Rica's prime destinations without having to go through San José.

This is Costa Rica's driest region. The rainy season starts later and ends earlier here, and overall it's more dependably sunny here than in other parts of the country. Combine this climate with a coastline that stretches from the Nicaraguan border to the southern tip of the Nicoya Peninsula and you have an equation that yields beach bliss.

There is one caveat: During the dry season (mid-Nov to Apr), when sunshine is most reliable, the hillsides in Guanacaste turn browner than the chaparral of southern California. Dust from dirt roads blankets the trees in many areas, and the vistas are far from tropical. Driving these dirt roads without air-conditioning and the windows rolled up tight can be extremely unpleasant.

On the other hand, if you happen to visit this area in the rainy season (particularly from May–Aug), the hillsides are a beautiful, rich green, and the sun usually shines all morning, giving way to an afternoon shower—just in time for a nice siesta.

Inland from the beaches, Guanacaste remains Costa Rica's "Wild West," a land of dry plains populated with cattle ranches and cowboys, who are known here as *sabaneros,* a name that derives from the Spanish word for "savanna" or "grassland." If it weren't for those rainforest-clad volcanoes in the distance, you might swear you were in Texas.

Guanacaste is home to several active volcanoes and some beautiful national parks, including **Santa Rosa National Park** 🐾, the home to massive sea turtle nestings and the site of a major battle to maintain independence, and **Rincón de la Vieja National Park** 🐾🐾, which features hot springs and bubbling mud pots, pristine waterfalls, and an active volcanic crater.

1 Liberia

217km (135 miles) NW of San José; 132km (82 miles) NW of Puntarenas

Founded in 1769, Liberia is the capital of Guanacaste province, and although it can hardly be considered a bustling metropolis, it does boast more colonial atmosphere than almost any other city in the country. Its narrow streets are lined with charming old adobe homes, many of which have ornate stone accents on their facades, carved wooden doors, and aged red-tile roofs. Many have beautiful large, shuttered windows (some don't even have iron bars for protection) opening onto the narrow streets. The central plaza, which occupies 2 square blocks in front of the church, is still the city's social hub and principal gathering spot.

Liberia is best as a base for exploring this region or as an overnight stop as part of a longer itinerary. You'll find several moderately priced hotels in the city and its outskirts. Still, all things considered, it's usually preferable to base yourself either at the beach or at one of the mountain lodges in the area, and to visit the city on a day trip.

ESSENTIALS

GETTING THERE & DEPARTING   By Plane   The **Daniel Oduber International Airport** (© **668-1010;** airport code LIR) in Liberia receives a steady stream of scheduled commercial and charter flights throughout the year. **Delta** (© **800/241-4141;** www.delta.com) has daily direct flights between its Atlanta hub and Liberia, and a once-weekly direct flight between Los Angeles and Liberia; **American Airlines** (© **800/433-7300;** www.aa.com) offers three weekly direct flights between Miami and Liberia, and twice weekly flights between Dallas-Ft. Worth and Liberia; **Continental** (© **800/231-0856;** www.continental.com) has daily direct flights between Houston and Liberia; **United Airlines** (© **800/538-2929;** www.united.com) has one weekly flight between Chicago O'Hare and Liberia; and **U.S. Airways** (© **800/622-1015;** www.usairways.com) has one weekly direct flight between Charlotte and Liberia. In addition, there are numerous commercial charter flights from various North American cities throughout the high season. Check with your travel agent.

Sansa (© **290-4100;** www.flysansa.com) has four daily flights to Liberia leaving at 6, 11:10, and 11:40am, and 2:30 and 2:40pm from San José's Juan Santamaría International Airport. Return flights depart for San José at 7am, and 12:15, 12:55, 3:25, and 3:35pm. The fare for the 50-minute flight is $82 (£41) each way.

Nature Air (© **800/235-9272** in the U.S. and Canada or 299-6000; www.natureair.com) has three flights daily to Liberia at 6:30 and 10am, and 2pm from Tobías Bolaños International Airport in Pavas. Return flights leave Liberia at 7:25 and 11:25am, and 3:25pm. Fares are $88 (£44) each way. Nature Air also has direct flights between Liberia and Arenal, Quepos, Tamarindo, and Tambor.

If you plan to fly here and rent a car to continue on to one of the nearby beaches and explore the region, the following companies all have local agencies: **Alamo** (© 800/432-5266, or 668-1111), **Avis** (© 668-1138), **Budget** (© 668-1118), **Dollar** (© 668-1061), **Economy** (© 666-2816), **Hertz** (© 668-1048), **Payless** (© 667-0511), **Sol** (© 666-2222), **Thrifty** (© 665-0787), and **Toyota** (© 668-1212). You can also reserve with these and most major international car-rental companies via their San José and international offices (see "Getting Around," in chapter 5).

Guanacaste & the Nicoya Peninsula

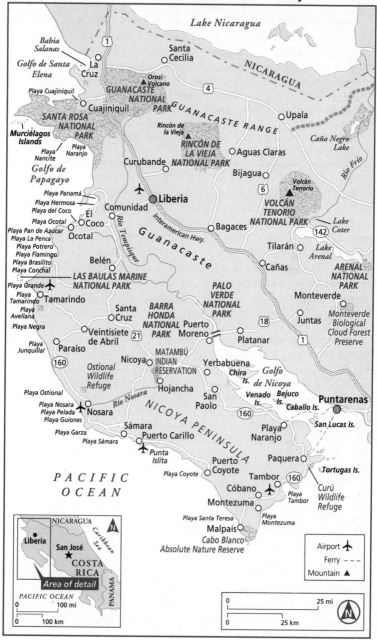

Lake Nicaragua

Bahía Salanas
Golfo de Santa Elena
1
La Cruz
Santa Cecilia
NICARAGUA
Playa Cuajiniquil
Orosi Volcano
GUANACASTE NATIONAL PARK
GUANACASTE RANGE
4
Upala
Cuajiniquil
SANTA ROSA NATIONAL PARK
Murciélagos Islands
Rincón de la Vieja
Caño Negro Lake
Playa Nancite
Playa Naranjo
RINCÓN DE LA VIEJA NATIONAL PARK
Aguas Claras
Curubande
Bijagua
Río Frío
Golfo de Papagayo
Volcán Tenorio
Playa Panamá
Playa Hermosa
Playa del Coco
Liberia
6
VOLCÁN TENORIO NATIONAL PARK
Comunidad
El Coco
Playa Ocotal
Playa Pan de Azúcar
Ocotal
Bagaces
Lake Coter
142
Playa La Penca
Playa Potrero
Playa Flamingo
Playa Brasilito
Playa Conchal
Belén
Río Tempisque
Guanacaste
Interamerican Hwy.
Tilarán
Cañas
Lake Arenal
ARENAL NATIONAL PARK
Playa Grande
LAS BAULAS MARINE NATIONAL PARK
Playa Tamarindo
Tamarindo
Playa Avellana
Santa Cruz
BARRA HONDA NATIONAL PARK
PALO VERDE NATIONAL PARK
Puerto Moreno
Monteverde
Playa Negra
Veintisiete de Abril
21
Platanar
18
Juntas
Monteverde Biological Cloud Forest Preserve
Playa Junquillal
Paraíso
MATAMBÚ INDIAN RESERVATION
Yerbabuena
1
160
Ostional Wildlife Refuge
Nicoya
Chira Is.
Golfo de Nicoya
Playa Ostional
Hojancha
San Paolo
Venado Is.
Bejuco Is.
Puntarenas
Playa Nosara
Playa Pelada
Playa Guiones
Nosara
Río Nosara
NICOYA PENINSULA
160
Caballo Is.
San Lucas Is.
Playa Garza
Sámara
Puerto Carillo
Playa Naranjo
Playa Sámara
Punta Islita
Paquera
Tortugas Is.
Puerto Coyote
Playa Coyote
Tambor
160
Curú Wildlife Refuge
Cóbano
Playa Tambor
Montezuma
PACIFIC OCEAN
Playa Santa Teresa
Playa Montezuma
Malpaís
Cabo Blanco Absolute Nature Reserve

Airport ✈
Ferry – – –
Mountain ▲

NICARAGUA
Liberia
San José ★
Caribbean Sea
COSTA RICA
PANAMA
Area of detail
PACIFIC OCEAN
0 —— 100 mi
0 —— 100 km

0 —— 25 mi
0 —— 25 km

Finds **An Interesting Stop on Your Way to Liberia**

If you're driving to or from Guanacaste, be sure to take a brief break to check out the **Iglesia de Cañas (Cañas Church)** ✪✪ in Cañas. Well-known painter, installation artist, and local prodigal son Otto Apuy has designed and directed the envelopment of the entire church in colorful mosaic. The work uses whole and broken tiles in glossy, vibrant colors to depict both religious and abstract themes. The church's central tower, which is entirely covered in mosaic, is nearly 30m (100 ft.) tall. It is estimated that more than a million pieces of ceramic were used in the work. The church is located in the center of town, just a few blocks off the highway.

Note: The official word is that the cramped, inefficient, and overcrowded terminals, for both arriving and departing passengers, at the Daniel Oduber International Airport will be replaced with a major, modern new facility by 2009. If experience is any guide, I wouldn't start holding my breath for a couple years beyond that date, although don't be surprised if there is ongoing construction when you arrive.

By Car Take the Interamerican Highway west from San José, and follow the signs for Nicaragua and the Guanacaste beaches. Liberia is about a 3½- to 4-hour drive.

By Bus **Pulmitan** express buses (© **222-1650** in San José, or 666-0458 in Liberia) leave **San José** roughly every hour between 6am and 7pm from Calle 24 between avenidas 5 and 7. The ride to Liberia takes 4 hours. A one-way fare costs $4.20 (£2.10).

 Gray Line (© **220-2126;** www.graylinecostarica.com) has a daily bus that leaves San José for Liberia at 7am. **Interbus** (© **283-5573;** www.interbusonline.com) has two daily buses that leave San José for Liberia at 7:45am and 2:30pm; the fare is $29 to Liberia. Each company's morning bus makes connections to Rincón de la Vieja and Santa Rosa national parks. The fare is $29 (£15) to Liberia on either line, and $38 (£19) to Rincón de la Vieja with Gray Line, and $39 (£20) with Interbus. Both companies will pick you up at most San José–area hotels.

 Buses depart for San José and most of the area beaches and national parks from the Liberia bus station on the edge of town, 200m (2 blocks) north and 100m (1 block) east of the main intersection on the Interamerican Highway. Express buses for San José leave roughly every hour between 4am and 8pm.

FAST FACTS There are several state and private bank offices clustered around downtown Liberia, as well as a branch of the **Banco de Costa Rica** inside the airport. The local **police** number is © **666-5656,** and the **Liberia Hospital** number is © **666-0011.** If you need a taxi, dial © **666-3330.** There are a host of Internet cafes on the blocks surrounding and just off of the central plaza.

 On the southern outskirts of the city is a modern shopping mall, the place to come for a food court fix or to catch a semi-late-run movie at the local multiplex.

EXPLORING THE TOWN

The central plaza in Liberia is a great place to people-watch, especially in the early evenings and on weekends. Grab a seat on one of the many concrete benches, or join the families and young lovers as they leisurely stroll around. If you venture off for a few blocks down **Calle Real** ✪, you'll see fine examples of the classic Spanish colonial architecture—adobe buildings with ornate wooden doors, heavy beams, central court-yards, and faded, sagging, red-tile roofs.

While the Catholic church that anchors the central plaza is unspectacular, if you head several blocks east of the plaza, you will come to **Iglesia La Ermita de la Agonía** ✦, which was built in 1865, and is still in pretty decent shape. The church is open daily for visits from 2:30 to 3:30pm.

OUTDOOR ADVENTURES NEAR LIBERIA
EXPLORING RINCON DE LA VIEJA NATIONAL PARK ✦✦
This national park begins on the flanks of the Rincón de la Vieja Volcano and includes this volcano's active crater. Down lower you'll find an area of geothermal activity similar to that of Yellowstone National Park in the United States. Fumaroles, geysers, and hot pools cover this small area, creating a bizarre, otherworldly landscape. In addition to hot springs and mud pots, you can explore waterfalls, a lake, and volcanic craters. The bird-watching here is excellent, and the views across the pasturelands to the Pacific Ocean are stunning.

The main entrance is 25km (16 miles) northeast of Liberia, down a badly rutted dirt road. The park entrance fee is $6 (£3) per person per day, and the park is open daily from 7am to 3pm.

Camping will cost you an extra $2 (£1) per person per day. There are actually two entrances and camping areas here: **Santa María** and **Las Pailas** (also called Las Espuelas; ✆ **661-8139**) ranger stations. The latter is by far the more popular and accessible, and it's closer to the action. These small camping areas are near each other. I recommend the one closer to the river, although the bathroom and shower facilities are about 90m (295 ft.) away, at the other site. For those seeking a less rugged tour of the park, there are several lodges located around the perimeter of the park; all offer guided hikes and horseback rides into the park.

GETTING THERE   To reach the Las Pailas (Las Espuelas) entrance, drive about 5km (3 miles) north of Liberia and turn right on the dirt road to the park. The turnoff is well marked. In about 12km (7½ miles), you'll pass through the small village of Curubandé. Continue on this road for another 6km (3¾ miles) until you reach the Hacienda Guachipelin. The lodge is private property, and the owners charge vehicles a $2 toll to pass through their gate and continue on to the park. I'm not sure if this is legal or mandatory, but it's not worth the hassle to protest. Pay the toll, pass through the gate, and continue for another 4km (2½ miles) until you reach the park entrance.

There are two routes to the **Santa María entrance.** The principal route heads out of the northeastern end of Liberia toward the small village of San Jorge. This route is about 25km (16 miles) long and takes about 45 minutes. A four-wheel-drive vehicle is required. Alternatively, you can reach the entrance on a turnoff from the Interamerican Highway at Bagaces. From here, head north through Guayabo, Aguas Claras, and Colonia Blanca. The road is paved up to Colonia Blanca, but again a four-wheel-drive vehicle is required for the final, very rough 10km (6¼ miles) of gravel road.

HIKING IN THE PARK   There are several excellent trails inside the Rincón de la Vieja National Park. More energetic hikers can tackle the 8km (5 miles) up to **the summit** and explore the several craters and beautiful lakes up here. On a clear day you'll be rewarded with a fabulous view of the plains of Guanacaste and the Pacific Ocean below. The easiest hiking is the gentle **Las Pailas loop** ✦. This 3km (1¾-mile) trail is just off the Las Espuelas park entrance and passes by several bubbling mud pots and steaming fumaroles. This trail crosses a river, so you'll have to either take off your shoes or get them wet. The whole loop takes around 2 hours.

My favorite hike here is to the **Blue Lake** and **La Cangrejo Waterfall** 🐦🐦. This 5km (3-mile) trail passes through several different life zones, including dry forest, transitional moist forest, and open savanna. A variety of birds and mammals are commonly sighted. Pack a lunch; at the end of your 2-hour hike in, you can picnic at the aptly named Blue Lake, where a 30m (98-ft.) waterfall empties into the small pond whose crystal-blue hues are amazing.

LLANO DE CORTES WATERFALL 🐦

Located about 25km (15.5 miles) south of Liberia, the Llano de Cortes Waterfall is a beautiful and wide jungle waterfall with an excellent pool at the base for cooling off and swimming. At roughly 12m (40 ft.) wide, the falls are actually slightly wider than they are tall. This is a great spot for a picnic. The turnoff for the dirt road to the falls is well marked and located about 3km (1.8 miles) north of the crossroads for Bagaces. From the turnoff, you must drive a rough dirt road to the parking area and then hike down a short steep trail to the falls. Admission is free.

BACK TO AFRICA

The landscape is postcard perfect, especially in the dry season, so you shouldn't be too surprised to see antelope, zebra, giraffe and elands roaming the grassy plains of Guanacaste. **Africa Mia** (My Africa) (🕐 357-5555; www.africamia.net) offers safari-style open-jeep tours through its 100-hectare (247-acre) private reserve, which is populated with a wide range of nonnative (predominantly African) species. All of the animals are herbivores, so don't expect to see any lions, hyenas, or cheetahs. Still, the trip does provide some of the sense of being on the Serengeti or some other African plain. The animals have plenty of room to roam. Admission, which is $15 (£7.50) for adults, and $10 (£5) for children under 12, includes a 90-minute guided tour. Africa Mia is located just of the Interamerican highway, 8km (5 miles) south of Liberia.

BIRDING

The **Río Tempisque Basin** 🐦, southwest of town, is one of the best places in the country to spot marsh and stream birds by the hundreds. This area is an important breeding ground for gallinules, jacanas, and limpkins, as well as a common habitat for numerous heron and kingfisher species. Several tour operators offer excursions and a wide range of tours in the region from Liberia. **Swiss Travel Services** (🕐 282-4898; www.swisstravelcr.com) is the largest and most reliable of the major operators here.

One of the most popular tours is a boat tour down the Bebedero River to **Palo Verde National Park** 🐦, which is south of Cañas and is best known for its migratory bird populations. Some of the best bird-watching requires no more than a little walking around the Biological Station in the park.

RAFTING TRIPS

Leisurely raft trips (with little white water) are offered by **Safaris Corobicí** (🕐/fax **669-6191;** www.nicoya.com), about 40km (25 miles) south of Liberia. It has 2-hour ($37/£19), 3-hour ($45/£23), and half-day ($60/£30) trips that are great for families and bird-watchers. Along the way you may see many of the area's more exotic animal residents: howler monkeys, iguanas, caimans, coatimundis, otters, toucans, parrots, motmots, trogons, and many other species of birds. Aside from your binoculars and camera, a bathing suit and sunscreen are the only things you'll need. Safaris Corobicí is based on the main highway, just before the Restaurant Rincón Corobicí (p. 157). For a much wetter and wilder ride, the folks at **Hacienda Guachipelin** (see below) offer white-water inner-tube trips on the narrow Río Negro.

HOT SPRINGS & MUD BATHS
Even if you're not staying at the Hacienda Guachipelin, you can take advantage of the hot spring pools, and hot mud pools at their **Simbiosis Spa** ★ (ⓒ **666-8075;** www.simbiosis-spa.com). A $15 (£7.50) entrance fee gets you free run of the pools and self-applications of the hot volcanic mud. And a wide range of massages, mud wraps, facials and other treatments are available at very reasonable prices.

SHOPPING
On the road to the beaches, just west of the airport, are several large souvenir shops. These are popular stopping points on organized tours throughout this region. The best of the bunch for a one-stop shop is **Kaltak Arts & Craft Market** (ⓒ **667-0696**). However, you might find better selection and prices, especially for Guaitíl pottery, at some of the smaller makeshift roadside kiosks that line the road between Liberia and the Guanacaste beaches.

WHERE TO STAY IN TOWN
MODERATE
Best Western El Sitio Hotel & Casino   Located just out of town, about 75m (¾ block) west of the main intersection on the road to Santa Cruz and the beaches, this hotel has a Spanish-influenced hacienda style, with an open and modern feel. Cool tile floors and original paintings of local Guanacaste scenes dominate the decor. There's a rancho-style bar/restaurant beside the large, shady pool, as well as a relatively well equipped little gym. This hotel is popular with Costa Ricans as both a conference site and a weekend getaway. This is the closest thing to a modern, midrange resort hotel in Liberia and is a decent deal.

Liberia (A.P. 134-5000), Guanacaste. ⓒ **800/780-7234** in the U.S. and Canada, or 666-1211 in Costa Rica. Fax 666-2059. www.bestwestern.com. 52 units. $65–$75 (£33–£38) double. Rates include full breakfast. AE, MC, V. **Amenities:** 2 restaurants; 2 bars; large pool; exercise room; Jacuzzi; tour desk; car-rental desk; room service; laundry service. *In room:* A/C, TV, dataport, free Wi-Fi, safe.

Hotel Boyeros (Value   This hotel isn't quite as modern or well-appointed as the El Sitio, but it's comfortable in its own right and a little closer to downtown. Arches with turned wooden railings and a red-tile roof give this two-story motel-style building a Spanish feel. The best and coolest rooms are on the second floor of the east wing. There's a large central courtyard with two swimming pools, some basic playground equipment, and a massive shade tree.

Liberia (A.P. 85-5000), Guanacaste. ⓒ **666-0722** or 666-0809. Fax 666-2529. www.hotelboyeros.com. 70 units. $65 (£33) double. AE, MC, V. **Amenities:** Restaurant; bar; midsize pool and children's pool; game room; free Wi-Fi; limited room service (6am–10pm); laundry service. *In room:* A/C, TV, safe.

INEXPENSIVE
In addition to the place listed below, the **Hotel Guanacaste** (ⓒ **666-0085;** www. higuanacaste.com) is another dependable budget option, affiliated with Hostelling International.

Posada del Tope   This humble little pension is nothing fancy, but the rooms and shared bathrooms are clean, the owners are friendly and helpful, and it's a real bargain. Only a couple of rooms have double beds; the rest have one, two, or three single beds.

The nicest thing about Posada del Tope is that it's housed in a wonderfully restored traditional colonial home with high ceilings, big shuttered windows facing the street, and hefty wooden trim all around. There's safe parking and Internet access, and every room comes with a television. These folks also run another simple hotel in another old home, Casa Real, located directly across the street. This annex has more rooms and a basic restaurant serving inexpensive Tico cuisine.

Calle Real (1½ blocks south of the central park), Liberia, Guanacaste. ℂ/fax **666-3876.** 22 units, 13 w/shared bathroom. $12 (£6) double w/shared bath; $18 (£9) double w/private bath. AE, MC, V. Free parking. **Amenities:** Restaurant; bike rental; tour desk, laundry service. *In room:* TV, no phone.

WHERE TO STAY NEAR RINCON DE LA VIEJA NATIONAL PARK

In addition to the hotels listed below, there are a couple of other good choices. Located on the Cañas Dulces road, **Buena Vista Lodge** ℱ (ℂ **690-1414;** www.buena vistalodgecr.com) is set on the edge of the national park and offers a wide range of activities and attractions. The delightful **La Carolina Lodge** ℱ (ℂ **380-1656;** www. lacarolinalodge.com) is on a working farm, next to a clear flowing river. This place is located on the road between the Interamerican Highway and Upala, and it affords excellent access to the Tenorio Volcano and Río Celeste Falls.

Hacienda Guachipelin ℱ   Located 23km (14 miles) northeast of Liberia on the edge of Rincón de la Vieja National Park, this lodge is centered on a 19th-century ranch house and a still-operational cattle-and-horse ranch. Most rooms are housed in rows of buildings just off the old ranch house. The newer rooms are quite spacious and modern and come with either a private patio or a wide shared veranda. Those in the older buildings are still clean and comfortable but much more rustic in feel.

This is one of the closest lodges to the thermal springs (10km/6¼ miles) and bubbling mud pots (5km/3 miles) of Rincón de la Vieja National Park. The lodge arranges horseback rides to the geothermal areas, various lakes, the top of a nearby dormant volcano, and some beautiful waterfalls. In addition to the lodge's good-size kidney-shape pool, nearby creeks and rivers feature a couple of natural swimming holes. It isn't easy to get to the lodge, so plan to take all your meals here and go on a few guided tours. These folks offer a "Canyon Tour" ℱℱ ($45/£23 per person) adventure in which you strap on a climbing harness and ride over a deep canyon while hanging from a cable—it's one of my favorite "canopy tours" in the country.

Rincón de la Vieja (A.P. 636-4050, Alajuela). ℂ **888/790-5264** in the U.S. and Canada, or 442-2818 for reservations in San José, or 666-8075 at the lodge. Fax 442-1910. www.guachipelin.com. 50 units. $140 (£70) standard double; $150 (£75) superior double. Rates include 3 meals and taxes. AE, MC, V. Follow the directions/signs to Curubandé and Rincón de la Vieja National Park. A 4WD vehicle is required in the rainy season (May to mid-Nov) and strongly recommended at other times. **Amenities:** Restaurant; pool; small spa; laundry service. *In room:* free Wi-Fi, no phone.

Hotel Borinquen Mountain Resort ℱ   This the fanciest resort in the Rincón de la Vieja area. Individual and duplex bungalows are set on a hillside above the main lodge, restaurants, and hot springs. While the individual bungalow units are slightly larger, every room is very spacious and comes with two queen-size beds, high ceilings, heavy wooden furniture (including a desk with chair plus two sitting chairs), a large TV, and a comfortable bathroom. Each has an ample wooden deck with a view over the valley and surrounding forests. Here again, the individual bungalow units get the nod because their covered decks provide protection from rain and bright sun.

In the foot of the valley are several natural hot-spring pools of varying temperatures, a natural sauna, and an area for full-body mud baths given with hot volcanic mud.

There's a good-size free-form man-made swimming pool as well. Everything is spread out over steep hillsides on the edge of the rainforest beside gentle creeks, with trails leading to the mud pots. There are good hiking and horseback riding here and some nice waterfalls nearby, and golf carts are available to shuttle you around. Despite the potential, spa services and facilities here have yet to be fully developed.

Cañas Dulces (A.P. 108-5000), Liberia. 🕿 253-5080 for reservations or 690-1900 at the lodge. Fax 253-50161. www.borinquenresort.com. 33 units. $210 (£105) double villa; $241 (£121) double bungalow; $356 (£178) double suite. Rates include breakfast and unlimited use of the hot springs, sauna, and mud baths. Rates lower in off season; higher during peak weeks. AE, MC, V. Drive 26km (16 miles) north of Liberia along the Interamerican Hwy., take the turnoff toward Cañas Dulces, and follow the signs. The hotel is approximately 18km (11 miles) from the highway and 3.5km (2¼ miles) beyond Cañas Dulces. **Amenities:** Restaurant; bar; large swimming pool; small spa; tour desk; laundry service. *In room:* A/C, TV, free Wi-Fi, minibar.

Rincón de la Vieja Mountain Lodge   This is the closest lodge to the Las Pailas mud pots and the Azufrale hot springs. Rooms vary in size, and the best are the individual cabins, which come with hammocks on their private balconies. In all rooms, the furnishings and decor are simple, rustic, and mostly pretty dated. Quite a few come with one queen-size and one set of bunk beds. Meals are served in a large open-air rancho in the middle of the complex. The lodge offers numerous day-long tours either on foot, by mountain bike, or on horseback. It also runs an extensive canopy tour, which takes you on a high-wire ride over a couple dozen different treetop platforms, beginning with a manual ascent up a towering ceiba tree. This place is geared toward backpackers, students, and nature enthusiasts.

Rincón de la Vieja (A.P. 164-5000, Liberia), Guanacaste. 🕿 666-0144. Fax 666-2441. www.rincondelaviejalodge.net. 40 units. $70–$80 (£35–£40) double. Student discounts and off-season rates available. AE, MC, V. If you're driving, follow the directions to the Hacienda Lodge Guachipelin and continue driving on this dirt road for another 7km (4½ miles), bearing right at the turnoff for the park entrance. **Amenities:** Restaurant; bar; small pool; laundry service. *In room:* No phone.

WHERE TO DINE

There are plenty of standard Tico dining choices in Liberia. In town the most popular alternatives are **Pizzería Pronto** (🕿 666-2098), which is located 100m (1 block) north of the visitor information center, and **Pizzería da Beppe** (🕿 666-0917), located near the highway on the road that leads into central Liberia. Both serve a wide range of pizzas and assorted pasta dishes. A favorite of mine is **Café Liberia** 🛠 (🕿 665-1660), a little French-style coffee shop and bistro that morphs into a sort of European-style hip lounge and bar at night. Another alternative is to choose one of the *sodas* around the central park. The best of these is **Restaurante Paseo Real** (🕿 666-3455). If you want fast food, you can find both **Burger King** and **Papa John's** in a small shopping complex on the northwest corner of the main intersection of the Interamerican Highway and the road to the beaches, as well as an even bigger food court with more fast-food options at the new mall on the southern outskirts of town.

Restaurant Rincón Corobicí COSTA RICAN/INTERNATIONAL   This roadside tourist restaurant can be packed with tour groups and the food is far from memorable. But the setting on the banks of the Corobicí River is wonderful. Although plenty of covered seating is available in the main open-air dining room, try to get a table on the wooden deck overlooking the river. The sound of rushing water tumbling over the rocks in the riverbed is a soothing accompaniment to the simple but filling meals. The whole fried fish is your best choice here, although you can also have steaks, lobster, shrimp, sandwiches, and even a couple of lamb dishes. This restaurant makes an ideal lunch stop if you're heading to or coming from Liberia, or if you have just done a rafting trip on the Corobicí River. Be sure to try the fried yuca chips; they're excellent.

Interamerican Hwy., 5km (3 miles) north of Cañas. © **669-6262.** Main courses $6–$17 (£3–£8.50). AE, DC, MC, V. Daily 8am–5pm.

2 La Cruz & Bahía Salinas

277km (172 miles) NW of San José; 59km (37 miles) NW of Liberia; 20km (12 miles) S of Peñas Blancas

Near the Nicaraguan border, La Cruz is a tiny hilltop town that has little to offer beyond a fabulous view of Bahía Salinas, but it does serve as a gateway to the nearly deserted beaches down below, a few mountain lodges bordering the nearby Santa Rosa and Guanacaste national parks, and the Nicaraguan border crossing at Peñas Blancas.

There's little reason to stay in La Cruz, but if you must, check out either **Amalia's Inn** (©/fax **679-9681**) or **Hotel Bella Vista** (© **679-8060**). Both are simple hotels, and both have small pools and good views of the bay. (Instead of staying in town, check out the listings below for places to stay in the environs of La Cruz.)

ESSENTIALS

GETTING THERE & DEPARTING   By Plane   The nearest airport with regular service is in Liberia (see "Liberia," earlier in this chapter).

By Car   Take the Interamerican Highway west from San José and follow the signs for Nicaragua and the Guanacaste beaches. When you reach Liberia, head straight through the major intersection, following signs to Peñas Blancas and the Nicaraguan border. Allow approximately 5 hours to get from San José to La Cruz.

By Bus   Transportes Deldú buses (© **256-9072**) leave San José daily for **Peñas Blancas** at 5, 7, 7:45, and 10:45am and 1:20 and 4:10pm from Calle 20 and Avenida 1. These buses stop in La Cruz and will also let you off at the entrance to Santa Rosa National Park. The ride to La Cruz takes 6 hours; a one-way fare costs $4.60 (£2.30). Additional buses are often added on weekends.

Local buses leave Liberia for Peñas Blancas periodically throughout the day. The ride to La Cruz takes about 1 hour and costs $2 (£1). Buses depart for San José from Peñas Blancas daily at 5, 7:30, and 10:30am, noon, and 3:30pm, passing through La Cruz about 20 minutes later. Buses leave Liberia for San José roughly every hour between 5am and 7pm.

ORIENTATION   The highway passes slightly to the east of town. You'll pass the turnoffs to Santa Rosa National Park and Playa Caujiniquil before you reach the town. To reach the beaches of Bahía Salinas, head into La Cruz to and take the road that runs along the north side of the small central park and then follow the signs down to the water and Bahía Salinas.

EXPLORING SANTA ROSA NATIONAL PARK

Known for its remote, pristine beaches (reached by several kilometers of hiking trails or a 4WD vehicle), **Santa Rosa National Park** (© **666-5051**) is a great place to camp on the beach, surf, or (if you're lucky) watch sea turtles nest. Located 30km (19 miles) north of Liberia and 21km (13 miles) south of La Cruz on the Interamerican Highway, Costa Rica's first national park blankets the Santa Elena Peninsula. Unlike other national parks, it was founded not to preserve the land but to save a building, known as **La Casona,** that played an important role in Costa Rican independence. It was here, in 1856, that Costa Rican forces fought the decisive Battle of Santa Rosa, forcing the U.S.-backed soldier of fortune William Walker and his men to flee into Nicaragua. La Casona was completely destroyed by arson in 2001, but it has been rebuilt, very accurately mimicking the original building, and houses a small museum.

It costs $6 (£3) per person to enter the park. Camping is allowed at several sites within the park. A campsite costs $2 (£1) per person per day. There's camping near the entrance and principal ranger station, as well as near La Casona and down by playas Naranjo and Nancite. For trail information, see the "Santa Rosa National Park" map in the color insert at the front of this book.

THE BEACHES 🏖🏖   Eight kilometers (5 miles) west of La Casona, down a rugged road that's impassable during the rainy season (it's rough on 4WD vehicles even in the dry season), is **Playa Naranjo.** Four kilometers (2½ miles) north of Playa Naranjo, along a hiking trail that follows the beach, you'll find **Playa Nancite. Playa Blanca** is 21km (13 miles) down a dirt road from Caujiniquil, which itself is 20km (12 miles) north of the park entrance. None of these three beaches has shower or restroom facilities. (Playa Nancite does have some facilities, but they're in a reservation-only camping area.) Bring along your own water, food, and anything else you'll need, and expect to find things relatively quiet and deserted.

Playa Nancite is known for its *arribadas* ("arrivals," grouped egg-layings) of olive ridley sea turtles, which come ashore to nest by the tens of thousands each year in October. Playa Naranjo is legendary for its perfect surfing waves. In fact, this spot is quite popular with day-trippers who come in by boat from the Playa del Coco area to ride the waves that break around **Witch's Rock,** which lies just offshore.

On the northern side of the peninsula is **Playa Blanca,** a beautiful, remote white-sand beach with calm waters. This beach is reached by way of the small village of Caujiniquil and is accessible only during the dry season.

If you reach Caujiniquil and then head north for a few kilometers, you'll come to a small annex to the national park system at **Playa Junquillal** (✆ 679-9692), not to be confused with the more-developed beach of the same name farther south in Guanacaste. This is a lovely little beach that is also often good for swimming. You'll have to pay the park entrance fee ($4/£2) to use the beach, and $2 (£1) more to camp here. There are basic bathroom and shower facilities.

FUN ON & OVER THE WAVES

The waters of Bahía Salinas are buffeted by serious winds from mid-November through mid-May, and this area is a prime spot for windsurfing and kiteboarding. The folks at **Ecoplaya Beach Resort** (see below) have the best windsurfing operation and rental equipment in the area. If you want to try your hand at the sport of kiteboarding, check in with the folks at the **Kitesurfing Center** (✆ 826-5221; www.suntour sandfun.com), who operate out of the **Blue Dream Hotel** in Playa Copal.

WHERE TO STAY NEAR LA CRUZ

Ecoplaya Beach Resort 🏖   This is by far the most comfortable, dare I say luxurious, beach hotel in the area. (However, aside from a facile attempt to cash in on a trend, I see no reason to use "eco" in the name.) The rooms are classified as either studios or junior, master, or luxury suites. Definitely opt for one of the suites because the studios are a bit cramped. The wide range in prices here reflects the wide range of room sizes. Inside they all have high ceilings, tile floors, and plenty of varnished wood accents. The beach here is calm and attractive, although the winter winds really howl. To take advantage of this, the hotel features a fully equipped windsurf center, offering rentals and classes. This is also a good option if you're looking to combine some beach time with excursions to Santa Rosa National Park, Los Inocentes Lodge, and/or neighboring Nicaragua. But if you're just looking for a beach-resort vacation, I recommend heading to one of the beaches farther south in Guanacaste.

La Coyotera Beach, Salinas Bay. ℂ **228-7146.** Fax 289-4536. www.ecoplaya.com. 35 units. $170–$322 (£81–£161) double. Rates lower in the off season, higher during peak weeks. AE, MC, V. From La Cruz, take the dirt road that passes to the right of El Mirador Ehecatl restaurant (as you face the water), and then follow signs to the hotel. **Amenities:** Restaurant; bar; midsize pool; 2 Jacuzzis; watersports equipment rental; tour desk; laundry service. *In room:* A/C, TV, kitchenette, fridge, coffeemaker.

3 Playa Hermosa, Playa Panamá & Papagayo ✦

258km (160 miles) NW of San José; 40km (25 miles) SW of Liberia

While most of Costa Rica's coast is highly coveted by surfers, the beaches here are mostly protected and calm. A good destination for families with kids, **Playa Hermosa** ✦ means "beautiful beach," which is an appropriate name for this crescent of sand. Surrounded by steep forested hills, this curving gray-sand beach is long and wide and the surf is usually quite gentle. Fringing the beach is a swath of trees that stays surprisingly green even during the dry season. The shade provided by these trees, along with the calm protected waters, is a big part of the beach's appeal. Rocky headlands jut out into the surf at both ends of the beach, and at the base of these rocks, you'll find fun tide pools to explore.

Beyond Playa Hermosa you'll find **Playa Panamá** ✦ and, farther on, the calm waters of **Bahía Culebra** ✦, a large protected bay dotted with small, private patches of beach and ringed with mostly intact dry forest. Around the north end of Bahía Culebra is the rapidly developing **Papagayo Peninsula** ✦. Currently the home to two large all-inclusive resorts and one championship golf course, this area is slated to expand and develop even more in the coming years and you'll see the visible signs (and hear the sounds) of construction all around. This peninsula has a half-dozen or so small to midsize beaches, the nicest of which might just be **Playa Nacascolo** ✦✦, which is inside the domain of the new Four Seasons Resort here—but all beaches in Costa Rica are public, so you can still visit, albeit after passing through security and parking at the public parking lot.

ESSENTIALS

GETTING THERE & DEPARTING   By Plane   The nearest airport with regularly scheduled service is in Liberia. From there you can arrange a taxi to bring you the rest of the way. The ride takes about 25 minutes and should cost $25 to $40 (£13–£20).

By Car   Follow the directions for getting to Liberia (described earlier in this chapter), and then head west toward Santa Cruz. The turnoff for the Papagayo Peninsula is prominently marked 8km (5 miles) south of the Liberia airport. At the corner here you'll see a massive Do It Center hardware store and lumber yard. If you're going on to Playa Hermosa and Playa Panamá, continue on a little farther and, just past the village of Comunidad, turn right. In about 11km (6¾ miles) you'll come to a fork in the road; take the right fork. These roads are relatively well marked, and a host of prominent hotel billboards should make it easy enough to find the beach. The drive takes about 4½ hours from San José.

By Bus   A **Tralapa** express bus (© 221-7202) leaves San José daily at 3pm from Calle 20 between avenidas 3 and 5, stopping at Playa Hermosa and Playa Panamá, 3km (1¾ miles) farther north. One-way fare for the 5-hour trip is $5 (£2.50).

Gray Line (© 220-2126; www.graylinecostarica.com) has a daily bus that leaves San José at 7am for all beaches in this area. **Interbus** (© 283-5573; www.interbus online.com) has two daily buses that leave San José at 7:45am and 2:30pm for all beaches in this area. Both companies charge $29 (£15) and will pick you up at most San José–area hotels.

You can take a bus from San José to Liberia (see "Essentials," earlier in this chapter) and then take a bus from Liberia to Playa Hermosa and Playa Panamá. Buses (© 666-0042) leave Liberia roughly every 2 hours or so throughout the day between 5am and 7pm. The trip lasts 40 minutes because the bus stops frequently to drop off and pick up passengers. The one-way fare costs $1.30 (65p). These bus schedules change from time to time, so it's always best to check in advance. During the high season and on weekends, extra buses from Liberia are sometimes added. You can also take a bus to Playa del Coco, from which playas Hermosa and Panamá are a relatively quick taxi ride away. Taxi fare should run between $5 and $7 (£2.50–£3.50).

One direct bus departs for San José daily at 5am from Playa Panamá, with a stop in Playa Hermosa along the way. Buses to Liberia leave Playa Panamá at 6, 7, and 10am and 2, 5, and 7pm, stopping in Playa Hermosa a few minutes later. Ask at your hotel where to catch the bus.

ORIENTATION   From the well-marked turnoff for the Papagayo Peninsula (near the prominent Do It Center hardware store), a paved road leads around to the Allegro Papagayo and Four Seasons resorts. If you are heading to the beaches a little farther south, continue on to the well-marked turnoff for Playa del Coco and Playa Hermosa. The road forks before reaching Playa del Coco. You'll come to Playa Hermosa first, followed by Playa Panamá a few kilometers farther along the same road. The road ends at the Fiesta Premier Resort & Spa. There is also a connecting road between the Papagayo Peninsula road and Playa Panamá. This 11km (6¾-mile) stretch of road is unpaved but well maintained and it's definitely your quickest route to Playa Panamá.

Playa Hermosa is about a 450m (1,476-ft.) stretch of beach, with all the hotels laid out along this stretch. From the main road, which continues on to Playa Panamá, three access roads head off toward the beach. All the hotels are well marked, with signs pointing guests down the right access road. Playa Panamá is the least developed of the beaches out here. Somewhat longer than Playa Hermosa, it also has several access roads heading in toward the beach from the main road, which is slightly inland.

FUN ON & UNDER THE WATER

Most of the beaches up here are usually quite calm and good for swimming.

If you want to do some diving, check in with **Diving Safaris de Costa Rica** ⚡ (© 672-1259; www.costaricadiving.net), which is headquartered on the principal access road into Playa Hermosa, about 137m (450 ft.) before you hit the beach. This is a long-established and respected dive operation. It has a large shop and offers a wide range of trips to numerous dive spots, and it also offers night dives, multiday packages, certification classes, and Nitrox dives. Alternatively, you can check out **Resort Divers** (© 672-0106; www.resortdivers-cr.com), which has set up shop at the Fiesta Premier Resort in Playa Panama. A two-tank dive should run between $65 and $130 (£33–£65) per person, depending primarily on the distance traveled to the dive sites.

In the middle of Playa Hermosa, **Aqua Sport** (© 672-0050) is where to go for watersports equipment rental in Playa Hermosa. Kayaks, sailboards, canoes, bicycles, beach umbrellas, snorkel gear, and parasails are available for rental at fairly reasonable rates. You'll also find here a small supermarket, public phones, and a restaurant.

Because the beaches in this area are relatively protected and generally flat, surfers should look into boat trips to nearby **Witch's Rock** 🏄🏄 and **Ollie's Point** 🏄. Diving Safaris de Costa Rica (© 672-1259), **Hotel Finisterra** (© 670-0293), and **Aqua Sport** (© 672-0050) all offer trips for up to six surfers for around $250 to $300 (£125–£150), including lunch. All of these companies also offer fishing trips for between $250 and $1,200 (£125–£600) for groups of two to four anglers.

If you're interested in wind power, a 5-hour cruise on the 14m (46-ft.) trimaran *Cool Runnings* (© 672-0103) costs $70 (£35) per person, including lunch and drinks. A shorter sunset tour costs $55 (£28) per person.

OTHER OPTIONS

Other activities in the area include horseback riding, all-terrain quad tours, canopy tours, and trips to other major attractions in the Guanacaste region. **Swiss Travel Service** (© 668-1020) has operations in the area and offers a wide range of activities and tours, including trips to Santa Rosa or Rincón de la Vieja national parks, and rafting on the Corobicí River. These folks have desks at many of the hotels around here and will pick you up at any hotel in the area.

The best zip-line canopy tour in this area is the **Witch's Rock Canopy Tour** (© 666-7546), just before the Allegro Papagayo Resort. The 2½-hour tour covers 3km (1¾ miles) of cables touching down on 24 platforms and costs $55 (£23).

Finally, the Arnold Palmer–designed championship course at the Four Seasons Resort is hands down the most beautiful and challenging **golf course** in the country. However, it is open only to guests at the Four Seasons.

WHERE TO STAY
VERY EXPENSIVE

Allegro Papagayo Resort 🏄   If you're looking for an affordable all-inclusive vacation at a large modern resort with a wide range of facilities and activities, this is the best choice in the region. The rooms are all identical in size—comfortable enough, but by no means extravagant—and housed in 14 different three-story buildings spread over a steep hillside overlooking the sea. Obviously, the rooms on the upper floors in the buildings higher up the hill have the best views. All come with two queen-size beds or one king-size bed, a small private balcony, and the full complement of modern amenities. The beach is an isolated patch of hard-packed salt-and-pepper sand that almost disappears at high tide. The waters here are very protected, and the drop-off is very gradual. The hotel has an extensive offering of activities throughout the day and a "Fun Club" on a nearby white sand beach, although only a limited number of guests are allowed at this fun club at anyone time, so you have to sign up early.

Playa Manzanillo, Guanacaste (A.P. 434-1150, La Uruca). © 800/858-2258 in the U.S. and Canada, 248-2323 for reservations inside Costa Rica, or 690-9900 at the resort. Fax 255-0919. www.occidentalhotels.com. 296 units. $155–$165 (£78–£83) per person double occupancy. Rates include food, drinks, a range of activities, and taxes. AE, DC, MC, V. **Amenities:** 3 restaurants; 3 bars; large free-form pool; small fitness center; 2 Jacuzzis; watersports equipment; children's programs; tour desk; massage; babysitting; laundry service. *In room:* A/C, TV, minibar, coffeemaker, hair dryer, safe.

Fiesta Premier Resort & Spa 🏄 *Kids*   This was the first all-inclusive resort in the Guanacaste region. It has changed its name and management at least three times, but it has finally settled down and for the past few years has been kept in the best shape of its career. Most of the duplex villas can be separated into two rooms or shared by a family or two couples. Inside, one room is equipped with a king-size bed; the other has two queen-size beds. All rooms have marble floors, large bathrooms, and small private patios or balconies. The resort is quite spread out, so if you don't want to do a lot of walking or wait for the minivan shuttles, ask for a room near the main pool and restaurants. If you want a good view, ask for one on the hill overlooking the bay. For those seeking more isolation, there are rooms located in the dry forest behind the resort. The hotel has a host of organized sports and activities, including daily programs for children. It also has its own small crescent-shape swath of beach, which is very calm and protected for swimming. A dinner theater and disco complex offers nightly entertainment revues and late-night dancing, and a small casino is on site.

Playa Panamá, Guanacaste. (C) 296-6263 or 672-0000. Fax 220-3409. www.fiestapremier.com. 202 units. $390–$590 (£195–£295) double. Rates include food, drinks, activities, and taxes. Rates lower in off season; higher during peak weeks. AE, MC, V. **Amenities:** 5 restaurants; 3 bars; casino; 3-tiered main pool, small lap pool, and resistance lap pool; tennis court; well-equipped fitness center and spa; Jacuzzi; sauna; watersports equipment; children's programs; tour desk; car-rental desk; shopping arcade; salon; babysitting; laundry service. In room: A/C, TV, free Wi-Fi, minibar, coffeemaker, hair dryer, safe.

Four Seasons Resort Costa Rica ★★★ (Kids)

Set near the very end of a long peninsula on a narrow spit of land between two white-sand beaches, this is the most luxurious and impressive large-scale resort in Costa Rica. Most of the rooms are in three long, four-story, oceanfront buildings. The architecture is stunning, with most buildings featuring flowing roof designs and other touches imitating the forms of turtles, armadillos, and butterflies. All the rooms are sufficiently spacious, with wood floors, rich wood furnishings, tasteful fixtures and decorations from around the world, marble bathrooms with deep tubs and separate showers, and luscious cotton sheets and bathrobes. The rooms on the third and fourth floors have the best views and are priced accordingly. The others have either garden views or partial ocean views, even though every room faces the sea. Each has a large private balcony with a sofa, a table and a couple of chairs, and a smooth-working roll-up screen system. On the rocky hill at the very end of the peninsula are the resort's suites and villas. These are all similarly appointed, but with even more space and often either a private pool, a Jacuzzi, or an open-air gazebo for soaking in the views. The resort also features the Four Seasons' renowned service (including family-friendly amenities such as kid-size bathrobes and childproof rooms), one of the best-equipped full-service spas in the country, and a truly spectacular golf course that offers ocean views from 15 of its 18 holes.

Papagayo Peninsula, Guanacaste. (C) 800/819-5053 in the U.S. or 696-0000. Fax 696-0010. www.fourseasons.com/costarica. 165 units. $470–$650 (£235–£325) double; $1,325–$6,500 (£663–£3,250) suites and villas. Rates lower in off season; higher during peak weeks. Children stay free in parent's room. AE, DC, DISC, MC, V. **Amenities:** 4 restaurants; 2 bars; lounge; 3 free-form pools; championship 18-hole golf course; 2 tennis courts; modern, full-service spa; watersports equipment; children's programs; tour desk; concierge; 24-hr. room service; massage; babysitting; laundry service; nonsmoking rooms. In room: A/C, TV/DVD, dataport, Wi-Fi, hair dryer, safe.

Grand Papagayo ★★

The Grand Papagayo is the highest-end all-inclusive resort of the Occidental Hotel chain in Costa Rica. The rooms are spread over a broad and contoured hillside overlooking the ocean, but not all rooms come with an ocean view. At the center of the complex is a large, free-form pool. The beach here is very protected and calm, although it almost entirely disappears at peak high tide. The resort is geared toward couples, and the vast majority of the rooms come with just one king-size bed, although there are some with two queens. All are quite roomy, with private terraces or balconies, and a host of amenities. I like the Grand Concierge rooms, which are close to the pool and restaurants, and feature marble floors. However, the Royal Club rooms and suites are the best rooms here, and they come with beefed up concierge services, separate check-in and check-out, as well as daily refills of the minibar—as opposed to every other day with the other rooms. The resort has several restaurants and dining options, although be sure to book your meals at the fancier a-la-carte options early. A host of scheduled activities and entertainment options are offered, and a wide range of additional tours and activities can be added on.

Papagayo Peninsula, Guanacaste (A.P. 434-1150, La Uruca). ✆ 800/858-2258 in the U.S. and Canada, 248-2323 for reservations inside Costa Rica, or 672-0191 at the hotel. Fax 255-0919. www.occidentalhotels.com. 169 units. $219–$489 (£110–£245) per person double occupancy. Rates include food, drinks, a range of activities, and taxes. AE, DC, MC, V. **Amenities:** 4 restaurants; 2 bars; lounge; 2 large free-form pools; 1 lighted tennis court; gym; spa; watersports equipment; tour desk; massage; babysitting; laundry service; nonsmoking rooms. *In room:* A/C, TV, stocked minibar, coffeemaker, hair dryer, safe.

Villas Sol Hotel & Beach Resort ✿   Set on a steep hillside at the north end of the beach, the Villas Sol is part of a long-standing project that has changed hands several times, divided, and grown over the past years. The hotel is at the top of the hill, about 270m (886 ft.) from the beach—you'll need to be in good shape to stay here, or you can spend some time waiting for the sporadic jitney service. Luckily, the two pools are both at the top of the hill if you want to opt out of the trip to and from the beach. The hotel rooms are all well maintained and most have excellent views. The villas are newer units located just off the entrance. All have kitchens, satellite TVs, and modern furnishings. About a third of them have their own small swimming pool or Jacuzzi. Given their placement, not all of the villas have spectacular views.

Playa Hermosa, Guanacaste. ✆ 800/572-9934 in the U.S. and Canada, or 257-0607 reservations in San José, or 672-0001 at the hotel. Fax 223-3036. www.villassol.com. 56 units, 106 villas. $232–$248 (£116–£124) double; $339–$576 (£170–£288) villa. Rates include food, drinks, activities, and taxes. Rates lower during off season; higher during peak weeks. AE, DC, MC, V. **Amenities:** 3 restaurants; 2 bars; 2 pools; small spa; 2 lighted tennis courts; limited watersports equipment rental; tour desk; laundry service; free Wi-Fi. *In room:* A/C, TV, minifridge, coffeemaker, hair dryer, safe.

MODERATE

El Velero Hotel ✿   This place is one of my top choices right on the beach in Playa Hermosa. White walls and polished tile floors give El Velero a Mediterranean flavor. The guest rooms are large, and those on the second floor have high ceilings. The furnishings are simple, though, and some of the bathrooms are a bit small. The hotel has its own popular little restaurant, which offers a good selection of meat, fish, and shrimp dishes, as well as weekly barbecue fests. Various tours, horseback riding, and fishing trips can be arranged through the hotel; however, the most popular excursions are the full-day and sunset cruises on the hotel's namesake sailboat.

Playa Hermosa (A.P. 49-5019), Guanacaste. ✆ 672-1017. Fax 672-0016. www.costaricahotel.net. 22 units. $79 (£40) double. Rates lower in off season; higher during peak periods. AE, MC, V. **Amenities:** Restaurant; bar; small pool by the beach; tour desk; laundry service. *In room:* A/C, TV, coffeemaker, hair dryer, safe.

Hotel Finisterra   This hillside hotel offers neat, spacious accommodations on the southern end of Playa Hermosa. All rooms are located on the second floor and come with either one queen-size bed or two double beds. Large picture windows face either a forested hillside or the Pacific Ocean. A large open-air restaurant and lounge takes up most of the first floor, and a refreshing little pool has good views. The beach is about 270m (886 ft.) away, down the steep driveway. The restaurant here serves a nightly mix of fresh seafood, steaks, and chicken prepared with fusion flare. The folks here can arrange a wide variety of tours, including sportfishing and surf trips to Witch's Rock.

Playa Hermosa, Guanacaste. Ⓒ/fax 672-0227. www.finisterra.net. 10 units. $90 (£45) double. Rates include full breakfast. Rates lower in off season; higher during peak periods. MC, V. **Amenities:** Restaurant; bar; small pool; tour desk; babysitting; laundry service. *In room:* A/C, free Wi-Fi, no phone.

Hotel Playa Hermosa Bosque del Mar ⒻⒻ ⒻⒾⓃⒹⓈ   Tucked away under shady trees, this sprawling beachfront spread has an envious location on the southern end of Playa Hermosa. The cool and cozy rooms have tile floors, air-conditioning, and contemporary furniture and fixtures. They also have firm beds, although some are a bit small. The suites are larger and newer and come with two queen-size beds, a minifridge and coffeemaker. The open-air restaurant has a rustic tropical feel, with unfinished tree trunks holding up the roof, and serves a range of Tico and international dishes. The pretty free-form pool sits in a shady spot under several tall trees, with a broad deck area and separate tepid Jacuzzi beside it.

Playa Hermosa, Guanacaste. Ⓒ 672-0046. Fax 672-0019. www.hotelplayahermosa.com. 32 units. $75–$120 (£48–£60) double. Rates lower in off season; higher during peak periods. MC, V. Turn left at the 1st road into Playa Hermosa; the hotel's white archway gate is about 1km (½ mile) down this dirt road. **Amenities:** Restaurant; bar; outdoor pool; Jacuzzi; tour desk; laundry service. *In room:* A/C, TV, free Wi-Fi.

Villa del Sueño Hotel Ⓕ   Although this hotel isn't right on the beach (it's about 90m/295 ft. from the sand), its well-groomed lawns and gardens feel like an oasis in the dust and heat of a Guanacaste dry season. Villa del Sueño offers clean and comfortable rooms at a good price, and the Villa del Sueño Restaurant here is one of the best in Playa Hermosa (p. 160). All the rooms have cool tile floors, high hardwood ceilings, ceiling fans, and well-placed windows for cross ventilation. The second-floor superior rooms have more space and larger windows. The more expensive rooms here come with air-conditioning and televisions. There's a small pool and open-air bar in the center courtyard. Meals are served in the main building's open-air restaurant or in their new open-air dinner theater, which features live music, by a variety of local acts, during much of the high season. The folks here manage the neighboring "El Oasis" condominium development, which has additional apartment and efficiency units available for nightly and weekly rentals, as well as its own pool.

Playa Hermosa, Guanacaste (Interlink 2059, P.O. Box 025635, Miami, FL 33102). Ⓒ **800/378-8599** in the U.S., or Ⓒ/fax 672-0026. www.villadelsueno.com. 45 units. $75–$130 (£48–£65) double; $195–$255 (£98–£128) condo. Rates lower in off season; higher during peak periods. AE, MC, V. **Amenities:** Restaurant; bar; small pool; tour desk; laundry service; free Wi-Fi. *In room:* A/C.

DINING & AFTER-DARK DIVERSIONS

For nightlife, find out whether the **Villa del Sueño Restaurant** (see below) has live music. Two Saturdays a month, Villa del Sueño hosts larger concerts, featuring prominent Costa Rican acts, in its spiffy open-air amphitheater. For something simpler, head inland to the **Monkey Bar** (Ⓒ **672-0267**), which is located off the main road to Playa Panamá, has a pool table and a satellite TV, and serves U.S.-style bar food.

In addition to the places listed below, you'll find good restaurants at both the **El Velero Hotel** and the **Hotel Finisterra** (see "Where to Stay," above).

Ginger ⒻⒻ ⒻⒾⓃⒹⓈ INTERNATIONAL/TAPAS   In this most creative restaurant in the area, the architecture and decor are stylish and modern, with sharp angles and loads of chrome and glass. The food is an eclectic mix of modern takes on wide-ranging international fare, all served as tapas, meant to be shared while sampling some of the many cocktails and wines served here. Still, it's easy to make a full meal. Order the house special ginger-glazed chicken wings, along with some spring rolls, and a plate of fresh mahimahi marinated in vodka and Asian spices. There are also more traditional Mediterranean and Spanish-style tapas, as well as delicious desserts.

On the main road, Playa Hermosa. 🕐 672-0041. Tapas $4–$7 (£2–£3.50). AE, MC, V. Tues–Sun 11:30am–10pm.

Villa del Sueño Restaurant 🏵 CONTINENTAL   A mellow yet refined atmosphere presides under slow-turning ceiling fans at this simple open-air restaurant. In addition to the regular menu, a small selection of nightly specials is provided. If you venture away from the fresh fish, there are well-prepared pasta dishes, as well as meat and poultry options. Live music is available many nights during high season.

At the Villa del Sueño Hotel. 🕐 672-0026. Main courses $8–$17 (£4–£8.50). AE, MC, V. Daily 7am–10pm.

4 Playa del Coco & Playa Ocotal

253km (157 miles) NW of San José; 35km (22 miles) W of Liberia

In the midst of a major construction boom, **Playa del Coco** is one of the busiest and most built-up beaches in this area. You'll pass through a tight jumble of restaurants, hotels, and souvenir shops several hundred meters before you hit the sand and sea, while homes, condos, and hotels are sprouting up along the beach in either direction. This has long been, and remains, a popular destination with middle-class Ticos and weekend revelers from San José. It's also a prime jumping-off point for some of Costa Rica's best scuba diving. The beach, which has grayish-brown sand and gentle surf, is quite wide at low tide and almost nonexistent at high tide. The crowds that come here like their music loud and constant, so if you're in search of a quiet retreat, stay away from the center of town. Still, if you're looking for a beach with a wide range of inexpensive hotels, lively nightlife, and plenty of cheap food and beer close at hand, you'll enjoy Playa del Coco.

Better still, in my opinion, head over to **Playa Ocotal** 🏵, which is a couple of kilometers to the south. This tiny pocket cove features a small salt-and-pepper beach bordered by high bluffs and is quite beautiful. When it's calm there's good snorkeling around some rocky islands close to shore here.

ESSENTIALS

GETTING THERE & DEPARTING   By Plane   The nearest airport with regularly scheduled flights is in Liberia. From there you can arrange for a taxi to take you to Playa del Coco or Playa Ocotal, which is about a 25-minute drive, for $30 to $40 (£15–£20).

By Car   From Liberia, head west toward Santa Cruz. Just past the village of Comunidad, turn right. In about 11km (6¾ miles) you'll come to a fork in the road. Take the left fork. It takes about 4½ hours from San José.

By Bus   **Pulmitan** express buses (🕐 222-1650) leave San José for Playa del Coco at 8am and 2 and 4pm daily from Calle 24 between avenidas 5 and 7. Allow 5 hours for the trip. A one-way ticket is $5.20 (£2.70). From Liberia, buses to Playa del Coco leave regularly throughout the day between 5am and 7pm. A one-way ticket for the 40-minute trip costs $1.50 (75p). These bus schedules change frequently, so it's always best to check in advance. During the high season and on weekends, extra buses from Liberia are sometimes added.

Gray Line (© **220-2126;** www.graylinecostarica.com) has a daily bus that leaves San José for Playa del Coco at 7am. **Interbus** (© **283-5573;** www.interbusonline.com) has two daily buses that leave San José for Playa del Coco at 7:45am and 2:30pm. Both companies charge $29 (£15), and will pick you up at most San José–area hotels.

The direct bus for San José leaves Playa del Coco daily at 4 and 8am and 2pm. Local buses for Liberia leave between 5am and 7pm.

Depending on demand, the Playa del Coco buses sometimes go as far as Playa Ocotal; it's worth checking beforehand if possible. Otherwise, a taxi should cost around $5 (£2.50).

ORIENTATION   Playa del Coco is a compact and busy beach town. Most of its hotels and restaurants are either on the water, on the road leading into town, or on the road that heads north, about 100m (328 ft.) inland from and parallel to the beach.

Playa Ocotal, which is south of Playa del Coco on a paved road that leaves the main road about 183m (600 ft.) before the beach, is a small collection of vacation homes, condos, and a couple of hotels. It has one bar and one restaurant on the beach.

FAST FACTS   There's a branch of the state-run **Banco Nacional** (© **670-0801**) on the main road into town, about 3 blocks before you hit the beach. If you can't flag down a **taxi** easily on the street, call © **670-0408.** For the local **police,** dial © **670-0258;** for the local **health clinic,** call © **670-0987;** and for the local **pharmacy** call © **670-1186.**

FUN ON & OFF THE BEACH

Plenty of boats are anchored here at Playa del Coco, and that means plenty of opportunities to go fishing, diving, or sailing. Still, the most popular activities, especially among the hordes of Ticos who come here, are hanging out on the beach, hanging out in the *sodas,* and cruising the bars and discos at night. If you're interested, you might be able to join a soccer match. (The soccer field is in the middle of town.) You can also arrange horseback rides; ask at your hotel.

BEACH CLUB   If you're staying at a hotel without a pool, or just want a sense of exclusivity on the beach, you might check out **Café de Playa Beach & Dining Club** (© **670-1621**). In addition to having an excellent restaurant (see below), this place offers up day passes for $10 (£5) that allow you access to their pool and private grassy lawn fronting the beach, and spread with comfortable teak chaise lounges. They also have a host of watersports equipment rental and tour options, and small spa on site, offering a broad range of massages and treatments.

SAILING   Several cruising sailboats and long-time local salts offer daily sailing excursions. The 50-foot *Drums of Bora* (© **670-1033** or 845-9448) is a large motor-sailer plying the waters off Playa del Coco. A full-day cruise with lunch and drinks runs $65 (£33) per person. The trip includes a couple of snorkel stops, and an open bar. You could also book a ride on the *Don Bosco* (© **670-0181**), a 65-foot ketch, that includes a beach barbeque and party, as part of its daily cruise itinerary ($90–$120/£45–£60 per person, full-day).

SCUBA DIVING   Scuba diving is the most popular watersport in the area, and dive shops abound. **Ocotal Diving** (© **670-0321;** www.ocotaldiving.com) and **Rich Coast Diving** (© **800/434-8464** in the U.S. and Canada, or 670-0176 in Costa

---

Fun Fact **Charlie Don't Surf, But Ollie Does**

Ollie's Point is named after Oliver North, the famous and felonious former lieutenant colonel at the center of the Iran-Contra scandal. The beaches and ports of northern Guanacaste were a staging ground for supplying the Nicaraguan Contra rebels. Legend has it that during a news broadcast of an interview with North, some surfers noticed a fabulous point break going off in the background. Hence, the discovery and naming of Ollie's Point.

Rica; www.richcoastdiving.com) are the most established and offer equipment rentals and dive trips. A two-tank dive, with equipment, should cost between $70 and $140 (£35–£70) per person, depending on the distance to the dive site. The more distant dive sites visited include the Catalina Islands and Bat Island. Both operators also offer PADI certification courses.

SPORTFISHING Full- and half-day sportfishing excursions can be arranged through any of the hotel tour desks, or with **Tranquilamar** (©/fax **670-0400** or 814-0994; www.tranquilamar.com). A half-day of fishing, with boat, captain, food, and tackle, should cost between $200 and $600 (£100–£300) for two to four passengers; a full day should run between $500 and $1,400 (£250–£700).

SURFING There's no surf whatsoever in Playa del Coco. But this is a popular jumping-off point for daily boat trips to Witch's Rock or Roca Bruja, and Ollie's Point up in Santa Rosa National Park. Most of the above-mentioned sportfishing and dive operations also offer trips to ferry surfers up to these two isolated surf breaks. Alternatively, you can contact **Roca Bruja Surf Operations** (© **670-1020**; www.costarica surftrips.com). A boat that carries six surfers for a full day, including lunch and beer, should run around $250 to $375 (£125–£188). *Tip:* Both Witch's Rock and Ollie's Point are technically within Santa Rosa National Park. Permits are sometimes required, and boats without permits are sometimes turned away. If you decide to go, be sure your boat captain is licensed and has cleared access to the park. You may also have to pay the park's $6 (£3) entrance fee.

WHERE TO STAY
EXPENSIVE
El Ocotal Beach Resort ♣ This is the most luxurious hotel in the Playa del Coco area. The guest rooms vary in size, styling, and age. Moving up the hillside leading to the reception and lobby areas are six large duplex bungalows. These are some of the better rooms here. Each of these duplex bungalows shares a small ocean-view plunge pool. The rooms with the best views are at the top of the hill, overlooking a dramatic stretch of rocky coastline, although if you want quick access to the beach, choose one of the lower units. These rooms feature pastel-wash painted walls and colorful floral bedspreads. The third-floor suite, no. 520, is the best room in the whole joint, with a large wraparound balcony and private Jacuzzi. *Note:* It's a steep, vigorous hike from bottom to top at this resort.

Scuba diving and sportfishing are the main draws here, and package tours are available. Diminutive Playa Ocotal is one of the prettiest beaches along this stretch of coast and offers good swimming. El Ocotal's hilltop Roca Bruja restaurant is also one of its greatest assets. The large open-air dining room opens onto an expansive, multilevel deck that has more seating, as well as a stunning view of Playa Ocotal and miles of coastline. This is a great place to come for sunset and a drink, and the meals are pretty good as well. There's also another restaurant down by the beach.

Playa del Coco (A.P. 1), Guanacaste. ☎ **670-0321.** Fax 670-0083. www.ocotalresort.com. 59 units, 12 bungalows, 5 suites. $172 (£86) double; $265 (£133) bungalow; $325 (£163) suite. Rates include full breakfast. Rates lower in off season; higher during peak weeks. AE, DC, MC, V. **Amenities:** 2 restaurants; 6 small pools; lighted tennis court; exercise room; Jacuzzi; tour desk; babysitting; laundry service. *In room:* A/C, TV, free Wi-Fi, minifridge, coffeemaker, hair dryer, safe.

MODERATE

In addition to the places listed below, **Villa Flores B&B** (☎ **670-0269;** www.hotel-villa-flores.com) is another good option in this price range, located north of downtown in Playa del Coco and just off the beach.

Coco Beach Hotel   This two-story hotel is the biggest thing in Playa del Coco and is an acceptable choice if you're looking for a clean, comfortable, modern room close to the beach and all the action. The very bland rooms are identical in size but have a variety of bedding options for singles, couples, and families. They all share a common veranda, which gets blasted by the hot afternoon sun. The casino here is the liveliest in Playa del Coco. You can't miss this green-and-white building on your right, on the main road into Playa del Coco, about 200m (656 ft.) before you hit the beach.

Playa del Coco (A.P. 61), Guanacaste. ☎ **670-0494.** Fax 670-0555. 33 units. $79 (£40) double. Rates lower in off season. V. **Amenities:** Restaurant; bar; casino; small pool; small spa; tour desk; laundry service. *In room:* A/C, TV, coffeemaker, hair dryer, safe.

Hotel Villa Casa Blanca ✦   With friendly, helpful owners, beautiful gardens, and attractive rooms, this bed-and-breakfast inn is one of my favorite options in the area. Located about 500m (1,640 ft.) inland from the beach at Playa Ocotal, it's built in the style of a Spanish villa. All the guest rooms feature fine furnishings and are well kept. Some are a tad small, but others are quite roomy and even have kitchenettes. The suites are higher up and have ocean views. My favorite has a secluded patio with lush flowering plants all around. A little rancho serves as an open-air bar and breakfast area, and beside this is a pretty little lap pool with a bridge over it. Another separate rancho serves as a sort of lounge/recreation area and has a satellite television. Not only do they offer free wireless Internet, but they'll also let you call anywhere in the U.S., Canada, or Europe for free on the VoIP connection.

Playa Ocotal (A.P. 176-5019), Playa del Coco, Guanacaste. ☎ **877/623-3198** in the U.S. and Canada, or 670-0518 in Costa Rica. Fax 670-0448. www.hotelvillacasablanca.com. 10 units. $90 (£45) double; $107 (£54) double suite. Rates include breakfast buffet. Rates lower in off season; higher during peak periods. AE, MC, V. **Amenities:** Outdoor lounge and bar; small pool; Jacuzzi; tour desk; laundry service; free Wi-Fi. *In room:* A/C.

Villa del Sol B&B   This small bed-and-breakfast, located 1km (½ mile) north of Playa del Coco village, is a friendly family-run joint. There are seven rooms in the original building here. All are spacious and clean and receive plenty of light. The most interesting room has a round queen-size bed, high ceilings, and views of the gardens. Still, the nicest rooms here are the six studios, each with a small kitchenette, private bathroom, television, and telephone. Those on the second floor even have a bit of ocean view from their shared veranda. There's an inviting small pool with a covered barbecue area. Tasty dinners from a small menu of European-influenced dishes are prepared nightly for guests. For me, the hotel's greatest attribute is its location on the quiet northern end of Playa del Coco. To find the hotel, turn onto the dirt road just beyond the Coco Beach Hotel, before you hit the beach.

Playa del Coco, (A.P. 52-5019) Guanacaste. © **866/793-9523** in the U.S. or ©/fax 670-0085 in Costa Rica. www.villa delsol.com. 13 units, 11 w/private bathroom. $70 (£35) double; $87 (£44) studio apt. Rates include full breakfast for rooms only, not studio apts. Rates lower in off season; higher during peak periods. AE, MC, V. **Amenities:** Restaurant; small pool; tour desk; free Wi-Fi. *In room:* A/C, no phone.

WHERE TO DINE

There are dozens of basic open-air *sodas* at the traffic circle in the center of El Coco village. These restaurants serve Tico standards, with an emphasis on fried fish. Prices are quite low—and so is the quality, for the most part.

In addition to the places listed below, you can get excellent Italian food at **Sol y Luna,** at the Hotel La Puerta del Sol (© **670-0195**), located 200m (2 blocks) north and 100m (1 block) east of the main road at the turnoff just beyond the Coco Beach Hotel, before you hit the beach, and at **La Dolce Vita** (© **670-1384**), located in the little El Pueblito strip mall on the road running north and parallel to the beach.

For a simple sandwich, salad, or fresh-fruit juice, check out **Chile Dulce** (© **670-0465**) on the main road in Playa del Coco. For something a little different, try **Oku Sushi** (© **670-0153**), at the Coco Palms hotel, right across from the soccer field.

Café de Playa ★★ *(Finds)* INTERNATIONAL/FUSION   This hip restaurant is the most elegant and enjoyable spot in Playa del Coco. The creative menu covers a lot of ground, with influence from Italy and across Asia quite prevalent. Appetizers range from an octopus carpaccio to a cold Thai beef salad. There's a range of pasta choices, and a very tasty oriental rice salad with smoked tuna, caviar and avocado. Lobster is served several ways, as are tender filets of sirloin. For dessert be sure to try the passion fruit ice cream. Heavy teak tables and chairs are spread around the ample open air dining room, or out under the open sky (either sun or stars, depending upon the hour). These folks have an excellent wine list, with plenty of Italian and French choices, in addition to the more common Chilean and Argentine fare. The bar—which is made from thick bamboo—and lounge are dimly lit, chic and very inviting.

On the beach, Playa del Coco. © **670-1621.** Reservations recommended. Main courses $6–$15 (£3–£7.50). MC, V. Daily 7am–11pm.

Picante ★ INTERNATIONAL   This is a large, open-air, poolside restaurant at Bahía Pez Vela resort and condominium project. Beyond the pool and down a steep little hill, you can see the Pacific Ocean. The menu is pretty simple and straightforward, with a selection of fresh fish and seafood dishes, big burgers, excellent fish sandwiches, and large creative salads. There are also daily chalkboard specials, which are usually more creative and eclectic, ranging from sesame-seared tuna to mahimahi topped with a homemade curry sauce.

At Bahía Pez Vela resort, Playa Ocotal. © **670-0901.** Reservations recommended. Main courses $5–$17 (£2.50–£8.50). MC, V. Daily 10am–10pm.

Tequila Bar & Grill ★ MEXICAN   This is a simple and rustic joint that serves good Mexican food and magnificent margaritas—in fact, there are 20 different types of margaritas on the menu here. Because this is a fishing town, I recommend the seafood tacos and fajitas, which are excellent, although they both come in chicken and beef varieties. Main-course meals include pork chops in a chipotle barbecue sauce and grilled chicken with tomatillo and lime. Definitely grab one of the open-air street-side tables if you get here early enough to snag one.

On the main road, 150m (1½ blocks) before the beach. © 670-0741. Reservations not necessary. Main courses $4–$12 (£2–£6). V. Thurs–Tues noon–10pm.

PLAYA DEL COCO AFTER DARK

Playa del Coco is one of Costa Rica's liveliest beach towns after dark. On the road into town, you'll find the **Lizard Lounge,** which has a popular pool table and a laid-back tropical vibe. Alternatively, you can head across the park to the **El Bohio Bar & Yacht Club,** which is popular with American expatriates and often shows sporting events on its TV. For a more European style, check out **Zouk Santana** ✹, which often has a DJ spinning electronic dance and lounge music. **Cocomar** is the main disco in town. It's located just off the little park fronting the beach. (If these directions don't get you there, just follow the loud music.) The **Café de Playa** often has live music and concerts, with major acts from San José, as well as local talent filling the bills. Finally, if you want to test your luck, head to the casino at the **Coco Beach Hotel** (see above).

5 Playas Flamingo ✹✹, Potrero, Brasilito & Conchal ✹✹

280km (174 miles) NW of San José; 66km (41 miles) SW of Liberia

For a time this was the epicenter of Costa Rica's beach tourism. The heart of Guanacaste's "Gold Coast." Then Tamarindo to the south and the Papagayo peninsula to the north stole much of its thunder, and things were dormant here for a long while. However, this is area is once again booming, and major construction and development are going on all over the place.

Playa Conchal ✹✹ is the first in a string of beaches stretching north along this coast. This beach is almost entirely backed by the massive Paradisus Playa Conchal resort complex. The unique beach here was once made up primarily of soft crushed shells. Nearly every place you could walk, turn, or lay down your towel was shell-collectors' heaven. Unfortunately, as Conchal has developed and its popularity spread, unscrupulous builders have brought in dump trucks to haul away the namesake seashells for landscaping and construction, and the impact is noticeable.

Just beyond Playa Conchal to the north, you'll come to **Playa Brasilito,** a tiny beach town and one of the few real villages in the area. The soccer field is the center of the village, and around its edges you'll find a couple of little *pulperías* (general stores). There's a long stretch of beach, and though it's of gray sand, it still has a quiet, undiscovered feel, although this is about to change, as the **Hyatt** hotel group has broken ground on a massive project here.

Playa Flamingo ✹✹ is a long, broad stretch of pinkish white sand, located on a long spit of land that forms part of Potrero Bay. At the northern end of the beach is a high rock outcropping upon which most of Playa Flamingo's hotels and vacation homes are built. There are great views from this rocky hill.

If you continue along the road from Brasilito without taking the turn for Playa Flamingo, you'll come to **Playa Potrero.** The sand here is a brownish gray, but the beach is long, clean, deserted, and very calm for swimming. You can see the hotels of Playa Flamingo across the bay. Drive a little farther north and you'll find the still-underdeveloped beaches of **Playa La Penca** ✹ and, finally, **Playa Pan de Azúcar** ✹, or **Sugar Beach.**

ESSENTIALS

GETTING THERE & DEPARTING   By Plane   The nearest airport with regularly scheduled flights is in Tamarindo (see "Essentials," later in this chapter), although it is also possible to fly into Liberia (see earlier in this chapter). From either of these places, you can arrange for a taxi to drive you to any of these beaches. Playas Brasilito and Conchal are about 25 minutes from Tamarindo and 40 minutes from Liberia (add about 5 min. for Flamingo and 10 min. for Potrero). A taxi from Tamarindo should cost around $30 (£15), and between $40 and $50 (£20–£25) from Liberia.

By Car   There are two major routes to the beaches. The most direct is by way of the Tempisque River bridge. Take the Interamerican Highway west from San José. Forty-seven kilometers (29 miles) past the turnoff for Puntarenas, you'll see signs for the turnoff to the bridge. After crossing the Tempisque River, follow the signs for Nicoya, continuing north to Santa Cruz. About 16km (10 miles) north of Santa Cruz, just before the village of Belén, take the turnoff for playas Flamingo, Brasilito, and Potrero. After another 20km (12 miles), at the town of Huacas, take the right fork to reach these beaches. The drive takes about 4½ hours.

Alternatively, you can drive here via Liberia. When you reach Liberia, turn west and follow the signs for Santa Cruz and the various beaches. Just beyond the town of Belén, take the turnoff for playas Flamingo, Brasilito, and Potrero, and continue following the directions given above. This route takes around 5 hours.

By Bus   Tralapa express buses (© 221-7202) leave San José daily at 8 and 10:30am and 3pm from Calle 20 between avenidas 3 and 5, stopping at playas Brasilito, Flamingo, and Potrero, in that order. The ride takes around 5½ hours. A one-way ticket costs $6 (£3).

Alternatively, the same company's buses to Santa Cruz (© **680-0392**) connect with one of the several buses from Santa Cruz to Playa Potrero. Buses depart San José for Santa Cruz roughly every 2 hours between 7am and 6pm from Calle 20 between avenidas 3 and 5. Trip duration is around 4 hours; the fare is $3.80 (£1.90). From Santa Cruz, the ride is about 90 minutes; the fare is $1.30 (65p).

Gray Line (© **220-2126;** www.graylinecostarica.com) has a daily bus that leaves San José for Playa Flamingo at 7am. **Interbus** (© **283-5573;** www.interbusonline.com) has two daily buses that leave San José for Playa Flamingo at 7:45am and 2:30pm. Both companies charge $29 (£15), and will pick you up at most San José–area hotels.

Express buses depart **Playa Potrero** for San José at 3 and 9am and 2pm, stopping a few minutes later in playas Flamingo and Brasilito. Ask at your hotel where to catch the bus. Buses to **Santa Cruz** leave Potrero at regular intervals throughout the day and take about 90 minutes. If you're heading north toward Liberia, get off the bus at Belén and wait for a bus going north. Buses leave Santa Cruz for San José roughly every hour between 6am and 6pm.

GETTING AROUND   Economy Rent A Car (© 654-4543) has an office in Playa Flamingo.

ORIENTATION   The pavement ends just beyond Playa Conchal as you leave the small village of Brasilito. The rest of these beaches are strung out over several kilometers of rough dirt roads. Playa Flamingo is by far the most developed town in this region. There's a small collection of shops at the crossroads in the center of Playa Flamingo. Here you'll find a branch of the **Banco de Costa Rica,** as well as the **Santa Fe Pharmacy and Medical Center** (© 654-9000).

FUN ON & OFF THE BEACH

Playa Flamingo ✹✹ is a long and beautiful stretch of soft white sand, although the surf can sometimes get a bit rough here. There isn't much shade on the beach, so be sure to use plenty of sunscreen and bring an umbrella if you can. If you're not staying here, there are parking spots all along the beach road where you can park your car for the day—although remember to never leave anything of value inside.

Playa Potrero has the gentlest surf and, therefore, is the best swimming beach. However, the beach is made up of hard-packed dark sand that is much less appealing than that found at other spots mentioned here. The water at **Playa Brasilito** is often fairly calm, which makes it another good swimming choice.

Playa Conchal ✹✹, which is legendary for its crushed seashells, is also stunningly beautiful, but the drop-off is quite steep, making it notorious for its strong riptides. My favorites for a full day of swimming and sunbathing are **Playa La Penca** ✹ and **Playa Pan de Azúcar** ✹, both of which are north of Playa Potrero.

Tip: All beaches in Costa Rica are public property. But the land behind the beaches is not, and the Meliá company owns almost all of it in Playa Conchal, so the only public access is along the soft-sand road that follows the beach south from Brasilito (see below). Before the road reaches Conchal, you'll have to ford a small river and then climb a steep, rocky hill, so four-wheel-drive is recommended.

GOLF   The **Paradisus Playa Conchal** ✹✹ (🕿 654-4123) is home to an excellent golf course featuring a few wonderful views of the ocean. This Robert Trent Jones–designed resort course is open to the walk-in public from neighboring hotels and resorts. It costs $160 (£80) in greens fees for as many rounds as you can squeeze into 1 day, including a cart. If you tee off after 1pm, it's just $110 (£55).

HORSEBACK RIDING   You can arrange a horseback ride with the **Flamingo Equestrian Center** (🕿 654-4089), **Casagua Horses** (🕿 653-8041), or **Brasilito Excursions** (🕿 654-4237). This latter place works out of the Hotel Brasilito. Depending on the size of your group, it should cost between $10 and $20 (£5–£10) per person per hour.

LEARN THE LANGUAGE   The **Centro Panamericano de Idiomas** (🕿 654-5002; www.cpi-edu.com), which has schools in San José and Monteverde, recently opened a branch in Flamingo, across from the Flamingo Marina, facing Potrero Bay. A 1-week course with 4 hours of classes per day, including a home stay, costs $415 (£208). Longer course options are available.

SCUBA DIVING   Scuba diving is quite popular here. The **Edge Adventure Company** (🕿 654-4946; www.theedgeadventure.com) and **Costa Rica Diving** (🕿/fax 654-4148; www.costarica-diving.com) both have shops in Flamingo and offer trips to the Catalina and Bat islands for between $75 and $150 (£38–£75). Both also offer PADI certification courses, as well as multiday packages. Alternatively, you can check in at the **Flamingo Marina Resort Hotel and Club** (p. 175).

SPORTFISHING & SAILBOAT CHARTERS   Although the Flamingo Marina remains in a state of legal limbo and turmoil, you still have plenty of sportfishing and sailboat charter options here. Jim McKee, the former force behind the Flamingo Marina, manages a fleet of boats. Contact him via his company, **Oso Viejo** (🕿 827-5533; www.flamingobeachcr.com). A full-day fishing excursion costs between $500 and $1,400 (£250–£700), depending on the size and quality of the boat, and distance traveled to the fishing grounds. Half-day trips cost between $200 and $700 (£100–£350).

If you're looking for a full- or half-day sail or sunset cruise, check in with **Oso Viejo** (see above) to see what boats are available, or ask about the 52-foot cutter *Shannon.* The 52-foot ketch *Samonique III* (© **388-7870;** www.costarica-sailing.com) is another good option. Prices range from around $50 to $110 (£25–£55) per person, depending on the length of the cruise. Multiday trips are also available.

Alternatively, you can contact the **Edge Adventure Company** or the **Flamingo Marina Resort Hotel and Club.**

OTHER ADVENTURE TOURS   You can sign up for a **sea kayaking or surf trip** with **The Edge Adventure Company.** Alternatively, check in with the tour desk at the **Flamingo Marina Resort Hotel and Club,** which offers a host of tours to other nearby destinations, as well as hiking and rafting trips.

WHERE TO STAY

If you plan to be here for a while or are coming down with friends or a large family, you might want to consider renting a condo or house. For information and reservations, contact the folks at **Costal Properties** (© **654-4912;** www.coastalproperties.co.cr), **Emerald Shores Realty** (© **654-4554;** www.emeraldshoresrealty.net) or **Pacific Coast Realty** (© **654-5050;** www.flamingobeach.com).

VERY EXPENSIVE

Paradisus Playa Conchal 🐾🐾   This sprawling hotel is the largest all-inclusive resort in Costa Rica. From the massive open-air reception building down to the free-form swimming pool (allegedly the largest in Central America), everything here is on a grand scale. There's a small-village feel to the layout; most of the rooms are located in 30 separate two-story buildings, reached by way of constantly circulating shuttles. All rooms are suites and come with either one king-size bed or two double beds in a raised bedroom nook. Down below there's a comfortable sitting area, with a couch, coffee table, and chairs with ottomans. The bathrooms are large and modern, with marble tiles, full tubs, bidets, and a telephone. Each unit has a garden patio or a small balcony. Although the rooms are exactly the same, the Royal level suites come with private butler service and VIP attention. Only three of the building units actually front the ocean, and two of these contain the Presidential suites, which have double the living area of the standard suites and even more luxurious appointments. Unlike most all-inclusives, only one of the restaurants here is buffet; the rest are sit-down a la carte affairs, although they are still decidedly mediocre.

The hotel has a beautiful **golf course** 🐾🐾🐾, with broad, open holes, rolling hills, and the occasional sea view. Because of the golf course and its ponds and wetlands, there's good bird-watching here, with healthy populations of parrots, roseate spoon-bills, and wood storks. Because the hotel owns so much land behind Playa Conchal, guests here have almost exclusive access to this crushed-seashell beach.

Playa Conchal (A.P. 499-4005, San Antonio de Belén), Guanacaste. © **888/336-3542** in the U.S. or 654-4123. Fax 654-4181. www.solmelia.com. 406 suites. $398–$482 (£199–£241) double; $482–$792 (£241–£396) Royal suites; $990 (£495) Presidential suite. Rates include all meals, drinks, taxes, a wide range of activities, and use of nonmotorized land and watersports equipment. Golf and spa services extra. AE, MC, V. **Amenities:** 8 restaurants; 3 bars; 2 lounges; casino, dance club, massive free-form pool w/several Jacuzzis, and another large outdoor pool for Royal Level suites; Robert Trent Jones II–designed 18-hole golf course and pro shop; 4 lighted tennis courts; exercise room; modest exercise facilities and spa; watersports equipment rental; bike rental; children's programs; concierge; tour desk; car-rental desk; modest business center; shopping arcade; 24-hr. room service; in-room massage; babysitting; laundry service; nonsmoking rooms. *In room:* A/C, TV, free Wi-Fi, minibar, fridge, coffeemaker, hair dryer, safe.

EXPENSIVE

Bahía del Sol ⚜   This small-scale resort sits right on the water's edge at the heart of Playa Potrero. The rooms are all large and feature contemporary decor with bright primary colors at every turn, although the furnishings are rather sparse. All have either a private balcony or shared veranda, and most of these are strung with hammocks. They also have fully equipped studio and two-bedroom apartments that are a good bet for longer stays. The midsize pool is set in a small grassy lawn, just beyond the beach. The pool features a Jacuzzi above it, whose water cascades down a faux-waterfall into it. The large open-air restaurant serves fresh seafood and international fare, and offers wonderful views of Potrero Bay.

Playa Potrero, Guanacaste. ℂ **654-4671.** Fax 654-5182. www.potrerobay.com. 25 units. $140–$155 (£70–£78) double; $195–$310 (£98–£155) suite. Rates include breakfast. Rates lower in off season; higher during peak periods. AE, MC, V. **Amenities:** Restaurant; bar; large pool; small spa; tour desk; laundry service. In room: A/C, TV.

Flamingo Beach Resort ⚜   Located right across the road from the best section of beach at Playa Flamingo, this large, modern facility is the best full-service hotel in Flamingo. The resort has an enviable locations fronting a gorgeous section of Playa Flamingo. The hotel is constructed in a horseshoe shape around a large pool and opens out onto the ocean. Half of the rooms have clear views of the ocean across a narrow dirt road. I definitely prefer the pool and oceanview rooms. Others, which are termede "mountain view" rooms, aren't quite as desirable. All the rooms are clean and cool, with tile floors and comfortable bathrooms, although many were in need of some upkeep when I last visited. The junior suites and suites are larger and better equipped, with full size refrigerators, kitchenettes and 27-inch television sets. There is a casino on site for the adults, as well as a children's center and play room for the kids.

Playa Flamingo, Guanacaste. ℂ **654-4444.** Fax 654-4060. www.resortflamingobeach.com. 130 units. $129 (£65) double; $165 (£83) junior suite; $185–$260 (£93–£130) suite. Rates lower in off-season. AE, MC, V. **Amenities:** 2 restaurants; 2 bars; casino; large pool; outdoor lighted tennis court; exercise room; game room; tour desk; limited room service (6:30am–10pm); laundry service. In room: A/C, TV, minifridge, coffeemaker, hair dryer, safe.

Flamingo Marina Resort Hotel and Club ⚜   Located up the hill from the beach, the Flamingo Marina Hotel is a midsize resort with a good mix of facilities and amenities. This place was built in several phases, and there's no overall sense of coherence or grand plan here. Still, the entire complex has received steady upkeep and upgrading over the years. The rooms have white tile floors, bright bedspreads, and lots of light. The suites have leather couches and a wet bar in the seating area, as well as private whirlpool tubs. Condo units have full kitchenettes. All the rooms have patios or balconies, and most have pretty good bay views. This place caters to fishermen and scuba divers, and a host of tours and adventures are offered here.

Playa Flamingo (A.P. 321-1002, San José), Guanacaste. ℂ **800/276-7501** in the U.S. and Canada, or 654-4141. Fax 654-4035. www.flamingomarina.com. 45 units, 44 apts. $119–$139 (£60–£70) double; $169 (£85) suite; $180–$280 (£90–£140) apt. Rates lower in the off season, slightly higher during peak periods. AE, DC, MC, V. **Amenities:** Restaurant; snack bar; bar; 4 small pools; tennis court; exercise room; Jacuzzi; watersports equipment rental; tour desk; laundry service. In room: A/C, TV, free Wi-Fi, safe.

Hotel Sugar Beach ⚜⚜   Hotel Sugar Beach is on a beautiful, semiprivate salt-and-pepper beach about a 10-minute drive north of Playa Potrero along a rough dirt road. It's one of the only hotels in the area, and that's what gives it most of its charm, in my opinion—lots of seclusion and privacy. The beach is on a small cove surrounded by rocky hills. The hotel itself is perched above the water. Nature lovers will be thrilled to find howler monkeys and iguanas almost on their doorsteps. Snorkelers should be happy here too; this cove has some good snorkeling in the dry season. Although this is a longstanding hotel, the rooms, which come in a variety of sizes and configurations, have received a good amount of remodeling and upgrading in recent years, and several newer suites and deluxe rooms have been added. My favorite rooms are the ocean-front standard rooms, which have great views and easy access to the beach. However, the deluxe rooms and suites are larger and more luxurious, and some have excellent ocean views from their private balconies. If you don't land one of the rooms with a sea view, the main lodge and restaurant have commanding views from a hillside perch.

Playa Pan de Azúcar (A.P. 90, Santa Cruz), Guanacaste. © 654-4242. Fax 654-4239. www.sugar-beach.com. 30 units. $125–$155 (£63–£78) double; $195 (£98) suite. Rates include breakfast. Rates lower in off season. AE, MC, V. **Amenities:** Restaurant; bar; small kidney-shape pool set on the hillside; watersports equipment rental; tour desk; laundry service. *In room:* A/C, TV, minifridge, safe.

INEXPENSIVE

There is a string of inexpensive *cabinas* on the main road leading into Brasilito, just before you hit the beach. It's also possible to camp on playas Potrero and Brasilito. At the former, contact **Maiyra's** (© **654-4213**); at the latter, try **Camping Brasilito** (© **654-4452**). Both of these places offer some budget rooms as well. Each charges around $3 to $6 (£1.50–£3) per person to make camp and use the basic bathroom facilities, or around $10 to $12 (£5–£6) per person to stay in a rustic room.

Hotel Brasilito *Value*   This hotel, just across a sand road from the beach, offers basic small rooms that are quite clean and well maintained. There's also a bar and a big open-air restaurant that is excellent. Even with Playa Brasilito's glut of budget options, this is one of the best values in town and is the closest to the water. The best rooms have nice balconies with ocean views, and air-conditioning. The hotel rents snorkeling equipment, kayaks, body boards, and horses and can arrange a variety of tours.

Playa Brasilito, Santa Cruz, Guanacaste. © **654-4237**. Fax 654-4247. www.brasilito.com. 15 units. $38–$45 (£19–£23) double. Rates include taxes. V. **Amenities:** Restaurant; watersports equipment rental; tour desk; laundry service. *In room:* Free Wi-Fi, no phone.

WHERE TO DINE

In addition to the places listed below, you'll find good fresh seafood and international fare at **The Happy Snapper** (© **654-4413**) in Brasilito. And for more elegant dining, try **Mar y Sol** (© **654-4151**), located high on the hill above Flamingo.

Camarón Dorado ★ *Finds*   SEAFOOD   With a series of tables and kerosene torches set right in the sand just steps from the crashing surf, this is one of my favorite beach restaurants in the country. There are more tables in a simple, open-air dining room, for those who don't want sand in their shoes. The service is semiformal, and at times can be anything from lax to rude. The seafood is fresh, excellently prepared, and reasonably priced. When I asked to see the wine list, two waiters came over carrying about 12 different bottles between them.

Playa Brasilito © **654-4028**. Reservations recommended in high season. Main courses $6–$21 (£3–£11). MC, V. Daily 11am–10pm.

Marie's ★   COSTA RICAN/SEAFOOD   This is a great place for a quick bite or a leisurely sit-down meal. The menu has grown steadily over the years, although the best option here is always some simply prepared fresh fish, chicken, or meat. Check the blackboard for the daily specials, which usually highlight the freshest catch, such as mahimahi *(dorado),* marlin, and red snapper. You'll also find such Tico favorites as *casados* (rice-and-bean dish) and ceviche, as well as burritos and quesadillas. Marie's is a free Wi-Fi hotspot. At press time, Marie's is in a temporary space behind the old restaurant, awaiting construction of a new location inside a larger commercial complex on the old site. Marie's should be in its new home sometime in 2008.

Playa Flamingo. © 654-4136. Reservations recommended for dinner during the high season. Sandwiches $4–$7 (£2–£3.50); main courses $7–$20 (£3.50–£10). V. Daily 6:30am–9:30pm.

Mar y Sol ⭐⭐ *Finds* INTERNATIONAL/SEAFOOD   Seventh-generation Catalan chef Alain Taulere has prepared food for the likes of Henry Kissinger and Prince Rainier of Monaco. For visitors to his hilltop restaurant in Flamingo Beach, he offers a small, well-executed, and pricey selection of fresh seafood and meats. The ambience is casually formal, with the open-air main dining room dimly lit by old-fashioned lamp posts and covered by a thatched roof. Along with a surf-and-turf combo featuring filet mignon and either lobster tails or jumbo shrimp, menu highlights include rich and creamy lobster bisque, and a hearty bouillabaisse. I enjoyed the tender duck served with passion fruit-cognac sauce. For dessert, the chocolate volcano was a little disappointing, but the homemade tropical fruit ice creams are sweet and refreshing. Call in advance for free transportation from and back to your hotel.

Playa Flamingo. © 654-4151. Reservations recommended for dinner in high season. Main courses $14–$30 (£7–£15). AE, DC, MC, V. Nov–Apr daily 10am–3:30pm, 5–10pm; May–Aug daily 2–10pm. Closed Sept–Oct.

PLAYA FLAMINGO AFTER DARK

With both a disco and casino, **Amberes** is the undisputed hotspot in this area; however, there's also now a casino at the **Flamingo Beach Resort.** You might also see if there's any live music or sports events on the televisions at **The Happy Snapper** or **Outback Jack's Australian Road Kill Grill & Beach Bar** (at the Hotel Brasilito). All of the other beaches and towns here are rather quiet.

6 Playa Tamarindo ⭐ & Playa Grande ⭐⭐

295km (183 miles) NW of San José; 73km (45 miles) SW of Liberia

Tamarindo is the biggest boomtown in Guanacaste—and personally, I think the boom has gone a bit too far a bit too fast. The main road into Tamarindo has turned into a seemingly helter-skelter jumble of strip malls, surf shops, hotels and random restaurants. Ongoing development is spreading up the hills inland from the beach and south beyond Punta Langosta. None of it seems regulated or particularly planned out. However, once you get off the road, the beach itself is a long, wide swath of white sand that curves gently from one rocky headland to another.

Still, the wide range of accommodations, abundant restaurants and active nightlife, along with very dependable surf have made Tamarindo one of the most popular beaches on this coast. Fishing boats bob at their moorings and brown pelicans fish just beyond the breakers. A sandy islet off the southern end of the beach makes a great destination if you're a strong swimmer; if you're not, it makes a great foreground for sunsets. Tamarindo is popular with surfers, who ply the break right here or use the town as a jumping-off place for playas Grande, Langosta, Avellanas, and Negra.

Just to the north of Tamarindo lies **Playa Grande,** one of the principal nesting sites for the giant leatherback turtle, the largest turtle in the world. This beach is often too rough for swimming, but the well-formed and consistent beach break is very popular with surfers. I almost hate to mention places to stay in Playa Grande because the steady influx of tourists and development has apparently doomed it as a turtle-nesting site.

Behind all the beaches in this area are low, dry hills that can be a dreary brown in the dry season but that instantly turn green with the first brief showers of the rainy season.

ESSENTIALS

GETTING THERE & DEPARTING   By Plane   Sansa (© 290-4100; www. flysansa.com) has 10 daily flights to Tamarindo from San José's Juan Santamaría International Airport, with the first flight leaving at 5am and the last flight departing at 2:40pm. The flight takes 55 minutes. The fare is $82 (£41) each way. The frequency of flights decreases in the off season.

Nature Air (© 800/235-9272 in the U.S. and Canada, or 299-6000; www.natureair.com) flies to Tamarindo daily at 6:30, 8:40 and 10am and 2pm from Tobías Bolaños International Airport in Pavas. The fare is $88 (£44) each way. The flight takes 55 minutes. As at Sansa, the number of flights is often reduced and the schedule changes during the off season. Nature Air also has connections between Tamarindo and Arenal, Liberia and Quepos.

Whether you arrive on Sansa or Nature Air, a couple of cabs or minivans are always waiting for arriving flights. It costs $3 to $6 (£1.50–£3) for the ride into town.

Sansa flights leave Tamarindo for San José between 6am and 5:35pm. Nature Air flights leave for San José at 7:50 and 11am, and 2:55 and 3pm.

If you're flying into Liberia, a taxi should cost around $40 to $60 (£20–£30). Alternately, you can use **Tamarindo Shuttle** (© 653-0885; www.tamarindoshuttle.com), which charges $15 (£7.50) per person.

By Car   The most direct route is by way of the Tempisque River bridge. Take the Interamerican Highway west from San José. Forty-seven kilometers (29 miles) past the turnoff for Puntarenas, you'll see signs for the turnoff to the bridge. After crossing the river, follow the signs for Nicoya and Santa Cruz. Continue north out of Santa Cruz, until just before the village of Belén, where you will find the turnoff for Tamarindo. In another 20km (12 miles) take the left fork for Playa Tamarindo at Huacas and continue on until the village of Villareal, where you make your final turn into Tamarindo. The trip should take around 4½ hours.

You can save a little time, especially in the dry season, by taking a more direct but rougher route: You turn left just after passing the main intersection for Santa Cruz at the turnoff for playas Junquillal and Ostional. The road is paved until the tiny village of Veintesiete de Abril. From here, it's about 20km (12 miles) on a rough dirt road until the village of Villareal, where you make your final turn into Tamarindo.

Alternatively, you can drive here via Liberia. When you reach Liberia, turn west and follow the signs for Santa Cruz and the various beaches. Just beyond the town of Belén, take the turnoff for playas Flamingo, Brasilito, and Tamarindo, and then follow the directions for the second option above. This route takes around 5½ hours.

By Bus   Alfaro express buses (© 222-2160) leave San José daily for Tamarindo at 8:30 and 11:30am and 3:30pm, departing from Calle 14 between avenidas 3 and 5. **Tralapa** (© 221-7202) also has one daily direct bus to Tamarindo leaving at 4pm from their main terminal at Calle 20 between avenidas 3 and 5. The trip takes 5 hours, and the one-way fare is around $5.50 (£2.25).

Alternatively, you can catch a bus to Santa Cruz from the either of the above bus companies. Buses leave both stations for Santa Cruz roughly every hour between 6am

Tamarindo

DINING ◆
Cala Moresco **5**
Dragonfly Bar & Grill **20**
Fiesta del Mar **11**
Fish & Meat **16**
La Laguna del
   Cocodrilo Bistro **31**
Nogui's Sunset Café **13**
Pachanga **18**
Sunset Lounge **13**
Taboo **2**

ATTRACTIONS ●
Agua Rica Diving Center **24**
Hightide Adventures **15**
Iguana Surf **9, 26**
Papagayo Excursions **24**
Tamarindo Tennis Club **23**
Tamarindo Tour/Rentals **29**
Wayra Instituto de Español **8**

NIGHTLIFE ●
Babylon **10**
Barceló Playa
   Langosta Casino **1**
Jazz Casino **24**
Mambo **12**
Monkey Bar **30**

ACCOMMODATIONS ■
Best Western Tamarindo
   Vista Villas **30**
Cabinas Arco Iris **17**
Cabinas Dolly **28**
Cabinas Marielos **27**
Cabinas Zully Mar **14**
El Diriá **25**
Hostel La Botella de Leche **21**
Hotel and Villas Cala Luna **5**
Hotel Capitán Suizo **6**
Hotel El Jardín del Edén **22**
Hotel Pasatiempo **19**
Sueño del Mar **4**
Tito's Camping **7**
Villa Alegre **3**

PACIFIC OCEAN

To Airport

Isla
Capitán

Punta
San Francisco

Playa
Tamarindo

Playa
Langosta

NICARAGUA
Caribbean
Sea
Monteverde
San José
COSTA
RICA
Tamarindo
PACIFIC
OCEAN
PANAMA
100 mi
100 km

and 6pm. The trip's duration is 4 hours; the one-way fare is around $4.80 (£2.40). Buses leave Santa Cruz (© **680-0392**) for Tamarindo roughly every 1½ hours between 6am and 6pm; the one-way fare is $1.60 (80p).

Gray Line (© **220-2126;** www.graylinecostarica.com) has a daily bus that leaves San José for Tamarindo at 7am. **Interbus** (© **283-5573;** www.interbusonline.com) has two daily buses that leave San José for Tamarindo at 7:45am and 2:30pm. Both companies charge $29 (£15) and will pick you up at most San José–area hotels.

Direct buses leave Tamarindo for San José daily at 3:30 and 5:45am and 2 and 4pm. Buses to Santa Cruz leave roughly every 1½ hours between 6am and 6pm. In Santa Cruz you can transfer to one of the frequent San José buses.

ORIENTATION   The road leading into town runs parallel to the beach and ends in a small cul-de-sac just past Zully Mar. A couple of side roads off this main road lead farther on, to playas Langosta, Avellanas, and Negra. You'll find several of the newer hotels mentioned below off these side roads.

FAST FACTS   The local **police** can be reached at © **653-0283.** There's a **Banco Nacional** (© **653-0376**) branch at the little mall across from El Diria, and a branch of the **Banco de Costa Rica** (© **653-1852**) in the Plaza Conchal mall. There are also several Internet cafes and a couple of pharmacies in town. You'll find the **Mariposa Laundry** (no phone) just past the turnoff for Playa Langosta.

GETTING AROUND   For a rental car, **Adobe** (© 653-0031), **Alamo** (© 800/ 432-5266, or 653-0727), **Budget** (© 653-4381), **Economy** (© 653-0728), **Hertz** (© 653-1358), **Payless** (© 653-0015), and **Thrifty** (© 653-0829) have offices in Tamarindo.

The town itself is very compact and you should be able to walk most places. If you need to, you can call a **taxi** at © **653-0751,** 834-4075, or 653-0586.

FUN ON & OFF THE BEACH

Tamarindo is a long, white-sand beach. Still, you have to be careful when and where you swim. The calmest water and best swimming are always down at the far southern end of the beach, toward Punta Langosta. Much of the sea in just off the busiest part of the town is best for surfing. When there's any swell, you'll find scores of surfers in the water here. Be careful: there are rocks just offshore in several places, some of which are exposed only at low tide. An encounter with one of these rocks could be nasty, especially if you're bodysurfing. I also advise that you avoid swimming near the estuary mouth, where the currents can carry you out away from the beach.

BIKING   Bikes are available for rent at several locations in Tamarindo. Check around; you'll probably find your best bikes at the **Blue Trax Bike Shop** ✦ (© **653-1705;** www.bluetraxcr.com), who rent everything from single gear beach cruisers for $10 (£5) per day, to high end Trek and Specialized mountain bikes for between $20 and $50 per day (£10–£25). These folks also offer guided mountain bike tours and excursions.

FOUR-WHEELING   **Hightide Adventures** (© **653-0108;** www.tamarindoadventures. net) has a fleet of four-wheel-drive all-terrain vehicles. They're available for the day ($99/£50) and half-day ($60/£30). A variety of guided ATV tours range in duration from 1 to 8 hours and in price from $40 to $140 (£20–£70) per person. This company also rents dirt bikes, snorkel equipment, surf and boogie boards, and jet skis and offers a full menu of other guided tours around the region.

> **Tips** **Yo Quiero Hablar Español**
>
> If you want to try an intensive immersion program or just brush up on your rusty high school Spanish, check in with the folks at **Wayra Instituto de Español** (©/fax **653-0359**; www.spanish-wayra.co.cr). This place is located up a side street from Iguana Surf.

GOLF   Hacienda Pinilla 🏌🏌 (© **680-7000**; www.haciendapinilla.com) is a beautiful 18-hole links-style course located south of Tamarindo. Hotel and residential development here is still in its infancy. The course is currently accepting golfers staying at hotels around the area, with advance reservation. Greens fees run around $150 for 18 holes, including a cart. Many folks staying in Tamarindo also play at the **Paradisus Playa Conchal** 🏌🏌, an excellent resort course (p. 174).

HORSEBACK RIDING   Although some will be disappointed, I think it's a very good thing that horses are no longer allowed on the beach. However, you'll find plenty of opportunities to ride in the hills and forests around Tamarindo. You can go riding with **Casagua Horses** 🐎 (© 653-8041), **Hightide Adventures** (© 653-0108; www.tamarindoadventures.net), **Iguana Surf** (© 653-0148; www.iguanasurf.net), or **Papagayo Excursions** (©/fax 653-0254; www.papagayoexcursions.com). Rates for horse rental, with a guide, are around $15 to $30 (£7.50–£15) per hour.

SAILBOAT CHARTERS   There are several boats offering cruises offshore from Tamarindo; the 50-foot schooner *Lemuria* (© **831-8875**; www.tamarindosailing.com), and the 40-foot catamaran *Blue Dolphin* (© **653-0867**; www.sailbluedolphin.com) are both good choices. Options range from sunset cruises to weeklong trips out to Isla del Coco. A half-day snorkel or shorter sunset cruise should cost $50 to $70 (£25–£35) per person, and a full day should run between $75 and $110 (£38–£55) per person. This usually includes an open bar and snacks on the half-day and sunset cruises, and all of that plus lunch on the full-day trip.

SCUBA DIVING   If you want to do any scuba diving or snorkeling while you're here, check in with **Agua Rica Diving Center** 🤿 (© 653-0094; www.aguarica.net). These folks are the best and longest running operators in Tamarindo, and have a full-service dive shop. They offer day trips, multiday dive cruises, and the standard resort and full-certification courses.

SPORTFISHING   A host of captains offer anglers a chance to go after the "big ones" that abound in the waters offshore here. From the Tamarindo estuary, it takes only 20 minutes to reach the edge of the continental shelf, where the waters are filled with mostly marlin and sailfish. Although fishing is good all year, the peak season for billfish is between mid-April and August. You can contact **Tamarindo Sportfishing** (© 653-0090; www.tamarindosportfishing.com) or **Capullo Sportfishing** (© 653-0048; www.capullo.com).

TENNIS   You can rent court time and equipment at the **Tamarindo Tennis Club** (© 653-0898), which features two lighted outdoor courts located on the back road on the way to the Hotel El Jardín del Edén. It is open from 6am to 10pm, and court time runs $15 (£7.50) per hour. You can also play out at **Hacienda Pinilla** (see above) for $5 (£2.50) per hour during the day, and $10 (£5) per hour at night.

TOURS GALORE **Hightide Adventures, Papagayo Excursions,** and **Iguana Surf** (see above for all) all offer a host of tour and activity options. Papagayo Excursions probably offers the widest selection of full- and multiday trips, including outboard or kayak tours through the nearby estuary and mangroves, excursions to Santa Cruz and Guaitíl, raft floats on the Corobicí River, and tours to Palo Verde and Rincón de la Vieja national parks. Rates run between $30 and $140 (£15–£70), depending on the length of the tour and group size.

There's no longer a canopy tour available right in Tamarindo. Both the **Santa Rosa Canopy Tour** (© 653-0926) and **Cartagena Canopy Tour** (© 675-0801) are nearby. Both charge $35 per person. Of these two, I recommend the Cartagena tour, which has a much more lush forest setting, but I think your best bet is to take a day trip to Hacienda Guachipelin (p. 156) and do the "Canyon Tour" there.

WATCHING NESTING SEA TURTLES On nearby **Playa Grande,** leatherback sea turtles nest between early October and mid-February. The turtles come ashore to lay their eggs only at night. During the nesting season, you'll be inundated with opportunities to sign up for nightly tours, which usually cost $35 to $50 (£18–£25) per person. No flash photography or flashlights are allowed because any sort of light can confuse the turtles and prevent them from laying their eggs; guides must use red-tinted flashlights.

Note: Turtle nesting is a natural, unpredictable, and increasingly rare event. Moreover, things have gotten worse in recent years. The number of nesting turtles was down severely in 2007. All indications are that excessive building and lighting close to the beach are the culprits. Even during heavy nesting years you sometimes have to wait your turn for hours, hike quite a ways, and even accept the possibility that no nesting mothers will be spotted that evening.

If your hotel can't set it up for you, you'll see signs all over town offering tours. Make sure you go with someone licensed and reputable. Do-it-yourselfers can drive over to Playa Grande and book a tour directly with the **National Parks Service** (© 653-0470; $13/£6.50). The Parks Service operates out of a small shack just before the beach, across from the hotel Las Tortugas. It opens each evening at around 6pm to begin taking reservations. They sometimes answer their phone during the day, and it's best to make a reservation in advance because only a limited number of people are allowed on the beach at one time. Spots fill up fast, and if you don't have a reservation, you may have to wait until really late, or you may not be able to go out onto the beach.

WATERSPORTS If you want to try snorkeling, surfing, or sea kayaking while in Tamarindo, **Iguana Surf** and **Hightide Adventures** (see above) both rent snorkeling equipment, boogie boards, sea kayaks, and surfboards. They have half-day and hourly rates for many of these items.

If you want to learn to catch a wave while in Tamarindo, check in with the **Tamarindo Surf School** (© 653-0923; www.tamarindosurfschool.com) or **Witch's Rock Surf Camp** ⊀ (© 653-1262; www.witchsrocksurfcamp.com).

WHERE TO STAY IN TOWN

In addition to the hotels listed below, Tamarindo and Playa Grande have a wide range of beach houses and condos for rent by the night, the week, or the month. For more information on this option, check out **Remax Tamarindo** (© 653-0073; www.remax-oceansurf-cr.com) or **Century 21** (© 866/978-4492 in the U.S. and Canada, or 653-0030 in Costa Rica; www.c21tamarindo.com).

EXPENSIVE

El Diriá 👈 This is Tamarindo's oldest and largest beachfront resort. Wedged into a narrow piece of land planted with tropical gardens and palm trees, the Diriá has an enviable spot, smack dab in the middle of Tamarindo's long beach. Regular remodeling and new construction have kept it in good shape. The rooms in the main building are done in contemporary pastel colors with red-tile floors. Some have separate seating areas, and all come with a small bathroom. I especially recommend the second- and third-floor "sunset deluxe" rooms, which feature oceanview private balconies. However, some rooms are across the street from the beach, so be sure you know what type of room you are booking when you reserve. The central location and modern rooms make this an excellent choice in town, although service here can be spotty. The hotel has several swimming pools, as well as a lighted outdoor tennis court. They also have a large, open-air amphitheater that they use for weddings, private parties and the occasional public concert.

Playa Tamarindo (A.P. 476-1007, San José), Guanacaste. (✆ 653-0031. Fax 653-0848. www.tamarindodiria.com. 182 units. $137–$178 (£69–£89) double. Rates include breakfast buffet. Rates lower in off season. AE, MC, V. **Amenities:** 2 restaurants; 2 bars; 3 pools; watersports equipment rental; game room; tour desk; car-rental desk; laundry service. *In room:* A/C, TV, minibar (in some units), fridge, hair dryer, safe.

Hotel and Villas Cala Luna 👈👈 If you're looking for serious luxury in Tamarindo, stay in one of the two- or three-bedroom villas here, which are the size of a small home and just as well equipped. The living rooms are huge, with high-peaked ceilings, couches, tables and chairs, satellite televisions, and complete sound systems. The full kitchens come with microwave ovens and cappuccino machines—even washing machines. If this isn't enough, each villa has its own private swimming pool. The bedrooms are spacious and elegant, with either a king-size bed or two double beds. Everything is done in soft pastels with hand-painted accents, and the red-tile roofs and Mexican tile floors add elegance while keeping things cool. Rooms in the hotel are spacious and similarly well done, with their own terraces, but you'll have to share the hotel's main swimming pool with the rest of the guests. The hotel isn't right on the beach; you have to cross the street and walk a short path to reach the ocean.

Playa Tamarindo, Guanacaste. (✆ 653-0214. Fax 653-0213. www.calaluna.com. 20 units, 18 villas. $185 (£93) double; $370–$470 (£185–£24) villa. Rates for rooms, but not villas, include continental breakfast. Rates lower in off season; slightly higher during peak weeks. AE, MC, V. **Amenities:** 2 restaurants; bar; large free-form pool w/poolside bar; watersports equipment rental; bike rental; tour desk; limited room service (6am–10pm); in-room massage; babysitting; laundry service; free Wi-Fi. *In room:* A/C, TV, minibar, hair dryer, safe.

Hotel Capitán Suizo 👈👈 *Kids* This well-appointed beachfront hotel sits on the quiet southern end of Tamarindo. The rooms are housed in a series of two-story buildings. The lower rooms have air-conditioning and private patios; the upper units have plenty of cross ventilation, ceiling fans, and cozy balconies. All have large bathrooms and sitting rooms with fold-down futon couches. In effect, all the rooms are really suites, with separate sitting/living room areas. The spacious bungalows are spread around the shady grounds; these all come with a tub in the bathroom and an inviting outdoor shower among the trees. The hotel's free-form pool is quite nice. The shallow end slopes in gradually, imitating a beach, and there's also a separate children's pool. Perhaps the greatest attribute here is that it's just

steps from one of the calmer and more isolated sections of Playa Tamarindo, making it a good family pick.

Playa Tamarindo, Guanacaste. ⓒ 653-0353 or 653-0075. Fax 653-0292. www.hotelcapitansuizo.com. 22 units, 8 bungalows. $175–$195 (£88–£98) double; $235–$275 (£118–£138) bungalow; $360 (£180) suite. Rates include breakfast buffet. Rates lower in off season; higher during peak periods. AE, MC, V. **Amenities:** Restaurant; bar; midsize pool and children's pool; small exercise room; tour desk; babysitting; laundry service. *In room:* Minifridge, coffeemaker, safe.

Hotel El Jardín del Edén ⭑   It isn't right on the beach, but this is one of the more luxurious and stylish hotels in Tamarindo. The French owners bring a touch of sophistication that's often lacking at beach hotels in Costa Rica. There are splendid views from many of the guest rooms, which are in Mediterranean-style buildings on a hill 136m (446 ft.) from and high above the beach. Most have been remodeled in the past few years, and there are a couple dozen new rooms to boot. Almost all have balconies or private terraces with views of the Pacific. The large stone-tiled terraces, in particular, give you the sense that you're staying at your own private villa.

Playa Tamarindo, Guanacaste. ⓒ **653-0137.** Fax 653-0111. www.jardindeleden.com. 36 units, 2 apts. $120–$160 (£60–£80) double; $145–$190 (£73–£85) apt or suite. Rates include full breakfast. Rates lower in off season; higher during peak weeks. AE, MC, V. **Amenities:** Restaurant; bar; 2 small adjoining pools; small exercise room; Jacuzzi; tour desk; limited room service (8am–5pm); laundry service. *In room:* A/C, TV, minibar, hair dryer, safe.

Sueño del Mar ⭑ *(Finds*   Located on Playa Langosta, Sueño del Mar has charming little touches and innovative design: four-poster beds made from driftwood; African dolls on the windowsills; Kokopeli candleholders; and open-air showers with sculpted angelfish, hand-painted tiles, and lush tropical plants. Fabrics are from Bali and Guatemala. Somehow all of this works well together, and the requisite chairs and lounges nestled under shade trees right on the beach add the crowning touch.

The two casitas have their own kitchens, veranda, and sleeping loft. The honeymoon suite is a spacious second-floor room, with wraparound screened-in windows, a delightful open-air bathtub and shower, and an ocean view. The beach right out front is rocky and a bit rough, but it does reveal some nice, quiet tidal pools at low tide; it's one of the better sunset-viewing spots in Costa Rica. Breakfasts are huge, elaborate, and delicious. No children under 12 are allowed unless your party rents out the whole hotel.

Playa Tamarindo, Guanacaste. ⓒ/fax **653-0284.** www.sueno-del-mar.com. 4 units, 2 casitas. $195 (£98) double; $220–$295 (£110–£148) suite or casita. Rates include full breakfast. Rates lower in off season; higher during peak periods. MC, V. **Amenities:** Small pool; free use of snorkel equipment and boogie boards; tour desk; laundry service. *In room:* A/C, free Wi-Fi, safe.

Villa Alegre   This small bed-and-breakfast on Playa Langosta is a well-located and homey option. The owners' years of globetrotting have inspired them to decorate each room in the theme of a different country. In the main house, Guatemala, Mexico, and the United States are all represented. Of these, Mexico is the most spacious, with a recently expanded open-air bathroom and shower. The smallest are Guatemala and the California casita. The latter room is quite small, in fact. Every room has its own private patio, courtyard, or balcony. The villas are spacious and luxurious, with kitchenettes. My favorite is the Japanese unit, with its subtle design touches and great woodwork. The Russian villa and the United States rooms are truly wheelchair accessible and equipped, with ramps and modified bathrooms with handrails. The beach is just 91m (298 ft.) away through the trees. Breakfasts are delicious and abundant.

Playa Tamarindo, Guanacaste. ⓒ **653-0270.** Fax 653-0287. www.villaalegrecostarica.com. 5 units; 2 villas. $170–$185 (£85–£93) double; $230 (£115) villa. Rates include full breakfast. AE, MC, V. **Amenities:** Small pool. *In room:* A/C, free Wi-Fi, safe, no phone.

MODERATE

Best Western Tamarindo Vista Villas   This place was originally conceived as a condo project and then was converted into a hotel and taken over by a local surfer and business man and now is marketed as part of the Best Western chain. There's a wide range of accommodations here, from the simple garden-view rooms to the Tropical and Corona suites. The former are basic budget motel-like affairs. The latter are split-level one-bedroom affairs with full kitchens, large living rooms (with two couches that can double as single beds), and either a private patio or a balcony with fabulous views of the Pacific Ocean. This hotel really caters to surfers, and there is often a lively, beach-party at spring break–like atmosphere around the pool and at the bar here.

Playa Tamarindo, Guanacaste. © 800/536-3241 in the U.S. and Canada, or 653-0114 in Costa Rica. Fax 653-0115. www.tamarindovistavillas.com. 33 units. $89–$119 (£45–£60) double; $139–$229 (£70–£115) suite. Rates lower in off season; higher during peak periods. AE, DC, MC, V. **Amenities:** Restaurant; bar; midsize free-form pool w/swim-up bar and a waterfall; tour desk; laundry service; free Wi-Fi. *In room:* A/C, TV, safe.

Hotel Pasatiempo *Value*   A longstanding and highly dependable option, this hotel is set back from the beach a couple of hundred meters in a grove of shady trees. Most rooms are housed in duplex buildings, but each room has its own private patio with a hammock or chairs. Every room has plenty of space, and all have received regular upkeep and remodeling over the years. The two suites are very comfortable and well equipped. Each room bears the name of a different beach, and the bedroom walls feature hand-painted murals. A small yet very inviting pool sits in the center of the complex. The restaurant serves excellent fresh fish, as well as pizza and Tex-Mex specialties. This popular rancho-style affair also has a pool table, a nightly happy hour, cable TV with live sporting events, good snacks, and occasional live music.

Playa Tamarindo, Santa Cruz, Guanacaste. © 653-0096. Fax 653-0275. www.hotelpasatiempo.com. 17 units. $79–$99 (£40–£50) double. Rates slightly lower in off season; slightly higher during peak periods. AE, MC, V. **Amenities:** Restaurant; bar; midsize pool; tour desk, laundry service; free Wi-Fi. *In room:* A/C, safe, no phone.

INEXPENSIVE

In addition to the *cabinas* listed below, **Tito's Camping** (no phone), out toward the Hotel Capitán Suizo in Tamarindo, costs $3 to $5 (£1.50–£2.50) per person. **Cabinas Dolly** (© 653-0017), a perennial budget favorite and decidedly basic, still has the best location right on the beach in the center of town. Also, **Cabinas Arco Iris** (© 653-0330; www.hotelarcoiris.com) and **Hostal La Botella de Leche** (© 653-0189; www.labotelladeleche.com) are two popular, if slightly inland, options.

Cabinas Marielos   This place is located up a palm-shaded driveway across the road from the beach. Rooms are clean and well maintained, although most are small and simply furnished. Most have air-conditioning. Some of the bathrooms are quite small, but they're clean. There's a kitchen that guests can use, and the lush gardens are beautiful and provide some welcome shade. Common verandas and balconies are cool places to sit and read a book. The staff and owners are incredibly helpful and will make you feel like part of the family—in fact many of them are already family to each other.

Playa Tamarindo, Guanacaste. ©/fax 653-0141. www.cabinasmmarieloscr.com. 20 units. $40–$55 (£20–£28) double. Rates lower in off season. AE, MC, V. **Amenities:** Tour desk; surfboard rentals. *In room:* No phone.

Cabinas Zully Mar   The Zully Mar has long been a favorite of budget travelers, although they've been steadily upgrading their rooms and upping their prices over the years. The best rooms here are in a two-story white-stucco building with a wide, curving staircase on the outside. They have air-conditioning, tile floors, long verandas or balconies, overhead or standing fans, large bathrooms, and doors that are hand-carved with pre-Columbian motifs. The older, less expensive rooms are smaller and darker and just have ceiling fans. There is a small free-form pool that's refreshing if you don't want to walk across the street to the beach, although there's not much landscaping or shade around it. This place is smack dab in the center of things, and noise can be a problem at times.

Tamarindo, Guanacaste. (© **653-0140.** Fax 653-0028. www.zullymar.com. 25 units. $50–$69 (£25–£35) double. Rates lower in off season; higher during peak periods. AE, MC, V. **Amenities:** Restaurant; small pool; laundry service. *In room:* Minifridge, no phone.

WHERE TO STAY IN PLAYA GRANDE

In addition to the places listed below, **Hotel Bula Bula** ✦ (© **877/658-2880** in the U.S. and Canada, or 653-0975 in Costa Rica; www.hotelbulabula.com) is another excellent inland option, while the **Playa Grande Surf Camp** (© **653-1074;** www.playagrandesurfcamp.com) is geared toward surfers and budget travelers.

Hotel Las Tortugas ✦ *(Finds)*   Playa Grande is best known for the leatherback turtles that nest here, and much of the beach is now part of Las Baulas National Park, which was created to protect the turtles. However, this beach is also very popular with surfers, who make up a large percentage of the clientele at this beachfront hotel. Several of the rooms are quite large, and most have interesting stone floors and shower stalls. The upper suite has a curving staircase that leads to its second room. A few canoes on the nearby estuary are available for gentle paddling among the mangroves.

The owners led the fight to have the area declared a national park and continue to do everything possible to protect the turtles. As part of the hotel's turtle-friendly design, a natural wall of shrubs and trees shields the beach from the restaurant's light and noise, and the swimming pool is fittingly shaped like a turtle. These folks also have a collection of fully equipped apartments located a few blocks inland from the water, and available for weekly or monthly rental.

Playa Grande (A.P. 164, Santa Cruz), Guanacaste. (© **653-0423** or (©/fax 653-0458. www.lastortugashotel.com. 12 units. $50–$80 (£25–£40) double; $120 (£60) suite. Rates lower in off season; slightly higher during peak weeks. V (5% surcharge). **Amenities:** Restaurant; bar; small pool; Jacuzzi. *In room:* A/C, no phone.

Ripjack Inn ✦   This hotel is located about 100m (328 ft.) inland from the beach, which is reached via a short path. The rooms are all clean and cool, with tile floors, air-conditioning, and private bathrooms. The rooms come in several sizes and a mix of bed arrangements. They feature various Indonesian-inspired and imported design touches. The hotel's restaurant and bar, which is located on the second floor of the octagonal main building, is one of the best restaurants in Playa Grande. The hotel has a large yoga studio, with regular classes for guests and the local community.

Playa Grande, Guanacaste. (© **800/808-4605** in the U.S. and Canada, or 653-0480 in Costa Rica. Fax 653-0575. www.ripjackinn.com. 8 units. $75–$85 (£38–£43) double. Rates lower in off season; slightly higher during peak weeks. MC, V. **Amenities:** Restaurant; bar; laundry service. *In room:* A/C, coffeemaker, no phone.

WHERE TO DINE

Tamarindo has a glut of stylish and creative restaurants. **Nogui's Sunset Café** (© **653-0029**) is one of the more popular places in town—and rightly so. This simple open-air cafe just off the beach on the small traffic circle serves hearty breakfasts and well-prepared salads, sandwiches, burgers, and casual meals. In the evenings—actually, beginning a bit before sunset—the second floor here becomes the **Sunset Lounge** ✦, serving up a regularly changing menu of international tapas, small entrees, and sunset views. The **Cala Moresco** ☆ (② 653-0214) restaurant, at the Hotel and Villas Cala Luna (p. 183), is the place to go if you're looking for some good Italian and Mediterranean cuisine served up in an elegant open-air atmosphere. The folks here at Cala Luna also have a new sushi bar, **La Caletta. Pachanga** ☆☆ (② 653-7983) is a perennially popular option specializing in fresh seafood and eclectic fare prepared with Mediterranean flair, while **Fish & Meat** ☆ (② 653-0535) is a dinner-only restaurant serving everything from sushi to grilled lamb chops.

At Playa Grande, try **Upstairs** ☆, the restaurant at the Ripjack Inn (see above), or **The Great Waltini's** ☆, at the Hotel Bula Bula (see above). Both are excellent restaurants serving fresh seafood and prime meats, cooked with care and creativity.

Dragonfly Bar & Grill ☆☆ INTERNATIONAL/FUSION

Tucked away on a back street, this restaurant has garnered fast praise and a loyal following with its excellent food and cozy ambience. The menu mixes and matches several cuisines, with the Southwestern United States and Pacific Rim fusion as the strongest influences. There are daily fish and seafood specials, which might range from wood-fired red snapper to pistachio crusted mahimahi. If you're in the mood for a steak, try the shiitake-crusted filet mignon served with a goat cheese bread pudding. The restaurant space itself is a simple open-air affair, with a concrete floor and rough wood tree trunks as support columns. There's an open wood-fired grill and oven on one side, and a popular bar toward the back. They even offer free Wi-Fi throughout the restaurant.

Down a dirt road behind the Hotel Pasatiempo. ② 653-1506. Reservations recommended. Main courses $9–$14 (£4.50–£7). AE, MC, V. Mon–Sat 6–10pm.

Fiesta del Mar SEAFOOD/COSTA RICAN

A popular local spot, located just across from the beach, on the popular traffic circle near the center of town, Fiesta del Mar specializes in seafood, steaks and chicken cooked over a raging wood fire and coals. Try the grilled steak or whole fish in garlic sauce. They also have typical Costa Rican–style roast chicken. The open-air dining area is edged with greenery and has a thatch roof, so it feels very tropical. There's live music by a local marimba band most nights. This is also a good place for an inexpensive Costa Rican breakfast.

On the traffic circle, at the end of the main road. ② 653-0914. Reservations not necessary. Main courses $4–$18 (£2–£9). MC, V. Daily 8am–11pm.

La Laguna del Cocodrilo Bistro ☆☆ INTERNATIONAL/FUSION

Yet another option for fine dining and fusion cuisine, this small open-air restaurant has impressed me every time I've eaten here. When weather permits, more tables are set up under the trees in their beachfront garden area. Beautiful presentations and creative use of ingredients are the norm here. The menu changes regularly, but the chefs always focus on using on the freshest and best ingredients available. Be sure to save room for dessert, as they are always excellent. One of the best ways to go here is to simply opt for the nightly tasting menu, which will feature anywhere from 5 to 7 courses, including dessert. The restaurant has a good wine list, and they keep their bottles properly cool, to compensate for the often unforgiving heat of Guanacaste.

On the main road, toward the north end of Tamarindo. ② 653-3897. Reservations recommended. Main courses $12–$25 (£6–£13). MC, V. Mon–Sat 7:30am–9pm.

Taboo ☆☆ *Finds* INTERNATIONAL

Located in a small shopping center on the main road into Playa Langosta, this open-air place has the feel of a contemporary urban bistro—if you ignore the tropical heat and overhead ceiling fans. The chalkboard menu changes regularly, but always features a broad mix of appetizers and main dishes to choose from. I've enjoyed everything from lobster and conch rolls wrapped in bacon to duck breast in a mango reduction. The wine list here is broad and fairly priced.

On the main road, Playa Langosta. ℂ **653-1422.** Reservations recommended. Main courses $10–$44 (£5–£22). MC, V. Mon–Sat noon–3pm and 6–10pm; Sun 3–10pm.

TAMARINDO AFTER DARK

As a popular surfer destination, Tamarindo has a sometimes raging nightlife. The most happening bars in town are **Babylon** and **Mambo.** Other popular spots that go off throughout the week include the **Monkey Bar** at the Best Western Vista Villas, and the bar at the **Hotel Pasatiempo** (p. 185). Both of these places have televisions for sporting events and sometimes feature live music.

For those looking for some gaming, there are two casinos in town: the **Jazz Casino,** across from the El Diriá hotel, and the casino at the **Barceló Playa Langosta** resort.

EN ROUTE SOUTH: PLAYA AVELLANAS & PLAYA NEGRA

Heading south from Tamarindo are several as-yet-undeveloped beaches, most of which are quite popular with surfers. Beyond Tamarindo and Playa Langosta are **Playa Avellanas** and **Playa Negra,** both with a few basic *cabinas* catering to surfers.

If you are in Avellanas, be sure to stop at **Lola's** ✦✦ (ℂ **658-8097**), a laid-back restaurant and bar right on the beach, whose namesake giant pet pig is a local legend. Lola's is particularly popular on Sundays, when Tamarindo locals and expats pack the tables here in a weekly informal community get-together.

WHERE TO STAY

In addition to the places listed below, the **Mono Congo Lodge** (ℂ **658-8261;** www.monocongolodge.com), located just outside of Playa Negra, is a rustically comfortable option in a lush, forested setting a few hundred yards from the water.

Cabinas Las Olas   This collection of duplex cabins is a popular surf lodge set in the shade of some tall trees, a couple hundred meters inland from the beach and bordering a mangrove reserve. The rooms are simple but clean and are a good value. Each comes with a private little veranda with a table and some chairs and a hammock. The beach is a long stretch of almost always uncrowded white sand. There are good beach breaks for surfers up and down the shoreline, especially toward the northern end and the Langosta estuary. Mountain bikes and sea kayaks are available for rent.

Playa Avellanas, Santa Cruz, Guanacaste. ℂ **658-8315.** Fax 658-8331. www.cabinaslasolas.co.cr. 10 units. $70 (£35) double. Rates lower in off season. MC, V. **Amenities:** Restaurant; bar; laundry service. *In room:* No phone.

Hotel Playa Negra   This collection of thatch-roofed bungalows is right in front of the famous Playa Negra point break. Even if you're not a surfer, you'll appreciate the beautiful beach and coast with its coral and rock outcroppings and calm tide pools. The round bungalows each have one queen-size and two single beds, two desks, a ceiling fan, and a private bathroom. Although they have concrete floors, everything is painted in contrasting pastels and feels quite comfortable. The restaurant is close to the ocean in a large open-air rancho and serves as a social hub for guests and surfers staying at more basic *cabinas* inland from the beach.

Playa Negra (A.P. 31-5150, Santa Cruz), Guanacaste. ℂ **652-9134.** Fax 652-9035. www.playanegra.com. 10 units. $80 (£40) double. Rates lower in off season; higher during peak periods. AE, MC, V. **Amenities:** Restaurant; bar; mid-size oval pool; laundry service. *In room:* No phone.

7 Playa Junquillal ⟨★

30km (19 miles) W of Santa Cruz; 20km (12 miles) S of Tamarindo

A long, windswept beach that, for most of its length, is backed by grasslands, Playa Junquillal, remains a nearly undiscovered gem on an increasingly crowded coast—although this could change at any time. There's really no village to speak of here and the road is rough, so it's a good place to get away from it all and enjoy some unfettered time on a nearly deserted beach. The long stretch of white sand is great for strolling, and the sunsets are superb. When the waves are big, this beach is great for surfing, but can be a little dangerous for swimming. When it's calm, jump right in.

ESSENTIALS
GETTING THERE & DEPARTING   By Plane   The nearest airport with regularly scheduled flights is in Tamarindo (see earlier in this chapter). You can arrange a taxi from the airport to Playa Junquillal. The ride should take around 40 minutes and cost about $35 to $40 (£18–£20).

By Car   Take the Interamerican Highway from San José. Forty-seven kilometers (29 miles) past the turnoff for Puntarenas, you'll see signs and the turnoff for the new Tempisque River Bridge. After crossing the river, follow the signs for Nicoya and Santa Cruz. Just after leaving the main intersection for Santa Cruz, you'll see a marked turnoff for Playa Junquillal, Ostional, and Tamarindo. The road is paved for 14km (8½ miles), until the tiny village of Veintesiete de Abril. From here, it's another rough 18km (11 miles) to Playa Junquillal.

By Bus   To get here by bus, you must first head to Santa Cruz and, from there, take another bus to Playa Junquillal. Buses depart San José for Santa Cruz roughly every hour between 6am and 6pm from the **Tralapa** bus station (© **221-7202**) at Calle 20 between avenidas 3 and 5, and from the **Tracopa** bus station (© **222-2666**) at Calle 14 between avenidas 3 and 5. Trip duration is around 4 hours; the fare is $5 (£2.50). Buses leave Santa Cruz for Junquillal at 10am and 2 and 5pm from the town's central plaza. The ride takes about 1 hour, and the one-way fare is $1.50 (75p). Buses depart Playa Junquillal for Santa Cruz daily at 6am and noon and 3pm. Always check with your hotel in advance as the schedule of buses between Junquillal and Santa Cruz is notoriously fickle. If you miss the connection, or there's no bus running, you can hire a taxi for the trip to Junquillal for $25 to $35 (£13–£18). From Tamarindo, a taxi should cost $35 to $45 (£18–£23).

WHAT TO DO IN JUNQUILLAL
Other than walking on the beach, surfing, swimming when the surf isn't too strong, and exploring tide pools, there isn't much to do here—which is just fine with me. This beach is ideal for anyone who wants to relax without any distractions. Bring a few good books. You can rent bikes at the Iguanazul Hotel, which is a good way to get up and down to the beach; horseback-riding tours are also popular. If you have a car you explore the coastline just north and south of here, as well.

For surfers, the beach break right in Junquillal is often pretty good. I've also heard that if you look hard enough, there are a few hidden reef and point breaks around.

Several sportfishing boats operate out of Playa Junquillal. Inquire at your hotel or ask at the Iguanazul Hotel (see below). If you want to rent a mountain bike, you can also check in at the Iguanazul.

Finally, if you want to do some diving, check in with Micke and Maarten at **El Lugarcito** (✆/fax **658-8436;** lugarcito@racsa.co.cr). These folks offer day trips to the Catalina Islands, as well as resort and full-certification courses.

WHERE TO STAY & DINE

All of the hotels listed below have their own restaurants. You can get good pizza, homemade pasta, and fresh seafood at **Pizzería Tatanka** (✆ **658-8426**), which also offers simple rooms at reasonable rates. It is located near the Iguanazul Hotel on your left as you come into Junquillal, and also has good ocean and sunset views. For a more elegant dining experience, also featuring Italian cuisine, try **La Puesta del Sol** (✆ **658-8442**), which is on a hillside overlooking the sea. This is a great place for sunsets. For a change of pace, try **Lak Ampu** (✆ **658-8339**), which serves up Peruvian fare.

MODERATE

Iguanazul Hotel ✪   Set on a windswept, grassy bluff above a rocky beach, Iguanazul is the biggest, best-equipped and most happening hotel in Junquillal. The pool—which features a tiny island with a palm tree growing on it—is large, as is the surrounding patio area, and there's also a volleyball court. If you're feeling mellow, head down to one of the quiet coves or grab a hammock set in a covered palapa on the hillside. Guest rooms are spacious and nicely decorated with basket lampshades, wicker furniture, red-tile floors, high ceilings, and blue-and-white-tile bathrooms. Even if you're not staying here, it's a good place to dine; the food is excellent and the sunset views are phenomenal. These folks can also rent out fully equipped houses and condos for longer stays at their neighboring residential project.

Playa Junquillal (A.P. 130-5150, Santa Cruz), Guanacaste. ✆ **658-8124** or ✆/fax 658-8235. www.iguanazul.com. 24 units. $110 (£55) double. Rates include continental breakfast. Rates lower in off season. AE, MC, V. **Amenities:** Restaurant; bar; pool; watersports equipment rental; bike rental; game room; tour desk; laundry service; free Wi-Fi. *In room:* A/C, TV.

INEXPENSIVE

In addition to the lodgings listed below, **Camping Los Malinches** (✆ **658-8429**) has wonderful campsites on fluffy grass amid manicured gardens set on a bluff above the beach. Camping costs $3 (£1.50) per person, and includes bathroom and shower privileges. You'll see a sign on the right as you drive toward Playa Junquillal, a little bit beyond the Iguanazul Hotel. The campground is located about 1km (½ mile) down this dirt road. These folks also have some simple, rustic rooms. You'll also find very basic rooms just steps from the beach at **Hotel Playa Junquillal** (✆ **888/666-2322** in the U.S., or 658-8432; www.playa-junquillal.com).

Hotel El Castillo Divertido   This fanciful hotel is a tropical rendition of a classic medieval castle (well, sort of). Ramparts and a turret with a rooftop bar certainly grab the attention of passersby. Guest rooms are fairly small, although rates are certainly fair. Ask for an upstairs room with a balcony. If you don't get one of these, you'll still have a good view from the hotel's rooftop bar, which sometimes features live music, ranging from Latin folk to reggae. The hotel is located on a hillside, about 500m (1,640 ft.) from the beach.

Playa Junquillal, Santa Cruz, Guanacaste. ✆/fax **658-8428.** www.costarica-adventureholidays.com. 6 units. $30–$45 (£15–£23) double. Rates lower in off season. AE, MC, V. **Amenities:** Restaurant; bar. *In room:* No phone.

Hotel Hibiscus *Value*   Although the accommodations here are simple, the friendly German owner makes sure that everything is always in top shape. The grounds are pleasantly shady, with plenty of flowering tropical flora, and the beach is just across the road. The rooms have cool Mexican-tile floors and firm beds. The service and ambience here are excellent for the price range. The restaurant serves very well-prepared international cuisine and fresh seafood at reasonable prices.

Playa Junquillal (A.P. 163-5150, Santa Cruz), Guanacaste. ©/fax 658-8437. www.adventure-costarica.com/hibiscus. 4 units. $50 (£25) double. Rates include full breakfast and taxes. MC, V. **Amenities:** Restaurant; laundry service. *In room:* No phone.

8 Playa Nosara ★★

55km (34 miles) SW of Nicoya; 266km (165 miles) W of San José

Playa Nosara is a bucket term used to refer to several neighboring beaches, spread along an isolated stretch of coast. In addition to the namesake beach, **Playa Guiones, Playa Pelada, Playa Garza,** and **Playa Ostional** are also lumped into this area. In fact, the village of Nosara itself is several kilometers inland from the beach. Playa Guiones is one of Costa Rica's most dependable beach breaks, and the surfing boom has led to a similar boom in Nosara. There's now a tiny strip mall at the crossroads to Playa Guiones, and a boom in hotels and restaurants is underway.

The best way to get to Nosara is to fly, but, with everything so spread out, that makes getting around difficult after you've arrived. The roads to, in, and around Nosara are almost always in very rough shape, and there's little sign that this will improve any time soon.

ESSENTIALS

GETTING THERE & DEPARTING   By Plane   Sansa (© **290-4100;** www.flysansa.com) has a daily flight to Nosara, departing from San José's Juan Santamaría International Airport at 8am. The one-way fare for the 50-minute flight is $82 (£41). **Nature Air** (© **800/235-9272** in the U.S. and Canada, or 299-6000; www.natureair.com) has one flight daily that leaves at 3:15pm from Tobías Bolaños International Airport in Pavas. The fare is $88 (£44) each way. Taxis are waiting for every arrival; fares range between $4 and $8 (£2–£4) to most hotels in Nosara. The return Sansa flight to San José departs Nosara at 9am, and the Nature Air flight leaves at 4:15pm.

By Car   Follow the directions for getting to Playa Sámara (see "Playa Sámara," below), but watch for a well-marked fork in the road a few kilometers before you reach that beach. The right-hand fork leads to Nosara over another 22km (14 miles) of rough dirt road.

By Bus   An **Alfaro** express bus (© **222-2666** in San José, or 682-0297 in Nosara) leaves San José daily at 5:30am from Calle 14 between avenidas 3 and 5. The trip's duration is 5½ hours; the one-way fare is $6 (£3).

You can also take an Alfaro bus from San José to Nicoya and then catch a second bus from Nicoya to Nosara. Alfaro buses leave San José roughly every hour between 5am and 5pm. The fare is $4.80 (£2.40). The trip can take between 4 and 5½ hours, depending on whether the bus goes via Liberia or the Tempisque bridge. The latter route is much faster. **Empresa Rojas** buses (© **686-9089**) leave Nicoya for Nosara daily at 5 and 10am and noon and 3pm. Trip duration is 2 hours; the one-way fare is $1.30 (65p).

The direct Alfaro bus to San José leaves daily at 12:30pm. Buses to Nicoya leave Nosara daily at 5 and 7am and noon and 3pm. Buses leave Nicoya for San José roughly every hour between 5am and 5pm.

Interbus (© **283-5573;** www.interbusonline.com) runs a daily bus from San José to Playa Nosara at 8:15am; the fare is $39 (£20).

ORIENTATION   The village of Nosara is about 5km (3 miles) inland from the beach. The small airstrip runs pretty much through the center of town; however, most hotels listed here are on or near the beach itself. You'll find the **post office** and **police station** right at the end of the airstrip. There's a small medical clinic and pharmacy in the village, as well. If you need a **taxi,** call © **682-0142** or 682-0236. There's an **Internet cafe** in the village and others at Café de Paris and Harbor Reef Lodge (p. 194). Both **Banco Popular** and **Banco Nacional** have offices in Nosara, with ATM machines. If you want to rent a car out here, both **Alamo** and **National** have offices here. Alternatively, you can rent an ATV from several operators around town.

This area was originally conceived and zoned as a primarily residential community. The maze of dirt roads and lack of any single defining thoroughfare can be confusing for first-time visitors. Luckily, a host of hotel and restaurant signs have gone up in recent years pointing lost travelers in the general direction of their final destination.

FUN ON & OFF THE BEACH

Among the several beaches at Nosara are the long, curving **Playa Guiones** ⟨★★⟩, **Playa Nosara** ⟨★⟩, and the diminutive **Playa Pelada** ⟨★⟩. Because the village of Nosara is several miles inland, these beaches tend to be clean, secluded, and quiet. Surfing and bodysurfing are good here, particularly at Playa Guiones, which is garnering quite a reputation as a consistent and rideable beach break. Pelada is a short white-sand beach with three deep scallops, backed by sea grasses and mangroves. There isn't too much sand at high tide, so you'll want to hit the beach when the tide's out. At either end of the beach, rocky outcroppings reveal tide pools at low tide.

With miles of excellent beach breaks and relatively few crowds, this is a great place to learn how to surf. If you want to try to stand up for your first time, check in with the folks at **Safari Surf School** (© **866/433-3355** in the U.S. and Canada, or 682-0573; www.safarisurfschool.com) or **Corky Carroll's Surf School** (© **888/454-7873** in the U.S. and Canada, or 682-0385; www.surfschool.net). Both places also rent boards.

BIRD- & SEA TURTLE–WATCHING   Bird-watchers should explore the mangrove swamps around the estuary mouth of the Río Nosara. Just walk north from Playa Pelada and follow the riverbank; explore the paths into the mangroves.

If you time your trip right, you can do a night tour to nearby **Playa Ostional** to watch nesting olive ridley sea turtles. These turtles come ashore by the thousands in a mass egg-laying phenomenon known as an *arribada*. These *arribadas* take place 4 to 10 times between July and December; each occurrence lasts between 3 and 10 days. Consider yourself very lucky if you happen to be around during one of these fascinating natural phenomena. Even if it's not turtle-nesting season, you might want to look into visiting Playa Ostional just to have a long, wide expanse of beach to yourself. However, be careful swimming here because the surf and riptides can be formidable. During the dry season (mid-Nov to Apr), you can usually get here in a regular car, but during the rainy season you'll need four-wheel-drive. This beach is part of Ostional National Wildlife Refuge. At the northwest end of the refuge is **India Point,** which is known for its tide pools and rocky outcrops.

The *arribadas* are so difficult to predict that no one runs regularly scheduled turtle-viewing trips, but when the *arribada* is in full swing, several local tour guides and agencies offer tours. Your best bet is to ask the staff at your hotel or check in with Joe at **Iguana Expeditions** (℃ 682-4089; www.iguanaexpeditions.com).

FISHING CHARTERS & OTHER OUTDOOR ACTIVITIES   All the hotels in the area can arrange fishing charters for $250 to $500 (£125–£250) for a half-day, or $400 to $1,200 (£200–£600) for a full day. These rates are for one to four people and vary according to boat size and accouterments. Despite its name, **Sunset Sails** (℃ 682-0509) offers full-day, half-day, and—of course—sunset cruises.

HORSEBACK RIDING   The folks at **Casa Río Nosara Excursions** (℃ 682-0117) have a large stable of well-cared-for horses and a range of beach, jungle, and waterfall rides to choose from. Rates run between $25 and $60 (£13–£30) per person, depending on the size of your group and the length of the tour.

KAYAK TOURS   Based out of the Gilded Iguana hotel and restaurant, **Iguana Expeditions** ☆ (℃ 682-4089; www.iguanaexpeditions.com) offers a range of full- and half-day tours around the area. Explore the inland coastal mangroves, or combine some open-water paddling with a snorkel break at San Juanillo. These folks also offer hikes to waterfalls and can arrange inexpensive fishing outings in a *panga* (small craft) with a local fisherman. Half-day tours cost between $25 and $50 (£13–£25); full-day tours run between $50 and $100 (£25–£50).

YOGA & MORE   If you want to spend some time getting mind and body together, check in with the **Nosara Yoga Institute** (℃ 682-0360; www.nosarayoga.com), which offers intensive and daily yoga classes, teacher trainings, and a host of custom-designed "retreat" options.

WHERE TO STAY

In addition to the places listed below, **Casa Romántica** ☆ (℃ 682-0272; www.casa-romantica.net) on Playa Guiones, has clean and comfortable rooms and a swimming pool—and it's right on the beach to boot. **Giardino Tropicale** (℃ 682-4000; www.giardinotropicale.com) is a similar choice, although a bit farther from the beach. For a more intimate option that's also a very good deal, check out the **Nosara B&B** (℃ 682-0209; www.nosarabandb.com). One final hotel that needs mentioning is the **Nosara Beach Hotel** (℃ 682-0121; www.nosarabeachhotel.com). You can't miss the giant Russian-style dome topping this hillside hotel. The location and view here are top notch. However, the place has been in a constant state of construction for over a decade, and service is gruff at times and spotty at best.

EXPENSIVE

Harmony Hotel & Spa ☆☆   This totally revamped resort hotel is set just off the beach, on the road that leads from the main Nosara road to Playa Nosara. This is easily the most complete, luxurious and best located option in the Nosara area. The room decor is simple but attractive, with white-tile floors, contemporary furnishings, and well-designed bathrooms. All the rooms have patios or wooden decks. In fact, even the most basic rooms here, their "Coco" rooms, feature quite large private wooden decks out back, with an outdoor shower. The hotel is geared toward couples, and all are equipped with just one king-size bed, although roll-in beds are available for families or buddies. The bungalows are two-bedroom affairs, with a king-size bed and fold-out sofa in each room and large shared deck area. The hotel has a well-run and pretty spa, with various treatment options and regular yoga classes. One of the best features here is the fact that the beach is only about 90m (295 ft.) away, reached via a short path through some sea grass and dunes.

Playa Nosara, Guanacaste. © 682-4113. Fax 682-4114. www.harmonynosara.com. 16 units, 10 bungalows. $185 (£93) double; $225 (£113) villa; $345 (£173) two-bedroom bungalow. Rates include breakfast buffet. Rates lower in off season. AE, MC, V. **Amenities:** Restaurant; bar; midsize pool; spa; lighted tennis court; watersports equipment rental; tour desk; laundry service. *In room:* A/C, TV, free Wi-Fi, minifridge, coffeemaker, safe.

MODERATE

Café de París ✿   Located on the main road into Nosara, where it branches off to Playa Guiones, this popular bakery and bistro (reviewed separately below) has some equally popular rooms out back, set behind the restaurant and pool in a series of duplex buildings. All have high ceilings and plenty of room; about half have kitchenettes. A few shady ranchos are spread around the grounds for afternoon lazing. These folks also rent a couple of luxury villas with fabulous views atop a steep hill across the street.

Playa Nosara, Guanacaste. © 682-0087. Fax 682-0089. www.cafedeparis.net. 14 units. $100 (£50) double; $300–$400 (£150–£200) per week. AE, MC, V. **Amenities:** Restaurant; bar; small pool; game room; tour desk; laundry service. *In room:* A/C, no phone.

Harbor Reef Lodge ✿   This hotel caters to both surfers and fishermen, with clean, spacious rooms close to the beach (about 182m/597 ft. inland from Playa Guiones). The suites come with separate sitting rooms, and a couple even have kitchenettes. There's a cool, oasis-like feel to the lush grounds. The best rooms are the new Surf City rooms and suites, which are set around the hotels second, and larger pool, which is reserved for hotel guests—the other pool, which is just off the restaurant, is open to diners and walk-ins. The hotel offers surf lessons and sportfishing outings and even has a small general store and Internet cafe on the grounds. They also rent out a variety of private homes and villas.

Playa Nosara, Guanacaste. © 682-0059. Fax 682-0060. www.harborreef.com. 22 units. $89–$130 (£45–£65) double; $110–$185 (£55–£93) suite. AE, MC, V. **Amenities:** Restaurant; bar; 2 small pools; watersports equipment rental; bike rental; tour desk; laundry service. *In room:* A/C, fridge, coffeemaker, no phone.

Lagarta Lodge   Located on a hillside high over the Nosara River, this small lodge is an excellent choice for bird-watchers and other travelers who are more interested in the flora and fauna than the beach. The rooms are spartan but acceptable. The lodge borders its own private reserve, which has trails along the riverbank and through the mangrove and tropical humid forests here. There are spectacular views from the restaurant and most rooms over the river and surrounding forest, with the beaches of Nosara and Ostional in the distance. You'll want to have your own vehicle if you stay here: The beach is a good 10- to 15-minute hike away, and it's uphill on the way back.

Playa Nosara (A.P. 18-5233), Guanacaste. © 682-0035. Fax 682-0135. www.lagarta.com. 6 units. $68 (£34) double. Rates lower in off season; higher during peak periods. AE, MC, V. **Amenities:** Restaurant; bar; midsize pool; tour desk. *In room:* No phone.

INEXPENSIVE

The Gilded Iguana ✿   This longstanding hotel and restaurant began with a few very basic budget rooms. However, it now has a swimming pool, with a high waterfall emptying into it, and six newer more luxurious rooms. The new rooms have very high ceilings, lots of space, air-conditioning, and minifridges. They are set back from the pool in a row, and sit amongst some shade trees. The older rooms are much more

> **Tips Yo Quiero Hablar Español**
>
> You can brush up on or start up your Spanish at the **Rey de Nosara Language School** (℃/fax **682-0215**; www.reydenosara.itgo.com). It offers group and private lessons according to demand, and can coordinate week or multiweek packages.

---

rustic, and located close to the road, just off the hotel's popular restaurant. These lack air-conditioning, but are obviously more economical. The restaurant here is deservedly popular (see below), and in addition to feeding its guests, draws a lot of the local expatriate community to watch sporting events and listen to the occasional live band.

Playa Guiones, Guanacaste. ℃ 682-0259. www.gildediguana.com. 12 units. $45–$80 (£23–£40) double. Rates lower in off season; higher during peak periods. AE, MC, V. **Amenities:** Restaurant; bar; midsize pool; tour desk; laundry service. *In room:* Minifridge, coffeemaker, no phone.

WHERE TO DINE

In addition to the places mentioned below, **Marlin Bill's** (℃ **682-0458**) is a popular and massive open-air haunt on the hillside on the main road, just across from Café de Paris (see below). You can expect to get good, fresh seafood and American classics here. For Mexican food, try **Pancho's** (℃ **682-0591**) or **Foony's** (℃ **682-0385**), both in Playa Guiones. For Italian, **La Dolce Vita** 𝆑 (℃ **682-0107**), located on the outskirts of town on the road to Playa Sámara, serves up excellent Italian fare nightly, while closer to town, **Giardino Tropicale** (℃ **682-4000**) also has good Italian fare and brick-oven pizzas. Finally, for local flavor, head to Doña Olga's (no phone), a simple Costa Rican *soda,* located right on the beach in Playa Pelada.

Café de Paris 𝆑 *Finds* BAKERY/BISTRO This popular place has wonderful fresh-baked goods and a wide assortment of light bites and full-on meals. You can get pizza or nachos or filling sandwiches on fresh baguettes. There are also hearty salads, as well as fish, meat, and chicken dishes. I enjoy stopping in for a cup of espresso and a fresh almond croissant, and breakfasts are excellent here. Sporting events or movie videos are shown nightly, and there's even a pool table and Internet cafe here.

On the main road into Nosara. ℃ 682-0087. Baked goods 60¢–$4 (30p–£2); main courses $4–$16 (£2–£8). AE, MC, V. Daily 7am–11pm.

The Gilded Iguana 𝆑 SEAFOOD/GRILL This simple restaurant serves fish so fresh that it's still wiggling: The owner's husband, Chiqui, is a local fisherman. There are also great burgers, Costa Rican *casados,* and a list of nightly specials. If you're in town fishing, they'll cook your catch. Sporting events are shown on a not-quite-big-enough television. There's a separate bar area, on the other side of their new pool, and you can also dine over there. Overall, the vibe is sociable and lively. Be careful, most of the tables and chairs here are low lying affairs, plus-size travelers might find the chairs a bit challenging to get in and out of.

About 90m (295 ft.) inland from the beach at Playa Guiones. ℃ 682-0259. Main courses $4–$14 (£2–£7). V. Daily 7am–9:30am, 11am–2pm, and 5–10pm.

La Luna 𝆑 *Finds* INTERNATIONAL With an enviable location and overlooking the water at Playa Pelada and a casually elegant ambience, this little restaurant is an excellent choice. I especially like grabbing one of the outdoor tables closest to the waves for breakfast or lunch. However, it's also quite beautiful at night, with candles spread around generously. Be forewarned, service here is frequently very, very slow. The chalkboard menu changes regularly, but will usually include some Thai or Indian curry, as well as pasta dishes, and hearty steaks. The mango-seafood salad is an excellent starter. Prices are high, and service and hospitality can be spotty at times, but this is still probably the best fine dining to be had in Nosara.

Playa Pelada. ✆ 682-0122. Main courses $9–$36 (£4.50–£18). MC, V. Daily 11am–10pm.

NOSARA AFTER DARK

When evening rolls around, don't expect a major party scene. Nightlife near the beach seems to center on the **Café de Paris, Marlin Bill's, Casa Tucán,** and the **Gilded Iguana.** The last two spots often have live music. In "downtown" Nosara, you'll probably want to check out either the **Tropicana,** the town's long-standing local disco, or the **Beatle Bar,** a U.S.-style bar that also has a branch in Jacó. Be forewarned, as with the Jacó branch, the Beatle Bar here is a popular prostitute pick-up spot.

NORTH OF NOSARA

Just north of Nosara lies Playa Ostional, famous for its massive nestings of olive ridley sea turtles (see above). At the northern edge of Playa Ostional where it meets Playa San Juanillo, a few new hotels have sprung up. The best of these is **Hotel Luna Azul** (✆ 821-0075; www.hotellunaazul.com), which features beautiful individual bungalows and a great view of the ocean—although the beach is a good distance away.

9 Playa Sámara

35km (22 miles) S of Nicoya; 245km (152 miles) W of San José

Playa Sámara is a long, broad beach on a gently curved horseshoe-shape bay. Unlike most of the rest of the Pacific coast, the water here is usually calm and perfect for swimming because an offshore island and rocky headlands break up most of the surf. Playa Sámara is easily accessible along a well-paved road, and it is popular both with Tico families seeking a quick and inexpensive getaway and with young Ticos looking to do some serious beach partying. On weekends, in particular, Sámara can get crowded and rowdy. Still, the calm waters and steep cliffs on the far side of the bay make this a very attractive spot, and the beach is so long that the crowds are usually well dispersed. Moreover, if you drive along the rugged coastal road in either direction, you'll discover some truly spectacular and isolated beaches.

ESSENTIALS

GETTING THERE & DEPARTING   By Plane   Sansa (✆ 290-4100; www. flysansa.com) flies to Carrillo (15 min. south of Sámara) daily at 8:40am from San José's Juan Santamaría International Airport. The flight might stop first at either Punta Islita or Nosara and takes approximately 1 hour; the fare is $82 (£41) each way. The Sansa flight leaves Carrillo for San José at 9:30am.

Most hotels will arrange to pick you up in Carrillo. If not, you'll have to hire a cab for between $8 and $10 (£4–£5).

Nature Air (✆ 800/235-9272 in the U.S. and Canada, or 299-6000; www.natureair.com) also has one flight daily to Punta Islita that leave at 9:15am from Tobías Bolaños International Airport in Pavas. The fare is $90 (£45) each way. The return flight for San José leaves at 3:30pm. Nature Air also flies between Liberia and Quepos, and Punta Islita.

By Car Take the Interamerican Highway from San José. Forty-seven kilometers (29 miles) past the turnoff for Puntarenas, you'll see signs and the turnoff for the new Tempisque River bridge. After crossing the bridge, continue north to Nicoya. In Nicoya, head more or less straight through town until you see signs for Playa Sámara. From here, it's a paved road almost all the way to the beach.

By Bus **Alfaro** express buses (𝒸 **222-2666**) leave San José daily at noon and 6:30pm from Calle 14 between avenidas 3 and 5. The trip lasts 5 hours; the one-way fare is $7 (£3.50). Extra buses are sometimes added on weekends and during peak periods, so it's always wise to check.

Alternatively, you can take a bus from this same station to Nicoya and then catch a second bus from Nicoya to Sámara. Alfaro buses leave San José roughly every hour between 5am and 5pm. The fare is $4.80 (£2.40). The trip can take between 4 and 5½ hours, depending if the bus goes via Liberia or the Tempisque bridge. The latter route is much faster. **Empresa Rojas** (𝒸 **685-5352**) buses leave Nicoya for Sámara and Carrillo regularly throughout the day, between 5am and 9pm. The trip's duration is 1½ hours. The fare to Sámara is $1.60 (80p); the fare to Carrillo is $2.20 (£1.10).

Express buses to San José leave daily at 4 and 8:30am. Buses for Nicoya leave throughout the day between 5am and 9pm. Buses leave Nicoya for San José roughly every hour between 5am and 5pm.

Gray Line (𝒸 **220-2126**; www.graylinecostarica.com) has a daily bus that leaves San José for Playa Sámara at 7am. **Interbus** (𝒸 **283-5573**; www.interbusonline.com) has a daily bus that leaves San José for Playa Sámara at 8:15am. Both companies charge $29 (£15) and will pick you up at most San José–area hotels.

ORIENTATION Sámara is a busy little town at the bottom of a steep hill. The main road heads straight into town, passing the soccer field before coming to an end at the beach. Just before the beach is a road to the left that leads to most of the hotels listed below. This road also leads to Playa Carrillo (see below) and Hotel Punta Islita (p. 200). If you turn right 3 blocks before hitting the beach, you'll hit the coastal road that goes to playas Buena Vista, Barrigona and eventually Nosara.

FAST FACTS In case of emergency, dial 𝒸 **911.** To reach the local police, dial 𝒸 **656-0436.** There's a small medical clinic in Samara (𝒸 **656-0166**). On the road to Playa Buena Vista, just outside of town, is a branch of the **Banco Nacional** (𝒸 **656-0086**). If you need a ride around town, or to one of the nearby beaches, you can hire a taxi by calling **Balto** (𝒸 **361-4167**) or **Jorge** (𝒸 **830-3002**).

FUN ON & OFF THE BEACH

Aside from sitting on the sand and soaking up the sun, the main activities in Playa Sámara seem to be hanging out in the bars and *sodas* and dancing into the early-morning hours. But if you're looking for something more, there's horseback riding either on the beach or through the bordering pastureland and forests. Other options include sea kayaking in the calm waters off Playa Sámara, sportfishing, snorkeling and scuba diving, boat tours, mountain biking, and tours to Playa Ostional to see the mass nesting of olive ridley sea turtles. You can inquire about and book any of these tours at your hotel.

You'll find that the beach is nicer and cleaner down at the south end. Better yet, head about 8km (5 miles) south to **Playa Carrillo** 𝔎𝔎, a long crescent of soft, white sand. There's almost no development here, so the beach is almost always deserted and there are loads of palm trees providing shade. If you've got a good four-wheel-drive vehicle, ask for directions at your hotel and set off in search of the hidden gems of

Playa Buena Vista and **Playa Barrigona** ⟨⟨, which are north of Sámara, less than a half-hour drive away. A taxi to Playa Carrillo should cost about $5 to $7 (£2.50–£3.50) each way. Because it's a bit farther and the roads are a little rougher, expect to pay a little more to reach Playa Buena Vista, and even more for Playa Barrigona.

Cavers will want to head 62km (38 miles) northeast of Playa Sámara on the road to the Tempisque bridge. If you don't have a car, your best bet is to get to Nicoya, which is about a half-hour away by bus, and then take a taxi to the park, which should cost about $12 (£6). Here, at **Barra Honda National Park** ⟨ (© 685-5267 or 686-6760), there's an extensive system of caves, some of which reach more than 200m (656 ft.) in depth. Human remains and indigenous relics have been found in other caves, but those are not open to the public. Because this is a national park, you'll have to pay the $6 (£3) entrance fee. If you plan to descend the one publicly accessible cave, you'll also need to rent (or bring your own) equipment and hire a local guide at the park entrance station. Depending upon your group size and bargaining abilities, expect to pay $10 to $30 (£5–£15) per person for a visit to the **Terciopelo Cave,** including the guide, harness, helmet, and flashlight. Furthermore, the cave is open only during the dry season (mid-Nov to Apr). Inside you'll see plenty of impressive stalactites and stalagmites while visiting several chambers of varying sizes. Even if you don't descend, the trails around Barra Honda and its prominent limestone plateau are great for hiking and bird-watching. If you visit this attraction, be sure to make a stop at **La Cascada,** a gentle waterfall that fills and passes through a series of calcium and limestone pools, some of them large enough to bathe in. The entire thing is slightly reminiscent of Ocho Rios in Jamaica.

The folks at **Wingnuts Canopy Tours** (© 656-0153) offer zip-line and harness "canopy tours." The 2-hour outing costs $55 (£28) per person. You'll find their office by the giant strangler fig tree, or *matapalo,* toward the southern end of the beach.

Almost every hotel in the area can arrange sportfishing trips, or you could contact **Samara Sport Fishing** (© 656-0589) or **Kingfisher** ⟨ (© 656-0091; www.costa ricabillfishing.com).

To learn how to surf, or to rent a board, check in with **C & C Surf Shop and School** (© 656-0628).

For a bird's-eye view of the area, head over to the **Flying Crocodile** (© 656-8048; www.flying-crocodile.com) in Playa Buena Vista. A 20-minute flight will run you $70 (£35).

If you want to acquire or polish some language skills while here, check in with the **Intercultura Language School** (© 866/978-6668 in the U.S. and Canada, or 656-0127 in Samara; www.samaralanguageschool.com). The facility here even features classes with ocean views, although that might be a detriment to your language learning. These folks offer a range of programs and private lessons and can arrange for a home stay with a local family.

All of the hotels here can help you arrange any number of tour options, including horseback rides, boat trips, scuba diving, and snorkeling outings. You might also contact **Tío Tigre Tours** (© 656-0098), a good all-around local tour company.

WHERE TO STAY

In addition to the places listed below, **Hacienda Dorada** ⟨ (© 318/387-5196 in the U.S., or 289-2211 in Costa Rica; www.dorada.com) rents three large and luxurious fully equipped villas on a hillside above and behind Playa Buenavista.

MODERATE

Fenix Hotel   Set right on the beach, the rooms here are all really studio apartments, with fully equipped kitchenettes. The rooms are simple, but they are kept fairly clean. For cooling off, the hotel has a postage stamp–size pool and some coconut trees for shade. In terms of services, amenities, and room decor, the entire operation is a bit spartan for my taste, but it is a good option for longer stays, and those looking to do some cooking in lieu of eating out all the time.

Playa Sámara, Nicoya, Guanacaste. ℰ **656-0158.** Fax 656-0162. www.fenixhotel.com. 6 units. $80 (£40) double. Rates lower in off season. No credit cards. **Amenities:** Small pool; laundry service. *In room:* A/C, kitchenette, no phone.

Hotel Giada   This neat little Italian-owned hotel is located on the left-hand side of the main road into town, about 150m (492 ft.) before the beach. The rooms are all very clean and comfortable and even have small balconies. Breakfast is served in a cool, shady central gazebo. The management is very helpful and can arrange diving or fishing expeditions and horseback-riding trips.

Playa Sámara, Nicoya, Guanacaste. ℰ **656-0132.** Fax 656-0131. www.hotelgiada.net. 24 units. $75 (£38) double. Rates include breakfast. Rates lower in off season; higher during peak periods. AE, DC, MC, V. **Amenities:** Restaurant; bar; small pool; tour desk; laundry service. *In room:* A/C, TV, safe.

Las Brisas del Pacífico Hotel ℱ   This is my top choice for a beach hotel in Playa Sámara. Located on a quiet stretch of sand, this hotel is set amid shady grounds and backs up on a steep hill. Most of the rooms are found in the three-story building, up a long and steep flight of stairs at the top of the hill. These have comfortable balconies and walls of glass that provide an excellent view of the bay. The third-floor rooms are the largest here, but the second-floor rooms actually have the best views. At the base of the hill are rooms in stucco duplexes with steeply pitched tile roofs and red-tile patios. The range in prices reflects the range in room size, location, and amenities. However, all of the rooms are rather plain, with decidedly uninspired decor. This lack of inspiration also sometimes bleeds over into the service. Depending on the season and demand, one or both of the restaurants here will be open. Regardless, you should find very fresh seafood and excellently prepared Italian pastas and entrees.

Playa Sámara (A.P. 11917-1000, San José), Guanacaste. ℰ **656-0250.** Fax 656-0248. www.brisas.net. 48 units. $65–$120 (£33–£60) double. Rates lower in the off season, higher during peak weeks. AE, MC, V. **Amenities:** 2 restaurants; 2 bars; 2 midsize pools; 2 unheated Jacuzzis; limited watersports equipment rental; tour desk; laundry service. *In room:* A/C (in some units), safe, no phone.

INEXPENSIVE

In addition to the places listed below, I like the tidy, German-run **Hotel Belvedere** (ℰ **656-0213;** www.samara-costarica.com), located on the hill overlooking the beach. You'll find a slew of very inexpensive places to stay along the road into town and around the soccer field. Many of the rooms at these places are less accommodating than your average jail cell. As an alternative, you can pitch a tent right by the beach for a few dollars at **Camping Coco's** (ℰ **656-0496**). You'll find Camping Coco's several hundred meters south of the downtown.

Casa del Mar *Value*   Located on the inland side of the beach-access road, 1 block south of the downtown, Casa del Mar is just 50m (164 ft.) from the beach. The rooms here are kept immaculate, and most of them are quite spacious. The place feels like a cool oasis from the harsh Guanacaste sun, with its open-air restaurant, shady central courtyard, and small pool/Jacuzzi. Although the units with shared bathrooms are the best bargains here, I'd opt for a second-floor room with a private bathroom. The owners and staff here are extremely friendly and helpful.

Playa Sámara, Nicoya, Guanacaste. ✆ 656-0264. Fax 656-0129. www.casadelmarsamara.com. 17 units, 11 w/private bathroom. $40 (£20) double w/shared bathroom; $75 (£38) double w/private bathroom and A/C. Rates include full breakfast. Rates lower in the off season; higher during peak periods. AE, MC, V. **Amenities:** Bar; unheated pool/Jacuzzi; tour desk; laundry service. *In room:* No phone.

Casa Valeria   This is the best beachfront budget option in town. The rooms are quite basic and much more rustic than those at either Belvedere or Casa del Mar, but they are just steps away from the sand and surf. The best bets here are the four individual bungalows. There's a basic restaurant, as well as some tables, chairs, and plenty of hammocks set in the shade of tall coconut palms. This place is popular with European backpackers, and there's a hostel feel to the whole operation.

Playa Sámara, Nicoya, Guanacaste. ✆ 656-0511. Fax 656-0317. 9 units. $30–$60 (£15–£30) double. Rates include breakfast. V. **Amenities:** Restaurant. *In room:* A/C, minifridge, no phone.

A NEARBY LUXURY HOTEL

Hotel Punta Islita ★★★ *Finds*   This is one of the most exclusive and romantic luxury resorts in Costa Rica. It's isolated on a high bluff between two mountain ridges that meet the sea. The rooms here are done in a Santa Fe style, with red Mexican floor tiles, neo-Navajo-print bedspreads, and adobe-colored walls offset with sky-blue doors and trim. Each room has a king-size bed and a private patio with a hammock; a few of these also have a Jacuzzi. The suites come with a separate sitting room and a private two-person plunge pool or Jacuzzi; the villas have two or three bedrooms, their own private swimming pools, and full kitchens.

The beach below the hotel is a small crescent of gray-white sand with a calm, protected section at the northern end. It's about a 10-minute hike, but the hotel will shuttle you up and back if you don't feel like walking. You can take the hotel's small "canopy tour," which leaves from just below the small exercise room and ends just steps from the beach. There's a rancho bar and grill down there for when you get hungry or thirsty, and a new lap pool for when the waves are too rough. A full range of spa treatments and services is offered, including yoga classes. This hotel is very involved with the local community, and has sponsored a wide ranging art program that brings in prominent Costa Rican artists to teach the local residents art and craft skills, while often creating large public works in the process. The hotel also has a top-notch little gallery, as well as a 9-hole executive course.

Although most guests opt to fly into the nearby airstrip, it's possible to drive here. Punta Islita is just two beaches south of Sámara. If you do drive, it's best to come over on the new Tempisque River bridge, follow the directions to Playa Sámara, and continue south.

Playa Islita (A.P. 242-1225, Plaza Mayor, San José), Guanacaste. ✆ 231-6122. Fax 231-0715. www.hotelpunta islita.com. 20 units, 17 villas. $300 (£150) double; $420–$480 (£210–£240) suite; $625–$720 (£313–£360) villa. Rates include continental breakfast. Rates lower in the off season; higher during peak periods. AE, MC, V. **Amenities:** 3 restaurants; bar; small tile pool and lap pool; 9-hole golf course and driving range; 2 tennis courts; small exercise room and spa; Jacuzzi; watersports equipment, bike, horse, and 4WD rentals; game room; tour desk; in-room massage; laundry service. *In room:* A/C, TV, free Wi-Fi, minibar, coffeemaker, hair dryer, safe.

DINING & AFTER-DARK DIVERSIONS

There are numerous inexpensive *sodas* in Sámara, and most of the hotels have their own dining rooms. If you want to eat overlooking the water, check out **El Ancla**

(📞 656-0716) or **Shake Joe's** (📞 656-0252). Both of these are located right on the beach a bit south of downtown. If you head out along the beach north of town, you'll find **El Lagarto** (📞 656-0750), which serves fresh fish and specializes in barbeque. If you're hot and steamy, stop in at **Coco Loco** (📞 656-0820), on the main street into town, for an ice cream treat or fresh-fruit smoothie.

After dark the most happening place in town is **La Góndola Bar,** which has a pool table, dartboards, and board games. My favorite spot is **El Lagarto** ✦ located on the beach a bit north of downtown. You might also try the lounge scene at **Shake Joe's, La Vela Latina,** or **Wana Wana Acuario.**

Las Brasas SPANISH/SEAFOOD   This two-story, open-air affair serves authentic Spanish cuisine and well-prepared fresh seafood. The whole fish *a la catalana* is excellent, as is the paella. For something lighter, try the gazpacho Andaluz, a refreshing lunch choice on a hot afternoon. If you have a big party, and order a day or so in advance, they'll roast a whole pig for you. There's a good selection of Spanish wines, a rarity in Costa Rica. Service is attentive yet informal.

On the main road into Sámara, about 90m (295 ft.) before the beach. 📞 656-0546. Reservations recommended in the high season. Main courses $8–$38 (£4–£19). V. Sat–Thurs noon–10pm.

10 Playa Tambor

150km–168km (93–104 miles) W of San José (not including ferry ride); 20km (12 miles) S of Paquera; 38km (24 miles) S of Naranjo

Playa Tambor was the site of Costa Rica's first large-scale all-inclusive resort, the Barceló Playa Tambor Beach Resort. Despite big plans, the resort and surrounding area have never really taken off. Playa Tambor itself is a long gently curving stretch of beach protected on either end by rocky headlands. These headlands give the waters ample protection from Pacific swells, making this a good beach for swimming. However, the sand is a rather hard-packed, dull gray-brown color, which often receives a large amount of flotsam and jetsam brought in by the sea. I find this beach much less attractive than those located farther south along the Nicoya Peninsula. This beach and the two hotels listed below were chosen as the prime locations for Fox's *Temptation Island 2.* But despite this publicity boon, Tambor still has a forgotten, isolated feel.

ESSENTIALS
GETTING THERE & DEPARTING   By Plane   Sansa (📞 290-4100; www.fly sansa.com) flies three times daily to Tambor from San José's Juan Santamaría International Airport at 8:25 and 10:30am and 12:55pm. These flights depart for San José at 9am and 12:10 and 1:40pm. Flight duration is 30 minutes; the fare is $65 (£33) each way.

Nature Air (📞 800/235-9272 in the U.S. and Canada, or 299-6000; www.natureair.com) flies to Tambor daily at 12:30 and 3:15pm from Tobías Bolaños International Airport in Pavas. Flight duration is 30 minutes; the fare is $69 (£35) each way. The return flights leave at 1:10 and 4:45pm.

By Car   The traditional route here is to take the Interamerican Highway from San José to Puntarenas and catch the ferry to either Naranjo or Paquera. Tambor is about 45 minutes south of Paquera and 2 hours south of Naranjo. The road from Paquera to Tambor is paved and usually in pretty good shape, and taking the Paquera ferry will save you time and some rough, dusty driving. The road from Naranjo to Paquera is all dirt and gravel and in bad shape.

Naviera Tambor (© **661-2084**) ferries to Paquera leave Puntarenas roughly every 2 to 3 hours between 5am and 8:30pm. The trip takes 1½ hours. The fare is around $9 (£4.50) for a car and driver, $1.20 (60p) for additional adults, 80¢ (40p) for children. I recommend arriving early during the peak season and on weekends because lines can be long; if you miss the ferry, you'll have to wait around 2 hours or more for the next one. Moreover, the ferry schedule changes frequently, with fewer ferries during the low season, and the occasional extra ferry during the high season to meet demand. It is always best to check in advance.

The **Naranjo ferry** (© **661-1069**) leaves daily at 6:30 and 10am and 2:30 and 7pm. The trip takes 1½ hours. The fare is $9 (£4.50) for cars, $1.60 (80p) for adults, and 80¢ (40p) for children.

Another option is to drive via the Tempisque River bridge. Although heading farther north and crossing the bridge is more circuitous, you will be driving the whole time, which at least feels faster than taking a seaborne ferry. Moreover, you will not be at the whim of the ferry schedule and the sometimes sold-out boats. To go this route, take the Interamerican Highway west from San José. Forty-seven kilometers (29 miles) past the turnoff for Puntarenas, turn left for the Tempisque River bridge. After you cross the Tempisque River, head to Quebrada Honda and then south to route 21, following signs for San Pablo, Jicaral, Lepanto, Playa Naranjo, and Paquera. This route is an option if you foresee waiting more than 2 hours for a ferry.

The car ferry from Paquera to Puntarenas leaves roughly every 2 hours between 8am and 10pm. *Note:* If you have to wait for the ferry, do not leave your car unattended, since break-ins are common.

By Bus & Ferry   **Transportes Rodriguez Hermanos** (© **642-0740**) runs three daily direct buses between San José and Montezuma, dropping passengers off in Tambor en route. The buses leave from the Coca Cola bus terminal at Calle 12 and Avenida 5 at 7:30am and 12:30 and 5pm. The fare is around $10 (£5), including the ferry ride, and the trip takes a little over 4 hours.

Alternately, it takes two buses and a ferry ride to get to Tambor. Express buses (© **222-0064**) for Puntarenas leave San José daily every hour between 6am and 8pm from Calle 16 and Avenida 12. Trip duration is 2½ hours; the fare is $2.80 (£1.40).

From Puntarenas, you can take one of the car ferries mentioned above or the passenger launch **Paquereña** (© **641-0515**), which leaves from the pier behind the market at 11:30am and 4pm. Ferry-trip duration is 1½ hours; the fare is 80¢ (40p). A bus south to Montezuma (this will drop you off in Tambor) will be waiting to meet the ferry when it arrives in Paquera. The bus ride takes about 45 minutes; the fare is $2 (£1). Be careful not to take the Naranjo ferry because it does not meet with regular onward bus transportation to Tambor.

When you're ready to head back, direct buses originating in Montezuma, pass through Tambor at approximately 6, 8:45, and 10:45am, and 4pm. Regular local buses to Paquera pass by Tambor roughly every 2 hours throughout the day. The Paquereña ferry returns for Puntarenas at 7:30am and 2pm. Total trip duration is 3½ hours. Buses to San José leave Puntarenas daily every hour between 5am and 8pm.

ORIENTATION   Although there's a small village of Tambor, through which the main road passes, the hotels themselves are scattered along several kilometers. You'll see signs for these hotels as the road circles around Playa Tambor.

FUN ON & OFF THE BEACH

Curú Wildlife Refuge ✮ (© 641-0004; www.curutourism.com), 16km (10 miles) north of Tambor, is a private reserve that has several pretty, secluded beaches, as well as forests and mangrove swamps. This area is extremely rich in wildlife. Howler and white-faced monkeys are often spotted here, as are quite a few species of birds. Admission for the day is $8 (£4) per person. There are some rustic cabins available with advance notice for around $30 (£15) per person per day, including the entrance and three square meals. If you don't have a car, you should arrange pickup with the folks who manage this refuge. Or you could hire a taxi in Paquera to take you there for around $7 (£3.50).

Both the hotels listed below offer horseback riding and various tours around this part of the peninsula and can arrange fishing and dive trips.

WHERE TO STAY & DINE

Aside from the hotels listed here, there are a few inexpensive *cabinas* available near the town of Tambor, at the southern end of the beach. Of these, your best bet is **Hotel Dos Largatos** (©/fax 683-0236), located right on the beach next to Tambor Tropical. Another option is **Costa Coral** ✮ (© 683-0105; www.costacoral.com), a very attractive place with a good restaurant. This place would be my top choice in Tambor, except it is unfortunately is set right off the busy main road here, several hundred meters from the beach.

The **Barceló Playa Tambor Beach Resort** (© 683-0303; www.barcelo.com) was Costa Rica's first all-inclusive resort, but its beach is mediocre at best, and the Barceló company has been accused of violating Costa Rica's environmental laws, ignoring zoning regulations, and mistreating workers. So although this resort is a major presence here, I don't recommend it; there are much better all-inclusive options available farther north in Guanacaste.

Tambor Tropical ✮   This is one of the more architecturally interesting hotels around. The rooms here are located in five two-story octagonal cabins, and the whole place is an orgy of varnished hardwoods, with purpleheart and cocobolo offsetting each other at every turn. The rooms are enormous and come with large, complete kitchens and a spacious sitting area. The walls are, in effect, nothing but shuttered picture windows, which give you the choice of gazing out at the ocean or shutting in for a bit of privacy. The upstairs rooms have large wraparound verandas, and the lower rooms have garden-level decks. The beach is only steps away. Plenty of coconut palms and flowering plants provide a very tropical feel.

Tambor, Puntarenas (mailing address: 867 Liberty St. NE, Salem, OR 97301). © **866/890-2537** in the U.S., or 683-0011 in Costa Rica. Fax 683-0013. www.tambortropical.com. 12 units. $165–$190 (£83–£95) double. Rates include continental breakfast. AE, MC, V. No children under 16. **Amenities:** Restaurant; bar; small free-form tile pool and Jacuzzi; small spa; tour desk; laundry service. *In room:* Free Wi-Fi, kitchenette, fridge, coffeemaker, iron, no phone.

Tango Mar Resort ✮✮   Tango Mar was *the* original luxury resort in this neck of the woods, and it's still a great place to get away from it all. With only 18 rooms and scattered suites and villas, there are never any crowds. The water is wonderfully clear, and the beach is fronted by coconut palms and luxuriant lawns. If you choose to go exploring, you'll find seaside cliffs and a beautiful nearby waterfall that pours into a tide pool. The rooms have big balconies and glass walls to soak up ocean views; some even have their own Jacuzzis. The suites are set back among shade trees and flowering vegetation. Most come with carved four-poster canopy beds and indoor Jacuzzis.

The villas are all different, spacious, and relatively secluded. Some suites and villas are a bit far from the beach and main hotel, so you'll need either your own car or one of the hotel's gas-powered golf carts. The suites closest to the beach are the five octagonal Tiki suites. In addition to a 9-hole par-3 golf course and two lighted tennis courts, the hotel has a small spa and yoga space to keep you fit and busy. Among the several pools is one beautiful free-form pool with a swim-up bar down by the beach.

Playa Tambor, Puntarenas. © 866/770-7383 in the U.S., or 683-0001 in Costa Rica. Fax 683-0003. www.tangomar.com. 18 units, 17 suites, 3 villas. $190 (£95) double; $190–$240 (£95–£120) suite; $450–$1,000 (£225–£500) villa. Rates include breakfast. Rates slightly lower during the off season, higher during peak weeks. AE, DC, MC, V. **Amenities:** Restaurant; bar; 3 small pools; small spa; 9-hole par-3 golf course ($25 full-day greens fee) w/wonderful sea views; 2 lighted tennis courts; limited watersports equipment rental; bike rental; tour desk; limited room service; in-room massage; laundry service. *In room:* A/C, TV, minibar, safe.

11 Playa Montezuma ★★

166km–184km (103–114 miles) W of San José (not including the ferry ride); 36km (22 miles) SE of Paquera; 54km (33 miles) S of Naranjo

Montezuma still isn't like most other beach destinations in Guanacaste and Nicoya, but it's getting there. For years, this remote village and its surrounding beaches, forests and waterfalls have enjoyed near-legendary status among backpackers, UFO seekers, hippie expatriates, and European budget travelers. Although it maintains its alternative vibe, Montezuma has emerged as a great destination for all manner of travelers looking for a beach retreat surrounded by some stunning scenery. As with the rest of Guanacaste and Nicoya, the town is booming, and there are lodgings of value and quality in all price ranges. Active pursuits abound, from hiking in the Cabo Blanco Absolute Nature Reserve to horseback riding to a beachside waterfall. As ever, it's the natural beauty, miles of almost abandoned beaches, rich wildlife, and jungle waterfalls that first made Montezuma famous, and they continue to make this one of my favorite beach towns in Costa Rica.

ESSENTIALS

GETTING THERE & DEPARTING   By Plane   The nearest airport is in Tambor, 17km (11 miles) away (see "Playa Tambor," above, for flight details). Some of the hotels listed below might pick you up in Tambor for a reasonable fee. If not, you'll have to hire a taxi, which could cost anywhere between $20 and $30 (£10–£15). **Taxis** are generally waiting to meet most regularly scheduled planes, but if they aren't, you can call Gilberto (© 642-0241) or Ronald (© 822-0610) for a cab.

By Car   The traditional route here is to take the Interamerican Highway from San José to Puntarenas and catch the ferry to either Naranjo or Paquera. Montezuma is about 50 minutes south of Tambor, 1¼ hours south of Paquera, and 2¾ hours south of Naranjo. The road from Paquera to Tambor is paved and usually in pretty good shape, and taking the Paquera ferry will save you time and some rough, dusty driving. The road from Naranjo to Paquera is all dirt and gravel and in bad shape.

Naviera Tambor (© 661-2084) ferries to Paquera leave Puntarenas roughly every 2 to 3 hours between 5am and 8:30pm. The trip takes 1½ hours. The fare is around $9 (£4.50) for a car and driver, $1.20 (60p) for additional adults, 80¢ (40p) for children. I recommend arriving early during the peak season and on weekends because lines can be long; if you miss the ferry, you'll have to wait around 2 hours or more for the next one. Moreover, the ferry schedule changes frequently, with fewer ferries during the low season, and the occasional extra ferry during the high season to meet demand. It is always best to check in advance.

The **Naranjo ferry** (© 661-1069) leaves daily at 6:30 and 10am and 2:30 and 7pm. The trip takes 1½ hours. The fare is $9 (£4.50) for cars, $1.60 (80p) for adults, and 80¢ (40p) for children.

Another option is to drive via the Tempisque River bridge. Although heading farther north and crossing the bridge is more circuitous, you will be driving the whole time, which at least feels faster than taking a seaborne ferry. Moreover, you will not be at the whim of the ferry schedule and the sometimes sold-out boats. To go this route, take the Interamerican Highway west from San José. Forty-seven kilometers (29 miles) past the turnoff for Puntarenas, turn left for the Tempisque River bridge. After you cross the Tempisque River, head to Quebrada Honda and then south to route 21, following signs for San Pablo, Jicaral, Lepanto, Playa Naranjo, and Paquera. This route is an option if you foresee waiting more than 2 hours for a ferry.

The car ferry from Paquera to Puntarenas leaves roughly every 2 hours between 8am and 10pm. *Note:* If you have to wait for the ferry, do not leave your car unattended, since break-ins are common.

By Bus & Ferry   **Transportes Rodriguez Hermanos** (© 642-0740, or 642-0219) runs three daily direct buses between San José and Montezuma. The buses leave from the Coca Cola bus terminal at Calle 12 and Avenida 5 at 7:30am and 12:30 and 5pm. The fare is around $10 (£5), including the ferry ride, and the trip takes around 5 hours.

Alternately, it takes two buses and a ferry ride to get to Montezuma. Express buses (© 222-0064) for Puntarenas leave San José daily every hour between 6am and 8pm from Calle 16 and Avenida 12. Trip duration is 2½ hours; the fare is $2.80 (£1.40).

From Puntarenas, you can take one of the car ferries mentioned above or the passenger launch *Paquereña* (© 641-0515), which leaves from the pier behind the market at 11:30am and 4pm. Ferry-trip duration is 1½ hours; the fare is 80¢ (40p). A bus south to Montezuma will be waiting to meet the ferry when it arrives in Paquera. The bus ride takes about 1½ hours; the fare is $2.50 (£1.25). Be careful not to take the Naranjo ferry because it does not meet with regular onward bus transportation to Montezuma.

Buses are met by hordes of locals trying to corral you to one of the many budget hotels. Remember, they are getting a commission for every body they bring in, so their information is biased.

When you're ready to head back, direct leave Montezuma at 5:15 and 8:15am, and 3:15pm. Regular local buses to Paquera leave Montezuma roughly every 2 hours throughout the day starting around 4am. The Paquereña ferry returns for Puntarenas at 7:30am and 2pm. Total trip duration is 3½ hours. Buses to San José leave Puntarenas daily every hour between 5am and 8pm.

ORIENTATION   As the winding mountain road that descends into Montezuma bottoms out, you turn left onto a small dirt road that defines the village proper. On this 1-block road, you will find El Sano Banano Village Cafe and, across from it, a small park with its own basketball court and children's playground. The bus stops at the end of this road. From here, hotels are scattered up and down the beach and around the village's few sand streets. If you're looking for Internet access, try the high-speed satellite connections offered at El Sano Banano's Internet cafe.

FUN ON & OFF THE BEACH

The ocean here is a gorgeous royal blue, and beautiful beaches stretch out along the coast on either side of town. Be careful, though: The waves can occasionally be too rough for casual swimming, and you need to be aware of stray rocks at your feet. Be sure you know where the rocks and tide are before doing any bodysurfing. The best places to swim are a couple hundred meters north of town in front of **El Rincón de los Monos,** or several kilometers farther north at Playa Grande.

If you're interested in more than simple beach time, head for the **Montezuma waterfall** ⚡ just south of town—it's one of those tropical fantasies where water comes pouring down into a deep pool. It's a popular spot, and it's a bit of a hike up the stream. There are actually a couple of waterfalls up this stream, but the upper falls are by far the more spectacular. You'll find the trail to the falls just over the bridge south of the village (on your right just past Las Cascadas restaurant). At the first major out-cropping of rocks, the trail disappears and you have to scramble up the rocks and river for a bit. A trail occasionally reappears for short stretches. Just stick close to the stream and you'll eventually hit the falls.

Note: Be very careful when climbing close to the rushing water, and also if you plan on taking any dives into the pools below. The rocks are quite slippery, and several people each year get very scraped up, break bones, and otherwise hurt themselves here.

Another popular local waterfall is **El Chorro** ⚡, located 8km (5 miles) north of Montezuma. This waterfall cascades down into a tide pool at the edge of the ocean. The pool here is a delightful mix of fresh- and seawater, and you can bathe while gazing out over the sea and rocky coastline. When the water is clear and calm, this is one of my favorite swimming holes in all of Costa Rica. However, a massive landslide in 2004 filled in much of this pool and also somewhat lessened the drama and beauty of the falls. Moreover, the pool here is dependent upon the tides—it disappears entirely at very high tide. It's about a 2-hour hike along the beach to reach El Chorro. Alternatively you can take a horseback tour here (see below).

HORSEBACK RIDING   Several people around the village will rent you horses for around $8 to $12 (£4–£6) an hour, although most people choose to do a guided 4-hour horseback tour for $30 to $40 (£15–£20). Luis, whose rental place is down the road that leads from town out to the beach, is a reliable source for horses, as is "Roger, the horse guy"—any local can direct you to him. All of the tour agencies in town also offer up these tours.

OTHER ACTIVITIES   There are some shops in the center of the village where you can rent a bicycle by the day or hour, as well as boogie boards and snorkeling equipment (although the water must be very calm for snorkeling).

A range of guided tour and adventure options is available in Montezuma. **CocoZuma Traveller** (© 642-0911; www.cocozuma.com) and **Montezuma Travel Adventures** (© 642-0808; www.montezumatraveladventures.com) can both arrange horseback riding, boat excursions, scuba-dive and snorkel tours, and rafting trips; car

---

Tips Buy the Book . . . or Just Borrow It

If you came unprepared or run out of reading material, check in at **Librería Topsy** (© 642-0576), which, in addition to selling books, runs a lending library.

and motorcycle rentals; airport transfers; international phone, fax, and Internet service; and currency exchange.

One popular tour option here is the **Waterfall Canopy Tour** ☆ (© 823-6111 or 642-0808), which is built right alongside Montezuma's famous falls. The tour, which features 9 cables connecting 11 platforms, includes a swim at the foot of the falls and costs $35 (£18) per person.

There are plenty of simple souvenir stores, as well as itinerant artisans selling their wares on the street, but it's worth stopping in at **Piedra Colorado** (© 841-5855) to check out their impressive silver, stone, and polished-shell creations. This place is located in the tiny strip mall in the center of Montezuma.

AN EXCURSION TO CABO BLANCO NATURE RESERVE

As beautiful as the beaches around Montezuma are, the beaches at **Cabo Blanco Absolute Nature Reserve** ☆☆, 11km (6¾ miles) south of the village, are even more stunning. Located at the southernmost tip of the Nicoya Peninsula, Cabo Blanco is a national park that preserves a nesting site for brown pelicans, magnificent frigate birds, and brown boobies. The beaches are backed by lush tropical forest that is home to howler monkeys. You can hike through the preserve's lush forest right down to the deserted, pristine beach, which is 4km (2½ miles) away. Or you can take a shorter 2km (1¼-mile) loop trail through the primary forest here. This is Costa Rica's oldest official bioreserve and was set up thanks to the pioneering efforts of conservationists Karen Mogensen and Nicholas Wessberg. Admission is $6 (£3); the reserve is closed on Monday and Tuesday.

On your way out to Cabo Blanco, you'll pass through the tiny village of **Cabuya.** Some very basic *cabinas* and hotels have sprung up out here, and there are a couple of hidden patches of beach to discover if you poke around some of the deserted dirt roads.

Shuttle buses head from Montezuma to Cabo Blanco roughly every 2 hours beginning at 8am, and then turn around and bring folks from Cabo Blanco to Montezuma; the last one leaves Cabo Blanco around 5pm. The fare is $2 (£1) each way. These shuttles often don't run during the off season. Alternatively, you can share a taxi: The fare is around $15 to $20 (£7.50–£10) per taxi, which can hold four or five passengers. Taxis tend to hang around Montezuma center. One dependable *taxista* is **Gilberto Rodríguez** (© 642-0241).

WHERE TO STAY

In addition to the places listed below, the **Hotel El Jardín** (© 642-0548; www. hoteleljardin.com), located at the crossroads to town at the bottom of the hill, has pleasant rooms and a swimming pool. The rooms here are spread up a steep hillside, which may call for a short but vigorous hike.

EXPENSIVE
Ylang Ylang Beach Resort ☆☆ *Finds*   This place is the sort of tropical retreat many travelers dream about finding. Set in a lush patch of forest just steps away from the sand, the hotel offers rooms that are about a 15-minute walk northeast of town along the beach. Rooms and cabins come in a variety of shapes and sizes. Coco Joe's Rancho is the largest cabin and features a luscious wraparound balcony and a small sleeping loft. But I also like the smaller cabins, which are yellow ferroconcrete geodesic domes that look like igloos. These have both indoor and outdoor garden showers which match the surroundings perfectly. There are also three spacious suites with private balconies and sleeping lofts in a separate building, with three standard rooms

on the ground floor below them. Many guests opt for extended stays. There's a beautiful little swimming pool with a sculpted waterfall, and the whole operation is set amid lush gardens planted with lots of banana, heliconia, and elephant-ear plants. Ylang Ylang is part of the El Sano Banano project and arrival and check-in are handled at the downtown El Sano Banano Village Café.

Montezuma, Cóbano de Puntarenas. ℭ 642-0636. Fax 642-0068. www.ylangylangresort.com. 20 units. $160–$255 (£80–£128) double. Rates include breakfast and dinner. Rates lower in off season. AE, MC, V. Amenities: Restaurant; bar; midsize outdoor pool; tour desk; in-room massage; laundry service. In room: Free Wi-Fi, fridge, coffeemaker, hair dryer, safe, no phone.

MODERATE

The El Sano Banano folks also run an in-town B&B (ℭ **642-0636;** www. elbanano.com), located just off the popular restaurant (see below). The rooms here feature air-conditioning and satellite televisions; because of the design, you are basically forced to use the air-conditioning. Rooms here go for $75 (£38) double.

Nature Lodge Finca Los Caballos ⭐   This remote lodge is located on a high ridge about 3km (1¾ miles) above Montezuma. The rooms are simple, yet elegant. Spanish-style tile roofs, hardwood trim, stone floors, and some pretty paintings and craft works add decorative accents. Every room has a private patio or balcony with either a garden, jungle or ocean view. The best rooms here are the Superior Pacific Rooms, which feature ocean views out across the forested hills below. There's a small pool here, and plenty of hammocks strung around for relaxing. The restaurant serves creative, well-prepared meals using fresh and natural ingredients.

Finca Los Caballos translates to "horse ranch," and riding is taken seriously here. The owners have 16 hectares (40 acres) of land and access to many neighboring ranches and trail systems. The horses are well tended and trained. The standard trips to Montezuma's waterfalls are available, as well as a host of other adventure-tour options. Be forewarned: if you stay here, it's a quick car ride, but very hefty hike, especially on the way back, to the beach.

Cóbano de Puntarenas (A.P. 22). ℭ **642-0664.** ℭ/fax 642-0124. www.naturelodge.net. 12 units. $86–$138 (£43–£69) double. Rates include breakfast. Rates lower in off season. MC, V. Amenities: Restaurant; small pool; horse rental and tours; tour desk; laundry service. In room: Minifridge, no phone.

INEXPENSIVE

Now that camping on the beach is discouraged (although many folks still get away with it), most campers make do at **El Rincón de los Monos** (ℭ 642-0048), which is about 90m (295 ft.) north of town along the beach. It charges about $3 (£1.50) per tent and provides showers and bathrooms. Others head south toward Cabuya and Cabo Blanco. **El Pargo Feliz** (ℭ 642-0065) and **Cabinas Mar y Cielo** (ℭ 642-0261) are two good budget options right in the center of town.

Amor de Mar ⭐ (Value   This hotel has a wonderful setting overlooking the ocean. With its wide expanse of neatly trimmed grass sloping down to the sea, tide pools (one of which is as big as a small swimming pool), and hammocks slung from the mango trees, this is the perfect place for anyone who wants to do some serious relaxing. The rooms are housed in a beautifully appointed two-story building, which abounds in varnished hardwoods. Although simply appointed, most rooms have plenty of space and receive lots of sunlight. The big porch on the second floor is a great place for reading or just gazing out to sea. Breakfast and lunch only are served here on a beautiful open-air patio overlooking the sea. The breakfast specialties include big banana pancakes and fresh homemade whole-wheat French bread. These folks also rent out a large fully equipped two-story, four-bedroom house next to the hotel.

Montezuma, (A.P. 22, Cóbano de Puntarenas). ©/fax 642-0262. www.amordemar.com. 11 units, 9 w/private bathroom. $45–$55 (£23–£28) double w/shared bathroom; $60–$90 (£30–£45) double w/private bathroom; $170 (£85) house. Rates lower in off season. V. **Amenities:** Restaurant; laundry service. *In room:* No phone.

Hotel La Aurora   Just to the left as you enter the village of Montezuma, you'll find this long-standing hotel. The rooms are spread out over two neighboring buildings fronting the village's small park and playground. All rooms are clean and well-kept. I prefer the older rooms, which are located in a spacious three-story wooden building. There's even a two-room apartment on the third floor here, with a private balcony and a bit of an ocean view through the treetops. The hotel also features a small lending library, some hammocks and comfortable chairs, a communal kitchen, and flowering vines growing up the walls. In fact, there are plants and vines all over La Aurora, which keeps things cool and gives the place a fitting tropical feel. Fresh coffee, tea, and hearty breakfasts are served each morning.

Montezuma (A.P. 2), Cóbano de Puntarenas. ©/fax 642-0051. www.playamontezuma.net. 16 units, 13 w/private bathroom. $25 (£13) double w/shared bathroom; $30–$65 (£15–£33) double w/bathroom. Rates include taxes. Rates lower in off season. AE, MC, V. **Amenities:** Laundry service. *In room:* A/C, no phone.

Hotel Los Mangos   Situated across the road from the water a bit before the waterfall on the road toward Cabo Blanco, this place takes its name from the many mango trees under which the bungalows are built. (If mango is your passion, come in May, when it's in season.) The shared-bathroom budget rooms are very basic, but they are a decent value and you get access to the pool to boot. However, the rooms are pretty run down, and the octagonal bungalows built of Costa Rican hardwoods are the better accommodations here. Each has a small porch with rocking chairs, a thatched roof, a good amount of space, and ceiling fans. The swimming pool is built to resemble a natural pond—there's even an artificial waterfall flowing into it—and there's a separate Jacuzzi. The old restaurant here has been converted into a yoga studio, and daily yoga classes are offered.

Montezuma, Cóbano de Puntarenas. © 642-0076. Fax 642-0259. www.hotellosmangos.com. 10 units, 6 w/private bathroom; 9 bungalows. $35 (£18) double w/shared bathroom; $70 (£35) double w/private bathroom; $82 (£41) bungalow. Rates lower in off season. AE, DC, MC, V. **Amenities:** Small pool; yoga studio, Jacuzzi; laundry service. *In room:* Safe, no phone.

WHERE TO DINE

In addition to the places listed below, you'll find several basic *sodas* and casual restaurants right in the village. My favorite of these is the simple **Restaurante Lucy** (© 642-0273), which has a few tables set on the sand a few feet from the ocean, right next to the Hotel Lucy. There's also **Pizzería Angulo Etrusco** (© 642-0489), which is located at the crossroads into town and serves good thin-crust pizzas, calzones, and pastas. You might also want to check out the Spanish cuisine at the downtown **Hotel Montezuma** (© 642-0657) or the varied international fare at **Cocolores** (© 642-0348) or the **Iguana Café** (© 642-0422).

El Sano Banano Village Cafe 🎔🎔 VEGETARIAN/INTERNATIONAL   Delicious vegetarian meals, including nightly specials, sandwiches, and salads, are the specialty of this ever-popular Montezuma restaurant, although there's also a variety of fish and chicken dishes. Lunches feature hefty sandwiches on whole-wheat bread and filling fish and vegetarian *casados* for around $5 (£2.50). The yogurt fruit shakes are fabulous, but I like to get a little more decadent and have one of the mocha chill shakes.

El Sano Banano also doubles as the local movie house. Nightly DVD releases are projected on a large screen; the selection ranges from first-run to quite artsy, and there's a constantly growing library of more than 800 movies. The movies begin at 7:30pm and require a minimum purchase of $6 (£3).

On the main road into the village. ℂ 642-0944. Main courses $5–$15 (£2.50–£7.50). AE, MC, V. Daily 7am–9:30pm.

Playa de los Artistas 𝒢𝒢𝒢 *Finds* ITALIAN/MEDITERRANEAN   This popular open-air restaurant is beside an old house fronting the beach, and there are only a few tables, so arrive early. If you don't get a seat and you feel hearty, try the low wooden table surrounded by tatami mats on the sand. Meals are served in large classy and creative plates, or in broad wooden bowls set on ceramic-ringed coasters or on large wooden planks lined with banana leaves. The menu changes nightly but always features several fish and seafood dishes. The fresh grouper in a black-pepper sauce is phenomenal. The outdoor grill is great for grilled fish and seafood. All meals come with plenty of fresh bread for soaking up the delicious sauces.

Across from Hotel Los Mangos. ℂ 642-0920. Reservations recommended. Main courses $7–$21 (£3.50–£11). No credit cards. Mon–Sat noon–10pm.

Ylang-Ylang 𝒢𝒢 INTERNATIONAL   Located at the Ylang Ylang Beach Resort, this pretty, open-air affair features a sculpted bar with indigenous and wildlife motifs. The menu is broad with a prominent Asian influence, ranging from sushi to jumbo shrimp in a pineapple-and-coconut sauce to vegetarian teriyaki stir-fry. There are also several crepe and pasta options and plenty of fresh seafood dishes. For lunch you can have a bruschetta or some cool gazpacho and be just a few steps from the sand when you're done.

At the Ylang Ylang Beach Resort. ℂ 642-0402 or 833-4106. Reservations recommended. Main courses $9–$20 (£4.50–£10). AE, MC, V. Daily 7am–10pm.

MONTEZUMA AFTER DARK

Montezuma has had a tough time coming to terms with its nightlife. For years, local businesses banded together to force most of the loud, late-night activity out of town. This has eased somewhat, and there's currently quite an active nightlife in Montezuma proper. The local action seems to base itself either at **Chico's Bar** 𝒢 or at the bar at the **Hotel Montezuma.** Both are located on the main strip in town facing the water. For real raging nightlife, head to the large disco at the **Barceló Playa Tambor Beach Resort,** located on the main road between Paquera and Cóbano, about 20km (12 miles) south of Paquera and about 16km (10 miles) north of Montezuma. Playa Tambor Beach Resort has even been known to offer free round-trip taxi service to lure partiers. Alternatively there's often something happening, either a live music or DJ, at **Playa Las Manchas,** located about a mile south of town on the road to Cabo Blanco. If your evening tastes are mellower, **El Sano Banano Village Cafe** (p. 209) doubles as the local movie house, with nightly late-run features projected on a large screen.

12 Malpaís/Santa Teresa 𝒢𝒢

150km (93 miles) W of San José; 12km (7½ miles) S of Cóbano

Malpaís (or Mal País) means "badlands," and, while this may have been an apt moniker many years ago, it no longer accurately describes this booming beach area. Malpaís is a bucket term often used to refer a string of neighboring beaches running from south to north, and including Malpaís, Playa Carmen, Santa Teresa and Playa Hermosa. These beaches are long, wide expanses of light sand dotted with rocky outcroppings. This area is one of Costa Rica's hottest spots, and hotels and restaurants are opening at a dizzying pace. Still, it will take time before this place is anything like more developed destinations like Tamarindo or Manuel Antonio. In Malpaís and Santa Teresa today, you'll find a just scattering of beach hotels and resorts, miles of nearly deserted beach, and easy access to some nice jungle and the nearby **Cabo Blanco Reserve** (p. 207).

ESSENTIALS

GETTING THERE & DEPARTING   By Plane   The nearest airport is in Tambor (see "Playa Tambor," above, for flight details). Some of the hotels listed below might be willing to pick you up in Tambor for a reasonable fee. If not, you'll have to hire a taxi, which could cost anywhere between $30 and $40 (£15–£20). **Taxis** are generally waiting to meet most regularly scheduled planes, but if they aren't, you can call Gilberto (© **642-0241**) or Ronald (© **822-0610**) for a cab.

By Car   Follow the directions above to Montezuma (see "Playa Montezuma," earlier in this chapter). At Cóbano follow the signs to Malpaís and Playa Santa Teresa. It's another 12km (7½ miles) down a rough dirt road that requires four-wheel-drive and is sometimes (although rarely) impassable during the rainy season.

By Bus & Ferry   Transportes Rodriguez Hermanos (© **642-0740** or 642-0219) has three daily buses from San José's Coca-Cola bus station to Malpaís. The buses leave at 7am and 12:30 and 3pm, and the fare is $10 (£5), including the ferry passage. The ride takes a little over 5 hours. The return buses leave Malpaís at 5:30 and 8am, and 3:15pm.

Alternately, you can follow the directions above for getting to Montezuma, but get off the Montezuma bus in Cóbano. From Cóbano, there are buses daily for Malpaís and Santa Teresa at 10:30am and 2:30pm. The fare is $1.50 (75p). Buses return daily to Cóbano at 7am and noon. *Be forewarned:* These bus schedules are subject to change according to demand, road conditions, and the whim of the bus company.

If you miss the bus connection in Cóbano, you can hire a cab to Malpaís for around $15 (£7.50).

ORIENTATION   Malpaís and Santa Teresa are two tiny beach villages. As you reach the ocean, the road forks; Playa Carmen is straight ahead, Malpaís is to your left, and Santa Teresa is to your right. If you continue beyond Santa Teresa, you'll come to the even-more-deserted beaches of playas Hermosa and Manzanillo (not to be confused with beaches of the same names to be found elsewhere in the country).

FAST FACTS   There are no banks, ATM machines, or medical clinics in Malpaís or Santa Teresa. All of that is in Cóbano. There are several general stores, public phones, and a few Internet cafes, however.

If you need a taxi, call **Miguel** (© **819-9021** or 640-0261). If you want to do the driving yourself, you can contact the local office of **Budget Rent A Car** (© **640-0418**), or the **Quad Rental Center** (© **640-0178**). The latter rents out ATVs, while the former has a fleet of more traditional cars and trucks.

FUN ON & OFF THE BEACH

If you decide to do anything here besides sunbathe on the beach and play in the waves, your options include nature hikes, horseback riding, ATV tours, scuba diving and snorkeling, which most hotels can help arrange. Surfing is a major draw here. There are miles of beach breaks to choose from and a few points to boot. If you want to rent a board or take a lesson, check out the **Santa Teresa Surf School** (✆ 640-0049; www.santateresasurfschool.com).

If you want try a canopy adventure here, head to **Canopy del Pacífico** (✆ **640-0091**), which is located toward the southern end of Malpaís and just slightly inland. A 2-hour tour over the nearly 1km (½ mile) of cables touches down on eight platforms, features two rappels, and offers good views of both the forest and the ocean below. The cost is $35 (£18).

If the waves aren't happening, or if you just want to complement your newfound surfing skills with some linguistic maneuvering, contact the folks at the **Santa Teresa Beach Spanish School** (✆ 640-0049; www.spanishandsurf.com), who run weeklong total-immersion classes with or without lodging, and are tied in to the Santa Teresa Surf School as well.

Finally, any hotel in the area can arrange a horseback-riding or ATV trip into the hills and along the beaches of this region, a guided hike through **Cabo Blanco Nature Reserve,** a sportfishing excursion out onto the high seas, or a trip over to Montezuma.

WHERE TO STAY
VERY EXPENSIVE
Flor Blanca Resort ✦✦✦ *Finds*   This intimate resort hotel is, hands down, the most luxurious option in this neck of the woods and one of the most luxurious boutique hotels in the country. The individual villas are huge, with a vast central living area opening onto a spacious veranda. The furnishings, decorations, and architecture boast a mix of Latin American and Asian influences, with some African adornments thrown in for good measure. Most overlook lush gardens, and about half have views through to the sea. Every unit features a large open-air bathroom with a garden shower and teardrop-shape tub set amid flowering tropical foliage. You can opt for either the one-bedroom villas with a four-poster king-size bed in the main bedroom, or a two-bedroom, two-bathroom villa, with two twin beds in a separate upstairs bedroom. You'll find several examples of the resort's namesake tree planted around the grounds.

The restaurant features wonderfully prepared creative fusion cuisine (see below). There's a modern, full-service spa, as well as a full-size and active dojo on the grounds, where complimentary yoga, kickboxing, and cardio-workout classes are regularly offered. The beautiful free-form pool is on two levels, with a sculpted waterfall connecting them and a shady Indonesian-style gazebo off to one side for lounging around in. Flor Blanca is located toward the northern end of Playa Santa Teresa.

Playa Santa Teresa, Cóbano, Puntarenas. ✆ **640-0232.** Fax 640-0226. www.florblanca.com. 11 units. $495–$525 (£248–£263) double; $725–$775 (£363–£388) 2-bedroom villa for 4; $850 (£425) villa deluxe. Rates include full breakfast. Rates lower during off season; higher during peak weeks. AE, DC, MC, V. No children under 6. **Amenities:** Restaurant; bar; pool; small open-air gym; spa; watersports equipment rental; bike rental; limited room service (7am–9:30pm); laundry service. *In room:* A/C, free Wi-Fi, kitchenette, coffeemaker, safe.

EXPENSIVE
Milarepa ✦   Named after a Buddhist sage, this small collection of individual bungalows is spread around shady grounds fronting the beach, just next door to Flor Blanca. The bungalows are simple, roomy, and understated. All have wooden floors, a mix of teak and bamboo furniture, beds with mosquito netting, and a private porch. An overhead fan keeps things cool, and there are plenty of windows for cross ventilation. The more expensive units are closest to the beach and have ocean views. There's a midsize pool here for when the surf is too rough. Service can be spotty, and I find

the rates a bit high for what you get. Still the setting is wonderful, and for many that's worth the price of admission right there. The restaurant here, Soma, is excellent.

Playa Santa Teresa, Cóbano, Puntarenas. ℂ 640-0023. Fax 640-0168. www.milarepahotel.com. 10 units. $154–$184 (£77–£92) double. Rates lower during off season; higher during peak weeks. AE, MC, V. **Amenities:** Restaurant; bar; pool; tour desk; laundry service. *In room:* Wi-Fi, no phone.

Trópico Latino Lodge 🌴   One of the first hotels out here, this beachfront spread is still a good choice. The nicest accommodations here are the new private bungalows, which have artistic tile work and finishings and views of the ocean. The original rooms here are housed in four duplex units. These are huge—the king-size bamboo bed barely makes a dent in the floor space. There's also a separate sofa bed, as well as a small desk, a wall unit of shelves, and closet space galore. Although none of the older rooms has any ocean view to speak of, they all have private patios with a hammock. The shady grounds are rich in the native pochote tree, which is known for its spiky trunk. The small restaurant here has excellent fresh fish and plenty of pasta dishes.

Playa Santa Teresa, Cóbano, Puntarenas. ℂ 640-0062. Fax 640-0117. www.hoteltropicolatino.com. 12 units. $100–$160 (£50–£80) double. Rates lower in off season. No credit cards. **Amenities:** Restaurant; bar; small free-form pool; small spa; Jacuzzi; laundry service; free Wi-Fi. *In room:* A/C, coffeemaker, safe, no phone.

INEXPENSIVE

Budget travelers can check out **Cabinas Bosque Mar** (ℂ **640-0074**), which is on the Malpaís road and has a few basic rooms and even a small swimming pool. You can also pitch a tent at several spots along the beaches here. Look for camping signs; you should get bathroom and shower access for a few bucks.

Frank's Place   Building on the perennial popularity of their long-standing restaurant, these folks also offer a hodgepodge of rooms in a variety of styles, price ranges, and configurations. Nine rooms are very basic and feature a shared bathroom; four units come with private bathrooms, a minifridge, and a tiny television set. Only four rooms here feature double beds, although a few come with complete kitchenettes, and some have air-conditioning. Although the midrange rooms are a decent value and the hotel is well located, I don't think the higher-priced rooms here are worth it—you can certainly do better for the money. There's a small pool at the center of the complex, as well as an unheated Jacuzzi. The restaurant here is a glorified *soda,* but it does serve good Costa Rican cuisine, fresh fish, and a smattering of international dishes. It's also one of the most popular hangouts in Malpaís. This place is located at the crossroads of Malpaís and Playa Carmen, just as you enter town.

Malpaís, Cóbano de Puntarenas. ℂ/fax 640-0096. www.franksplacehotel.com. 30 units, 9 w/shared bathroom. $24 (£12) double w/shared bathroom; $36–$65 (£18–£33) double w/private bathroom. AE, MC, V. **Amenities:** Restaurant; bar; small pool; Jacuzzi; watersports equipment rental; bike rental; tour desk; laundry service; free Wi-Fi. *In room:* No phone.

Malpaís Surf Camp & Resort   There's a wide range of accommodations here, reflected in the equally wide range of prices. The most basic rooms are open-air ranchos with gravel floors, lathe-and-bamboo walls, bead curtains for a door, and shared bathrooms. From here, your options get progressively more comfortable, ranging from shared-bathroom bunk-bed rooms to new deluxe poolside villas, to private houses with all the amenities. There's a refreshing free-form tile pool in the center of the complex, and the large, open main lodge area serves as a combination restaurant, bar, lounge, and surfboard-storage area. There's satellite TV with surf videos playing most of the day, as well as pool, Ping-Pong, and foosball tables. As the name implies, this place is run by and caters to surfers. The overall vibe here is loose and funky, as it should be. The restaurant serves filling, fresh, and, at times, quite creative cuisine, depending on how accomplished the itinerant surf-chef-of-the-month is. Surf rentals, lessons, and video sessions are all available.

Malpaís, Cóbano de Puntarenas. ℂ 640-0031. ℂ/fax 640-0061. www.malpaissurfcamp.com. 16 units, 8 w/shared bathroom. $10–$15 (£5–£7.50) per person w/shared bathroom; $95–$135 (£48–£68) double w/private bathroom. AE, MC, V. **Amenities:** Restaurant; bar; midsize pool; small exercise room; watersports equipment rental; bike rental; game room; tour desk; babysitting; laundry service. *In room:* Safe, no phone.

Point Break Hotel   The simple cabins here feature polished concrete floors, inset with cross-sections of tree trunks, two twin beds, and three walls comprised largely of screening. They also come with a refrigerator and a small patio area with a couple of chairs. The shared bathrooms and showers are kept quite clean and there's a large lounge area strung with hammocks and featuring a television. Several newer cabins have their own bathrooms. The greatest attraction here is the fact that this hotel sits just steps away from one of the best breaks along this stretch of coast. Hence the name and the steady stream of surfers who choose this simple place.

Playa Santa Teresa, Cóbano de Puntarenas. ℂ/fax **640-0190.** www.surfing-malpais.com. 7 units, 2 w/shared bathroom. $40 (£20) double w/shared bathroom; $50–$60 (£25–£30) double w/private bathroom and kitchenette. MC, V. **Amenities:** Bar; lounge. *In room:* No phone.

WHERE TO DINE
In addition to the places listed below, you might try **La Bella Napoli** (ℂ **640-0073**), a homey Italian restaurant located across the street from Cabinas Bosque Mar, or **Mary's** (ℂ **640-0153**), which features wood-oven baked pizzas and is located toward the northern end of Malpaís. For another fine dining option, in addition to Nectar, head to **Soma** at Milarepa (see above).

Nectar ★★★ *Finds*   FUSION   The dimly lit open-air setting of this poolside and beachfront restaurant is elegant yet casual. There's a Pacific Rim influence to the fusion cuisine served up here. You can almost always start with some sushi or sashimi made with the daily catch. In addition to fresh seafood and several vegetarian entrees, you might also find lamb, rabbit, or duck on the regularly changing menu. The creativity, service, and presentation are some of the best you'll find in Costa Rica.

At Flor Blanca Resort in Santa Teresa. ℂ 640-0232. Reservations recommended. Main courses $8–$42 (£4–£21). AE, MC, V. Daily 7am–9:30pm.

Soda Piedra Mar *Finds*   COSTA RICAN/SEAFOOD   This simple open-air restaurant is set on a rocky outcropping just steps away from the sea. The place is little more than a zinc-roofed shack that seems as if a stiff breeze would quickly level it. There are only a few tables here under the low roof; weather permitting, more tables are set in the sand under the sun or stars. The fare is simple, but the fish is guaranteed fresh, the portions are hearty, and the setting and sunsets are wonderful.

On the beach in Malpaís. ℂ 640-0069. Main courses $3–$14 (£1.50–£7). No credit cards. Daily 8am–8pm.

MALPAIS & SANTA TERESA AFTER DARK
There's not much in the way of raging nightlife here. Some folks make the long and arduous journey over to Montezuma. The most popular bar in Malpaís is **Night & Day,** which used to be called Tabu. Surfers and other travelers also tend to gather in the evenings at **Frank's Place** and the **Malpaís Surf Camp.**

The Northern Zone: Mountain Lakes, Cloud Forests & a Volcano

While many visitors to Costa Rica covet the country's beaches, the northern zone is home to several prime ecotourist destinations, including the **Monteverde Cloud Forest Reserve** 𝒸𝒸𝒸 and **Arenal Volcano** 𝒸𝒸. There are rainforests and cloud forests, jungle rivers, mountain lakes, lowland marshes, and an unbelievable wealth of birds and other wildlife. Slight changes in elevation create unique microclimates and ecosystems throughout the region. In addition to these natural wonders, this region also provides an intimate glimpse into the rural heart and soul of Costa

Rica. Small, isolated lodges abound, and towns and villages remain predominantly small agricultural communities.

This area is also a must for adventure travelers. The northern zone has one of the best windsurfing spots in the world, on **Lake Arenal** 𝒸, as well as excellent opportunities for mountain biking, hiking, canyoning and river rafting. And if you partake in any number of adventure activities, you'll also find several soothing natural hot springs in the area to soak your tired muscles.

1 Puerto Viejo de Sarapiquí 𝒸

82km (51 miles) N of San José; 102km (63 miles) E of La Fortuna

The Sarapiquí region, named for the river that drains this area, lies at the foot of the Cordillera Central mountain range. To the west is the rainforest of **Braulio Carrillo National Park,** and to the east are **Tortuguero National Park** 𝒸𝒸 and **Barra del Colorado National Wildlife Refuge** 𝒸. In between these protected areas lay thousands of acres of banana, pineapple, and palm plantations. Here you see the great contradiction of Costa Rica: On the one hand, the country is known for its national parks, which preserve some of the largest tracts of rainforest left in Central America; on the other hand, nearly every acre of land outside of these parks, save a few private reserves, has been clear-cut and converted into plantations—and the cutting continues.

Within the remaining rainforest are several lodges that attract naturalists (both amateur and professional). Two of these lodges, La Selva and Rara Avis, are famous for the research that's conducted on their surrounding reserves. Bird-watching and rainforest hikes are the primary attractions, but more adventure-oriented travelers will find plenty of activities available here, including canopy tours and boating and rafting trips along the Sarapiquí River.

ESSENTIALS
GETTING THERE & DEPARTING   By Car   The Guápiles Highway, which leads to the Caribbean coast, heads north out of downtown San José on Calle 3 before

heading east. Turn north before reaching Guápiles on the road to Río Frío, and continue north through Las Horquetas, passing the turnoffs for Rara Avis, La Selva, and El Gavilán lodges before reaching Puerto Viejo.

A more scenic route goes through Heredia, Barva, Varablanca, and San Miguel before reaching Puerto Viejo. This route passes very close to the Poás Volcano and directly in front of the La Paz waterfall. If you want to take this route, head west out of San José, then turn north to Heredia and follow the signs for Varablanca. *Tip:* If you plan to stop on the way to see the **La Paz Waterfall Gardens** (p. 126) or ride the **Rain Forest Aerial Tram** (p. 140), budget *at least* 2 hours to visit either attraction.

By Bus   **Empresarios Guapileños** buses (© 257-6859 in San José, or 710-7780 in Puerto Viejo) leave San José roughly every hour between 6am and 6pm from the **Gran Terminal del Caribe,** on Calle Central, 1 block north of Avenida 11. The buses are marked RIO FRIO, PUERTO VIEJO, or both. There are two routes to Puerto Viejo de Sarapiquí. The faster route heads out on the Guápiles Highway, through Braulio Carrillo National Park and then past Las Horquetas. The slower but more scenic route heads out through Heredia, Varablanca, and La Virgen, passing between the Barva and Poás volcanoes. If you're heading to La Selva, Rara Avis, or El Gavilán lodges, be sure you're on a bus going through Braulio Carrillo and Las Horquetas. The trip takes between 2 and 4 hours, depending on the route taken, the condition of the roads, and the frequency of stops; the fare is around $2.40 (£1.20). Buses for San José leave Puerto Viejo roughly every hour between 6am and 6pm.

ORIENTATION   Puerto Viejo is a very small town, at the center of which is a soccer field. If you continue past the soccer field on the main road and stay on the paved road, and then turn right at the Banco Nacional, you'll come to the Río Sarapiquí and the dock, where you can look into arranging a boat trip.

WHAT TO SEE & DO

BOAT TRIPS   For the adventurous, Puerto Viejo is a jumping-off point for trips down the Río Sarapiquí to Barra del Colorado National Wildlife Refuge and Tortuguero National Park on the Caribbean coast. A boat for up to 10 people will cost you around $200 to $250 (£100–£125) to Barra del Colorado or $250 to $350 (£125–£175) to Tortuguero. If you're interested in this trip, it's worth checking at your hotel or with **Oasis Nature Tours** (© 766-6108; www.oasisnaturetours.com). Alternatively, you can head down to the town dock on the bank of the Sarapiquí and see if you can arrange a less expensive boat trip on your own by tagging along with another group or, better yet, with a bunch of locals.

In addition to the longer trips, you can take shorter trips on the river for between $10 and $20 (£5–£10) per person per hour. A trip down the Sarapiquí, even if it's for only an hour or two, provides opportunities to spot crocodiles, caimans, monkeys, sloths, and dozens of bird species.

CANOPY TOUR & MORE   Hacienda Pozo Azul (© 761-1360; www.pozoazul. com) is a working cattle farm and one-stop shop for a wide range of adventure activities. These folks have an extensive zip-line canopy tour operation, with 17 platforms connected by 12 different cable runs. They also offer white-water rafting and kayaking, horseback riding, guided hikes, and mountain bike tours. These folks even run a tent-camp and separate rustic lodge, in deep rainforest sites here.

HIKING & GUIDED TOURS   Anyone can take advantage of the 56km (35 miles) of well-maintained **trails at La Selva** ✸✸ (p. 216). If you're not staying there, however,

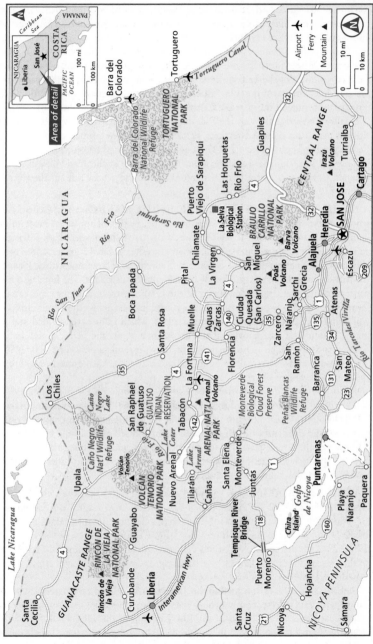

you'll have to take a guided hike, led by experienced and well-informed naturalists. Half- and full-day hikes ($28/£14 and $36/£18, respectively) are offered daily, but you must reserve in advance (© **766-6565;** www.ots.ac.cr). The half-day tours leave at 8am and 1:30pm daily.

My favorite hike starts off with the Cantarrana ("singing frog") trail, which includes a section of low bridges over a rainforest swamp. From here, you can join up with either the near or far circular loop trails—**CCC** and **CCL.** Another good hiking option is the trails and suspended bridges at the **Centro Neotrópico Sarapiquís** (p. 220).

Finally, if you want to visit the Sarapiquí region on a day trip from San José, call either **Costa Rica Fun Adventures** (© **290-6015;** www.crfunadventures.com) or **Ecoscapes Highlights Tour** (© **297-0664;** www.costaricasbesttour.com), which run jam-packed day trips that combine a bus ride and stop at the Poás Volcano, La Paz waterfall, a visit to a coffee farm, a rainforest hike, and a boat ride on the river for around $79 (£40) per person.

A NATURAL-HISTORY THEME PARK IN THE MAKING   The **Centro Neotrópico Sarapiquís** (p. 220) is working toward the creation of one of the most unique natural-history projects in the region. The Alma Ata Archaeological Park is basically an ongoing dig of a modest pre-Columbian gravesite; so far, 12 graves, some petroglyphs, and numerous pieces of ceramic and jewelry have been unearthed. Plans for the park include the reconstruction of a small indigenous village. The hotel also has a small museum that displays examples of the ceramics, tools, clothing, and carvings found here, as well as other natural-history exhibits. Just across the hotel's driveway, you'll find the Chester Field Biological Gardens, which feature well-tended and displayed examples of local medicinal and ornamental plants and herbs, as well as food crops. Admission to the archaeological park, museum, and gardens costs $20 (£10). If you just want to visit the small museum, the cost is $8 (£4). A self-guided walk through the botanical gardens is free.

Across the Sarapiquí River from the Centro Neotrópico is the 300-hectare (741-acre) private **Tirimbina Rainforest Center** ⚞ (© **761-1579;** www.tirimbina.org), which features a small network of trails and several impressive suspension bridges, both over the river and through the forest canopy. A self-guided walk of the bridges and trails of the reserve costs $15 (£7.50) per person, and a 2-hour guided tour costs $18 (£9) per person—definitely worth the extra few bucks. Night tours and specialized bird-watching tours are also available.

RAFTING & KAYAKING   If you want a fast, wild ride on the river, check in with **Aguas Bravas** (© **292-2072;** www.aguas-bravas.co.cr) or **Aventuras del Sarapiquí** ⚞ (© **766-6768;** www.sarapiqui.com). Both companies run trips on a variety of sections of the Sarapiquí River, ranging from Class III to Class V. Trips cost between $45 and $75 (£23–£38) per person. Aventuras del Sarapiquí also runs mountain-biking tours in the area, and they rent kayaks, give kayaking classes, and offer kayak trips for more experienced and/or daring river rats.

Another option is to stay at **Rancho Leona,** in La Virgen de Sarapiquí (© **761-1019;** www.rancholeona.com), a small stained-glass workshop, kayaking center, and rustic guesthouse on the banks of the Río Sarapiquí in the village of La Virgen. Its trips are offered as a package that includes lodging in simple dormitory-style accommodations, all meals, and extensive kayak instruction on the river. They even throw in an hour of Spanish lessons per day. No experience is necessary, and the river here is very calm. Trips for experienced kayakers can also be arranged.

SNAKES UNDER GLASS   Just a few blocks west of the Centro Neotrópico Sara-piquís, you'll find **Jardin de Seprientes** (**Snake Garden**; ✆ **761-1059**), a collection of over 50 local snakes, both venomous and non-venomous, and other reptiles and amphibians. All are kept in clean, well-lit displays. Admission is $6 (£3) adults, $3 (£1.50) children.

TWO MAJOR ATTRACTIONS EN ROUTE   If you're driving to Puerto Viejo de Sarapiquí via the Guápiles Highway, you might want to stop at the **Rain Forest Aerial Tram** 🐾. You'll see the entrance on your right shortly after passing through the Zurquí tunnel. If you're traveling via Varablanca and La Virgen, you'll want to visit the **La Paz Waterfall Gardens** 🐾🐾, which is right on the winding road to Puerto Viejo de Sarapiquí, about 6km (3¾ miles) beyond Varablanca. For more information, see "What to See & Do" and "Side Trips from San José," in chapter 5.

WHERE TO STAY & DINE

All the lodges listed below arrange excursions throughout the region, including boat trips on the Sarapiquí, guided hikes in the rainforest, and horseback or mountain-bike rides. Also note that rates for the lodges in the "Expensive" category include all meals, taxes, and usually a tour or two, greatly reducing their real cost. In addition to the hotels listed below, **Peace Lodge** (p. 111), located at the La Paz Waterfall Gardens, is almost close enough to be considered lodging in this region.

EXPENSIVE

La Selva Biological Station 🐾   Located a few kilometers south of Puerto Viejo, La Selva Biological Station caters primarily to students and researchers but also accepts visitors seeking a rustic rainforest adventure. The atmosphere is definitely that of a scientific research center. La Selva, which is operated by the Organization for Tropical Studies (OTS), covers 1,480 hectares (3,656 acres) and is contiguous with Braulio Carrillo National Park. There are miles of well-maintained hiking trails to explore. Researchers estimate that more than 2,000 species of flora exist in this private reserve, and 400-plus species of birds have been identified here, making this a great choice if you want to do some serious bird-watching. Rooms are basic but large, and the high ceilings help keep them cool. Most have bunk beds and shared bathrooms, although the eight newest rooms have private bathrooms and twin beds, while the two-room family units have a mix of twin and queen-size beds. There's no price difference, so be specific when reserving a room. The dining hall is a big, bright place where students and scientists swap data over fried chicken or fish with rice and beans.

Because scientific research is the primary objective of La Selva, researchers receive priority over casual, short-term visitors. However, informative guided tours are available most days, even if you are staying at another hotel in the area. Call the local number (✆ **766-6565**) at least a day in advance to arrange one of these. If you want to stay overnight at La Selva, you should have a reservation with the San José office—they try to discourage walk-in traffic. Moreover, because there are very few rooms here, it pays to book in advance. Rates are quite high for the actual accommodations, but you can take some solace in the fact that you're helping to support valuable and valiant research and conservation efforts.

Puerto Viejo (A.P. 676-2050, San Pedro, Costa Rica). ✆ **524-0628** for reservations office in San José, or 766-6565 at the lodge. Fax 524-0629. www.ots.ac.cr. 24 units, 16 w/shared bathroom. $82 (£41) per person double occupancy. Rates include all meals, half-day tour, and taxes. Rates lower for researchers and student groups. MC, V. **Amenities:** Restaurant; kayak rentals; laundry service. *In room:* No phone.

Rara Avis *(Finds)*   Rara Avis is one of the first, most responsible, biologically rich, and isolated ecolodge operations in Costa Rica. There are several lodging options here, but the Waterfall Lodge is by far the most comfortable and popular. It has rustic but comfortable rooms in a two-story building near the main lodge and dining room and just 200m (656 ft.) from its namesake two-tiered waterfall. Each unit here is a corner room with a wraparound porch. For those who want closer communion with nature, Rara Avis has a two-room cabin set deep in the forest beside a river, about a 10-minute hike from the main lodge, as well as three more rustic two-bedroom cabins with shared bathrooms, located in a small clearing about a 5-minute walk from the lodge. Meals are basic Tico-style dishes with lots of beans and rice.

The grounds of Rara Avis are adjacent to Braulio Carrillo National Park, and together the two areas have many miles of trails for you to explore. *Bird-watchers, take note:* More than 367 species of birds have been sighted here, and the lodge consistently has excellent guides and naturalists.

When making reservations, be sure to get directions for how to get to Las Horquetas and information on coordinating your ride on the lodge's tractor. Be forewarned, it's a long, slow, bumpy and muddy ride in a small buggy pulled by a tractor up to the lodge. The tractor leaves just once daily for the 3-hour ride to the lodge.

15km (9½ miles) from Las Horquetas (A.P. 8105-1000, San José). ℭ 764-1111 for reservations or 710-8032 at the lodge. Fax 764-1114. www.rara-avis.com. 16 units, 10 w/private bathroom. $50 (£25) per person w/shared bathroom; $150–$170 (£75–£85) double w/private bathroom. Rates include transportation from Las Horquetas (you can't get there by car), guided hikes, all meals, and taxes. AE, MC, V. **Amenities:** Restaurant. *In room:* No phone.

Selva Verde Lodge *(F)*   This long-standing rainforest lodge is another of the early ecotourist ventures in Costa Rica. Expansion and remodeling have kept things comfortable and up-to-date. The lodge buildings are made of varnished hardwoods inside and out and are built on pilings so that the rooms are on the second floor. They're connected by covered walkways that keep you dry even though this area receives more than 150 inches of rain each year. The bungalows are across the road and 500m (1,640 ft.) into the forest; they're not nearly as plush and comfortable as the rooms in the main compound, but they offer quite a bit more privacy. Still, I definitely recommend the lodge rooms; all rooms are nonsmoking. Most meals are served buffet style in a beautiful large dining room that overlooks the river. Selva Verde is located right between the main road (a few kilometers west of Puerto Viejo) and by the Río Sarapiquí. Across the river is a large rainforest preserve. There are several trails on the grounds, a wonderful suspension bridge, and a separate little zip-line adventure across the river to more trails, a nice little swimming hole on the river, and modest butterfly and botanical gardens.

Chilamate (A.P. 55-3069), Sarapiquí. ℭ 800/451-7111 in the U.S. and Canada, or 766-6800. Fax 766-6011. www.selvaverde.com. 45 units, 5 bungalows. $162 (£81) double. Rates include 3 meals daily and taxes. Rates lower in off season. AE, DC, DISC, MC, V. **Amenities:** Restaurant; bar; outdoor pool; tour desk; laundry service. *In room:* Hair dryer, safe.

MODERATE

Although I highly recommend you choose one of the more atmospheric nature lodges listed in this section, if you absolutely must, or for some reason prefer to, stay in Puerto Viejo de Sarapiquí proper, **Hotel El Bambú** (ℭ **766-6005;** www.elbambu. com) is a clean, comfortable, and modern option.

Centro Neotrópico Sarapiquís *(F)*   Located on a high bluff fronting the Sarapiquí River, this complex is the most unique project in the Sarapiquí region. The deluxe

rooms are housed in three large, round buildings, or *palenques*. Based on the traditional pre-Columbian constructions of the area, each of the three *palenques* has a towering thatch roof rising some 18m (59 ft.). All rooms are comfortable and spacious
although a little dark, and each has a door leading out to the shared veranda that encir-
cles the building. The 12 standard rooms are housed in the main lodge building, are
somewhat smaller and less luxurious, and lack the veranda. Smoking is permitted only
in the bar and restaurant. The hotel has several interesting attractions, including a
small natural-history museum, an on-site excavation of a pre-Columbian graveyard,
and a well-marked botanical garden. Just across the river lies the 300-hectare (741-
acre) Tirimbina Rainforest Center, with a small network of trails and several impressive suspension bridges, both over the river and through the forest canopy. Tours of
the museum and reserve cost extra and are open to guests at other hotels.

A.P. 86-3069, La Virgen de Sarapiquí. © 761-1004. Fax 761-1415. www.sarapiquis.org. 47 units. $85–$99 (£43–
£50) double. Rates lower in off season. V. **Amenities:** Restaurant; bar; tour desk; limited room service; babysitting;
laundry service; nonsmoking rooms.

Sueño Azul Resort ⚜ This nature lodge and wellness retreat offers the top accommodations in the area. Set at the juncture of two rivers and backed by rainforest and
forested mountains, the setting's pretty darn nice as well. All rooms are spacious, with
high ceilings, two double beds, large bathrooms, and a private porch overlooking either
one of the rivers or a small lake. Ten of the rooms come with air-conditioning, and one
large junior suite has its own outdoor Jacuzzi. Meals are served in an open-air dining
room set to take in the view, and a pool, Jacuzzi, bar, and rancho are down by the rivers'
edge. The best place to cool off is in the massive outdoor pool, fed and filled by river
water from a small waterfall. There's also a good-size spa and yoga facility.

A wide range of tours and activities is offered, including rainforest hikes, horseback
riding, mountain biking, and fly-fishing, as well as trips to the area's major attractions.

Las Horquetas de Sarapiquí (A.P. 3630-1000, San José). © 253-2020 reservation number in San José, 764-1000 at
the lodge. Fax 224-3552. www.suenoazulresort.com. 56 units. $98 (£49) double; $140 (£70) suite. Rates lower in off
season. MC, V. **Amenities:** Restaurant; small pool; activities desk; room service (7am–10pm); laundry service. *In
room:* Minibar, hair dryer, safe, no phone.

INEXPENSIVE

In addition to the places listed below, budget travelers might want to check out the
Posada Andrea Cristina (© 766-6265; www.andreacristina.com), which is located
just on the outskirts of Puerto Viejo and is run by Alex Martínez, an excellent local
guide and pioneering conservationist in the region. You may also consider staying at
the jungle tent camp or isolated Magsasay Lodge at **Hacienda Pozo Azul** (© 877/
810-6903 in the U.S. and Canada, or 761-1360; www.pozoazul.com).

Gavilán Sarapiquí River Lodge Located on the banks of the Río Sarapiquí just
south of Puerto Viejo on the road to Río Frío, Gavilán is surrounded by 100 hectares
(247 acres) of forest reserve (secondary forest) and 14 hectares (35 acres) of gardens
planted with lots of flowering ginger, heliconia, orchids, and bromeliads. Guest rooms
are basic and simply furnished, and the beds are a bit soft for my taste. Still, all have
fans and hot water, and there are always fresh-cut flowers. Most have one single and
one double bed. What Gavilán lacks in luxurious comfort, it makes up for in friend-
liness and attentive service. There's an unheated Jacuzzi in the garden and several
open-air ranchos, some of which have hammocks strung up for afternoon siestas. Tico
and Continental meals are served buffet style, and there are always plenty of fresh

fruits and juices. Guided hikes through the forest, horseback rides, and river trips are all offered for around $30 (£15) per person.

Puerto Viejo de Sarapiquí (A.P. 445-2010, San José). ℂ **234-9507** or 766-6743. Fax 253-6556. www.gavilanlodge.com. 13 units. $50 (£25) double. MC, V. **Amenities:** Restaurant; bar; Jacuzzi; laundry service. *In room:* No phone.

La Quinta de Sarapiquí Country Inn This small, family-run lodge makes a good base for exploring the Sarapiquí region. Located on the banks of the Sardinal River about 15 minutes west of Puerto Viejo, La Quinta caters primarily to nature lovers and bird-watchers. The rooms are located in a half-dozen buildings dispersed around the grounds among richly flowering gardens and connected by covered walkways. They're simple but clean, with good lighting and comfortable bathrooms. Each room has a small patio with a sitting chair or two for gazing out into the garden. The superior rooms have air-conditioning. There are also a small gift shop, a butterfly garden, a frog garden, an extensive insect display, and a vegetable garden and reforestation project on hand. If you don't have a car, call the hotel to see if you can arrange a pickup in Puerto Viejo. Meals are served either buffet or family style in the main lodge and will run you an extra $31 (£16) per day.

Chilamate (A.P. 43-3069), Sarapiquí. ℂ **761-1300.** Fax 761-1395. www.laquintasarapiqui.com. 31 units. $65 (£33) double; $80 (£40) superior double. Children under 12 stay free in parent's room. AE, MC, V. **Amenities:** Restaurant; bar; small pool; tour desk; laundry service.

A REMOTE NATURE LODGE

La Laguna del Lagarto Lodge 𝒜 *Finds* It's hard to get much more remote than this. Located near the Nicaraguan border, La Laguna del Lagarto Lodge is bordered by more than 480 hectares (1,186 acres) of virgin rainforest that is home to a rich variety of tropical flora and fauna. The accommodations are simple yet comfortable. Most rooms open onto a balcony or veranda with sitting chairs and hammocks. Meals, which will run you around $28 (£14) per person per day, are served family style in the open-air dining room and are filling affairs.

The hotel is named after the two man-made lagoons that sit below the lodge buildings; canoes are available for paddling around these and several other nearby jungle waterways. There are more than 10km (6¼ miles) of well-maintained hiking trails, and the lodge offers trips on the San Carlos River ($25/£13), as well as horseback riding tours ($20/£10). More than 380 species of birds have been spotted here, and the hotel is involved in efforts to preserve the rare great green macaw, which is frequently sighted here. In addition to the rainforest, the lodge sits on a small pepper plantation and has other lands planted with palmito, pineapple, and other tropical fruits.

To get here, you head first to Pital and then continue on dirt roads to the town of Boca Tapada. It's another 6km (3¾ miles) to the lodge on more bumpy dirt roads. It's also possible to get here on public transportation (call for directions), or you can arrange for the lodge to handle your transportation from San José. The lodge's transfers cost $220 (£110) round-trip for two people, or $70 (£35) per person for more than three. But anyone with four-wheel-drive can make the trip here independently, so you're best off driving on your own.

Boca Tapada (A.P. 995-1007, San José). ℂ **289-8163.** Fax 289-5295. www.lagarto-lodge-costa-rica.com. 20 units. $68 (£34) double. AE, MC, V (5% surcharge). **Amenities:** Restaurant; bar. *In room:* No phone.

2 Arenal Volcano & La Fortuna ★★

140km (87 miles) NW of San José; 61km (38 miles) E of Tilarán

I never tire of watching red lava rocks tumble down the flanks of **Arenal Volcano** and listening in awe to its deep rumbling. If you've never experienced them firsthand, the sights and sounds of an active volcano are awesome. Arenal is one of the world's most regularly active volcanoes. In July 1968, the volcano, which had lain dormant for hundreds of years, surprised everybody by erupting with sudden violence. The nearby village of Tabacón was destroyed, and nearly 80 of its inhabitants were killed. Since that eruption, 1,607m (5,271-ft.) Arenal has been Costa Rica's most active volcano. Frequent powerful explosions send cascades of red-hot lava rocks down the volcano's steep slopes. During the day these lava flows smoke and rumble. However, at night the volcano puts on its most mesmerizing show. If you are lucky enough to be here on a clear and active night—not necessarily a guaranteed occurrence—you'll see the night sky turned red by lava spewing from Arenal's crater. In the past few years, the forests to the south of the volcano have been declared Arenal National Park. Eventually, this park should stretch all the way to Monteverde Biological Cloud Forest Reserve.

Lying at the eastern foot of this natural spectacle is the tiny farming community of **La Fortuna.** In recent years this town has become a magnet for volcano watchers from around the world. A host of moderately priced hotels are in and near La Fortuna, and from here you can arrange night tours to the best volcano-viewing spots, which are 17km (11 miles) away on the western slope, on the road to and beyond the Tabacón Grand Spa Thermal Resort.

ESSENTIALS

GETTING THERE & DEPARTING   By Plane   Nature Air (© **800/235-9272** in the U.S. and Canada, or 299-6000; www.natureair.com) flies to Arenal/La Fortuna daily at 11:30 from Tobías Bolaños International Airport in Pavas. The flight duration is 30 minutes. Return flights depart for San José at 12:10pm. Nature Air also has a daily flight from Tamarindo to Arenal at 10am, stopping at Liberia en route, and making the return flight at 11:25am. One-way fares are $65 (£33) between Arenal and San Jose or Liberia, and $85 (£43) between Arenal and Tamarindo.

By Car   There are several routes to La Fortuna from San José. The most popular is to head west on the Interamerican Highway and then turn north at Naranjo, continuing north through Zarcero to Ciudad Quesada. From Ciudad Quesada, one route goes through Jabillos, while the other goes through Muelle. The former route is better marked, more popular, slightly shorter, and generally better maintained, but the severe weather and heavy traffic quickly take their toll, and the roads up here can be notoriously bad for long stretches. This route offers wonderful views of the San Carlos valley as you come down from Ciudad Quesada, and Zarcero, with its topiary gardens and quaint church, makes a good place to stop, stretch your legs, and snap a few photos (see "Side Trips from San José," in chapter 5, for more information).

You can also stay on the Interamerican Highway until San Ramón (west of Naranjo) and then head north through La Tigra. This route is also very scenic and passes the Villablanca Cloud Forest & Spa (p. 236). The travel time on any of the above routes is between 2½ and 3½ hours.

Finally, if you combine your visit here with a stop at the Poás Volcano and La Paz Waterfall, or if you stay at a lodge closer to Aguas Zarcas, you can go first to Alajuela

Tips Boats, Horses & Taxis

You can travel between La Fortuna and Monteverde by boat and taxi, or on a combination boat, horseback, and taxi trip. A 10- to 20-minute boat ride across Lake Arenal cuts out hours of driving around its shores. From La Fortuna to the put-in point is about a 25-minute taxi ride. It's about a 1½-hour four-wheel-drive taxi ride between the Río Chiquito dock on the other side of Lake Arenal and Santa Elena. These trips can be arranged in either direction for between $20 and $40 (£10–£20) per person, all-inclusive.

You can also add on a horseback ride on the Santa Elena/Monteverde side of the lake. There are several routes and rides offered. The steepest heads up the mountains and through the forest to the town of San Gerardo, which is only a 30-minute car ride from Santa Elena. Other routes throw in shorter sections of horseback riding along the lakeside lowlands. With the horseback ride, this trip runs around $50 to $70 (£25–£35) per person.

Warning: The riding is often rainy, muddy, and steep. Many find it much more arduous than awe-inspiring. Moreover, I've received numerous complaints about the condition of the trails and the treatment of the horses, so be very careful and demanding before signing on for this trip. Find out what route you will be taking, as well as the condition of the horses if possible. **Desafío Expeditions (© 479-9464;** www.desafiocostarica.com) is one of the more reputable operators. They will even drive your car around for you while you take the scenic (and sore) route.

or Heredia and then head north to Varablanca before continuing on to San Miguel, where you turn west toward Río Cuarto and Aguas Zarcas. From Aguas Zarcas, continue west through Muelle to the turnoff for La Fortuna. This is the longest route.

By Bus   Buses (© **256-8914**) leave San José for La Fortuna roughly every 2 hours between 6am and 5:30pm from the **Atlántico del Norte** bus station at Avenida 9 and Calle 12. The trip lasts 4½ hours; the fare is $3.40 (£1.70). The bus you take might be labeled TILARAN. Make sure it passes through Ciudad Quesada. If so, it passes through La Fortuna; if not, you'll end up in Tilarán via the Interamerican Highway, passing through the Guanacaste town of Cañas, a long way from La Fortuna.

Alternatively, you can take a bus from the same station to Ciudad Quesada and transfer there to another bus to La Fortuna. These buses depart roughly every 30 minutes between 5am and 7:30pm. The fare for the 2½-hour trip is $2.80 (£1.40). Local buses between Ciudad Quesada and La Fortuna run regularly through the day, although the schedule changes frequently, depending on demand. The trip lasts 1 hour; the fare is $1.50 (75p).

Buses depart **Monteverde/Santa Elena** for Tilarán every day at 7am. This is a journey of only 35km (22 miles), but the trip lasts 2½ hours because the road is in such horrendous condition. People with bad backs should think twice about making this trip, especially by bus. The return bus from Tilarán to Santa Elena leaves at 12:30pm. The fare is $2.15 (£1.10). Buses from Tilarán to La Fortuna depart daily at 7am and 12:30pm (hence, a person coming from Monteverde would have to wait for the

12:30pm bus) and make the return trip at 8am and 2:30pm. The trip is 3 to 4 hours; the fare is $2.70 (£1.35).

Buses depart La Fortuna for San José roughly every 2 hours between 5am and 5:30pm; in some instances, you might have to transfer in Ciudad Quesada. From there, you can catch one of the frequent buses to San José.

Gray Line (⊘ 220-2126; www.graylinecostarica.com) has two daily buses from San José to La Fortuna at 8am and 3:30pm. **Interbus** (⊘ 283-5573; www.interbus online.com) has two buses daily leaving San José for La Fortuna at 8am and 2:30pm. Both companies charge $29 (£15) and will pick you up at most San José–area hotels. Both companies also run routes from La Fortuna with connections to most other major destinations in Costa Rica.

ORIENTATION & FAST FACTS   As you enter La Fortuna, you'll see the massive volcano directly in front of you. La Fortuna is only a few streets wide, with almost all the hotels, restaurants, and shops clustered along the main road that leads out of town toward Tabacón and the volcano. There are several information and tour-booking offices and Internet cafes, as well as a laundromat, on the streets that surround the small central park that fronts the Catholic church. There's a Banco de Costa Rica as you enter La Fortuna, just over the Río Burío bridge, and a Banco Nacional in the center of town, across the park from the church. Both have ATMs.

GETTING AROUND   If you don't have a car, you'll need to either take a cab or go on an organized tour if you want to visit the hot springs or view the volcano eruption. There are tons of taxis in La Fortuna (you can flag one down practically anywhere), and there is always a line of them ready and waiting along the main road beside the central park. A taxi between La Fortuna and Tabacón should cost around $5 (£2.50). Another alternative is to rent a car when you get here. **Alamo** (⊘ 479-9090; www. alamocostarica.com) and **Poás** (⊘ 479-9400; www.carentals.com) both have offices in La Fortuna.

There are also several places to rent scooters and ATVs around town. Provided it's not raining too heavily, this is a good way to get around. Rates run around $35 to $45 (£18–£23) per day for a scooter, and $40 to $65 (£20–£33) for an ATV.

WHAT TO SEE & DO

While in the town of La Fortuna, be sure to spend some time simply people-watching from a bench or grassy spot on the central plaza. It's also worth a quick visit to tour the town's **Catholic church.** This modern church was designed by famous Costa Rican artist Teodorico Quirós, and features an interesting soaring front steeple and clock tower of concrete. In town, you'll find the tiny **Los Abuelos Museum** (⊘ 479-7306), a very modest collection of old currency, tools, clothing, and household items, collected over several generations by a local family. Admission is $8 (£4), which I think is just a bit ridiculous.

EXPERIENCING THE VOLCANO 🐸🐸

The first thing you should know is that Arenal Volcano borders a region of cloud forests and rainforests, and the volcano's cone is often socked in by clouds and fog. Many people come to Arenal and never get to see the exposed cone. Moreover, the volcano does go through periods when it is relatively quiet.

The second thing you should know is that you can't climb Arenal Volcano—it's not safe due to the constant activity. Several foolish people who have ignored this warning

Taking a Soothing Soak in Hot Springs

Arenal Volcano has bestowed a terrific fringe benefit on the area around it: several naturally heated thermal springs. Located at the site of the former village that was destroyed by the 1968 eruption, **Tabacón Grand Spa Thermal Resort** 𝒦𝒦𝒦 (© 519-1900; www.tabacon.com) is the most extensive, luxurious, and expensive spot to soak your tired bones. A series of variously sized pools, fed by natural springs, are spread out among lush gardens. At the center is a large, warm, spring-fed swimming pool with a slide, a swim-up bar, and a perfect view of the volcano. One of the stronger streams flows over a sculpted waterfall, with a rock ledge underneath that provides a perfect place to sit and receive a free hydraulic shoulder massage. The resort also has an excellent spa on the grounds offering professional massages, mud masks, and other treatments, as well as yoga classes (appointments required.) The spa here even has several permanent sweat lodges, based on a Native American traditional design.

In addition to the poolside swim-up bar, you'll find a restaurant and separate snack bar and grill here. You can sign a credit card voucher when you enter and charge your food and drinks throughout your stay. This sure beats pulling soggy bills from your bathing suit.

Entrance fees are $55 (£28) for adults and $20 (£10) for children under 12. The hot springs are open daily from noon to 10pm (spa treatments can actually be scheduled as early as 8am, and hotel guests can enter at 10am). Packages can be purchased with meals and/or treatments. There's a slight discount for entering after 6pm. Management enforces a policy of limiting visitors, so reservations (which can be made online or by phone) are recommended.

Baldi Hot Springs (© 479-9651), next to the Volcano Look Disco, are the first hot springs you'll come to as you drive from La Fortuna toward Tabacón. This place has grown substantially over the years, with many different pools and lush gardens, similar to those found at Tabacón. However, their prices have also gone up accordingly, and I find this place far less attractive than either of the other two options mentioned here. Planned for 2008 were a couple of massive water slides. Admission is $25 (£13).

Just across the street from Baldi Termae is the unmarked entrance of a new hot spring option, **Eco Termales** 𝒦𝒦 (© 479-8484). Smaller and more intimate than Tabacón, this series of pools set amid lush forest and gardens is almost as picturesque and luxurious, although the spa services are much less extensive and there is no view of the volcano. Reservations are absolutely necessary here. Admission is $16 (£8).

have lost their lives, and others have been severely injured. The most recent fatalities occurred in August 2000.

Still, waiting for and watching Arenal's regular eruptions is the main activity in La Fortuna and is best done at night when the orange lava glows against the starry sky. Although it's possible simply to look up from the middle of town and see Arenal erupting, the view is best from the north and west sides of the volcano along the road to Tabacón and toward the national park entrance. If you have a car, you can drive along this road, but if you've arrived by bus, you will need to take a taxi or tour.

Arenal National Park constitutes an area of more than 2,880 hectares (7,114 acres), which includes the viewing and parking areas closest to the volcano. The park is open daily from 8am to 10pm and charges $6 (£3) admission per person. The trails through forest and over old lava flows inside the park are gorgeous and fun. (Be careful climbing on those volcanic boulders.) However, at night the view from inside the park is no better than on the roads just outside it.

If you don't have a car and are staying in La Fortuna, every hotel in town and several tour offices offer night tours to the volcano. (They don't actually enter the park; they stop on the road that runs between the park entrance and the Arenal Observatory Lodge.) These tours generally cost between $10 and $20 (£5–£10) per person. Often these volcano-viewing tours include a stop at one of the local hot springs, and the price goes up accordingly (see "Taking a Soothing Soak in Hot Springs," below, for a description of the different options and fees).

Note: Although it's counterintuitive, the rainy season is often a better time to see the exposed cone of Arenal Volcano, especially at night. I don't know why this is, but I've had excellent volcano-viewing sessions at various points during the rainy season; during the dry season the volcano can often be socked in solid for days at a time. The bottom line is that catching a glimpse of the volcano's cone is never a sure thing.

OTHER ADVENTUROUS PURSUITS IN THE AREA

Aside from the impressive volcanic activity, the area around Arenal Volcano is packed with other natural wonders.

ATV The folks at **Fourtrax Adventures** (© 479-8444; www.fourtraxadventure.com) offer a 3-hour adventure through the forests and farmlands around La Fortuna. The tour includes a stop at a jungle swimming hole, where you can cool off, as well as a visit to a butterfly farm. You get good views of the volcano, as well as the La Fortuna Waterfall. Cost is $75 (£38) per ATV. A second rider on the same ATV costs $15 (£7.50).

CANOPY TOURS & CANYONING There are numerous ways to get up into the forest canopy here. Perhaps the simplest way is to hike the trails and bridges of **Arenal Hanging Bridges** (© 253-5080; www.hangingbridges.com). Located just over the Lake Arenal dam, this attraction is a complex of gentle trails and suspension bridges through a beautiful tract of primary forest. It's open daily from 7am to 4pm; admission is $20 (£10). Guided tours and night tours are also available.

Another option is the **Sky Tram** ★★ (© 479-9944; www.skytrek.com), an open gondola-style ride that begins near the shores of Lake Arenal and rises up, providing excellent views of the lake and volcano. From here you can hike their series of trails and suspended bridges. In the end you can hike down, take the gondola, or strap on a harness and ride their zip-line canopy tour down to the bottom. The zip-line tour here features several very long and very fast sections, with some impressive views of the lake and volcano. The cost is $60 (£30).

If you'd like a bigger rush than the canopy tours offer, you could go "canyoning" with **Pure Trek Canyoning** (© 866/569-5723 in the U.S. and Canada, or 461-2110; www.puretrekcostarica.com) and **Desafío Expeditions** ★★ (© 479-9464; www.desafiocostarica.com); both offer canyoning adventures. This adventure sport is a mix of hiking through and alongside a jungle river, punctuated with periodic rappels through and alongside the faces of rushing waterfalls. Pure Trek's trip is probably better for first-timers and families with kids, while Desafío's tour is just a bit more rugged and adventurous. Both of these companies charge $90 (£45) for a canyoning tour, and offer various possible combination, full-day tours.

Finally, while nowhere near as natural, you can also take a bungee jump in La Fortuna at **Arenal Bungee** (© 479-7440). The bungee jump here is a 40m (130 ft.) fall from a steel tower constructed on the outskirts of downtown La Fortuna. You can also try a water landing, as well as a "rocket launch," which is kind of the equivalent of becoming a human sling shot. Jumps, falls and rocket shots cost $39 (£20). This attraction is open 9am to 10pm daily, so you can even partake in this fun after dark.

FISHING   With Lake Arenal just around the corner, fishing is a popular activity here. The big action is *guapote,* a Central American species of rainbow bass. However, you can also book fishing trips to Caño Negro, where snook, tarpon, and other game fish can be stalked. Most hotels and adventure-tour companies can arrange fishing excursions. Costs run around $100 to $200 (£50–£100) for a half-day, $200 to $400 (£100–£200) for a full day.

HIKING & HORSEBACK RIDING   Horseback riding is a popular activity in this area, and there are scores of good rides on dirt back roads and through open fields and dense rainforest. Volcano and lake views come with the terrain on most rides. Horseback trips to the Río Fortuna waterfall are perhaps the most popular tours sold, but remember, the horse will get you only to the entrance; from there, you'll have to hike a bit. A horseback ride to the falls should cost between $20 and $40 (£10–£20), including the entrance fee.

One popular and strenuous hike is to **Cerro Chato,** a dormant volcanic cone on the flank of Arenal. There's a pretty little lake up here. **Desafío Expeditions** ✶ (© 479-9464; www.desafiocostarica.com) leads a 4- to 5-hour hike for $65 (£33), including lunch.

Aventuras Arenal (© 479-9133; www.arenaladventures.com), **Desafío Expeditions** ✶✶ (© 479-9464; www.desafiocostarica.com), **Jacamar Tours** (© 479-9767; www.arenaltours.com), and **Sunset Tours** (© 479-9800; www.sunsettourcr.com) are the main tour operators. In addition to the above tours, each of these companies offers most of the tours listed in this section, as well as fishing trips and sightseeing excursions on the lake.

LA FORTUNA FALLS   Leading the list of side attractions in the area is the impressive **Río Fortuna Waterfall** ✶ (© 479-8360), located about 5.5km (3½ miles) outside of town in a lush jungle setting. There's a sign in town to indicate the road that leads out to the falls. You can drive or hike to just within viewing distance. When you get to the entrance to the lookout, you'll have to pay a $6 (£3) entrance fee to actually check out the falls. It's another 15- to 20-minute hike down a steep and often muddy path to the pool formed by the waterfall. The hike back up will take slightly longer. You can swim, but stay away from the turbulent water at the base of the falls—several people have drowned here. Instead, check out and enjoy the calm pool just around the bend, or join the locals at the popular swimming hole under the bridge on the paved road, just after the turnoff for the road up to the falls. The trail to the falls is open daily from 8am to 4pm.

MOUNTAIN BIKING   This region is very well suited for mountain biking. Rides range in difficulty from moderate to extremely challenging. You can combine a day on a mountain bike with a visit to one or more of the more popular attractions here. **Bike**

Arenal ⚲ (✆ **866/465-4114** in the U.S. and Canada, or 479-9454; www.bikearenal. com) is the only dedicated operator in the field, with an excellent collection of top-notch bikes and equipment and a wide range of tour possibilities.

WHITE-WATER RAFTING & CANOEING   For adventurous tours of the area, check out **Desafío Expeditions** ⚲⚲ (✆ **479-9464;** www.desafiocostarica.com) or **Wave Expeditions** ⚲⚲ (✆ **479-7262;** www.waveexpeditions.com). Both companies offer daily raft rides of Class I to II, III, and IV to V on different sections of the Toro, Peñas Blancas, and Sarapiquí rivers. A half-day trip on the Peñas Blancas leaving from La Fortuna costs around $45 (£23) per person; a full day of rafting costs $70 to $90 (£35–£45) per person, depending on what section of what river you ride. Both companies also offer mountain biking and most of the standard local guided trips. If you want a wet and personal ride, try Desafío's tour in inflatable kayaks, or "duckies," down the pristine Arenal River.

A more laid-back alternative is to take a canoe tour with **Canoa Aventura** (✆ **479-8200;** www.canoa-aventura.com), which offers half-, full-, and multiday excursions on a variety of rivers in the region.

SIDE TRIPS FROM LA FORTUNA

La Fortuna is a great place from which to make a day trip to the **Caño Negro National Wildlife Refuge** ⚲. This vast network of marshes and rivers (particularly the Río Frío) is 100km (62 miles) north of La Fortuna near the town of Los Chiles. This refuge is best known for its amazing abundance of bird life, including roseate spoonbills, jabiru storks, herons, and egrets, but you can also see caimans and crocodiles. Bird-watchers should not miss this refuge, although keep in mind that the main lake dries up in the dry season (mid-Apr to Nov), which reduces the number of wading birds. Full-day tours to Caño Negro average between $45 and $60 (£23–£30) per person. However, most of the tours run out of La Fortuna that are billed as Caño Negro never really enter the refuge but instead ply sections of the nearby Río Frio, which features similar wildlife and ecosystems. If you're interested in staying in this area and really visiting the refuge, check out the **Caño Negro Natural Lodge** (see "Where to Stay & Dine Farther Afield," later in this chapter).

You can also visit the **Venado Caverns,** a 45-minute drive away. In addition to plenty of stalactites, stalagmites, and other limestone formations, you'll see bats and cave fish. Tours here cost around $45 (£23). All of the tour agencies and hotel tour desks can arrange or directly offer trips to Caño Negro and Venado Caverns.

Kids and the young at heart may enjoy the pool, fountain, and water slide at **Jungla y Senderos Los Lagos** (✆ **461-1818;** www.hotelloslagos.com). I come here more for the network of trails and small lakes that are also on this property. It recently added a small crocodile hatchery and tilapia farm, a canopy tour, and some basic hot springs. They've also got rooms and cabins that range widely in size, amenities, and price. You'll find Los Lagos on the road to Tabacón, a few kilometers out of La Fortuna. It charges $15 (£7.50) per person—adults and children—for daily use of its facilities.

SHOPPING

La Fortuna is chock full of simple souvenir shops selling standard tourist fare. However, you'll find one of my favorite craft shops here. There's no real name or sign to the store, and they don't have a phone number, but you won't be able to miss it. As you leave the town of La Fortuna toward Tabacón, keep your eye on the right-hand side of the road. When you see a massive collection of **wood sculptures,** slow down and pull over. The local artisan and his family produce works in a variety of styles and sizes. They specialize in faces, many of them larger than a typical home's front door. You can also find a host of animal figures, ranging in style from purely representational to rather abstract. Another good shop for higher end arts and crafts is **Galería Lunática** (© 479-8255), located on the main road in La Fortuna.

WHERE TO STAY IN LA FORTUNA
MODERATE
Hotel San Bosco *Value* Located a block off La Fortuna's main street, the San Bosco offers the best rooms to be found right in town. The hotel actually has two styles of rooms. The least expensive rooms are all well maintained and feature tile floors and fans. However, these are standard budget-hotel affairs. The more expensive rooms are much more attractive and have stone walls, tile floors, reading lights, televisions, and benches on the veranda in front. There's an observation deck for volcano viewing on the top floor of the hotel, as well as a helpful front desk staff.

La Fortuna, San Carlos (200m/656 ft. north of the central park). © 479-9050. Fax 479-9109. www.arenal-volcano. com. 34 units. $72–$77 (£36–£39) double. Rates include breakfast. Rates lower in off season. AE, MC, V. **Amenities:** Small pool and separate children's pool; small exercise room; Jacuzzi; tour desk; laundry service. *In room:* A/C, TV, free Wi-Fi, no phone.

INEXPENSIVE
La Fortuna is a tourist boomtown; basic hotels have been popping up here at a phenomenal rate for several years running. Right in La Fortuna you'll find a score of budget options. If you have time, it's worth walking around and checking out a couple. One of the newer options is **Arenal Backpackers Resort** (© 479-7000; www. arenalbackpackers.com), which bills itself as a 5-star hostel. It has both shared-bathroom dorm rooms, and more upscale private rooms, but even backpackers get to enjoy the large pool, free Wi-Fi, and volcano views.

There are a couple places both in town and right on the outskirts of La Fortuna that allow camping, with access to basic bathroom facilities, for around $5 to $7 (£2.50–£3.50) per person per night. If you have a car, drive a little bit out of town toward Tabacón and you'll find several more basic cabins and camping sites, some that even offer views of the volcano.

Hotel Fortuna *Value* Centrally located just 1 block south of the gas station, this perennial budget favorite has been totally rebuilt following a 1997 fire. Accommodations are very basic, but are clean and have private bathrooms. There is a popular open-air restaurant at the front of the hotel, and the helpful and friendly owners can arrange a wide variety of tours.

La Fortuna, San Carlos. © 479-9197. Fax 479-8563. www.fortunainn.com. 13 units. $26 (£13) double. Rates include breakfast and taxes. V. **Amenities:** Restaurant; tour desk; free Wi-Fi. *In room:* No phone.

Hotel Las Colinas This three-story building in the center of town offers clean but basic rooms. You'll need to be in good shape if you stay in one of the third-floor rooms, but it's worth it if you can snag room no. 33, which has a private balcony and a great view of the volcano. However, most of the other rooms are much less desirable, considering the wear and tear they've received over the years, so look at one or two before settling in. There are a few rooms on the ground floor, but they don't even have windows to the outside and are very dark.

La Fortuna (A.P. 06), San Carlos. © 479-9305. Fax 479-9160. www.lascolinasarenal.com. 17 units. $30–$35 (£15–£18) double. Rates include breakfast. Rates lower in off season. MC, V. *In room:* A/C, no phone.

WHERE TO DINE IN & AROUND LA FORTUNA

Dining in La Fortuna is nowhere near as spectacular as volcano viewing, although, given the area's popularity, there's no lack of options. The favorite meeting places in town are the **El Jardín Restaurant** (© 479-9360) and **Lava Rocks** (© 479-8039); both are on the main road, right in the center of La Fortuna. Other choices include **La Choza de Laurel** (© 479-9231), **Rancho La Cascada** (© 479-9145), and **Restaurante Nene's** (© 479-9192). For Mexican fare, try **Las Brasitas** (© 479-9819). For a quiet coffee break or snack, try the **Rainforest Cafe** (© 365-6370). Heading out of town, you'll find **El Vagabundo** ⭐ (© 479-9565), a good Italian pizza-and-spaghetti joint. For some fine and fancy dining, you can try the **Los Tucanes** ⭐⭐ (© 460-2020) restaurant at the Tabacón Grand Spa resort.

Don Rufino ⭐ COSTA RICAN/INTERNATIONAL   Set on a busy corner in the heart of town, this restaurant is easily the best—and the busiest—option right in town. The front wall and bar area open on to the street and are often filled both with local tour guides and tourists. Try the *pollo al estilo de la abuela* (Grandma's chicken), which is baked and served wrapped in banana leaves, or one of the excellent cuts of meat. It's a good choice for breakfast, and the bar stays open most nights until 2am.

Downtown La Fortuna. © **479-9997.** Main courses $8–$12 (£4–£6). Reservations recommended during the high season. AE, MC, V. Daily 10am–11pm.

El Novillo *(Finds)* STEAKHOUSE/COSTA RICAN   After more than a decade as a simple open joint with a high zinc roof over a concrete slab, this successful local steakhouse has been forced to relocate. The new location is no longer so close to the volcano, and there's little or no view to speak of. However, it's still a simple, open-air joint, and the steaks are still big, tender, and well prepared. The chicken and fish dishes are huge as well and also nicely done. Meals come with garlic bread, fries, and some slaw. If you want a local treat, skip the French fries and order some fried yuca as a side.

On the road to Ciudad Quesada, 4km (2½ miles) outside of La Fortuna. © **849-1508.** Reservations not necessary. Main courses $5–$10 (£2.50–£5). No credit cards. Daily 10am–midnight.

Lava Lounge ⭐ *(Finds)* INTERNATIONAL   This downtown La Fortuna open-air restaurant combines a very simple setting, with a sleek and somewhat eclectic menu. Healthy and hearty sandwiches, wraps, and salads are the main offerings here. You can get a traditional burger, or one made with fresh grilled tuna. For more substantial fare, there's traditional Costa Rican *arroz con pollo,* and a *casado,* built around a thick pork chop. You can also get several different pasta dishes, and every evening there are dinner specials, which may include some coconut battered shrimp with a mango salsa, or a prime sirloin steak in a green pepper or red wine sauce. The decor consists of a series of rustic wooden tables with mostly bench seats.

Downtown La Fortuna, on the main road. © **479-7365.** Reservations not necessary. Main courses $6.50–$13 (£3.25–£6.50). AE, MC, V. Daily noon–midnight.

LA FORTUNA AFTER DARK

La Fortuna's biggest after-dark attraction is the volcano, but the **Volcano Look Disco** on the road to Tabacón is trying to compete. If you get bored of the eruptions and seismic rumbling, head here for heavy dance beats and mirrored disco balls. In town the folks at Luigi's Hotel have opened a midsize **casino** next door to their hotel and restaurant, while the open-to-the-street bar at **Don Rufino** is a popular spot for a drink.

WHERE TO STAY NEAR THE VOLCANO

One other very unique alternative is to stay aboard the **Rain Goddess** (© 866/593-3168 in the U.S., or 231-4299; www.bluwing.com). This luxurious houseboat has four staterooms, ample lounge and dining areas, and cruises around Lake Arenal.

VERY EXPENSIVE *stayed here*

Arenal Kioro ✦✦   Set on 27 acres of hilly land with two rivers and a small patch of forest, this place is very close to Arenal Volcano. The views from the rooms, grounds, pool, and restaurant of this hotel are truly astounding. The rooms themselves are massive and opulent, with soaring high ceilings, large picture windows and glass doors, and a private balcony or patio facing the action. Each has its own four-person modern Jacuzzi tub, with sculpted seats and numerous jets, set below a large picture window with a volcano view, and is an attempt to compensate for the fact that there are no natural hot springs right on the grounds, as you will find at Tabacón Grand Spa Thermal Resort. The beds are also set to take in the view. The spa is well designed and offers a wide range of treatment options. There are trails through the grounds and a host of tours and activities are offered. The restaurant serves excellent international cuisine in a beautiful setting, with a giant wall of windows facing the volcano.

On the main road between La Fortuna and Lake Arenal, 10km (6 miles) from La Fortuna. © 888/866-5027 in the U.S. and Canada, or 461-1700. Fax 461-1710. www.hotelarenalkioro.com. 53 units. $345 (£173) double. Rates include buffet breakfast. Rates lower in off season; higher during peak periods. AE, DC, MC, V. **Amenities:** Restaurant; bar; large outdoor pool; exercise room; spa; Jacuzzi; tour desk; in-room massage; laundry service. *In room:* A/C, TV, mini-bar, coffeemaker, hair dryer, safe.

Tabacón Grand Spa Thermal Resort ✦✦✦   This is the most-established, extensive, and popular resort in the Arenal area. Steady improvements in service and amenities have only made this a better option over the years. Many rooms have excellent, direct views of the volcano. Rooms on the upper floors of the 300-block building have the best vistas. However, quite a few of the rooms have obstructed, or no, views. My advice: Book a "Standard Superior," which will come with a view that is definitely worth the $30 (£15) splurge over the straight "Standard."

All rooms are very spacious, with heavy, dark-stained wooden furniture. Most come with a private terrace or balcony with a table and a couple of chairs. Nine of the rooms are truly accessible to travelers with disabilities, and 11 are suites with separate sitting rooms, many with a private volcano-view Jacuzzi. The newer Forest Deluxe rooms are perhaps some of the plusher rooms here, with a private mosaic tile Jacuzzi and plasma screen television, but, as the name suggests, they come with forest and not volcano views. Guests enjoy privileges at the spectacular hot-springs complex and spa across the street (see "Taking a Soothing Soak in Hot Springs" on p. 226), including slightly extended hours.

As you drive along the main road between La Fortuna and Lake Arenal, you'll see the resort on your right. About 90m (295 ft.) or so later, around a sharp bend, the hot springs and spa will be on your left.

On the main road between La Fortuna and Lake Arenal, Tabacón (P.O. Box 181-1007, Centro Colón, San José). © 877/277-8291 in the U.S. and Canada, or 519-1900 reservations in San José, or 460-2020 at the resort. Fax 519-1940. www.tabacon.com. 114 units. $215–$295 (£108–£148) double; $305–$395 (£153–£198) suite. Rates include buffet breakfast. AE, DC, MC, V. **Amenities:** 2 restaurants; 2 bars; large pool w/swim-up bar; exercise room; extensive hot springs and spa facilities; Jacuzzi; tour desk; in-room massage; laundry service; Wi-Fi. *In room:* A/C, TV, dataport, coffeemaker, hair dryer, safe.

EXPENSIVE

La Selva Resort ⭐ This newer option offers wonderful views from each of its spacious individual cabins. The cabins are arranged in two parallel rows. My favorites are nos. 1 and 2, at the far end of the higher row. All have varnished wood walls, heavy wood beds, and large bathrooms, as well as a small front porch with a bench seat or a couple of chairs. They come with one king or two queen-size beds. Some offer views of the volcano from the bed, and a few come with bathtubs. The bedding has high thread-count cotton sheets and soft down pillows. The hotel is set back from the road a bit, with a small patch of forest on site. The pool sits on a high spot on the property with a great view of the volcano, and there's a large heated Jacuzzi next to it.

La Fortuna de San Carlos, about 5 minutes outside La Fortuna on the main road. ℂ 461-2345. Fax 460-8898. www.laselvaadventureresort.com. 14 units. $85–$125 (£42.5–£62.5) double. Rates include full breakfast. Rates lower in off season; higher during peak periods. AE, MC, V. **Amenities:** Restaurant; bar; midsize pool; Jacuzzi; tour desk; in-room massage; laundry service. *In room:* A/C, TV, minifridge, coffeemaker.

Lost Iguana Resort ⭐⭐ This resort offers large and luxurious rooms with great views of the volcano, although you're a little farther away from the action here than you are at the hotels closer to Tabacón and La Fortuna. The rooms are housed in a series of two-story buildings set on a hillside facing the volcano, and are quite spacious, with either one king or two twin beds on bamboo frames, attractive handmade wooden furniture, and interesting decorative touches. All feature a wall of glass letting out on a private balcony or porch, which in itself lets out onto the view. The suites are even larger and feature a Jacuzzi tub on the porch or balcony. Just below the open-air restaurant are a pretty two-tiered swimming pool and poolside bar. You can also reserve one of several villas, which are in effect two-bedroom suites, with a full kitchenette and an extra-long balcony. The hotel has a small network of trails on its own 40 hectares (100 acres) of land. By the time this book goes to press, they should have a large spa opened in the lush grounds below the hotel.

As you drive along the main road from La Fortuna to Lake Arenal, you'll cross over the dam and make an almost immediate right. The hotel is located about a mile up this road, which is rough gravel in parts.

On the road to Arenal Hanging Bridges, just over the Lake Arenal dam (mailing address: A.P. 63-4417, La Fortuna de San Carlos). ℂ 267-6148 reservations office in San José, or 461-0122 at the lodge. Fax 267-7672. www.lostiguana resort.com. 41 units. $135 (£68) double; $185 (£93) suite; $215 (£108) villa. Rates include breakfast. AE, MC, V. **Amenities:** Restaurant; bar; midsize pool w/swim-up bar; spa; tour desk; in-room massage; room service (7:30am–9:30pm); laundry service. *In room:* A/C, TV, free Wi-Fi, minifridge, coffeemaker, hair dryer, safe.

Montaña de Fuego Inn ⭐ This large spread started out as a small collection of cabins with a great view and great prices. As its popularity has grown, the prices and a whole host of new rooms have quickly gone up. Inside, the individual cabins are all varnished wood, with sparse appointments. Still, there's no denying that the rooms here have amazing volcano views from their spacious glass-enclosed porches. The deluxe rooms all have minifridges, and some even have back balconies overlooking a forested ravine, in addition to the volcano-facing front porch. The newest suites are large units set over a small artificial lake. Behind the hotel are some rolling hills that lead down to a small river surrounded by patches of gallery forest, where they conduct an adventurous horseback, hiking, and rappel loop tour.

If this place is full, check next door at the **Cabañas Arenal Paraíso** (ℂ **460-5333;** www.arenalparaiso.com), which has very similar accommodations and is run by the same family. (The owners of the two lodges are brothers.) Both of these hotels are located 8km (5 miles) outside La Fortuna on the road to Tabacón.

La Palma de la Fortuna (A.P. 82-4417), San Carlos. ⓒ **460-1220.** Fax 460-1455. www.montanadefuego.com. 66 units. $116–$140 (£58–£70) double; $222 (£111) suite. Rates include buffet breakfast. MC, V. **Amenities:** Restaurant; 2 bars; small pool; small spa; 2 Jacuzzis; tour desk; massage; laundry service. *In room:* A/C, TV, coffeemaker.

MODERATE

In addition to the places listed below, there has been ongoing construction along the entire length of the road between La Fortuna and Tabacón over the past few years. If you have a car and some time, you might want to stop and check out any new or interesting hotels or cabins that strike your fancy along the way.

Arenal Observatory Lodge 𝒦𝒦   This place is incredibly close to the volcano and is built on a high ridge, with a spectacular view of the cone. Lying in bed at night listening to the eruptions, it's easy to think you're in imminent danger (don't worry—you're not). The best rooms here are the junior suites built below the restaurant and main lodge, as well as the four rooms in the Observatory Block, and the White Hawk villa. The "Smithsonian" rooms feature massive picture windows, with a direct view of the volcano. The lodge offers a number of guided and unguided hiking options, including a free morning guided hike through their trails and gardens, as well as a wide range of other tours. Meals are served in a dining room with a full wall of glass facing the volcano. This is one of the better nature lodges for travelers with disabilities: five rooms are truly equipped for wheelchair access, and a paved path extends almost 1km (½ mile) into the rainforest. When you're not hiking or touring the region, you can hang by the volcano-view swimming pool and Jacuzzi.

To get here, head to the national park entrance, stay on the dirt road past the entrance, and follow the signs to the Observatory Lodge. A four-wheel-drive vehicle used to be required for the 9km (5½-mile) dirt road up to the lodge, but two bridges now eliminate the need to ford any major rivers, and a traditional sedan will usually make it even in the rainy season—although you'll always be better off with the clearance afforded by a four-wheel-drive vehicle.

On the flanks of Arenal Volcano (A.P. 13411-1000, San José). ⓒ **290-7011** reservations number in San José, or 692-2070 at the lodge. Fax 290-8427. www.arenal-observatory.co.cr. 42 units. $81–$108 (£41–£54) standard double; $142 (£71) Smithsonian; $163 (£82) junior suite. Rates include breakfast buffet. Rates lower in off season. AE, MC, V. **Amenities:** Restaurant; bar; pool; Jacuzzi; tour desk; laundry service. *In room:* No phone.

Volcano Lodge   This lodge is a collection of duplexes across the road from and facing the volcano. All of the rooms come with two double beds, a private bathroom, two wicker chairs inside, and a small terrace with a couple of wooden rocking chairs for volcano viewing outside. The appointments are simple, but the rooms are spacious and get plenty of light through big picture windows. There are a swimming pool and heated Jacuzzi, both with volcano views, and a wide range of tours is available.

La Fortuna de San Carlos. ⓒ **866/208-9819** in the U.S. and Canada, or 460-6080. Fax 460-6020. www.volcanolodge.com. 68 units. $110 (£55) double. Rates include continental breakfast. Rates lower in off season. AE, MC, V. **Amenities:** Restaurant; bar; small free-form pool; Jacuzzi; tour desk; laundry service. *In room:* A/C, free Wi-Fi, hair dryer, safe.

INEXPENSIVE

In addition to the inexpensive options in La Fortuna, if you have a car, **Cabinas Los Guayabos** (ⓒ/fax **460-6644**) and **Cabinas Palo Verde** (ⓒ **460-9791**) are good, economical options, with views and locations that rival some of the more expensive lodgings listed above.

WHERE TO STAY & DINE FARTHER AFIELD

All of the hotels listed in the following three sections are at least a half-hour drive from La Fortuna and the volcano. Most, if not all, offer both night and day tours to Arenal and Tabacón, but they also hope to attract you with their own natural charms.

EAST OF LA FORTUNA

In addition to the places listed below, the quaint, little **Hotel La Garza** (© 475-5222; www.hotellagarza.com) is another good choice.

Termales del Bosque *(Finds*   This simple hotel and lodge features some wonderful **natural hot springs** 🅰🅰 set in rich rainforest. The series of sculpted pools is set on the banks of a small river. Down by the pools are a natural steam room (scented each day with fresh eucalyptus), a massage room, and a snack-and-juice bar. The trail down here winds through the thick forest, and, if you want to keep on walking, you can take guided or self-guided tours on a network of well-marked trails. Most rooms are plain, modern affairs with little in the way of style or personality. Still, they are clean and spacious, and most feature a private or shared veranda, with view over gardens and rolling hills. There is also a three-bedroom bungalow with a shared bathroom and kitchenette. You can rent horses at the lodge, and a variety of tours are offered. If you aren't staying here, you can use the pools and hike the trails for $10 (£5).

On the road from San Carlos to Aguas Zarcas, just before El Tucano; Ciudad Quesada (A.P. 243-4400), San Carlos. © 460-4740. Fax 460-1356. www.termalesdelbosque.com. 51 units. $61–$71 (£31–£36) double. Rates include full breakfast, unlimited use of the hot springs, and taxes. AE, DC, MC, V. **Amenities:** Restaurant; several hot-spring pools set beside a forest river; tour desk; massage; laundry service. *In room:* A/C, TV, no phone.

Tilajari Resort Hotel 🅰 *(Kids*   This sprawling 12-hectare (30-acre) resort on the banks of the San Carlos River just outside the farming community of Muelle (28km/17 miles from La Fortuna) makes a good base for exploring this area and offers terrific bird-watching. The Tilajari offers some of the more luxurious accommodations in the region. Most rooms have views of the river; others open onto rich flowering gardens. All have a private balcony or terrace. Large iguanas are frequently sighted on the grounds, and crocodiles live in the river. There's also an orchid garden, a tropical fruit-and-vegetable garden, a medicinal herb garden, and a well-maintained butterfly garden. The large open-air dining room has both formal and informal sections and a bar.

Tilajari is quite popular with Tico families, especially on weekends. This is a great place for your kids to have a chance to interact and play with their Costa Rican counterparts. The lodge arranges tours of the region, including trips to Caño Negro, Arenal Volcano and some hot springs, and Fortuna Falls, for around $60 (£30) per person. Trips into the nearby rainforest (on foot, on horseback, or by tractor), can also be arranged, as can gentle floats on the Peñas Blancas River. Tennis is quite popular and important; the hotel frequently hosts local tournaments.

Tilajari is almost directly between La Fortuna, Aguas Zarcas, and Ciudad Quesada, and there are roads leading here from each of these towns.

Muelle (A.P. 81-4400), San Carlos. © 469-9091. Fax 469-9095. www.tilajari.com. 76 units. $96–$105 (£48–£53) double; $110–$120 (£55–£60) suite. Rates include full breakfast. Rates lower in off season. AE, MC, V. **Amenities:** Restaurant; bar; large pool; 6 lighted tennis courts (2 indoors); exercise room; Jacuzzi; sauna; bike rental; game room; tour desk; laundry service. *In room:* A/C, TV, hair dryer, safe.

NORTH OF LA FORTUNA

Caño Negro Natural Lodge 🅰   This small nature lodge is the best option in the tiny village of Caño Negro, and it's well located right near the canals and lagoons. If you really want to visit the Caño Negro Wildlife Refuge, either for bird-watching and wildlife viewing or for fishing, this is a good choice. The hotel has spacious grounds full of flowering plants, tropical palms, and fruit trees. The rooms, housed in a series of duplex buildings, are all simple but roomy, clean, and comfortable, with much needed air-conditioning and tasteful decor. To get here, drive toward Los Chiles; several kilometers before Los Chiles, you'll see signs for this hotel and the wildlife refuge. From here, it's 18km (11 miles) on a flat dirt road to the village, refuge, and hotel.

Caño Negro. ✆ 265-3302 for reservations, or 471-1426 direct to the lodge. Fax 265-4310. www.canonegrolodge. com. 22 units. $95 (£48) double. Rates include continental breakfast. Rates lower in off season. AE, DC, MC, V. Amenities: Restaurant; bar; midsize pool; game room; tour desk; laundry service. In room: A/C, safe.

SOUTH OF LA FORTUNA

Villablanca Cloud Forest & Spa 🌟🌟   Formerly owned and operated by an ex-president of Costa Rica and his family, this lodge is currently part of a group of "Green Hotels" that includes Si Como No in Manuel Antonio and Aguila de Osa in Drake Bay. The hotel consists of a series of Tico-style casitas surrounded by 800 hectares (1,976 acres) of farm and forest. Each casita is built of adobe and has tile floors, open beamed ceilings, and whitewashed walls. Inside you'll find a fireplace in one corner, comfortable hardwood chairs, and either one queen or two twin beds covered with colorful bedspreads. The deluxe units and suites have a separate sitting area with a fold-out couch and bathrooms with a whirlpool bathtub and a separate shower. In many rooms the bathroom tubs look out through a wall of windows onto lush gardens. Some have private patios.

The main lobby features two restaurants, a bar, and large common areas. Movies are projected nightly on a screen in their THX theater. Four of the old casitas were converted into a modest little spa, and there are plans for a rather major new spa facility in the near future. Adjacent to the lodge are 11km (6¾ miles) of trails through the **Los Angeles Cloud Forest Reserve.** You can also rent horses or take an adventurous swing through the canopy on a canopy tour here. Villablanca is off the beaten track, but it is relatively close to San José, and if you're interested in bird-watching or exploring a cloud forest and want to avoid the crowds of Monteverde, this is a good choice.

If you're driving, head west out of San José to San Ramón and then head north, following the signs to Villablanca. Or you can take a public bus from San José to San Ramón and then take a taxi for around $15 (£7.50).

San Ramón, Alajuela. ✆ 461-0300. Fax 461-0302. www.villablancacr.com. 34 units. $155 (£78) double; $175 (£88) deluxe; $195 (£98) suite. Rates include buffet breakfast. Rates lower in off season. AE, DC, MC, V. Amenities: 2 restaurants; bar; spa; tour desk; laundry service, Wi-Fi. In room: Stocked minifridge, coffeemaker, safe.

3 Along the Shores of Lake Arenal 🌟

200km (124 miles) NW of San José; 20km (12 miles) NW of Monteverde; 70km (43 miles) SE of Liberia

Despite possessing ample resources and charms, this remains one of the least-developed tourism regions in Costa Rica. Lake Arenal, the largest lake in Costa Rica, is the centerpiece here. A long beautiful lake, it is surrounded by rolling hills that are partly pastured and partly forested. There are loads of activities and adventures available both on the lake, and in the hills and forests around it. While the towns of Tilarán and Nuevo Arenal remain quiet rural communities, there are several excellent hotels spread out along the shores of the lake.

Locals here used to curse the winds, which often come blasting across this end of the lake at 60 knots or greater. However, since the first sailboarders caught wind of

Lake Arenal's combination of warm, fresh water, steady blows, and spectacular scenery, things have been changing quickly. Even if you aren't a fanatical sailboarder, you might enjoy hanging out by the lake, hiking in the nearby forests, riding a mountain bike on dirt farm roads and one-track trails, and catching glimpses of Arenal Volcano.

The lake's other claim to fame is its rainbow-bass fishing. These fighting fish are known in Central America as *guapote* and are large members of the cichlid family. Their sharp teeth and fighting nature make them a real challenge.

ESSENTIALS

GETTING THERE & DEPARTING   By Car   From San José, take the Interamerican Highway west toward Puntarenas, and then continue north to Cañas. In Cañas, turn east toward Tilarán. The drive takes 4 hours. If you're continuing on to Nuevo Arenal, follow the signs in town, which will put you on the road that skirts the shore of the lake. Nuevo Arenal is about a half-hour drive from Tilarán. You can also drive here from La Fortuna, along a scenic road that winds around the lake. From La Fortuna, it's approximately 1 hour to Nuevo Arenal and 1½ hours to Tilarán.

By Bus   Transportes Tilaran buses (© 222-3854) leave San José for Tilarán daily at 7:30 and 9:30am and 12:45, 3:45, and 6:30pm from Calle 14 between avenidas 7 and 9. The trip lasts from 4 to 5½ hours, depending on road conditions; the fare is $3.20 (£1.60).

There are also morning and afternoon buses from **Puntarenas** to Tilarán. The ride takes about 3 hours; the fare is $2.80 (£1.40). (For details on getting to Puntarenas, see "Puntarenas," in chapter 8.) From **Monteverde** (Santa Elena), there is a bus daily at 7am. The fare for the 2-hour trip is $2.15 (£1.10). Buses from **La Fortuna** leave for Tilarán daily at 8am and 5pm, returning at 7am and noon. The trip takes around 2 to 3 hours; the fare is $2.50 (£1.25).

Direct buses to San José leave from Tilarán daily at 5, 7, and 9:30am and 2 and 5pm. Buses to Puntarenas leave at 6am and 1pm daily. The bus to Santa Elena (Monteverde) leaves daily at 12:30pm. Buses also leave regularly for Cañas, where you can catch buses north or south along the Interamerican Highway.

ORIENTATION & FAST FACTS   Tilarán is about 5km (3 miles) from Lake Arenal. All roads into town lead to the central park, which is Tilarán's main point of reference for addresses. If you need to exchange money, check at one of the hotels listed here, or go to the Banco Nacional. If you need a taxi to get to a lodge on Lake Arenal, call **Taxis Unidos Tilarán** (© 695-5324). For a taxi in Nuevo Arenal, call **Taxis Nuevo Arenal** (© 694-4415).

WHAT TO SEE & DO

ARTS, CRAFTS & DOWN-HOME COOKING   If you're in the area, don't miss **Toad Hall** 👍👍 (© 692-8020; www.toadhall-gallery.com). Located 9km (5½ miles) outside of Nuevo Arenal, toward La Fortuna, this roadside gallery and cafe serves up excellent breakfasts, light lunches, and a wide range of coffee drinks and desserts. It also has one of the better-stocked galleries in the country. You'll find the works of Lil Mena, Cecilia Figueres, Patricia Erickson, and Barry Biesanz, among others, as well as a good selection of craftworks.

Located about halfway between Nuevo Arenal and Tilarán is **Casa Delagua** (© 692-2101; www.casadelaguacr.com) the studio, gallery and coffee shop of Costa Rican

CHAPTER 7 · THE NORTHERN ZONE

artist Juan Carlos Ruiz. **The Lucky Bug Gallery** is an excellent roadside arts-and-crafts and souvenir shop, attached to Willy's Caballo Negro restaurant (p. 240).

FISHING   Ask at your hotel if you want to try your hand at fishing for *guapote*. A half-day fishing trip should cost around $150 (£75) per boat, and a full day goes for around $250 to $350 (£125–£175). The boats used will usually accommodate up to three people fishing.

HORSEBACK RIDING   Any of the hotels in the area can hook you up with a horseback-riding tour for around $10 to $15 (£5–£7.50)per hour.

MOUNTAIN BIKING   This is a great area to explore on a mountain bike. You can rent bikes from the **Hotel Tilawa** (see "Where to Stay," below).

A PRIVATE GARDEN   Continuing clockwise on the road around Lake Arenal will bring you to the town of Nuevo Arenal, where the pavement ends. If you continue another 4km (2½ miles) on the dirt road, you'll come to the **Arenal Botanical Gardens & Butterfly Sanctuary** (© **694-4305;** Nov–May daily 9am–5pm; $8/£4 admission). This private garden was started in 1991, and is quite beautiful and extensive. You can see many tropical plants and flowers, the butterfly garden is large and well-stocked, and there are usually scores of hummingbirds to be seen here.

SWIMMING & HIKING   Up above Lake Arenal on the far side of the lake from Tilarán, you'll find the beautiful little heart-shape **Lake Coter.** This lake is surrounded by forest and has good swimming. (UFO watchers also claim that this is a popular pit stop for extraterrestrials.) A taxi to Lake Coter costs around $10 (£5).

If you feel like strapping on your boots, there are some hiking trails on the far side of Lake Arenal, near the smaller Lake Coter.

WINDSURFING & KITEBOARDING   If you want to try windsurfing, **Tilawa Windsurfing Center** (© **695-5050;** www.windsurfcostarica.com) rents equipment at its facilities on one of the lake's few accessible beaches, about 8km (5 miles) from Tilarán on the road along the west end of the lake. Boards rent for around $55 (£28) per day, and lessons are available. These folks also offer classes and rentals for the new high-octane sport of kiteboarding. Another option that is especially popular with serious sailboarders is **Tico Wind** (© **692-2002;** www.ticowind.com), which sets up shop on the shores of the lake each year from December 1 to the end of April, when the winds blow. Rates run around $65 (£33) per day, including lunch, with multiday packages available. If you can't reach them via the phone or website, the folks at **Mystica** (see "Where to Stay," below) can hook you up.

WHERE TO STAY

In addition to the places listed below, the **Ceiba Tree Lodge** (© **692-8050;** www.ceibatree-lodge.com) is a small, simple lodge with a beautiful view and lovely gardens, located on a hill above the lake. **La Mansion Inn Arenal** (© **692-8018;** www.lamansionarenal.com) is an upscale option with a great setting and cozy cabins.

MODERATE

Hotel Tilawa *Kids*   Built to resemble the Palace of Knossos on the island of Crete, the Hotel Tilawa sits high on the slopes above the lake and has a sweeping vista down to the water. It's primarily a windsurfers' and kiteboarders' hangout. Unusual colors and antique paint effects give the hotel a weathered look; inside there are wall murals and other artistic paint treatments throughout. Rooms have dyed cement floors,

Guatemalan bedspreads, and big windows. Some have kitchenettes. Tilawa can arrange windsurfing, kiteboarding, mountain-biking, horseback-riding, and fishing trips. There's even a small skate park for radical skateboarders and BMX freestyle bikers, which makes this a good place to bring teenagers. The hotel also features a small spa, an outdoor pool, and one of the few microbrew operations in Costa Rica.

On the road between Tilarán and Nuevo Arenal (A.P. 92-5710, Tilarán). ⓒ 695-5050. Fax 695-5766. www.hotel-tilawa.com. 28 units. $68–$98 (£34–£49) double. Rates lower in off season; higher during peak periods. MC, V. **Amenities:** Restaurant; bar; outdoor pool; tennis court; small spa and hot spring Jacuzzi; sailboard, kiteboard, and bike rental nearby; tour desk; laundry service; free Wi-Fi. *In room:* No phone.

Mystica ⓖ *Value*   Set on a high hill above Lake Arenal (about midway between Nuevo Arenal and Tilarán), this establishment has simple but spacious and cheery rooms. The painted cement floors are kept immaculate, and the rooms get good ventilation from their large windows. All rooms open onto a long and broad shared veranda with a great view of the lake. There's also one private villa, with a kitchenette, fireplace, and beautiful open deck area. The owners can help you book a wide range of adventures and tours. The hotel has a large open-air yoga platform and sometimes hosts retreats. Perhaps the star attraction here is the hotel's excellent little Italian restaurant and pizzeria by the same name (p. 240).

On the road between Tilarán and Nuevo Arenal (A.P. 29-5710, Tilarán). ⓒ 692-1001. Fax 692-2097. www.mystica lodge.com. 7 units. $75 (£38) double; $125 (£63) villa. Rates include continental breakfast. Rates lower in off season. MC, V. **Amenities:** Restaurant; bar; laundry service. *In room:* No phone.

Villa Decary ⓖ *Finds*   Named after a French explorer (and a rare palm species that he discovered and named), this small bed-and-breakfast is nestled on a hill above Lake Arenal, midway between the town of Nuevo Arenal and the Arenal Botanical Gardens. Each room comes with one queen-size and one twin bed, large picture windows, and a spacious private balcony with a lake view. The rooms get plenty of light, and the bright Guatemalan bedspreads and white-tile floors create a vibrant look. The separate casitas have full kitchens, more room, and even better views of the lake from their slightly higher perches. Breakfasts are extravagant and memorable, with a steady stream of fresh fruits; fresh juice; strong coffee; homemade pancakes, waffles, or muffins; and usually an excellent omelet or soufflé. There's great bird-watching on the hotel grounds, and howler monkeys are common guests here as well.

Nuevo Arenal (5717 Tilarán, Guanacaste). ⓒ 383-3012 or ⓒ/fax 694-4330. www.villadecary.com. 5 units, 3 casitas. $89 (£45) double; $119–$139 (£60–£70) casita for 2. Rates include full breakfast. Extra person $15. MC, V. *In room:* No phone.

INEXPENSIVE

Cabinas Mary   Located right on Tilarán's large and sunny central park, Cabinas Mary is basic but clean lodging. It's upstairs from the restaurant of the same name and has safe parking in back. Rooms are large, and most have plenty of windows. The restaurant downstairs is a popular hangout.

Tilarán (A.P. 89), Guanacaste. ⓒ/fax 695-5479. 18 units. $18 (£9) double. V. **Amenities:** Restaurant; bar. *In room:* TV, no phone.

Chalet Nicholas *Value*   This friendly American-owned bed-and-breakfast is located 2.5km (1½ miles) west of Nuevo Arenal and sits on a hill above the road. There are great views from the garden, and all three rooms have a view of Arenal Volcano in the distance. This converted home is set on 6 hectares (15 acres) and has pretty flower gardens, an organic vegetable garden, and an orchid garden. Behind the property are acres of forest through which you can hike in search of birds, orchids, butterflies, and other tropical beauties. The upstairs loft room is the largest unit, with its own private deck. No smoking is allowed in the house or on the grounds. A 3-hour horseback-riding tour costs $25 (£13) per person. Owners John and Catherine Nicholas go out of their way to make their guests feel at home, although their five Great Danes might intimidate you when you first drive up. All around, it's a really good deal.

Tilarán (A.P. 72-5710), Guanacaste. (℃) 694-4041. www.chaletnicholas.com. 3 units. $58 (£29) double. Rates include full breakfast. No credit cards. *In room:* No phone.

WHERE TO DINE

There are numerous inexpensive places to eat in the town of Tilarán, including the restaurant at Cabinas Mary. In Nuevo Arenal, try the pizzas and pastas at **Tramonti** (℃ 694-4282) or **Café del Lago Pizzeria** (℃ 694-4780). For breakfast, snacks, and fresh-baked goods, check out **Tom's Pan German Bakery** (℃ 694-4547). Also worth mentioning is **Equus BBQ** (℃ 692-1101), a small open-air restaurant in front of the Xiloe Lodge with a view of the lake. It specializes in roast chicken and steaks.

Mystica ℱ PIZZA/ITALIAN   The restaurant in this Italian-run hotel has a wonderful setting high on a hill overlooking the lake. The large dining room features rustic wooden chairs and tables, varnished wood floors, colorful tablecloths, and abundant flower arrangements. The most striking features, aside from the view, are the large open fireplace on one end and the large brick oven, in the shape of a small cottage, on the other that turns out pizzas. The pastas and delicious main dishes are authentically northern Italian. Whenever possible, Mystica uses fresh ingredients from its own garden.

On the road between Tilarán and Nuevo Arenal. (℃) 692-1001. Main courses $5–$12 (£2.50–£6). MC, V. Daily noon–9pm.

Willy's Caballo Negro ℱ ⟨finds⟩ INTERNATIONAL/VEGETARIAN   The German owners of this attractive little roadside cafe serve up two different types of schnitzel, bratwurst, veal cordon bleu, and a host of other old-world dishes. However, vegetarians are well served here, and will find several tasty and filling options here, including stuffed potatoes, garden burgers, and eggplant Parmesan. The delicious pesto is made with locally grown organic macadamia nuts and cilantro. Wooden tables are set around the edges of the round dining room, with a high peaked roof. Candles and creative lighting give the place a cozy and warm feel. There's a small, picturesque lake behind the restaurant, a few rooms, and the very interesting Lucky Bug Gallery, run by the owner's triplet daughters.

Nuevo Arenal (about 3km/1¾ miles out of town on the road to Tilarán). (℃) 694-4515. Main courses $5–$14 (£2.50–£7). MC, V. Daily 7:30am–8pm.

4 Monteverde ⟨★⟩⟨★⟩

167km (104 miles) NW of San José; 82km (51 miles) NW of Puntarenas

Monteverde translates as "green mountain," and that's exactly what you'll find at the end of the steep and windy rutted dirt road that leads here. It's a rough ride up, and the roads remain rough and bumpy once you've made it and begin touring the area.

Next to Manuel Antonio, this is Costa Rica's most internationally recognized ecotourism destination. The fame, rapid growth and accompanying traffic have led some to dub it the Monteverde Crowd Forest. Nevertheless, the reserve itself and the extensive network of private reserves around it are incredibly rich in biodiversity, and

Monteverde

ACCOMODATIONS ■
Arco Iris Lodge **2**
Finca Valverde **10**
Hotel Belmar **25**
Hotel El Establo **22**
Hotel El Sapo Dorado **19**
Hotel El Viandante **18**
Hotel Fonda Vela **20**
Hotel Heliconia **20**
Hotel Poco a Poco **14**
Monteverde Lodge
  & Gardens **15**
Pension Flor de
  Monteverde **12**
Pension Santa Elena **1**
Treehouse Hotel **4**

DINING ◆
Café Cuzuco **8**
Chunches **3**
El Sapo Dorado **19**
Lazy Frog Cafe **28**
Moon Shiva **23**
Morpho's Café **6**
Pizzeria de Johnny **17**
Rainforest Café **5**
Restaurante De Lucia **16**
Sofia **21**
Stella's Bakery **32**
Tramonti **29**

ATTRACTIONS ●
Bajo del Tigre Trail **31**
Bat Jungle **33**
Butterfly Garden **27**
Centro Panamericano
  de Idiomas **24**
Ecological Sanctuary **26**
Frog Pond of Monteverde **13**
Monteverde Cheese Factory **35**
Monteverde Conservation
  League **30**
Monteverde Serpentarium **11**
Orchid Garden **9**
Reserva Sendero Tranquilo **34**
World of Insects **7**

a well-organized infrastructure helps guarantee a rewarding experience for both first-time and experienced ecoadventurers.

The village of Monteverde was founded in 1951 by Quakers from the United States who wanted to leave behind a constant fear of war as well as an obligation to support continued militarism through paying U.S. taxes. They chose Costa Rica primarily because it had no standing army. Although Monteverde's founders came here to farm the land, they wisely recognized the need to preserve the rare cloud forest that covered the mountain slopes above their fields, and to that end they dedicated the largest adjacent tract of cloud forest as the Monteverde Biological Cloud Forest Reserve.

Cloud forests are a mountaintop phenomenon. Moist, warm air sweeping in off the ocean is forced upward by mountain slopes, and as this moist air rises, it cools, forming clouds. The mountaintops of Costa Rica are blanketed almost daily in dense clouds, and as the clouds cling to the slopes, moisture condenses on forest trees. This constant level of moisture has given rise to an incredible diversity of innovative life forms and a forest in which nearly every square inch of space has some sort of plant growing. Within the cloud forest, the branches of huge trees are draped with epiphytic plants: orchids, ferns, and bromeliads. This intense botanic competition has created an almost equally diverse population of insects, birds, and other wildlife. Monteverde Biological Cloud Forest Reserve covers 10,400 hectares (25,688 acres) of forest, including several different life zones characterized by different types of plants and animals. Within this small area are more than 2,500 species of plants, including 400 types of orchids, 400 species of birds, and 100 species of mammals. It's no wonder that the reserve has been the site of constant scientific investigations since its founding in 1972.

Tip: For many, the primary goal in visiting Monteverde is to glimpse the rare and elusive **quetzal,** a bird once revered by the pre-Columbian peoples of the Americas. However, if you just care about seeing a quetzal, you should also consider visiting other cloud forest areas. In particular, San Gerardo de Dota and Cerro de la Muerte areas are home to several specialty lodges (see "San Isidro de El General: A Base for Exploring Chirripó National Park" in chapter 8), where you'll find far fewer crowds and often better chances of seeing the famed quetzal.

ESSENTIALS

GETTING THERE & DEPARTING   By Car   From San José, take the Interamerican Highway north. About 20km (12 miles) past the turnoff for Puntarenas, there will be a marked turnoff for Sardinal, Santa Elena, and Monteverde. From this turnoff, the road is paved almost as far as the tiny town of Guacimal. From here it's another 20km (12 miles) to Santa Elena. It should take you a little over 2 hours to reach the turnoff and another 1 hour or so from there.

An alternative route is to continue on the Interamerican Highway until just before the Río Lagarto Bridge. This turnoff isn't always well marked. From the Río Lagarto turnoff, it's 38km (24 miles) to Santa Elena and Monteverde.

Whichever route you take, the final going is slow because the roads into Santa Elena are rough, unpaved dirt and gravel affairs. Just before you enter the town of Santa Elena, you'll be stopped at a little tollbooth collecting 200 colones. The money is ostensibly going to maintain the road, and payment is actually optional.

By Bus   **Transmonteverde** express buses (© **222-3854** in San José, or 645-5159 in Santa Elena) leave San José daily at 6:30am and 2:30pm from Calle 12 between avenidas 7 and 9. The trip takes around 4 hours; the fare is $4.20 (£2.10). Buses arrive

---

Tips   Alternative Transport

You can travel between Monteverde and La Fortuna by boat and taxi, or on a combination boat, horseback, and taxi trip. See "Boats, Horses & Taxis" on p. 224 for details. Any of the trips described there can be done in the reverse direction departing from Monteverde. Most hotels and **Desafío Expeditions** (© 645-5874; www.monteverdetours.com) can arrange this trip for you. Desafío also offers multiday hikes from Monteverde to Arenal; you spend the night in rustic research facilities inside the Bosque Eterno de los Niños.

---

at and depart from Santa Elena. If you're staying at one of the hotels or lodges toward the reserve, you'll want to arrange pickup if possible, or take a taxi or local bus.

There are two daily buses that depart Puntarenas for Santa Elena at 1:15 and 2:15pm. The bus stop in Puntarenas is across the street from the main bus station. The fare for the 2½-hour trip is $2.60 (£1.30).

There is a daily bus from Tilarán (Lake Arenal) at 12:30pm. Trip duration, believe it or not, is 2 hours (for a 40km/25-mile trip); the fare is $2.15 (£1.10).

Gray Line (© 220-2126; www.graylinecostarica.com) has a daily bus that leaves San José for Monteverde at 7am; the fare is $38 (£19). **Interbus** (© 283-5573; www.interbusonline.com) has two daily buses that leave San José for Monteverde at 8:15am and 2:30pm; the fare is $29 (£15). Another option is to take **Costa Rica Expeditions'** van (© 257-0766; www.costaricaexpeditions.com) from San José; the fare is $40 (£20). Any of the above companies will pick you up and drop you off at most San José and Monteverde area hotels.

The express bus departs for San José daily at 6:30am and 2:30pm. Buses from Santa Elena to Puntarenas leave daily at 4:15 and 6am. If you're heading to Manuel Antonio, take one of the Santa Elena/Puntarenas buses and transfer in Puntarenas. To reach Liberia, take any bus down the mountain and get off at the Río Lagarto Bridge, where you hit the paved road. You can then flag down a bus bound for Liberia (almost any bus heading north). The Santa Elena/Tilarán bus leaves daily at 7am. Both **Gray Line** and **Interbus** offer routes with connections to most major destinations in Costa Rica.

GETTING AROUND   There are six buses daily between the town of Santa Elena and the Monteverde Biological Cloud Forest Reserve. The first bus leaves Santa Elena for the reserve at 6am and the last bus from the reserve leaves there at 4pm. Fare is $1.50 (75p). There's also periodic van transportation between the town of Santa Elena and the Santa Elena Cloud Forest Reserve. Ask around town and you should be able to find the current schedule and book·a ride for around $2 (£1) per person. A **taxi** (© 645-6969 or 645-5148) between Santa Elena and either the Monteverde Reserve or the Santa Elena Cloud Forest Reserve costs around $8 to $10 (£4–£5) for up to four people. Count on paying between $4 and $10 (£2–£5)for the ride from Santa Elena to your lodge in Monteverde. Finally, several places around town rent ATVs, or all-terrain vehicles, for around $45 to $60 (£23–£30) per day. Hourly rates and guided tours are also available. If this is up your alley, try **Aventura** (© 645-6959) or **Monteverde Offroader** (© 645-6463).

ORIENTATION   As you approach Santa Elena, take the right fork in the road if you're heading directly to Monteverde. If you continue straight, you'll come into the little village of **Santa Elena,** which has a bus stop, a health clinic, a bank, a general store, a laundromat, and a few simple restaurants, budget hotels, souvenir shops, and tour offices. **Monteverde,** on the other hand, is not a village in the traditional sense of the word. There's no center of town—only dirt lanes leading off from the main road to various farms. This main road has signs for all the hotels and restaurants mentioned here, and it dead-ends at the reserve entrance.

FAST FACTS   The telephone number for the **local clinic** is ○ **645-5076;** for the **Red Cross,** ○ **645-6128;** and for the **local police,** ○ **911** or 645-6248. There's a 24-hour gas station located about halfway between the town of Santa Elena and the Monteverde Biological Cloud Forest Reserve. The **Farmacia Monteverde** (○ **645-7110)** is right downtown. There's a **Banco Nacional** (○ **645-5610)** in downtown Santa Elena and **Coopemex** (○ **645-6948)** on the road out to Santa Elena, near Finca Valverde; both have 24-hour ATM machines.

EXPLORING THE MONTEVERDE BIOLOGICAL CLOUD FOREST RESERVE ⚘⚘⚘

The **Monteverde Biological Cloud Forest Reserve** (○ 645-5122; www.cct.or.cr) is one of the most developed and well-maintained natural attractions in Costa Rica. The trails are clearly marked, regularly traveled, and generally gentle in terms of ascents and descents. The cloud forest here is lush and largely untouched. Still, keep in mind that most of the birds and mammals are rare, elusive, and nocturnal. Moreover, to all but the most trained of eyes, those thousands of exotic ferns, orchids, and bromeliads tend to blend into one large mass of indistinguishable green. However, with a guide hired through your hotel, or on one of the reserve's official guided 2- to 3-hour hikes, you can see and learn far more than you could on your own. At $15 (£7.50) per person, the reserve's tours might seem like a splurge, especially after you pay the entrance fee, but I strongly recommend that you go with a guide.

Perhaps the most famous resident of the cloud forests of Costa Rica is the quetzal, a robin-size bird with iridescent green wings and a ruby-red breast, which has become extremely rare due to habitat destruction. The male quetzal also has two long tail feathers that can reach nearly .6m (2 ft.) in length, making it one of the most spectacular birds on earth. The best time to see quetzals is early morning to midmorning, and the best months are February through April (mating season).

Other animals that have been seen in Monteverde, although sightings are extremely rare, include jaguars, ocelots, and tapirs. After the quetzal, Monteverde's most famous resident was the golden toad *(sapo dorado),* a rare native species. However, the golden toad has disappeared from the forest and is feared extinct. Competing theories of the toad's demise include adverse effects of a natural drought cycle, the disappearing ozone

---

Tips **Seeing the Forest for the Trees, Bromeliads, Monkeys, Hummingbirds . . .**

Because the entrance fee to Monteverde is valid for a full day, I recommend taking an early-morning walk with a guide and then heading off on your own either directly after that hike or after lunch. A guide will certainly point out and explain a lot, but there's also much to be said for walking quietly through the forest on your own or in very small groups. This will also allow you to stray from the well-traveled paths in the park.

layer, pesticides, and acid rain. Photos of the golden toad abound in Monteverde. (I particularly like the shots of amphibian group sex.)

ADMISSION, HOURS & TOURS The reserve is open daily from 7am to 4pm, and the entrance fee is $15 (£7.50) for adults and $7.50 (£3.75) for students and children. Because only 160 people are allowed into the reserve at any one time, you might be forced to wait for a while. Most hotels can reserve a guided walk and entrance to the reserve for the following day for you, or you can get tickets in advance directly at the reserve entrance.

Some of the trails can be very muddy, depending on the season, so ask about current conditions. If the mud is heavy, you can rent rubber boots at the reserve entrance for $2 (£1) per day. They might make your hike much more pleasant. Before venturing into the forest, have a look around the information center. There are several guidebooks available, as well as posters and postcards of some of the reserve's more famous animal inhabitants.

Night tours of the reserve leave every evening at 7:15pm. The cost is $15 (£7.50), including admission to the reserve, a 2-hour hike, and, most important, a guide with a high-powered searchlight. For an extra $2 (£1), they'll throw in round-trip transportation to and from your area hotel.

WHAT TO SEE & DO OUTSIDE THE RESERVE
BIRD-WATCHING & HIKING

You can also find ample bird-watching and hiking opportunities outside the reserve boundaries. Avoid the crowds at Monteverde by heading 5km (3 miles) north from the village of Santa Elena to the **Santa Elena Cloud Forest Reserve** 𝆺𝅥 (𝄐 **645-5390;** www.reservasantaelena.org). This 310-hectare (765-acre) reserve has a maximum elevation of 1,680m (5,510 ft.), making it the highest cloud forest in the Monteverde area. There are 13km (8 miles) of hiking trails, as well as an information center. Because it borders the Monteverde Reserve, a similar richness of flora and fauna is found here, although quetzals are not nearly as common. The $9 (£4.50) entry fee at this reserve goes directly to support local schools. The reserve is open daily from 7am to 4pm. Three-hour guided tours are available for $15 (£7.50) per person, not including the entrance fee. (Call the number above to make a reservation for the tour.) A night tour ($15/£7.50) is also offered each evening at 7pm.

Sky Walk 𝆺𝅥 (𝄐 **645-5238;** www.skytrek.com) is a network of forest paths and suspension bridges that provides visitors with a view previously reserved for birds, monkeys, and the much more adventurous traveler. The bridges reach 39m (128 ft.) above the ground at their highest point, so acrophobia could be an issue. The Sky Walk and its sister attraction, **Sky Trek** (see "Canopy Tours & Canyoning," below), are located about 3.5km (2¼ miles) outside of the town of Santa Elena, on the road to the Santa Elena Cloud Forest Reserve. The Sky Walk is open daily from 7am to 4pm; admission is $17 (£8.50). For an extra $10 (£5), a knowledgeable guide will point out the diverse flora and fauna on the walk. For $50 (£25) per person, you can do the Sky Trek canopy tour and then walk the trails and bridges of the Sky Walk. Reservations are recommended for the Sky Trek; round-trip transportation from Santa Elena is just $2 (£1) per person.

To learn even more about Monteverde, stop in at the **Monteverde Conservation League** (𝄐 **645-5003;** www.acmcr.org), which administers the 22,000-hectare (54,000-acre) private reserve **Bosque Eterno de Los Niños (Children's Eternal Forest),** as well as the Bajo del Tigre Trail. The Conservation League has its office on the Cerro Plano road, 50m (164 ft.) before the Butterfly Garden. In addition to being a good source for information, it also sells books, T-shirts, and cards, and all proceeds go to purchase more land for the Bosque Eterno de Los Niños. The **Bajo del Tigre Trail** 𝆏 is a 3.5km (2¼-mile) trail that's home to several different bird species not usually found within the reserve. You can take several different loops, lasting anywhere from 1 hour to several hours. The trail starts a little past the CASEM artisans' shop (see "Other Attractions in Monteverde," below) and is open daily from 8am to 5pm. Admission is $7 (£3.50) general and $4 (£2) for students.

You can also go on guided 3-hour hikes at the **Reserva Sendero Tranquilo** 𝆏 (© 645-5010), which is run by the folks at the Sapo Dorado and has 80 hectares (198 acres) of land, two-thirds of which is in virgin forest. This reserve is located up the hill from the cheese factory, charges $22 (£11) for its tours, and is open daily from 7am to 3pm seasonally.

Finally, you can walk the trails and grounds of the **Ecological Sanctuary** 𝆏 (© 645-5869), a family-run wildlife refuge and private reserve located down the Cerro Plano road. This place has four main trails through a variety of ecosystems, and wildlife viewing is often quite good here. There are a couple of pretty waterfalls off the trails. It's open daily from 6:30am to 7pm; admission is $9 (£4.50) for self-guided hiking on the trails; $24 (£12) during the day for a 2-hour guided tour; and $15 (£7.50) for the 1½ hour guided night tour that leaves at 5:30pm.

CANOPY TOURS

One of the oldest canopy tours in the country is run by **The Original Canopy Tour** 𝆏 (© 645-5243; www.canopytour.com), which has an office right in the center of Santa Elena. This is one of the more interesting canopy tours in Costa Rica because the initial ascent is made by climbing up the hollowed-out interior of a giant strangler fig. This tour has 11 platforms and two rappels. The 2- to 2½-hour tours run three times daily and cost $45 (£23) for adults, $35 (£18) for students, and $25 (£13) for children under 12.

Another popular option is offered by the folks at **Sky Trek** 𝆏𝆏 (© 645-5238; www.skytrek.com), a growing complex of aerial adventures and hiking trails. This is one of the more extensive canopy tours in the country, with two very long cables to cross. The longest of these is some 770m (2,525 ft.) long, high above the forest floor. There are no rappel descents here, and you brake using the pulley system for friction. This tour costs $44 (£22).

One of the most complete additions to the field is **Selvatura Park** 𝆏𝆏 (© 645-5929; www.selvatura.com). Located close to the Santa Elena Cloud Forest Reserve, this place is the best one-stop shop for various adventures and attractions in the area. In addition to an extensive canopy tour, with 15 cables connecting 18 platforms, they also have a network of trails and suspended bridges, a huge butterfly garden, a hummingbird garden, a snake exhibit, and a wonderful insect display and museum. Prices vary depending upon how much you want to see and do. Individually, the canopy tour costs $40 (£20); the walkways and bridges, $20 (£10); and the butterfly garden and the insect museum, $10 (£5) each. Packages to combine the various exhibits are available, although it's definitely confusing, and somewhat annoying, to pick the perfect package. For $108 (£54), you get the run of the entire joint, all the tours, lunch, and round-trip transportation from your Monteverde hotel.

There's currently a glut of canopy tours in the Monteverde area, and I can only recommend those mentioned above. Anybody in average physical condition can do any of the adventure tours in Monteverde, but they're not for the faint-hearted or acrophobic. Try to book directly with the companies listed above or through your hotel.

Beware of touts on the streets of Monteverde, who make a small commission and frequently try to steer tourists to the operator paying the highest percentage.

HORSEBACK RIDING

There's excellent terrain for horseback riding all around Monteverde. **Meg's Riding Stables** (© 645-5560), **La Estrella Stables** (© 645-5075), **Palomina Horse Tours** (© 645-5479), and **Sabine's Smiling Horses** (© 645-6894; www.smilinghorses.com) are the more established operators, offering guided rides for around $10 to $15 (£5–£7.50) per hour. As I mentioned earlier in "Boats, Horses & Taxis" (p. 224), there are horseback/boat trips linking Monteverde/Santa Elena with La Fortuna. This is certainly an exciting and adventurous means of connecting these two popular destinations, but I've received numerous complaints about the state of the trails and the treatment of the horses, so be very careful before undertaking this trip.

Another option is to set up a day tour and sauna at **El Sol** ✦ (© **645-5838;** www.elsolnuestro.com). Located about a 10-minute car ride down the mountain from Santa Elena, these folks take you on a roughly 3-hour ride either to San Luis or to an isolated little waterfall with an excellent swimming hole. After the ride back, you'll find the wood-burning traditional Swedish sauna all fired up, with a refreshing and beautiful little pool beside it. The tour costs around $60 (£30) per person, including lunch. These folks also have two very rustically luxurious private cabins ($95–$125/ £48–£63 double), with excellent views.

OTHER ATTRACTIONS IN MONTEVERDE

Birds are not the only colorful fauna in Monteverde. Butterflies abound here, and the **Butterfly Garden** ✦ (© 645-5512), located near the Pensión Monteverde Inn, displays many of Costa Rica's most beautiful species. Besides the hundreds of preserved and mounted butterflies, there are a garden and a greenhouse where you can watch live butterflies. The garden is open daily from 9:30am to 4pm, and admission is $8 (£4) for adults and $6 (£3) for students and children, including a guided tour. The best time to visit is between 9:30am and 1pm, when the butterflies are most active.

It seems as if Monteverde has an exhibit or attraction dedicated to almost every type of tropical fauna. If your taste runs toward the slithery, you can check out the **Monteverde Serpentarium** (© **645-5238;** www.snaketour.com), on the road to the reserve. This place was recently remodeled and the new enclosures and informative displays are a vast improvement. It's open daily from 8am to 8:30pm and charges $8 (£4) for admission. The **Frog Pond of Monteverde** (© 645-6320; www.ranario.com), a couple of hundred meters north of the Monteverde Lodge, is probably a better bet. The $9 (£4.50) entrance gets you a 45-minute tour, and your ticket is good for 2 days. A variety of species populates a series of glass terrariums. This place is open daily from 9am to 8:30pm. I especially recommend that you stop by at least once after dark, when the tree frogs are active. Fans of invertebrates will want to head to **World of Insects** (© **645-6859**), which features more than 30 terrariums filled with some of the area's more interesting creepy crawlers. My favorites are the giant horned beetles. This place is located 300m (984 ft.) west of the supermarket in Santa Elena. It's open daily from 9am to 7pm; admission is $7 (£3.50). Finally, the newest entry in the field is **The Bat Jungle** (© **645-6566**) an in-depth look into the world life and habits of these odd flying mammals. A visit here includes several different types of exhibits, from skeletal remains, to large enclosures where you get to see various live species in action—the enclosures and rooms are kept dark, and the bats have had their biological clocks tricked into thinking that it's night. The Bat Jungle is open daily from 9:30am to 8:30pm. Admission is $8 (£4).

If you've had your fill of birds, snakes, bugs, butterflies, and bats, you might want to stop at the **Orchid Garden** $\mathscr{R}$ (© **645-5308**), in Santa Elena across from the Pension El Tucano. This small botanical garden boasts more than 450 species of orchids. The tour is fascinating, especially the fact that you need (and are given) a magnifying glass to see some of the flowers in bloom. Admission is $7 (£3.50) for adults and $5 (£2.50) for students. It's open daily from 8am to 5pm.

Because the vegetation in the cloud forest is so dense, most of the forest's animal residents are rather difficult to spot. If you were dissatisfied with your sightings, even with a naturalist guide leading you, you might want to consider attending a slide show of photographs taken in the reserve. There is a host of daily slide shows around Monteverde. The longest running of these takes place at the **Monteverde Lodge, Hotel El Sapo Dorado, Hotel Belmar** (see "Where to Stay," below, for phone numbers), and **Hummingbird Gallery** (see below). Dates, showtimes, and admissions vary, so inquire at your hotel or one of the places mentioned above.

The **Centro Panamericano de Idiomas** $\mathscr{R}$ (© **645-5441;** www.spanishlanguage school.com) offers immersion language classes in a wonderful setting. A 1-week program with 4 hours of class per day and a home stay with a Costa Rican family costs $415 (£208).

Almost all of the area hotels can arrange a wide variety of other tours and activities, including guided night tours of the cloud forest and night trips to the Arenal Volcano (a tedious 4-hr. ride, each way).

SHOPPING

The best-stocked gift shop in Monteverde is the **Hummingbird Gallery** $\mathscr{R}$ (© **645-5030**). You'll find the gallery just outside the reserve entrance. Hanging from trees around it are several hummingbird feeders that attract more than seven species of these tiny birds. At any given moment, there might be several dozen hummingbirds buzzing and chattering around the building and your head. Inside you will find many beautiful color prints of hummingbirds and other local flora and fauna, as well as a wide range of craft items, T-shirts, and other gifts. The Hummingbird Gallery is open daily from 8:30am to 4:30pm.

Another good option is **CASEM** (© **645-5190**), located on the right side of the main road, just across from Stella's Bakery. This crafts cooperative sells embroidered clothing, T-shirts, posters, and postcards with photos of the local flora and fauna, Boruca weavings, locally grown and roasted coffee, and many other items to remind you of your visit to Monteverde. CASEM is open Monday through Saturday from 8am to 5pm and Sunday from 10am to 4pm (closed Sun May–Oct). There is also a well-stocked **gift shop** at the entrance to the Monteverde Biological Cloud Forest Reserve. You'll find plenty of T-shirts, postcards, and assorted crafts here, as well as a well-stocked selection of science and natural-history books.

Over the years, Monteverde has developed a nice little community of artists. Around town you'll see paintings by local artists such as Paul Smith and Meg Wallace, whose works are displayed at the Fonda Vela Hotel and Stella's Bakery, respectively. You might also check out **Casa de Arte** $\mathscr{R}$ (© **645-5275**), which has a mix of arts and crafts in many media and is located just off the main road to the reserve. Another nice place to visit is the **Community Arts Center** $\mathscr{R}$ (© **645-6121**), which is located just beyond the Cheese Factory (see below) on the right-hand side of the road. In addition to studio space, there's a small gallery and gift shop here selling the work of local artists and artisans.

Finally, it's also worth stopping by the **Monteverde Cheese Factory** to pick up some of the best cheese in Costa Rica. (You can even watch it being processed and get homemade ice cream.) The cheese factory is located right on the main road about midway between Santa Elena and the reserve. It's open Monday through Saturday from 7:30am to 4pm and Sunday from 7:30am to noon.

WHERE TO STAY

When choosing a place to stay in Monteverde, be sure to check whether the rates include a meal plan. In the past almost all the lodges included three meals a day in their prices, but this practice is waning. Check before you assume anything.

EXPENSIVE *Stayed here*

Hotel El Establo ✿   *El Establo* translates as "the stable." From a working stable owned by a local Quaker family, with just a handful of budget rooms, this place has morphed into what is certainly the largest and most luxurious hotel in Monteverde. It is still owned and managed by the same family. However, in many ways, I find the scale, design, and decor of this place somewhat out of place with the vibe and aesthetic of Monteverde. A series of buildings are spread up a steep hill. The rooms are all quite large and have private balconies or patios taking in spectacular views. All rooms come with cable television, and all rooms are nonsmoking. The luxurious honeymoon suites have fabulous views and a private Jacuzzi. The 400-block of rooms are my favorites. There's one midsize outdoor swimming pool and another slightly smaller pool built under a high-open air roof, for when it's raining. El Establo owns 48 hectares (119 acres) of land backing the hotel, and half of that is primary forest. The also have an on-site canopy tour, and extensive spa.

Monteverde (A.P. 549-2050, San Pedro). ☎ 645-5110. Fax 645-5041. www.hotelelestablo.com. 115 units. $159 (£80) double; $193–$243 (£97–£122) suite. Rates include breakfast. AE, MC, V. **Amenities:** Restaurant; bar; 2 pools; spa; tour desk; babysitting; laundry service. *In room:* TV, minifridge, hair dryer, coffeemaker, safe.

MODERATE

In addition to the hotels listed below, **Hotel Heliconia** (☎ **645-5109;** www.hotel heliconia.com) is another good option in this price range. Or you can try **El Sol** ✿ (☎ **645-5838;** www.elsolnuestro.com), which is located about 10 minutes south of Santa Elena, on the road to the Interamerican Highway.

Finca Valverde ✿   This place is located right on the outskirts of Santa Elena, yet once you head uphill to the rooms, you'll feel far from the hustle and bustle of the tiny burg. The standard rooms are set behind the main lodge and restaurant and are reached via a small suspension bridge over a small forest creek. Most have one queen-size and two twin beds. All share a broad common veranda. The junior suites and cabins are larger, more private, and feature bathtubs. The junior suites are the highest up the hill and also have televisions, small refrigerators, and coffeemakers. The grounds are lush and well tended. A buffet breakfast and all other meals are served in the large restaurant just off the lobby.

Monteverde (A.P. 2-5655), Puntarenas. ☎ 645-5157. Fax 645-5216. www.monteverde.co.cr. 20 units. $65–$85 (£33–£43) double. Rates lower in off season. MC, V. **Amenities:** Restaurant; bar; tour desk; laundry service; free Wi-Fi.

Hotel Belmar ✿   You might think you're in the Alps when you stay at this beautiful Swiss Chalet–style hotel. Set on the top of a grassy hill, the Belmar has stunning views of the Nicoya Gulf and the Pacific. Afternoons in the dining room or lounge are idyllic, with bright sunlight streaming in through a west-facing glass wall. Sunsets are spectacular. Most of the guest rooms are fitted with wood paneling, French doors, and little balconies that open onto splendid views. There are actually two buildings here. My favorite rooms are in the main building; those in the Chalet building are a bit smaller. The restaurant serves a mix of well-prepared Tico and international cuisine. The Belmar is up a dirt road that passes to the left of the gas station as you come into the village of Monteverde.

Monteverde (A.P. 17-5655), Puntarenas. © 645-5201. Fax 645-5135. www.hotelbelmar.net. 28 units. $85–$95 (£43–£48) double. Rates lower in off season. V. **Amenities:** Restaurant; bar; Jacuzzi; game room; tour desk; laundry service. *In room:* Free Wi-Fi.

Hotel El Sapo Dorado 🐸🐸   Located on a steep hill between Santa Elena and the reserve, El Sapo Dorado (named for Monteverde's famous golden toad) offers some of the most charming and comfortable accommodations in Monteverde. The spacious cabins are built of hardwoods both inside and out and are surrounded by a grassy lawn. Big windows let in lots of light, and high ceilings keep the rooms cool during the day. Some of the cabins have fireplaces, a welcome feature on chilly nights and during the peak parts of the rainy season. My favorite rooms are the sunset suites, which have private terraces with views to the Gulf of Nicoya and wonderful sunsets.

There's an excellent restaurant here (see "Where to Dine," below), and the quiet yet jovial bar stays open until 10pm. The hotel has a combination conference/game room, where it sometimes shows slide shows at night. Not only does El Sapo Dorado own and manage the Reserva Sendero Tranquilo, but it also has a network of well-maintained trails into primary forest on-site. To find the hotel and restaurant, watch for the sign on the left-hand side of the main road to the reserve, a few hundred yards outside of the town of Santa Elena.

Monteverde (A.P. 9-5655), Puntarenas. © 645-5010. Fax 645-5180. www.sapodorado.com. 30 units. $112–$122 (£56–£61) double. MC, V. **Amenities:** Restaurant; bar; tour desk; massage; laundry service; free Wi-Fi. *In room:* Coffeemaker, hair dryer, safe.

Hotel Fonda Vela 🐸🐸   Although it's one of the older hotels here, Fonda Vela remains one of my top choices in Monteverde. Moreover, this is one of the closer lodges to the Cloud Forest Reserve, a relatively easy 15-minute walk away. Guest rooms are in nine separate buildings scattered among the forests and pastures of this former farm, and most have views of the Nicoya Gulf. The junior suites all come with cable television. The newer junior suites, some of which have excellent views, are the best rooms in the house, and I prefer them to the older and larger junior suites. The dining room has great sunset views, and it sometimes even features live music. There's a popular bar here, as well as a small system of private trails. Throughout the hotel, you'll see paintings by co-owner Paul Smith, who also handcrafts violins and cellos and is a musician himself.

Monteverde (A.P. 70060-1000, San José). © 257-1413 reservations in San José, or 645-5125 at the lodge. Fax 257-1416. www.fondavela.com. 40 units. $103 (£52) double; $121 (£61) junior suite. Extra person $9 (£4.50). AE, MC, V. **Amenities:** Restaurant; bar; horse rental; tour desk; laundry service. *In room:* TV, minibar, coffeemaker, hair dryer.

Hotel Poco A Poco 🐸   Located just outside of the town of Santa Elena, this newer hotel provides many of the perks and comforts of a luxury hotel, at good prices. Some rooms are on the small size, and the decor is rather inconsistent, but the beds are firm, and everything is kept neat and contemporary. The best rooms are higher up, away from the road, and have a small little balcony. All rooms come with DVD players, and the hotel maintains a movie-lending library of over 4,000 titles. There are a heated pool, children's pool, and Jacuzzi on site, and the small restaurant is excellent.

Monteverde, Puntarenas. © **645-6000**. Fax 645-6264. www.hotelpocoapoco.com. 30 units. $80 (£40) double. Rates include breakfast. Rates lower in off season; higher during peak periods. MC, V. **Amenities:** Restaurant; bar; small outdoor pool; tour desk; laundry service. *In room:* TV, free Wi-Fi, hair dryer, safe.

Monteverde Lodge & Gardens ⭐⭐ *Kids*   Operated by Costa Rica Expeditions, the Monteverde Lodge was one of the first ecolodges in Monteverde, and it remains one of the most popular. It's located 5km (3 miles) from the reserve entrance in a secluded setting near Santa Elena. Guest rooms are large and comfortable, and thanks to ongoing upkeep and remodeling are some of the best in town. Most feature angled walls of glass with chairs and a table placed so that avid bird-watchers can do a bit of birding without leaving their rooms. The gardens and secondary forest surrounding the lodge have some gentle groomed trails and are also home to quite a few species of birds. Perhaps the lodge's most popular attraction is the large hot tub in a big atrium garden just off the lobby.

The hotel's dining room offers great views, good food, and excellent formal service provided by bow-tied waiters. The adjacent bar is a popular gathering spot, and there are regular evening slide shows focusing on the cloud forest. Scheduled bus service to and from San José is available ($40/£20 each way), as is a shuttle to the reserve ($6/£3 each way), horseback riding, and a variety of optional tours. The excellent guides here have lots of experience with family groups.

Monteverde (mailing address: SJO 235, P.O. Box 25216, Miami, FL 33102-5216). © **257-0766** reservations office in San José, or 645-5057 at the lodge. Fax 257-1665. www.monteverdelodge.com. 28 units. $95–$125 (£48–£63) double. Rates slightly lower in off season; higher during peak periods. AE, MC, V. **Amenities:** Restaurant; bar; Jacuzzi; tour desk; laundry service. *In room:* Coffeemaker, safe.

INEXPENSIVE

In addition to the hotels listed below, there are quite a few *pensiones* and backpacker specials in Santa Elena and spread out along the road to the reserve. The best of these are **Pensión Flor de Monteverde** (© 645-5758), and **Pensión Santa Elena** (© 645-5051;** www.pensionsantaelena.com). Both charge from $8 to $15 (£4–£7.50) per person. A slightly more expensive and modern alternative is the new **Hotel El Viandante** (© 645-6475; www.hotelelviandante.com), which is located near El Sapo Dorado.

Finally, it is possible to stay in one of the very basic dormitory rooms right at the **Monteverde Biological Cloud Forest Reserve** (© 645-5122; www.cct.or.cr). A bunk bed and three meals per day here run $32 (£16) per person. Admission to the reserve is extra.

Arco Iris Lodge ⭐ *Value*   This is the best hotel right in Santa Elena and an excellent value to boot. The rooms are spread out in a variety of separate buildings, including several individual cabins. All have wood or tile floors and plenty of wood accents. My favorite is the "honeymoon cabin," which has a Jacuzzi tub and its own private balcony with a forest view and good bird-watching, although rooms 16 and 17 are good choices, also with their own small private balconies. There's a two-bedroom, one-bathroom house for families. Budget travelers can inquire about the two rooms equipped with bunk beds ($20–$25/£10–£13 per person). The management here is helpful, speaks five languages, and can arrange a wide variety of tours. Although they don't serve lunch or dinner, breakfast is offered in the new and spacious dining and lounge building, and refreshments are available throughout the day and evening.

Monteverde (A.P. 003-5655), Puntarenas. © **645-5067**. Fax 645-5022. www.arcoirislodge.com. 19 units. $35–$70 (£18–£35) double; $115 (£58) house; $180 (£90) honeymoon cabin. AE, MC, V. **Amenities:** Lounge; tour desk; laundry service. *In room:* No phone.

Treehouse Hotel   Housed in Santa Elena's first, and only, high-rise building, this hotel offers spanking-clean and spacious rooms in the center of town. Taking up the third—and highest—floor of this building, the seven rooms vary in size and the number of beds they feature. The best rooms come with small balconies overlooking the town, although these are also susceptible to street noise, particularly early in the morning and on weekend nights. All rooms feature bright white tile floors, colorful bedspreads, and sparse furnishings. Although the building is new, it is built around a massive old fig tree, hence the hotel's name.

Santa Elena, Puntarenas. ⓒ 645-7475 or 389-2573. 7 units. $45 (£23) double. MC, V. **Amenities:** Restaurant; tour desk; laundry service. *In room:* TV, hair dryer, safe, no phone.

WHERE TO DINE

Most lodges in Monteverde have their own dining rooms, and these are the most convenient places to eat, especially if you don't have a car. Because most visitors want to get an early start, they usually grab a quick breakfast at their hotel. It's also common for people to have their lodge pack them a bag lunch to take with them to the reserve, although there's now a decent little *soda* at the reserve entrance. If you're in the mood to eat out, there are several inexpensive restaurants scattered along the road between Santa Elena and Monteverde.

In addition to the places listed below, you can get good pizzas and pastas at **Tramonti** (ⓒ 645-6120) and **Pizzeria de Johnny** (ⓒ 645-5066), both located out along the road to the reserve. In the heart of tiny downtown Santa Elena, the **Café Cuzuco** (ⓒ 645-7090) has emerged as the best breakfast joint and casual spot for lunch or dinner. Vegetarians will probably want to head to **Flor de Vida** (ⓒ 645-6328) in its new, larger digs on the road out to the reserve. Also, the restaurant at the **Hotel Poco a Poco** (ⓒ 645-6000) gets good marks with a wide range of international dishes, including some Chinese and Japanese fare. Finally, **Moon Shiva** (ⓒ 645-6270), located in Cerro Plano, serves a limited menu of Mediterranean and international fare and often features live music or movies.

A popular choice for lunch is **Stella's Bakery** (ⓒ 645-5560), across the road from the CASEM gift shop. Stella's is open daily from 6am to 9pm. The restaurant is bright and inviting, with lots of varnished woodwork, as well as a few outdoor tables. The selection changes regularly but might include vegetarian quiche, eggplant parmigiana, and different salads. Stella's also features a daily supply of decadent baked goods.

El Sapo Dorado ✪ INTERNATIONAL   Located high on a hill above the main road, El Sapo Dorado offers up great sunsets and food. The menu is more imaginative than at most restaurants in Monteverde, which makes it worth a visit even if you miss the sunset. The regularly changing menu might include grilled corvina in heart-of-palm sauce, shrimp in a sambuca mushroom sauce, or filet mignon in pepper-cream sauce. The emphasis is on fresh ingredients and healthful preparation, and there are always vegetarian and vegan options as well. If you come for lunch or a sunset dinner, definitely grab a table in the large, covered dining room, which has full walls of picture windows for taking in the views, or, weather permitting, on their outdoor terrace.

On the left as you go from Santa Elena toward the reserve. ⓒ 645-5010. Reservations recommended during high season. Main courses $8–$18 (£4–£9). AE, MC, V. Daily 6:30am–9:30pm.

Morpho's Café *(Value* COSTA RICAN/INTERNATIONAL   Probably the best and most popular restaurant in the town of Santa Elena, this simple second-floor affair serves up hearty and economical meals. There are soups, sandwiches, and *casados* (plates of the

---

Tips **Take a Break**

If all of the activities in Monteverde have worn you out, stop in at **Lazy Frog Cafe** ☆ (© 645-5567), a delightful coffeehouse, restaurant and gift shop located about midway between Santa Elena and the Monteverde Cloud Forest Reserve. In downtown Santa Elena, you could try the **Rainforest Cafe** (© 645-5841) or **Chunches** (© 645-5147), a bookstore with a small coffee shop and espresso bar that also doubles as a laundromat.

---

day) for lunch and dinner, and delicious fresh-fruit juices, ice-cream shakes, and home-baked desserts throughout the day. The tables and chairs are made from rough-hewn lumber and whole branches and trunks, and the place brims with a light convivial atmosphere. This place is a very popular hangout for backpackers and budget travelers.

In downtown Santa Elena, across from the supermarket. © 645-5607. Main courses $5–$10 (£2.50–£5). MC, V. Daily 11am–9pm.

Restaurante De Lucía COSTA RICAN/INTERNATIONAL De Lucía has earned a loyal following for its grilled-to-order meats and fresh fish. All meals come with fresh homemade tortillas and a full accompaniment of side orders and vegetables. The sweet *plátanos* prepared on the open grill are delicious. Service is informal and friendly. The heavy wood tables and chairs are spread comfortably around the large dining room. They have a good wine selection.

On the road down to the Butterfly Farm, on your right. © 645-5337. Reservations recommended during high season. Lunch $6–$12 (£3–£6); main courses $7–$15 (£3.50–£7.50). AE, MC, V. Daily noon–9pm.

Sofia ☆☆ *Finds* COSTA RICAN/FUSION This restaurant is the most exciting and eclectic dining option in the Monteverde area. Start everything off with a mango-ginger mojito and then try one of their colorful and abundant salads. Main courses range from seafood *chimichangas* to chicken breast served in a guava reduction. The tenderloin comes with a chipotle butter sauce over a bed of mashed sweet potato. Everything is very well prepared and reasonably priced. There are two good-size dining rooms here, with heavy wood furniture. The best seats are close to the large arched picture windows overlooking the neighboring forest and gardens.

Cerro Plano, just past the turnoff to the Butterfly Farm, on your left. © 645-7017. Reservations recommended during high season. Main courses $9–$16 (£4.50–£8). MC, V. Daily 11:30am–9:30pm.

MONTEVERDE AFTER DARK

The most popular after-dark activities in Monteverde are night hikes in one of the reserves and a natural-history slide show (see "Other Attractions in Monteverde," earlier in this chapter). However, if you want a taste of the local party scene, head to **La Taberna** ☆, which is just outside of downtown Santa Elena before the Serpentarium. This place attracts a mix of locals and tourists, cranks its music loud, and often gets people dancing. Alternatively, **Flor de Vida, Lazy Frog Café, Kaffa Café Art** and **Moon Shiva** sometimes feature live music or open-mic jam sessions.

You'll certainly want to check to see if there's any live music or other performance at the **Monteverde Amphitheater,** a beautiful open-air performance space, located up a steep driveway up from Stella's Bakery, next to Bromelia's. However, be forewarned: The concrete seats here are uncomfortable, so try to bring something soft to sit on.

8

The Central Pacific Coast: Where the Mountains Meet the Sea

The closest beaches to San José, and some of the country's most popular, are found on Costa Rica's central Pacific coast. Options here range from the somewhat seedy Puntarenas and the cut-rate, fun-in-the-sun Jacó, to the jungle-clad hillsides of Dominical, and the ecotourist mecca of Manuel Antonio. The climate here is considerably more humid than that farther north in Guanacaste, but it's not nearly as steamy as along the south Pacific or Caribbean coasts.

Jacó and Manuel Antonio are two of Costa Rica's more developed beaches, while Puntarenas, a former seaport, is just a little over 2 hours from San José. If you're looking to get away from it all without traveling too far or spending too much, **Dominical** and the **beaches south of Dominical** ★ should be your top choice on this coast.

This is also where you'll find some of Costa Rica's most popular and spectacular national parks and biological reserves: **Manuel Antonio National Park** ★★, home of three-toed sloths and white-faced monkeys; **Chirripó National Park** ★★, a misty cloud forest that becomes a barren *páramo* (a region above 3,000m/9,840 ft.) at the peak of its namesake, Mount Chirripó; and **Carara National Park** ★★, one of the last places in Costa Rica where you can see the disappearing dry forest join the damp, humid forests that extend south down the coast. You might even glimpse a scarlet macaw.

1 Puntarenas

115km (71 miles) W of San José; 191km (118 miles) S of Liberia; 75km (47 miles) N of Playa de Jacó

They say you can't put lipstick on a pig, and this may just be an apropos motto for Puntarenas. Despite serious investment and the steady influx of cruise ship passengers, Puntarenas has yet to shed its image as a rough-and-tumble port town. While the seafront **Paseo de los Turistas (Tourist Walk)** has been spruced up some, there's little in this town to interest visitors, and the beach here pales in comparison to almost any other beach destination in the country.

A 16km (10-mile) spit of land jutting into the Gulf of Nicoya, Puntarenas was once Costa Rica's busiest port, but that changed drastically when the government inaugurated nearby Puerto Caldera, a modern container port facility. After losing its shipping business, the city has survived primarily on commercial fishing.

There's a good highway leading all the way from San José, so you can reach Puntarenas (on a good day, with little traffic) in a little more than 2 hours by car, which makes

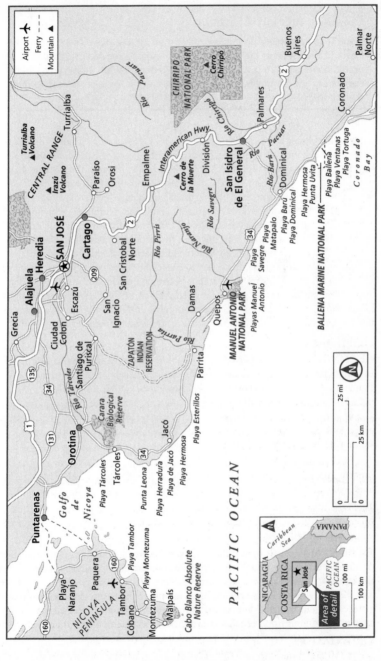

The Central Pacific Coast

Moments A Colorful Festival

If you're in Puntarenas on the Saturday closest to July 16, you can witness the **Fiesta of the Virgin of the Sea.** During this festival a regatta of colorfully decorated boats carries a statue of Puntarenas's patron saint. Boats run all along the waterfront, but the Paseo de los Turistas makes for a good place to catch the action.

---

it one of the closest beaches to San José (at least in elapsed time, if not in distance. A long, straight stretch of sand with gentle surf, the beach is backed for most of its length by the Paseo de los Turistas. Across a wide boulevard from the paseo are hotels, restaurants, bars, discos, and shops. The sunsets and the views across the Gulf of Nicoya are quite beautiful, and there's usually a cooling breeze blowing in off the water. All around town you'll find unusual old buildings, reminders of the important role that Puntarenas once played in Costa Rican history. It was from here that much of the Central Valley's coffee crop was once shipped, and while the coffee barons in the highlands were getting rich, so were the merchants of Puntarenas.

Still, Puntarenas is primarily a place to spend the night during transit. Here you must pick up the ferries to the southern Nicoya Peninsula, and many folks like to arrive the night before and get an early start. It's also a good place to break up the longer trip up to or back from Guanacaste. Puntarenas is also popular as a weekend holiday spot for Ticos from San José and is at its liveliest on weekends.

ESSENTIALS

GETTING THERE & DEPARTING   By Car   Head west out of San José on the Interamerican Highway, passing the airport and Alajuela, and follow the signs to Puntarenas. The drive takes between 2 and 2½ hours.

By Bus   Express buses (© 222-0064) leave San José daily every hour between 6am and 8pm from Calle 16 and Avenida 12. Trip duration is 2½ hours; the fare is $2.80 (£1.40). The main Puntarenas bus station is catty-cornered to the main pier on the Paseo de los Turistas. Buses to **San José** leave daily every hour between 5am and 8pm. The bus to **Santa Elena** leaves daily at 2pm from a stop across the railroad tracks from the main bus station. Buses to **Quepos** (Manuel Antonio) leave daily at 5 and 11am and 2:30 and 4:30pm.

By Ferry   See "Playa Tambor" or "Playa Montezuma" in chapter 6 for information on crossing to and returning from Puntarenas from Paquera or Naranjo on the Nicoya Peninsula.

By Train   One unique option for getting here is to take the train. Although Costa Rica's train system is for the most part nonoperational, the **Tico Train Tour** (© 233-3300; www.americatravelcr.com) runs the 87km (54-mile) stretch between San José and the nearby port city of Caldera. The train runs very infrequently, and only when there's sufficient demand, but it usually runs most weekends, especially in the high season. The 4-hour ride, including a snack and refreshments, costs $12 (£6).

ORIENTATION   Puntarenas is built on a long, narrow sand spit that stretches 16km (10 miles) out into the Gulf of Nicoya and is marked by only five streets at its widest. The ferry docks for the Nicoya Peninsula are near the far end of town, as are the bus station and market. The north side of town faces an estuary, and the south side faces the mouth of the gulf. The Paseo de los Turistas is on the south side of town, beginning at the pier and extending out to the point.

FAST FACTS   Check out the **Millennium Cibercafé** (© **661-4759**), on the Paseo de los Turistas, if you need to send or check e-mail. If you need a taxi, call **Coopetico** (© **663-2020**).

WHAT TO SEE & DO

Take a walk along the **Paseo de los Turistas,** which feels rather like a Florida beach town out of the 1950s. The hotels across the street range in style from converted old wooden homes with bright gingerbread trim to modern concrete monstrosities to tasteful Art Deco relics that need a new coat of paint.

If you venture into the center of the city, be sure to check out the **central plaza around the Catholic church.** The large, stone church itself is interesting because it has portholes for windows, reflecting the city's maritime tradition. It's also one of the few churches in the country with a front entry facing east, as most face west. Here you'll also find the city's cultural center, **La Casa de la Cultura** (© **661-1394**), and the **Museo Histórico Marino** (© **661-5036**), a small museum on the city's maritime history, with exhibits in both English and Spanish. Admission is free.

The newest attraction in town is the **Parque Marino del Pacífico (Pacific Marine Park)** (© **661-5272;** www.parquemarino.org), a modest collection of saltwater aquariums highlighting the sea life of Costa Rica. There are 21 separate tanks, with the largest dedicated to re-creating the undersea environment of Isla del Coco. This place is located 2 blocks east of the main cruise ship terminal and is open Tuesday through Sunday from 9am to 5pm. Admission is $4 (£2) for adults, and $2 (£1) for children under 14.

If you want to go swimming, the ocean waters are now said to be perfectly safe (pollution was a problem for many years), although the beach is still not very attractive. Your best bet is to head back down the spit; just a few kilometers out of town, you'll find **Playa Doña Aña,** a popular beach with picnic tables, restrooms and changing rooms, and a couple of *sodas* (diners). If you head a little farther south, you will come to **Playa Tivives,** which is virtually unvisited by tourists but quite popular with Ticos, many of whom have beach houses up and down this long, brown-sand beach. Surfers can check out the beach break here or head to the mouth of the Barranca River, which boasts an amazingly long left break. Still, surfers and swimmers should be careful; there are crocodiles in both the Barranca and Tivives river mouths, and, despite improvements, I'd be wary of pollution in the waters emptying out of the rivers here.

Puntarenas isn't known as one of Costa Rica's prime sportfishing ports, but a few charter boats are usually available. Check at your hotel or head to the docks and ask around. Rates (for up to six people) are usually between $400 and $600 (£200–£300) for a half-day and between $800 and $1,600 (£400–£800) for a full day.

You can also take a yacht cruise through the tiny, uninhabited islands of the Guayabo, Negritos, and Pájaros Islands Biological Reserve. These cruises include a lunch buffet and a relaxing stop on beautiful and undeveloped **Tortuga Island** ⚓, where you can swim, snorkel, and sunbathe. The water is clear blue, and the sand is bright white. However, this trip has surged in popularity, and many of the tours here have a cattle-car feel. Several San José–based companies offer these excursions, with round-trip transportation from San José, but if you're already in Puntarenas, you might receive a slight discount by boarding here.

Diving Trips to Isla del Coco (Cocos Island)

This little speck of land located some 480km (300 miles) off the Pacific coast was a prime pirate hideout and refueling station. Robert Louis Stevenson most likely modeled *Treasure Island* on Cocos. Sir Francis Drake, Captain Edward Davis, William Dampier, and Mary Welch are just some of the famous corsairs who dropped anchor in the calm harbors of this Pacific pearl. They allegedly left troves of buried loot, although scores of treasure hunters over several centuries have failed to unearth more than a smatter-ing of the purported bounty. The Costa Rican flag was first raised here on September 15, 1869. Throughout its history, Isla del Coco has provided anchorage and fresh water to hundreds of ships and has entertained divers and dignitaries. (Franklin Delano Roosevelt visited it three times.) In 1978 it was declared a national park and protected area.

The clear, warm waters around Cocos are widely regarded as one of the most rewarding **dive destinations** ✪✪✪ on this planet. This is a prime place to see schooling herds of scalloped hammerhead sharks. On a recent shal-low-water checkout dive—normally, a perfunctory and uninspiring affair—I spotted my first hammerhead lurking just 4.5m (15 ft.) below me within 15 seconds of flipping into the water. Soon there were more, and soon they came much, much closer.

Other denizens of the waters around Isla del Coco include white- and sil-ver-tipped reef sharks; marbled, manta, eagle, and mobula rays; moray and spotted eels; octopi; spiny and slipper lobsters; hawksbill turtles; squirrel fish, trigger fish, and angelfish; surgeon fish, trumpet fish, grouper, grunts, snapper, jack, and tangs; and more. Two of the more spectacular underwa-ter residents here include the red-lipped batfish and the frogfish.

Most diving at Cocos is relatively deep (26–35m/85–115 ft.), and there are often strong currents and choppy swells to deal with—not to mention all those sharks. This is not a trip for novice divers.

The perimeter of Isla del Coco is ringed by steep, forested cliffs punctuated by dozens of majestic waterfalls cascading down in stages or steady streams for hundreds of feet. The island itself has a series of trails that climb its steep hills and wind through its rain-forested interior. There are several endemic bird, reptile, and plant species here, including the ubiquitous Cocos finch, which I spotted soon after landing onshore, and the wild Isla del Coco pig.

With just a small ranger station housing a handful of national park guards, Isla del Coco is essentially uninhabited. Visitors these days come on private or charter yachts, fishing boats, or one of the few live-aboard dive vessels that make regular voyages out here. It's a long trip: Most dive ves-sels take 30 to 36 hours to reach Cocos. Sailboats are even slower.

Both **Aggressor Fleet Limited** (© **800/348-2628** in the U.S. and Canada, or 257-0191 in Costa Rica; www.aggressor.com) and **Undersea Hunter** (© **800/ 203-2120** in the U.S., or 228-6613 in Costa Rica; www.underseahunter.com) regularly run dive trips to Isla del Coco from Puntarenas.

Calypso Tours ★ (📞 256-8585; www.calypsotours.com) is the most reputable company that cruises out of Puntarenas. In addition to **Tortuga Island** trips, Calypso Tours takes folks to its own private nature reserve at **Punta Coral** and even on a sunset cruise that includes dinner and some guided stargazing. Any of these cruises cost $99 (£50) per person, whether you join them in San José or Puntarenas. If you check at the docks, you might find some other boats that ply the waters of the Nicoya Gulf. Some of these companies also offer sunset cruises with live music, snacks, and a bar.

WHERE TO STAY
EXPENSIVE
Hotel Las Brisas Out near the end of the Paseo de los Turistas, you'll find this well-kept hotel with large air-conditioned rooms, a small pool out front, and the beach right across the street. All the rooms have tile floors, double or twin beds, and small televisions and tables. Large picture windows keep the rooms sunny and bright during the day. There's complimentary coffee and a secure parking lot. The hotel's small open-air restaurant serves Greek and other international fare.

Paseo de los Turistas (A.P. 83-5400), Puntarenas. 📞 661-4040. Fax 661-2120. www.lasbrisashotelcr.com. 27 units. $115–$195 (£58–£98) double. Rates include breakfast. Rates lower in off season. AE, DC, MC, V. **Amenities:** Restaurant; bar; small pool; small gym; Jacuzzi; laundry service. *In room:* A/C, TV, free Wi-Fi, safe.

MODERATE
Hotel Alamar ★ This hotel is easily the most luxurious option in town, and a better deal than Las Brisas. Located toward the end of the Paseo de los Turistas, more than half of its units are one- or two-bedroom apartments, with fully equipped kitchens. All the rooms are roomy, clean, and modern. Walls are painted in bright primary colors and pastels. The furniture and decor are contemporary. In the center of the hotel complex are a refreshing pool and Jacuzzi. Ample breakfast buffets are served poolside. The best rooms here feature water-facing balconies and Jacuzzi tubs.

Paseo de los Turistas (A.P. 195-5400), Puntarenas. 📞 661-4343. Fax 661-2726. www.alamarcr.com. 34 units. $81–$128 (£41–£64) double. Rates include buffet breakfast. Rates lower in off season. AE, DC, MC, V. **Amenities:** Restaurant; bar; small pool; Jacuzzi; tour desk; laundry service. *In room:* A/C, TV, free Wi-Fi, minifridge, coffeemaker, hair dryer, iron, safe.

Hotel Tioga This 1950s-style hotel has long been the standard-bearer beachfront accommodation in Puntarenas. It's still dependable, but it's showing its age. There's a courtyard with a pool that's been painted a brilliant shade of blue. Rooms vary in size and view. The larger, most expensive rooms are attractive, with huge closets, modern bathrooms, and private balconies with a view of the ocean. The smaller, less expensive rooms have louvered, frosted-glass windows to let in lots of light and air while maintaining some privacy. The hotel runs a small casino next door. The beach is across the street, and plenty of restaurants are nearby.

Paseo de los Turistas (A.P. 96-5400), Puntarenas. 📞 661-0271 or 255-3115. Fax 661-0127. www.hoteltioga.com. 52 units. $64–$99 (£32–£50) double. Rates include breakfast. Rates lower in off season and for extended stays. AE, DC, MC, V. **Amenities:** Restaurant; bar; casino; small pool; tour desk; room service; laundry service. *In room:* A/C, TV, free Wi-Fi, safe.

INEXPENSIVE
Hotel La Punta Most budget lodgings in Puntarenas are real port-town dives. This place isn't for rock-bottom backpackers, but it's the most appealing and comfortable hotel I've found here for those looking for an inexpensive room. The rooms are spread around the two-story building here. Some are a bit small and spartan. You'll pay a little

more for air-conditioning, but you'll likely need it. There's a small pool for cooling off in the day, as well as safe parking and easy access to the ferry terminal and docks.

A.P. 228, Puntarenas (50m/164 ft. south of the ferry terminal). ⓒ 661-0696. 11 units. $20–$25 (£10–£13) double. MC, V. **Amenities:** Restaurant; bar; small pool; laundry service. *In room:* A/C (extra fee), no phone.

WHERE TO DINE

Because you're in a seaport, try some of the local catch. Corvina (sea bass) is the most popular offering, and it's served in various forms and preparations. My favorite dish on a hot afternoon is ceviche, and you'll find that just about every restaurant in town serves this savory marinated seafood concoction.

The most economical option is to pull up a table at one of the many open-air *sodas* along the Paseo de los Turistas, serving everything from sandwiches, drinks, and ice cream to ceviche and fish meals. Sandwiches are priced at around $2 (£1), and a fish filet with rice and beans should cost around $4 (£2). If you want some seafood in a slightly more formal atmosphere, try the **Caribbean Breeze** or **Capitán Moreno,** or the open-air **Restaurant Aloha,** all located on the Paseo de los Turistas.

La Yunta Steakhouse 🔆 *(Finds* STEAKS/SEAFOOD   This airy place bills itself as a steakhouse, but it has an ample menu of seafood dishes as well. Most of the tables are located on a two-tiered covered veranda at the front of the restaurant, overlooking the street and the ocean just beyond. Overall, this restaurant has the nicest ambience in town. The portions are immense, and the meat is tender and well prepared.

Paseo de los Turistas. ⓒ 661-3216. Reservations recommended in high season and on weekends. Main courses $8.60–$21 (£4.30–£11). AE, MC, V. Daily 24 hours.

EN ROUTE TO JACO: AN ISOLATED BOUTIQUE BEAUTY

If you're planning on heading to the beaches of the central Pacific coast via Ciudad Colón and Puriscal, you might consider a stop at **AmeTierra Hotel & Retreat** 🔆 (ⓒ 866/659-3805 in the U.S. and Canada, or 419-0110 in Costa Rica; www.amatierra. com), a lovely little boutique hotel located about 1½ hours out of San José along this route, and approximately 1 hour from Jacó.

2 Playa de Jacó 🔆 & Playa Herradura

117km (73 miles) W of San José; 75km (47 miles) S of Puntarenas

These beach towns are booming. Construction is either already underway or in advanced planning stages for Sonesta, St. Regis, and Ramada resort developments here. On top of these major players, scores of smaller hotels and condominium projects are being built. The big resorts probably won't open until 2009 or so. Today, Playa de Jacó is a long stretch of beach strung with a dense hodgepodge of hotels in all price categories, cheap souvenir shops, seafood restaurants, pizza joints, rowdy bars, and a miniature-golf course. In apparent anticipation of the larger boom, the main strip here is already an overcrowded and congested collection of restaurants, shops, and small strip malls.

The number-one attraction here is the surf, and this is definitely a surfer-dominated beach town. Surfers love the consistent beach break here (and at neighboring Playa Hermosa). However, the beach itself is not particularly appealing. It consists of dark-gray sand with lots of little rocks, and it's often very rough. Still, given its proximity to San José, Jacó is almost always packed with a mix of foreign and Tico vacationers.

Just north of Jacó, is Playa Herradura, a once-forgotten patch of brown sand that is now home to the large Los Sueños Marriott Ocean & Golf Resort. North of Herradura, you'll find a few other small beaches and resorts. The high-end St. Regis is taking over one of these beaches, and the elegant boutique hotel Villa Caletas is located on a high hill above another.

In contrast to the dryness of Guanacaste, these are the first beaches on the Pacific coast to have a tropical feel. The humidity is palpable, and the lushness of the tropical forest is visible on the hillsides surrounding town. In hotel gardens, flowers bloom profusely throughout the year.

ESSENTIALS

GETTING THERE & DEPARTING   By Car   There are several routes to this region. The most popular one is a narrow and winding two-lane road, the "old highway," over and through mountains, known locally as *La Cuesta del Aguacate* (Avocado Hill). This route is equal parts scenic and harrowing—it's not uncommon to encounter buses and trucks passing on blind curves, or to find yourself in a long line of cars stuck behind a slow-moving truck crawling up one of the steep hills. Begin this route by taking the Interamerican Highway west out of San José and exiting just west of Alajuela near the town of Atenas. Follow the numerous signs to any hotel in Jacó or Manuel Antonio. The old highway meets the Costanera Highway a few kilometers west of Orotina. From here it's a straight and flat shot down the coast to Jacó.

Alternatively, you can head out of San José on the highway to Escazú and Santa Ana. Continue to the town of Ciudad Colón; from here, follow signs to Puriscal and then Orotina. This is a similarly scenic and winding route through the mountains, with the same caveats, but it is less traveled and slightly more direct than the more popular route mentioned above. Finally, if you're coming from anywhere in northern Costa Rica, take the Interamerican Highway and get off at the Puntarenas exit and follow signs to Caldera. From here, head south on the Costanera.

By Bus   Transportes Jacó express buses (© **223-1109** or 643-3135) leave San José daily at 7:30 and 10:30am and 1, 3:30, and 6:30pm from the Coca-Cola bus terminal at Calle 16 between avenidas 1 and 3. The trip takes between 2½ and 3 hours; the fare is $2.50 (£1.25). On weekends and holidays, extra buses are often added, so it's worth calling to check.

Moments Don't Feed the Crocs

The Costanera Highway passes over the Tárcoles River just outside the entrance to **Carara National Park,** about 23km (14 miles) south of Orotina. This is a popular spot to pull over and spot some gargantuan crocodiles. Some can reach 3.7 to 4.6m (12–15 ft.) in length. There are usually anywhere from 10 to 20 easily visible, either swimming in the water or sunning on the banks. But be careful. First, you'll be walking on a narrow sidewalk along the side of the bridge with cars and trucks speeding by. And second, there have been numerous car break-ins here, although a new police post has somewhat reduced the risk. Still, don't leave your car or valuables unguarded for long, or better yet, leave someone at the car and take turns watching the crocs.

Gray Line (© 220-2126; www.graylinecostarica.com) has two buses that leave San José for Jacó daily at 8am and 2pm; the fare is $21 (£11). **Interbus** (© 283-5573; www.interbusonline.com) has two buses that leave San José for Jacó daily at 8:15am and 2:30pm; the fare is $19 (£9.50). Both companies will pick you up at most San José–area hotels.

Buses from San José to **Quepos** and Manuel Antonio also pass by Jacó. (They let passengers off on the highway about 1km/½ mile from town.) These buses leave San José daily at 6, 7, and 10am, noon, and 2, 4, 6, and 7:30pm. Trip duration is 2½ to 3 hours; the fare to Jacó is $3 (£1.50) on the indirect bus to Quepos and $5 (£2.50) on the direct bus to Manuel Antonio. However, during the busy months, some of these buses will refuse passengers getting off in Jacó or will accept them only if they pay the full fare to Quepos or Manuel Antonio.

From **Puntarenas,** you can catch Quepos-bound buses at 5 and 11am and 2:30 and 4:30pm. The buses drop you off on the highway outside of town. The trip's duration is 1 hour; the fare is $2 (£1).

The Jacó bus station is at the north end of town, at a small mall across from the Jacó Fiesta Hotel. Buses for San José leave daily at 5, 7:30, and 11am and 3 and 5pm. Buses returning to San José from Quepos pass periodically and pick up passengers on the highway. Because schedules can change, it's best to ask at your hotel about current departure times.

ORIENTATION   Playa de Jacó is a short distance off the southern highway. One main road runs parallel to the beach, with a host of arteries heading toward the water; off these roads you'll find most of the hotels and restaurants.

GETTING AROUND   Almost everything is within walking distance in Jacó, but you can rent a bicycle or scooter from several shops on the main street or call **Jacó Taxi** (© 643-2020). A bike rental should run you around $8 to $12 (£4–£6) per day, and a scooter should cost between $30 and $50 (£15–£25) per day. **Rent @ Me** (© 643-1809) offers free shuttle service to and from your hotel.

For longer excursions, you can rent a car from **Budget** (© 643-2265), **Economy** (© 643-1098), **National** (© 643-1752), **Payless** (© 643-3224), or **Zuma** (© 643-3207). Expect to pay approximately $50 (£25) for a 1-day rental. You might also consider talking to a local taxi driver, who'd probably take you wherever you want to go for about the same price, saving you some hassle and headache.

FAST FACTS   The **Banco Nacional** (© 643-3072) and the **Banco de Costa Rica** (© 643-3695) have branches in town on the main road and are open Monday through Friday from 8:30am to 3pm. Also on the main road, you can find the **Farmacia Jacó** (© 643-3205) and the well-stocked **Farmacia Fischel** (© 643-2683), which is in the El Galeone shopping center. A gas station is on the main highway, between Playa Herradura and Jacó, and a 24-hour gas station, **El Arroyo,** is on the highway on the southern edge of Jacó. The **health center** (© 643-3667) and **post office** (© 643-2175) are at the Municipal Center at the south end of town.

A **public phone office,** where you can make international calls, is located in the ICE building on the main road. This office is open Monday through Saturday from 8am to noon and 1 to 5pm. There are half a dozen or more **Internet cafes** in town, as well as several inexpensive full-service laundromats; a **Western Union office** in a small strip mall across from La Hacienda restaurant; a large **Más × Menos** supermarket on the main drag in the center of town; and an even larger and more modern

Automercado supermarket in the new strip mall on the main highway near the entrance to Playa Herradura.

FUN ON & OFF THE BEACH

Unfortunately, this beach has a reputation for dangerous riptides (as does most of Costa Rica's Pacific coast). Even strong swimmers have been known to drown in the power rips. At times, storms far offshore cause huge waves to pound on the beach, making it impossible to go into the water much beyond your waist. If this is the case, you'll have to be content with the hotel pool. In general, the far southern end of the beach is the calmest and safest place to swim.

OTHER BEACHES AROUND JACO

As an alternative to Playa de Jacó, you may want to visit other nearby beaches. These beaches are easily reached by car, moped, or bicycle—if you've got a lot of energy. All are signposted, so you'll have no trouble finding them. **Playa Hermosa,** 10km (6¼ miles) southeast of Jacó, where sea turtles lay eggs from July to December, is also well known for its great surfing waves. This beach is dark, made of nearly black, yet fine, volcanic sand. **Playa Herradura,** about 6.5km (4 miles) northwest of Jacó, is a hard-packed brown-sand-and-rock beach ringed by lush hillsides. This is home to the Los Sueños Marriott Ocean & Golf Resort. However, the Marriott occupies only one end of the beach here; despite its presence, Playa Herradura still feels a lot more isolated and deserted than Jacó. **Playa Esterillos,** 22km (14 miles) southeast of Jacó, is long and wide and almost always nearly deserted. Playa Esterillos is so long, in fact, that there are three separate entrances and sections, Esterillos Oeste, Centro, and Este—West, Center, and East, in order as you head away from Jacó. Just beyond Playa Esterillos is **Playa Bejuco,** another long, wide, nearly deserted stretch of sand.

Finally, **Punta Leona,** just a few kilometers north of Playa Herradura, is a cross between a hotel, a resort, and a private country club, and it has some of the nicer beaches in the area. Although they effectively have restricted access to their beaches for years, this is technically illegal in Costa Rica, and you have the right to enjoy both playas **Manta** and **Blanca,** two very nice white-sand beaches inside the Punta Leona complex. The public access road to these beaches is located south of the main Punta Leona entrance and is not very well marked.

CARARA NATIONAL PARK 🐾🐾

A little more than 15km (9⅓ miles) north of Jacó is **Carara National Park,** a world-renowned nesting ground for **scarlet macaws.** It has a few kilometers of trails open to visitors. There's a loop trail that takes about an hour, and another trail that's open only to tour groups. The macaws migrate daily, spending their days in the park and their nights among the coastal mangroves. It's best to view them in the early morning when they arrive, or around sunset when they head back to the coast for the evening, but a good guide can usually find them for you during the day. Whether or not you see them, you should hear their loud squawks. Among the other wildlife that you might see here are caimans, coatimundis, armadillos, pacas, peccaries, and, of course, hundreds of species of birds.

Be sure to bring along insect repellent or, better yet, wear light cotton long sleeves and pants. (I was once foolish enough to attempt a quick hike while returning from Manuel Antonio, still in beach clothes and flip-flops.) The reserve is open daily from 8am to 4pm. Admission is $8 (£4) per person at the gate.

Several companies offer tours to Carara National Park for around $30 to $40 (£15–£20). Check at your hotel or contact **Gray Line Tours** (*C* 643-3231) or **Superior Sightseeing** (*C* 393-6626) to set one up. If you're looking for a more personalized tour, contact Lisa Robertson, a knowledgeable and amiable guide who runs **Happy Trails** (*C* 643-1894), or you can hike the trails of Carara independently, but my advice is to take a guided tour; you'll learn a lot more about your surroundings.

The muddy banks of the Tárcoles River are home to a healthy population of American crocodiles. Just north of the entrance to the park is a bridge that's a prime spot for viewing both the crocs and the macaw migrations. In Jacó, several operators run daily crocodile tours on the Tárcoles River. These are simple tours in open skiffs or Boston whalers. Most of these companies bring along plenty of freshly killed chicken to attract the reptiles and pump up the adrenaline. Don't expect a highly trained naturalist guide or any semblance of respect for the natural world. Do expect to pay between around $20 to $40 (£10–£20) per person for the trip.

Finally, just beyond Carara National Park on the Costanera Sur in the direction of Jacó is a turnoff for some spectacular waterfalls (including a 180m/590-ft. fall) around the town of **Bijagual.** There are several ways to visit these falls and people run tours from Jacó or from entrances both at the top and bottom of the falls. At the top a local family runs the **Complejo Ecológico La Catarata** (*C* 661-8263), which features a basic restaurant and a campground, and also offers horseback tours down to the falls for around $35 (£18). Alternatively, you can hike in from an entrance lower down. The hike takes about 45 minutes each way, and entrance costs $10 (£5) per person. While you're in this area, you can also visit **Pura Vida Botanical Gardens** (*C* 200-5040). Admission for the gardens is $15 (£7.50). To get here, turn off at the signs for Hotel Villa Lapas. From there, it's a rough 8km (5 miles) up to the top of the falls.

ACTIVITIES & TOURS

ATV TOURS   Several operations take folks out on ATV tours through the surrounding countryside. Tours range in length from 2 to 6 hours and cost between $65 and $125 (£33–£63) per person. Contact **Paraíso Adventures** (*C* 643-2920) or **Jaguar Riders** (*C* 393-6626).

BIKING   You can rent a bike for around $8 to $12 (£4–£6) per day or $1.50 (£0.75) per hour. Bikes are available from a slew of shops along the main road. Shop around, and make sure you get a bike that is in good condition and that is comfortable to ride.

CANOPY TOURS   The easiest way to get up into the canopy here is on the **Rain Forest Aerial Tram Pacific** (*C* 257-5961; www.rainforestram.com). A sister project to the original Rain Forest Aerial Tram, this attraction features modified ski-lift type gondolas that take you through and above the transitional forests bordering Carara National Park. The $55 (£28) entrance fee includes the guided 40-minute tram ride, and a guided 45-minute hike on a network of trails. You can also hike the company's trails for as long as you like. These folks also offer guided tours, including transportation from both San José and any hotel in the area. The Aerial Tram is located a few kilometers inland from an exit just north of the first entrance into Jacó.

There are quite a few zip-line and harness-style canopy tours in this area. **Chiclets Tree Tour** (*C* 643-1879) offers up a canopy adventure ($60/£30 per person) in nearby Playa Hermosa. This is an adventurous tour, with 13 platforms set in transitional forest, with some sweeping views of the Pacific. **Villa Lapas** (p. 269) has two different tours through the treetops outside of Jacó. The better and cheaper option is a guided hike on its network of trails and five suspended bridges ($20/£10 per person). The operator also has a relatively low-adrenaline zip-line canopy tour ($35/£18 per person), with seven platforms connected by six cables.

Finally, Jacó is also a good jumping-off point for a trip to **Turu BaRi Tropical Park** (© **250-0705;** www.turubari.com), near Orotina. See chapter 5 for details.

GOLF The excellent **La Iguana,** an 18-hole golf course at the **Los Sueños Marriott Ocean & Golf Resort** (© **630-9000;** www.golflaiguana.com), is open to nonguests. Greens fees are $155 (£78) for a full round. The price drops to $130 (£65) if you tee off after noon. Club and shoe rentals are available. Marriott guests pay slightly less to play here.

HORSEBACK RIDING Horseback-riding tours give you a chance to get away from all the development in Jacó and see a bit of nature. Contact **Happy Trails** (© **643-1894**) or **Hermanos Salazar** (© **643-3203**) to make a reservation. Over in Playa Herradura, you can try the **Jacó Equestrian Center** (© **643-1569**). Tours lasting 3 to 4 hours cost anywhere from $35 to $70 (£18–£35).

KAYAKING **Kayak Jacó** (© **643-1233;** www.kayakjaco.com) runs a couple of different trips. Tours range from gentle paddles and floats on the Tulin River to combination ocean-kayaking/snorkeling trips on calm Herradura Bay, to full-on kayak surfing at one of the local beach breaks. You can also do some moderate white-water kayaking in easy-to-use inflatable kayaks or try your hand in the ocean on one of the eight-person outrigger canoes. Most options run around 4 hours and include transportation to and from the put-in, as well as fresh fruit and soft drinks during the trip. The tours cost between $50 and $100 (£25–£50) per person, depending on the particular trip and group size.

ORGANIZED TOURS FARTHER AFIELD If you'll be spending your entire Costa Rican visit in Jacó but would like to see some other parts of the country, you can arrange tours through the local offices of **Gray Line Tours** (© **643-3231**), which operates out of the Best Western Jacó Beach Hotel (p. 266). Gray Line offers day tours to Arenal, Poás, and Irazú volcanoes; white-water rafting trips; cruises to Tortuga Island; and trips to Braulio Carrillo National Park and other places. Rates range from $35 to $120 (£18–£60) for day trips. Overnight trips are also available. Thanks to improvements to the road, you can now reach **Manuel Antonio** in about 1 hour from Jacó. In addition to the above-mentioned companies, many local operators offer a variety of tour options in Manuel Antonio, including trips to the national park, the Rainmaker Nature Refuge, and the Damas Island estuary. See the "Manuel Antonio National Park" section (later in this chapter) for more details on the types of tours and activities available there.

SPA The **Serenity Spa** (© **643-1624**) offers massages, as well as mud packs, face and body treatments, and manicures and pedicures. The spa's Jacó branch is located on the first floor, among a tiny little cul-de-sac of shops next to Zuma Rent-A-Car. These folks also have operations at Villa Caletas.

SPORTFISHING, SCUBA DIVING & SEABORNE FUN Since the Los Sueños Marriott resort (p. 268) and its adjacent 250-slip marina opened, most local maritime activity has shifted over here. If you're interested in doing some sportfishing, scuba diving, or any other waterborne activity, I recommend that you check with your hotel or at the marina. Two dependable operators that have set up here are **Spanish Fly**

Sportfishing (© **866/888-6426** in the U.S., or 637-8824 in Costa Rica; www.spanish flysportfishing.com) and **Costa Rica Fishing Charters** (© **800/634-0012** in the U.S. and Canada, or 282-7215; www.4costaricafishing.com). A half-day fishing trip for four people costs around $250 to $600 (£125–£300), and a full day costs between $600 and $1,800 (£300–£900).

SURFING   The same waves that often make Playa de Jacó dangerous for swimmers make it one of the most popular beaches in the country with surfers. Nearby **Playa Hermosa, Playa Tulin,** and **Playa Escondida** are also excellent surfing beaches. Those who want to challenge the waves can rent surfboards for around $3 (£1.50) an hour or $10 to $15 (£5–£7.50) per day, and boogie boards for $2 (£1) an hour, from any one of the numerous surf shops along the main road. If you want to learn how to surf, check in with Johnny (© **393-6626**) at **Superior Sightseeing,** or ask for him at Club del Mar.

SHOPPING

If you try to do any shopping in Jacó, you'll be overrun with shops selling T-shirts, cut-rate souvenirs, and handmade jewelry and trinkets. Most of the offerings are of pretty poor quality. Two notable exceptions are **Guacamole** ✿ (© **643-1120**), a small clothing store that produces its own line of batik beachwear, and **La Galería Heliconia** ✿✿ (© **643-3613**), which carries a superb selection of artworks and pottery.

WHERE TO STAY IN PLAYA DE JACO

Because Punta Leona, Playa Herradura, Playa Hermosa de Jacó (not to be confused with Playa Hermosa in Guanacaste), Playa Esterillos, and Playa Bejuco are close, many people choose accommodations in these beach towns as well. Selected listings for these towns follow this section.

EXPENSIVE

Best Western Jacó Beach Resort   This remains Jacó's largest and most popular resort hotel. Situated right on the beach, this five-story hotel offers all the amenities and services you could want at a pretty good price. Still, this is a cut-rate resort, and there's little in the way of charm, romance, or true ambience here. The hotel is often packed throughout the high season, and a party atmosphere pervades the place. The open-air lobby is surrounded by lush gardens, and covered walkways connect the hotel's buildings. Rooms are adequate and have tile floors and walls of glass facing balconies; however, not all of the rooms have good views (some face another building), and many of them show the wear and tear of age and heavy occupancy. Ask for a room on a higher floor and with an ocean view. Bathrooms tend to be a bit battered, but they do have bathtubs. A large percentage of guests opt for an all-inclusive package.

Playa de Jacó (A.P. 962-1000, San José), Puntarenas. © **800/528-1234** in the U.S. and Canada, or 643-1000 in Costa Rica. Fax 643-3833. www.bestwestern.com. 125 units. $132–$157 (£66–£79) double. Rates include breakfast buffet. AE, DC, MC, V. **Amenities:** 2 restaurants; 2 bars; 2 circular pools; tennis court; well-equipped gym; watersports equipment rental; complimentary bike use; tour desk; limited room service (7am–9pm); laundry service. *In room:* A/C, TV, free Wi-Fi, coffeemaker, safe.

Club del Mar Condominiums & Resort ✿✿ (Kids)   This has long been my top choice in Playa de Jacó, and it still is. It has a fabulous location, friendly management, and attractively designed rooms. Club del Mar is at the far southern end of the beach, where the rocky hills meet the sand, and where the swimming is probably the safest in town. Most of the rooms are actually one- or two-bedroom condo units, with full

kitchens. All are spacious and feature private balconies or porches. There are also eight rooms on the second floor of the large main building, as well as two huge and luxurious penthouse suites up on the third floor. All units come with an ocean view, although some are more open and expansive than others. The grounds are lush and chock-full of flowering heliconia and ginger. There's a midsize multipurpose pool and a good open-air restaurant, as well as some modest spa facilities.

Playa de Jacó (A.P. 107-4023), Puntarenas. © 866-978-5669 in the U.S. and Canada, or 643-3194 in Costa Rica. Fax 643-3550. www.clubdelmarcostarica.com. 32 units. $146 (£73) double; $212–$356 (£106–£178) condo; $364 (£182) penthouse. Rates lower in off season; higher during peak weeks. AE, DC, MC, V. **Amenities:** Restaurant; bar; midsize free-form pool; small spa; tour desk; concierge; free Wi-Fi in main building and around pool; room service (8am–9pm); in-room massage; babysitting. *In room:* A/C, TV, fridge, safe.

MODERATE

In addition to the places listed below, the oceanfront **Apartotel Girasol** ✦ (© **800/ 923-2779** or 643-1591; www.girasol.com), with 16 fully equipped one-bedroom apartments, is a good option, especially for longer stays. **Hotel Poseidon** (© **888/ 643-1242** in the U.S. and Canada, or 643-1642; www.hotel-poseidon.com) is a pretty boutique hotel in the heart of downtown, while **Hotel Catalina** (© **643-1237;** www.hotelcatalinacr.com) is another good beachfront choice.

Arenal Pacífico ✦   This is a good midrange option, and it's right on the beach to boot. The rooms are nothing special—and almost none offer an ocean view—but they are clean and cool, and most are pretty spacious. The grounds are pretty lush for Jacó—you even have to cross a shady bridge over a little stream to get from the parking lot and reception to the rooms and restaurant. I like the newer second floor rooms, which have private balconies. The superior rooms are larger, and come with coffeemakers and minifridges. There are two outdoor pools—one with a little waterfall filling it, another with a round children's pool. The open-air restaurant serves standard Tico and international fare.

Playa de Jacó (A.P. 962-1000, San José), Puntarenas. © 643-3419. Fax 643-3770. www.arenalpacifico.com. 22 units. $98 (£49) double; $121 (£61) superior double. Rates include continental breakfast. Rates lower in off season; higher during peak weeks. AE, MC, V. **Amenities:** Restaurant; bar; pool; bike rental; surf and boogie board rental; tour desk; laundry service. *In room:* A/C, TV, free Wi-Fi, safe.

Hotel Mar de Luz ✦ ⓥalue   This is one of Playa de Jacó's best deals and a comfortable alternative to the typical string of cut-rate *cabinas* you'll find crowding this popular beach town. All the rooms are immaculate and comfortable. Some feature stone walls, small sitting areas, and one or two double beds placed on a raised sleeping nook. My only complaint is that the windows are too small and mostly sealed, forcing you to use air-conditioning. In the gardens just off the pools are a couple of grills for guest use. A comfortable common sitting area has a selection of magazines and books. Dutch owners Victor and Carmen Keulen seem driven to offer as much comfort, quality, and service as they can for the price. The hotel lies 50m (164 ft.) east of the Hotel Tangeri, right in the center of Jacó. In mid-2007, these folks opened a sister hotel in nearby Playa Bejuco (see review of Hotel Playa Bejuco, below).

Playa de Jacó (A.P. 143), Puntarenas. ©/fax 643-3259. www.mardeluz.com. 29 units. $80 (£40) double. Rates include breakfast. Rates lower in off season; higher during peak weeks. V. **Amenities:** 2 small-to-midsize adult pools and children's pool; Jacuzzi; game room; tour desk; babysitting; laundry service; nonsmoking rooms. *In room:* A/C, TV, free Wi-Fi, kitchenette (in some units), minifridge, coffeemaker, safe.

Pochote Grande ⓥalue   Named for a huge old pochote tree on the grounds, this well-kept and attractive hotel is located right on the beach toward the far north end of Jacó. The grounds are shady and lush, and there's a refreshing little pool. All of the rooms are quite large, although sparsely furnished, and have white-tile floors, one queen-size and one single bed, a small fridge, and a balcony or patio. I prefer the second-floor rooms, which are blessed with high ceilings. The modest restaurant and snack bar serve a mixture of Tico, German, and American meals. (The owners are German by way of Africa.)

Playa de Jacó (A.P. 42), Puntarenas. ✆ 643-3236. Fax 220-4979. www.hotelpochotegrande.net. 24 units. $80 (£40) double; $95 (£48) triple. Add $15 for a room with A/C. Rates lower in off season; higher during peak weeks. AE, MC, V. **Amenities:** Restaurant; bar; pool. *In room:* TV, free Wi-Fi, fridge, safe, no phone.

INEXPENSIVE

There are quite a few budget hotels around town. Most cater to itinerant surfers, backpackers, and Ticos. If you're looking to stay on the cheap, your best bet is to simply walk the strip and see who's got the best room at the best price. If you walk slightly inland from the center of town, the **Blue Palms** (✆ 643-0099; www.blue-palms.net) offers immaculate rooms and a small swimming pool at budget prices.

There are also several campgrounds in or near Playa de Jacó. **Madrigal** (✆ 643-3230), at the south end of town at the foot of some jungley cliffs, is my favorite. You can also try **El Hicaco** (✆ 643-3004), which is close to the beach but also pretty close to the Disco La Central, so don't expect to get much sleep if you stay here. Campsites run between $3 and $6 (£1.50–£3) per night.

Hotel Zabamar *(Kids)*   The Zabamar is set back about 1 block from the beach in a shady compound. The best rooms are in a two-story building closest to the road. These are quite roomy and feature cool tile floors and air-conditioning. The older rooms are also large and have red-tile floors, small refrigerators, ceiling fans, hammocks on their front porches, and *pilas* (laundry sinks) in little gravel-and-palm gardens behind them. Travelers on budgets will appreciate the size of the older, less-expensive rooms. There's a small swimming pool with two separate children's sections that's quite popular with Tico families staying here.

Playa de Jacó, Puntarenas. ✆ 643-3174. Fax 643-2645. www.hotelzabamar.com. 20 units. $45–$60 (£23–£30) double. Rates include breakfast. Rates lower in off season; discounts for long-term stays. No credit cards. **Amenities:** Restaurant; small pool. *In room:* No phone.

WHERE TO STAY IN PLAYA HERRADURA & NORTH OF PLAYA DE JACO

VERY EXPENSIVE

In addition to the hotel listed below, there are scores of condominium units for rent at the Los Sueños resort. All come with kitchens, access to swimming pools, and rights to use the golf course here. These are excellent options for families, who want to do some cooking, and for longer stays. If you want to rent a condo here, contact **Costa Rica Luxury Rentals** (✆ 866/525-2188 in the U.S. and Canada, or 637-7105 in Costa Rica; www.crluxury.com). Rates run between $350 and $450 (£175–£225) nightly for one- and two-bedroom units, to over $1,000 (£500) for some of the more luxurious three-bedroom units.

Los Sueños Marriott Ocean & Golf Resort *(★★ Kids)*   This is the closest large-scale resort to San José and is one of the nicest in the country. The hotel is a massive, four-story horseshoe facing the beach. The entire thing is done in a Spanish colonial style, with stucco walls, heavy wooden doors, and red-clay roof tiles. The rooms are all spacious and tastefully done. They come with one king-size or two queen-size beds, a large armoire, a desk, and a sitting chair with an ottoman. The bathrooms are large and have plenty of counter space. Every room has a balcony, but all are not created equal. Most have only small Juliet-style balconies. Those facing the ocean are clearly superior, and a few of the ocean-facing rooms even have large, comfortable balconies with chaise longues and tables and chairs. (You'll have to specifically request these.)

The expansive lobby area opens out onto a large terrace and the Puesta del Sol bar, with its panoramic views of the beach and the bluffs bordering Playa Herradura. The pool is a vast, intricate maze built to imitate the canals of Venice (in miniature), with private nooks and grottos; kids love exploring it. Parents will appreciate the excellent children's program. The beach here is calm and good for swimming, although it's one of the least attractive beaches on this coast, with a mix of rocks and hard-packed, dark-brown sand. The Ted Robinson–designed 18-hole golf course winds through some of the neighboring forest and is an excellent, if not particularly challenging, resort course. The Stellaris Casino is the largest and most comfortable I've found at a beach resort in Costa Rica.

Playa Herradura (A.P. 502-4005), San Antonio de Belén. ℰ 888/236-2427 in the U.S., 298-0844, or 630-9000 in Costa Rica. Fax 630-9090. www.marriott.com. 201 units. $219–$319 (£110–£160) double; $449–$650 (£225–£325) suite; $1,250–$1,500 (£625–£750) presidential suite. Rates lower in off season. AE, MC, V. **Amenities:** 4 restaurants; coffee shop; 2 bars; lounge; large pool; golf course and pro shop; 9-hole miniature golf course; 4 outdoor lit tennis courts; large health club and spa; children's program; game room; concierge; tour desk; car-rental desk; salon; 24-hr. room service; in-room massage; babysitting; laundry service; nonsmoking rooms; Wi-Fi (for a fee) in most public areas. *In room:* A/C, TV, minibar, dataport, coffeemaker, hair dryer, iron, safe.

Villa Lapas   Located on a lush piece of property along the Río Tarcolitos and bordering Carara National Park, Villa Lapas is a good choice if you're looking to combine a bit of ecoadventure and bird-watching with some beach time. The rooms here are spacious, with two double beds, cool red-clay tile floors, air-conditioning, ceiling fans, and a shady veranda with wooden benches for taking in the scenery. The hotel's best feature is its massive, open-air restaurant and deck, which overlooks the river and where buffet-style meals are served. Villa Lapas has 217 hectares (536 acres) of land with excellent trails, a series of suspended bridges crossing the river, and its own canopy tour. The hotel also features a small re-creation of a typical Costa Rican rural village of times gone by. This riverside attraction also has three massive gift shops, an atmospheric old-style Costa Rican bar, and a small chapel. You'll see the signs for Villa Lapas on the left, just after passing Carara National Park. The hotel is about 15 to 20 minutes from the beaches of Jacó, Hermosa, and Herradura.

Tárcoles (A.P. 419-4005, San Antonio de Belén). ℰ 637-0232. Fax 637-0227. www.villalapas.com. 55 units. $116 (£58) per person. Rates include 3 meals daily and taxes. Rates lower in off season; higher during peak weeks. AE, MC, V. **Amenities:** 2 restaurants; 2 bars; small pool; 2 Jacuzzis; laundry service. *In room:* A/C, coffeemaker, safe.

EXPENSIVE

Villa Caletas ★★★ *Finds*   It's hard to find a luxury hotel in Costa Rica with a more spectacular setting than this. Perched 350m (1,148 ft.) above the sea, Villa Caletas enjoys commanding views of the Pacific over forested hillsides. The regular rooms are all elegantly appointed and spacious, but you'll definitely want to stay in a villa or suite here. Each individual villa is situated on a patch of hillside facing the sea or forests. Inside you'll find a main bedroom with a queen-size bed and a comfortable sitting room with couches that convert into two single beds. The villas feature white-tile floors, modern bathrooms, and a private terrace for soaking up the views. The larger junior suites come with their own outdoor Jacuzzis. The suites and master suites are larger still—and even come with their own private swimming pools. There are only two master suites, and one is a vigorous hike downhill from the main hotel building and restaurants. The same is true of some of the villas and juniors.

Opened in 2007, **Zephyr Palace** is a new 7-suite addition, located a little bit below the main hotel and villas. The rooms here are immense and thematically designed—you can choose from an African suite, an Arabian suite, an Oriental suite, and more. The Imperial suite has its own gym and sauna. All have beautiful ocean views, home theater systems, Jacuzzis, and private balconies.

Although most guests are happy to lounge around and swim in the free-form "infinity" pools that seem to blend into the sea below and beyond, Villa Caletas offers hourly shuttle service to its own little private beach, as well as a host of tour options. A Greek-style amphitheater hosts periodic sunset concerts of jazz or classical music.

A.P. 12358-1000, San José. © **637-0505.** Fax 637-0303. www.hotelvillacaletas.com. 42 units. $165–$180 (£83–£90) double; $210 (£105) villa; $320–$425 (£160–£213) suite; $450–$1,500 (£225–£750) Zephyr Palace suites. Rates slightly lower in off season. Extra person $35. AE, MC, V. **Amenities:** 2 restaurants; bar; 2 midsize pools w/spectacular view; spa; concierge; tour desk; beach shuttle; in-room massage; laundry service. *In room:* A/C, TV, minibar, coffeemaker, hair dryer, safe.

WHERE TO DINE

Playa de Jacó has a wide range of restaurants. Many cater to surfers and budget travelers. In addition to the places listed below, if you're looking for simply prepared fresh seafood, **El Barco de Mariscos** (© 643-2831) and **El Recreo** (© 643-3012) are both good bets that serve standard Tico beach fare—fresh seafood, sandwiches, chicken, and steak. For a filling American-style breakfast, try the **Sunrise Breakfast Place** (© 643-3361). For a coffee break, cappuccino, and fresh pastries and breads, head to either **Pachi's Pan** (© 643-1153) or **Café del M@r** (© 643-1250). **Restaurante Wahoo** (© 643-1876) offers fresh seafood and Mexican fare. The small restaurant at the **Hotel Poseidon** ★ (© 643-1642) serves a regularly changing small menu of high-end fusion cuisine. And sushi lovers should head to **Tsunami Sushi** (© 643-3678), inside the El Galeone strip mall.

Over in Playa Herradura are several restaurants, including the Peruvian chain **Inka Grill,** in the new strip mall on the highway near the entrance to the beach. Also, at the Los Sueños marina, you'll find several options, including the **Hook Up** (© 637-8284), an excellent American-style grill and restaurant with a second-floor perch and good views of the boats bobbing at their berths.

Steve & Lisa's (© 637-0594), located several miles outside of town, around Tárcoles, is a good place for lunch. The food here is standard Tico fare, but the oceanside setting and views set it apart from other simple *sodas*. *Note:* There's another restaurant on this road calling itself "Steve & Lisa's," but it's located inland with no view. Definitely head to the one on the water's edge.

EXPENSIVE

El Hicaco *(Overrated* SEAFOOD/COSTA RICAN   This beachside restaurant has gotten too popular for its own good. There's now a cattle-car feel to the entire operation and the food is overpriced and average. But the setting is simply wonderful: right on the edge of the beach, with the majority of the tables outdoors. At night you sit under the stars, surrounded by tall palm trees, with some interesting lighting overhead. If you do come here, stick with the freshly caught grilled seafood or lobster, although there are plenty of meat and chicken selections on the menu as well.

On the beach in downtown Jacó. © **643-3226.** Reservations recommended during high season. Main courses $14–$40 (£7–£20). AE, MC, V. Daily 11am–11pm.

Pacific Bistro ✿✿ ASIAN/FUSION   Chef Kent Green changes the menu almost nightly, but fresh seafood and top-quality cuts of meat are always the building blocks for his creative Asian-influenced creations. You'll usually find some fresh tuna, mahimahi, and jumbo shrimp on the menu, but on any given night the sauces will range from a homemade teriyaki to a spicy Thai sauce to coconut curry. Portions are large, but it's worth saving some room for dessert. Set just off the sidewalk on the main drag in town, the restaurant only has six or so tables, so reservations are often essential.

On the main road in Jacó. ✆ 643-3771. Reservations recommended. Main courses $8–$20 (£4–£10). AE, MC, V. Wed–Mon 6–10pm.

MODERATE

Los Amigos SEAFOOD/INTERNATIONAL   Set on a large corner of a busy intersection in the heart of Jacó, this restaurant serves fresh seafood and adventurous international fare at very reasonable prices. Sturdy wooden tables are spread around the small dining room and open-air patio here. I prefer the patio seating which looks out over flowering heliconia to the bustle of Jacó's main drag. Fresh tuna can be had Cajun style or with a spicy mango salsa. There are also several traditional Thai dishes on the menu, as well as some wraps and hearty salads. At night, they play electronic music and are developing a lively bar scene.

On the main road in Jacó. ✆ 643-2961. Main courses $8–$33 (£4–£17). AE, MC, V. Daily noon–3pm and 6–11pm.

INEXPENSIVE

Caliche's Wishbone ✿ (Finds) SEAFOOD/MEXICAN   This casual spot is popular with surfers and offers Tex-Mex standards and homemade pizzas. However, you can also get excellent fresh fish and perfectly prepared seafood dishes, as well as a variety of sandwiches served in homemade pita bread. The portions are huge. It almost always has fresh tuna lightly seared and served with a soy-wasabi dressing. The nicest tables are street-side on a covered veranda. Inside are more tables, as well as a bar with television sets showing surf videos.

On the main road in Jacó. ✆ 643-3406. Reservations not accepted. Main courses $4.20–$15 (£2.10–£7.50). V. Thurs–Tues 12–3pm and 6–10pm.

El Pelicano (Finds) SEAFOOD/COSTA RICAN   This simple beachfront restaurant is a lot like El Hicaco was before success went to its head. Heavy wooden tables and chairs are spread around a large, open-air dining room facing the beach and boats bobbing at anchor off of Playa Herradura. The menu features a range of ceviches, salads, and main courses, with a heavy—and logical—emphasis on fresh seafood. The *corvina al ajillo* (sea bass in garlic sauce) is excellent here, as is the *arroz con mariscos* (rice with seafood). To get here, drive the Playa Herradura road until you hit the beach, and then turn left on the narrow sandy access road.

On the beach in Playa Herradura. ✆ 637-8910. Reservations recommended during high season. Main courses $5.50–$22 (£2.75–£11). MC, V. Daily 11am–10pm.

Rioasis PIZZA/MEXICAN   Rioasis serves hearty burritos, simple pasta dishes, and a wide array of freshly baked wood-oven pizzas. My favorite item is the Greek pizza, with olives, feta cheese, and anchovies, but the barbecue chicken pizza is also delicious. There is both indoor and terrace seating, as well as a bar area, complete with a pool table, dartboards, and a couple of TVs for sports events and surf videos.

On the main road in Jacó. ✆ 643-3354. Reservations not accepted. Main courses $4–$22 (£2–£11). V. Wed–Mon noon–midnight.

Taco Bar ⚓ *(Finds* TACOS   This casual little open-air joint serves up excellent food at great prices. The best option here is to order a one-, two- or three-taco plate with the accompanying salad bar. Choose from fresh fish, chicken, shrimp, calamari, or any combination of them. My favorites are the coconut shrimp and spicy fish fillings. The well-stocked salad bar features a wide range of stand-alone salads, as well as numerous toppings to finish off your tacos. You won't leave here hungry. There are a few wooden tables outdoors under large umbrellas, but most of the seating is around a large "U"-shaped bar. The seats are either high stools or wood-planks hung from ropes, like swings. They also serve breakfast, as well as pizzas and a small selection of full entrees, and offer free Wi-Fi for diners.

A half-block inland from Pop's, central Jacó. ⓒ 643-0222. Reservations not accepted. Main courses $5–$10 (£2.50–£5). MC, V. Daily 11am–10pm.

PLAYA DE JACO AFTER DARK

Playa de Jacó is the central Pacific's party town, with tons of bars and several discos. **Disco La Central** is packed every night of the high season and every weekend during the off season. La Central is right on the beach near the south end of town. There's a huge open-air hall that features the requisite 1970s flashing lights and suspended mirrored ball, as well as a garden bar in a thatch-roofed building that's a slightly quieter place to have a drink. The disco charges a nominal cover charge. Other popular bars in town are the **Beatle Bar, Club Olé, Jungle Bar** and **Monkey Bar.** All of the aforementioned bars are located along the main strip through town. *Note:* There's a good amount of prostitution in Jacó. It's not uncommon to find working women at any of the above-mentioned places, as well as cruising other bars around town.

For a more casual atmosphere, head to either **Los Amigos** or **Tabacón** ⚓. Los Amigos has nightly movies projected on a large outdoor wall, while Tabacón has popular pool and foosball tables, and often has live music.

Sports freaks can catch the latest games at **Clarita's Beach Bar & Grill, Hotel Copacabana,** or **Hotel Poseidon.** The last serves up good, reasonably priced burritos, burgers, and other assorted bar food.

If you're into gaming, head to the **Stellaris Casino** ⚓ at the Los Sueños Marriott resort (p. 268) or the **Jazz Casino** (ⓒ 643-2316), located at the Hotel Amapola. The latter is a modest casino situated toward the southern end of the main road through Jacó (Av. Pastor Díaz), about a block beyond where it takes a sharp turn inland toward the Costanera Sur.

EN ROUTE SOUTH: PLAYAS HERMOSA, ESTERILLOS AND BEJUCO

Playa Hermosa is the first beach you'll hit as you head south from Playa de Jacó. This is primarily a surfers' beach, but it is still a lovely spot to spend some beach time. In fact, even though the surf conditions here can be rather rough and unprotected, and the beach is made of dark volcanic sand, I find Playa Hermosa and the beaches south of it much more attractive than Jacó. After Playa Hermosa you will hit Esterillos, which is actually divided up by rivers into three sections, Esterillos Oeste, Esterillos Centro, Esterillos Este, each with a separate well marked entrance. Farther south (which because of how the coast turns here, is actually more easterly), lies Playa Bejuco.

At night most folks in Playa Hermosa find their way to **The Backyard,** a raucous surfer bar with a pool table, darts, and hearty food.

Note: While beautiful, isolated and relatively undeveloped, the beaches of Hermosa, Esterillos, and Bejuco can be quite rough at times and dangerous for swimming. Caution is highly advised here.

WHERE TO STAY

In addition to the hotels listed below, there are a host of simple hotels and *cabinas* catering to surfers in Playa Hermosa. Prices, conditions, and upkeep can vary greatly. If you've got the time, your best bet is to visit a few until you find the best deal on the cleanest room. **Costa Nera** (© 643-7044) and **Cabinas Las Arenas** (© 643-7013; www.cabinaslasarenas.com) are two good options.

If you're looking for something more remote and undeveloped, head to Playa Esterillos Este for the **Pelican Hotel** (© 778-8105; www.pelicanbeachfronthotel.com), or head slightly farther south to the nearly deserted Playa Bejuco and the small **Delfin Beach Resort** (© 778-8054; www.delfinbeachfront.com).

VERY EXPENSIVE

Xandari by the Pacific 🎖🎖 *(Finds)*   This place has definitely upped the ante along this stretch of coast. A sister to the popular, upscale boutique Xandari Resort & Spa (p. 112) in Alajuela, this beachfront boutique resort is very similar in terms of design, style, and aesthetics. All the accommodations here are large, private villas, with high, curved ceilings and loads of artistic touches. I especially like the open, mosaic tile showers that let out on to lush gardens. The Maxima villas here are the top option and come with their own private plunge pool. Most of the villas are beachfront, but those that aren't have large gardens and a wonderful sense of seclusion and romance. *Note:* In order to encourage the enjoyment of the villas, beach, and surrounding nature, the rooms have no televisions. The open-air seafront restaurant serves excellent international fare, with an equal emphasis on healthy fresh ingredients and creative cooking combinations. By early 2008, they expect to have a full spa built and operational, again, similar to their wonderful spa in Alajuela.

Playa Esterillos Centro (mailing address: A.P. 10-6300), Parrita. © 866/363-3212 in the U.S. and Canada, or 778-7070 in Costa Rica. Fax 778-7878. www.xandari.com. 20 units. $235–$370 (£118–£185) double. Rates include continental breakfast. Rates lower in off season; higher during peak periods. AE, MC, V. **Amenities:** Restaurant; bar; two lap pools; Jacuzzi; tour desk; room service (7am–9pm); laundry service; all rooms nonsmoking. *In room:* A/C, free Wi-Fi, kitchenette, minibar, coffeemaker, hair dryer, safe.

EXPENSIVE

The Backyard   This perennially popular bar and restaurant also has some of the most modern and comfortable rooms in Playa Hermosa, although they're overpriced for what you get, and you'll definitely do better at the hotels listed below. The two-story building features spacious rooms with dark red terra-cotta tile floors and simple furnishings. The second-floor rooms are definitely nicer than those on the ground floor. The oceanfront end units are classified as suites. They are a bit bigger and do have excellent ocean views. The small pool features a little sculpted-rock waterfall and is quite refreshing on the hot days here. Despite the more elaborate facilities and amenities, this place is still quintessentially a surfer joint, and the main reason to stay here is that this hotel sits directly in front of the principal peaks on Playa Hermosa.

Playa Hermosa de Jacó (A.P. 132), Jacó, Puntarenas. ©/fax 643-7011. www.backyardhotel.com. 8 units. $135–$185 (£68–£93) double. Rates lower in off season. AE, MC, V. **Amenities:** Restaurant; bar; small pool; laundry service. *In room:* A/C, TV, safe.

Hotel Playa Bejuco ⟨★⟩   Located just off the beach at Playa Bejuco, this is a younger sister to the popular Mar de Luz hotel in Jacó (p. 267). The two-story hotel is an "L" shape around a central swimming pool and gardens and facing the ocean. The construction features various walls and details made from heavy, smooth river stones. Rooms are spacious, cool and modern, with red tile floors, simple wooden furnishings, and spacious bathrooms. The second-floor rooms are quite large, and feature high ceilings with sleeping lofts, making them good options for families with children. The Belgian chef here serves excellent continental cuisine.

Playa Bejuco, Puntarenas. ℂ/fax **778-8181**. www.mardeluz.com. 20 units. $150 (£75) double. Rates include breakfast and taxes. Lower rates in off season. AE, MC, V. **Amenities:** Restaurant; bar; outdoor pool; tour desk; laundry service. *In room:* A/C, TV, minifridge, coffeemaker, safe.

MODERATE

Hotel Fuego del Sol ⟨★⟩   This place is located right on the beach and offers good value for someone looking for a clean, cool, and comfortable room, as well as easy access to the waves. Most of the rooms are housed in a long, two-story block set perpendicular to the beach. Each comes with a queen-size and twin bed and a private balcony overlooking the free-form pool. Those closest to the water will also give you a glimpse of the sea. The suites come with king-size beds, a separate sitting room, and fully stocked kitchenette. Everything is well maintained, and the restaurant here boasts a good view of the beach action.

Playa Hermosa, Jacó, Puntarenas. ℂ **800/850-4532** in the U.S. and Canada, 289-6060 reservations office in San José, or 643-3737 at the hotel. Fax 288-0123. www.fuegodelsolhotel.com. 22 units. $89 (£45) double; $146–$165 (£73–£83) suite. Rates include breakfast. Lower rates in off season. AE, MC, V. **Amenities:** Restaurant; bar; surf- and boogie-board rental; tour desk; laundry service. *In room:* A/C, TV (in some), safe.

Terraza del Pacífico ⟨★⟩   Located just over the hill at the start of Playa Hermosa, this hotel has a wonderful setting on a mostly undeveloped section of beach. In the middle of the complex is a circular pool with a swim-up bar and plenty of chaise longues for sunbathing and siestas. Red-tile roofs and faux-stucco walls give the buildings a Mediterranean look, and hardwood balcony railings add a touch of the tropics. Each guest room has two double beds, a private bathroom, and either a patio or balcony. A couple of suites are considerably larger and even include a kitchenette. The hotel's restaurant and open-air bar are located within a few feet of the high-tide mark. The hotel offers a range of tours, including a nearby canopy tour. Surfing is still the major draw here, and the Terraza hosts several major tournaments each year and has even installed klieg lights on the beach for night surfing.

Playa Hermosa de Jacó (A.P. 168-4023), Jacó, Puntarenas. ℂ **643-3222** or 440-6862. Fax 430-7571. www.terraza delpacifico.com. 62 units. $112 (£56) double; $189–$221 suite (£95–£111). Rates include full breakfast. Rates lower in off season; higher during peak weeks. AE, MC, V. **Amenities:** Restaurant; bar; pool w/swim-up bar; laundry service. *In room:* A/C, TV, free Wi-Fi, minibar, safe.

3 Manuel Antonio National Park ⟨★⟩⟨★⟩

140km (87 miles) SW of San José; 69km (43 miles) S of Playa de Jacó

Manuel Antonio was Costa Rica's first major ecotourist destination and it remains one of its most popular. The views from the hills overlooking Manuel Antonio are spectacular, the beaches (particularly those inside the national park) are idyllic, and its jungles are crawling with howler, white-faced, and squirrel monkeys, among other forms of exotic wildlife. The downside is that you'll have to pay more to see it, and you'll

Manuel Antonio

To San José
To Airport, Hospital and Dominical

Estuario Boca Vieja

Area of inset at right

Quepos

To Airport

Market & Bus Terminal

Soccer Field

Quepos

To Manuel Antonio

PACIFIC OCEAN

Fincas Naturales

Quebrada Camaronera

0   1/2 mi
0   0.5 km

N

Punta Quepos

Playa Espadilla

Park Entrance

PARQUE NACIONAL MANUEL ANTONIO

Park Entrance

Playa Espadilla Sur

Punta Catedral

Playa Manuel Antonio

Playa Puerto Escondido

Punta Surrucho

Bank
Church
Post Office
Trails

NICARAGUA

Caribbean Sea

COSTA RICA

San José

Quepos

Area of detail

PACIFIC OCEAN

PANAMA

N

0   100 mi
0   100 km

ACCOMMODATIONS ■
Arenas del Mar **18**
Best Western Kamuk **4**
Cabinas Vela-Bar **29**
El Mono Azul Hotel **10**
Gaia Hotel & Reserve **13**
Hotel and Cabinas
   Playa Espadilla **30**
Hotel Costa Verde **25**
Hotel La Mariposa **19**
Hotel Malinche **7**
Hotel Parador **17**
Hotel Plinio **11**
Hotel Sí Como No **23**
Hotel Verde Mar **28**
Karahé **26**
Makanda by the Sea **16**
Villas Nicolas **22**
The Widemouth Frog **8**

DINING ◆
Agua Azul **21**
Café Milagro **2, 20**
El Avión **24**
El Gran Escape **3**
El Patio Bistro Latino **2**

La Hacienda **14**
Marlin Restaurant **31**
Mar Luna **15**
Plinio Restaurant **11**
Ronny's Place **9**
Sunspot Bar & Grill **16**
Tropical Sushi **3**

NIGHTLIFE/SHOPPING ●
Arco Iris **1**
El Banco Bar **6**
Guacamole **12**
Kamuk Casino **4**
La Buena Nota **27**
L'Aventura Boutique **5**

have to share it with more fellow travelers than you would at other rainforest destinations around the country. In fact, development here is threatening to destroy what makes this place so special. What was once a smattering of small hotels tucked into the forested hillside has become a long string of lodgings along the 7km (4⅓ miles) of road between Quepos and the national park entrance. Hotel roofs now regularly break the tree line, and there seems to be no control over zoning and unchecked ongoing construction. A jumble of snack shacks, souvenir stands, and makeshift parking lots line the beach road just outside the park, making the entrance road look more like a shanty than a national park.

Still, this remains a beautiful destination, with a wide range of attractions and activities. Gazing down on the blue Pacific from high on the hillsides of Manuel Antonio, it's almost impossible to hold back a gasp of delight. Offshore, rocky islands dot the vast expanse of blue, and in the foreground, the rich, deep green of the rainforest sweeps down to the water. Even cheap disposable cameras regularly produce postcard-perfect snapshots. It's this superb view that keeps people transfixed on decks, patios, and balconies throughout the area.

One of the most popular national parks in the country, Manuel Antonio is also one of the smallest, covering fewer than 680 hectares (1,680 acres). Its several nearly perfect small beaches are connected by trails that meander through the rainforest. The mountains surrounding the beaches quickly rise as you head inland from the water; however, the park was created to preserve not its beautiful beaches but its forests, home to endangered squirrel monkeys, three-toed sloths, purple-and-orange crabs, and hundreds of other species of birds, mammals, and plants. Once this entire stretch of coast was a rainforest teeming with wildlife, but now only this small rocky outcrop of forest remains.

Those views that are so bewitching also have their own set of drawbacks. If you want a great view, you aren't going to be staying on the beach—in fact, you probably won't be able to walk to the beach. This means that you'll be driving back and forth, taking taxis, or riding the public bus. Also keep in mind that it's hot and humid here, and it rains a lot. However, the rain is what keeps Manuel Antonio lush and green, and this wouldn't be the tropics if things were otherwise.

If you're traveling on a rock-bottom budget or are mainly interested in sportfishing, you might end up staying in the nearby town of **Quepos,** which was once a quiet banana port; the land to the north was used by Chiquita to grow its bananas. Disease wiped out most of the banana plantations, and now the land is planted primarily with African oil-palm trees. To reach Quepos by road, you pass through miles of these oil-palm plantations. Quepos is coming of age, and now features a wide variety of restaurants, souvenir and crafts shops, and lively bars.

ESSENTIALS

GETTING THERE & DEPARTING   By Plane   Sansa (✆ **290-4100;** www.flysansa.com) has 6 daily flights to Quepos beginning at 6am, with the final flight departing at 1:30pm from San José's Juan Santamaría International Airport. The flight's duration is 30 minutes; the fare is $49 (£25) each way.

Nature Air (✆ **800/235-9272** in the U.S. and Canada, or 299-6000; www.natureair.com) flies to Quepos daily at 9am and 1 and 4:25pm from Tobías Bolaños International Airport in Pavas. The flight duration is 30 minutes; the fare is $54 (£27) each way.

Both Sansa and Nature Air provide airport-transfer service coordinated with their arriving flights. The service costs around $4 (£2) per person each way, depending on

> ## *Tips* Travel Tips
>
> Despite the above caveats, Manuel Antonio is still a fabulous destination with a wealth of activities and attractions for all types and all ages. If you plan carefully, you can avoid many of the problems that detract from its appeal. If you steer clear of the peak months (Dec–Mar), you'll miss most of the crowds. If you must come during the peak months, try to avoid weekends, when the beach is packed with families and young Ticos from San José. If you visit the park early in the morning, you can leave when the crowds begin to show up at midday. In the afternoon you can lounge by your pool or on your patio.

where exactly your hotel is located. Speak to your airline's agent when you arrive to confirm your return flight and coordinate a pickup at your hotel for that day if necessary. Taxis occasionally meet incoming flights as well. Expect to be charged between $8 and $12 (£4–£6) per car for up to four people, depending on the distance to your hotel and your bargaining abilities.

When you're ready to depart, **Sansa** (*©* 777-**0683** in Quepos) flights begin departing at 6:40am, with the final flight leaving at 2:10pm.

Nature Air (*©* 777-2548 in Quepos) flights leave for San José daily at 7:40 and 10:45am and 1:35 and 5pm.

By Car   From San José, the most popular route is to take the narrow and winding old highway, which turns off the Interamerican Highway just west of Alajuela near the town of Atenas and joins the Costanera Highway near Orotina. Just follow the many signs to hotels in either Jacó or Manuel Antonio. When you reach Jacó, it's a straight shot and another hour to Manuel Antonio.

Alternatively, you could try the route beginning in Ciudad Colón, a western suburb of San José, and then head out to Puriscal and join the Costanera Highway either near Parrita or Orotina. The route that heads to Parrita is the shortest route, but some sections are not paved and others are in rough shape. Nevertheless, locals often use it, especially during the dry season. Four-wheel-drive vehicles are recommended, but normal two-wheel-drive sedans can usually make it. The route to Orotina is paved the entire way. It is slightly longer than the more popular route mentioned above and not as well marked, but since it passes over a narrow suspension bridge, there are never any trucks or commercial traffic.

If you're coming from Guanacaste or any point north, take the Interamerican Highway to the Puntarenas turnoff and head south on the Costanera Highway, the coastal road to Jacó.

By Bus   **Express buses** (*©* 223-5567) to Manuel Antonio leave San José daily at 6am, noon, and 6 and 7:30pm from the Coca-Cola bus terminal at Calle 16 between avenidas 1 and 3. Trip duration is 3½ hours; the fare is $4.80 (£2.40). These buses go all the way to the park entrance and will drop you off at any of the hotels along the way.

Regular buses (*©* 223-5567) to Quepos leave San José daily at 7 and 10am and 2 and 4pm. Trip duration is 4½ hours; the fare is $4 (£2). These buses stop in Quepos. From here, if you're staying at one of the hotels on the road to Manuel Antonio, you must take a local bus or taxi to your hotel.

Gray Line (*©* 220-2126; www.graylinecostarica.com) has two daily buses that leave San José for Quepos and Manuel Antonio at 8am and 2pm; the fare is $29

(£15). The return bus leaves at 8am and 1pm for San José. **Interbus** (© **283-5573;** www.interbusonline.com) has two daily buses that leave San José for Quepos and Manuel Antonio at 8:15am and 2:30pm; the fare is $29 (£15). Return buses leave at 8:30am and 1:45pm. Both companies will pick you up at most San José– and Manuel Antonio–area hotels and also offer connections to various other popular destinations around Costa Rica.

Buses leave **Puntarenas** for Quepos daily at 5 and 11am and 2:30 and 4:30pm. The ride takes 2½ hours; the fare is $3 (£1.50).

Many of the buses for Quepos stop to unload and pick up passengers in **Playa de Jacó.** If you're in Jacó heading toward Manuel Antonio, you can try your luck at one of the covered bus stops out on the Interamerican Highway (see "Playa de Jacó & Playa Herradura," earlier in this chapter).

From Quepos, buses leave for Manuel Antonio daily, roughly every half-hour, from 6am to 7pm, with one late bus at 10pm. The fare is 30¢ (15p). The ride takes about 15 minutes. When you're ready to depart, the Quepos bus station (© 777-0263) is next to the market, which is 3 blocks east of the water and 2 blocks north of the road to Manuel Antonio. Express buses to San José leave daily at 6 and 9:30am, noon, and 3 and 5pm. Local buses to San José (duration is 4 hr.) leave at 5 and 8am and 2 and 4pm.

In the busy winter months, tickets sell out well in advance, especially on weekends; if you can, purchase your ticket several days in advance. However, you must buy your Quepos-bound tickets in San José and your San José return tickets in Quepos. If you're staying in Manuel Antonio, you can buy your return ticket for a direct bus in advance in Quepos and then wait along the road to be picked up. There is no particular bus stop; just make sure you are out to flag down the bus and give it time to stop—you don't want to be standing in a blind spot when the bus comes flying around a tight corner.

Buses for **Puntarenas** leave daily at 4:30, 7:30, and 10:30am and 3pm. Any bus headed for San José or Puntarenas will let you off in Playa de Jacó.

ORIENTATION   Quepos is a little port town at the mouth of the Boca Vieja Estuary. After crossing the bridge into town, take the lower road (to the left of the high road). In 4 blocks, turn left; you'll be on the road to Manuel Antonio. This road winds through town a bit before starting over the hill to all the hotels and the national park.

GETTING AROUND   A taxi between Quepos and Manuel Antonio (or any hotel along the road toward the park) costs between $3 and $6 (£1.50–£3), depending upon the distance. At night or if the taxi must leave the main road (for hotels such as La Mariposa, Parador, Makanda, and Arenas del Mar), the charge is a little higher. If you need to call a taxi, dial © 777-3080 or 777-0425. Taxis are supposed to use meters, although this isn't always the case. If your taxi doesn't have a meter, or the driver won't use it, try to negotiate in advance. Ask your hotel desk what a specific ride should cost, and use that as your guide.

The bus between Quepos and Manuel Antonio takes 15 minutes each way and runs roughly every half-hour from 6am to 7pm daily, with one late bus leaving Quepos at 10pm and returning from Manuel Antonio at 10:30pm. The buses, which leave from the main bus terminal in Quepos, near the market, go all the way to the national park entrance before turning around and returning. You can flag down these buses from any point on the side of the road. The fare is 30¢ (15p).

You can also rent a car from **Adobe** (© 777-4242), **Alamo** (© 777-3344), **Economy** (© 777-5260), **Hertz** (© 777-3365), or **Payless Rent-a-Car** (© 777-0115) for around $50 (£25) a day. All have offices in downtown Quepos, but with advance notice, someone will meet you at the airport with your car for no extra charge.

If you rent a car, never leave anything of value in it unless you intend to stay within sight of the car at all times. Car break-ins are common here. There are now a couple of parking lots just outside the park entrance that cost around $3 (£1.50) for the entire day. You should definitely keep your car in one of these while exploring the park or soaking up sun on the beach. And although these lots do offer a modicum of protection and safety, you should still not leave anything of value exposed in the car. The trunk is probably safe, though.

FAST FACTS   The telephone number of the **Quepos Hospital** is ☏ 777-0922; for the **local police,** call ☏ 777-1511. The **post office** (☏ 777-1471) is located in downtown Quepos. There are several pharmacies in Quepos, as well as a pharmacy at the hospital, and another close to the park entrance. There are also a half-dozen or so laundromats and laundry services in town. For film, batteries, and any urgent developing, try **Todo Foto Quepos** (☏ 777-1442).

There are a handful of **Internet cafes** around Quepos and along the road to Manuel Antonio, and many hotels have them as well.

EXPLORING THE NATIONAL PARK

Manuel Antonio is a small park with three major trails. Most visitors come primarily to lie on a beach and check out the white-faced monkeys, which sometimes seem as common as tourists. A guide is not essential here, but unless you're experienced in rainforest hiking, you'll see and learn a lot more with one. A 2- or 3-hour guided hike should cost between $25 and $40 (£13–£20) per person. Almost any of the hotels in town can help you set up a tour of the park. If you decide to explore the park on your own, a basic map is usually available at the park entrance for $1 (50p).

ENTRY POINT, FEES & REGULATIONS   The park (☏ 777-5185) is closed on Monday but is open Tuesday through Sunday from 8am to 4pm year-round. You'll find the principal park entrance at **Playa Espadilla,** the beach at the end of the road from Quepos. To reach the park station, you must cross a small, sometimes polluted stream that's little more than ankle-deep at low tide but that can be knee- or even waist-deep at high tide. It's even reputed to be home to a crocodile or two. For years there has been talk of building a bridge over this stream; in the meantime you'll have to either wade it or pay a boatman a small voluntary tip for the very quick crossing. Just over the stream, you'll find the small ranger station where you can pick up the small park map I mentioned above. You can also sometimes enter the park at an inland entrance located at the end of the side road that leads off perpendicular to **Playa Espadilla** just beyond Marlin Restaurant. Whichever entrance you choose, you will have to pay a fee of $8 (£4) per person to enter. The Parks Service allows only 600 visitors to enter each day, which could mean that you won't get in if you arrive in midafternoon during the high season. Camping is not allowed.

THE BEACHES   **Playa Espadilla Sur** (as opposed to Playa Espadilla, which is just outside the park; see "Hitting the Water," below) is the first beach within the actual park boundaries. It's usually the least-crowded and one of the best places to find a quiet shade tree to plant yourself under. However, if there's any surf, this is also the roughest beach in the park. If you want to explore further, you can walk along this soft-sand beach or follow a trail through the forest parallel to the beach. **Playa Manuel Antonio,** which is the most popular beach inside the park, is a short, deep

---

Tips Helping Out

If you want to help efforts in protecting the endangered squirrel monkey (*mono titi*), make a donation to **ASCOMOTI** (© **777-2306;** www.ascomoti.org), which is working in conjunction with a host of local tourism businesses to protect this pint-size primate.

---

crescent of white sand backed by lush rainforest. The water here is sometimes clear enough to offer good snorkeling along the rocks at either end, and it's usually fairly calm. At low tide Playa Manuel Antonio shows a very interesting relic: a circular stone turtle trap left by its pre-Columbian residents. From Playa Manuel Antonio, there's another slightly longer trail to **Puerto Escondido,** where a blowhole sends up plumes of spray at high tide.

THE HIKING TRAILS   From either Playa Espadilla Sur or Playa Manuel Antonio, you can take a circular hike around a high promontory bluff. The farthest point on this hike, which takes about 25 minutes round-trip, is **Punta Catedral** , where the view is spectacular. The trail is a little steep in places, but anybody in average shape can do it. I have done it in sturdy sandals, but you might want to wear good hiking shoes. This is a good place to spot monkeys, although you're more likely to see a white-faced monkey than a rare squirrel monkey. Another good place to see monkeys is the **trail inland** from Playa Manuel Antonio. This is a linear trail and mostly uphill, but it's not too taxing. It's great to spend hours exploring the steamy jungle and then take a refreshing dip in the ocean.

Finally, there's a trail that leads first to Puerto Escondido (see above) and **Punta Surrucho,** where there are some sea caves. Be careful when hiking beyond Puerto Escondido: What seems like easy beach hiking at low tide becomes treacherous to impassable at high tide. Don't get trapped.

HITTING THE WATER

BEACHES OUTSIDE THE PARK   **Playa Espadilla,** the gray-sand beach just outside the park boundary, is often perfect for board surfing and bodysurfing. At times it's a bit rough for casual swimming, but with no entrance fee, it's the most popular beach with locals and visiting Ticos. Some shops by the water rent boogie boards and beach chairs and umbrellas. A full-day rental of a beach umbrella and two chaise longues costs around $10 (£5). (These are not available inside the park.) This beach is actually a great spot to learn how to surf. There are several open-air shops renting surfboards and boogie boards along the road fronting this beach. Rates run between $5 to $10 (£2.50–£5) per hour, and around $30 to $40 (£15–£20) per day. If you want a lesson, check in with the **Manuel Antonio Surf School** (© **777-4842;** www.masurfschool.com), which has a roadside kiosk on the road to Manuel Antonio.

BOATING, KAYAKING, RAFTING & SPORTFISHING TOURS   Adventure **Manuel Antonio** (© **800/401-5944** in the U.S. and Canada, or 777-1084 in Costa Rica; www.adventuremanuelantonio.com) and **Iguana Tours** (© **777-2052;** www. iguanatours.com) are the most established and dependable tour operators in the area; both offer river rafting, sea kayaking, mangrove tours, and guided hikes.

The two above companies, as well as **Rios Tropicales** (© **777-4092;** www. aventurash2o.com), offer full-day rafting trips for around $85 to $110 (£43–£55).

Large multiperson rafts are used during the rainy season, and single-person "duckies" are broken out when the water levels drop. All of the above companies also offer half-day rafting adventures and sea-kayaking trips for around $65 (£33). Depending on rainfall and demand, they will run either the Naranjo or Savegre rivers. I very much prefer the Savegre River for its stunning scenery.

Another of my favorite tours in the area is a mangrove tour of the Damas Island estuary. These trips generally include lunch, a stop on Damas Island, and roughly 3 to 4 hours of cruising the waterways. You'll see loads of wildlife. The cost is usually around $60 to $70 (£30–£35).

Among the other boating options around Quepos/Manuel Antonio are excursions in search of dolphins and sunset cruises. **Iguana Tours** (see above) and **Planet Dolphin** (©/fax 777-1647; www.planetdolphin.com) offer these tours for $40 to $70 (£20–£35) per person. Most tours include a snorkel break and, if lucky, dolphin sightings. **Jungle Coast Jets** (© 777-1706; www.junglecoastjets.com) offers 2-hour jet-ski tours for $99 (£50) per person. This tour plies the same waters and includes some snorkeling and the possibility of a dolphin encounter.

Quepos is one of Costa Rica's billfish centers, and sailfish, marlin, and tuna are all common in these waters. In the past year or so, fresh and brackish water fishing in the mangroves and estuaries has also become popular. If you're into sportfishing, try hooking up with **Blue Fin Sportfishing** (© 777-1676; www.bluefinsportfishing.com), **Blue Water** (© 800/807-1585 in the U.S. and Canada or 777-4841; www.sportfishing incostarica.com), **High Tec Sportfishing** (© 777-3465; www.hightecsportfishing. com), or **Luna Tours Sportfishing** (© 777-0725; www.lunatours.net). A full day of fishing should cost between $400 and $1,800 (£200–£900), depending on the size of the boat, distance traveled, tackle provided, and amenities. There's a lot of competition here, so shop around.

SCUBA DIVING & SNORKELING   Manuel Antonio Scuba Divers (© 777-3483; www.manuelantoniodivers.com) and **Oceans Unlimited** ★ (© 777-3171; www.oceansunlimitedcr.com) offer both scuba diving and snorkel outings, as well as certification and resort courses. Because of river run-off and often less than stellar visibility close to Quepos, the best trips involve some travel time. However, **Isla del Caño** (p. 258) is only about a 90-minute ride (each way). This is one of the best dive sites in Costa Rica, and I highly recommend it.

OTHER ACTIVITIES IN THE AREA

ATV   If you want to try riding a four-wheel ATV (all-terrain vehicle), check in with the folks at **Fourtrax Adventures** (© 777-1825; www.fourtraxadventure.com). Their principal tour is a 3-hour adventure through African palm plantations, rural towns, and secondary forest to a jungle waterfall, where you stop for a dip. You cross several rivers and a long suspension bridge. Either breakfast or lunch is served, depending on the timing. Cost is $95 (£48) per ATV. A second rider on the same ATV costs $20 (£10).

BIKING   If you want to do some mountain biking while you're here, check in with **Estrella Tour** (©/fax 777-1286) in downtown Quepos. Well-maintained bikes rent for around $24 (£12) per day. You can also do a number of different guided tours according to skill level for between $45 and $90 (£23–£45) per day, as well as multi-day expeditions.

BUTTERFLY GARDEN   Fincas Naturales/The Nature Farm Reserve ★ (© 777-1043; www.butterflygardens.co.cr) is just across from (and run by) Hotel Sí Como No

> **Tips Yo Quiero Hablar Español**
>
> Escuela D'Amore (©/fax **777-1143**; www.escueladamore.com) runs language-immersion programs out of a former hotel with a fabulous view on the road to Manuel Antonio. A 2-week conversational Spanish course, including a home stay and two meals daily, costs $995 (£498). Or you can try the **Costa Rica Spanish Institute (COSI)** (© **800/771-5184** in the U.S. and Canada; 234-1001 or 777-0021 in Costa Rica; www.cosi.co.cr), which charges $305 (£153) per week, with room and board extra.

(p. 285). A lovely bi-level **butterfly garden** ☆ is the centerpiece attraction here, but there is also a private reserve and a small network of well-groomed trails through the forest. A 1-hour guided tour of the butterfly garden costs $15 (£7.50) per person, or $35 (£18) when combined with a 1-hour guided hike through the forest. This is also a good place to do a night tour ($30/£15).

CANOPY & CANYONING ADVENTURES   There are several canopy tours in the area. The most adventurous is offered by **Canopy Safari** ☆ (© 777-0100; www.canopysafari.com), which features 21 tree-top platforms connected by a series of cables and suspension bridges. Adventurers use a harness-and-pulley system to "zip" between platforms, using a leather-gloved hand as their only brake. The **Titi Canopy Tour** (© 777-3130; www.titicanopytours.com) is a similar but mellower setup. A canopy tour should run you between $55 and $65 (£28–£33) per person.

HORSEBACK RIDING   If your tropical fantasy is to ride a horse down a beach between jungle and ocean, contact **Stable Equus** (© 777-0001), which charges $35 (£18) for a 2-hour ride in Manuel Antonio. This stable treats its animals more humanely than other stables in the immediate Manuel Antonio area and is also concerned with keeping horse droppings off the beaches. Back in the hills, **Brisas del Nara** (© 779-1235; www.horsebacktour.com) offers full- and half-day horseback excursions that pass through both primary and secondary forest and feature a swimming stop at a jungle waterfall. A full-day tour with these folks, including breakfast and lunch, costs $55 (£28) per person; and $45 (£23) for a similar half-day tour, with less time on the horse.

SOOTHE YOUR BODY & SOUL   There are quite a few massage therapists around Manuel Antonio and a couple of day spas. The best of these are **Raindrop Spa** (© 777-2880; www.raindropspa.com), **Sea Glass Spa** ☆ (© 777-2607; www.seaglassspa.com), and **Serenity Spa** ☆ at the Hotel Sí Como No (p. 285). A wide range of treatments, wraps, and facials are available at all of the above.

   Sivana Yoga (© 356-7492; www.sivanayoga.com) has open classes ($12/£6) Monday through Friday at 8am above the Anaconda restaurant, across from the Hotel Costa Verde. Private classes are also offered.

ULTRALIGHT TOUR   If you want a really good view of Manuel Antonio's spectacular scenery, you might sign up with the folks at **Costa Rica Flying Boat** (© 777-9208; www.flyingboatcostarica.com), who offer ultralight flights out of the Quepos airport. A 20-minute flight runs around $70 (£35).

SHOPPING

If you're looking for souvenirs, you'll find plenty of beach towels, beachwear, and handmade jewelry in a variety of small shops in Quepos and at impromptu stalls down near the national park. For a good selection, try **La Buena Nota** (© 777-1002), which is on the road to Manuel Antonio, right near the Karahé hotel (p. 288). The shop is jam-packed with all sorts of beachwear, souvenirs, used books, and U.S. magazines and newspapers. It also has a few basic rooms located above the store; if you'd like to find out about renting a house, ask here.

If you're looking for higher-end gifts, check out **L'Aventura Boutique** (© 777-1019), on Avenida Central in Quepos. This small shop has a nice collection of woodwork by Barry Biesanz, banana-fabric works by Lil Mena, and pottery by Cecilia "Pefi" Figueres. The Hotel Sí Como No's **Regálame** (www.regalameart.com) gift shop is also pretty well stocked. Finally, one of my favorite shops from Jacó has opened a branch in Manuel Antonio. Look for handmade batik and tie-dye clothing at the new **Guacamole** (© 777-2071) in the small Plaza Yara shopping center.

One of my favorite hangouts has always been **Café Milagro** ★★ (© 777-1707; www.cafemilagro.com), a homey coffeehouse and gift shop with two locations in the area. The folks here roast their own beans and also have a mail-order service to keep you in Costa Rican coffee year-round. The menu includes a daily selection of freshly baked sweets, simple sandwiches and breakfast items, and a wide range of coffee drinks. You'll find local art for sale on the walls and a good selection of Cuban cigars and international newspapers, too. The original storefront, just over the bridge on your left as you enter Quepos, is now expanded and there's another branch on the main road to Manuel Antonio right across from the turnoff for Hotel La Mariposa.

WHERE TO STAY

Take care when choosing your accommodations in Quepos/Manuel Antonio. There are very few true beachfront hotels in Manuel Antonio, so you won't have much luck finding a hotel where you can walk directly out of your room and onto the beach. In fact, most of the nicer hotels here are 1km (½ mile) or so away from the beach, high on the hill overlooking the ocean.

If you're traveling on a rock-bottom budget, you'll get more for your money by staying in Quepos and taking the bus to the beaches at Manuel Antonio every day. The rooms in Quepos might be small, but they're generally cleaner and more appealing than those available in the same price category closer to the park.

VERY EXPENSIVE

If you're coming for an extended stay with your family or a large group, look into **Escape Villas** ★★ (© 877/533-8988 in the U.S., or 777-5258 in Costa Rica; www.villascostarica.com), which rents a broad selection of very large and luxurious private villas with all the amenities and some of the best views in Manuel Antonio.

Arenas del Mar ★★★ *(Finds)*   Finally, there's Manuel Antonio that combines the best of all worlds, direct beach access, rainforest setting and surroundings, fabulous views, and luxurious accommodations. Designed and built by the folks behind Finca Rosa Blanca (p. 110), this place features 7 three-story units, with large, luxurious 1- and 2-bedroom units. Not all have ocean views, so be sure to specify if you want one. The top-floor units of the highest building (no. 7) would be my first choice. Buildings nos. 1, 2, and 3 are closest to the beach. All rooms are very spacious, with tasteful decor, cool yellow tile floors, and plenty of wood and tile accents. Most have outdoor Jacuzzi tubs on their private balconies. The apartments are immense two-bedroom, three-bath affairs with a kitchenette, perfect for families and longer stays. The restaurant, lobby, and main pool are set on the highest point of land here, and several spots have fabulous views of Manuel Antonio's Punta Catedral. The owners are truly concerned about the environment and promoting sustainable tourism. Very little was done to disturb the land or surrounding ecosystems during construction. Free daily yoga classes and loads of relaxing treatments can be enjoyed at the hotel's spa.

Manuel Antonio. ℂ/fax **777-2777**. www.arenasdelmar.com. 38 units. $220–$360 (£110–£180) double; $580 (£290) apartment. Rates lower in off season; higher during peak periods. Rates include full breakfast. AE, MC, V. **Amenities:** Restaurant; bar; snack bar; 2 small outdoor pools; spa; concierge; tour desk; 24-hr. room service; in-room massage; babysitting; laundry service. In room: A/C, TV, dataport, free Wi-Fi, minibar, coffeemaker, safe.

Gaia Hotel & Reserve ✦✦

Making a play for the high-end luxury market, this hotel features chic, post-modern minimalist design and decor, with large, well-equipped rooms, tons of amenities, and personalized service. Set on a hilly patch of land, with its own private reserve, the rooms, spa, and restaurant are housed in a series of tall, blocky buildings. The large rooms feature wooden floors, contemporary furnishings, plasma screen televisions with complete home theater systems, and elaborate bathrooms with massive Jacuzzi tubs. Each guest is assigned a personal concierge. The deluxe suites feature a private rooftop terrace, with a reflecting pool, and shaded lounge chairs. The immense Gaia suite features soaring ceilings, a huge sitting room, and a private pool. The spa here is extensive and well-run, with a wide range of treatment options and free daily yoga classes. The restaurant serves excellent fusion cuisine crafted by an energetic young Costa Rican chef, Eduardo Florian.

Manuel Antonio. ℂ **800/226-2515** in the U.S., or 777-9797 in Costa Rica. Fax 777-9126. www.gaiahr.com. 17 units. $330 (£165) double; $440–$495 (£220–£248) suite; $800 (£400) Gaia suite. Rates lower in off season; higher during peak periods. Rates include full breakfast. No children under 16 allowed. AE, MC, V. **Amenities:** Restaurant; bar; multilevel outdoor pool; small gym; extensive spa; concierge; tour desk; 24-hr. room service; in-room massage; laundry service. In room: A/C, TV, free Wi-Fi, minibar, coffeemaker, safe.

Hotel La Mariposa ✦

Perched on a ridge at the top of the hill between Quepos and Manuel Antonio, La Mariposa (The Butterfly) commands a mountains-to-the-sea vista of more than 270 degrees. The sunsets here are knockouts, and the daytime views are pretty captivating, too. However, La Mariposa has been transformed from an intimate and elegant boutique hotel—with 10 large villas set discreetly into the hillside—into a cluster of rooms, suites, and villas crowned by an awkward behemoth of a building towering over everything in sight. Although this is still one of Manuel Antonio's premier accommodations, expansion and growth have cost this place much of its charm.

The best accommodations are the Premier Suites, housed in two three-story buildings constructed over the foundation of a couple of the original villas. These rooms are large, well equipped, and tastefully decorated, with excellent views. Most of the surviving older villas have been split into separate junior suites and deluxe rooms. Each junior suite has a Jacuzzi out on the small balcony or just inside its sliding glass door. There are rooms in the four-story addition to the hotel's main building; they're quite spacious and have great views, but they don't have much charm or personality. There are also a few standard rooms which are certainly comfortable but have no view to speak of.

Manuel Antonio (A.P. 4, Quepos). ℂ **800/549-0157** in the U.S. and Canada, or 777-0355 in Costa Rica. Fax 777-0050. www.lamariposa.com. 62 units. $205–$225 (£103–£113) double; $280–$390 (£140–£195) suite or villa; $450 (£225) penthouse suite. Rates lower in off season. Extra person $40. Children under 10 stay free in parent's room. AE, MC, V. **Amenities:** Restaurant; bar; 4 small pools; concierge; tour desk; complimentary shuttle to and from the national park; in-room massage; babysitting; laundry service. *In room:* A/C, TV, free Wi-Fi, safe.

Hotel Parador ⭐ This hotel is spread out over more than 4.8 hectares (12 acres) of land on a low peninsula, down a dirt road from Hotel La Mariposa. Its design aims to imitate Spanish Mediterranean grandeur, and the main building is loaded with antiques, including 17th-century Dutch and Flemish oil paintings, a 300-year-old carved wooden horse, and 16th-century church and castle doors. The standard rooms are well appointed but far too small for this price range. All have private patios, but few have any view to speak of. Deluxe rooms offer slightly more space, and the second-floor units have private balconies.

The spacious junior suites are located on the top of a hill, giving a good view of the sea and Punta Catedral in the distance. Note that it's a bit of a hike up to these units, although the hotel offers an on-call golf-cart shuttle service. The premium rooms, located in a newer three-story building built on a high spot on the grounds, have the best views and are my first choice here. The hotel runs a shuttle van to the national park, and there's a small, secluded beach about 500m (1,640 ft.) from the hotel.

Manuel Antonio (A.P. 284, Quepos). © 777-1414. Fax 777-1437. www.hotelparador.com. 108 units. $180 (£90) standard double; $205–$245 (£103–£123) deluxe double; $280–$300 (£140–£150) premium double; $330 (£165) junior suite; $920 (£460) presidential suite. Rates include breakfast buffet. Rates slightly higher during peak weeks; significantly lower in off season. AE, MC, V. **Amenities:** 2 restaurants; 2 bars; large free-form pool w/swim-up bar and central fountain; tennis court; modern gym and spa; Jacuzzi; concierge; tour desk; room service; free Wi-Fi in main building and around pool; in-room massage; babysitting; laundry service. *In room:* A/C, TV, minibar, coffeemaker, hair dryer, safe.

Hotel Sí Como No ⭐⭐ *(Finds)* *(Kids)* Owner Jim Damalas has done a great job creating a lively, upscale, midsize resort that blends in with and respects the rainforests and natural wonders of Manuel Antonio. Sí Como No offers an array of facilities and modern amenities with an ecologically conscious attitude. This is a place equally suited to families traveling with children and to couples looking for a romantic getaway.

All the wood used is farm-grown, and while all the rooms have energy-efficient air-conditioning units, guests are urged to use them only when necessary. The standard rooms (housed in the hotel's main building or in the ground floor of a villa) are quite acceptable, but it's worth the splurge for a superior or deluxe room or a suite. Most of these are on the top floors of the two- to three-story villas, with spectacular tree-top views out over the forest and onto the Pacific. These units all have a bedroom with an adjoining living-room area, a private balcony, and either a kitchenette or a wet bar. There are a series of deluxe suites with lots of space and large garden bathrooms, some of which have private Jacuzzis. A separate building set on a high patch of land has a more Art Deco style to it. They also have a wonderful butterfly garden and frog farm just across the street.

Manuel Antonio (mailing address: Mail Stop SJO 297, P.O. Box 025216, Miami, FL 33102). © 777-0777. Fax 777-1093. www.sicomono.com. 58 units. $190–$310 (£95–£155) double. Rates include breakfast. Rates lower in off season. Extra person $30. Children under 6 stay free in parent's room. AE, MC, V. **Amenities:** 2 restaurants; 2 bars; 2 midsize pools, including 1 w/small water slide; modest spa; 2 Jacuzzis; concierge; tour desk; free beach shuttle; in-room massage; babysitting; laundry service; free Wi-Fi. *In room:* A/C, minibar, coffeemaker, hair dryer, iron, safe.

Makanda by the Sea ⭐⭐ *(Finds)* A wonderfully luxurious collection of studio apartments and private villas, Makanda is easily the best option for anyone looking for an intimate, romantic getaway in Manuel Antonio. Each is individually decorated with flair. If you combine villa no. 1 with the three studios, you get one very large four-bedroom villa, great for a family or a small group (although children under 16 are not allowed, unless you rent out the entire hotel). Every choice comes with a full kitchenette, cable television, CD player, and either a terrace or a balcony. The grounds are well tended, intermixed with tropical flowers and Japanese gardens. A full breakfast is delivered to your room each morning. The hotel's pool and Jacuzzi combine intricate and colorful tile work with a view of the jungle-covered hillsides and the Pacific Ocean.

Makanda's **Sunspot Bar & Grill** ✸✸ is one of the better restaurants in Manuel Antonio, with just a few tables set under open-sided cloth tents, serving creative continental dishes and rich desserts. Be sure to make reservations in the high season. Makanda is located halfway down the road to Hotel Parador and Punta Quepos.

Manuel Antonio (A.P. 29, Quepos). ✆ 888/625-2632 in the U.S., or 777-0442 in Costa Rica. Fax 777-1032. www.makanda.com. 11 units. $265 (£133) studio; $400 (£200) villa. Rates include full breakfast. Rates lower in off season; higher during peak periods. AE, MC, V. No children under 16. **Amenities:** Restaurant; bar; midsize pool; Jacuzzi; watersports equipment and bike rental; concierge; tour desk; limited room service (11am–10pm); in-room massage and spa services; laundry service. *In room:* TV, kitchenette, stocked minibar, coffeemaker, safe.

EXPENSIVE   *Stayed here*

Hotel Costa Verde ✸   This long-standing hotel has consistently offered up good values, ocean views, and reasonable proximity to the beaches and national park. Located more than halfway down the hill to Manuel Antonio, about a 10-minute walk from the beach, Costa Verde has continued to add new rooms and new buildings over the years, even swallowing up a neighboring project or two. Today there are rooms in a wide range of sizes and prices. Some of the buildings are located quite a hike from the hotel's reception and restaurants, so be sure you know exactly what type of room you'll be staying in and where it's located. The best rooms here have ocean views, kitchenettes, private balconies, and loads of space; some of these don't have air-conditioning, but that's no problem because they feature huge screened walls to encourage cross ventilation. There is also an enormous penthouse suite with a commanding view of the spectacular surroundings. Three small pools are set into the hillside, with views out to the ocean, and the hotel has a couple of miles of private trails through the rainforest.

Manuel Antonio (mailing address: SJO 1313, P.O. Box 025216, Miami, FL 33102). ✆ 866/854-7958 in the U.S. and Canada, or 777-0584 in Costa Rica. Fax 777-0560. www.costaverde.com. 63 units. $104–$185 (£52–£93) double. Rates lower in off season; higher during peak weeks. AE, MC, V. **Amenities:** 2 restaurants; 3 bars; 3 small pools; tour desk; laundry service. *In room:* A/C and TV (in some units), free Wi-Fi, no phone.

Villas Nicolás ✸✸ *Value*   These large villas offer a lot of bang for your buck. Built as terraced units up a steep hill in deep forest, they really give you the feeling that you're in the jungle. Most are quite spacious and well appointed, with wood floors, throw rugs, and comfortable bathrooms; some rooms even have separate living rooms and full kitchenettes, which make longer stays comfortable. My favorite features, though, are the balconies, which come with sitting chairs and a hammock. Some of these balconies are massive and have incredible views. In fact, the rooms highest up the hill have views that I'd be willing to pay a lot more for, and a few of them even have air-conditioning. During the high season the hotel opens an informal restaurant/bar near the pool that serves breakfast and sometimes lunch and dinner, depending on demand.

Manuel Antonio (A.P. 236, Quepos). ✆ 777-0481. Fax 777-0451. www.villasnicolas.com. 20 units. $110–$163 (£55–£82) double. Weekly, monthly, and off season (May–Nov) rates available. AE, MC, V. **Amenities:** Small pool; laundry service. *In room:* A/C (in some units), fridge.

MODERATE

In addition to the hotels mentioned below, the **Best Western Kamuk Hotel** (✆ 777-0811; www.kamuk.co.cr) is a dependable option right in downtown Quepos; it's popular with sportfishing enthusiasts.

El Mono Azul Hotel _(Value)_   Located on the road to Manuel Antonio, just outside of Quepos, the "Blue Monkey" offers clean and comfortable rooms at a good price. The more expensive rooms feature air-conditioning and/or a small television with cable. The new villas have red-tile floors, separate sitting rooms, and a kitchenette. One room even has a Jacuzzi tub. The place has a lively, hostel-like feel. The owner is active in a children's arts program aimed at helping preserve the local rainforest and the endangered squirrel monkey. In fact, 10% of your bill goes to this program. The restaurant/pizzeria here is quite popular. These folks can also arrange longer-term rentals of fully equipped apartments and villas.

Manuel Antonio (A.P. 297-6350, Quepos). ℂ 800/381-3578 in the U.S., or 777-2572 in Costa Rica. Fax 777-1954. www.monoazul.com. 29 units. $80 (£40) double; $125 (£63) villa. Rates lower in off season; higher during peak weeks. AE, DC, MC, V. **Amenities:** Restaurant; bar; lounge; 3 small pools; small gym; game room; tour desk; laundry service. *In room:* A/C, TV, free Wi-Fi, no phone.

Hotel and Cabinas Playa Espadilla   These are actually two separate sister projects located across the street from each other. The hotel has rooms with air-conditioning, cable television, and in-room phones. Most of these have full kitchenettes. There's a tennis court here, as well as a bordering private reserve with a small trail system. The older (and less expensive) _cabinas_ are more basic, although most have been well maintained and a few have air-conditioning. Ask about bed distribution before making a reservation because a fair number of rooms have one double and a bunk bed. There are a small swimming pool and well-tended green areas at each site. This place started out as a popular budget option down near the national park entrance. Despite the expansion and improvements, I'm not sure that the facilities and amenities merit the prices they're charging. You'll find both of these places a hundred yards or so down the side road that runs inland perpendicular to Playa Espadilla, the first beach outside the national park.

Manuel Antonio (A.P. 195, Quepos). ℂ/fax 777-0903. www.espadilla.com. 32 units. $91–$103 (£46–£52) cabina; $130–$163 (£65–£82) double. Rates for hotel rooms include a full breakfast. Rates lower in off season. AE, MC, V. **Amenities:** Restaurant; bar; 2 small pools; tennis court; tour desk; laundry service. *In room:* A/C and TV (in some units), fridge, safe, no phone in cabinas.

Hotel Plinio _★ (Value)_   The hotel is built into a steep hillside, so it's a bit of a climb from the parking lot up to the guest rooms and restaurant. The rooms have the feel of a treehouse. Floors and walls are polished hardwood, and there are even rooms with tree-trunk pillars. The hotel's suites are the best value. These are built on either two or three levels. Both options have sleeping lofts; the three-story rooms also have rooftop decks. The whole complex is set in lush forest. Behind the hotel is a private reserve with 15km (9⅓ miles) of trails and, at the top of the hill, a 15m-tall (49-ft.) observation tower with an incredible view. In addition to the popular **Plinio Restaurant** _★★_ (p. 290), there's a poolside grill where lunches are served. Plinio is located just outside of Quepos on the road toward the national park, so it's a bit far from the park entrance and beaches.

Manuel Antonio (A.P. 71-6350, Quepos). ℂ 777-0055. Fax 777-0558. www.hotelplinio.com. 13 units. Dec–Apr $65–$75 (£33–£38) double; $85–$110 (£43–£105) suite or house. Rates include breakfast buffet in high season. Rates lower May–Nov. V (7% surcharge). **Amenities:** Restaurant; bar; small pool in lush garden setting; laundry service. *In room:* No phone.

Hotel Verde Mar _★ (Value)_   This hotel is a great choice for proximity to the national park and the beach. From your room it's just a short walk to the beach (Playa Espadilla) via a raised wooden walkway. All the rooms here have plenty of space, nice wrought-iron queen-size beds, tile floors, a desk and chair, a fan, and a small porch.

All but two of the rooms come with a basic kitchenette. Some of the larger rooms even have two queen-size beds. The hotel has no restaurant, but plenty are within walking distance. There's a small pool here, for when the surf is too rough. You'll find Verde Mar on the beach side of the road just before the Mar y Sombra.

Manuel Antonio (A.P. 348-6350), Quepos. ℂ **777-1805.** Fax 777-1311. www.verdemar.com. 24 units. $90–$100 (£45–£50) double; $105–$120 (£53–£60) suite. Rates lower in off season. AE, MC, V. **Amenities:** Small pool. *In room:* A/C, kitchenette, no phone.

Karahé   The Karahé has long been one of the few beachfront hotels in Manuel Antonio. If you stay in one of the more expensive beachfront units, you'll have a newer room with cool tile floors, two double beds, and a small patio. The least-expensive rooms are located just off the reception and offer neither views nor easy access to the ocean. Be aware that if you opt for one of the villas, you'll have a steep uphill climb from the beach; on the other hand, a couple of these have great views. The gardens here are quite lush and have flowering ginger that often attracts hummingbirds. The hotel can arrange a wide variety of tours and charters, including sportfishing ($850/£425 for a full day). Karahé is located on both sides of the road about 450m (1,476 ft.) before you reach Playa Espadilla.

Manuel Antonio (A.P. 100-6350, Quepos). ℂ **877/623-3198** in the U.S. and Canada, or 777-0170 in Costa Rica. Fax 777-1075. www.karahe.com. 33 units. $90–$125 (£45–£63) double. Rates include continental breakfast. Rates lower in off season. AE, MC, V. **Amenities:** Restaurant; bar; small pool; exercise room; Jacuzzi; tour desk; laundry service. *In room:* A/C, no phone.

INEXPENSIVE

In addition to the places listed below, **The Widemouth Frog** (ℂ **777-2798;** www. widemouthfrog.org) is a hostel-like option in downtown Quepos, which even has its own swimming pool.

Hotel Malinche   A good choice for budget travelers, the Hotel Malinche is my top choice in this category right in Quepos. The standard rooms are small but have hardwood or tile floors and clean bathrooms. Some of those on the second floor even have small private balconies that open on to a small interior courtyard. The more expensive rooms are newer and larger and have air-conditioning, TVs, and carpets.

75m (246 ft.) west of downtown bus terminal, Quepos. ℂ **777-1833.** Fax 777-0093. 24 units. $25–$55 (£13–£28) double. AE, MC, V. *In room:* No phone.

Hotel Vela-Bar   You'll find this little hotel up the narrow road that leads off to the left just before the end of the road to Manuel Antonio National Park. It has a wide variety of room choices: If you're on a tight budget, you can stay in a tiny room, or if you have a little more money to spend, you can opt for a spacious one-bedroom house that has tile floors and arched windows. All rooms have double beds and tiled bathrooms. Quite a few rooms come with air-conditioning and small refrigerators, and a couple have full kitchenettes. The open-air restaurant/bar is pretty good, and serves creative international cuisine. Check the chalkboard for the day's special. If you can bear the soft beds and slightly dated feel, this is one of the better budget options in Manuel Antonio, and it's only 100m (328 ft.) from the beach.

Manuel Antonio (A.P. 13, Quepos). ℂ **777-0413.** Fax 777-1071. www.velabar.com. 13 units. $40–$115 (£20–£58) double. Rates lower in off season. AE, MC, V. **Amenities:** Restaurant; bar; laundry service. *In room:* A/C, no phone.

WHERE TO DINE

Scores of dining options are available around Manuel Antonio and Quepos, and almost every hotel has some sort of restaurant. For the cheapest meals around, try a simple *soda* in Quepos, or head to one of the open-air joints on the beach road before the national park entrance. The standard Tico menu prevails, with prices in the $3 to $8 (£1.50–£4) range. Of these, **Marlin Restaurant** (© 777-1134), right in front of Playa Espadilla, and **Mar Luna** (© 777-5107), on the main road just beyond Hotel La Colina, are your best bets. For simple pasta, pizzas, and Italian gelato, head to **Escalofrío** (© 777-0833) or **Pizza de Marco** (© 777-9400), both located in downtown Quepos. In addition to the places listed below, another good option, on the outskirts of Quepos, is **Ronny's Place** (© 777-5120). There's now a selection of sushi restaurants, as **Tsunami Sushi** (© 777-2159) has opened up on the second floor of a building on the main street fronting the bay in Quepos, almost directly across the street from Tropical Sushi (see below).

For a taste of the high-life, head to the **La Luna** restaurant at Gaia Hotel & Reserve (see above) for their sunset *tapa* menu. The views are great and the creative tapas are very reasonably priced.

Agua Azul 𝒜 *(Finds)* INTERNATIONAL   With a fabulous perch and panoramic view, this open-air restaurant has changed names and owners steadily over the years. It finally seems to have settled down with a menu and management that may just be able to make this place live up to its fantastic setting. Tables by the railing fill up fast, so get here well before sunset if you want to snag one. Start things off with a Tuna Margarita, an inventive version of ceviche with a lime and tequila marinade. Main dishes include coconut crusted mahimahi and Panko crusted tuna. For lunch there are giant burgers and fresh fish sandwiches. The long wooden bar is a popular hangout, and a good place to order up some appetizers and drinks.

Manuel Antonio, near Villas del Parque. © 777-5082. Reservations not accepted. Main courses $13–$18 (£6.50–£9). V. Thurs–Tues 11am–10pm.

El Avión SEAFOOD/INTERNATIONAL   Set on the edge of Manuel Antonio's hillside with a great view of the ocean and surrounding forests, this restaurant is actually housed under some permanent tents and the starboard wing of a retired army transport plane, hence the name El Avión, which means "The Plane." This specific plane was actually shot down by the Sandinista army, leading to a scandal that uncovered illegal CIA supply missions to the Contra rebels in Nicaragua. Today you can enjoy well-prepared seafood and steaks as you take in the unique surroundings and glow of history. Inside the fuselage you'll also find a small bar.

Manuel Antonio. © 777-3378. Reservations recommended. Main courses $8–$23 (£4–£12). MC, V. Daily noon–11pm.

El Gran Escape 𝒜𝒜 SEAFOOD   This Quepos landmark is consistently one of the top restaurants in the region. The fish is fresh and expertly prepared, and the prices are reasonable. If that's not enough of a recommendation, the atmosphere is lively, the locals seem to keep coming back, and the service is darn good for a beach town in Costa Rica. Sturdy wooden tables and chairs fill up the large indoor dining room, and sportfishing photos and an exotic collection of masks fill up the walls. If you venture away from the fish, the menu features hearty steaks, giant burgers, and a wide assortment of delicious appetizers, including fresh tuna sashimi. El Gran Escape's Fish Head Bar is usually crowded and spirited, and if there's a game going on, it will be on the television here. Breakfasts here are also excellent.

On the main road into Quepos, on your left just after the bridge. ℂ **777-0395.** Reservations recommended in high season. Main courses $5–$21 (£2.50–£11). V. Daily 7am–11pm.

El Patio Bistro Latino 🌾🌾🌾 NUEVO LATINO/FUSION   This small bistro-style restaurant is an outgrowth of the popular coffeehouse and roasting company Café Milagro. The same attention to detail and focus on quality carries over here. By day you can get a wide range of coffee drinks and specialties, as well as full breakfasts, fresh-baked sweets, and a variety of salads, sandwiches, and light lunch dishes. By night, things get more interesting and this humble little spot serves up some of the best food in Manuel Antonio. Their regularly changing menu features inventive main dishes that take advantage of local ingredients and various regional culinary traditions. So the fresh red snapper may come steamed in a banana leaf with a spicy *mojo,* and the tenderloin could feature a tamarind glaze and be served over some roasted local sweet potatoes *(camote).* Start things off with the calamari sautéed with spicy sausage and fresh corn and served over a spicy flat bread. You may even find some of their home-roasted coffee used as an ingredient in a glaze, sauce, or dessert.

Manuel Antonio. ℂ **777-4982.** Reservations recommended. Main courses $6–$18 (£3–£9). AE, MC, V. Daily 6am–10pm.

La Hacienda 🌾 INTERNATIONAL   Located on a jungle-facing open-air back patio of the Plaza Yara strip mall, this place is surprisingly intimate and atmospheric, especially at night. Subdued lighting and vines draping down from the high ceiling make you feel as if you are almost in the jungle. The menu is inventive and eclectic. I highly recommend starting things off with the quesadilla of caramelized onions, brie, and fresh mango. For a main dish, the mixed seafood grill for two, features shrimp, squid, and fresh fish prepared on a wood-fired grill with a tropical fruit salsa on the side. The dessert menu changes regularly, but almost always features some rich chocolate concoction, as well as a flavored crème brulee.

In the Plaza Yara, on the road between Quepos and Manuel Antonio. ℂ **777-3473.** Reservations recommended in high season. Main courses $10–$18 (£5–£9). AE, MC, V. Daily 11am–10pm.

Plinio Restaurant 🌾🌾 INTERNATIONAL   This is a long-standing, popular restaurant in Manuel Antonio, located at an equally popular hotel. The open-air restaurant is about three stories above the parking lot, so be prepared to climb some steps. It's worth it, though. The broad menu features an enticing mix of international dishes, with a smattering of German and Italian dishes, and a distinct emphasis on Asian fare. The chef uses locally organically grown herbs and veggies. Thai, Indian, and Indonesian dishes are all excellently prepared, and there are always vegetarian options. The shrimp in coconut milk curry sauce is excellent.

In the Hotel Plinio, 1km (½ mile) out of Quepos toward Manuel Antonio. ℂ **777-0055.** Reservations recommended in high season. Main courses $8.30–$19 (£4.15–£9.50). V. Daily 5–10pm.

Sunspot Bar & Grill 🌾🌾 *Finds* INTERNATIONAL   Dining by candlelight under a purple canvas tent at one of the few poolside tables here is one of the most romantic dining experiences to be had in Manuel Antonio. The food's some of the best in town as well. The menu changes regularly but features prime meats and poultry and fresh fish, excellently prepared. The rack of lamb might get a light jalapeño-mint or tamarind glaze, and the chicken breast might be stuffed with feta cheese, kalamata olives, and roasted red peppers and topped with a blackberry sauce. There are nightly specials and a good selection of salads, appetizers, and desserts.

At Makanda by the Sea (p. 285). ℂ 777-0442. Reservations recommended. Main courses $10–$20 (£5–£10). V. Daily 11am–10pm.

Tropical Sushi 🔍 SUSHI/JAPANESE   As the name implies, the ambience here is decidedly tropical, with lively pastel colors and Caribbean architectural highlights, but don't let the surroundings fool you: This is still an excellent sushi joint. In addition to fresh tuna and grouper brought in daily by local fishermen, you can get maki, sushi, and sashimi made with Chilean salmon, smoked eel, and deep-fried soft-shell crabs. The sushi bar itself is tiny, and the main dining room is similarly small. The nicest seating here is in the open-air patio. Start things off with some edamame, an appetizer of steamed soybeans in their husks, and be sure to try the Crocodile Roll, with its mix of crab, eel, and avocado. The biggest problem here is that, when busy, the service can be excruciatingly slow.

On a side street next to El Gran Escape, Quepos. ℂ 777-1710. Reservations recommended. Maki rolls $4–$10 (£2–£5); main courses $5–$20 (£2.50–£10). V. Daily noon–2:30pm and 4:30–11pm.

MANUEL ANTONIO AFTER DARK

The bars at the **Barba Roja** restaurant and the **Hotel Sí Como No** are good places to hang out and meet people in the evenings. For shooting pool, I head to the **Billfish Sportbar & Grill** at the Byblos Resort. For *tapas* and local *bocas,* try **Salsipuedes,** which translates as "get out if you can." If you want to find some live music, **Bambu Jam,** and **Juan Tucan's** 🔍 are your best bets. Back in Quepos, **El Banco Bar, Mar y Blues, Dos Locos, Sargento Garcia's, Wacky Wanda's,** and the **Fish Head Bar** at El Gran Escape are all popular hangouts.

Night owls and dancing fools have several of choices here, although the bulldozing of Mar y Sombra down by the beach has really hurt the scene. The live music at **Bambu Jam** is often salsa and merengue, perfect for dancing. For real late-night action, the local favorite appears to be the **Arco Iris,** which is located just before the bridge heading into town. Admission is usually around $3 (£1.50).

If you enjoy gaming tables, the **Hotel Kamuk** in Quepos and the **Byblos Resort** on the road to Manuel Antonio both have small casinos and will even foot your cab bill if you try your luck and lay down your money.

If you want to see a flick, check what's playing at **Hotel Sí Como No**'s little theater, although you have to eat at the restaurant or spend a minimum at the bar to earn admission.

EN ROUTE TO DOMINICAL: PLAYA MATAPALO

Playa Matapalo is a long expanse of flat beach that's about midway between Quepos and Dominical. It's an easy but bumpy 26km (16 miles) south of Quepos on the Costanera Sur. It's nowhere near as developed as either of those two beaches, but that's part of its charm. The beach here seems to stretch on forever, and it's usually deserted. The surf and strong riptides frequently make Matapalo too rough for swimming, although surfing and boogie-boarding can be good. Foremost among this beach's charms are peace and quiet.

WHERE TO STAY

Matapalo is basically a little village; the beach is about 1km (½ mile) away. A few very small and intimate lodges are right on the beach. One of the more interesting is **Bahari Beach Bungalows** (ℂ 787-5014; www.baharibeach.com), which offers deluxe tents, with private bathrooms, and more standard rooms, right on the beach.

If you're looking for a longer stay, check out **Jungle House** (©/fax **787-5005;** www. junglehouse.com), which has a variety of private houses and bungalows for rent.

El Coquito del Pacifico *(Value* This hotel is located right on the beach. The rooms are all quite large and have white-tile floors, high ceilings and get plenty of natural light. The open-air restaurant here is popular with guests and locals alike. El Coquito has a small kidney-shaped pool and ample grounds planted with coconut palms and other shade trees. When you hit the beach at Matapalo, turn right, and the hotel will be 100m (328 ft.) or so north. Starting in late 2007, this place was slated to begin a major overhaul, with modern condo units and a new restaurant to be added.

Playa Matapalo (Apdo. 6783-1000, San José). © **787-5028.** Fax 787-5029. www.elcoquito.com. 8 units. $50–$60 (£25–£30) double. Rates lower in the off season. AE, MC, V. **Amenities:** Restaurant; bar; outdoor pool; laundry service. *In room:* A/C, no phone.

4 Dominical ⟨⋆

29km (18 miles) SW of San Isidro; 42km (26 miles) S of Quepos; 160km (99 miles) S of San José

With a stunning setting, and miles of nearly deserted beaches backed by rainforest covered mountains, Dominical and the coastline south of it are excellent places to find uncrowded stretches of sand, spectacular views, remote jungle waterfalls, and abundant budget lodgings. The beach at Dominical itself is one of the prime surf destinations in Costa Rica, with both right and left beach breaks. When the swell is big, the wave here is a powerful and hollow tube, and the town is often packed with surfers. In fact, while the beach at Dominical gets broad, flat, and beautiful at low tide, its primary appeal is to surfers. It is often too rough for casual bathers. However, you will find excellent swimming, sunbathing, and strolling beaches just a little farther south at **Dominicalito, Playa Hermosa,** and inside **Ballena Marine National Park** ⟨⋆.

Leaving Manuel Antonio, the road south to Dominical runs by mile after mile of oil-palm plantations. However, just before Dominical, the mountains again meet the sea. From Dominical south, the coastline is dotted with tide pools, tiny coves, and cliffside vistas. Dominical is the largest village in the area and has several small lodges both in town and along the beach to the south. The village enjoys an enviable location on the banks of Río Barú, right where it widens considerably before emptying into the ocean. There's good bird-watching along the banks of the river and throughout the surrounding forests.

ESSENTIALS

GETTING THERE & DEPARTING   By Plane   The nearest airport with regular service is in Quepos (see "Essentials" under "Manuel Antonio National Park," earlier in this chapter). From there you can hire a taxi, rent a car, or take the bus.

By Car   From San José, head south (toward Cartago) on the Interamerican Highway. Continue on this road all the way to San Isidro de El General, where you turn right and head down toward the coast. The entire drive takes about 4 hours.

You can also drive here from Manuel Antonio/Quepos. Just take the road out of Quepos toward the hospital and airport. Follow the signs for Dominical. It's a straight, albeit bumpy, shot that takes a bit over an hour due to the poor state of the washboard rutted dirt road. For nearly a decade, this road has been scheduled for paving. I actually have heard this may happen by early 2008. If this happens, it should take only a half-hour to cover the 40km (25 miles).

The road from Dominical heading south to Palmar Norte, passing all the beaches mentioned below, is in excellent shape.

By Bus To reach Dominical, you must first go to San Isidro de El General or Quepos. Buses leave San José for San Isidro roughly every hour between 5:30am and 6:30pm. See "Getting There & Departing" in "San Isidro de El General: A Base for Exploring Chirripó National Park," later in this chapter. The trip takes 3 hours; the fare is $2.80 (£1.40). Leave no later than 9am if you want to be sure to catch the 1:30pm bus to Dominical.

From **San Isidro de El General,** buses (© **257-4121** or 771-4744) leave for Dominical at 7 and 9am and 1:30 and 4pm. The bus station for Dominical is 1 block south of the main bus station and 2 blocks west of the church. Trip duration is 1½ hours; the fare is $1.50 (£0.75).

From **Quepos,** buses leave daily at 5 and 9:30am and 1:30 and 7pm. Trip duration is 2 hours; the fare is $3 (£1.50).

When you're ready to leave, buses depart Dominical for San Isidro at 6:45 and 7:15am and 2:30 and 3:30pm. If you want to get to San José the same day, you should catch the morning bus. Buses leave San Isidro for San José roughly every hour between 5am and 6pm. Buses to Quepos leave Dominical at approximately 5:45 and 8am and 1 and 2:30pm.

ORIENTATION Dominical is a very small village on the banks of Río Barú. The village is to the right after you cross the bridge and stretches out along the main road parallel to the beach. As you first come into town, you'll see a soccer field and a general store, which has a couple of public telephones. Just beyond the turnoff into town, on the Costanera Highway heading south, is a little strip mall, **Plaza Pacífica,** with a couple of restaurants, a pharmacy, and a grocery store.

FAST FACTS Taxis tend to congregate in front of the soccer field. The gas station is located about 2km (1¼ miles) north of town on the road to Quepos. You can purchase stamps and send mail from the **San Clemente Bar & Grill.** In the little mall built beside the San Clemente Bar & Grill, you'll also find an Internet cafe, and they'll change dollars. There's also a small branch of the **Banco de Costa Rica,** with an ATM, at the Plaza Pacifica.

EXPLORING THE BEACHES & BALLENA MARINE NATIONAL PARK

Because the beach in the village of Dominical itself is unprotected and at the mouth of a river, it's often too rough for swimming. However, you can go for a swim in the calm waters at the mouth of the Río Barú, or head down the beach a few kilometers to the little sheltered cove at **Roca Verde.**

If you have a car, you should continue driving south, exploring beaches as you go. You will first come to **Dominicalito,** a small beach and cove that shelters the local fishing fleet and can be a decent place to swim, but continue on a bit. You'll soon hit **Playa Hermosa,** a long stretch of desolate beach with fine sand. As in Dominical, this is unprotected and can be rough, but it's a nicer place to sunbathe and swim than Dominical.

At the village of Uvita, 16km (10 miles) south of Dominical, you'll reach the northern end of the **Ballena Marine National Park** ✦ (© **743-8236**), which protects a coral reef that stretches from Uvita south to Playa Piñuela and includes the little Isla Ballena, just offshore. To get to **Playa Uvita** (which is inside the park), turn in at the village of Bahía and continue until you hit the ocean. The beach here is actually well protected and good for swimming. At low tide an exposed sandbar allows you to walk about and explore another tiny island. This park is named for the whales that are sometimes sighted close to shore in the winter months. If you ever fly over this area, you'll also notice that this little island and the spit of land that's formed at low tide compose the perfect outline of a whale's tail. A parks office at the entrance here regulates the park's use and even runs a small turtle-hatching shelter and program. Entrance to the national park is $6 (£3) per person. Camping is allowed here for $2 (£1) per person per day, with access to a public bathroom and shower.

Dominical is a major surf destination. The long and varied beach break here is justifiably popular. In general, the beach boasts powerful waves best suited for experienced surfers. Nevertheless, beginners should check in with the folks at the **Green Iguana Surf Camp** (© 787-0157; www.greeniguanasurfcamp.com), who offer lessons and comprehensive "surf camps."

OTHER ACTIVITIES IN THE AREA

Although the beaches stretching south from Dominical should be beautiful enough to keep most people content, there are lots of other things to do. Several local farms offer horseback tours through forests and orchards, and at some of these farms you can even spend the night. **Hacienda Barú** ♠ (© **787-0003;** fax 787-0057; www.hacienda baru.com) offers several different hikes and tours, including a walk through mangroves and along the riverbank (for some good bird-watching), a rainforest hike through 80 hectares (198 acres) of virgin jungle, an all-day trek from beach to mangrove to jungle that includes a visit to some Indian petroglyphs, an overnight camping trip, and a combination horseback-and-hiking tour. It even has tree-climbing tours and a small canopy platform 30m (98 ft.) above the ground, as well as one of the more common zip-line canopy tours. Tour prices range from $20 (£10) for the mangrove hike to $60 (£30) for the jungle overnight. If you're traveling with a group, you'll be charged a lower per-person rate, depending on the number of people in your group. Hacienda Barú also has six comfortable cabins with two bedrooms each, full kitchens, and even a living room ($60/£30 double). Hacienda Barú is located about 1.5km (1 mile) north of Dominical on the road to Manuel Antonio.

The jungles just outside of Dominical are home to two spectacular waterfalls. The most popular and impressive is the **Santo Cristo** or **Nauyaca Waterfalls** ♠, a two-tiered beauty with an excellent swimming hole. Most of the hotels in town can arrange for the horseback ride up here, or you can contact **Don Lulo** (© **787-8013;** www.cataratasnauyaca.com) directly. A full-day tour, with both breakfast and lunch, should cost around $45 (£23) per person, including transportation to and from Dominical. The tour is a mix of hiking, horseback riding, and hanging out at the falls. It is also possible to reach these falls by horseback from an entrance near the small village of Tinamaste. (You will see signs on the road.) Similar tours (at similar prices) are offered to the **Diamante Waterfalls,** which are a three-tiered set of falls with a 360m (1,180-ft.) drop, but not quite as spacious and inviting a pool as the one at Santo Cristo.

If you're looking for a bird's-eye view of the area, **Skyline Ultralights** (© 743-8037; www.flyultralight.com) offers a variety of airborne tours of the area. Located near the beach in Uvita, these folks offer options ranging from a 20-minute introductory flight for $65 (£33) to a circuit exploring the Ballena Marine National Park and neighboring mangrove forests lasting a bit over 45 minutes for $120 (£60).

If you want to take a scuba-diving trip out to the rocky sites off of Ballena National Park or all the way out to Isla del Caño, call **Mystic Dive Center** (© **786-5217;** www.mysticdivecenter.com), which has its main office in a small roadside strip mall down toward Playa Tortuga and Ojochal. These folks are only open from December 1 through April 15.

Other adventure activities offered in Dominical include kayak tours of the mangroves, river floats in inner tubes, and sportfishing. To arrange any of these activities, check in with **Dominical Adventures** (© 787-0191; at the San Clemente Bar & Grill), **Southern Expeditions** (© 787-0100; www.southernexpeditionscr.com), or the folks at the **Hotel Roca Verde** (© 787-0036).

For a fun side trip for anyone interested in snakes and other little critters, head to **Parque Reptilandia** (© 787-8007), located a few miles outside of Dominical on the road to San Isidro. This place features over 50 terrariums or enclosed exhibits of snakes, frogs, turtles, and lizards, as well as crocodiles and caimans. It's open daily from 9am to 4:30pm; admission is $10 (£5).

Finally, if you're looking to learn or bone-up on your Spanish, **Adventure Education Center** (© 787-0023; www.adventurespanishschool.com), located right in the heart of town, offers a variety of immersion-style language programs.

WHERE TO STAY

In addition to the places listed below, there are a host of beautiful private homes built on the hillsides above Dominical that are regularly rented out. Most come with several bedrooms and full kitchens, and quite a few have private pools. If you're here for an extended stay and have a four-wheel-drive vehicle (a must for most of these), check in with **Paradise Costa Rica** (© 388-0155; www.paradisecostarica.com) or with the folks at **Cabinas San Clemente** or **Hotel Roca Verde** (see below for both of these).

MODERATE

Hotel Diuwak   This little complex offers the most modern accommodations right near the surf break, although that's not necessarily saying much. The rooms are clean and bright. About half the rooms come with air-conditioning, and there are a few bigger suites and bungalows for larger groups and families. Most have some sort of private or semiprivate veranda facing lush gardens. At the center of the complex, you'll find a refreshing pool, and in the adjacent shopping center, there's a minimarket. Located about 50m (164 ft.) inland from the beach, this place is a decent option for surfers seeking a little extra comfort just steps away from the waves.

Dominical (mailing address: A.P. 7737-1000, San José). © 787-0087. Fax 787-0089. www.diuwak.com. 18 units. $75–$110 (£38–£55) double. Rates lower in off season; higher during peak weeks. MC, V. **Amenities:** Restaurant; bar; midsize pool; Jacuzzi; tour desk; laundry service. *In room:* Free Wi-Fi, safe.

Hotel Roca Verde ⋆   This popular hotel offers the best beachfront accommodations in Dominical. The setting is superb—on a protected little cove with rocks and tide pools. The rooms are located in a two-story building beside the swimming pool. Each room comes with one queen-size and one single bed, and a small patio or balcony. A large open-air restaurant with a popular bar really gets going on Saturday nights. The rooms are a bit close to the bar, so it can sometimes be hard to get an early night's sleep, especially during the high season if the bar is raging.

1km (½ mile) south of Barú River Bridge in Dominical, just off the coastal highway. © 787-0036. Fax 787-0013. www.rocaverde.net. 10 units. $85 (£43) double. Rates lower in off season; higher during peak weeks. MC, V. **Amenities:** Restaurant; bar; small pool; tour desk; laundry service. *In room:* A/C, no phone.

Pacific Edge ⋆ *(Finds)*   This place is away from the beach, but the views from each individual bungalow are so breathtaking that you might not mind. Spread along a lushly planted ridge on the hillside over Dominical, these comfortable cabins have wood floors, solar-heated water, and solar reading lights. Their best feature is surely the private porch with a comfortable hammock in which to laze about and enjoy the view. The restaurant serves breakfast. Dinners are also served upon request, with an emphasis on well-prepared international cuisine. A wide range of tours and activities can be arranged here, and there's a refreshing swimming pool if you're too tired or lazy to head down to the beach. Pacific Edge is 4km (2½ miles) south of Dominical and then another 1.2km (¾ mile) up a steep and rocky road; four-wheel-drive vehicles are highly recommended.

Dominical (A.P. 531-8000, Pérez Zeledón). ©/fax **787-8010**. www.pacificedge.info. 4 units. $60 (£30) double. AE, MC, V (7% surcharge). **Amenities:** Restaurant; midsize pool. *In room:* Kitchenette, no phone.

INEXPENSIVE

As a popular surfer destination, budget lodgings abound in Dominical. I've tried to list the best below, but if you're really counting pennies, it's always a good idea to walk around and check out what's currently available. There are plenty of camping options as well. I recommend **Piramys** (© **787-0196;** piramys@gmail.com), which is right on the beach and offers reasonably clean bathroom and shower facilities.

Cabinas San Clemente *(Value* In addition to running the town's most popular restaurant (see below) and serving as the social hub for the surfers, beach bums, and expatriates passing through, this place offers a variety of accommodations to fit most budgets. Located about 1km (½ mile) from the in-town restaurant, San Clemente offers rooms in three separate buildings, right on the beach. Some of the newer second-floor rooms have wood floors and wraparound verandas and are a real steal in this price range. The grounds are shady, and there are plenty of hammocks. The cheapest rooms are bunk-bed hostel-style affairs in a separate building dubbed the **Dominical Backpacker's Hostel.** Rooms here come with access to a communal kitchen.

Dominical (A.P. 703-8000, Pérez Zeledón). © **787-0026** or 787-0055. Fax 787-0158. 19 units, 16 w/private bathroom. $10 (£5) per person w/shared bathroom; $25–$65 (£13–£33) double w/private bathroom. AE, MC, V. **Amenities:** Restaurant; bar; surf- and boogie-board rental; bike rental; tour desk; laundry service. *In room:* No phone.

Tortilla Flats This long-standing surfer hotel is another good budget option on the beach. There are several styles of rooms located in a cluster of buildings, including rooms with fans, rooms with air-conditioning, and larger rooms fitted out for groups of surfers. I recommend the second-floor rooms with ocean views. Because the rooms differ so much in size and comfort levels, you should definitely take a look at a few of them before choosing.

Dominical. ©/fax **787-0168**. www.tortillaflatsdominical.com. 18 units. $30–$55 (£15–£28) double. Rates lower in off season. AE, MC, V (7% surcharge). **Amenities:** Restaurant; bar; laundry service. *In room:* No phone.

WHERE TO DINE

Right in town, in front of the soccer field, there's **Su Raza** (© **787-0105**), which serves basic Tico meals and good seafood, and even has a nice view of the river mouth. A little farther down the main road is the **Soda Nanyoa** (© **787-0164**). Dishes at these places range in price from $2 to $7 (£1–£3.50).

On the beach **Tortilla Flats** (© **787-0033**) is the best and most happening spot, and their menu features some excellent fresh-fish dishes and a touch of fusion cuisine. If you head a little bit south of town, you can check out the restaurant at the **Hotel Roca Verde** (p. 295), which is usually pretty good for freshly grilled fish, steaks, and burgers. For good Italian food head, to **ConFusione** (© **787-0244**) at the **Domilocos Hotel;** for healthy fare, try the new **Maracatú** (© **787-0091**), located toward the southern end of town.

Coconut Spice ✦ THAI/INDIAN   Housed in a new location, near the river mouth, this place continues to serve up dependable and reasonably authentic Thai and Indian cuisine. The lemon-grass soups and pad Thai are both excellent, and there's a broad selection of different curries and other main dishes. There are several open-air dining spaces, and the best seats actually have a view of the Río Baru.

In the Pueblo del Rio shopping complex, Dominical. ℂ 787-0073. Reservations not accepted. Main courses $8–$13 (£4–£6.50). V. Daily 7:30–9pm.

La Parcela ✦ SEAFOOD/INTERNATIONAL   This open-air restaurant has a lovely setting on a rocky bluff overlooking the ocean. Try to get one of the tables by the railing and you'll be able to watch the waves crashing on the rocks below. The menu features fresh seafood, meat, and poultry dishes, as well as a selection of pastas. The sauces and presentation are all interesting. Start things off with a tuna tartare tower, and then try either their fresh mahimahi with a mango relish, or the filet mignon in a porcini mushroom sauce. The restaurant is a free Wi-Fi hot spot; in fact, I'll say this is one of the prettiest views you'll ever have while surfing the Web.

At Punto Dominical. ℂ 787-0016. Reservations recommended. Main courses $7–$30 (£3.50–£15). V. Daily 7:30am–9pm.

San Clemente Bar & Grill ✦ MEXICAN/INTERNATIONAL   The large wooden tables and bench seats here fill up fast most nights. A convivial atmosphere pervades this place. The menu has a large selection of Mexican-American fare ranging from tacos and burritos to sandwiches. You can get any of the former with fresh fish. There are also more substantial plates, as well as nightly specials. Breakfasts here are also excellent. Just off the restaurant is a large indoor space that has a pool and foosball table, and which becomes one of the town's more popular nightspots, particularly on Friday nights. An interesting (and sobering) decorative touch here is the ceiling full of broken surfboards. If you break a board out on the waves, bring it in; they'll hang it and even buy you a bucket of beer.

Next to the soccer field, Dominical. ℂ 787-0055. Reservations not accepted. Main courses $4–$16 (£2–£8). MC, V. Daily 7am–10pm.

DOMINICAL AFTER DARK

The big party scenes shift from night to night. **Maracutú** hosts an open jam session every Tuesday and a reggae night every Thursday. The loud and late-night dancing scene usually takes place Fridays at **San Clemente** and Saturdays at **Roca Verde.** In addition, **Thrusters** is a popular surfer bar with pool tables and dartboards.

SOUTH OF DOMINICAL

The beaches south of Dominical are some of the nicest and most unexplored in Costa Rica. With the paving of the Costanera Sur, hotels and *cabinas* have begun popping up all along this route. This is a great area to roam in a rental car—it's a **beautiful drive** ✦✦. One good itinerary is to make a loop from San Isidro to Dominical, down the Costanera Sur, hitting several deserted beaches and then returning along the Interamerican Highway.

Among the beaches you'll find are **Playa Ballena, Playa Uvita, Playa Piñuela, Playa Ventanas,** and **Playa Tortuga.** *Tip:* Most of these beaches are considered part of **Ballena Marine National Park** and are subject to the national park entrance fee of $6 (£3) per person. If you're visiting several of these beaches in 1 day, save your ticket—it's good at all of them.

WHERE TO STAY DOWN SOUTH

In addition to the places listed here, you'll find a campground at Playa Ballena and a couple of basic *cabinas* in Bahía and Uvita. The most popular of these is **El Coco Tico**

Ecolodge (© 743-8032; $38 (£19) double), owned and operated by Jorge Díaz, a local legend and enjoyable raconteur who also arranges trips to a nearby waterfall. Coco Tico allows camping as well for around $4 (£2) per person. You'll see a sign for Coco Tico on your left as you reach Uvita, traveling south from Dominical. However, if you want to be closer to the beach, check out **Canto de Ballenas** (© 743-8085), an interesting local cooperative with neat rooms located about .7km (a little less than a half-mile) from the national park entrance at Playa Uvita.

Expensive
Cuna del Angel 🌟🌟   This new hotel has the plushest accommodations along this stretch of coast. The name of this place translates roughly as The Angel's Cradle. All rooms are named after angels, and angel motifs are abundant, as are stained glass windows and lampshades, carved wood details, tile mosaics, and other artistic touches. The hotel is a bit set in, away from the ocean, but there are pretty good sea views from many rooms and common areas, over the thick forest and gardens here. Rooms come with either an open front patio fronting the pool, or a private balcony. I prefer the second floor rooms, with the balconies. A wide range of treatments is available at the spa here.

9km (5½ miles) south of Dominical, just off the coastal hwy. ©/fax 787-8012. www.cunadelangel.com. 16 units. $153 (£77) double. Rates include full breakfast. Rates lower in off season; higher during peak periods. AE, MC, V. **Amenities:** Restaurant; bar; midsize outdoor pool; small spa; Jacuzzi; sauna; steam room; tour desk; laundry service. *In room:* A/C, TV, free Wi-Fi, minifridge, coffeemaker, hair dryer, safe.

La Cusinga Lodge 🌟 *Finds*   This should be a top choice for bird-watchers and those looking for a comfortable lodge that also feels entirely in touch with the natural surroundings. The individual and duplex cabins feature lots of varnished woodwork and large screened windows on all sides for cross ventilation. Most have interesting stone and tile work in their bathrooms. The small complex is set on a hill overlooking Ballena National Park and Playa Uvita. Heavy stone paths connect the main lodge to the various individual cabins. The "honeymoon cabin" is large, has a private garden sitting area, and a large bathroom with rustic stone masonry and its own Jacuzzi tub.

Bahía Ballena (A.P. 41-8000). ©/fax 770-2549. www.lacusingalodge.com. 7 units. $134–$160 (£67–£80) double. Rates include breakfast. MC, V. **Amenities:** Restaurant; bar; tour desk; laundry service. *In room:* No phone.

Moderate
Costa Paraiso Lodge   This hotel offers spacious and clean individual cabins on a rocky point at the north end of Dominicalito beach. All but one of the units come with either a full kitchen or kitchenette, and most have high ceilings and plenty of light and ventilation. Dolphin Lodge and Pelican Roost are the two best rooms here, with spacious living and dining areas. Though it's not quite as large and lacks the cooking facilities, the Toucan Nest is the most private of the accommodations, with an inviting shaded patio. All of the rooms are nonsmoking. There is a small swimming pool, as well as some beautiful tide pools right in front of the hotel; the beach is just a short walk away. There's no restaurant here, but several dining options are close by.

2km (1¼ mile) south of Dominical, just off the coastal hwy., Dominicalito (A.P. 578-8000, Pérez Zeledón). © 787-0025. Fax 787-0338. www.costaparaisodominical.com. 5 units. $110–$140 (£55–£70) double. Rates include full breakfast. Rates lower in off season. AE, DC, MC, V. **Amenities:** Small pool; laundry service. *In room:* A/C, free Wi-Fi, fridge, coffeemaker, no phone.

Cristal Ballena 🌟   Set on a high hill overlooking the ocean, every room here boasts fabulous views. The suites and master suites in the main building are quite large, and feature a host of modern amenities, although I find the decor somewhat lacking in style and taste. The suites all have a large, private balcony with sea view. Four much more rustic "adventure cabins" are, in fact, quite comfortable, but only come with ceiling fans, and lack the televisions, air-conditioning, and other accoutrements found in the suites. One of the prime attractions here is the massive pool, which is set so as to best take advantage of the hotel's high perch and expansive vistas.

7km (4⅓ miles) south of Playa Uvita, just off the coastal hwy. ✆ 786-5354. Fax 786-5355. www.cristal-ballena.com. 23 units. $67 (£34) double cabin; $144–$184 (£72–£92) double suite. Rates include full breakfast. Rates lower in off season; higher during peak periods. AE, MC, V. **Amenities:** Restaurant; bar; large outdoor pool; tour desk; laundry service. *In room:* A/C, TV, free Wi-Fi, minifridge, hair dryer, safe.

Hotel Villas Gaia 🄰   Located off the Costanera Sur just before the town of Ojochal, this small hotel is a collection of separate, spacious wood bungalows. Each bungalow has one single and one double bed, a private bathroom, a ceiling fan, and a small veranda with a jungle view. A few have air-conditioning. I prefer the bungalows farthest from the restaurant, up on the high hill by the swimming pool. The pool and pool area have wonderful views over forest to the sea. A large, open-air dining room down by the parking lot is too close to the highway for my taste but serves tasty, well-prepared international fare. A wide range of tours is available, including trips to Isla del Caño, Corcovado National Park, and Wilson Botanical Gardens.

Playa Tortuga (A.P. 11516-1000, San José). ✆/fax 244-0316. www.villasgaia.com. 14 units. $75 (£38) double. AE, MC, V. **Amenities:** Restaurant; bar; small pool; tour desk; laundry service. *In room:* A/C ($10 surcharge), no phone.

WHERE TO DINE DOWN SOUTH

Exotica 🄰🄰 *(Finds)* FRENCH/INTERNATIONAL   This place is tucked away deep along the dirt road that runs through Ojochal. With polished concrete floors, roll-up bamboo screens for walls, and only a few tree-trunk slab tables and plastic lawn chairs for furniture, it is nonetheless one of the most popular restaurants in the area. The chalkboard menu changes regularly but might feature such dishes as shrimp in a coconut curry sauce. The Chicken Exotica is stuffed with bacon, prunes, and cheese and topped with a red-pepper coulis. The lunch menu is much more limited, with a selection of fresh salads and a few more filling mains.

1km (½ mile) inland from the turnoff for Ojochal. ✆ 786-5050. Reservations not accepted. Lunch $3–$6 (£1.50–£3); main courses $6–$20 (£3–£10). No credit cards. Mon–Sat 11am–9:30pm.

5 San Isidro de El General: A Base for Exploring Chirripó National Park

120km (74 miles) SE of San José; 123km (76 miles) NW of Palmar Norte; 29km (18 miles) NE of Dominical

San Isidro de El General is located just off the Interamerican Highway in the foothills of the Talamanca Mountains and is the largest town in this region. Although there isn't much to do right in town, this is the jumping-off point for trips to Chirripó National Park. This is also the principal transfer point if you're coming from or going to Dominical, and most buses traveling the Interamerican Highway stop here.

ESSENTIALS

GETTING THERE & DEPARTING   By Car   The long and winding stretch of the Interamerican Highway between San José and San Isidro is one of the most difficult sections of road in the country. Not only are there the usual car-eating potholes and periodic landslides, but you must also contend with driving over the 3,300m (10,824-ft.) **Cerro de la Muerte (Mountain of Death).** This aptly named mountain

Tips **Little Devils**

If you're visiting the San Isidro area in February, head out to the nearby **Rey Curré** village for the **Fiesta of the Diablitos,** where costumed Boruca Indians perform dances representative of the Spanish conquest of Central America. The 3-day event also includes fireworks and an Indian handicraft market—this is *the* best place in Costa Rica to buy hand-carved Boruca masks. The date varies, so it's best to call the **Costa Rica Tourist Board** (© **800/327-7033**) for more information.

pass is legendary for its dense afternoon fogs, blinding torrential downpours, steep drop-offs, severe switchbacks, and unexpectedly breathtaking views. (Well, you wanted adventure travel, so here you go!) Drive with extreme care, and bring a sweater or sweatshirt—it's cold up at the top. It'll take you about 3 hours to get to San Isidro.

Tip: If you want a break from the road, stop for a coffee or meal at **Mirador Vista del Valle** (© **384-4685;** at Km 119) a rustic roadside joint, with a great view, gift shop, hiking trails, and orchid collection.

By Bus   Plenty of daily buses will take you to San Isidro. **Musoc** buses (© **222-2422** in San José, or 771-3829 in San Isidro) leave from their modern terminal at Calle Central and Avenida 22 roughly hourly between 5:30am and 6:30pm. **Tracopa** (© **221-4214** or 771-0468) also runs express buses between San José and San Isidro that leave roughly every hour between 5am and 6pm from Calle 5, between Avenidas 18 and 20. Whichever company you choose, the trip takes a little over 3 hours, and the fare is roughly $3 (£1.50). Buses from **Quepos** to San Isidro leave daily at 5am and 1:30pm. Trip duration is 3½ hours; the fare is $3 (£1.50). Buses to or from **Golfito** and **Puerto Jiménez** will also drop you off in San Isidro. Buses depart San Isidro for **San José** roughly every hour between 5am and 6pm.

ORIENTATION   Downtown San Isidro is just off the Interamerican Highway. A large church fronts the central park. The main bus station is 2 blocks west of the north end of the central park.

EXPLORING CHIRRIPO NATIONAL PARK 🐾🐾

At 3,759m (12,330 ft.) in elevation, Mount Chirripó is the tallest mountain in Costa Rica. If you're headed up this way, come prepared for chilly weather. Actually, dress in layers and come prepared for all sorts of weather: Because of the great elevations, temperatures frequently dip below freezing, especially at night. However, during the day, temperatures can soar—remember, you're still only 9 degrees from the equator. The elevation and radical temperatures have produced an environment here that's very different from the Costa Rican norm. Above 3,000m (9,840 ft.), only stunted trees and shrubs survive in *páramos.* If you're driving the Interamerican Highway between San Isidro and San José, you'll pass through a *páramo* on the Cerro de la Muerte.

Hiking up to the top of Mount Chirripó is one of Costa Rica's great adventures. On a clear day (usually in the morning), an unforgettable **view** 🐾🐾🐾 is your reward: You can see both the Pacific Ocean and the Caribbean Sea from the summit. You can do this trip fairly easily on your own if you've brought gear and are an experienced backpacker. Although it's possible to hike from the park entrance to the summit and back down in 2 days (in fact, some daredevils even do it in 1 day), it's best to allow 3 to 4 days for the trip in order to give yourself time to enjoy your hike fully and spend some time on top because that's where the glacier lakes and *páramos* are. For much of the way, you'll be hiking through cloud forests that are home to abundant tropical fauna, including the spectacular **quetzal,** Costa Rica's most beautiful bird. However, quetzal sightings on summit climbs are rare. If you really want to see one of these birds, head to one of the specialized lodges listed below. These cloud forests are cold and damp, so come prepared for rain and fog.

There are several routes to the top of Mount Chirripó. The most popular, by far, leaves from **San Gerardo de Rivas.** However, it's also possible to start your hike from the nearby towns of **Herradura** or **Canaan.** All these places are within a mile or so of each other, reached by the same major road out of San Isidro. San Gerardo is the most popular because it's the easiest route to the top and has the greatest collections of small hotels and lodges, as well as the National Parks office. Information on all of these routes is available at the parks office.

When you're at the summit lodge, there are a number of hiking options. Just in front of the lodge are Los Crestones (The Crests), an impressive rock formation, with trails leading up and around them. The most popular, however, is to the actual summit (the lodge itself is a bit below), which is about a 2-hour hike that passes through the Valle de los Conejos (Rabbit Valley) and the Valle de los Lagos (Valley of Lakes). Other hikes and trails lead off from the summit lodge, and it's easy to spend a couple of days hiking around here. A few trails will take you to the summits of several neighboring peaks. These hikes should be undertaken only after carefully studying an accurate map and talking to park rangers and other hikers.

ENTRY POINT, FEES & REGULATIONS   Although it's not that difficult to get to Chirripó National Park from nearby San Isidro, it's still rather remote. And to see it fully, you have to be prepared to hike. To get to the trail head, you have three choices: car, taxi, or bus. If you choose to drive, take the road out of San Isidro, heading north toward San Gerardo de Rivas, which is some 20km (12 miles) down the road. Otherwise, you can catch a bus in San Isidro that will take you directly to the trail head in San Gerardo de Rivas. Buses leave daily at 5am from the western side of the central park in San Isidro. It costs 80¢ (40p) one-way and takes 1½ hours. Another bus departs at 2pm from a bus station 200m (656 ft.) south of the park. Buses return to San Isidro daily at 7am and 4pm. A taxi from town should cost around $15 to $20 (£7.50–£10). Because the hike to the summit of Mount Chirripó can take between 6 and 12 hours, depending on your physical condition, I recommend taking the earlier bus so that you can start hiking when the day is still young or, better still, arriving the day before and spending the night in San Gerardo de Rivas (there are inexpensive *cabinas* there) before setting out early the following morning.

Before climbing Mount Chirripó, you must check in with the National Parks office (© **200-5348**) in San Gerardo de Rivas. The office is open from 6am to 4pm daily. I highly recommend checking in the day before you plan to climb if possible. If you plan to stay at the lodge near the summit, you must make reservations in advance because accommodations there are limited (see "Staying at the Summit Lodge," below). Note that camping is not allowed in the park. It's possible to have your gear carried up to the summit by horseback during the dry season (Dec–Apr). Guides work outside the park entrance in San Gerardo de Rivas. They charge between $20 and $25 (£10–£13) per pack, depending on size and weight. In the rainy season the same guides work, but they take packs up by themselves, not by horseback. The guides like to take up the packs well before dawn, so arrangements are best made the day before.

STAYING AT THE SUMMIT LODGE   Reservations for lodging on the summit of Mount Chirripó must be made with the **National Parks office** in San Isidro de El General (ⓒ/fax **771-3155** or 771-5116). This is an increasingly popular destination, and you must reserve well in advance during the dry season. The lodge holds only 60 people and fills up quite frequently. *Tip:* Many of the local tour agencies prebook the lodge beds, making it often difficult to impossible to do so on your own. If you can't book a bed by yourself, ask at your hotel, or contact one of the tour agencies listed below in "Other Adventures in & around San Isidro."

Once you get to the lodge, you'll find various rooms with bunk beds, several bathrooms and showers, and a common kitchen area complete with pots, pans, plates, and silverware. There is good drinking water at the lodge, and blankets, lanterns, and cook stoves for rent, although you have to pack your own food and water for the hike up. *Note:* It gets cold up here at night, and the lodge seems to have been designed to be as cold, dark, and cavernous as possible. No consideration was made to take advantage of the ample passive solar potential. The showers are freezing. It costs $10 (£5) per person per night to stay here; the entrance fee to the national park is $15 (£7.50) for your first 2 days, and then $10 (£5) for each additional day.

Warning: It can be dangerous for more inexperienced or out-of-shape hikers to climb Chirripó, especially by themselves. It's not very technical climbing, but it is a long, arduous hike. If you're not sure you're up for it, you can just take day hikes out of San Isidro and/or San Gerardo de Rivas, or ask at your hotel about guides.

OTHER ADVENTURES IN & AROUND SAN ISIDRO

If you want to undertake any other adventures while in San Isidro, contact **Costa Rica Trekking Adventures** (ⓒ **771-4582;** fax 771-8841; www.chirripo.com), or **CIPRO-TUR** (ⓒ **771-6096;** www.ecotourism.co.cr). Both offer organized treks through Chirripó National Park, as well as white-water rafting trips and other adventure tours and activities.

Just 7km (4⅓ miles) from San Isidro is **Las Quebradas Biological Center** (ⓒ/fax **771-4131**), a community-run private reserve with 2.7km (1¾ miles) of trails through primary rainforest. There's a rustic lodge for visitors and researchers ($25/£13 per person; $15/£7.50 students, including three meals), and camping is also permitted. There's an information center here and a small souvenir store. You can hike the trails here and visit the small information center for $5 (£2.50). From San Isidro, you can take a local bus to Quebradas, but you'll have to walk the last mile to the entrance. You can also take a taxi for around $8 (£4). If you're driving, take the road to Morazán and Quebradas.

WHERE TO STAY & DINE

In addition to the hotels listed below, there's a modern, yet soulless, three-story business-class option, **Hotel Diamante** (ⓒ **770-6230;** www.hoteldiamantereal.com), located 1 block west of the main bus station.

There are no notable restaurants in San Isidro. The town has its fair share of local joints, but most visitors are content at their hotel restaurant. If you do venture beyond your hotel, your best options are the **México Lindo** (ⓒ **771-8222**) and the **Pizzería El Tenedor** (ⓒ **771-0881**), both located just off the central park. Although the food is mediocre, the second-floor, open-air balcony seating at **La Cascada** (ⓒ **771-6479**) offers some excellent opportunities for people-watching, and is a great place to mingle with locals.

Hotel Iguazú   This is a good, clean, safe choice in San Isidro. The rooms are basic and come in different sizes with different arrangements of beds, but all have small televisions. The rooms are definitely in better shape than those at the more popular budget choice, the Hotel Chirripó. The hotel is half a block away from the Musoc bus station. Some might find this convenient; others might find it too noisy. The hotel is actually on the second and third floors of the Gallo Mas Gallo department store.

San Isidro de El General (above the Gallo Mas Gallo store). © 771-2571. Fax 771-4451. 22 units, 17 w/private bathroom. $8 (£4) double w/shared bathroom; $23 (£12) double w/private bathroom. V. *In room:* TV.

Hotel Los Crestones   This two-story hotel offers the newest, cleanest and most comfortable rooms in San Isidro. All rooms are relatively large and come with air-conditioning, but it costs an extra $10 (£5) to use it. I prefer the units on the second floor, which share a broad tiled veranda. These folks have recently added a midsize outdoor swimming pool and separate Jacuzzi. Hotel Los Crestones is located 4 blocks south of San Isidro's central park.

San Isidro de El General (southwest side of the stadium). © 770-1500. Fax 770-5047. www.hotelloscrestones.com. 27 units. $47–$52 (£24–£26) double. Rates include breakfast. MC, V. **Amenities:** Restaurant; outdoor pool; tour desk; laundry service. *In room:* A/C, TV, free Wi-Fi.

WHERE TO STAY CLOSER TO THE TRAIL HEAD

If you're climbing Mount Chirripó, you'll want to spend the night as close to the trail head as possible. As mentioned above, several basic *cabinas* right in San Gerardo de Rivas charge between $5 and $10 (£2.50–£5) per person. The best of these are **El Descanso** (© **369-0067**) and **Roca Dura** (© **363-7318;** luisrocadura@hotmail.com). If you're looking for a little more comfort, check out the lodge listed below.

Talari Mountain Lodge ⭐   This small mountain getaway is nothing fancy, but it is one of the nicer options right around San Isidro, and it also makes a good base for exploring or climbing Mount Chirripó. The rooms are in two separate concrete-block buildings. Most come with one double and one single bed, although one room can handle a family of four in one double and two single beds. Each room comes with a small fridge and a small patio. I prefer the four rooms that face the Talamanca Mountains. There are plenty of fruit trees around and good bird-watching right on the grounds. (They've identified more than 200 bird species here.) The hotel borders the Río General and maintains some forest trails. Talari is located 8km (5 miles) outside of San Isidro, and a staff member picks you up in town for free with advance notice. Remember, if you're here just to climb the mountain, this lodge is about 11km (6¾ miles) from San Gerardo de Rivas, so you'll probably also have to arrange transportation to and from the park entrance.

Rivas, San Isidro (A.P. 517-8000, Pérez Zeledón). ©/fax **771-0341.** www.talari.co.cr. 8 units. $56 (£28) double. Rates include full breakfast. AE, MC, V. Closed Sept 16–Oct 31. **Amenities:** Restaurant; bar; small pool and separate children's pool; tour desk; laundry service. *In room:* Fridge, no phone.

ⓘ Tips   Rest Your Weary Muscles Here

If you're tired and sore from so much hiking, be sure to check out the small **Herradura Hot Springs** (© **391-8107**) located off the road between San Gerardo de Rivas and Herradura. The entrance to the springs is 1km (½ mile) beyond San Gerardo de Rivas. The entrance fee is $3 (£1.50).

EN ROUTE TO SAN JOSE: THREE PLACES
TO SEE QUETZALS IN THE WILD

Between San Isidro de El General and San José, the Interamerican Highway climbs to its highest point in Costa Rica and crosses over the Cerro de la Muerte. This area is one of the best places in Costa Rica to see quetzals. March, April, and May is nesting season for these birds, and this is usually the best time to see them. However, it's often possible to spot them year-round here. On my first visit here, a 2-hour hike without a guide, my small group spotted eight of these amazing birds. I was hooked.

In addition to the places listed below, **Dantica Cloud Forest Lodge** (© 740-1067; www.dantica.com) is a small collection of private bungalows, in a beautiful forested setting in this region, near the town of San Gerardo de Dota.

Mirador de Quetzales   This family-run lodge is also known as Finca Eddie Serrano. The rooms in the main lodge are quite basic, with wood floors, bunk beds, and shared bathrooms. Eight separate A-frames provide a bit more comfort and a private bathroom. Meals are served family style in the main lodge. But quetzals, not comfort, are the main draw here, and if you come between December and May, you should have no trouble spotting plenty of them. There are good hiking trails through the cloud forest, and the Serrano family members are genial hosts and good guides. On a clear day you can see the peaks of five volcanoes from the hotel's lookout—but it's not that clear often. The lodge is about 1km (½ mile) down a dirt road from the highway.

Carretera Interamericana Sur Km 70 (A.P. 985-7050, Cartago). ©/fax **381-8456**. 11 units. $47 (£24) per person. Rate includes 3 meals, a 2-hr. tour, and taxes. AE, MC, V. **Amenities:** Restaurant; bar. *In room:* No phone.

Savegre Mountain Hotel   This working apple-and-pear farm, which also has more than 240 hectares (593 acres) of primary forest, has acquired a reputation for superb birdwatching—it's one of the best places in the country to see quetzals. The rooms are basic, but if you're serious about birding, this shouldn't matter. In addition to the quetzals, some 170 other species have been spotted here. Hearty Tico meals are served, and if you want to try your hand at trout fishing, you might luck into a fish dinner. You'll find this lodge 9km (5½ miles) down a dirt road off the Interamerican Highway. This road is steep and often muddy, and four-wheel-drive is recommended, although not necessary.

Carretera Interamericana Sur Km 80, San Gerardo de Dota (A.P. 482, Cartago). © **740-1028**. Fax 740-1027. www.savegre.co.cr. 41 cabins. $161–$217 (£81–£109) double. Rates include all meals, nonalcoholic drinks, entrance to their reserve, and taxes. AE, MC, V. **Amenities:** Restaurant; bar; tour desk; laundry service.

Trogon Lodge 🐸 *(Finds*   This is the most attractive and comfortable of the lodges in the area. The rooms are rather basic, but the grounds, setting, and amenities are much nicer than at the lodges listed above. The rooms are all of good size, with wood floors, wood walls, a shared veranda, and one double and one twin bed. Room nos. 15 and 16 are my favorites; they are the farthest from the main lodge and have great views of the river. The family-style meals often feature fresh trout from their well-stocked trout ponds; as at Savegre Mountain Hotel, more than half the fun is catching it yourself. These folks have their own little zip-line canopy tour.

Carretera Interamericana Sur Km 80, San Gerardo de Dota (A.P. 10980-1000, San José). © **293-8181** in San José, or 740-1051 at the lodge. Fax 239-7657. www.grupomawamba.com/trogonlodge. 23 units. $74 (£37) double; $120 (£60) junior suite w/Jacuzzi. A full meal package runs $33 (£17) per person. AE, MC, V. **Amenities:** Restaurant; bar; tour desk; laundry service; pool table; TV room in lodge. *In room:* No phone.

The Southern Zone

Costa Rica's southern zone is an area of rugged beauty, with vast expanses of virgin lowland rainforest and few cities or settlements. Lushly forested mountains tumble into the sea, streams still run clear and clean, scarlet macaws squawk raucously in the treetops, and dolphins frolic in the Golfo Dulce. The Osa Peninsula is the most popular attraction in this region and one of the premier ecotourism destinations in the world. It's home to **Corcovado National Park** ✶✶✶, the largest single expanse of lowland tropical rainforest in Central America, and its sister, **Piedras Blancas National Park** ✶✶. Scattered around the edges of these national parks and along the shores of the Golfo Dulce are some of the country's finest nature lodges. These lodges, in general, offer comfortable to nearly luxurious accommodations, attentive service, knowledgeable guides, and a wide range of activities and tours, all close to the area's many natural wonders.

But this beauty doesn't come easy. You must have plenty of time (or plenty of money—or, preferably, both) and a desire for adventure. It's a long way from San José, and many of the most fascinating spots can be reached only by small plane or boat—although hiking and four-wheeling will get you into some memorable surroundings as well. In many ways, this is Costa Rica's final frontier, and the cities of Golfito and Puerto Jiménez are nearly as wild as the jungles that surround them. Tourism is still underdeveloped here; there are no large resorts in this neck of the woods. Moreover, the heat and humidity are more than many people can stand. So it's best to put some forethought into planning a vacation down here, and it's usually wise to book your rooms and transportation in advance.

1 Drake Bay ✶✶

145km (90 miles) S of San José; 32km (20 miles) SW of Palmar

While Drake Bay remains one of the most isolated places on the planet, the small town located at the mouth of the **Río Agujitas** is experiencing a definite construction and tourism boom. Most of that is due to the opening of a small airstrip here, and the sometimes passable condition of the rough dirt road connecting Drake Bay to the coastal highway—just a few years ago there was no road, and the nearest airstrip was in Palmar Sur. That said, the lodges listed here remain quiet and remote getaways catering to naturalists, anglers, scuba divers, and assorted vacationers. Located on the northern edge of the Osa Peninsula, Drake Bay is a great place to get away from it all.

The bay is named after Sir Francis Drake, who is believed to have anchored here in 1579. Emptying into a broad bay, the tiny Río Agujitas acts as a protected harbor for small boats and is a great place to do a bit of canoeing or swimming. It's here that many of the local lodges dock their boats. Stretching south from Drake Bay are miles of deserted beaches and dense primary tropical rainforest. Adventurous explorers will

> **⟨Tips⟩ Helping Out**
>
> If you want to help local efforts in protecting the fragile rainforests and wild areas of the Osa Peninsula, contact the **Corcovado Foundation** (© 297-3013; www.corcovadofoundation.org) or the **Friends of the Osa** (© 735-5756; www. osaconservation.org).

find tide pools, spring-fed rivers, waterfalls, forest trails, and some of the best bird-watching in all of Costa Rica. If a paradise such as this appeals to you, Drake Bay makes a good base for exploring the peninsula.

South of Drake Bay lay the wilds of the **Osa Peninsula,** including **Corcovado National Park.** This is one of Costa Rica's most beautiful regions, yet it's also one of its least accessible. Corcovado National Park covers about half of the peninsula and contains the largest single expanse of virgin lowland rainforest in Central America. For this reason, Corcovado is well known among naturalists and researchers studying rainforest ecology. If you come here, you'll learn firsthand why they call them rainforests: Some parts of the peninsula receive more than 250 inches of rain per year.

Puerto Jiménez (see later in this chapter) is the best base to choose if you want to spend a lot of time hiking in and camping inside Corcovado National Park. Drake Bay is primarily a collection of mostly high-end hotels, very isolated and mostly accessible only by boat. Travelers using these hotels can have great day hikes and guided tours into Corcovado Park, but Puerto Jiménez is the place if you want to have more time in the park or to explore independently. (It has a range of budget hotels, the parks office, and "taxi/bus" service to Carate and Los Patos, from which visitors can hike into the various stations.) From the Drake Bay side, you're much more dependent on a boat ride/organized tour from one of the lodges to explore the park; these lodges offer many other guided outings in addition to visits to the park.

ESSENTIALS

Because Drake Bay is so remote, I recommend that you have a room reservation and transportation arrangements (usually arranged with your hotel) before you arrive. Most of the lodges listed here are scattered along several kilometers of coastline, and it is not easy to go from one to another looking for a room.

Tip: A flashlight and rain gear are always useful to have on hand in Costa Rica; they're absolutely essential in Drake Bay.

GETTING THERE   By Plane   Most people are flying directly into the little airstrip at Drake Bay, although some tourists still fly to Palmar Sur. Most lodges include transportation in their packages, so check with them about where you will be flying into. **Sansa** (© 290-4100; www.flysansa.com) flies directly to Drake Bay daily at 6 and 10:30am and 1:05 and 1:40pm from San José's Juan Santamaría International Airport. The return flights leave Drake Bay at 7 and 11:30am and 2 and 2:30pm. The flight takes 50 minutes; the fare is $84 (£42) each way. Another flight departs San José daily at 9:30am for Palmar Sur; the fare is $75 (£38) each way. Note that Sansa frequently alters its schedule and routing; this flight might stop in Quepos on the way down and thus could take slightly longer.

Nature Air (© 800/235-9272 in the U.S. and Canada, or 299-6000; www.natureair. com) has direct flights to Drake Bay departing daily from Tobías Bolaños International

Tapantí National Park

↖To San José

Cerro de la Muerte

CHIRRIPÓ INDIAN RESERVATION

TALAMANCA INDIAN RESERVATION

BRIBRI INDIAN RESERVATION

PANAMA

Cerro Chirripó

TALAMANCA RANGE (CORDILLERA DE TALAMANCA)

LA AMISTAD INTERNATIONAL PARK

Cerro Kámuk

San Isidro de El General

Peñas Blancas

Interamerican Hwy.

Río Pacuare

SALITRE INDIAN RESERVATION

Dominical

↖To Quepos & Manuel Antonio

Buenos Aires

Punta Uvita

BALLENA MARINE NATIONAL PARK

El Brujo

Playa Ballena

Playa Píñuela

Ojochal

Ciudad Cortes

Palmar Norte

Boca Brava

Palmar Sur Airport

CURRÉ INDIAN RESERVATION

Coronado Bay

Río Sierpe

Sierpe

Sabanilla

Sabalito

Piedras Blancas

San Vito

Río Chocuaco

PIEDRAS BLANCAS NATIONAL PARK

Wilson Botanical Garden

Drake Bay

Golfito Airport

Río Claro

Caño Island

Chocuaco Lake

Rincón

La Palma

Golfito

↖To Panama

Caño Island Biological Reserve

OSA PENINSULA

OSA INDIAN RESERVATION

Playa Cativa

Ciudad Neily

Corcovado Lake

Los Patos Ranger Station

Lake Colorado

San Pedrillo

El Tigre

Playa Zancudo

Río Colorado

Zancudo

CORCOVADO NATIONAL PARK

Puerto Jiménez

Playa Sirena

La Leona Ranger Station

Carate

Playa Tamale

Playa Pavones

Pavones

Cabo Matapalo

Punta Banco

PANAMA

PACIFIC OCEAN

NICARAGUA

COSTA RICA

Caribbean Sea

San José

PACIFIC OCEAN

Area of detail

PANAMA

0   100 mi
0   100 km

Airport ✈
Ferry 🚢
Mountain ▲
Ranger Station 🏠

0   50 mi
0   50 km

Punta Buríca

N

Airport in Pavas at 8:10am and 3pm. Flight duration is 50 minutes; the fare is $92 (£46) each way. The return flights leave Drake Bay at 9am and 3:50pm. It also has a daily flight to Palmar Sur that departs at 9am and sometimes stops at Quepos en route. The flight takes a little over an hour, and the fare is $80 (£40) each way.

If your travels take you to Drake Bay via Palmar Sur, you must then take a 15-minute bus or taxi ride over dirt roads to the small town of **Sierpe**. This bumpy route runs through several banana plantations and quickly past some important archaeological sites. In Sierpe you board a small boat for a 40km (25-mile) ride to Drake Bay; see "By Taxi & Boat from Sierpe," below. The first half of this trip snakes through a maze of mangrove canals and rivers before heading out to sea for the final leg to the bay. *Warning:* Entering and exiting the Sierpe River mouth is often treacherous; I've had several very white-knuckle moments here.

By Bus **Tracopa** express buses (© **221-4214**) leave San José daily for Palmar Norte at 5, 7, 8:30, and 10am, and 1, 2:30, and 6pm from Calle 5 between avenidas 18 and 20. Bus trips take 6 hours; the fare is $6.35 (£3.20).

You can also catch any Golfito-bound bus from this same station and get off in Palmar Norte. Once in Palmar Norte, ask when the next bus goes out to Sierpe. If it doesn't leave for a while (buses aren't frequent), consider taking a taxi (see below).

By Taxi & Boat from Sierpe When you arrive at either the Palmar Norte bus station or the Palmar Sur airstrip, you'll most likely first need to take a taxi to the village of Sierpe. The fare should be around $15 (£7.50). If you're booked into one of the main lodges, chances are your transportation is already included. Even if you're not booked into one of the lodges, a host of taxi and minibus drivers offer the trip. When you get to Sierpe, head to the dock and try to find space on a boat. This should run you another $15 to $30 (£7.50–£15). If you don't arrive early enough, you might have to hire an entire boat, which usually runs around $80 to $120 (£40–£60) for a boat that can carry up to six passengers. Make sure that you feel confident about the boat and skipper, and, if possible, try to find a spot on a boat from one of the established lodges in Drake Bay.

By Car Driving to Drake Bay isn't recommended. But if you insist, take the Interamerican Highway east out of San José (through San Pedro and Cartago) and continue south on this road. In about 3 hours you'll reach San Isidro de El General. Although you can continue on the Interamerican Highway all the way south, it is faster, smoother, and safer to turn off in San Isidro and head to Dominical, picking up the Southern Highway or Costanera Sur in Dominical. From here it's a fast and smooth shot down Palmar Norte, where you meet up again with the Interamerican Highway. South of Palmar take the turnoff for La Palma and Puerto Jiménez (at the town of Chacarita; it's clearly marked). Then at Rincón, turn onto the rough road leading into Drake Bay. This road fords some 10 rivers and is often not passable during the rainy season. Moreover, it only reaches into the small heart of the village of Drake Bay, whereas almost all of the hotels I've listed below are farther out along the peninsula, where only boats reach. In fact, the only hotels that you can actually drive up to are very basic cabins in town. For the rest, you'd have to find someplace secure to leave your car and either haul your bags quite a way or get picked up in a boat.

DEPARTING If you're not flying directly out of Drake Bay, have your lodge arrange a boat trip back to Sierpe for you. Be sure that the lodge also arranges for a taxi to meet you in Sierpe for the trip to Palmar Sur or Palmar Norte. (If you're on a budget, you can ask around to see whether a late-morning public bus is still running from Sierpe to Palmar Norte.) In the two Palmars you can make onward plane and bus connections. At the Palmar Norte bus terminal, almost any bus heading north will take you to San José, and almost any bus heading south will take you to Golfito.

WHAT TO SEE & DO

Beaches, forests, wildlife, and solitude are the main attractions of Drake Bay. Although Corcovado National Park (see "Puerto Jiménez: Gateway to Corcovado National Park," later in this chapter) is the area's star attraction, there's plenty to soak up in Drake Bay. The Osa Peninsula is home to an unbelievable variety of plants and animals: more than 140 species of mammals, 380 species of birds, and 120 species of amphibians and reptiles. You aren't likely to see a high percentage of these animals, but you can expect to see quite a few, including several species of monkeys, coatimundis, scarlet macaws, parrots, and hummingbirds. Other park inhabitants include jaguars, tapirs, sloths, and crocodiles. If you're lucky, you might even see one of the region's namesake *osas,* the giant anteaters.

Around Drake Bay and within the national park are many miles of trails through rainforests and swamps, down beaches, and around rock headlands. All of the lodges listed below offer guided excursions into the park. It's also possible to begin a hike around the peninsula from Drake Bay.

One of the most popular excursions from Drake Bay is a trip out to **Isla del Caño** and the **Caño Island Biological Reserve** ⚜⚜ for a bit of exploring and snorkeling or scuba diving. The island is located about 19km (12 miles) offshore from Drake Bay and was once home to a pre-Columbian culture about which little is known. A trip to the island will include a visit to an ancient cemetery, and you'll also be able to see some of the stone spheres believed to have been carved by this area's ancient inhabitants (see the nearby box, "Those Mysterious Stone Spheres"). Few animals or birds live on the island, but the coral reefs just offshore teem with life and are the main reason most people come here. This is one of Costa Rica's prime **scuba spots** ⚜⚜. Visibility is often quite good, and there's even easily accessible snorkeling from the beach. All of the lodges listed below offer trips to Isla del Caño.

All lodges in the area also offer a host of half- and full-day tours and activities, including hikes in Corcovado National Park, horseback rides, and sportfishing. In some cases, tours are included in your room rate or package; in others, they must be bought a la carte. Other options include mountain biking and sea kayaking. Most of these tours run between $60 and $110 (£30–£55), depending on the activity, with scuba diving ($100–$120/£50–£60 for a two-tank dive) and sportfishing ($450–$1,200/£225–£600), depending on the size of the boat and other amenities) costing a bit more.

One of the most interesting tour options in Drake Bay is a 2-hour **night tour** ⚜⚜ (www.thenighttour.com; $35/£18 per person) offered by Tracie Stice, who is affectionately known as the "Bug Lady." Equipped with flashlights, participants get a bug's-eye view of the forest at night. You might see reflections of some larger forest dwellers, but most of the tour is a fascinating exploration of the nocturnal insect and arachnid world. Consider yourself lucky if she finds the burrow of a trap-door spider or large tarantula. Avoid this tour if you are helplessly arachnophobic. Also, the folks from the **Original Canopy Tour** (© 291-4465; www.canopytour.com) have set up an operation in Drake Bay in the forest behind the Hotel Jinetes de Osa. The 2½-hour tour costs $45 (£23) per person. Any hotel in the area can book either of the above tours for you.

Those Mysterious Stone Spheres

Although Costa Rica lacks the great cities, giant temples, and bas-relief carvings of the Maya, Aztec, and Olmec civilizations of northern Mesoamerica, its pre-Columbian residents did leave a unique legacy that continues to cause archaeologists and anthropologists to scratch their heads and wonder. Over a period of several centuries, hundreds of painstakingly carved and carefully positioned granite spheres were left by the peoples who lived throughout the Diquís Delta, which flanks the Terraba River in southern Costa Rica. The orbs, which range from grapefruit size to more than 2m (6½ ft.) in diameter, can weigh up to 15 tons, and many reach near-spherical perfection.

Archaeologists believe that the spheres were created during two defined cultural periods. The first, called the Aguas Buenas period, dates from around A.D. 100 to 500. Few spheres survive from this time. The second phase, during which spheres were created in apparently greater numbers, is called the Chiriquí period and lasted from approximately A.D. 800 to 1500. The "balls" believed to have been carved during this timeframe are widely dispersed along the entire length of the lower section of the Terraba River. To date, only one known quarry for the spheres has been discovered, in the mountains above the Diquís Delta, which points to a difficult and lengthy transportation process.

Some archaeologists believe that the spheres were hand-carved in a very time-consuming process, using stone tools, perhaps aided by some sort of firing process. However, another theory holds that granite blocks were placed at the bases of powerful waterfalls, and the hydraulic beating of the water eventually turned and carved the rock into these near-perfect spheres. And more than a few proponents have credited extraterrestrial intervention for the creation of the stone balls.

Most of the stone balls have been found at the archaeological remains of defined settlements and are associated with either central plazas or known burial sites. Their size and placement have been interpreted to have both social and celestial importance, although their exact significance remains a mystery. Unfortunately, many of the stone balls have been plundered and are currently used as lawn ornaments in the fancier neighborhoods of San José. Some have even been shipped out of the country. The **Museo Nacional de Costa Rica** (p. 124) has a nice collection, including one massive sphere in its center courtyard. It's a never-fail photo op. You can also see the stone balls near the small **airports in Palmar Sur** and **Drake Bay,** and on **Isla del Caño** (which is located 19km/12 miles off the Pacific coast near Drake Bay).

WHERE TO STAY & DINE

Given the remote location and logistics of reaching Drake Bay, as well as the individual isolation of each hotel, nearly all of the hotels listed below deal almost exclusively in package trips that include transportation, meals, tours, and taxes. I've listed the

> ### ⌒Tips Combing for Beaches
>
> While the beach at Drake Bay itself is acceptable and calm for swimming, it's far
> from spectacular. The most popular swimming beach is a pretty small patch of
> sand about a 7-minute hike down from La Paloma Lodge. The nicest beaches
> around involve taking a day trip to either Isla del Caño or San Josesito, a beau-
> tiful beach farther south on the peninsula with excellent snorkeling possibilities.

most common packages, although all the lodges will work with you to accommodate
longer or shorter stays. I've listed nightly room rates only where they're available and
practical, generally at the more moderately priced hotels.

In addition to the places listed below, **Guaria de Osa** ⋆ (© **358-9788;** www.guaria
deosa.com) is a beautiful lodge near the Río Claro that specializes in yoga, spiritual,
and educational retreats.

VERY EXPENSIVE

Aguila de Osa Inn ⋆   This luxurious hillside lodge is a great choice for serious
sportfishers and scuba divers. Situated high on a hill overlooking Drake Bay and the
Pacific Ocean, the Aguila de Osa Inn offers large, attractively decorated rooms (with
hardwood or tile floors, ceiling fans, large bathrooms, and excellent views), located a
vigorous hike up a steep hillside. This could pose a problem for those with mobility
or health issues because the restaurant, reception, and docks are located far below,
around river level. A bar is built atop some rocks on the bank of the Río Agujitas, and
the open-air dining room is set amidst lush foliage with a partial view of the bay
through the leaves. Meals are simply prepared but tasty and filling, and the kitchen
leaves a fresh Thermos of coffee outside each room every morning.

Because most folks are out for the day fishing or taking one of the organized tours,
lunches are often picnic affairs on the boat, in Corcovado National Park, or on Isla del
Caño. Dinners feature fresh fish, meat, and chicken, often prepared with a tropical or
Caribbean flair.

Drake Bay (mailing address: Interlink 898, P.O. Box 025635, Miami, FL 33102). © **866/924-8452** in the U.S., or
296-2190 in Costa Rica. Fax 232-7722. www.aguiladeosainn.com. 13 units. $541–$613 (£271–£307) for 3 days/2
nights; $809–$917 (£405–£459) for 4 days/3 nights. Rates are per person based on double occupancy and include
round-trip transportation from Palmar Sur, all meals, and taxes. Lower rates in off season. AE, MC, V. **Amenities:**
Restaurant; bar; fleet of sportfishing and dive vessels; laundry service. *In room:* No phone.

Casa Corcovado Jungle Lodge ⋆   This very isolated jungle lodge is the closest
accommodation to Corcovado National Park on this end of the Osa Peninsula. The
rooms are all private bungalows built on the grounds of an old cacao plantation on
the jungle's edge. The bungalows are very spacious, with one or two double beds (each
with mosquito netting) and a large tiled bathroom. Electricity and hot water are sup-
plied by a combination solar and hydroelectric energy system. Family-style meals are
served in the main lodge, although most guests take lunch with them to the beach or
on one of the various tours available. Late afternoons are usually enjoyed from a high
point overlooking the sea and sunset, with your beverage of choice in hand. Access is
strictly by small boat, and sometimes the beach landing can be a bit rough, so it's recommended that guests be in decent physical shape. When the sea is calm, the beach
is great for swimming; when it is rough, it's a great place to grab a hammock in the

shade and read a book. The lodge has two pretty swimming pools, both surrounded by thick rainforest, and a wide range of tours and activities is available.

Osa Peninsula (mailing address: Interlink 253, P.O. Box 526770, Miami, FL 33152). © **888/896-6097** in the U.S., or 256-3181 in Costa Rica. Fax 256-7409. www.casacorcovado.com. 14 units. $765–$795 (£383–£398) per person for 3 days/2 nights w/1 tour; $925–$955 (£463–£478) for 4 days/3 nights w/2 tours. Rates are based on double occupancy and include round-trip transportation from San José, all meals, park fees, and taxes. Rates slightly higher during peak weeks; lower in off season. AE, MC, V. **Amenities:** Restaurant; 2 bars; 2 outdoor pools; laundry service. *In room:* Stocked minibar, safe, no phone.

La Paloma Lodge ★★★ (Finds   Set on a steep hill overlooking the Pacific, with Isla del Caño in the distance, the luxurious individual bungalows at La Paloma offer expansive ocean views that, combined with the attentive and amiable service, make this my top choice in Drake Bay. The main lodge building is a large, open-air structure with a long veranda that has a sitting area and swing chairs where you can mingle with other guests. All of the cabins are built on stilts, feature private verandas, and are set among lush foliage facing the Pacific. The large two-story Sunset Ranchos are the choice rooms here: Sliding screen windows and doors keep you in touch with nature and let the ocean breezes blow through, and the views are to die for. The other cabins are a tad smaller, but all are plenty spacious and beautifully appointed, and feature luxurious bathrooms and pretty good ocean views as well. The standard rooms, which are located in a row in one long building, are smaller and less private than the cabins, but they're still quite attractive and have good views from their verandas (which, like the cabins, have hammocks). The beach is about a 7-minute hike down a winding jungle path, and the lodge also offers scuba certification courses. Single and double kayaks, boogie boards, and surfboards are available and free for guests to use.

Hearty and delicious meals are served family style in the restaurant; with advance notification, the kitchen will accommodate vegetarians and others with special dietary needs. There's scrumptious freshly baked bread served with almost every meal here.

Drake Bay (mailing address: SJO Dept. 229, Box 025216, Miami, FL 33102-5216). © **293-7502** or ©/fax 239-0954. www.lapalomalodge.com. 11 units. $1,100–$1,400 (£550–£700) per person for 4 days/3 nights w/2 tours; $1,245–$1,625 (£623–£813) per person for 5 days/4 nights w/2 tours. Rates are based on double occupancy and include round-trip transportation from San José, all meals, park fees, indicated tours, and taxes. Rates slightly lower in off season. AE, MC, V. **Amenities:** Restaurant; bar; small tile pool w/spectacular view; free Wi-Fi around the main lodge; laundry service. *In room:* Minibar, safe, no phone.

EXPENSIVE

Drake Bay Wilderness Resort ★   This is one of the best-located lodges at Drake Bay. It backs onto the Río Agujitas and fronts the Pacific. The rooms here are less fancy than those at the more expensive resort lodges listed above, but they are clean and comfortable, with ceiling fans, small verandas, good mattresses on the beds, and private bathrooms. All of the rooms have been well maintained and periodically upgraded over the years, and they have a pretty deluxe honeymoon suite on a little hill toward the rear of the property, with a great view of the bay. There are also five budget cabins that share bathroom and shower facilities. The family-style meals are filling, with an emphasis on fresh seafood and fresh fruits. My favorite treats here are the freshly baked chocolate-chip cookies frequently served for dessert.

Because it's on a rocky spit, there isn't a good swimming beach on-site (it's about a 15-min. walk away), but there's a saltwater pool in front of the bay, and, depending on the tide, you can bathe in a beautiful small tide pool formed by the rocks. The resort offers a wide range of tour options. The lodge runs a small butterfly farm and iguana-breeding project on some land inland from Drake Bay, and you can even spend the night there if you want.

Drake Bay (A.P. 13710-1000, San José). © 770-8012 or 825-4130. Fax 250-1145. www.drakebay.com. 25 units. $85 (£43) per person per day w/shared bathroom; $120–$155 (£60–£78) per person per day standard and deluxe. Rates include all meals and taxes. $662 (£331) per person for 4 days/3 nights w/2 tours, including all meals, and taxes. Rates lower in off season. AE, MC, V. **Amenities:** Restaurant; bar; small saltwater pool; free use of canoes and kayaks; free same-day laundry service. *In room:* Hair dryer, no phone.

Hotel Jinetes de Osa   This is the best option right in the village of Drake Bay, and a good choice for serious divers and adventure tourists. Although no longer a budget lodging, it does offer a reasonable alternative to the more upscale options in the area. The nicest rooms here are spacious and well-appointed, and even have a view of the bay. The hotel is pretty close to the docks on the Río Agujitas, which is a plus for those traveling independently or with heavy bags. A wide range of tours and activities is available, as are dive packages, weekly packages, and PADI certification courses. For true budget travelers, camping is allowed on some land up a hill and just behind the main lodge.

Drake Bay (mailing address: 831 S. Newcombe Way, Lakewood, CO 80226). © 866/553-7073 in the U.S. and Canada, or 231-5806 in Costa Rica. Fax 241-2906. www.drakebayhotel.com. 9 units, 7 w/private bathroom. $130–$160 (£65–£80) double. Rates include 3 meals daily. MC, V. **Amenities:** Restaurant; bar. *In room:* Free Wi-Fi, no phone.

2 Puerto Jiménez ⟨★⟩: Gateway to Corcovado National Park

35km (22 miles) W of Golfito by water (90km/56 miles by road); 85km (53 miles) S of Palmar Norte

Despite its small size and languid pace, Puerto Jiménez is a bustling little burg, where rough jungle gold-panners mix with wealthy ecotourists, budget backpackers, and a smattering of celebrities seeking a small dose of anonymity and escape. Located on the southeastern tip of the Osa Peninsula, the town itself is just a couple of gravel streets with the ubiquitous soccer field, a block of general stores, some inexpensive *sodas* (diners), a butcher shop, and several bars. Scarlet macaws fly overhead, and mealy parrots provide wake-up calls.

   Corcovado National Park has its headquarters here, and this town makes an excellent base for exploring this vast wilderness. Signs in English on walls around town advertise a variety of tours, including a host of activities outside of the park. If the in-town accommodations are too budget-oriented, you'll find several far more luxurious places farther south on the Osa Peninsula. This is also a prime surf spot. **Cabo Matapalo** (the southern tip of the Osa Peninsula) is home to several very dependable right point breaks. When it's working, Pan Dulce and Backwash can provide rides almost as long and tiring as those to be had in more famous Pavones (see "Playa Pavones: A Surfer's Mecca," later in this chapter).

ESSENTIALS
GETTING THERE & DEPARTING   By Plane   Sansa (© **290-4100;** www.fly sansa.com) has flights to Puerto Jiménez daily at 6 and 10:30am and 1:05 and 1:40pm from San José's Juan Santamaría International Airport. The flight takes 55 minutes; the cost is $82 (£41) each way. Sansa flights depart Puerto Jiménez for San José daily at 7 and 11:30am and 2 and 2:30pm.

   Nature Air (© **800/235-9272** in the U.S. and Canada, or 299-6000; www.nature air.com) has flights to Puerto Jiménez departing from Tobías Bolaños International Airport in Pavas at 6, 8:30, and 10:50am and 3pm daily. The flight takes between 55 minutes and 1½ hours, depending on whether it stops en route; the fare is $92 (£46) each way. Nature Air flights to San José depart daily at 7, 9:30am, and 11:50am and 4:15pm.

Note that due to the remoteness of this area and the unpredictable flux of traffic, both Sansa and Nature Air frequently improvise on scheduling. Sometimes this means an unscheduled stop in Quepos or Golfito either on the way to or from San José, which can add some time to your flight. Less frequently it might mean a change in departure time, so it's always best to confirm. Also, lodges down here sometimes run charters, so it pays to ask them as well.

By Car   Take the Interamerican Highway east out of San José (through San Pedro and Cartago) and continue south on this road. In about 3 hours, you'll reach San Isidro de El General. Although you can continue on the Interamerican Highway all the way south, it is currently faster, smoother, and safer to turn off in San Isidro and head to Dominical, picking up the Southern Highway or Costanera Sur in Dominical. From here it's a fast and smooth shot down Palmar Norte, where you meet up again with the Interamerican Highway. Take the turnoff for La Palma, Rincón, and Puerto Jiménez. This road is paved at first, but at Rincón it turns to gravel. The last 35km (22 miles) are slow and rough, and, if it's the rainy season (mid-Apr to Nov), it'll be too muddy for anything but a four-wheel-drive vehicle.

By Bus   **Transportes Blanco-Lobo** express buses (© **257-4121** in San José or 771-4744 in Puerto Jiménez) leave San José daily at 6am and noon from Calle 12 between avenidas 7 and 9. The trip takes 8 hours; the fare is $6 (£3). Buses depart Puerto Jiménez for San José daily at 6 and 11am.

By Boat   There is daily passenger launch service from Golfito to Puerto Jiménez at 11:30am. The boat leaves from the municipal dock. Trip duration is 1½ hours; the fare is $3 (£1.50). The return trip departs Puerto Jiménez for Golfito from the public dock at 6am. It's also possible to charter a water taxi in Golfito for the trip across to Puerto Jiménez. You'll have to pay between $40 and $60 (£20–£30) for an entire launch, some of which can carry up to 12 people.

ORIENTATION   Puerto Jiménez is a dirt-lane town on the southern coast of the Osa Peninsula. The public dock is over a bridge past the north end of the soccer field; the bus stop is 2 blocks east of the center of town. You'll find a couple of Internet cafes in town; the best of these is **Cafe Net El Sol** (© **735-5719;** www.soldeosa.com), which is a great place to book tours and get information, and is also a Wi-Fi hot spot.

Four-wheel drive taxis are actually fairly plentiful in Puerto Jiménez. You can usually find them cruising or parked along the main street in town. Alternatively, you can call **Federico** (© **735-5678**), **Luis** (© **837-3120**), or **Orlando** (© **836-8241**). You can actually even rent a car down here from **Solid Car Rental** (© **735-5777;** www.solidcarrental.com).

EXPLORING CORCOVADO NATIONAL PARK 🐾🐾🐾

Exploring Corcovado National Park is not something to be undertaken lightly, but neither is it the expedition that some people make it out to be. The weather is the biggest obstacle to overnight backpacking trips through the park. Within a couple of hours of Puerto Jiménez (by 4WD vehicle) are several entrances to the park; however, there are no roads in the park, so once you reach any of the entrances, you'll have to start hiking. The heat and humidity are often quite extreme, and frequent rainstorms can make trails fairly muddy. If you choose the alternative—hiking on the beach—

(Tips Trail Distances in Corcovado National Park

It's 14km (8½ miles) from La Leona to Sirena. From Sirena to San Pedrillo, it's 23km (14 miles) along the beach. From San Pedrillo, it's 20km (12½ miles) to Drake Bay. It's 19km (12 miles) between Sirena and Los Patos.

you'll have to plan your hiking around the tides when often there is no beach at all and some rivers are impassable.

Because of its size and remoteness, Corcovado National Park is best explored over several days; however, it is possible to enter and hike a bit of it for day trips. The best way to do this is to book a tour with your lodge on the Osa Peninsula, from a tour company in Puerto Jiménez, or through a lodge in Drake Bay (see "Where to Stay & Dine," above).

GETTING THERE & ENTRY POINTS   The park has four primary entrances, which are really just ranger stations reached by rough dirt roads. When you've reached them, you'll have to strap on a backpack and hike. Perhaps the easiest one to reach from Puerto Jiménez is **La Leona ranger station,** accessible by car, bus, or taxi.

If you choose to drive, take the dirt road from Puerto Jiménez to Carate (Carate is at the end of the road). From Carate, it's a 3km (1¾-mile) hike to La Leona. To travel there by "public transportation," pick up one of the collective buses (actually, a 4WD pickup truck with a tarpaulin cover and slat seats in the back) that leave Puerto Jiménez for Carate daily at 6am and 1:30pm, returning at 8am and 4pm. Remember, these "buses" are very informal and change their schedules regularly to meet demand or avoid bad weather, so always ask in town. One-way fare is around $7 (£3.50). A small fleet of these pickups leaves just south of the new bus terminal, and will stop to pick up anyone who flags them down along the way. Your other option is to hire a taxi to suit your schedule, which will charge approximately $60 to $70 (£30–£35) each way to or from Carate.

En route to Carate, you will pass several campgrounds and small lodges as you approach the park. If you are unable to get a spot at one of the campsites in the park, you can stay at one of these and hike the park during the day.

You can also travel to **El Tigre,** about 14km (8¾ miles) by dirt road from Puerto Jiménez, where there's another ranger station. But note that trails from El Tigre go only a short distance into the park.

The third entrance is in **Los Patos,** which is reached from the town of La Palma, northwest of Puerto Jiménez. From here, there's a 19km (12-mile) trail through the center of the park to **Sirena,** a ranger station and research facility (see "Beach Treks & Rainforest Hikes," below). Sirena has a landing strip that is used by charter flights.

The northern entrance to the park is **San Pedrillo,** which you can reach by hiking from Sirena or by taking a boat from Drake Bay or Sierpe (see "Beach Treks & Rainforest Hikes," below). It's 14km (8¾ miles) from Drake Bay.

If you're not into hiking in the heat, you can charter a plane in Puerto Jiménez to take you to Carate or Sirena. A five-passenger plane should cost around $200 to $300 (£100–£150) one-way, depending on your destination. Contact **Alfa Romeo Air Charters** (© 735-5353 or 735-5112; www.alfaromeoair.com) for details.

FEES & REGULATIONS   Park admission is $8 (£4) per person per day, or you can buy a 5-day pass for $17 (£8.50). Only the Sirena station is equipped with dormitory-style lodgings and a simple *soda,* but the others have basic campsites and toilet facilities. All must be reserved in advance by contacting the **ACOSA (Area de Conservacion de**

Tips **Important Corcovado Tips**

If you plan to hike the beach trails from La Leona or San Pedrillo, be sure to pick up a tide table at the park headquarters' office in Puerto Jiménez. The tide changes rapidly; when it's high, the trails and river crossings can be dangerous or impassable.

If you plan to spend a night or more in the park, you'll want to stock up on food, water, and other essentials while you're in Puerto Jiménez. There's a mini-market in Carate, but the selection is limited. Although most of the stations have simple *sodas,* you need to reserve in advance if you plan to take your meals at any of these.

Osa) in Puerto Jiménez (© **735-5036;** fax 735-5276; www.corcovado.org). Its offices are adjacent to the airstrip. Only a limited number of people are allowed to camp at each ranger station, so make your reservations well in advance.

BEACH TREKS & RAINFOREST HIKES   The park has quite a few good hiking trails. Two of the better-known ones are the beach routes, starting at either the La Leona or San Pedrillo ranger stations. None of the hikes is easy, but the forest route from the Los Patos ranger station to Sirena, although long, is less taxing than either of the beach treks, which can be completed only when the tide is low. The route between the Los Patos/Sirena hike is 19km (12 miles) through beautiful rainforest.

Sirena is a fascinating destination. As a research facility and ranger station, it's frequented primarily by scientists studying the rainforest. One of the longest hikes, from San Pedrillo to Sirena, can be done only during the dry season. Between any two stations, the hiking is arduous and takes all day, so it's best to rest for a day or so between hikes if possible.

Remember, this is quite a wild area. Never hike alone, and take all the standard precautions for hiking in the rainforest. In addition, be especially careful about swimming in any isolated rivers or river mouths because most rivers in Corcovado are home to crocodiles.

WHERE TO STAY & DINE IN THE PARK: CAMPSITES, CABINS & CANTINAS
Reservations are essential at the various ranger stations if you plan to eat or sleep inside the park (see "Fees & Regulations," above). **Sirena** has a modern research facility with dormitory-style accommodations for 28 persons, as well as a campground, *soda,* and landing strip for charter flights. There is also camping at the **La Leona, Los Patos,** and **San Pedrillo** ranger stations. Every ranger station has potable water, but it's advisable to pack in your own; whatever you do, don't drink stream water. Campsites in the park are $4 (£2) per person per night. A dorm bed at the Sirena station will run you $12 (£6)—you must bring your own sheets, and a mosquito net is highly recommended— and meals here are another $29 (£15) per day. Everything must be reserved in advance.

ACTIVITIES OUTSIDE THE PARK
While Puerto Jiménez has typically been a staging ground for adventures much farther out toward Carate and the park, quite a few activities and tours can be undertaken closer to town.

If you're looking to spend some time on the beach, head just east of town for a long pretty stretch of sand called **Playa Plantanares.** The waves here are generally fairly gentle, and quite a few hotels have begun to pop up here. If you head farther out the peninsula, you'll come to the beaches of **Pan Dulce, Backwash,** and **Matapalo,** all major surf spots with consistently well-formed right point breaks. When the waves aren't too big, these are excellent places to learn how to surf.

Kayaking trips around the estuary and up into the mangroves and out into the gulf are popular. Contact **Escondido Trex** ☆ (© 735-5210; www.escondidotrex.com), which has an office in the Soda Carolina (see "Where to Dine in Puerto Jiménez," below). There are daily paddles through the mangroves, as well as sunset trips where you can sometimes see dolphins. These folks also do guided rainforest hikes and can have you rappelling down the face of a jungle waterfall. More adventurous multiday kayak and camping trips are also available, in price and comfort ranges from budget to luxury (staying at various lodges around the Golfo Dulce and Matapalo). They'll even take you gold-panning (although there are no guarantees that your panning will pay for the trip).

Closer to town, be sure to check out the **Herrera Botanical Gardens** ☆ (© 735-5210). These gardens are located just outside of town, and the entrance is across from Crocodile Bay. The whole project encompasses over 260 acres of botanical gardens, working permaculture gardens, and secondary forest. There are even a few platforms built high in the trees here and reached by climbing a ladder. A 2½-hour guided tour of the gardens costs $15 (£7.50), although you can wander the gardens yourself, with a self-guiding map, for just $4 (£2).

For a real adventure, check in with **Everyday Adventures** ☆☆ (© 353-8619; www.psychotours.com). These folks, who also call themselves Psycho Tours, run a variety of adventure tours, but their signature combo trip features a free climb up (with a safety rope attached) the roots and trunks of a 200-foot-tall strangler fig. You can climb as high as your ability allows, but most try to reach a natural platform at around 60 feet, where you take a leap of faith into space and are belayed down by your guide. This is preceded by an informative hike through primary rainforest, often wading through a small river, and followed by a couple of rappels down jungle waterfalls, the highest of which is around 100 feet. The 5- to 6-hour tour costs $110 (£55).

If you're interested in doing some **bill-fishing** or **deep-sea fishing,** you'll probably want to stay at or fish with **Crocodile Bay Lodge** (© 800/733-1115 in the U.S. and Canada, or 735-5631; www.crocodilebay.com). This upscale fishing lodge is close to the Puerto Jiménez airstrip. Alternatively, call Mike Hennessy at **Cabo Matapalo Sportfishing** ☆ (© 382-7796; www.cabo-matapalo.com). Mike is a longtime resident and one of the best captains around. You can also check around the public dock for notices put up by people with charter boats. Rates can run between $250 and $1,200 (£125–£600) for a full day, or between $100 and $600 (£50–£300) for a half-day, depending on the boat, tackle, number of anglers, and fishing grounds.

If you want to learn to surf, contact **Tres Amigos** ☆ (© 382-7796), which is also run by Mike Hennessy, and located near some excellent learning waves on Pan Dulce beach.

Osa Aventura (©/fax 735-5758, or 830-9832; www.osaaventura.com), **Sol de Osa** (© 735-5702; www.soldeosa.com), and **Tom Kayak's Osa Info** (© 838-2314) also offer a host of guided tours around the Osa Peninsula and into Corcovado National Park.

SHOPPING
Jagua Arts & Craft Store ☆☆ (© 735-5267) is located near the airstrip, and is definitely worth a visit. Owner Karen Herrera has found excellent local and regional art and craft works, including some excellent jewelry and blown glass. *Tip:* Many folks

head to this store while waiting for their departing flight out of Puerto Jiménez. Be sure to give yourself enough time, as the store has a wonderful and somewhat extensive collection.

WHERE TO STAY IN PUERTO JIMENEZ
EXPENSIVE
Parrot Bay Village 🏕 This collection of individual cabins is located on a spit of land jutting out into the gulf, just east of town and the airstrip. The smaller cabins are octagonal and have just one double bed, while the larger ones each feature a sleeping loft with a double and single bed above and a double bed below. There's a small restaurant and bar here and a large central deck with a view of the gulf. The grounds also include a pretty patch of beach and a semigroomed trail through the mangroves. There's a small-resort feel to the entire operation, and despite being just a short walk from town, it feels miles away.

A.P. 91, Puerto Jiménez. ✆ **866/551-2003** in U.S., or 735-5180 in Costa Rica. Fax 735-5568. www.parrotbayvillage. com. 9 units. $145 (£73) double. Rates include breakfast. Rates lower in off season; higher during peak weeks. MC, V. **Amenities:** Restaurant; bar; watersports equipment rental and free kayak use; tour desk; laundry service. *In room:* A/C, hair dryer, no phone.

MODERATE
Agua Luna Agua Luna is located right at the foot of the town's public dock and backs up to a mangrove forest. The older rooms directly face the gulf across a fenced-in gravel parking area. The most surprising feature in each of these rooms is the bathroom, which includes both a shower and a tub facing a picture window that looks into the mangroves. There are two double beds in each room, and on the tiled veranda out front, you'll find hammocks for lounging. The newer rooms are located a half-block away and are smaller and less attractive than those in the original building, although room nos. 4 and 5 in this building do overlook the mangroves.

In front of the public dock, Puerto Jiménez. ✆/fax **735-5393**. 20 units. $65 (£33) double. V. **Amenities:** Restaurant; laundry service. *In room:* A/C, TV, minifridge.

La Choza del Manglar Located a short distance from the airstrip, this long-standing hotel is one of the better in-town options. The rooms here are clean and comfortable, probably the most modern and tastefully decorated rooms you'll find in Puerto Jiménez proper. The hotel has several acres of mangroves and gardens, and the bird-watching and wildlife viewing are pretty good. The restaurant serves Costa Rican and international fare in a large, open-air space with colorful murals covering all of the walls. While this is a good in-town option, you're still several hundred meters or more from the water and from downtown Puerto Jiménez.

125m (410 ft.) west of the airstrip, Puerto Jiménez. ✆/fax **735-5605**. www.manglares.com. 10 units. $49–$119 (£25–£60) double. Rates higher during peak weeks; lower in off season. MC, V (5% surcharge). **Amenities:** Restaurant; bar; tour desk; laundry service; free Wi-Fi. *In room:* A/C, no phone.

INEXPENSIVE
In addition to the places listed below, you can camp or take advantage of some simple screened-in rooms at the beautiful **Herrera Botanical Gardens and Tent Camp** (✆ **735-5210**). Rates run around $12 to $15 (£6–£7.50) per person to camp; it's $20 (£10) per person in a screened-in room, with access to a communal kitchen, bathroom, and shower facilities, and unlimited access to the trails and gardens. If you don't have your own tent, they can rent you one.

Cabinas Jiménez *Value*   Located right on the waterfront at the north end of the soccer field, this perennial budget favorite is now much improved. All of the rooms have air-conditioning, tile floors, small fridges, coffeemakers, hot-water showers, and hand-carved headboards and Guatemalan bedspreads on the beds. Three units even have views of the water, with new wooden decks in front, and there's one private bungalow that's the choice room in the house. The wide range in prices, in fact, reflects the range in size and location of the rooms, and the fact that using the air-conditioning costs an extra $10. But even the most basic standard room here is a good option.

Downtown, 50m (164 ft.) north of the soccer field, Puerto Jiménez, Puntarenas. ℂ 735-5090. www.cabinasjimenez. com. 10 units. $45–$80 (£23–£40) double. A/C $10 (£5) extra. MC, V. *In room:* A/C, minifridge, coffeemaker, no phone.

Cabinas Oro Verde   The rooms at this budget hotel are on the second floor of a basic restaurant of the same name. The rooms are kept clean and have fans and fresh sheets. The five rooms in the front of the hotel share a narrow veranda over a sleepy street in Puerto Jiménez. The owners can help arrange a variety of tour and adventure options.

On a cross street in the center of town, 50m (164 ft.) east of the main road, Puerto Jiménez. ℂ 735-5241. 10 units. $20 (£10) double. MC, V. **Amenities:** Restaurant; laundry service. *In room:* No phone.

WHERE TO STAY IN PLAYA PLANTANARES
VERY EXPENSIVE
Iguana Lodge *⋆*   This place has a collection of large two-story bungalows set among palm trees and flowering gardens, just a few steps from the sand. Hardwood floors, bamboo furniture, and mosquito netting over orthopedic mattresses all add up to rustic tropical elegance. The lower units have delightful semi-outdoor garden showers, and all come with either a large covered balcony or veranda. Still, I prefer the second-floor rooms for their views and elevation. These folks also offer less-expensive rooms at the neighboring Pearl of the Osa Lodge, as well as a separate, private three-bedroom villa.

Playa Plantanares. ℂ 829-5865 or 848-0752. Fax 735-5436. www.iguanalodge.com. 8 units. $240 (£120) double. Rates include 3 meals daily. Rates lower in off season; higher during peak weeks. MC, V. **Amenities:** Restaurant; bar; watersports equipment rental; laundry service. *In room:* No phone.

WHERE TO DINE IN PUERTO JIMENEZ
In addition to the places listed below, locals also seem to enjoy the pizzas and occasional sushi at the open-air downtown Italian joint, **Il Giardino** (ℂ 735-5129).

Jade Luna *⋆⋆* FUSION   I can't quite figure out how a high-end fusion restaurant ended up at the end of a dirt road on the outskirts of this backwater town, but it has— and it's worth a visit. Heavy wooden tables are spread around the open-air first floor of this converted home. The small kitchen is clearly visible through the serving bar. Everything is softly lit and casually elegant. The menu changes regularly but might include Cajun blackened mahimahi with a fresh pineapple salsa, or grilled pork chops seasoned with a black pepper, star anise, and coffee rub. The appetizers and desserts are equally creative and unexpected. The small wine list features French and Italian wines, reasonably priced.

500 meters (5 blocks) east of the airstrip, Puerto Jiménez. ℂ 735-5739. Reservations recommended. Main courses $12–$16 (£6–£8). No credit cards. Mon–Sat 5–9pm.

Juanita's Mexican Bar & Grille *⋆* *Value* MEXICAN   This place offers good, hearty California-style Mexican food and seafood served up in a lively, convivial atmosphere. You can get fajitas with chicken, beef, fish, or even grilled vegetables. Juanita's also has pizza by the slice or pie, and will deliver, although I'm not sure how far out the peninsula their drivers will go. There are nightly specials and a popular happy hour. You can also order breakfast a la carte, or you can load up on an abundant breakfast buffet.

Downtown, Puerto Jiménez. (C) 735-5056. Reservations not accepted. Main courses $3–$8 (£1.50–£4). V. Daily 7am–midnight.

Soda Carolina COSTA RICAN   Set in the center of the town's main street, and otherwise known as the "Bar, Restaurante y Cabinas Carolina," this is the town's budget travelers' hangout and also serves as an unofficial information center. The walls are painted with colorful jungle and wildlife scenes. As for the fare, seafood is the way to go. There's good fried fish as well as a variety of ceviches. The black bean soup is usually tasty, and the *casados* (plates of the day) are filling and cost around $3.50 (£1.75).

On the main street. (C) 735-5185. Reservations not accepted. Main courses $3.50–$8.50 (£1.75–£4.25). V. Daily 7am–10pm.

WHERE TO STAY & DINE AROUND THE OSA PENINSULA

As with most of the lodges in Drake Bay, the accommodations listed in this section include three meals a day in their rates and do a large share of their bookings in package trips. Per-night rates are listed, but the price categories have been adjusted to take into account the fact that all meals are included. Ask about package rates if you plan to take several tours and stay a while: They could save you money.

In addition to the lodges listed below, there are several other options, ranging from small bed-and-breakfasts to fully equipped home rentals. Surfers, in particular, might want to inquire into one of the several rental houses located close to the beach at Matapalo. Your best bet for any of the above is to contact Isabel at **Osa Tropical** ((C) 735-5062).

Finally, there's been a small boom of lodges out in Carate. In addition to the tent lodge listed below you can look into **La Leona Eco-Lodge** ((C) 735-5705; www.laleona lodge.com), another tent camp option on the outskirts of the national park, and **Lookout Inn** ((C) 735-5431; www.lookout-inn.com), a more traditional lodge option right in Carate. Predominantly used for yoga retreats, **Luna Lodge** (★ ((C) 888/409-8448 in the U.S., or 380-5036; www.lunalodge.com) has luxurious rooms and private cabins with great views over the jungle, and they even have some permanent, large tents for the more budget-conscious travelers.

VERY EXPENSIVE

Bosque del Cabo Rainforest Lodge (★★★ *Finds*   This secluded jungle lodge is my favorite place in this neck of the woods. The individual cabins are all spacious and attractively furnished, have wooden decks or verandas to catch the ocean views, and are set amid beautiful gardens. Bosque del Cabo is located on top of a steep ridge overlooking the water at the southern tip of the Osa Peninsula, where the Golfo Dulce meets the Pacific Ocean. The deluxe cabins come with king-size beds and slightly larger deck space. The Congo cabin is my choice for its spectacular view of the sunrise from your bed. All cabins have indoor bathrooms; tiled showers are set outdoors amid flowering heliconia and ginger. About half of the units also have outdoor bathtubs.

There's a trail down to a secluded beach that has some tide pools and ocean-carved caves. Another trail leads to a jungle waterfall, and several others wind through the rainforests of the lodge's 650-acre private reserve. The wildlife viewing here is excellent. If you're too lazy to hike down to the beach, there's a beautiful pool by the main lodge. Surfing is a popular activity here, as are hiking and horseback riding. Attractions include a canopy platform 36m (118 ft.) up a Manu tree, reached along a 90m

(295-ft.) zip line, as well as a bird- and wildlife-watching rancho set beside a little lake on the edge of their tropical gardens and surrounded by forest. Local naturalists and environmental activists give talks each Wednesday night on various conservation and wildlife subjects. Trips to the national park or fishing excursions can be arranged, as can guided hikes, sea kayaking, and a host of other activities and tours. These folks also rent out two separate, fully equipped houses that are quite nice and popular, along with a couple of cabins set inland by their gardens.

Osa Peninsula (mailing address: Interlink 528, P.O. Box 02-5635, Miami, FL 33102). ©/fax **735-5206** or 389-2846. www.bosquedelcabo.com. 10 units. $350–$390 (£175–£195) double. Rates include 3 meals daily and taxes. $30 (£15) round-trip transportation from Puerto Jiménez. MC, V. **Amenities:** Restaurant; bar; midsize pool; surfboard rental; in-room or rainforest massage; laundry service. *In room:* No phone.

El Remanso ★★ This small collection of individual cabins and two-story units is set in a deep patch of primary forest bordering Bosque del Cabo. The best view of the ocean, over and through thick forest, can be had from the two-story deluxe La Vanilla unit, which can be rented whole, or split into two separate one-bedroom affairs. The upstairs room here is the best in the house, with plenty of space, varnished wood floors and a spacious balcony. If you want an individual cabin, Azul de Mar has the best view. All of the private cabins feature polished cement floors, a queen bed, and separate fold-down futon. There is a host of adventure activities available on the grounds here, including tree climbing, waterfall rappelling, and a zip-line canopy tour. They also have a large, open-air yoga platform, and frequently host yoga groups. The newest addition here is a small oval pool set in a stone deck area with great views to the ocean. The meals here are fresh, filling, and expertly prepared. Breakfasts can even be taken on a platform high atop a rainforest tree. The owners are committed to environmental protection. In fact, Joel and Belen Stewart met aboard the Greenpeace vessel *Rainbow Warrior,* which Joel captained for a number of years.

Osa Peninsula. © **735-5569.** Fax 735-5126. www.elremanso.com. 14 units. $290–$320 (£145–£160) double. Rates include 3 meals daily and all taxes. Rates lower in off season; slightly higher during peak periods. MC, V (6% surcharge). **Amenities:** Restaurant; bar; small pool; tour desk; laundry service. *In room:* No phone.

Lapa Ríos ★★ This is Costa Rica's most famous ecolodge. The hotel consists of eight duplex buildings perched along a steep ridge. Each spacious room is totally private and oriented toward the view. Walls have open screenings, and the ceiling is a high-peaked thatched roof. Mosquito nets drape languidly over the rooms' two queensize beds. A large deck and small tropical garden, complete with a hammock and outdoor shower, more than double the living space. There's an indoor shower in each room, which features open screen walls letting out on the view, so it's not all that different from being outdoors. *Note:* It's a bit of a hike back and forth from the main lodge to the farthest rooms.

The centerpiece of the lodge's large open-air dining room is a 15m (49-ft.) spiral staircase that leads to an observation deck tucked beneath the peak of the building's thatched roof. There's also another wonderful open-air yoga platform, where classes are sometimes offered. Lapa Ríos is surrounded by its own 400-hectare (988-acre) private rainforest reserve, which is home to scarlet macaws, toucans, parrots, hummingbirds, monkeys, and myriad other wildlife. However, keep in mind that there are no TVs, no telephones, no air-conditioning, no discos, no shopping, no paved roads, and no crowds. Moreover, the beach is a good 15-minute hike away. In fact, other than a beautiful little pool, miles of hiking trails, an array of adventure tours and activities, and a quiet tropical bar, there is little to distract your attention from the stupendous views of the rainforest all around and the ocean far below.

Osa Peninsula (mailing address: SJO-706, Box 025216, Miami, FL 33102). ℭ **735-5130.** Fax 735-5179. www.laparios. com. 16 units. $590 (£295) double. Rates include 3 meals daily, round-trip transportation between the lodge and Puerto Jiménez, and taxes. Discounts for children under 11. AE, MC, V. **Amenities:** Restaurant; bar; small pool; tour desk; massage; laundry service; nonsmoking rooms. *In room:* Safe, no phone.

EXPENSIVE

Corcovado Lodge Tent Camp ℛ   If you're looking for a balanced blend of comfort and adventure, check out Corcovado Lodge Tent Camp, which is built on a low bluff right above the beach. Forested mountains rise up behind the tent camp, and just a few minutes' walk away is the entrance to the national park. Accommodations are in large tents pitched on wooden decks. Each tent has two twin beds, a table, a couple of plastic garden chairs on the front deck, and an ocean view. Toilets and showers are a short walk away, but there are enough that there's usually no waiting.

Meals are served family style in a large open-air dining room furnished with picnic tables. A separate screen-walled building is furnished with hammocks, a small bar, a Ping-Pong table, and a few board games. Services at the lodge include guided walks and excursions, including hikes through the national park and horseback rides on the beach. The latest addition to the lodge is a canopy platform located 36m (118 ft.) up an ancient guapinol tree. If you're truly adventurous, you can spend the night in a tent atop the platform. (Just don't wake up on the wrong side of the tent.) Package rates that include transportation and tours are also available and are the way most people come here.

Just reaching this lodge is an adventure in itself. Most guests take a five-seat chartered plane to the gravel landing strip at Carate and then walk for around 30 minutes along the beach to the lodge. Don't worry: Your bags are hauled in on a mule-drawn cart. If you have a four-wheel-drive vehicle, you can get as far as Carate, arrange for safe parking, and then walk the remaining 1.6km (1 mile). When you're there, you have a real sense of being very away from it all.

Osa Peninsula (mailing address: SJO 235, P.O. Box 025216, Miami, FL 33102-5216). ℭ **257-0766.** Fax 257-1665. www.corcovadolodge.com. 20 tents, all w/shared bathrooms. $126 (£63) double. Rates include 3 meals daily. 3-day/2-night package $1,356 (£678) double, including air transportation (pickup and delivery from any San José hotel), 1 treetop/canopy tour, park entrance fee, and all taxes. Add $65 (£33) per person per day for extra days. Rates lower in off season; slightly higher during peak periods. AE, MC, V. **Amenities:** Restaurant; bar; laundry service. *In room:* No phone.

PUERTO JIMENEZ AFTER DARK

If you're looking for any after tours action in Puerto Jiménez, I recommend you start off at either **Juanita's Mexican Bar & Grille** or the **Soda Carolina.** If you want to dance, there's basically just one option, the **Delfines Discoteque,** which is located near the bus station.

3 Golfito: Gateway to the Golfo Dulce

87km (54 miles) S of Palmar Norte; 337km (209 miles) S of San José

Despite being the largest and most important city in Costa Rica's southern zone, Golfito, in and of itself, is neither a popular nor a particularly inviting tourist destination. In its prime, this was a major banana port, but United Fruit pulled out in 1985 following a few years of rising taxes, falling prices, and labor disputes. Things may change in a few years, as rumors abound about the potential addition of an international airport and major marina operation down here.

Golfito is a major sportfishing center and a popular gateway to a slew of nature lodges spread along the quiet waters, isolated bays, and lush rainforests of the Golfo Dulce, or "Sweet Gulf." In 1998, much of the rainforest bordering the Golfo Dulce was officially declared the **Piedras Blancas National Park** *GG*, which includes 12,000 hectares (29,640 acres) of primary forests, as well as newly protected secondary forests and pasturelands.

Golfito is set on the north side of the Golfo Dulce, at the foot of lush green mountains. The setting alone is enough to make this one of the most attractive cities in the country, but Golfito also has a certain charm all its own. Sure, the areas around the municipal park and public dock are somewhat seedy and the "downtown" section is quite run-down, but if you go a little bit farther along the bay, you come to the old United Fruit Company housing. Here you'll find well-maintained wooden houses painted bright colors and surrounded by neatly manicured gardens. Toucans are commonly sighted. It's all very lush and green and clean—an altogether different picture from that painted by most port towns in this country. When a duty-free zone was opened here, these old homes experienced a minor renaissance and several were converted into small hotels. Ticos come here in droves on weekends and throughout December to take advantage of cheap prices on name-brand goods and clothing at the duty-free zone; sometimes all these shoppers make finding a room difficult.

ESSENTIALS
GETTING THERE & DEPARTING   By Plane   Sansa (© 290-4100; www.fly sansa.com) has four daily flights to Golfito departing at 5:30, 5:45, and 11am, and 1pm from San José's Juan Santamaría International Airport. Trip duration is 1 hour; the fare is $82 (£41) each way. Sansa flights return to San José daily at 6:40 and 7am, and 12:15 and 2:15pm.

By Car   Take the Interamerican Highway east out of San José (through San Pedro and Cartago) and continue south on this road. In about 3 hours, you'll reach San Isidro de El General. Although you can continue on the Interamerican Highway all the way south, it is currently faster, smoother, and safer to turn off in San Isidro and head to Dominical, picking up the Southern Highway or Costanera Sur in Dominical. From here it's a fast and smooth shot down to Palmar Norte, where you meet up again with the Interamerican Highway. When you get to Río Claro, you'll notice a couple of gas stations and quite a bit of activity. Turn right here and follow the signs to Golfito. If you end up at the Panama border, you've missed the turnoff by about 32km (20 miles). The complete drive takes about 6 hours. On most of the Interamerican Highway, you'll have to contend with potholes of sometimes gargantuan proportions. Just remember, if the road is suddenly smooth and in great shape, you can bet that around the next bend there will be a bottomless pothole that you can't swerve around. Take it easy.

By Bus   Express buses leave San José daily at 7am and 3pm from the **Tracopa** station on the Plaza Viquez at Calle 5 between avenidas 18 and 20 (© 221-4214). The trip takes 7½ hours; the fare is $5 (£2.50). Buses depart Golfito for San José daily at 5am and 1:30pm from the bus station near the municipal dock.

By Boat   A passenger launch leaves **Puerto Jiménez,** on the Osa Peninsula, for Golfito daily at 6am. The trip takes 1½ hours; the fare is $3 (£1.50). You can also hire a boat to take you across the Golfo Dulce to Golfito. However, there are often not very many boats available in Puerto Jiménez; they tend to be based in Golfito. You're likely to have to pay between $40 and $60 (£20–£30) for a boat that can carry up to 12 passengers. The passenger launch departs Golfito for Puerto Jiménez daily at 11:30am.

GETTING AROUND   If you can't get to your next destination by boat, bus, commuter airline, or car, **Alfa Romeo Air Charters** (© **735-5353** or 735-5112; www.alfa romeoair.com) runs charters to most of the nearby destinations, including Carate, Drake Bay, Sirena, and Puerto Jiménez. A regular taxi ride anywhere in town should cost around 75¢ (40p). If you drive down here and head out to one of the remote lodges on the gulf, you can leave your car at Samoa del Sur (see "Where to Stay" below) for around $10 (£5) per day.

FAST FACTS   To avoid the bureaucracy and frequently long lines at the banks, you can **exchange money** at the gas station, or "La Bomba," in the middle of town. A **laundromat** on the upper street of the small downtown charges around $3 (£1.50) for an average-size load.

EXPLORING THE AREA
You won't find any really good swimming beaches right in Golfito. The closest spot is **Playa Cacao,** a short boat ride away, although this is not one of my favorite beaches in Costa Rica. You should be able to get a ride here for around $5 (£2.50) per person from one of the boat taxis down at the public docks. However, you might have to negotiate hard because these boatmen like to gouge tourists whenever possible. If you really want some beach time, I recommend staying at one of the hotels in the Golfo Dulce (see "Where to Stay," below) or heading over to **Playa Zancudo** (see "Playa Zancudo," later in this chapter).

About a 20-minute drive over rough dirt road from Golfito will bring you to the **Avellana Waterfall & Trails.** Admission to the site costs $8 (£4) and includes a 2-hour guided hike through the forests and a visit to a beautiful forest waterfall, with several refreshing pools perfect for swimming. A taxi should charge around $10 (£5) for the ride, one way. Horseback riding is available, camping is allowed, and meals are served by the friendly owners of the land, the local Gamba family. However, your best bet for visiting this site is to go as part of an organized trip with **Land Sea Tours** (© 775-1614).

The waters off Golfito also offer some of the best **sportfishing** in Costa Rica. If you'd like to try hooking into a possible world-record marlin or sailfish, contact **Banana Bay Marina** (© 775-0838; www.bananabaymarina.com) or **King and Bartlett** (© 775-1624; www.kingandbartlettsportfishing.com). Both of these operators have a full-service marina, a few waterside rooms for guests, and a fleet of sportfishing boats and captains. A full-day fishing trip costs between $800 and $1,600 (£400–£800). You can also try **The Zancudo Lodge** (© 776-0008; www.thezancudolodge.com), which is based in nearby Playa Zancudo. The lodge can arrange pickup in Golfito, and I prefer the lodgings and scenery out in Zancudo to what you'll find in Golfito.

There's no steady charter fleet here, but itinerant sailors often set up shop here for a season or so. If you're looking to charter a sailboat, you should check with **Banana Bay Marina, King and Bartlett,** or **Las Gaviotas Hotel** (p. 326).

About 30 minutes by boat out of Golfito, you'll find **Casa Orquídeas** ★★, a private botanical garden lovingly built and maintained by Ron and Trudy MacAllister. Most hotels in the area offer trips here, including transportation and a 2-hour tour of the gardens. During the tour, you'll sample a load of fresh fruits picked right off the trees. If your hotel can't, you can book a trip out of Golfito with **Land Sea Tours**

(📞 775-1614). The entrance and guided tour is only $5 (£2.50) per person, but it will cost you between $50 and $60 (£25–£30) to hire a boat for the round-trip ride.

If you have a serious interest in botanical gardens or bird-watching, consider an excursion to **Wilson Botanical Gardens** 🌟🌟🌟 at the Las Cruces Biological Station (📞 **524-0628** in San José, or 773-4004 at the gardens; www.ots.ac.cr), located just outside the town of San Vito, about 65km (40 miles) to the northeast. The gardens are owned and maintained by the Organization for Tropical Studies and include more than 7,000 species of tropical plants from around the world. Among the plants grown here are many endangered species, which make the gardens of interest to botanical researchers. Despite the scientific aspects of the gardens, there are so many beautiful and unusual flowers amid the manicured grounds that even a neophyte can't help but be astounded. All this luscious flora has attracted at least 330 species of birds. A full-day guided walk, including lunch, costs $36 (£18); a half-day guided walk costs $18 (£9). If you'd like to stay the night here, there are 12 well-appointed rooms. Rates, which include one guided walk, three meals, and taxes, run around $82 (£41) per person; you definitely need to make reservations if you want to spend the night, and it's usually a good idea to make a reservation for a simple day visit and hike. The gardens are about 6km (3¾ miles) before San Vito. To get here from Golfito, drive out to the Interamerican Highway and continue south toward Panama. In Ciudad Neily, turn north. A taxi from Golfito should cost around $40 (£20) each way.

WHERE TO STAY
IN GOLFITO

Centro Turístico Samoa del Sur   This is the best located hotel on the waterfront, and it features a popular restaurant and bar. The rooms are spacious and clean. Varnished wood headboards complement two firm and comfortable queen-size beds. With red-tile floors, modern bathrooms, and carved-wood doors, the rooms all share a long, covered veranda that's set perpendicular to the gulf, so the views aren't great. If you want to watch the water, you're better off grabbing a table at the restaurant, or walking out to the docks at their small marina. The hotel also has a swimming pool, a volleyball court, and a large gift shop with an extensive shell-and-coral collection that they bill as a museum.

100m (328 ft.) north of the public dock, Golfito. 📞 **775-0233.** Fax 775-0573. www.samoadelsur.com. 14 units. $60 (£30) double. AE, MC, V. **Amenities:** Restaurant; bar; midsize outdoor pool; tour desk; kayak rental; laundry service. *In room:* A/C, TV.

El Gran Ceibo *(Value)*   This little motel-like option at the entrance to Golfito is a good choice. It's named after the giant ceibo tree you'll see standing over it near the entrance. The rooms are clean, bright, comfortable, and relatively spacious. All feature small verandas with some sitting chairs. About half of them come with air-conditioning and cable TV; although you pay more for these, they're still quite affordable. The others have just fans and cold-water showers. There are nice views over the gulf from the grounds and some of the rooms.

On the left, just as you enter Golfito. 📞 **775-0403.** Fax 775-2303. www.hotel-elgranceibo.com. 27 units. $25–$38 (£13–£19) double. AE, MC, V. **Amenities:** Restaurant; bar; pool; laundry service. *In room:* A/C and TV in some units, no phone.

Hotel Sierra 🌟   This resort-style hotel is the most luxurious option in Golfito. Located right beside the airstrip and walking distance to the duty-free zone, the Hotel Sierra was originally built as a business-class option geared toward middle-class Ticos in town to shop. It is currently trying to reinvent itself as a sportfishing and eco-tourism lodge, but it's not particularly well located for either. The Sierra is constructed to be as open and breezy as possible, and covered walkways connect the hotel's various buildings. The rooms are spacious and have windows on two sides to let in plenty of light. The swimming pool is the largest and most appealing in town, and the restaurant serves good international fare at reasonable prices. One of the big draws here is the small casino, which is popular with guests and locals alike.

Beside the airstrip (A.P. 37), Golfito. © 775-0666. Fax 775-0506. www.hotelsierra.com. 72 units. $70 (£35) double. AE, MC, V. **Amenities:** Restaurant; bar; casino; midsize outdoor pool; tour desk; car rental; laundry service. *In room:* A/C, TV, safe.

Las Gaviotas Hotel   Situated just at the start of Golfito proper—a short taxi or bus ride from the "downtown"—Las Gaviotas has long been a popular choice. The waterfront location is this hotel's greatest asset. There is a long pier that attracts the sailboat and sportfishing crowd. For landlubbers, there's a small pool built out near the gulf. Guest rooms, which are set amid attractive gardens, all face the ocean, and although they're quite large, they're spartan and show their age. There are small, tiled patios in front of all the rooms, and the cabanas have little kitchens. A large, open-air restaurant looks over the pool to the gulf; it's a great view, but the food leaves much to be desired. Just around the corner is a large, open-air bar.

A.P. 12-8201, Golfito. © 775-0062. Fax 775-0544. 18 units, 3 cabanas. $42 (£21) double; $85 (£43) cabana. AE, DC, MC, V. **Amenities:** Restaurant; bar; small pool; tour desk; laundry service. *In room:* A/C, TV.

FARTHER AFIELD ON THE GOLFO DULCE

The lodges listed here are located on the shores of the Golfo Dulce. There are no roads into this area, so you must get to the lodges by boat. I recommend that you have firm reservations when visiting this area, so your transportation should be arranged. If worse comes to worst, you can hire a boat taxi at the *muellecito* (little dock), which is located on the water just beyond the gas station, or "La Bomba," in Golfito, for between $25 and $40 (£13–£20), depending on which lodge you are staying at.

In addition to the lodges listed below, **Villas Corcovado** (★ (© **817-6969;** www.villacorcovado.com) is another excellent option.

VERY EXPENSIVE

Playa Nicuesa Rainforest Lodge (★★ (Finds   Set on its own private bay, with a large stretch of black-sand beach, this is the most luxurious and impressive lodge located along the shores of the Golfo Dulce. While the four Mango Manor rooms are certainly very comfortable, you'll definitely want to snag one of the individual cabins. These are all set amidst dense forest and are made almost entirely of wood, with large open-air showers, private verandas, and a true sense of being in touch with nature. The main lodge building is a huge, open-air affair with an abundance of varnished wood and a relaxed inviting vibe that induces one to grab a book, board game, or chat with other guests. There's an excellent network of trails on the lodge's 165 acres, and a whole host of tours and activities is offered. Guests have unlimited use of the lodge's kayaks and windsurfing, snorkeling, and fishing gear. Meals are served family style, and are well prepared and tasty.

Golfo Dulce (A.P. 56, Golfito). © 866/504-8116 in the U.S., or 258-8250 in Costa Rica. Fax 735-5043. www.nicuesa lodge.com. 8 units. $320–$360 (£160–£180) double. Rates include all meals, taxes, and transfers to and from either Golfito or Puerto Jiménez. A 2-night minimum stay is required. Closed Oct 1–Nov 15. MC, V. **Amenities:** Restaurant; bar; watersports equipment; laundry service. *In room:* Safe, no phone.

EXPENSIVE

Golfo Dulce Lodge ✿   This small, Swiss-run lodge is just down the beach from Casa Orquídeas, about a 30-minute boat ride from Golfito. The five separate cabins and main lodge buildings are all set back away from the beach about 500m (1,640 ft.) into the forest. The cabins are spacious and airy, and feature either a twin and a double bed or three single beds. In addition, there are large bathrooms, solar hot-water showers, a small sitting area, and a porch with a hammock. The rooms are all comfortable and well appointed, and even feature private verandas, but they are not nearly as nice as the cabins. Meals are served in a two-story open rancho with an observation deck, located beside the small swimming pool. The lodge offers jungle hikes, river trips, and other guided tours.

Golfo Dulce (A.P. 137-8201, Golfito). (✆ **821-5398**. Fax 775-0573. www.golfodulcelodge.com. 8 units. $190–$230 (£95–£115) double. Rates include 3 meals daily and taxes. Add $25 (£13) per person for transportation to and from Golfito. Rates lower in off season; higher during peak weeks. No credit cards. **Amenities:** Restaurant; bar; small outdoor pool; nature trails; laundry service. *In room:* No phone.

WHERE TO DINE
MODERATE

Bilge Bar, Restaurant & Grill ✿ INTERNATIONAL/SEAFOOD   The open-air restaurant attached to the Banana Bay Marina is the best restaurant in Golfito. The seafood is fresh and excellently prepared, but you can also get hearty steaks and great burgers. I personally recommend the fresh-fish burger. Grab a table toward the water and watch the boats bob up and down while you enjoy your meal.

At the Banana Bay Marina, on the waterfront in downtown Golfito. ✆ **775-0838**. Reservations not accepted. Main courses $6–$15 (£3–£7.50). AE, MC, V. Daily 7am–9pm.

Samoa del Sur CONTINENTAL   This large, open-air place features an extensive menu of Continental and French dishes (the owners are French), including such specialties as onion soup, salad Niçoise, filet of fish meunière, and, in a nod to their southern neighbor, paella. There are also pizzas and spaghetti. In addition to the food, the giant rancho houses a pool table, several high-quality dartboards, and two big-screen TVs. The bar sometimes stays open all night.

100m (328 ft.) north of the public dock. ✆ **775-0233**. Reservations not accepted. Main courses $6.50–$32 (£3.25–£16). AE, MC, V. Daily 7am–midnight.

INEXPENSIVE

Bar & Restaurant La Cubana COSTA RICAN   This small, open-air restaurant with a basic menu commands a good view of the gulf from its location on the bluff of a small hill. It serves hearty meals at rock-bottom prices. A fresh whole fish in garlic sauce costs around $4 (£2). The bar is a quiet spot to have a drink in the evening.

150m (492 ft.) east of the gas station, on the upper road through downtown Golfito. No phone. Main courses $4–$10 (£2–£5). No credit cards. Tues–Sun 6am–10pm.

GOLFITO AFTER DARK

Golfito is a rough-and-tumble port town, and it pays to be a bit careful here after dark. Right in town, about 1½ blocks inland and uphill from the *muellecito*, **Latitude 8** is the most popular spot. Most folks stick pretty close to their hotel bar and restaurant. Of these, the bar/restaurants at **Las Gaviotas** and **Samoa del Sur** are, by far, the liveliest. If you're feeling lucky, you can head to the **casino** at the **Hotel Sierra.**

4 Playa Zancudo ⭐

19km (12 miles) S of Golfito by boat; 35km (22 miles) S of Golfito by road

Playa Zancudo is one of Costa Rica's most isolated beach destinations. If you're look-ing for a remote and low-key beach getaway, it's hard to beat Zancudo. There are rel-atively few places to stay, and the better ones, such as those listed here, can fill up fast in the high season. The beach itself is long and flat, and because it's protected from the full force of Pacific waves, it's one of the calmest beaches on this coast and rela-tively good for swimming, especially toward the northern end. There's a splendid view across the Golfo Dulce, and the sunsets are hard to beat. Because there's a mangrove swamp directly behind the beach, mosquitoes and biting sand flies can be a problem when the winds die down, so be sure to bring insect repellent.

ESSENTIALS
GETTING THERE   By Plane   The nearest airport is in Golfito. See "Golfito: Gateway to the Golfo Dulce," earlier in this chapter, for details. To get from the air-port to Playa Zancudo, your best bets are by boat or taxi.

By Boat   Water taxis can be hired in Golfito to make the trip out to Playa Zancudo; however, trips depend on the tides and weather conditions. When the tide is high, the boats take a route through the mangroves. This is by far the calmest and most scenic way to get to Zancudo. When the tide is low, they must stay out in the gulf, which can get choppy at times. It costs around $12 (£6) per person for a water taxi, with a minimum charge of $25 (£13). If you can round up any sort of group, be sure to negotiate. The ride takes about 30 minutes.

Also, there's a passenger launch from the *muellecito* (little dock) in Golfito, which normally leaves daily at around noon. Because the schedule sometimes changes, be sure to ask in town about current departure times. The trip lasts 40 minutes; the fare is $5 (£2.50). The *muellecito* is located next to the town's principal gas station, or "La Bomba."

If you plan ahead, you can call **Zancudo Boat Tours** (𝒞 776-0012; www.loscocos.com) and arrange for pickup in Golfito or Puerto Jiménez. The trip costs $15 (£7.50) per person each way from Golfito or Puerto Jiménez, with a $30 (£15) minimum from Golfito and $60 (£30) minimum from Puerto Jiménez. Zancudo Boat Tours also includes land transportation to your hotel in Playa Zancudo—a very nice perk because there are so few taxis in town.

By Car   If you've got a four-wheel-drive vehicle, you can make it out to Zancudo even in the rainy season. To get here, follow the directions for driving to Golfito, but don't go all the way into town. The turnoff for playas Zancudo and Pavones is at El Rodeo, about 4km (2½ miles) outside of Golfito, on the road in from the Interameri-can Highway. About 20 minutes past the turnoff, you'll have to wait and take a small diesel-operated crank ferry. The fare is $1 (50p) per vehicle. The ferry generally oper-ates from around 5am until 8pm; however, the hours can be erratic. Moreover, at very low tides the ferry can't run, so sometimes you must wait a couple of hours. After the ferry, you should follow the few signs and the flow of traffic (if there is any) or stick to the most worn route when in doubt.

When the ferry's not running, or waiting for the tide to come in, there's an alterna-tive route from Paso Canoas (at the border), via the towns of La Cuesta and Laurel. This route meets the route mentioned above at the small village of Conte.

> *Tips* **Park It**
>
> If you drive down to Golfito, you can leave your car at Samoa del Sur (see "Where to Stay," earlier in this chapter) and take one of the waterborne routes mentioned above. They charge around $10 (£5) per day, and the lot is very secure.

A four-wheel-drive **taxi** costs around $40 (£20) from Golfito. It takes about 1 hour when the road is in good condition, and about 2 hours when it's not. To get here from San José, see "By Car" under "Essentials" in "Golfito: Gateway to the Golfo Dulce," earlier in this chapter.

By Bus   It's possible to get to Zancudo by bus, but I highly recommend coming by boat from Golfito, or your own car. If you insist, you can catch one of the Pavones buses in front of the gas station "La Bomba" in downtown Golfito and get off in the village of Conte (at around 4pm). In theory, a Zancudo-bound bus should be waiting. However, this is not always the case, and you may have to wait, hitchhike, or spring for a cab, if any can be found. The entire trip takes about 3 hours; the fare is $3 (£1.50).

DEPARTING   The public launch to Golfito leaves daily at 7am from the dock near the school, in the center of Zancudo. You can also arrange a water taxi back to Golfito, but it's best to work with your hotel owner and make a reservation at least 1 day in advance. **Zancudo Boat Tours** will take you for $15 (£7.50) per person, with a $30 (£15) minimum. If you're heading to **Pavones** or the **Osa Peninsula** next, **Zancudo Boat Tours** will also take you to these two places. It costs the same $15 (£7.50) per person, but there's a minimum charge of $60 (£30). The bus to Golfito leaves Zancudo each morning at 5:30am. You can catch the bus anywhere along the main road.

ORIENTATION   Zancudo is a long, narrow peninsula (sometimes only 90m/295 ft. or so wide) at the mouth of the Río Colorado. On one side is the beach; on the other is a mangrove swamp. There is only one road that runs the length of the beach, and along this road, spread out over several kilometers of long, flat beach, you'll find the hotels I mention here. It's about a 20-minute walk from the public dock near the school to the popular Cabinas Sol y Mar.

WHAT TO SEE & DO (OR HOW NOT TO DO ANYTHING)

The main activity at Zancudo is relaxing, and people take it seriously. There are hammocks at almost every lodge, and if you bring a few good books, you can spend quite a number of hours swinging slowly in the tropical breezes. The beach along Zancudo is great for swimming. It's generally a little calmer on the northern end and gets rougher (good for bodysurfing) as you head south. There are a couple of bars and even a disco, but visitors are most likely to spend their time just hanging out at their hotel or in restaurants meeting like-minded folks, reading a good book, or playing board games. If you want to take a horseback ride on the beach, ask at your hotel; they should be able to arrange it for you.

Susan and Andrew Robertson, who run Cabinas Los Cocos, also operate **Zancudo Boat Tours** (© 776-0012; www.loscocos.com), which offers snorkeling trips, kayaking tours, trips to the Casa Orquídeas Botanical Garden, hikes on the Osa peninsula, a trip up the Río Coto to watch birds and wildlife, and more. Tour prices are $45 to $75 (£23–£38) per person per tour, with discounts available for larger groups.

For fishing, contact **The Zancudo Lodge** (see below). A full day of fishing with lunch and beer should cost between $600 and $1,200 (£300–£600) per boat.

WHERE TO STAY

If you're planning on an extended stay, there are quite a few fully equipped beach houses for rent. Once again, Susan and Andrew at Los Cocos (© 776-0012; www.loscocos.com) are your best bet for lining up one of these houses.

VERY EXPENSIVE

The Zancudo Lodge ✦✦   Still widely known as Roy's Zancudo Lodge, this place is under new and enthusiastic management as of 2006. Primarily a fishing lodge, this hotel is located at the north end of Zancudo, and is, by far, the most luxurious option around. All of the rooms look out onto a bright green lawn of soft grass and the small swimming pool and Jacuzzi; the beach is just a few steps beyond. Most of the rooms are in a long two-story building and feature tile floors, clean, modern bathrooms, and small verandas. There are four suites that have separate sitting rooms, hardwood floors, and more space. The lodge offers many different types of fishing excursions and packages, and boasts more than 50 world-record catches.

Playa Zancudo (A.P. 41, Golfito). © **877/529-6980** in the U.S., or 776-0008 in Costa Rica. Fax 776-0011. www.the zancudolodge.com. 26 units. $150 (£75) per person nonfishing; $400–$500 (£200–£250) including full-day fishing. Rates are per person double occupancy and include all meals, drinks (alcoholic and carbonated), and taxes. Multiday packages available. V. **Amenities:** Restaurant; bar; pool; Jacuzzi; laundry service. *In room:* A/C, TV, dataport, stocked minibar, coffeemaker, hair dryer.

MODERATE

Cabinas Los Cocos ✦ *Finds*   If you've ever pondered throwing it all away and setting up shop in a simple house by the beach, these kitchen-equipped cabins might be a good place for a trial run. Set under the trees and only a few meters from the beach, the four cabins are quiet and semi-isolated from one another. Two of them served as banana-plantation housing in a former life, until they were salvaged and moved here. These wood houses have big verandas and bedrooms, and large eat-in kitchens. Bathrooms are down a few steps in back and have hot water. The two newer cabins also offer plenty of space, small kitchenettes, and a private veranda, as well as comfortable sleeping lofts. If you plan to stay in Zancudo for a while, this is a perennially good choice. The owners, Susan and Andrew Robertson, run Zancudo Boat Tours, so if you want to do some exploring or need a ride into Golfito or Puerto Jiménez, they're the folks to see. Finally, these folks also rent out several wonderful beach houses around Zancudo.

Playa Zancudo (A.P. 88, Golfito). ©/fax **776-0012.** www.loscocos.com. 4 units. $60 (£30) double. Rates lower in off season. Weekly discounts available. No credit cards. *In room:* Kitchenette, no phone.

Oasis on the Beach ✦   Located toward the southern end of Zancudo, this place is an intimate and isolated option. My favorite rooms here are the three individual bungalows. Although they are simple and lack the air-conditioning of the villa rooms, they are plenty spacious and I like their wood floors, private front porches, large bathrooms, and rustic yet comfortable feel. The villa is a two-story building with rooms upstairs and down that feature tile floors and air-conditioning. The upstairs unit has a high peaked ceiling and a great view over the Golfo Dulce to Cabo Matapalo from its private balcony. The restaurant here is quite good, with weekly pizza nights featuring homemade pizzas made in a wood-fired brick oven.

Playa Zancudo (A.P. 17, Golfito). ℰ/fax **776-0087**. www.oasisonthebeach.com. 5 units. $62–$75 (£31–£38) double. Rates lower in off season. Weekly discounts available. V. **Amenities:** Restaurant; bar; laundry service. *In room:* Minifridge, no phone.

INEXPENSIVE

Cabinas Sol y Mar ⟨★⟩ ⟨*Value*⟩   This friendly owner-run establishment is one of the most popular lodgings in Zancudo. There are two individual bungalows and two rooms in a duplex building with a shared veranda. I prefer the individual rooms for their privacy. The bathrooms in these have unusual showers that feature a tiled platform set amid smooth river rocks. There's also a small budget cabin that is quite a good deal, as well as a fully equipped house for longer stays. You can even camp here for a few bucks per night. All of the options are just steps away from the sand. The hotel's open-air restaurant is one of the most popular places to eat in Zancudo.

Playa Zancudo (A.P. 87-8201, Golfito). ℰ **776-0014**. www.zancudo.com. 6 units. $22–$42 (£11–£21) double. Rates lower in off season. No credit cards. **Amenities:** Restaurant; bar. *In room:* No phone.

WHERE TO DINE

In addition to the place listed below, you'll do well to try the wood-oven pizza and nightly specials at the **Oasis on the Beach** ⟨★⟩ (ℰ 776-0087). You might also try the tasty Italian meals at **Restaurante Macondo** (ℰ 776-0157) or **Alberto's Puerta Negra** (ℰ 776-0181). And if you want basic Tico fare and some local company, head to **Soda Sussy** (ℰ 776-0107) or **Soda Katherine** (ℰ 776-0124).

Finally, for a good breakfast, lunch, or dinner, or perhaps just a midday ice cream treat, check out the little open-air cafe at **Oceanos Cabinas** ⟨★⟩ (ℰ 776-0921; www. oceanocabinas.com).

Sol y Mar ⟨★★⟩ ⟨*Value*⟩ INTERNATIONAL/SEAFOOD   This is the best and most popular restaurant in Playa Zancudo. The reasonably priced menu is heavy on seafood, but features some items you won't find at most places in town, including thick-cut pork chops in a teriyaki sauce. You can also get the daily catch served in your choice of a delicious Veracruz sauce or homemade coconut curry. The fresh seared tuna is always excellent, as are the twice-weekly barbecues on Monday and Friday. This is also my top choice for breakfast—the breakfast burrito should get you through most of the day. A regular horseshoe tournament takes place on Sundays throughout the high season.

At Cabinas Sol y Mar. ℰ **776-0014**. Reservations not necessary. Main courses $3–$8 (£1.50–£4). No credit cards. Daily 7am–9pm.

5 Playa Pavones: A Surfer's Mecca ⟨★⟩

40km (25 miles) S of Golfito

Hailed as the world's longest rideable left point break, Pavones is a legendary destination for surfing. It takes around 1.8m (6 ft.) of swell to get this wave cranking, but when the surf's up, you're in for a long, long ride—so long, in fact, that it's much easier to walk back through town to where the wave is breaking than to paddle back. The swells are most consistent during the rainy season, but you're likely to find surfers here year-round. Locals tend to be pretty possessive around here (both the wave and local properties have engendered bitter disputes), so don't be surprised if you receive a cool welcome in Pavones.

Other than surfing, nothing much goes on here; however, the surrounding forests are quite nice, and the beaches feature some rocky coves and points that give Pavones a bit more visual appeal than Zancudo. If you're feeling energetic, you can go for a horseback ride or hike into the rainforests that back up this beach town, or stroll south on the beaches that stretch toward Punta Banco and beyond, all the way to the Panamanian border. This is a forgotten and isolated destination catering almost exclusively to backpackers. So be prepared, Pavones is a tiny village with few amenities, and most of the accommodations here are quite basic.

ESSENTIALS

GETTING THERE & DEPARTING By Plane The nearest airport with regularly scheduled flights is in Golfito (see earlier in this chapter). See "By Car" and "By Bus," below, for how to get to Pavones from the Golfito airport. There is a private strip at Tiskita Jungle Lodge (see below). Depending on space, you might be able to arrange transportation to Pavones on one of its charter flights even if you are not staying there.

By Car If you've got a four-wheel-drive vehicle, you can make it out to Pavones even in the rainy season. To get here, follow the directions for driving to Golfito, but don't go all the way into town. The turnoff for playas Zancudo and Pavones is at El Rodeo, about 4km (2½ miles) outside of Golfito, on the road in from the Interamerican Highway. About 20 minutes past the turnoff, you'll have to wait and take a small diesel-operated crank ferry. Fare is $1 (50p) per vehicle. The ferry generally operates from around 5am until 8pm; however, the hours can be erratic. Moreover, at very low tides the ferry can't run, so sometimes you must wait a couple of hours. A four-wheel-drive taxi from Golfito to Pavones will cost between $50 and $60 (£25–£30). It takes around 2 hours.

When the ferry's not running, or waiting for the tide to come in, there's an alternative route from Paso Canoas (at the border), via the towns of La Cuesta and Laurel. This route meets the route mentioned above at the small village of Conte.

By Bus There are two daily buses (© 775-0365) to Pavones from Golfito at 10am and 2pm. Trip duration is 3 hours; the fare is $2.50 (£1.25). Buses to Golfito depart Pavones daily at 5am and 12:30pm. This is a very remote destination, and the bus schedule is subject to change, so it always pays to check in advance.

ORIENTATION You can now find an Internet connection at **Esquina del Mar** (© 394-7676) in the heart of the village. If there are no waves, or you want some other form of exercise, check in with the folks at **Shooting Star Yoga** (© 393-6982; www.yogapavones.com).

WHERE TO STAY & DINE

Right in Pavones, there are several very basic lodges catering to itinerant surfers and renting rooms for between $10 and $20 (£5–£10) per night for a double room; most take walk-in reservations since they don't have phones. There are also a couple of *sodas* where you can get Tico meals. The most popular spot for both cheap meals and cheap rooms is **Esquina del Mar** (© 394-7676), which is located right on the beach's edge, in front of the fattest part of the surf break. However, for in-town lodgings, I prefer **Mira Olas** (© 393-7742; www.miraolas.com), located about 2 blocks uphill from the soccer field. A little bit out of town, on the way to Punta Banco, is **Cabinas La Ponderosa** (© 824-4145; www.cabinaslaponderosa.com), a small, beachfront collection of cabins and private, rustic villas.

For meals, I recommend **Café de la Suerte,** a lively little joint located across from Esquina del Mar that serves breakfasts and lunches and specializes in vegetarian items, freshly baked goods, and fresh-fruit smoothies. For dinner, check out either the pizzas and Italian cuisine at **Pizzeria Alessandro** or the falafel and Mediterranean cuisine at **La Manta Club,** where the day's surf action or a first-run movie is usually broadcast on a large screen.

EXPENSIVE

Tiskita Jungle Lodge *(Finds*   This small ecolodge is nearly on the Panamanian border, with the beach on one side and rainforest-clad hills behind. Originally an experimental fruit farm growing exotic tropical fruits from around the world, Tiskita has become a great place to get away from it all. The lodge itself is set on a hill a few hundred meters from the beach and commands a superb view of the ocean. There's a dark-sand swimming beach, tide pools, jungle waterfalls, a farm and forest to explore, and great bird-watching—285 species have been sighted. Of the 160 hectares (395 acres) here, 100 hectares (247 acres) are in primary rainforest; the rest are in secondary forest, reforestation projects, orchards, and pastures.

Accommodations are in deluxe rustic cabins with screen walls and verandas. Constructed of local hardwoods, the cabins have a very tropical feel. If you're a birdwatcher, you can just sit on the veranda and add to your life list. My favorite cabin is no. 6, which has a great view and ample deck space. Some cabins have two or three rooms, making them great for families but less private for couples. Most of the bathrooms are actually outdoors, although they are private and protected, allowing you to take in the sights and sounds as you shower and shave.

Meals are served family style in the open-air main lodge. Although they're not fancy, they're certainly tasty and filling, and you'll be eating plenty of ingredients straight from the gardens.

The lodge is more than 8 hours from San José by car, so most guests take advantage of the package tours, which can even include air transportation to Tiskita's private landing strip. If you've already driven all the way to Pavones, Tiskita is only 6km (3¾ miles) farther down the road.

Pavones (A.P. 13411-1000, San José). © **296-8125.** Fax 296-8133. www.tiskita-lodge.co.cr. 17 units. $260 (£130) double. Rates include 3 meals and 1 guided walk daily, and all taxes. Packages w/transportation to and from Golfito or Puerto Jiménez are available. AE, MC, V. **Amenities:** Restaurant; bar; small pool; limited watersports equipment; laundry service. *In room:* No phone.

MODERATE

Casa Siempre Domingo   This small hillside inn offers up the best accommodations right in Pavones. The rooms all feature high ceilings, tile floors, and two double beds (one room has two doubles and a twin). The high beds are custom-made constructions, and they're uncommonly high off the ground. The owner says the design helps capture every bit of breeze from the picture windows, but if there's not enough breeze, you can always crank up the air-conditioning. Meals are served on picnic tables in the large interior common space, and there is also a separate sitting room with satellite TV. The nicest feature is the huge deck, with its ocean view. Casa Siempre Domingo is located several hundred meters south and then several hundred more uphill from downtown Pavones.

Pavones (A.P. 91, Golfito). © **820-4709.** www.casa-domingo.com. 4 units. $80 (£40) double. Rate includes breakfast and taxes. No credit cards. *In room:* A/C, no phone.

The Caribbean Coast

Costa Rica's Caribbean coast is a world apart from the rest of the country. The pace is slower, the food is spicier, the tropical heat is more palpable, and the rhythmic lilt of patois and reggae music fills the air.

This remains one of Costa Rica's least discovered and explored regions. More than half of the coastline here is still inaccessible except by boat or small plane. This inaccessibility has helped preserve large tracts of virgin lowland rainforest, which are now set aside as **Tortuguero National Park** ✿✿ and **Barra del Colorado National Wildlife Refuge** ✿. These two parks, on the northern reaches of this coast, are among Costa Rica's most popular destinations for adventurers and eco-travelers. Of particular interest are the sea turtles that nest here. Farther south, **Cahuita National Park** ✿ is another popular national park in this area, located just off its namesake beach village. It was set up to preserve 200 hectares (494 acres) of coral reef, but its palm tree–lined beaches and gentle trails are stunning.

So remote was the Caribbean coast from Costa Rica's population centers in the Central Valley that it developed a culture all its own. The original inhabitants of the area included people of the Bribri, Cabécar, and Kéköldi tribes, and these groups maintain their cultures on indigenous reserves in the Talamanca Mountains. In fact, until the 1870s, there were few non-Indians in this area. However, when Minor Keith built the railroad to San José and began planting bananas, he brought in black laborers from Jamaica and other Caribbean islands to lay the track and work the plantations. These workers and their descendants established fishing and farming communities up and down the coast. Today dreadlocked Rastafarians, reggae music, Creole cooking, and the English-based patois of this Afro-Caribbean culture give this region a quasi-Jamaican flavor. Many visitors find fascinating this striking contrast with the Spanish-derived Costa Rican culture.

Today, the Caribbean coast's main city of **Limón** is a major commercial port and budding cruise ship port of call.

Over the years, the Caribbean coast has garnered a reputation as being a dangerous, drug-infested zone, rife with crime and danger. Although there have been several high-profile crimes in the area, overall this reputation is exaggerated. The same crime and drug problems found here exist in San José and most of the more popular beach destinations on the Pacific coast. Use common sense and take normal precautions and you should have no problems on the Caribbean coast.

1 Barra del Colorado ✿

115km (71 miles) NE of San José

Most visitors to Barra del Colorado come for the fishing. Tarpon and snook fishing are world class, or you can head farther offshore for some deep-sea action. Barra del Colorado is part of the same ecosystem as Tortuguero National Park (see below); as in

The Caribbean Coast

NICARAGUA

Barra del Colorado Airport
Barra del Colorado
*Boca del
Río Colorado*
Río Colorado
Río San Juan
Río Chirripó
Barra del Colorado
National Wildlife
Refuge

Boca del Río Tortuguero
Tortuguero Airport
Tortuguero

*Caribbean
Sea*

TORTUGUERO
NATIONAL PARK

*Tortuguero
Canal*

To Puerto
Viejo de
Sarapiquí
Cariari

Río Frío

32 Guapiles

Río Reventazón

Río Pacuare

Boca del Río Pacuare

BRAULIO CARRILLO
NATIONAL PARK

Turrialba
Volcano

Guayabo
National
Monument

Siquírres

*Playa
Bonita*
Moín
Limón

Limón Airport

Irazú
Volcano

CENTRAL RANGE

Turrialba

Paraiso

Tapantí
National
Park

Río Chirripó Atlántico

CHIRRIPÓ
NATIONAL
PARK

LA AMISTAD
NATIONAL
PARK

*Playa
Cahuita*

36 CAHUITA
NATIONAL
PARK

Cahuita

*Puerto
Viejo*

Cerro de
la Muerte

CORDILLERA DE TALAMANCA

Cerro
Chirripó

San Isidro
de El General

BriBri

*Punta
Uva*

TALAMANCA
INDIAN
RESERVATION

BRIBRI INDIAN
RESERVATION

Hitoy-
Cerere
Biological
Reserve

Gandoca-
Manzanillo
National
Wildlife Refuge

0   50 mi
0   50 km

NICARAGUA

COSTA
RICA

San José

PACIFIC
OCEAN

Area of detail

*Caribbean
Sea*

PANAMA

0   100 mi
0   100 km

Tortuguero, there's an abundance of wildlife and rainforest fauna in the rivers and canals, which are accessible only by boat.

Named for its location at the mouth of the Río Colorado up near the Costa Rica–Nicaragua border, Barra del Colorado can be reached only by boat or small plane. There are no roads in or out of Barra del Colorado. The town itself is a small, ramshackle collection of raised stilt houses, and it supports a diverse population of Afro-Caribbean and Miskito Indian residents, Nicaraguan emigrants, and transient commercial fishermen.

It's hot and humid here most of the year, and it rains a lot, so although some of the lodges have at times risked offering a "tarpon guarantee," they're generally hesitant to promise anything in terms of the weather.

ESSENTIALS

GETTING THERE & DEPARTING   By Plane   Sansa (✆ **290-4100;** www.fly sansa.com) has a daily flight that departs at 5:45am for Barra del Colorado from San José's Juan Santamaría International Airport. The return flight to San José leaves Barra del Colorado daily at 6:55am. Flight duration is one hour, with a stop in Tortuguero en route; the fare is $66 (£33) each way.

Nature Air (✆ **800/235-9272** in the U.S. and Canada, or 299-6000; www.natureair. com) has a daily flight that departs the Tobías Bolaños International Airport in Pavas at 6:15am. Flight duration is 1 hour and 20 minutes, with stops in Limón and Tortuguero en route. The fare is $70 (£35) each way. The return flight leaves Barra del Colorado at approximately 7:50am and flies directly back to San José.

Most folks come here on multiday fishing packages, and most of the lodges in this area either operate charter flights as part of their package trips or will book you a flight.

By Boat   It is also possible to travel to Barra del Colorado by boat from **Puerto Viejo de Sarapiquí** (see chapter 7). Expect to pay $200 to $275 (£100–£138) each way for a boat that holds up to 10 people. Check at the public dock in Puerto Viejo de Sarapiquí. **Río Colorado Lodge** (✆ **800/243-9777** in the U.S. and Canada, or 232-4063) runs its own launch between Barra del Colorado and Puerto Viejo de Sarapiquí (and some-times between Barra and Limón), including land transportation between Puerto Viejo de Sarapiquí and San José. If you're staying at the Río Colorado Lodge, be sure to ask about this option (for at least one leg of your trip) when booking; the hotel doesn't dis-criminate—you can arrange transportation even if you aren't staying there. For $198 (£99) per person, you can arrange a pickup in San José, a minibus to the boat, a trip down the river to Barra, overnight accommodations at Río Colorado Lodge, and a return trip the next day, all meals and taxes included.

ORIENTATION   The Río Colorado neatly divides the town of Barra del Colorado. The airstrip is in the southern half of town, as are most of the lodgings. The lodges that are farther up the canals will meet you at the airstrip with a small boat.

FISHING, FISHING & MORE FISHING

Almost all the lodges here specialize in fishing and fishing packages. If you don't fish, you may wonder just what in the world you're doing here. Even though there are excellent opportunities for bird-watching and touring jungle waterways, most lodges still merely pay lip service to ecotourists and would rather see you with a rod and reel.

Fishing takes place year-round. You can do it in the rivers and canals, in the very active river mouth, or offshore. Most anglers come in search of the tarpon, or silver king. **Tarpon** can be caught year-round, both in the river mouth and, to a lesser extent, in the canals; however, they are much harder to land in July and August—the 2 rainiest months—probably because the river runs so high and is so full of runoff and debris. **Snook,** an aggressive river fish, peak in April, May, October, and November; fat snook, or **calba,** run heavy November through January. Depending on how far out to sea you venture, you might hook up with **barracuda, jack, mackerel** (Spanish and king), **wahoo, tuna, dorado, marlin,** or **sailfish.** In the rivers and canals, fishermen regularly bring in **mojarra, machaca,** and **guapote** (rainbow bass).

Following recent developments in fishing, anglers have been using traditional rod-and-reel setups, as well as fly rods, to land just about all the fish mentioned above. To fish here, you'll need both salt- ($24/£12) and freshwater ($30/£15) fishing licenses. The lodges here either include these in your packages or can readily provide the licenses for you.

Nonfishers should see whether their lodge has a good naturalist guide or canoes or kayaks for rent or use.

WHERE TO STAY & DINE

Almost all of the hotels here specialize in package tours, including all your meals, fishing and tackle, taxes, and usually your transportation and liquor too, so rates are high. There are no dependable budget hotels here, and Barra remains a remote and difficult destination for independent and budget travelers. In addition to the places listed below, **Casa Mar Lodge** (© 800/543-0282 in the U.S. and Canada, or 710-8093 in Costa Rica; www.casamarlodge.com) is a long-standing fishing lodge that is popular with hard-core anglers.

Río Colorado Lodge ⊙ This rustic lodge is one of the country's oldest and best-known fishing lodges. It was founded and built more than 30 years ago by local legend Archie Fields. The rooms are comfortable but decidedly rustic, with many showing the wear and tear of the years. All have air-conditioning, several have televisions, and two are wheelchair accessible. There's even a "honeymoon suite," which is basically a standard room with a small mirror hung by ropes over the bed. As at Silver King Lodge, the whole complex is tied together by covered walkways.

The nicest feature here is the large covered deck out by the river, where breakfast is served. Dinner is served family style in the second-floor dining room. There's also a large bar (where lunch is served) with satellite TV, pool table, and dartboard, as well as a conference room and a well-stocked tackle shop. The lodge runs a small "zoo" and participates in a macaw breeding project, as well as local education efforts. While their hearts may be in the right place, I find zoo and cage conditions rather desultory.

This lodge runs riverboat tours (see "Essentials," above) for those interested in cruising to either Puerto Viejo de Sarapiquí or Limón, as well as several other smaller launches for a variety of tours and outings.

Barra del Colorado (A.P. 5094-1000, San José). © 800/243-9777 in the U.S. and Canada, or 232-4063 in Costa Rica. Fax 231-5987. www.riocolorodolodge.com. 18 units. $2,245 (£1,123) per person double occupancy for 7 days/6 nights w/4 full days of fishing, including 2 nights lodging in San José, all meals and drinks at the lodge, boat, guide, fuel, licenses, and taxes. Nonfishing guests $120–$170 (£60–£85) per person per day. AE, MC, V. **Amenities:** Restaurant; bar; Jacuzzi; laundry service. *In room:* A/C, no phone.

Silver King Lodge ⊙⊙ *(Finds* This is the most upscale lodge in Barra del Colorado. They take their fishing seriously here—there's a large selection of modern boats and equipment, as well as a full tackle shop—but Silver King also emphasizes comfort.

The rooms are immense, with two double beds, a desk and chair, luggage racks, fishing racks, air-conditioning, an overhead fan, and a roomy closet. The floors and walls are all varnished hardwood, and the ceilings are finished in bamboo. The entire complex is built on raised stilts and connected by covered walkways (useful during the frequent downpours).

The meals here are truly exceptional, with some of the best buffet-style lodge cooking I've ever had. Each all-you-can-eat meal is anchored with at least two main dishes and a wide variety of appetizers, salads, side dishes, and desserts. You should be eating plenty of fish during your stay—coconut-battered snook nuggets with a pineapple-wasabi dip were just one of the highlights of my culinary indulgences here. These folks also have a photographer snapping away digital shots of all the offshore action and give you a personalized CD of photos from your stay at no extra cost. The newest addition here is a small, for fee, Internet cafe on site.

Barra del Colorado (mailing address: Interlink 399, P.O. Box 02-5635, Miami, FL 33102). © **800/847-3474** in the U.S., or ©/fax 711-0708 in Costa Rica. www.silverkinglodge.net. 10 units. $1,525–$2,150 (£763–£1,075) per person double occupancy for 3 full days of fishing, air transportation to and from Barra del Colorado from San José, all meals at the lodge, liquor, and taxes; $350 (£175) per person per extra day, including all fishing, meals, liquor, and taxes; $175 (£88) per person for nonfishers. AE, MC, V. Closed June 16–Aug 31 and Nov 11–Dec 31. **Amenities:** Restaurant; bar w/satellite TV; small pool; enclosed Jacuzzi; massage; free daily laundry service. *In room:* A/C, coffeemaker, no phone.

2 Tortuguero National Park ★★

250km (155 miles) NE of San José; 79km (49 miles) N of Limón

Sometimes dubbed "the Venice of Costa Rica," Tortuguero is connected to Limón, and the rest of mainland Costa Rica, by a series of rivers and canals. This aquatic highway is lined almost entirely with a dense tropical rainforest that is home to howler and spider monkeys, three-toed sloths, toucans, and great green macaws. A trip through the canals is nothing like touring around Venice in a gondola, but it is a lot like cruising the Amazon basin—on a much smaller scale.

"Tortuguero" comes from the Spanish name for the giant sea turtles *(tortugas)* that nest on the beaches of this region every year from early March to mid-October. The chance to see this nesting attracts many people to this remote region, but just as many come to explore the intricate network of jungle canals that serve as the region's main transportation arteries.

Very important: More than 200 inches of rain fall annually, so you can expect a downpour at any time of the year. Most of the lodges will provide you with rain gear (including ponchos and rubber boots), but it can't hurt to carry your own.

Independent travel is not the norm here, although it's possible. Most travelers rely on their lodge for boat transportation through the canals and into town. At most of the lodges around Tortuguero, almost everything (bus rides to and from, boat trips through the canals, and even family-style meals) is done in groups. This group feeling can be intimate and rewarding, or overwhelming and impersonal.

ESSENTIALS

GETTING THERE & DEPARTING   By Plane   Nature Air (© **800/235-9272** in the U.S. and Canada, or 299-6000; www.natureair.com) has one flight that departs daily at 6:15am for Tortuguero from Tobías Bolaños International Airport in Pavas. The flight takes approximately 55 minutes with a stop in Barra del Colorado en route; the fare is $70 (£35) each way. The return flight leaves Tortuguero daily at around 7:30am for San José.

Sansa (© **290-4100;** www.flysansa.com) has one flight daily that departs at 5:45am for Tortuguero from San José's Juan Santamaría International Airport. The flight duration is 55 minutes; the fare is $66 (£33) each way. The return flight leaves Tortuguero daily at 6:50am for San José, stopping in Barra del Colorado en route.

It always pays to check with both Sansa and Nature Air. Additional flights are often added during the high season, and departure times can vary according to weather or the whim of the airline. In addition, many lodges in this area operate charter flights as part of their package trips.

By Car   It is not possible to drive to Tortuguero. If you have a car, your best bet is either to leave it in San José and take an organized tour; or drive it to Limón or Moín, find a secure hotel or public parking lot, and then follow the directions for arriving by boat below. You can also leave your car at the lot at Caño Blanco Marina, but you should try to arrange your boat transportation and lodging in advance. There is a road sign declaring TORTUGUERO at the turnoff for Caño Blanco Marina. There is also secure parking in La Pavona, which is useful for those meeting the boats plying the Cariari and La Pavona route outlined below.

By Boat   Flying to Tortuguero is convenient if you don't have much time, but a boat trip through the canals and rivers of this region is often the highlight of any visit to Tortuguero. However, be forewarned: Although this trip can be stunning and exciting, it can also be long, tiring, and uncomfortable. You'll first have to ride by bus or minivan from San José to Moín, Caño Blanco, or one of the other embarkation points; then it's 2 to 3 hours on a boat, usually with hard wooden benches or plastic seats. All of the more expensive lodges listed offer their own bus and boat transportation packages, which include the boat ride through the canals. However, if you're coming here on the cheap and plan to stay at one of the less expensive lodges or at a budget *cabina* in Tortuguero, you will have to arrange your own transportation. In this case, you have a few options.

The most traditional option is to get yourself first to Limón and then to the public docks in **Moín,** just north of Limón, and try to find a boat on your own. You can reach Limón easily by public bus from San José (see "Getting There & Departing" under "Limón: Gateway to Tortuguero National Park & Southern Coastal Beaches," later in this chapter). If you're coming by car, make sure you drive all the way to Limón or Moín, unless you have arrangements out of Cariari or Caño Blanco Marina.

If you arrive in Limón by bus, you might be able to catch one of the periodic local buses to Moín right there at the main bus terminal; it costs 50¢ (25p). Otherwise, you can take a taxi for around $5 (£2.50), for up to four people. At the docks, you should be able to negotiate a fare of between $40 and $60 (£20–£30) per person round-trip. These boats tend to depart between 8 and 10am every morning. You can stay as many days as you like in Tortuguero, but be sure to arrange with the captain to be there to pick you up when you're ready to leave. The trip from Moín to Tortuguero takes between 3 and 4 hours.

As I mentioned above, it is possible to get to Tortuguero by bus and boat from Cariari. This is the cheapest and currently most reliable means of reaching Tortuguero from San José. To take this route, begin by catching the 9am direct bus to Cariari from the **Gran Terminal del Caribe,** on Calle Central, 1 block north of Avenida 11 (© **222-0610**). The fare is $2 (£1). This bus will actually drop you off at the main bus terminal in Cariari, from which you'll have to walk 5 blocks north to a separate small bus station. Look for a booth marked COOPETRACA. At this booth you can buy your bus ticket for La Pavona. The bus fare is around $2 (£1). Buy a ticket for the noon bus (a later bus leaves at 3pm). A boat will be waiting to meet the bus at the dock at the edge of the river at around 1:30pm (and again at 4:30pm). Check with each of the two boat services you will find at the dock in La Pavona and pay on board. The boat fare to Tortuguero is not regulated, and the price sometimes varies for foreigners. It can be as low as $3 (£1.50) each way, which is what locals pay. However, the boat captains often try to gouge tourists. Stand firm, you should not have to pay more than $5 (£2.50). Return boats leave Tortuguero for La Pavona every morning at 6 and 11:30am, and 3:00pm, making return bus connections to Cariari.

Warning: Be careful if you decide to take this route. I've received reports of unscrupulous operators providing misinformation to tourists. Be especially careful if the folks selling you boat transportation aggressively steer you to a specific hotel option, claim that your first choice is full, or insist that you must buy a package with them that includes the transportation, lodging, and guide services. If you have doubts or want to check on the current state of this route, contact Daryl Loth in Tortuguero (© **833-0827;** safari@racsa.co.cr). Or you can check out the site www.geocities.com/tortugueroinfo/main.html, which has extremely detailed directions about how to get to Tortuguero by a variety of routes.

Finally, it's also possible, albeit expensive, to travel to Tortuguero by boat from **Puerto Viejo de Sarapiquí** (see chapter 7). Expect to pay $250 to $350 (£125–£175) each way for a boat that holds up to 10 people. Check at the public dock in Puerto Viejo de Sarapiquí if you're interested. The ride usually takes about 3 to 4 hours, and the boats tend to leave in the morning.

ORIENTATION   Tortuguero is one of the most remote locations in Costa Rica. There are no roads into this area and no cars in the village, so all transportation is by boat or foot. Most of the lodges are spread out over several kilometers to the north of the village of Tortuguero on either side of the main canal; the small airstrip is at the north end of the beachside spit of land. At the far northern end of the main canal, you'll see the **Cerro de Tortuguero (Turtle Hill),** which, at some 119m (390 ft.), towers over the area. The hike to the top of this hill is a popular half-day tour and offers some good views of the Tortuguero canals and village, as well as the Caribbean Sea.

Tortuguero Village is a tiny collection of houses connected by footpaths. The village is spread out on a thin spit of land, bordered on one side by the Caribbean Sea and on the other by the main canal. At most points, it's less than 300m (984 ft.) wide. In the center of the village, you'll find a small children's playground and a soccer field, as well as a kiosk that has information on the cultural and natural history of this area.

If you stay at a hotel on the ocean side of the canal, you'll be able to walk into and explore the village at your leisure; if you're across the canal, you'll be dependent on the lodge's boat transportation. However, some of the lodges across the canal have their own network of jungle trails that might appeal to naturalists.

FAST FACTS   There are no banks, ATMs, or currency-exchange houses in Tortuguero, so be sure to bring sufficient cash in colones to cover any expenses and incidental charges. The local hotels and shops generally charge a hefty commission to exchange dollars. There is an **information center** (© **833-0827**) in town in front of the Catholic church. This is a good place for independent travelers looking to arrange local tours and onward travel. You'll find a dependable Internet cafe at **La Casona** (© **709-8092**), a small restaurant and budget hotel in the heart of the village.

Turtle Tips

- Visitors to the beach at night must be accompanied by a licensed guide. Tours generally last between 2 and 4 hours.
- Sometimes you must walk quite a bit to encounter a nesting turtle. Wear sneakers or walking shoes rather than sandals. The beach is very dark at night, and it's easy to trip or step on driftwood or other detritus.
- Wear dark clothes. White T-shirts are not permitted.
- Flashlights, flash cameras, and lighted video cameras are prohibited on turtle tours.
- Smoking is prohibited on the beach at night.

EXPLORING THE NATIONAL PARK

According to existing records, sea turtles have frequented Tortuguero National Park since at least 1592, largely due to its extreme isolation. Over the years, turtles were captured and their eggs were harvested by local settlers; by the 1950s this practice became so widespread that turtles faced extinction. Regulations controlling this mini-industry were passed in 1963, and in 1970 Tortuguero National Park was established.

Today four different species of sea turtles nest here: the green turtle, the hawksbill, the loggerhead, and the giant leatherback. The prime nesting period is from **July to mid-October** (Aug–Sept are peak months). The park's beaches are excellent places to watch sea turtles nest, especially at night. Appealingly long and deserted, however, the beaches are not appropriate for swimming. The surf is usually very rough, and the river mouths have a nasty habit of attracting sharks that feed on the turtle hatchlings and many fish that live here.

Green turtles are perhaps the most common turtle found in Tortuguero, so you're more likely to see one of them than any other species if you visit during the prime nesting season. **Loggerheads** are very rare, so don't be disappointed if you don't see one. The **giant leatherback** is perhaps the most spectacular sea turtle to watch laying eggs. The largest of all turtle species, the leatherback can grow to 2m (6½ ft.) long and weigh well over 1,000 pounds. It nests from early March to mid-April, predominantly in the southern part of the park.

You can explore the park's rainforest, either by foot or by boat, and look for some of the incredible varieties of wildlife that live here: jaguars, anteaters, howler monkeys, collared and white-lipped peccaries, some 350 species of birds, and countless butterflies, among others. Boat tours are far and away the most popular way to visit this park, although one frequently very muddy trail starts at the park entrance and runs for about 2km (1¼ miles) through the coastal rainforest and along the beach.

ENTRY POINT, FEES & REGULATIONS   The Tortuguero National Park entrance and ranger station are at the south end of Tortuguero Village. Admission to the park is $7 (£3.50); a 3-day pass is $10 (£5). However, most people visit Tortuguero as part of a package tour. Be sure to confirm whether the park entrance is included in the price. Moreover, only certain canals and trails leaving from the park station are actually within the park. Many hotels and private guides take their tours to a series of canals that border the park and are very similar in terms of flora and fauna but don't require a park entrance. When the turtles are nesting, you will have to arrange a night tour in advance with either your hotel or one of the private guides working in town. These guided tours generally run between $10 and $15 (£5–£7.50). Flashlights and flash cameras are not permitted on the beach at night because the lights discourage the turtles from nesting.

ORGANIZED TOURS   Most visitors come to Tortuguero on an organized tour. All of the lodges listed below, with the exception of the most inexpensive accommodations in Tortuguero Village, offer package tours that include various hikes and river tours; this is generally the best way to visit the area.

In addition, several San José–based tour companies offer budget 2-day/1-night excursions to Tortuguero, including transportation, all meals, and limited tours around the region. Prices for these trips range between $90 and $200 (£45–£100) per person, and—depending on price—guests are lodged either in one of the basic hotels in Tortuguero Village or one of the nicer lodges listed below. Reputable companies offering these excursions include **Expediciones Tropicales** (© 257-4133; www. costaricainfo.com) and **Caño Blanco Marina** (© 256-9444). There are even 1-day trips that spend almost all their time coming and going but that do allow for a quick tour of the canals and lunch in Tortuguero. These trips are good for travelers who like to be able to say, "Been there, done that," and they generally run between $80 and $90 (£40–£45) per person. However, these trips spend most of their time traveling to and from Tortuguero. If you really want to experience Tortuguero, I recommend staying for at least 2 nights.

Alternately, you could go with **Fran and Modesto Watson** ✋ (© 226-0986; www.tortuguerocanals.com), who are pioneering guides in this region and operate their own boat. The couple offers a range of overnight and multiday packages to Tortuguero, with lodging options at most of the major lodges here.

BOAT CANAL TOURS   Aside from watching the turtles nest, the unique thing to do in Tortuguero is tour the canals by boat, keeping your eye out for tropical birds and native wildlife. Most lodges can arrange a canal tour for you, but you can also arrange a tour through one of the operators in Tortuguero Village. I recommend **Ernesto Castillo,** who can be reached through Cabinas Sabina or by asking around the village. I also recommend **Daryl Loth** (© 833-0827; safari@racsa.co.cr), who runs the Casa Marbella (see below) in the center of the village. If neither of these guides is available, ask for a recommendation at the **Jungle Shop** (© 709-8072) or at the **Caribbean Conservation Corporation's Museum** (© 709-8091). Most guides charge between $10 and $15 (£5–£7.50) per person for a tour of the canals. If you travel through the park, you'll also have to pay the park entrance fee ($7/£3.50 per person).

EXPLORING THE VILLAGE

The most popular attraction in town is the small **Caribbean Conservation Corporation's Visitors' Center and Museum** ✋ (© 709-8091; www.cccturtle.org). The museum has information and exhibits on a whole range of native flora and fauna, but its primary focus is on the life and natural history of the sea turtles. Most visits to the museum include a short, informative video on the turtles. There's a small gift shop here, and all the proceeds go toward conservation and turtle protection. The museum is open Monday through Saturday from 10am to noon and 2 to 5:30pm, and Sunday from 2 to 5pm. There's a $1 (50p) admission charge, but more generous donations are encouraged.

In the village you can also rent dugout canoes, known in Costa Rica as *cayucos* or *pangas.* Be careful before renting and taking off in one of these; they tend to be heavy, slow, and hard to maneuver, and you might be getting more than you bargained for. **Miss Junie** (✆ 709-8102) rents lighter and more modern fiberglass canoes for around $10 (£5) for a half-day.

You'll find a couple of souvenir shops on the main footpath near the center of the village. About 182m (597 ft.) of this path was recently paved with concrete. The **Paraíso Tropical Gift Shop** has the largest selection of gifts and souvenirs, by far. But I prefer **The Jungle Shop,** which has a higher-end selection of wares and donates 10% of its profits to local schools.

WHERE TO STAY & DINE
Although the room rates below may appear high, keep in mind that they usually include round-trip transportation from San José (which amounts to approximately $100–$140 (£50–£70) per person), plus all meals, taxes, and usually some tours. When broken down into nightly room rates, most of the lodges are really charging only between $60 and $100 (£30–£50) for a double room.

Most visitors take all their meals, as part of a package, at their hotel. There are a couple of simple *sodas* (diners) and local restaurants in town. The best of these are **La Casona** (✆ 709-8092) and the **Buddha Café** (✆ 709-8084).

EXPENSIVE
Laguna Lodge ✦ This comfortable lodge is located 2km (1¼ miles) north of Tortuguero Village, on the ocean side of the main canal (which allows you to walk along the beach and into town at your leisure). All rooms are spacious and attractive. Most have wood walls, waxed hardwood floors, and tiled bathrooms with screened upper walls to let in air and light. Each room also has a little shared veranda overlooking flowering gardens.

The large dining room, where basic buffet-style meals are served, is on a free-form deck that extends out over the Tortuguero Canal. Another covered deck, also over the water, is strung with hammocks for lazing away the afternoons. Several covered palapa huts also strung with hammocks have been built among the flowering ginger and hibiscus. There's a large and refreshing pool, with a poolside bar and grill, as well as a butterfly garden and botanical garden. All the standard Tortuguero tours are available.

Tortuguero (A.P. 173-2015, San José). ✆ 225-3740 for reservations, or 709-8082 at the lodge. Fax 283-8031. www.lagunatortuguero.com. 80 units. $398 (£199) double for 2 days/1 night; $498 (£249) double for 3 days/2 nights. Rates include round-trip transportation from San José, tours, taxes, and 3 meals daily. AE, DC, MC, V. **Amenities:** Restaurant; 2 bars; large free-form pool; laundry service. *In room:* No phone.

Mawamba Lodge ✦ Located just north of Tortuguero Village on the ocean side of the canal, Mawamba is quite similar to Laguna Lodge—perhaps because the two lodges are owned by brothers. Rooms have varnished wood floors, twin beds, hot-water showers, ceiling fans, and verandas with rocking chairs. The rooms are painted in bright Caribbean colors. The gardens are lush and overgrown with flowering ginger, heliconia, and hibiscus. There are plenty of hammocks around for anyone who wants to kick back and a beach volleyball court for those who don't. The family-style meals are above average for Tortuguero. Rates include a 4-hour boat ride through the canals and a guided forest hike. These folks also offer an extensive menu of kayaking tours and excursions, including one package in which you actually kayak part of the way into Tortuguero. On premises are a small gift shop a small butterfly garden, a game room, and nightly lectures and slide shows that focus on the natural history of this area.

Tortuguero (A.P. 10980-1000, San José). ⓒ **293-8181** or 709-8100. Fax 239-7657. www.grupomawamba.com. 54 units. $446 (£223) double for 2 days/1 night; $560 (£280) double for 3 days/2 nights. Rates include round-trip transportation from San José, 3 meals daily, taxes, and some tours. Rates lower in off season. AE, MC, V. **Amenities:** Restaurant; bar; free-form pool; laundry service. *In room:* No phone.

Pachira Lodge ⚐   The rooms in this lodge are in a series of fourplex buildings perched on stilts and connected by covered walkways in a dense section of secondary forest set in a little bit from the main canal. Each room is spacious and clean, with varnished wood floors, painted wood walls, two double beds, ceiling fans, and plenty of cross ventilation. The covered walkways come in handy when it rains. Standard buffet meals are served in a large, screened-in dining room. There's a large, cool pool in the shape of a turtle, with children's wading pools built into the flippers. Bilingual guides and all the major tour options are available.

Tortuguero (A.P. 1818-1002, San José). ⓒ **800/644-7438** in the U.S. and Canada, or 256-7080 in Costa Rica. Fax 223-1119. www.pachiralodge.com. 34 units. $376 (£188) double for 2 days/1 night; $518 (£259) double for 3 days/2 nights. Rates include round-trip transportation from San José, 3 meals daily, taxes, and tours. AE, MC, V. **Amenities:** Restaurant; bar; pool; laundry service. *In room:* No phone.

Tortuga Lodge ⚐⚐ *(Kids*   This is Costa Rica Expeditions' oldest hotel and one of the oldest hotels in Tortuguero, but thanks to steady renovations, maintenance, and additions, it has not only aged well but also has improved over time. The best feature here is the long multilevel deck located off the main dining room, where you can sit and dine, sip a cool tropical drink, or just take in the view as the water laps against the docks at your feet. There's also a lovely little pool built by the water's edge and designed to create the illusion that it blends into Tortuguero's main canal. All the rooms feature contemporary furniture, Caribbean-influenced decor, and loads of freshly varnished hardwood. They come with one double and one twin bed—or one king-size bed only—ceiling fans, and a comfortable private bathroom. If possible, I'd opt for the second-floor rooms, which feature varnished wood walls and floors and come with a small, covered veranda. There's also a new two-bedroom, two-bathroom second-floor penthouse suite for families or those wanting more space.

Service here is top notch, as are the family-style meals. The meal package here will run you $64 (£32) per person. There are several acres of forest behind the lodge, and a few kilometers of trails wind their way through the trees. This is a great place to look for howler monkeys and colorful poison-arrow frogs.

Tortuguero (mailing address: SJO 235, P.O. Box 025216, Miami, FL 33102-5216). ⓒ **257-0766** in San José or 710-8016 at the lodge. Fax 257-1665. www.tortugalodge.com. 27 units. $99 (£50) double; $155 (£78) penthouse. Rates lower in off season; slightly higher during peak periods. Package rates w/transportation, meals, and tours are available. AE, MC, V. **Amenities:** Restaurant; bar; small pool; game room; laundry service. *In room:* No phone.

Turtle Beach Lodge   This isolated ecolodge is located 5 miles north of the village of Tortuguero, about 20 minutes away by boat. The grounds are set on a narrow strip of land between the Caribbean Sea and the Caño Palma canal. The accommodations are somewhat more spartan than those at the lodges listed above, but they are still clean and comfortable. The rooms are housed in a series of long buildings. Most feature exterior walls that are solid on the bottom half and pure screening above. The best rooms are the corner units, which get the most air-flow and circulation. All have some form of shared or private veranda. Given its location, this is one of the more convenient lodges for viewing the turtle nestings. There's a small, turtle-shaped pool in the center of the grounds, and they have a stable of horses available for riding tours. The lounge area features a television with a satellite feed, and they even have an Internet cafe here.

Caño Palma, Tortuguero. © **248-0707** in San José, or 383-1652 at the lodge. Fax 257-4409. www.turtlebeachlodge.com. 47 units. $380 (£190) double for 2 days/1 night; $510 (£255) double for 3 days/2 nights. Rates include round-trip transportation from San José, 3 meals daily, and tours. AE, MC, V. **Amenities:** Restaurant; bar; pool; laundry service. *In room:* No phone.

INEXPENSIVE

Several basic *cabinas* in the village of Tortuguero offer budget lodgings for between $7 and $15 (£3.50–£7.50) per person. **Cabinas Miss Junie** (© **709-8102**) and **Cabinas Miss Miriam** (© **709-8107**) are the traditional favorites, although in my opinion, the best of the batch are the **Cabinas Aracari** (© **709-8006**), **Cabinas La Casona** (© **709-8092**), and **Cabinas Caribbean Dreams** (© **882-3161**).

Alternately, you could check out **El Manati Lodge** (©/fax **383-0330**), a small, rustic lodge located across the canal from Laguna Lodge, that offers a taste of the ecolodge experience at budget prices.

Casa Marbella *Value*   This in-town house is an excellent option for budget travelers looking for a bit more comfort and care than that offered at most of the other inexpensive in-town options. The rooms here all have high ceilings, tile floors, firm mattresses, and white walls with varnished wood trim. Owner Daryl Loth is a longtime resident and well-respected naturalist guide. Breakfast is served on a little patio facing the main Tortuguero canal in back of the house. A library and lounge area complement the facilities, and a wide range of tours and onward travels can be arranged.

Tortuguero, Limón. ©/fax **709-8011** or © **833-0827**. http://casamarbella.tripod.com. 5 units. $35–$40 (£18–£20) double. Rates include breakfast. No credit cards. *In room:* No phone.

3 Limón: Gateway to Tortuguero National Park & Southern Coastal Beaches

160km (99 miles) E of San José; 55km (34 miles) N of Puerto Viejo

It was just offshore from present-day Limón, in the lee of Isla Uvita, that Christopher Columbus is said to have anchored in 1502, on his fourth and final voyage to the New World. Believing that this was potentially a very rich land, he named it Costa Rica ("Rich Coast"). While never supplying the Spanish crown with much in the way of gold or jewels, the spot where he anchored has proved over the centuries to be the best port on Costa Rica's Caribbean coast—so his judgment wasn't all bad. From here the first bananas were shipped to North America in the late 19th century. Today Limón is primarily a rough-and-tumble port city that ships millions of pounds of bananas northward every year. It also receives a fair share of the country's ocean-borne imports and a modest number of cruise ship callings. On days when a cruise ship is in port, you'll find the city bustling far beyond the norm.

Limón is not generally considered a tourist destination, and few tourists take the time to tour the city, except those stopping here on cruise ships. Very few choose to stay here, and I don't recommend it except during Carnaval. Most travelers use it primarily as a gateway to Tortuguero to the north or the beaches of Cahuita and Puerto Viejo to the south. However, if you do spend some time in Limón, take a seat in Parque Vargas along the seawall and watch the city's citizens go about their business. You may even spot some sloths living in the trees here. Take a walk around town if you're interested in architecture. When banana shipments built this port, many local merchants erected

---

Tips **A Fall Festival**

The biggest event of the year in Limón, and one of the liveliest festivals in Costa Rica, is the annual **Carnaval,** which is held around Columbus Day (Oct 12). For a week, languid Limón shifts into high gear for a nonstop bacchanal orchestrated to the beat of reggae, soca, and calypso music. During the revelries, residents don costumes and take to the streets in a dazzling parade of color. If you want to experience Carnaval, make your reservations early because hotels fill up fast. (This advice goes for the entire coast.)

---

elaborately decorated buildings, several of which have survived the city's many earthquakes, humid weather, and salty sea air. There's a certain charm in the town's fallen grace, drooping balconies, rotting woodwork, and chipped paint. Just be careful, particularly after dark and outside of the city center—Limón has earned a reputation for frequent muggings and robberies.

If you want to get in some beach time while you're in Limón, hop in a taxi or a local bus and head north a few kilometers to **Playa Bonita,** a small public beach. Although the water isn't very clean and is usually too rough for swimming, the setting is much more attractive than downtown. This beach is popular with surfers.

ESSENTIALS

GETTING THERE & DEPARTING   By Plane   The small Limón airstrip received a major face-lift and expansion in 2003 and 2004. **Nature Air** (© **800/235-9272** in the U.S. and Canada, or 299-6000; www.natureair.com) has one flight that departs daily at 6:15am for Limón from the Tobías Bolaños International Airport in Pavas. The flight takes 45 minutes. The return flight leaves Limón for San José at 7am. The fare is $70 (£35).

By Car   The Guápiles Highway heads north out of San José on Calle 3 before turning east and passing close to Barva Volcano and through the rainforests of Braulio Carrillo National Park en route to Limón. The drive takes about 2½ hours and is spectacularly beautiful, especially when it's not raining or misty. Alternately, you can take the old highway, which is also scenic but much slower. This highway heads east out of San José on Avenida Central and passes through San Pedro before reaching Cartago. From Cartago on, the road is narrow and winding and passes through Paraíso and Turrialba before descending out of the mountains to Siquirres, where the old highway meets the new. This route takes around 4 hours, more or less, to get to Limón.

By Bus   **Transportes Caribeños** buses (© **222-0610** in San José, or © 758-2575 in Limón) leave San José roughly every half-hour daily between 5am and 7pm from the Caribbean bus terminal (Gran Terminal del Caribe) on Calle Central, 1 block north of Avenida 11. Friday through Sunday, the last bus leaves an hour later at 8pm. Trip duration is 2½ to 3 hours. The buses are either direct or local *(corriente),* and they don't alternate in any particularly predictable fashion. The local buses are generally older and less comfortable and stop en route to pick up passengers from the roadside. I highly recommend taking a direct bus, if possible. The fare is $3.50 (£1.75) for the local and $5 (£2.50) for the direct.

Buses leave Limón for San José roughly every half-hour between 6am and 7:30pm, and similarly alternate between local and direct, with the last bus leaving 1 hour later

Friday through Sunday. The new Limón bus terminal is on the main road into town, several blocks west of the downtown area and Parque Vargas. Buses (© 758-1572) to **Cahuita** and **Puerto Viejo** leave from this terminal roughly every hour from 5am to 6pm daily. Buses to **Punta Uva** and **Manzanillo,** both of which are south of Puerto Viejo, leave Limón daily at 6 and 10:30am and 3 and 6pm, from the same station.

ORIENTATION   Nearly all addresses in Limón are measured from the central market, which is aptly located smack-dab in the center of town, or from Parque Vargas, which is at the east end of town fronting the sea. The cruise ship dock is located just south of Parque Vargas. A pedestrian mall runs from Parque Vargast to the west for several blocks.

FAST FACTS   A host of private and national banks is located in the small downtown area. You can reach the **local police** at © 758-1148 and the **Red Cross** at © 758-0125. The **Tony Facio Hospital** (© 758-0580) is just outside of the downtown area on the road to Playa Bonita.

WHERE TO STAY & DINE

In addition to the hotels listed below, if you want to be right on the beach at Playa Bonita, check out the **Hotel Cocori** (© 795-1670; fax 795-2930).

Hotel Maribu Caribe   Located on top of a hill overlooking the Caribbean and built to resemble an Indian village, the Maribu Caribe is a pleasant (if not overly luxurious) choice if you're looking to spend some time close to Limón. The hotel is popular with Tico families from San José because it's easy to get to for weekend trips. The guest rooms are in circular bungalows with white-tile floors and varnished wood ceilings. The furnishings are comfortable but a bit old.

The hotel's restaurant has the best view in or around Limón. It's built out over the edge of a steep hill, with tide pools and the ocean below. In addition to the formal dining room, there are tables outside on a curving veranda that make the most of the view. The Maribu Caribe can help you with tour arrangements and also has a gift shop. *Note:* This hotel is several kilometers out of town, on the road to Playa Bonita.

Playa Bonita, Limón (mailing address: A.P. 623-7300, San José). © 795-2543 or 253-1838. Fax 234-0193. 52 units. $68 double (£34). Rates lower in off season. AE, DC, MC, V. **Amenities:** Restaurant; bar; attractive pool; laundry service. *In room:* A/C, free Wi-Fi.

Park Hotel 𝒜   This is easily the best option in Limón proper—although there really isn't any competition. The hotel has an excellent location fronting the ocean, across the street from the fire station. Unlike much of Limón, which feels to be in a state of prolonged and steady decay, this place has received constant and fairly competent upkeep over the years. Ask for a room on the ocean side of the hotel because these are brighter, quieter, and cooler than those that face the fire station, although they're also slightly more expensive. The suites have private oceanview balconies and larger bathrooms with tubs. The large, sunny dining room off the lobby serves standard Tico fare at very reasonable prices.

Av. 3, between calles 1 and 3 (A.P. 35-7300), Limón. © 758-3476 or 798-0555. Fax 758-4364. 32 units. $51–$60 double (£26–£30). AE, MC, V. **Amenities:** Restaurant. *In room:* A/C, TV.

EN ROUTE SOUTH

Staying at the place listed below is a great way to combine some quiet beach time on the Caribbean coast with a more active ecolodge and bird-watching experience into one compact itinerary.

Selva Bananito Lodge ★★ *(Finds)*   This remote nature lodge allows you to combine some rainforest adventuring with some serious beach time in Cahuita or Puerto Viejo. The individual raised-stilt cabins are spacious and comfortable, with an abundance of varnished woodwork. Inside are two double beds, a desk and chair, and some fresh flowers, as well as a large private bathroom. Outside is a wraparound veranda with a hammock and some chairs. It all adds up to what I call rustic luxury. Half the cabins have views of the Bananito River and a small valley; the other half have views of the Matama Mountains, part of the Talamanca mountain range.

There are no electric lights at Selva Bananito, but each evening as you dine by candlelight, your cabin's oil lamps are lit for you. Hot water is provided by solar panels. Tasty family-style meals are served in the large, open rancho, which is also a great spot for morning bird-watching. There's a wide range of tours and activities, including rainforest hikes and horseback rides in the jungle, tree climbing, self-guided trail hikes, and even the opportunity to rappel down the face of a jungle waterfall. The owners are very involved in conservation efforts in this area, and approximately two-thirds of the 840 hectares (2,100 acres) here are primary forest managed as a private reserve. You'll need a four-wheel-drive vehicle to reach the lodge itself, although most folks leave their rental cars in Bananito and let the lodge drive them the final bit. You can also arrange to be picked up in San José.

Bananito (A.P. 2333-2050, San Pedro). ℂ **253-8118.** Fax 280-0820. www.selvabananito.com. 11 units. $240 double (£120). Rates include 3 meals daily and all taxes. Rates lower in off season. No credit cards. **Amenities:** Restaurant; activity desk. *In room:* No phone.

4 Cahuita ★

200km (124 miles) E of San José; 42km (26 miles) S of Limón; 13km (8 miles) N of Puerto Viejo

Cahuita is a sleepy Caribbean beach village and the first "major" tourist destination heading south out of Limón. Nevertheless, the boom going on in Puerto Viejo and the beaches south of Puerto Viejo have in many ways passed Cahuita by. Depending on your point of view, that can be a reason to stay here, or to decide to head farther south. Any way you slice it, Cahuita is one of the most laid-back villages in Costa Rica. The few dirt and gravel streets here are host to a languid parade of pedestrian traffic, parted occasionally by a bicycle, car, or bus. After a short time, you'll find yourself slipping into the heat-induced torpor that affects anyone who ends up here.

The village traces its roots to Afro-Caribbean fishermen and laborers who settled in this region in the mid-1800s, and today the population is still primarily English-speaking blacks whose culture and language set them apart from other Costa Ricans.

People come to Cahuita for its miles of pristine beaches, which stretch both north and south from town. The southern beaches, the forest behind them, and the coral reef offshore (one of just a handful in Costa Rica) are all part of **Cahuita National Park.** Silt and pesticides washing down from nearby banana plantations have taken a heavy toll on the coral reefs, so don't expect the snorkeling to be world-class. But on a calm day, it can be pretty good, and the beaches are idyllic every day. It can rain almost any time of year here, but the most dependably dry season is in September and October.

ESSENTIALS

GETTING THERE & DEPARTING   By Plane   The closest airport to Cahuita is found in Limón (see above). A taxi from the airport to Cahuita should cost around

$15 (£7.50). You can also just walk the long block from the airport terminal to the main road south and flag down any of the frequent buses that pass by.

By Car   Follow the directions above for getting to Limón. As you enter Limón, about 5 blocks before the busiest section of downtown, watch for a paved road to the right, just before the railroad tracks. Take this road south to Cahuita, passing the airstrip and the beach on your left as you leave Limón. Alternatively, there's a turnoff with signs for Sixaola and La Bomba several miles before Limón. This winding short-cut skirts the city and puts you on the coastal road several miles south of town.

Tip: As you drive along the coastal road between Limón and Cahuita, keep your eye out for roadside stands selling fresh, green coconuts, or *pipas* in Spanish. Green coconuts have very little meat, but are filled with copious amounts of slightly sweet, clear liquid that is amazingly refreshing. According to local legend, this liquid is pure enough to be used as plasma in an emergency situation. Armed with a machete, the pipa seller will cut of the top and stick in a straw. In the best of cases, the pipa will have been cooled over ice. The entire thing should cost around $1 (50p).

By Bus   **Mepe** express buses (© 257-8129) leave San José daily at 6 and 10am, noon, and 2 and 4pm from the new Caribbean bus terminal (Gran Terminal del Caribe) on Calle Central, 1 block north of Avenida 11. The trip's duration is 4 hours; the fare is $6.30 (£3.15). During peak periods, extra buses are often added. However, it's wise to check because this bus line **(Mepe)** is one of the most fickle.

Alternatively, you can catch a bus to **Limón** (see above) and then transfer to a Cahuita- or Puerto Viejo–bound bus (© 758-1572) in Limón. These latter buses leave roughly every hour between 5am and 6pm from in front of Radio Casino, which is 1 block north of the municipal market. Buses from Limón to Manzanillo also stop in Cahuita and leave from the same spot daily at 6 and 10am and 3 and 6pm. The trip takes 1 hour; the fare is $1.50 (75p).

Gray Line (© 220-2126; www.graylinecostarica.com) has a daily bus that leaves San José for Cahuita at 6:30am. The return bus leaves Cahuita at 11:30pm. **Interbus** (© 283-5573; www.interbusonline.com) has a daily bus that leaves San José for Cahuita at 7:50am. The return bus leaves Cahuita at 1:40pm. Both companies will pick you up at most area hotels in both San José and Cahuita, and both charge $29 (£15) for a one-way fare.

Buses departing **Puerto Viejo** and Sixaola (on the Panama border) stop in Cahuita at approximately 7, 9:30, and 11:30am, and 4:30pm en route to San José. However, this schedule is far from precise, so it's always best to check with your hotel. Moreover, these buses are often full, particularly on weekends and throughout the high season. To avoid standing in the aisle all the way to San José, it is sometimes better to take a bus first to Limón and then catch one of the frequent Limón–San José buses. Buses to Limón pass through Cahuita regularly throughout the day. Another tactic I've used is to take a morning bus to Puerto Viejo, spend the day down there, and board a direct bus to San José at its point of origin, thereby snagging a seat.

ORIENTATION   There are only about eight dirt streets in Cahuita. The highway runs parallel to the coast, with three main roads running perpendicular. The north-ernmost of these roads bypasses town and brings you to the northern end of Playa Negra. It's marked with signs for the Magellan Inn and other hotels up on this end. The second road in brings you to the southern end of Playa Negra, a half-mile closer to town. Look for signs for Atlantida Lodge. The third road is the principal entrance into town. The village's main street in town, which runs parallel to the highway, dead-ends at the entrance to the national park (a footbridge over a small stream).

Buses drop their passengers by a small public park in front of Coco's Bar. Across from the park you'll find a helpful large-scale map of the town. If you come in on the bus and are staying at a lodge on Playa Negra, ask around town for a cab, or head out walking north on the street that runs between Coco's Bar and the small park. This road curves to the left and continues a mile or so out to Playa Negra.

FAST FACTS You can wash your clothes at the self-service **laundromat** in front of Cabinas Vaz. One load in the washer or dryer costs $1.50 (75p). The **police station** (© 755-0217) is located where the road from Playa Negra turns into town. The **post office,** next door to the police station, is open Monday through Friday from 8am to 5pm.

If you can't find a **cab** in town, try calling **René** (© 755-0243), **Wayne** (© 755-0078), or **Dino** (© 755-0012). You can also rent a scooter from **Sucurucú** (© 755-0218), which is located in village, at Cabinas Vaz.

EXPLORING CAHUITA NATIONAL PARK 🔆

On arrival, you'll immediately feel the call of the long scimitar of beach that stretches south from the edge of town. This beach can be glimpsed through the trees from Cahuita's sun-baked main street and extends a promise of relief from the heat. Although the lush coastal forest and picture-perfect palm lines are a tremendous draw, the park was actually created to preserve the 240-hectare (787-acre) **coral reef** that surrounds it. The reef contains 35 species of coral and provides a haven for hundreds of brightly colored tropical fish. You can walk on the beach itself or follow the trail that runs through the forest just behind the beach to check out the reef.

The best place to swim is just before or beyond the **Río Perezoso (Lazy River),** several hundred meters inside Cahuita National Park. The trail behind the beach is great for bird-watching, and if you're lucky, you might see some monkeys or a sloth. The loud grunting sounds you hear off in the distance are the calls of howler monkeys, which can be heard from more than a kilometer away. Nearer at hand, you're likely to hear crabs scuttling amid the dry leaves on the forest floor—a half-dozen or so species of land crabs live in this region—my favorites are the bright orange-and-purple ones.

The trail behind the beach stretches a little more than 6.4km (4 miles) to the southern end of the park at **Puerto Vargas,** where you'll find a beautiful white-sand beach, the park headquarters, and a primitive campground with showers and outhouses. It's a nice, flat walk, but a rewarding one because there's good wildlife viewing and access to the beach. The reef is off the point just north of Puerto Vargas, and you can snorkel here. If you don't dawdle, the hike to Puerto Vargas should take no more than 2 hours each way. Bring plenty of mosquito repellent because this area can be buggy.

Although there's snorkeling at Puerto Vargas, the nicest coral heads are located several hundred meters offshore, and it's best to have a boat take you out. A 3-hour **snorkel trip** costs between $15 and $25 (£7.50–£13) per person with equipment. You can arrange one with any of the local tour companies listed below. *Note:* These trips are best taken when the seas are calm—for safety's sake, visibility, and comfort.

ENTRY POINTS, FEES & REGULATIONS The **in-town park entrance** is just over a footbridge at the end of the village's main street. It has bathroom facilities, changing rooms, and storage lockers. This is the best place to enter if you just want to spend the day on the beach and maybe take a little hike in the bordering forest.

The alternate park entrance is at the southern end of the park in **Puerto Vargas.** This is where you should come if you plan to camp at the park or if you don't feel up to hiking a couple of hours to reach the good snorkeling spots. The road to Puerto Vargas is approximately 5km (3 miles) south of Cahuita on the left.

Officially, **admission** is $6 (£3) per person per day, but this is collected only at the Puerto Vargas entrance. You can enter the park from the town of Cahuita for free or with a voluntary contribution. The park is open from dawn to dusk for day visitors.

Camping is an extra $2 (£1) per person. Fifty campsites at Puerto Vargas stretch along for several kilometers and are either right on or just a few steps from the beach. My favorite are those farthest from the entrance. A small ranger station has basic shower and bathroom facilities, but they're a bit far from some of the better campsites.

GETTING THERE   By Car   The turnoff for the Puerto Vargas entrance is clearly marked 7km (4⅓ miles) south of Cahuita.

By Bus   Your best bet is to get off a Puerto Viejo– or Sixaola-bound bus at the turnoff for the Puerto Vargas entrance (well marked, but tell the bus driver in advance). The guard station/entrance is only about 500m (1,640 ft.) down this road. However, the campsites are several kilometers farther, so it's a long hike with a heavy pack.

BEACHES & ACTIVITIES OUTSIDE THE PARK

Outside the park the best place for swimming is **Playa Negra.** The stretch right in front of the Atlantida Lodge is my favorite spot.

There are plenty of options for organized adventure trips or tours while in Cahuita. I recommend **Cahuita Tours and Adventure Center** (© 755-0000), on the village's main street heading out toward Playa Negra. Cahuita Tours offers glass-bottom-boat and snorkeling trips ($25/£13 per person), jungle tours ($40/£20), white-water rafting trips ($100/£50), and Jeep tours to the Bribri Reservation ($70/£35).

Turística Cahuita Information Center (©/fax 755-0071), also on the main road heading toward Playa Negra, and **Roberto Tours** (© 755-0117), 50m (164 ft.) south of the bus stop, offer similar tours at similar prices. Most of the companies offer multiday trips to Tortuguero, as well as to Bocas del Toro, Panama.

Brigitte (© 755-0053; www.brigittecahuita.com) rents horses for $12 (£6) per hour (you must have experience riding) and offers guided horseback tours for $35 to $40 (£18–£20). She also rents mountain bikes for $8 (£4) per day, and even has a few rooms available.

On the main highway, just north of the main entrance to Cahuita is the new **Mariposario Cahuita** (© 755-0361), a large, informative butterfly farm attraction that charges $8 (£4) and is open daily from 8:30am to 3:30pm. It's best to come in the early morning on a sunny day, when the butterflies are most active.

Bird-watchers and sloth lovers should head north 9km (5½ miles) to **Aviarios del Caribe and the Buttercup Sloth Rescue Center** 🐾🐾 (©/fax 750-0775; www.slothrescue.org). The folks here run a sloth rehabilitation project and also offer guided canoe tours through the surrounding estuary and river system. More than 330 species of birds have been spotted here. The 3½-hour canoe tour costs $30 (£15) per person and leaves at 6am and 3pm. There's also a 1¼-hour canoe tour combination that includes a visit to the sloth rehabilitation center and a self-guided hike on its trails for $20 (£10) per person. This option is available between 8am and 2:30pm. It's best to make reservations in advance.

SHOPPING

For a wide selection of beachwear, local crafts, cheesy souvenirs, and batik clothing, try **Boutique Coco Miko** or **Boutique Bambata,** which are both on the main road near the entrance to the park. The latter is also a good place to have your hair wrapped in colorful threads and strung with beads. Out toward Playa Negra, similar wares are offered at the gift shop at **Cahuita Tours.** Handmade jewelry and crafts are sold by local and itinerant artisans in makeshift stands near the park entrance.

Ask around town for a copy of Paula Palmer's *What Happen: A Folk-History of Costa Rica's Talamanca Coast* (Zona Tropical; 2005). The book is a history of the region based on interviews with many of the area's oldest residents. Much of it is in the traditional Creole language, from which the title is taken. It makes fun and interesting reading, and you just might bump into someone mentioned in the book.

If you are interested in the local music scene, pick up a disc by Walter "Gavitt" Ferguson. The local 86-year-old calypso singer and songwriter is a living legend and has two CDs of original songs, *Babylon* and *Dr. Bombodee.* Ask around town and you should be able to find a copy. If you're lucky, you might even bump into Gavitt.

WHERE TO STAY
MODERATE
Atlantida Lodge   This quiet, midsize hotel has definitely seen better days. While it is still an option to consider if you want to be just steps away from the beach, with a pool and a few basic amenities, the lodge really is overdue for some maintenance and upkeep. The guest rooms have a decidedly rustic feel to them and some are a bit small, with pale-yellow stucco walls, red-tile floors, ceiling fans, and plenty of bamboo trim. Each has a small patio with a bamboo screen divider for privacy, which opens onto the hotel's lush gardens. A host of different tours can be arranged here, from snorkeling to horseback riding to white-water rafting.

Beside the soccer field on the road to Playa Negra, .8km (½ mile) north of town, Cahuita, Limón. (C) 755-0115. Fax 755-0213. 34 units. $60 double (£30). Rates lower in off season. AE, MC, V. **Amenities:** Restaurant; bar; midsize tile pool; small gym; tour desk; massage; laundry service. *In room:* No phone.

El Encanto Bed and Breakfast ★★ (Value   The individual bungalows at this little bed-and-breakfast are set in from the road on spacious and well-kept grounds. The bungalows themselves are also spacious and have attractive touches such as wooden bed frames, arched windows, Mexican-tile floors, Guatemalan bedspreads, and framed Panamanian molas hanging on the walls. There is a separate two-story, three-bedroom, two-bathroom house with a full kitchen at the rear of the grounds, as well as a new deluxe room. Hearty breakfasts are served in the small open dining room surrounded by lush gardens. Nice extra touches here include a small kidney-shaped pool, a wood-floored meditation hall, a covered garden gazebo, and an open-air massage room.

Cahuita (A.P. 7302-7), Limón (just outside of town on the road to Playa Negra). (C) 755-0113. Fax 755-0432. www.elencantobedandbreakfast.com. 7 units. $65 (£33) double. Rates include full breakfast. Rates slightly lower in off season; higher during peak weeks. MC, V. **Amenities:** Small pool. *In room:* No phone.

Hotel La Diosa ★   Located close to the sea north of Playa Negra, this newer option has some of the coziest and most inviting rooms around, with excellent facilities and friendly hosts. The best rooms here have air-conditioning and private Jacuzzis. All have cool tile floors, rattan furnishings, and plenty of ventilation. There's a midsize pool, as well as a yoga and meditation room. While breakfast is served daily, there's no restaurant here. The hotel is just steps from the sea, but the coast here is rugged and made up mostly of sharp coral, and not very suitable for swimming. Still, the gardens are lush and beautiful, and a relaxed and welcoming vibe pervades this place.

Cahuita, Limón (north of town, inland from the Playa Negra road). © 877/632-3198 in the U.S. and Canada, or 755-0055 in Costa Rica. Fax 755-0321. www.hotelladiosa.net. 18 units. $55–$85 (£28–£43) double. Rates include full breakfast. Rates slightly lower in off season; higher during peak weeks. MC, V. **Amenities:** Midsize pool. *In room:* No phone.

Magellan Inn ✦ This small inn is the most sophisticated hotel in the area. The rooms are all carpeted and have French doors, vertical blinds, tiled bathrooms with hardwood counters, and two joined single beds. Each room has its own tiled veranda with a Persian rug and bamboo sitting chairs. About half of the rooms have air-conditioning. Although there's a ceiling fan over each bed, the non-air-conditioned rooms could use a bit more ventilation. The combination bar/lounge and dining room features even more Persian-style rugs and wicker furniture. Most memorable of all are the hotel's sunken pool and lush gardens, both of which are built into a crevice in the ancient coral reef that underlies this entire region—which leads to good bird-watching.

At the far end of Playa Negra (about 2km/1¼ miles north of Cahuita), Cahuita (A.P. 1132), Limón. ©/fax 755-0035. www.magellaninn.com. 6 units. $69 (£35) double; $99 (£50) double with A/C. Rates include continental breakfast. Rates slightly lower in off season; higher during peak weeks. AE, MC, V. **Amenities:** Bar; lounge; small pool; tour desk; laundry service. *In room:* Free Wi-Fi, no phone.

INEXPENSIVE

In addition to the places listed below, **Spencer's Seaside Cabinas** (© 755-0027; hernanspencer@hotmail.com) is a somewhat funky collection of budget rooms worth considering. Rooms are set just a few feet from the water in the heart of town, **Hotel Belle Fleur** (© 755-0283; hotelbellefleur@hotmail.com) has neat and cheery new rooms set just a few feet back from the main road, close to the national park entrance.

Alby Lodge ✦ *Value* With the feel of a small village, Alby Lodge is a fascinating little place hand-built by its German owners. Although the four small cabins are close to the center of the village, they're surrounded by a large lawn and feel secluded. The cabins are quintessentially tropical, with thatched roofs, mosquito nets, hardwood floors and beams, big shuttered windows, tile bathrooms, and a hammock slung on the front porch. There's no restaurant here, but you may cook your own meals in a communal kitchen area if you wish. The turnoff for the lodge is on your right just before you reach the national park entrance; the hotel is located about 136m (446 ft.) down a narrow, winding lane from here.

Cahuita (A.P. 840), Limón. ©/fax 755-0031. www.albylodge.com. 4 units. $40 (£20) double; $45 (£23) triple; $50 (£25) quad. Children under 12 stay free in parent's room. No credit cards. *In room:* Free Wi-Fi, safe, no phone.

Cabinas Arrecife Located near the water, next to Restaurant Edith (p. 354), this row of basic rooms is an excellent budget choice in Cahuita. Each room comes with a double and a single bed, a table fan, and tile floors. There's not a lot of room to move around, but they are pretty clean and well kept for this price range. There's a shared veranda with some chairs for sitting, where you can catch a glimpse of the sea through a dense stand of coconut palms. If you want to be closer to the sea, grab one of the hammocks strung on those palms or sit in the small, open restaurant, which serves breakfast every day and dinners according to demand.

Cahuita (about 100m/328 ft. east of the post office), Limón. ©/fax 755-0081. 12 units. $25 (£13) double; $30 triple (£15). AE, MC, V. **Amenities:** Restaurant. *In room:* No phone.

WHERE TO DINE

Coconut meat and milk figure in a lot of the regional cuisine. Most nights, local women cook up pots of various local specialties and sell them from the front porches of the two discos or from street-side stands around town; a full meal will cost you around $2 to $4 (£1–£2).

In addition to the places listed below, **Don Corleone** (© 755-0341) serves good thin-crust pizzas and Italian cuisine, and **Caribbean Roots & Culture** (© 811-9351) cooks up excellent Pan-Caribbean and vegetarian fare. Another local favorite is **Relax** (© 755-0322), which serves a mix of local, Italian, and Mexican food in a lovely open-air dining room above **Ricky's Bar.**

Casa Creole 🍷🍷 FRENCH/FUSION   Under new management, this place remains an excellent option for upscale dining in this small, remote village. The menu and vibe are contemporary French chic. Tables in the open first-floor dining room are set with linen tablecloths and candles in glass lanterns. There's a sense of relaxed elegance, with the feel of an upscale lounge. Start with the crab and mango salad or the grilled shrimp and litchi nut shish-kebab. Main course selections are more traditional, with grilled lobster, steak au poivre, beef bourguignon, and sautéed shrimp or squid anchoring the menu. More adventurous diners can try chicken in a coconut milk curry sauce. For dessert, I recommend the homemade tart tatin.

Next to the Magellan Inn, Playa Negra Rd., 2.5km (1½ miles) north of Cahuita. © **755-0104.** Reservations recommended during the high season. Main courses $12–$20 (£6–£10). AE, MC, V. Mon–Sat 5–11pm.

Cha Cha Cha 🍷🍷 SEAFOOD/INTERNATIONAL   Fresh seafood and grilled meats, simply and expertly prepared. What more could you ask from a casual, open-air restaurant in a funky beach town? In addition to the fresh catch of the day and filet mignon, the eclectic menu here includes everything from jerk chicken and Thai shrimp salad to pasta primavera and fajitas. The grilled squid salad with a citrus dressing is one of the house specialties and a great light bite. The restaurant occupies the ground floor of an old wooden building. Everything is painted pure white, with some blue trim and accents. The restaurant has only a half-dozen or so tables that fill up fast.

On the main road in town, 3 blocks north of Coco's Bar. © **394-4153** or 755-0476. Reservations recommended during the high season. Main courses $6–$20 (£3–£10). MC, V. Tues–Sun 2–10pm.

Restaurant Edith 🍷 *Finds* CREOLE/SEAFOOD   This place is a local institution, and deservedly so. Many years ago, Miss Edith decided to serve home-cooked meals to all the hungry visitors hanging around. If you want a taste of the local cuisine in a homey, sit-down environment, this is the place. Miss Edith's daughters do most of the cooking and serving today, but you might just find her on hand. The menu is long, with lots of local seafood dishes and Creole combinations such as yuca in coconut milk with meat or vegetables. The sauces have spice and zest and are a welcome change from the typically bland fare served up elsewhere in Costa Rica. After you've ordered, it's usually no more than 45 minutes until your meal arrives. It's often crowded, so don't be bashful about sitting down with total strangers at any of the big tables. Hours can be erratic; it sometimes closes without warning. Miss Edith's place is at the opposite end of town from the park entrance.

By the police station, Cahuita. © **755-0248.** Reservations not accepted. Main courses $5–$20 (£2.50–£10). No credit cards. Mon–Sat 11am–10pm; Sun 4–9pm.

Sobre Las Olas 🍷 SEAFOOD/ITALIAN   Set on a slight rise of rocks above a coral cove and breaking waves, this place has by far the best location in Cahuita. The Italian owners serve a mix of local and Italian fare. They serve excellent fresh squid or shrimp in a tangy local coconut milk sauce, as well as a host of pasta dishes. The fresh grilled snapper is also always a good way to go. I especially like this place for lunch, when you can really enjoy the view of the clear blue Caribbean Sea. If weather permits, grab one of the outdoor tables set in the shade of coconut palms. After you finish eating, slide over and into one of the hammocks strung between those palms.

Just north of town on the road to Playa Negra. ℂ 755-0109. Reservations not necessary. Main courses $8–$18 (£4–£9). MC, V. Wed–Mon noon–10pm.

CAHUITA AFTER DARK

Coco's Bar 𝄪, a classic Caribbean watering hole, has traditionally been the place to spend your nights (or days, for that matter) if you like cold beer and very loud reggae and soca music. **Ricky's Bar,** located just across the street, is also popular. Check them both out; on any given night, you might be more drawn to one or the other. There are usually local women hanging out on the front porches of each establishment selling fresh *paty* pies or bowls of rundown stew (see "That Rundown Feeling" on p. 365). Toward the park entrance, the **National Park Restaurant** has a popular bar and disco on most nights during the high season and on weekends during the off season.

5 Puerto Viejo 𝄪𝄪

200km (124 miles) E of San José; 55km (34 miles) S of Limón

Puerto Viejo is the hottest spot on Costa Rica's Caribbean coast. And I'm not just talking about the weather. Puerto Viejo is farther down the road from Cahuita, it's but much more popular, with a livelier atmosphere and more ongoing development. Much of this is due to the many surfers who come here to ride the town's famous and fearsome Salsa Brava wave, and only slightly mellower Playa Cocles beach break. Nonsurfers will appreciate excellent swimming beaches, plenty of active adventure options, nearby rainforest trails, and some great local and international restaurants.

As you head still farther south, you will come to the most beautiful beaches on this coast, with white sand and turquoise seas. When it's calm (Aug–Oct), the waters down here are some of the clearest anywhere in the country, with good snorkeling among the nearby coral reefs.

This is the end of the line along Costa Rica's Caribbean coast. After the tiny town of Manzanillo, some 15km (9⅓ miles) south of Puerto Viejo, a national wildlife reserve stretches a few final kilometers to the Panamanian border.

This area gets plenty of rain, just like the rest of the coast (Sept–Oct are your best bets for sun, although it's not guaranteed even in those months).

ESSENTIALS

GETTING THERE & DEPARTING   By Plane   The closest airport to Puerto Viejo is in Limón (see "Limón: Gateway to Tortuguero National Park & Southern Coastal Beaches," earlier in this chapter). A taxi from the airport to Cahuita should cost around $20 (£10). Alternately, you can just walk the long block from the airport terminal to the main road south and flag down any of the frequent buses that pass by.

By Car   To reach Puerto Viejo, continue south from Cahuita for another 16km (10 miles). Watch for a prominent fork in the highway. The right-hand fork continues on to Bribri and Sixaola. The left-hand fork (it actually appears to be a straight shot) takes you into Puerto Viejo on 5km (3 miles) of paved road.

By Bus   **MEPE** express buses (© **257-8129** in San José, or 750-0023 in Puerto Viejo) to Puerto Viejo leave San José daily at 6 and 10am, noon, and 2 and 4pm from the new Caribbean terminal (Gran Terminal del Caribe) on Calle Central, 1 block north of Avenida 11. The trip's duration is 4½ to 5 hours; the fare is $6.80 (£3.40). During peak periods extra buses are sometimes added. Always ask if the bus is going into Puerto Viejo (you do not want to get dropped off at the turnoff for Sixaola) and if it's continuing on to **Manzanillo** (especially helpful if you're staying in a hotel south of town). Regardless, don't be surprised if it doesn't do exactly what you were told.

   Gray Line (© **220-2126;** www.graylinecostarica.com) has a daily bus that leaves San José for Puerto Viejo at 6:30am. This bus returns for San José at 11am. **Interbus** (© **283-5573;** www.interbusonline.com) has a daily bus that leaves San José for Puerto Viejo at 7:50am. The Interbus return bus leaves daily from Puerto Viejo at 2:30pm. Both companies will pick you up at most hotels, both in San José and in Puerto Viejo, and charge $29 (£15) for a one-way fare.

   Alternatively, you can catch a bus to **Limón** (see earlier in this chapter for details) and then transfer to a Puerto Viejo–bound bus in Limón. These latter buses (© **758-1572**) leave roughly every hour between 5am and 6pm from in front of Radio Casino, which is 1 block north of the municipal market. Buses from Limón to Manzanillo also stop in Puerto Viejo and leave daily at 6 and 10:30am and 3 and 6pm. The trip takes 1½ hours; the fare is $2 (£1).

   If you arrive in Puerto Viejo by bus, be leery of hucksters and touts offering you hotel rooms. In most cases, they just work on a small commission from whatever hotel or *cabina* is hiring, and, in some cases, they'll steer you away from one of my recommended hotels or falsely claim that it is full.

   Express buses leave Puerto Viejo for San José daily at 7:30, 9, and 11am, and 4pm. Buses for Limón leave daily at 6 and 9am, and 1, 4, and 5pm. Buses to **Punta Uva** and **Manzanillo** leave Puerto Viejo daily around 7:30am, noon, and 4:30 and 7:30pm. These buses return from Manzanillo at 5 and 8:15am and 12:45 and 5pm.

ORIENTATION   The road in from the highway runs parallel to Playa Negra, or Black Sand Beach (this is not the same one I talked about in Cahuita), for a couple hundred meters before entering the village of Puerto Viejo, which has all of about 10 dirt streets. The sea is on your left and forested hills on your right as you come into town. It's another 15km (9⅓ miles) south to Manzanillo. This road is paved all the way to Manzanillo, although some sections are nonetheless in fairly rough shape.

FAST FACTS   **Public phones** are located around town and at several hotels. Those looking to change money should head to the **Banco de Costa Rica** branch located on the main road in town. There's also a **Banco Nacional** branch in **Bribri,** about 10km (6 miles) away. Both of these banks have ATM machines. You'll find the **post office** in the tiny strip mall behind Café Viejo. There is a **Guardia Rural police** (© **750-0230**) post on the beach, near Johnny's Place.

   There are several little Internet cafes around town. There are also a couple of full-service laundromats—the one at **Café Rico** (© **750-0325**) will give you a free cup of coffee, cappuccino, or espresso while you wait.

   The town's main **taxi** driver is named **Bull** (© **750-0112** or 836-8219). You might find him hanging around the *parquecito* (little park), or you can ask a local to point you to his house. If Bull's not around or he's busy, you could try **Delroy** (© **750-0132**). You can rent scooters and bicycles from several operators in town. I like **Sucurucú**

(© 750-0700), which is located just south of the bus stop, and **Dragon Scooter Rentals** (© 750-0728), which is across from the restaurant Salsa Brava, at the stand for **Aventuras Bravas.**

WHAT TO SEE & DO

CULTURAL & ADVENTURE TOURS   The **Asociación Talamanqueña de Ecoturismo y Conservación (ATEC)** 🐾, across the street from the Soda Tamara (© **750-0398** or ©/fax 750-0191; www.greencoast.com/atec.htm), is concerned with preserving the environment and cultural heritage of this area and promoting ecologically sound development. (If you plan to stay in Puerto Viejo for an extended period of time and would like to contribute to the community, ask about volunteering.) In addition to functioning as the local information center, Internet cafe, and traveler's hub, ATEC runs a little shop that sells T-shirts, maps, posters, and books.

ATEC also offers quite a few tours, including **half-day walks** that focus on nature and either the local Afro-Caribbean culture or the indigenous Bribri culture. These walks pass through farms and forests, and along the way you'll learn about local history, customs, medicinal plants, and Indian mythology, and have an opportunity to see sloths, monkeys, iguanas, keel-billed toucans, and other wildlife. There is a range of different walks through the nearby Bribri Indians' Kéköldi Reserve, as well as more strenuous hikes through the primary rainforest. **Bird walks** and **night walks** will help you spot more of the area wildlife; there are even overnight treks. The local guides have a wealth of information and make a hike through the forest a truly educational experience. Half-day walks (and night walks) are $20 (£10), and a full-day tour costs between $30 and $50 (£15–£25). ATEC can arrange snorkeling trips to the nearby coral reefs, as well as snorkeling and fishing trips in dugout canoes. A half-day of snorkeling or fishing costs around $20 to $40 (£10–£20) per person.

ATEC can also help you arrange overnight and multiday **camping trips** into the Talamanca Mountains and through neighboring indigenous reserves, as well as trips to Tortuguero and even a 7- to 10-day transcontinental trek to the Pacific coast. Some tours require minimum groups of 5 or 10 people and several days' advance notice. The ATEC office is open daily from 8am to 9pm.

Atlántico Tours (© 750-0004), **Exploradores Outdoors** 🐾 (© 750-2020; www.exploradoresoutdoors.com), **Puerto Viejo Tours & Rentals** (© 750-0411), and **Terraventuras** 🐾 (© 750-0750; www.terraventuras.com) all offer a whole host of half- and full-day adventure tours into the jungle or sea for between $30 and $90 (£15–£45) per person. One popular tour is Terraventuras' zip-line canopy tour, which features 23 treetop platforms, a large harnessed swing, and a rappel.

One of the more educational tours is the 2-hour **Chocolate Tour** (© **750-0075;** chocoart@racsa.co.cr) through a working organic cacao plantation and chocolate production facility. The tour shows you the whole process of growing, harvesting, and processing cacao, and of course there's a tasting at the end. The tour is run by reservation only, and costs $15 (£7.50) per person, with a four-person minimum.

Scuba divers can check in with **Aquamor** 🐾 (© **759-9012**) or **Reef Runners Dive Shop** (© 750-0480). Both operations frequent a variety of dive sites between Punta Uva and Manzanillo, and when the seas are calm and visibility is good, this is some good diving, although throughout most of the year it can be a bit rough and murky here. Aquamor is based down in Manzanillo (where you'll find the best reefs), while Reef Runners has an office in downtown Puerto Viejo.

Tips South Caribbean Music Festival

Each year, the folks at Playa Chiquita Lodge (p. 364) organize a month-long festival of concerts and workshops featuring local and national musical groups
and solo artists. The dates vary, but the festival tends to fall somewhere during
the months of March and April and always ends the week before Easter. Concerts are usually held on Friday and weekends at Playa Chiquita Lodge and
other venues around the area.

A LITTLE MIND & BODY REVITALIZATION   If you're looking for some day spa
pampering, check out **Pure Jungle Spa** (� (© 750-0536; www.purejunglespa.com).
Located at La Costa De Papito (see below), these folks have a wide range of massage and
treatment options at reasonable rates. They make many of their own oils, masks, wraps,
and exfoliants.

Better suited to a longer stay, **Samasati** � (© **800/563-9643** in the U.S., or
756-8015 in Costa Rica; www.samasati.com) is a lovely jungle yoga retreat and spa,
with spectacular hillside views of the Caribbean Sea and surrounding forests. Rates
here run between $75 and $162 (£38–£81) per person per day, depending on occupancy and room type, and include three vegetarian meals per day, and taxes. A wide
range of tour, massage, and yoga packages is available. If you're staying elsewhere in
Puerto Viejo or Cahuita, you can come up for yoga classes ($12/£6), meditations
($5/£2.50), or private massages ($60–$110/£30–£55) with advance notice. Samasati
is located a couple of kilometers before Puerto Viejo (near the turnoff for Bribri) and
roughly 1.6km (1 mile) up into the jungle.

NOT YOUR EVERYDAY GARDENS   One of the nicest ways to spend a day in
Puerto Viejo is to visit the **Finca La Isla Botanical Gardens** (�� (© **750-0046;**
crgarden@mac.com), located a couple hundred meters inland from the Black Sand
Beach on a side road just north of El Pizote lodge. Peter Kring and his late wife Lindy
have poured time and love into the creation of this meandering collection of native
and imported tropical flora. You'll see medicinal, commercial, and just plain wild
flowering plants, fruits, herbs, trees, and bushes. Visitors get to gorge on whatever is
ripe at the moment. There is also a rigorous rainforest loop trail leaving from the
grounds. The gardens are generally open Friday through Monday from 10am to 4pm,
but visits can sometimes be arranged for other days with advance notice. Entrance to
the garden or loop trail is $5 (£2.50) per person, or $10 (£5) with the guided tour.

Cacao Trails � (© **756-8186;** www.cacaotrails.com) is a one-stop attraction featuring botanical gardens, a small serpentarium, an open-air museum demonstrating
the tools and techniques of cacao cultivation and processing, and a series of trails.
There's also a large open-air restaurant, and a swimming pool for cooling off. You can
also take canoe rides on the bordering Carbon River, and even watch sea turtles lay
their eggs during the nesting season. Admission to the attraction is $25 (£13) for
adults and $10 (£5) for children, including a guided tour. During turtle nesting sea-
son, they do night tours to watch sea turtles lay their eggs.

Near Punta Uva, you'll find the **Punta Uva Butterfly Garden** � (© **750-0086**).
This small yet well-run facility is the only butterfly-breeding and production facility
along the coast, and it's open daily from 8am to 4pm. Admission is $5 (£2.50) for
adults; children enter free.

SUNNING & SURFING **Surfing** has historically been the main draw here, but increasing numbers of folks are coming for the miles of beautiful and uncrowded **beaches** 𝒢𝒢, acres of lush rainforests, and laid-back atmosphere. If you aren't a surfer, the same activities that prevail in any quiet beach town are the norm here—sunbathe, go for a walk on the beach, read a book, or take a nap. If you have more energy, there's a host of tours and hiking options, or you can rent a bicycle or a horse. (Watch for signs.) For swimming and sunbathing, locals like to hang out on the small patches of sand in front of Stanford's Disco and Johnny's Place. There are small, protected tide pools in front of each of these bars for cooling off.

If you want a more open patch of sand and sea, head north out to **Playa Negra,** along the road into town, or, better yet, to the beaches south of town around Punta Uva and all the way down to Manzanillo, where the coral reefs keep the surf much more manageable (see "Manzanillo & the Manzanillo-Gandoca Wildlife Refuge," below).

Just offshore from the tiny village park is a shallow reef where powerful storm-generated waves sometimes reach 6m (20 ft.). **Salsa Brava,** as it's known, is the prime surf break on the Caribbean coast. Even when the waves are small, this spot is recommended only for very experienced surfers because of the danger of the reef. Other popular beach breaks are south of town on Playa Cocles. If you're interested in surf lessons or want to rent a board, check in with **Aventuras Bravas** (© 849-7600).

Several operators and makeshift roadside stands offer bicycles, scooters, boogie boards, surfboards, and snorkel gear for rent. Shop around and compare prices and the quality of the equipment before settling on any one.

ANOTHER WAY TO GET WET & WILD **Exploradores Outdoors** 𝒢 (© 222-6262 in San José, or 750-2020 in Puerto Viejo; www.exploradoresoutdoors.com) runs daily white-water rafting trips on the Pacuare and Reventazón rivers. The full-day trip, including transportation, breakfast, and lunch, is $95 (£48). If you want to combine white-water rafting with your transportation to or from the Caribbean coast, they can pick you up at your hotel in San José with all your luggage, take you for a day of white-water rafting, and drop you off at day's end at your hotel anywhere on the Caribbean coast from Cahuita to Manzanillo. You can also choose to use the option in the other direction.

MANZANILLO & THE MANZANILLO-GANDOCA WILDLIFE REFUGE 𝒢𝒢

If you continue south on the coast road from Puerto Viejo, you'll come to a couple of even smaller villages. **Punta Uva** 𝒢𝒢 is 8km (5 miles) away, and **Manzanillo** 𝒢𝒢 is about 15km (9⅓ miles) away. For a good day trip, you can catch the 7:30am bus from Puerto Viejo down to Manzanillo and then catch the 5pm bus back. (It's always wise to check with ATEC about current local bus schedules.) You could also hire a cab for around $6 (£3) to Punta Uva or $10 (£5) to Manzanillo. Alternatively, it's about 1½ hours each way by bicycle, with only two relatively small hills to contend with. Although the road is ostensibly paved all the way to Manzanillo, between the near constant potholes and washed out sections, it's almost like riding an off-road trail. It's also possible to walk along the beach all the way from Puerto Viejo to Manzanillo, with just a couple of short and well-worn detours inland around rocky points. However, I recommend you catch a ride down to Manzanillo and save your walking energies for the trails and beaches inside the refuge.

Manzanillo is a tiny village with only a few basic *cabinas* and funky *sodas,* although this has been changing in recent years. The most popular place to eat and hang out is **Restaurant Maxi** (✯ (*©* **759-9086**), an open-air joint located on the second floor of an old wooden building facing the sea. This place gets packed on weekends, especially for lunch.

The **Manzanillo-Gandoca Wildlife Refuge** (✯✯ encompasses the small village and extends all the way to the Panamanian border. Manatees, crocodiles, and more than 350 species of birds live within the boundaries of the reserve. The reserve also includes the coral reef offshore—when the seas are calm, this is the best **snorkeling** and **diving** spot on this entire coast. Four species of **sea turtles** nest on one 8.9km (5½-mile) stretch of beach within the reserve between March and July. Three species of dolphins also inhabit and frolic in the waters just off Manzanillo. Many local tour guides and operators offer boat trips out to spot them.

If you want to explore the refuge, you can easily find the single, well-maintained trail by walking along the beach just south of town until you have to wade across a small river. On the other side, you'll pick up the trail head. Otherwise, you can ask around the village for local guides or check out **Aquamor** (✯ (*©* **759-9012**), a kayak and dive operation located on the one main road in town. These folks rent kayaks for $6 (£3) per hour and offer a variety of guided excursions for between $15 and $55 (£7.50–£28) per person. Depending on tides and sea conditions, this is a great way to explore the mangroves and estuaries, visit several nearby beaches, and even snorkel or dive the nearby coral reef. A one-tank beach dive, with equipment and guide, costs $30 (£15) per person. They have a variety of tour and diving options, including PADI dive-certification courses, hikes into the Talamanca Mountains, dolphin-watching excursions, and trips to Bocas del Toro, Panama.

Sportfishers should check in with **Bacalao Tours** (*©* **759-9116**).

(ORGANIC) PEAS & LOVE (✯ Inside the Manzanillo-Gandoca refuge is the **Punta Mona Center For Sustainable Living & Education** (*©* **222-4568;** www. puntamona.org). With organic permaculture gardens and a distinctly alternative vibe, this place is open for day visits, overnight stays, and work-exchange and educational programs. A day trip to visit the center, its garden, and facilities, including a vegetarian organic lunch, costs $40 (£20).

SHOPPING

Puerto Viejo attracts a lot of local and international bohemians, who seem to survive solely on the sale of handmade jewelry, painted ceramic trinkets (mainly pipes and cigarette-lighter holders), and imported Indonesian textiles. You'll find them at makeshift stands set up by the town's *parquecito* (little park), a few wooden benches in front of the sea between Soda Tamara and Stanford's.

In addition to the makeshift outdoor stands is a host of well-stocked gift and crafts shops in town. **The Jewelry Factory** and **Color Caribe,** both on the main road into town, sell a wide range of jewelry, crafts, and gift items, as well as Costa Rican hammocks. **Luluberlu** (✯, located inland across from Cabinas Guaraná, features locally produced craftwork, including shell mobiles and mirrors with mosaic-inlaid frames, as well as imports from Thailand and India. For ceramics, head south to Playa Chiquita and check out the traditional Japanese-style works at **Raku Art.**

Tip: My favorite local purchase is locally produced chocolate, which comes wrapped in wax paper the size and shape of a roll of quarters. They come plain or flavored with coconut, peanuts, mint, ginger, or raisins, and can be found for sale at many gift shops and restaurants around town.

Finally, if you need a book to read on the beach, head just south of town to **Echo Books,** which has a good supply of new and used books, as well as a small cafe and gift shop. The owner also specializes in making homemade truffles and other chocolate treats from local cacao.

WHERE TO STAY IN PUERTO VIEJO

For a longer stay, close to town, you might want to check out **Cashew Hill Jungle Cottages** (© 750-0256; www.cashewhilllodge.co.cr). Located on a hill just on the outskirts of town, these are simple, but immaculate individual one- and two-bedroom bungalows, with kitchenettes.

True budget hounds will find a host of basic *cabinas* in downtown Puerto Viejo in addition to the hotels listed below. Of these, **Hotel Pura Vida** (© 750-0002; fax 750-0296) and **Cabinas Maritza** (© 750-0003; fax 750-0313) are both good bets; however, the most popular spot for backpackers, surfers, and students is **Rocking J's** (© 750-0657; www.rockingjs.com), a sprawling compound offering simple rooms, camping spaces, and a "hammock hotel."

For more isolated options, try **Kaya's Place** (© 750-0690; www.kayasplace.com), just before the bridge into town, or **Escape Caribeño** (© 750-0103; www.escape caribeno.com), just south of Salsa Brava.

Cabinas Casa Verde ☆ *Value*   This is my favorite hotel right in Puerto Viejo, regardless of price. A quiet sense of tropical tranquillity pervades this place. The rooms are spread around this small, but growing complex. Most are large, with high ceilings, tile floors, private bathrooms, and a private veranda. The rooms with shared bathrooms are housed in a raised building with a wide, covered breezeway between the rooms. The front and back porches of this building are hung with hammocks and surrounded by lush gardens, where you'll find the showers and toilets. There are also two fully equipped apartments available in a neighboring duplex. Everything is very well maintained, and even the shared bathrooms are kept immaculate. There are also a small but well-stocked gift shop, and a poison-dart-frog garden. The newest additions here include a good-size outdoor pool with waterfall, and a separate outdoor massage hut. Even though it's an in-town choice, there's great bird-watching all around the grounds.

A.P. 1115, Puerto Viejo, Limón. © **750-0015.** Fax 750-0047. www.cabinascasaverde.com. 17 units, 9 w/private bathroom. $34–$36 (£17–£18) double w/shared bathroom; $56 (£28) double w/private bathroom. Rates slightly lower in off season; higher during peak weeks. AE, MC, V. **Amenities:** Restaurant; pool; tour desk. *In room:* No phone.

Cabinas Guaraná *Value*   This is one of the better options in town, although it is several blocks from the water. The spacious rooms are painted in bright primary colors, with equally bright and contrasting trim. Rooms come with either two or three full-size beds, or a queen with one or two full beds. All come with tile floors, a ceiling fan, and mosquito netting. Guests can use the hotel's fully equipped kitchen to whip up meals, and there's an interesting little sitting area on a platform high up a tree on the property.

1½ blocks inland from Café Viejo, Puerto Viejo, Limón. ©/fax **750-0244.** www.hotelguarana.com. 12 units. $35–$45 (£18–£23) double. Rates slightly lower in off season; higher during peak weeks. AE, DC, MC, V. *In room:* No phone.

Cabinas Jacarandá *Value*   This small hotel has a few nice touches that set it apart from the others. Guatemalan bedspreads add a dash of color and tropical flavor, as do the tables made from sliced tree trunks. Most rooms and walkways feature intricate and colorful tile work, Japanese paper lanterns cover the lights, mosquito nets hang over the beds, and covered walkways connect the various buildings in this budding compound. Massage and yoga classes are offered on site. If you're traveling in a group, you'll enjoy the space and atmosphere of the big room. If the hotel is full, the owners also rent a few nearby bungalows.

1½ blocks inland from Café Viejo, Puerto Viejo, Limón. Ⓒ/fax **750-0069**. 14 units, 13 w/private bathroom. $30–$40 (£15–£20) double. MC, V. *In room:* No phone.

El Pizote El Pizote is a quiet hotel on the northern edge of town. The hotel has a large, free-form pool, and some of the most expansive grounds around. The four deluxe bungalows are modern concrete-block affairs, with a small kitchenette, two separate bedrooms, one small bathroom, air-conditioning, and a private porch. Although older and funkier, the standard bungalows have much more character. These raised wooden buildings have dark, stained wood walls; steeply pitched roofs; ceiling fans; private porches; and larger step-down bathrooms. The standard rooms are housed in a U-shape wooden building near the pool. These rooms are cool, and come with two double beds, a ceiling fan, and a shared wraparound veranda. The hotel is located 100m (328 ft.) or so inland from a long, quiet stretch of Playa Negra, about 400m (1,312 ft.) before you reach downtown proper. Everything is set amid lush gardens, assorted tropical fruit trees, and a few towering rainforest trees. For activity, there are hiking trails in the adjacent forest, and there's good bird-watching here, too.

Just off the main road, about 275m (902 ft.) before you enter downtown, Puerto Viejo, Limón. Ⓒ **750-0088**. Fax 750-0226. www.pizotelodge.com. 22 units. $57 (£29) double; $72 (£36) double bungalow; $99 (£50) double deluxe. Rates lower in off season. AE, MC, V. **Amenities:** Restaurant; bar; pool and adjacent kid's pool; laundry service. *In room:* No phone.

WHERE TO STAY BETWEEN PUERTO VIEJO & MANZANILLO

All the hotels listed below are located along the road south of Puerto Viejo heading toward Manzanillo. This is one of the most beautiful and isolated stretches of beach in Costa Rica. The single coastal road here has been paved all the way to Manzanillo, greatly improving access to this area. I recommend that you have a vehicle if you plan to stay at one of these hotels because public transportation is sporadic and taxis aren't always available. If you arrive by bus, however, a rented bicycle or scooter might be all you need to get around once you are settled.

VERY EXPENSIVE

In addition to the place listed below, the former tent camp **Almonds & Corals Hotel** (Ⓒ **272-2024** reservations in San José, or 759-9057 at the lodge; www.almondsand corals.com) is a totally revamped and reinvented new hotel, with rustically luxurious bungalows and suites in a lush forest setting near Manzanillo.

Tree House Lodge ★★★ *Finds* The three individual houses here are easily the most unique and stylish options on this coast. All three are distinct and quite large, with fluid and fanciful architectural details and tons of brightly varnished woodwork. As the name implies, the Tree House is built into and around a large *sangrillo* tree. The Beach House is closest to the sea and actually features an ocean view from its kitchen and broad deck. However, the crowning achievement here is the three-bedroom, two-bath Beach House Suite, with its spectacular domed bathroom, which during the day is lit by sunlight streaming through scores of colored glass skylights. All of the houses are beautiful, and you'll spend much of your time here marveling at the creative touches and one-off furniture. This property is set right off Punta Uva, one of the nicest swimming beaches on this coast. Two of the units here come with air-conditioning.

Punta Uva, Puerto Viejo, Limón. © **750-0706.** www.costaricatreehouse.com. 3 units. $200–$225 (£100–£113) double. Rates lower in off season, higher during peak weeks. No credit cards. *In room:* Full kitchen, safe.

MODERATE

Aguas Claras ⊀ *Finds*   These brightly painted individual bungalows are built on raised stilts and feature fancy gingerbread trim. They are all of wood construction, and all come with private verandas and fully equipped kitchens—although some have just a two-burner cooktop, while others come with a full stove and oven. Inside, they are bright and airy, with either wood or tile floors. There are two one-bedroom cottages, two two-bedroom affairs, and one three-bedroom house. The compound is just a few steps away from a lovely section of Playa Chiquita, and the restaurant here, Miss Holly's Kitchen (see later in chapter), is excellent. Maid service is provided every other day. If you book five nights, the sixth night is free.

Playa Chiquita, Puerto Viejo, Limón. © **750-0131.** Fax 750-0368. www.aguasclaras-cr.com. 5 bungalows. $70–$220 (£35–£110) bungalow. Rates lower in off season; higher during peak weeks. AE, DC, MC, V. **Amenities:** Restaurant; laundry service. *In room:* Kitchenette, no phone.

Azania Bungalows ⊀ *Finds*   This collection of private bungalows is an excellent option for those seeking a quiet, romantic tropical getaway. The spacious bungalows are set apart from each other amid the hotel's high flowering gardens, giving each a sense of seclusion. All come with one queen-size bed and one double bed downstairs and another double bed in the small loft. The thatch roofs are high-pitched and, combined with large screened windows, allow for good cross ventilation. The lounge area features a television with DirecTV, a small lending library, and a collection of board games. Some of the best features here include the refreshing free-form swimming pool and the open-air thatch-roofed poolside restaurant.

Playa Cocles, Puerto Viejo, Limón. © **750-0540.** Fax 750-0371. www.azania-costarica.com. 10 bungalows. $85 (£43) double. Rates include full breakfast. Rates lower in off season; higher during peak weeks. AE, DC, MC, V. **Amenities:** Restaurant; lounge; pool; bike rental; laundry service. *In room:* Fridge, safe, no phone.

Cariblue Bungalows ⊀⊀   This Italian-owned miniresort is a wonderful choice in this neck of the woods. The rooms are spread around the well-tended and lush grounds. My favorites are the raised-stilt wood bungalows, with spacious bedrooms featuring either one king-size bed and one single bed or two queen-size beds. The beds are covered with mosquito nets, and there's a small veranda with a hammock. The nicest features here are the bathrooms, with their intricate mosaic tile designs. The standard rooms are in a couple of concrete-block buildings with high-pitched thatch roofs. They are also spacious and comfortable, but not quite as private or charming as the bungalows. Another option is a two-bedroom house with a full kitchen, for families or for longer stays. A very inviting free-form swimming pool has a swim-up bar, and the restaurant here tends to serve excellent Italian and local cuisine. Cariblue is located about 90m (295 ft.) or so inland from the southern end of Playa Cocles.

Playa Cocles, Puerto Viejo (A.P. 51-7304), Limón. © **750-0035** or ©/fax 750-0057. www.cariblue.com. 16 units, 1 house. $85 (£43) double; $200 (£100) house. Rates include breakfast buffet. Rates slightly lower in off season. AE, MC, V. **Amenities:** Restaurant; bar/lounge; pool; bike rental; laundry service. *In room:* Hair dryer, safe, no phone.

Casa Camarona   Casa Camarona has the enviable distinction of being one of the very few hotels in this area right on the beach. There's no road to cross and no path through the jungle—just a small section of shady gardens separates you from a quiet section of Playa Cocles and the Caribbean Sea. The rooms are in two separate two-story buildings. Definitely get a room on the second floor. Up there you'll find spacious rooms painted in pleasant pastels, with plenty of cross-ventilation and a wide shared veranda. I don't know who designed the first-floor rooms, but several of them have such low ceilings that I felt as tall as Yao Ming—and believe me, I'm not. About half the rooms have air-conditioning units, and it'll cost you an extra $13 (£6.50) per day if you want to fire it up. The hotel keeps some chaise longues on the beach under the shade of palm trees, and a beach bar is open during the day, so you barely have to leave that chaise to quench your thirst.

Playa Cocles, Puerto Viejo, Limón (mailing address: A.P. 2270-1002, Paseo de los Estudiantes, San José). © 283-6711 or 750-0151. Fax 222-6184. www.casacamarona.co.cr. 17 units. $65 (£33) double. Rates include continental breakfast and taxes. AE, MC, V. **Amenities:** Restaurant; bar. *In room:* No phone.

La Costa de Papito ★ (Value   This small collection of individual and duplex cabins offers some of the same feel and character as Shawandha and Cariblue, with fewer amenities and less luxury—but at lower rates. La Costa de Papito is located just across from Playa Cocles, about 1.6km (1 mile) south of Puerto Viejo. The wooden bungalows come with one or two double beds, artfully tiled bathrooms, and an inviting private porch with a table and chairs and either a hammock or a swing chair. There's also a larger, two-bedroom unit. In 2007, they added a restaurant, as well as a small gym. The Pure Jungle Spa (see earlier in chapter), located on the premises here, is an excellent little day spa.

Playa Cocles, Puerto Viejo, Limón. ©/fax 750-0080. www.lacostadepapito.com. 13 units. $50–$69 (£25–£35) double. Rates lower in off season. AE, DISC, MC, V. **Amenities:** Restaurant; bar; small spa; bicycle rental; laundry service. *In room:* No phone.

Playa Chiquita Lodge (Kids   Set amid the shade of large old trees a few kilometers south of Puerto Viejo toward Punta Uva (watch for the sign), this lodge has several wooden buildings set on stilts and connected by a garden walkway. Wide verandas offer built-in seating and rocking chairs. The spacious rooms have received steady upkeep and upgrading and are painted in bright colors. The bathrooms have also been remodeled, with gas water heaters replacing the electric showerhead elements. A short trail leads down to a semiprivate little swimming beach with tide pools and beautiful turquoise water. This stretch of beach is the site of a daily 4pm volleyball game.

Throughout the day, free bananas and coffee are available. The owners have three children, ranging from a young child to a couple of teenagers. Guests are invited to join in the nightly family-style dinners, and travelers, especially those with kids, often feel like part of the family. These folks also rent out fully equipped houses for those interested in longer stays or more privacy and independence.

Puerto Viejo, Limón. © 750-0062 or ©/fax 750-0408. www.playachiquitalodge.com. 12 units. $60 (£30) double. Rates lower in off season; slightly higher during peak weeks. Rates include breakfast. AE, MC, V. **Amenities:** Restaurant. *In room:* Free Wi-Fi, no phone.

Shawandha Lodge ★★ (Finds   If you're looking for an isolated and romantic getaway, in a style best described as rustic luxury, this collection of individual bungalows is a great choice. Set in a lush patch of forest about 180m (590 ft.) or so inland from Playa Chiquita, Shawandha has the feel of a small village. Creative flourishes abound. The thatch-roofed, raised bungalows feature high-pitched ceilings, varnished wood floors, and either one king-size bed or a mix of queen-size and single beds. The bathrooms are practically works of art, each with original, intricate mosaics of hand-cut tile highlighting a large, open shower. Every bungalow has its own spacious balcony, with both a hammock and a couch, where you can lie and look out on the lush, flowering gardens. The beach is easily accessed by a private path, and a host of activities and tours can be arranged. I have it on reasonable authority they plan on adding a pool by early 2008. There's a large open-air restaurant and lounge where meals and drinks are served. The menu is an eclectic mix, featuring fresh fish and meats in a variety of French, Caribbean, and Polynesian sauces.

Puerto Viejo, Limón. Ⓒ **750-0018**. Fax 750-0037. www.shawandhalodge.com. 13 units. $100 (£50) double. Rates lower in off season; higher during peak weeks. Rates include full breakfast. AE, MC, V. **Amenities:** Restaurant; laundry service. *In room:* No phone.

INEXPENSIVE
Budget travelers can also check out **La Isla** (Ⓒ/fax **750-0109**), a simple hotel catering to surfers, located at the start of Playa Cocles. The neighboring **Totem** (Ⓒ **750-0758;** www.totemsite.com) offers slightly more comfort and the same access to the waves. Farther down in Manzanillo, the simple and clean **Cabinas Something Different** (Ⓒ **759-9014**) is a good option, while **Congo Bongo** (Ⓒ **759-9016;** www.congo-bongo.com) offers fully equipped houses in a lush forest setting.

Cabinas Selvyn   The atmosphere here is friendly and funky. Rooms are located in a few two-story buildings behind the small open-air restaurant. All rooms come with mosquito nets and fans, but beyond that, the accommodations are spartan and a bit worn. If you land a second-floor room facing the sea, you might get a bit of a breeze. The hotel is located about 100m (328 ft.) down a dirt lane from one of the most isolated and beautiful beaches in Costa Rica. The hotel's owner, Selvyn Brown, is a great cook and wonderful raconteur.

Punta Uva, Limón. No phone. 10 units, all w/shared bathroom; 2 apts. $15–$25 (£7.50–£13) double; $200–$325 (£100–£163) per month for apt. No credit cards. **Amenities:** Restaurant. *In room:* No phone.

WHERE TO DINE IN PUERTO VIEJO
To really sample the local cuisine, you need to look up a few local women. Ask around for **Miss Dolly, Miss Sam, Miss Isma,** and **Miss Irma,** who all serve up sit-down meals in their modest little *sodas.* In addition to locally seasoned fish and chicken served with rice and beans, these joints are usually a great place to find some *pan bon* (a local sweet, dark bread), ginger cakes, *paty* (meat-filled turnovers), and *rondon* (see below). Just ask around for these women, and someone will direct you to them. In a similar vein, but with a new, large restaurant space, is **Elena Brown,** who has set up shop on the outskirts of downtown, on the road heading south.

If you're looking for a light bite for breakfast, lunch, or a snack, check out **Pan Pay,** a French-run bakery and sandwich shop located next to Johnny's Place (see "Puerto Viejo After Dark," below). Also, **Jammin' Juice and Jerk Center,** in the same building,

---

Tips   That Rundown Feeling
Rundown (or *rondon*) soup is a spicy coconut milk–based soup or stew made with anything the cook can run down—it usually includes a mix of local tubers (potato, sweet potato, or yuca), other vegetables (carrots or corn), and often some fish and/or seafood. Be sure to try this authentic taste of the Caribbean.

specializes in jerk chicken, salads, and fresh juices. For casual fare, try **E-Z Times,** which is right in front of the water near the heart of town.

Finally, Puerto Viejo has a glut of excellent Italian restaurants; in addition to the places listed below, **Amimodo** (© 750-0257) and **Trattoria da Cesare** (© 750-0161) are both fine restaurants.

Café Viejo ⭐ ITALIAN   This place is set right on the busiest little corner of "downtown" Puerto Viejo. White gauze curtains help to slightly shield this open-air spot from the hustle and bustle just outside. Still, it's often loud and crowded inside as well, and that's part of the charm of this popular place. You can get a wide range of pastas and thin-crust wood-oven pizzas here, as well as more substantial fish, chicken, and meat entrees. The grilled whole fresh fish is an especially good option. On weekends, a late night lounge often develops here, with electronic music and dancing.

On the main road. © 750-0817. Main courses $10–$30 (£5–£15). MC, V. Wed–Mon noon–1am.

El Loco Natural ⭐⭐ (Finds) INTERNATIONAL   A funky, hippy vibe pervades this second-floor open-air restaurant. Seating is at heavy wooden tables, and if the few smaller, more private tables are taken, you can take any empty seat at one of the larger communal tables. The short menu features several vegetarian items, as well as fresh fish and some chicken and meat dishes, prepared in curry, Thai, and Mexican sauces. There's often live music here, ranging from reggae to jazz to Latin American folk.

On the main road. © 750-0263. Main courses $4–$12 (£2–£6). No credit cards. Thurs–Mon 6–10pm.

Salsa Brava ⭐⭐ SPANISH/MEDITERRANEAN   Fresh grilled seafood and meats are the specialty here, and everything is simply yet expertly prepared. There's usually a wide range of fresh-caught fish available, grilled either whole or in filets, plus grilled calamari, shrimp, or filet mignon, as well as several hearty vegetarian options. Wash down whatever you choose with the homemade sangria. The dozen or so wooden tables are painted bright primary colors and are set on a gravel floor under an open-air thatched roof. Service is attentive and informal.

On the left-hand side of the main road heading south of Puerto Viejo, just after El Bambú. © 750-0241. Main courses $8–$16 (£4–£8). MC, V. Tues–Sun noon–10pm.

Soda Tamara (Value) COSTA RICAN   This little restaurant has long been popular with budget-conscious travelers and has an attractive setting for such an economical place. Its open-air dining area is larger and more comfortable than the somewhat cramped indoor dining room. The painted picket fence in front gives the restaurant a homey feel. The menu features standard fish, chicken, and meat entrees, served with a hefty helping of Caribbean-style rice and beans. You can also get *patacones* (fried chips made out of plantains) and a wide selection of fresh-fruit juices. At the counter inside, you'll find homemade cocoa candies and unsweetened cocoa biscuits made by several women in town. They're definitely worth a try. Soda Tamara also has a second-floor open-air bar that's open nightly from 6pm until the last straggler calls it quits.

On the main road. © 750-0148. Main courses $4–$15 (£2–£7.50). AE, MC, V. Daily 11am–11pm.

WHERE TO DINE BETWEEN PUERTO VIEJO & MANZANILLO

As the beaches stretching south of Puerto Viejo keep getting more popular, there has been a corresponding increase in the number of places to grab a meal. In addition to the restaurants listed above and below, **Johanna Restaurante** (© 887-6203) in Playa Cocles, and **Cabinas Selvyn** (no phone) at Punta Uva, are both excellent options for local cuisine and fresh seafood. Another good option along this road is the small **Jungle Love Garden Café** (© 823-6708), which serves a regularly changing daily menu of creative international fare.

Finally, if you make it as far south as Manzanillo, **Restaurant Maxi** ℱ (© 759-9086) is your best bet. This open-air spot is always packed, especially for lunch. A fresh-fish plate will cost you between $5 and $7 (£2.50–£3.50); lobster, in season, will cost around $12 (£6). Whatever you order comes with rice and beans, *patacones* (fried plantain chips), and a small side of cabbage salad.

Gatta Ci Cova ℱ *Value* ITALIAN   Opened as an extension and variation on their nearby and extremely popular restaurant, La Pecora Nera (see below), this simple place serves a range of panini sandwiches and thin-crust pizzas. Located in an open, two-story building, the main dining room is on the second floor, watched over by a giant stuffed black jaguar on the stairway railing. Downstairs, is a more informal bar area. Try the four-cheese pizza with fresh pear slices and pine nuts, or the fresh fish panino with grilled zucchini and olive paste. There's always a two-course daily plate of an antipasto and pasta dish, with a glass of wine or beer for around $10 (£5). This is a great place for lunch or a light dinner.

Just beyond the soccer field on the main road through Cocles. © 750-0490. Reservations not necessary. Pizzas and panini $3–$9 (£1.50–£4.50). AE, MC, V. Tues–Sun noon–10:30pm.

La Pecora Nera ℱℱℱ *Finds* ITALIAN   This open-air joint on the jungle's edge has earned its reputation as the finest Italian restaurant in the region, if not the country. Owner Ilario Giannoni is a whirlwind of enthusiasm and activity, switching hats all night long from maitre d' to chef to waiter to busboy in an entertaining blur. Sure, he's got some help, including his grandmother, who makes gnocchi, but it seems like he's doing it single-handedly. The menu has a broad selection of pizzas and pastas, but your best bet is to just ask Ilario what's fresh and special for that day, and to trust his instincts and inventions. I've had fabulous fresh pasta dishes and top-notch appetizers every time I've visited. The gnocchi here is light and mouthwatering. The main dishes come with a variety of side dishes.

50m (164 ft.) inland from a well-marked turnoff on the main road south just beyond the soccer field in Cocles. © 750-0490. Reservations recommended. Main courses $7–$26 (£3.50–£13). AE, MC, V. Tues–Sun 5:30–11pm.

Miss Holly's Kitchen ℱ *Finds* INTERNATIONAL   Although they only serve breakfast and lunch, this new little cafe has quickly become a favorite spot for locals and visitors alike. Breakfasts feature fresh baked goods, omelets and local favorites such as rice and beans with eggs. For lunch the menu shifts to a range of green and hearty salads, and various sandwiches. I like grabbing one of the tables on the small wooden cottage's wrap-around veranda. But you can also just order at the deli counter inside and have a picnic on the beach. If you're traveling with a laptop, this is a great place to take advantage of some free Wi-Fi.

At Aguas Clara, Playa Chiquita. © 750-0131. Breakfast $4–$6 (£2–£3); sandwiches and salads $3–$5 (£1.50–£2.50). MC, V. Wed–Mon 8am–4pm.

PUERTO VIEJO AFTER DARK

There are two main disco/bars in town. **Johnny's Place** ℱℱ is near the Rural Guard station, about 100m (328 ft.) or so north of the ATEC office. You'll find **Stanford's** overlooking the water out near Salsa Brava just as the main road heads south of town. Both have small dance floors with ground-shaking reggae, dub, and rap rhythms blaring. The

On to Panama

Costa Rica's southern zone, particularly Puerto Viejo, is a popular jumping-off point for trips into Panama. The nearest and most popular destination is the island retreat of Bocas del Toro. Most tour agencies and hotel desks in the area can arrange tours to Panama. If you're doing it yourself, it's easiest to fly directly from Limón on **Nature Air** (✆ **800/235-9272** in the U.S. and Canada, or 299-6000; www.natureair.com), which has a daily flight that departs the Tobías Bolaños International Airport in Pavas at 1pm, stopping in Limón en route to pick up and discharge passengers. The one-way fare from Limón is $65 (£33). You can also take the local buses to the border at Sixaola. All the border formalities can be handled easily at the border, and onward bus connections wait on the Panamanian side to take you to Bocas del Toro.

If you're planning on spending any time touring around Panama, be sure to pick up a copy of *Frommer's Panama*.

---

action usually spills out from the dance floor at both joints on most nights. I like the atmosphere better at Johnny's, although both have tables, chairs and candles set out on the sand, near the water's edge.

One of the more popular places in town is **Hot Rocks,** a large dirt lot with some canvas catering tents over its bar and some of its table area. This place, which is located right where the main road hits the water, has a huge screen upon which several late-run movies are projected each night. Another option is the **Sunset Bar,** which is near the water, beside the bus station, and sometimes features live music. For a more sophisticated ambience try the downtown **Baba Yaga,** or the ocean-side **E-Z Times.** An open-air bar on the second floor of **Soda Tamara** (p. 366) is a casual and quiet place to gather after dark.

You can also take advantage of the pool table, board games, and DirecTV (usually showing sporting events) at **El Dorado,** in front of the ATEC office, as an alternative to the loud music and dance scenes of the other joints mentioned above.

Heading just south out of town, the **Cut Back** is a popular spot with backpackers and bohemians, with a solid after-hours scene. Farther south of town, at the start of Playa Cocless, **El Tesoro** shows large-screen movies every night.

Appendix A:
Costa Rica in Depth

Pura Vida! (Pure Life!) is Costa Rica's unofficial national slogan. You'll hear it exclaimed, proclaimed, and simply said by Ticos from all walks of life, from children to octogenarians. It is symbolic of the relatively easygoing and gentle nature of this country's people, politics, and personality. Often called the "Switzerland of Central America," Costa Rica is, and historically has been, a sea of tranquillity in a region that has been troubled by turmoil for centuries. For over 100 years, it has enjoyed a stable democracy and a relatively high standard of living for Latin America. The literacy rate is high, as are medical standards and facilities. Perhaps most significant, at least for proud and peace-loving Costa Ricans, is that this country does not have an army.

1 The Natural Environment

Costa Rica occupies a central spot in the isthmus that joins North and South America. For millennia, this land bridge served as a migratory thoroughfare and mating ground for species native to the once-separate continents. It was also where the Mesoamerican and Andean pre-Columbian indigenous cultures met.

The country comprises only .01% of the earth's landmass, yet it is home to 5% of the planet's biodiversity. More than 10,000 identified species of plants, 850 species of birds, 800 species of butterflies, and 500 species of mammals, reptiles, and amphibians are found here.

The key to this biological richness lies in the many distinct life zones and ecosystems found in Costa Rica. It might all seem like one big mass of green to the untrained eye, but the differences are profound.

In any one spot in Costa Rica, temperatures remain relatively constant year-round. However, they vary dramatically according to altitude, from tropically hot and steamy along the coasts to below freezing at the highest elevations.

Costa Rica's **lowland rainforests** are true tropical jungles. Some are deluged with more than 200 inches of rainfall per year, and their climate is hot and humid. Trees grow tall and fast, fighting for sunlight in the upper reaches. In fact, life and foliage on the forest floor are surprisingly sparse. The action is typically 30m (98 ft.) up, in the canopy, where long vines stream down, lianas climb up, and bromeliads grow on the branches and trunks of towering hardwood trees. You can find these lowland rainforests along the southern Pacific coast and Osa Peninsula, as well as along the Caribbean coast. **Corcovado, Cahuita,** and **Manuel Antonio** national parks, as well as the **Manzanillo-Gandoca Wildlife Refuge,** are fine examples of lowland rainforests.

At higher altitudes you'll find Costa Rica's famed **cloud forests.** Here the steady flow of moist air meets the mountains and creates a nearly constant mist. Epiphytes—resourceful plants that live cooperatively on the branches and trunks of other trees—grow abundantly in the cloud forests, where they must extract moisture and nutrients from the air. Because cloud forests are found in generally steep, mountainous terrain, the canopy here is lower and less uniform than in lowland rainforests, providing better chances for viewing elusive fauna. Costa Rica's most spectacular cloud forest is the **Monteverde Biological Cloud Forest Reserve** in Guanacaste province (see chapter 7).

At the highest reaches, the cloud forests give way to **elfin forests** and *páramos.* More commonly associated with the South American Andes, a *páramo* is characterized by a variety of tundralike shrubs and grasses, with a scattering of twisted, wind-blown trees. Reptiles, rodents, and raptors are the most common residents here. **Mount Chirripó, Chirripó National Park,** and the **Cerro de la Muerte (Mountain of Death)** are the principal areas of *páramo* in Costa Rica.

In a few protected areas of Guanacaste, you will still find examples of the otherwise vanishing **tropical dry forest.** During the long and pronounced dry season (late Nov–late Apr), no rain relieves the unabated heat. In an effort to conserve much-needed water, the trees drop their leaves but bloom in a riot of color: purple jacaranda, scarlet *poró,* and brilliant orange flame-of-the-forest are just a few examples. Then during the rainy season, this deciduous forest is transformed into a lush and verdant landscape. Because the foliage is not so dense, the dry forests are excellent places to view a variety of wildlife species, especially howler monkeys and *pizotes* (coati). Dry forests are found in **Santa Rosa** and **Guanacaste** national parks.

Along the coasts, primarily where river mouths meet the ocean, you will find extensive **mangrove forests** and **swamps.** Around these seemingly monotonous tangles of roots exists one of the most diverse and rich ecosystems in the country. All sorts of fish and crustaceans live in the brackish tidal waters. Caimans and crocodiles cruise the maze of rivers and unmarked canals, and hundreds of herons, ibises, egrets, and other marsh birds nest and feed along the silted banks. Mangrove swamps are often havens for water birds: cormorants, frigate birds, pelicans, and herons. The larger birds tend to nest up high in the canopy, while the smaller ones nestle in the underbrush. The **Gulf of Nicoya** is particularly popular among frigate birds and brown pelicans, as well as all manner of terns and seagulls.

Over the last decade or so, Costa Rica has taken great strides toward protecting its rich biodiversity. Thirty years ago it was difficult to find a protected area anywhere, but now more than 11% of the country is protected within the national park system. Another 10% to 15% of the land enjoys moderately effective preservation as part of private and public reserves, Indian reserves, and wildlife refuges and corridors. Still, Costa Rica's precious tropical hardwoods continue to be harvested at an alarming rate, often illegally, while other primary forests are clear-cut for short-term agricultural gain. Many experts predict that Costa Rica's unprotected forests will be gone within the early part of this century.

This is also a land of high volcanic and seismic activity. There are three major **volcanic mountain ranges** in Costa Rica, and many of the volcanoes are still active, allowing visitors to experience the awe-inspiring sight of steaming fumaroles and intense lava flows during their stay. Two volcanoes near the capital—Poás and Irazú—are currently active, although relatively quiet. The best places to see volcanic activity are farther north in **Rincón de la Vieja National Park** and at **Arenal Volcano** (see chapters 6 and 7).

SEARCHING FOR WILDLIFE

Animals in the forests are predominantly nocturnal. When they are active in the daytime, they are usually elusive and on the watch for predators. Birds are easier to spot in clearings or secondary forests than they are in primary forests. Unless you have lots of experience in the tropics, your best hope for enjoying a walk through the jungle lies in employing a trained and knowledgeable guide. (By the way, if it's been raining a lot and the trails are muddy, a good pair of rubber boots comes in handy. These are usually provided by the lodges or at the sites, where necessary.)

Here are a few helpful hints:

- **Listen.** Pay attention to rustling in the leaves; whether it's monkeys up above or pizotes on the ground, you're most likely to hear an animal before seeing one.
- **Keep quiet.** Noise will scare off animals and prevent you from hearing their movements and calls.
- **Don't try too hard.** Soften your focus and allow your peripheral vision to take over. This way you can catch glimpses of motion and then focus in on the prey.
- **Bring binoculars.** It's also a good idea to practice a little first to get the hang of them. It would be a shame to be fiddling around and staring into space while everyone else in your group oohs and aahs over a quetzal.

- **Dress appropriately.** You'll have a hard time focusing your binoculars if you're busy swatting mosquitoes. Light, long pants and long-sleeved shirts are your best bet. Comfortable hiking boots are a real boon, except where heavy rubber boots are necessary. Avoid loud colors; the better you blend in with your surroundings, the better your chances are of spotting wildlife.
- **Be patient.** The jungle isn't on a schedule. However, your best shots at seeing forest fauna are in the very early-morning and late-afternoon hours.
- **Read up.** Familiarize yourself with what you're most likely to see. Most lodges and hotels have a copy of *A Guide to the Birds of Costa Rica* (Cornell University Press, 1990) and other wildlife field guides, although it's always best to have your own. A good all-around book to have is Carrol Henderson's *The Field Guide to the Wildlife of Costa Rica* (University of Texas Press, 2002).

2 Costa Rica Today

Costa Rica has a population of some four million, more than half of whom live in the Central Valley and are considered as urban. Nearly 96% of the population is of Spanish or otherwise European descent, and it is not at all unusual to see fair-skinned and blond Costa Ricans. This is largely because the indigenous population in place when the first Spaniards arrived was small and thereafter was quickly reduced to even more of a minority by wars and disease. There are still some remnant indigenous populations, primarily on reservations around the country; the principal tribes include the Bribri, Cabécar, Boruca, and Guaymí. In addition, on the Caribbean coast and in the big cities, there is a substantial population of English-speaking black Creoles who came

over from the Antilles to work on the railroad and on the banana plantations. Racial tension isn't palpable, but it exists, perhaps more out of standard ignorance and fear rather than an organized or articulated prejudice.

In general, Costa Ricans are a friendly and outgoing people. In conversation and interaction with visitors, Ticos are very open and helpful. Time has relative meaning to Ticos. Although most tour companies and other establishments operate efficiently, don't expect punctuality, in general.

In a region plagued by internal strife and civil wars, Costa Ricans are proud of their peaceful history, political stability, and relatively high level of development.

However, this can also translate into arrogance and prejudice toward immigrants from neighboring countries, particularly Nicaraguans, who make up a large percentage of the workforce on the banana and coffee plantations.

Roman Catholicism is the official religion of Costa Rica, although freedom to practice any religion is guaranteed by the country's constitution. More than 90% of the population identifies itself as Roman Catholic, yet there are small but visible evangelical Christian, Protestant, and Jewish communities. By and large, Ticos are relatively religious. Although many city-dwellers lead quite secular lives, those in small villages and towns attend Mass regularly.

Costa Rica is the most technologically advanced and politically stable nation in Central America, and it has the largest middle class. Even the smallest towns have electricity, the water is mostly safe to drink, and the phone system is relatively good. Still, the gap between rich and poor has been widening for years. Government, banking, and social institutions are regularly embroiled in scandal. The roads, hospitals, and school systems have been in a slow but steady state of decay for decades. And there are no immediate signs of this condition changing. Several "Free Zones" and some high-tech investments and production facilities have dramatically changed the face of Costa Rica's economy. Intel, which opened two side-by-side assembly plants in Costa Rica, currently accounts for more than 20% of the country's exports, compared with traditional exports such as coffee (3.5%) and bananas (10%). Although Intel and other international companies are used to trumpet a growing gross domestic product, very little of the profits actually make their way into the Costa Rican economy. In early 2004, Costa Rican and U.S. negotiators hammered out a Free Trade Agreement, although it has yet to be ratified by the Costa Rican legislature, and there is widespread opposition to it.

Tourism is the nation's true principal source of income, surpassing both cattle ranching and exports of coffee, pineapples, and bananas. Over a million tourists visit Costa Rica each year. Increasingly, Ticos whose fathers and grandfathers were farmers and ranchers find themselves hotel owners, tour guides, and waiters. Although most have adapted gracefully and regard the industry as a source of new jobs and opportunities for economic advancement, restaurant and hotel staff can seem gruff and uninterested at times, especially in rural areas. And, unfortunately, an increase in the number of visitors has led to an increase in crime, prostitution, and drug trafficking. Common sense and street savvy are required in San José and in many of the more popular tourist destinations.

3 History 101

EARLY HISTORY Little is known of Costa Rica's history before its colonization by Spanish settlers. The pre-Columbian Indians who made their home in this region of Central America never developed the large cities or advanced culture that flowered farther north in what would become Guatemala, Belize, and Mexico. However, ancient artifacts indicating a strong sense of aesthetics have been unearthed from scattered excavations around the country. Beautiful gold and jade jewelry, intricately carved grinding stones, and artistically painted terra-cotta objects point to a small but highly skilled population.

SPAIN SETTLES COSTA RICA In 1502, on his fourth and last voyage to the New World, Christopher Columbus anchored just offshore from present-day Limón. Whether he actually gave the country its name—"the rich coast"—is open to discussion, but the Spaniards never did find much gold or minerals to exploit here.

The earliest Spanish settlers found that, unlike settlements to the north, the native population of Costa Rica was unwilling to submit to slavery. Despite their small numbers, scattered villages, and tribal differences, they fought back against the Spanish until they were overcome by superior firepower and European diseases. When the fighting ended, the European settlers in Costa Rica found that very few Indians were left to force into servitude. The settlers were thus forced to till their own lands, a situation unheard of in other parts of Central America. Few pioneers headed this way because they could settle in Guatemala, with its large native workforce. Costa Rica was nearly forgotten, as the Spanish crown looked elsewhere for riches to plunder and souls to convert.

It didn't take long for Costa Rica's few Spanish settlers to head for the hills, where they found rich volcanic soil and a climate that was less oppressive than in the lowlands. Cartago, the colony's first capital, was founded in 1563, but it was not until the 1700s that additional cities were established in this agriculturally rich region. In the late 18th century, the first coffee plants were introduced, and because these plants thrived in the highlands, Costa Rica began to develop its first cash crop. Unfortunately, it was a long and difficult journey transporting the coffee to the Caribbean coast and then onward to Europe, where the demand for coffee was growing.

FROM INDEPENDENCE TO THE PRESENT In 1821, Spain granted independence to its colonies in Central America. Costa Rica joined with its neighbors to form the Central American Federation; but in 1838, it withdrew to form a new nation and pursue its own interests. By the mid-1800s, coffee was the country's main export. Free land was given to anyone willing to plant coffee on it, and plantation owners soon grew wealthy and powerful, creating Costa Rica's first elite class. Coffee plantation owners were powerful enough to elect their own representatives to the presidency.

This was a stormy period in Costa Rican history. In 1856, the country was invaded by William Walker, a soldier of fortune from Tennessee who, with the backing of U.S. President James Buchanan, was attempting to fulfill his grandiose dreams of presiding over a slave state in Central America (before his invasion of Costa Rica, he had invaded Nicaragua and Baja, California). The people of Costa Rica, led by their own president, Juan Rafael Mora, marched against Walker and chased him

---

Dateline

- **13,000 B.C.** Earliest record of human inhabitants in Costa Rica.
- **1000 B.C.** Olmec people from Mexico arrive in Costa Rica searching for rare blue jade.
- **1502** Columbus lands in Costa Rica in September, at what is now Limón.
- **1563** City of Cartago is founded in the Central Valley.
- **1737** San José is founded.

- **Late 1700s** Coffee is introduced as a cash crop.
- **1821** On September 15, Costa Rica, with the rest of Central America, gains independence from Spain.
- **1823** San José is named the capital. The decision is disputed and isn't officially settled until 1835.
- **1848** Costa Rica is proclaimed an independent republic.

- **1856** Battle of Santa Rosa: Costa Ricans defeat the United States, which backed proslavery advocate William Walker.
- **1870s** First banana plantations are established.
- **1889** First election is won by an opposition party, establishing democratic process in Costa Rica.
- **1899** The United Fruit Company is founded by railroad builder Minor Keith.

continues

back to Nicaragua. Walker eventually surrendered to a U.S. warship in 1857, but, in 1860, he attacked Honduras, claiming to be the president of that country. The Hondurans, who had had enough of Walker's shenanigans, promptly executed him.

Until 1890, coffee growers had to transport their coffee either by oxcart to the Pacific port of Puntarenas or by boat down the Río Sarapiquí to the Caribbean. In the 1870s, a progressive president proposed a railway from San José to the Caribbean coast to facilitate the transport of coffee to European markets. It took nearly 20 years for this plan to reach fruition, and more than 4,000 workers lost their lives constructing the railway, which passed through dense jungles and rugged mountains on its journey from the Central Valley to the coast. Partway through the project, as funds were dwindling, the second chief engineer, Minor Keith, proposed an idea that not only enhanced his fortunes but also changed the course of Central American history. Banana plantations would be developed along the railway right-of-way (land on either side of the tracks). The export of this crop would help to finance the railway, and, in exchange, Keith would get a 99-year lease on 1,976,000 hectares (800,000 acres) of land with a 20-year tax deferment. The Costa Rican government gave its consent, and in 1878 the first bananas were shipped from the country. In 1899, Keith and a partner formed the United Fruit Company, a business that eventually became the largest landholder in Central America and caused political disputes and wars throughout the region.

In 1889, Costa Rica held what is considered the first free election in Central American history. The opposition candidate won the election, and the control of the government passed from the hands of one political party to those of another without bloodshed or hostilities. Thus, Costa Rica established itself as the region's only true democracy. In 1948, this democratic process was challenged by Rafael Angel Calderón, who had served as the country's president from 1940 to 1944. After losing by a narrow margin, Calderón, who had the backing of the communist labor unions and the Catholic Church, refused to concede the country's leadership to the rightfully elected president, Otillio Ulate, and a civil war ensued. Calderón was eventually defeated by José "Pepe" Figueres. In the wake of this crisis, a new constitution was drafted; among other changes, it abolished Costa Rica's army so that such a revolution could never happen again.

In 1994, history seemed to repeat itself—peacefully this time—when José

- **1941** Costa Rica's social security and health system is instituted by President Rafael Angel Calderón.
- **1948** After aborted revolution and short civil war, the Costa Rican army is abolished.
- **1949** Women and blacks are given the right to vote.
- **1963** Cabo Blanco Reserve becomes Costa Rica's first national park.
- **1987** President Oscar Arias Sánchez is awarded the Nobel Peace Prize for orchestrating the Central American Peace Plan.
- **1994** President Rafael Angel Calderón hands over the reigns of government to José María Figueres, in a peaceful replay of their fathers' less amenable and democratic transfer of power in 1948.
- **2002** For the first time in history, the presidential elections are forced into a second-round runoff. Abel Pachecho of the Social Christian Unity Party (PUSC) emerges as the winner.
- **2004** An aggressive public prosecutor and national press expose massive governmental scandals, landing two former presidents in jail and leaving another on the lam.
- **2006** In an intensely close election, Oscar Arias Sánchez is elected President. However, more importantly, the new upstart Citizen's Action Party has forever changed the face of the country's long-standing bi-party system.

María Figueres took the reins of government from the son of his father's adversary, Rafael Angel Calderón. In 2001, Otton Solís and his new Citizen's Action Party (PAC) forced the presidential elections into a second round, opening a crack in a two-party system that had become seemingly entrenched for good. Although Solis himself finished third and didn't make it to the runoff, his upstart Citizen's Action Party won quite a few deputy slots.

The battered traditional two-party system was further threatened in 2004, when major corruption scandals became public. Two former presidents are currently under house arrest (Miguel Angel Rodríguez and Rafael Angel Calderón), and another (José María Figueres) is in Switzerland refusing a legislative call to return and testify, as well as avoiding an Interpol warrant for his capture and arrest. All are implicated, as well as a long

list of high-level government employees and deputies, in one way or another, in various financial scandals or bribery cases. While it's unclear how these various scandals and trials will play out in the courts, they have already had a profound effect on the country's political landscape.

In 2006, former president Oscar Arias Sánchez, a Nobel Peace Prize laureate who had presided over the country during the mid-1980s, was reelected, defeating Otton Solís by an incredibly slim margin. The election was historic on two fronts. First, Arias needed to amend national law prohibiting reelection—it still prohibits consecutive terms. More importantly, spurred on by all the scandals, the traditional two-party system fractured into a multitude of smaller parties, with Solis' PAC emerging as the second political power in the country, behind Arias's PLN, with the traditional PUSC party almost disintegrating.

4 Recommended Books

Some of the books mentioned below might be difficult to track down in U.S. bookstores, but you'll find them all in abundance in Costa Rica. A good place to check for most of these titles is **Seventh Street Books,** on Calle 7 between avenidas 1 and Central in San José (© **256-8251**).

GENERAL INTEREST For a straightforward, albeit somewhat dry, historical overview, there's *The History of Costa Rica,* by Ivan Molina and Steven Palmer (University of Costa Rica, 2001). For a more readable look into Costa Rican society, pick up *The Ticos: Culture and Social Change,* by Richard, Karen, and Mavis Biesanz (Lynne Rienner Publishers, 1999), an examination of the country's politics and culture, by the authors of the out-of-print *The Costa Ricans.* Another option worth checking out is *The Costa Rica Reader: History, Culture, Politics,* a broad selection of stories, essays, and excerpts edited by Steven

Palmer and Ivan Molina (Duke University Press, 2004).

To learn more about the life and culture of Costa Rica's Talamanca coast, an area populated by Afro-Caribbean people whose forebears emigrated from Caribbean islands in the early 19th century, look for *What Happen: A Folk-History of Costa Rica's Talamanca Coast,* by Paula Palmer. This book is a collection of oral histories taken from a wide range of local characters. A new and improved edition was published in 2005 by Distribuidores Zona Tropical.

Costa Rica: A Traveler's Literary Companion, edited by Barbara Ras and with a foreword by Oscar Arias Sánchez (Whereabouts Press, 1994), is a collection of short stories by Costa Rican writers, organized by region of the country. If you're lucky, you might find a copy of *Stories of Tatamundo* (University of Costa Rica Press, 1998), by Fabian Dobles.

Young adults will enjoy Kristin Joy Pratt's *A Walk in the Rainforest* (Dawn Publications, 1992), while younger children will like the beautifully illustrated *The Forest in the Clouds,* by Sneed Collard and Michael Rothman (Charlesbridge Publishing, 2000), and *The Umbrella,* by Jan Brett (Putnam Juvenile, 2004).

NATURAL HISTORY I think that everyone coming to Costa Rica should read *Tropical Nature,* by Adrian Forsyth and Ken Miyata (Touchstone Books, 1987). My all-time favorite book on tropical biology, this is a wonderfully written and lively collection of tales and adventures by two Neotropical biologists who spent quite some time in the forests of Costa Rica.

Mario A. Boza's beautiful *Costa Rica National Parks* (INCAFO, 2004) has been reissued in an elegant coffee-table edition. *Wildlife of the National Parks and Reserves of Costa Rica,* by Michael and Patricia Fogden (Fundacion Neotropical, 1997), features some impressive photography by this prolific couple. *Costa Rica's National Parks and Preserves,* by Joseph Franke (The Mountaineers, 1999), is similar but with fewer photos.

For an introduction to a wide range of Costa Rican fauna, there's *The Field Guide to the Wildlife of Costa Rica,* by Carrol Henderson (University of Texas Press, 2002), or *Costa Rica: Traveller's Wildlife Guides,* by Les Beletsky (Interlink Books, 2004). Both pack a lot of useful information into a concise package and make great field guides for amateur naturalists and inquisitive tourists.

A Guide to the Birds of Costa Rica, by F. Gary Stiles and Alexander Skutch (Cornell University Press, 1989), is an invaluable guide to identifying the many birds you'll see during your stay. Most guides and nature lodges have a copy of this book on hand. This classic faces competition from the newly released, *Birds of Costa Rica,* by Richard Garrigues and Robert Dean (Cornell University Press, 2007). Bird-watchers might also enjoy Dennis Rodgers's *Site Guides: Costa Rica & Panama* (Cinclus Publications, 1997), which details each country's bird-watching bounty by site and region.

Other interesting natural-history books that will give you a look at the plants and animals of Costa Rica include *Costa Rica Natural History,* by Daniel Janzen (University of Chicago Press, 1983); *A Guide to Tropical Plants of Costa Rica,* by Willa Zuchowsky (Distribuidores Zona Tropical, 2005); *The Natural History of Costa Rican Mammals,* by Mark Wainwright (Distribuidores Zona Tropical, 2003); the new *A Guide to the Amphibians and Reptiles of Costa Rica,* by Twan Leenders (Distribuidores Zona Tropical, 2001); and the classic *A Neotropical Companion,* by John C. Kricher (Princeton University Press, 1999), which was recently reissued in an expanded edition with color photos.

5 *Gallo Pinto,* Ceviche & *Frescos:* Costa Rican Food & Drink

Costa Rican food is not especially memorable. Perhaps that's why there's so much international food available here. However, if you really want to save money, Costa Rican, or *típico,* food is always the cheapest nourishment available. It's primarily served in *sodas,* Costa Rica's equivalent of diners.

MEALS & DINING CUSTOMS

Rice and beans are the bases of Costa Rican meals—all three of them. At breakfast, they're called *gallo pinto* and come with everything from eggs to steak to seafood. At lunch or dinner, rice and beans are an integral part of a *casado* (which translates as "married" and is the name for the local version of a blue-plate special). A *casado* usually consists of cabbage-and-tomato salad, fried plantains (a starchy, banana-like fruit), and a chicken, fish, or meat dish of some sort.

Dining hours in Costa Rica are flexible but generally follow North American customs. Some downtown restaurants in San José are open 24 hours; however, expensive restaurants tend to be open for lunch between 11am and 3pm and for dinner between 6 and 11pm.

APPETIZERS Known as *bocas* in Costa Rica, appetizers are served with drinks in most bars. Often the *bocas* are free, but even if they aren't, they're very inexpensive. Popular *bocas* include *gallos* (tortillas piled with meat, chicken, cheese, or beans), ceviche (a marinated seafood salad), tamales (stuffed cornmeal patties wrapped and steamed inside banana leaves), *patacones* (fried green plantain chips), and fried yuca.

SANDWICHES & SNACKS Ticos love to snack, and there's a large variety of tasty little sandwiches and snacks available on the street, at snack bars, and in sodas. *Arreglados* are little meat-filled sandwiches, as are *tortas,* which are served on little rolls with a bit of salad tucked into them. Tacos, tamales, and *empanadas* (turnovers) also are quite common. *Gallos* (see above) are popular snacks as well.

MEAT Costa Rica is beef country, having converted much of its rainforest land to pastures for raising beef cattle. Consequently, beef is cheap and plentiful, although it might be a bit tougher—and cut and served thinner—than it is back home. One typical local dish is called *olla de carne,* a bowl of beef broth with large chunks of meat, local tubers, and corn. Spit-roasted chicken is also very popular here and is surprisingly tender.

SEAFOOD Costa Rica has two coasts, and, as you'd expect, plenty of seafood is available everywhere in the country. Corvina (sea bass) is the most commonly served

fish and is prepared innumerable ways, including as ceviche. (*Be careful:* In many cheaper restaurants, particularly in San José, shark meat is often sold as corvina.) You should also come across *pargo* (red snapper), dorado (mahimahi), and tuna on some menus, especially along the coasts. Although Costa Rica is a major exporter of shrimp and lobster, both are relatively expensive and in short supply here.

VEGETABLES On the whole, you'll find vegetables surprisingly lacking in the meals you're served in Costa Rica—usually nothing more than a little pile of shredded cabbage topped with a slice or two of tomato. For a much more satisfying and filling salad, order *palmito* (hearts of palm salad). The heart (actually the stalk or trunk of these small palms) is first boiled and then chopped into circular pieces and served with other fresh vegetables, with a salad dressing on top. If you want something more than this, you'll have to order a side dish such as *picadillo,* a stew or purée of vegetables with a bit of meat in it. Though they are giant relatives of bananas and are technically considered a fruit, *plátanos* (plantains) are really more like vegetables and require cooking before they can be eaten. Green plantains have a very starchy flavor and consistency, but they become as sweet as candy as they ripen. Fried *plátanos* are one of my favorite dishes. Yuca (manioc root or cassava in English) is another starchy staple root vegetable in Costa Rica.

One more vegetable worth mentioning is the *pejibaye,* a form of palm fruit that looks like a miniature orange coconut. Boiled *pejibayes* are frequently sold from carts on the streets of San José. When cut in half, a *pejibaye* reveals a large seed surrounded by soft, fibrous flesh. You can eat it plain, but it's usually topped with a dollop of mayonnaise.

FRUITS Costa Rica has a wealth of delicious tropical fruits. The most common are mangoes (the season begins in May), papayas, pineapples, melons, and bananas. Other fruits include *marañón*, which is the fruit of the cashew tree and has orange or yellow glossy skin; *granadilla* or *maracuyá* (passion fruit); *mamón chino*, which Asian travelers will immediately recognize as rambutan; and carambola (star fruit).

DESSERTS   *Queque seco*, literally "dry cake," is the same as pound cake. *Tres leches* cake, on the other hand, is so moist that you almost need to eat it with a spoon. Flan is a typical custard dessert. It often comes as either *flan de caramelo* (caramel) or *flan de coco* (coconut). Numerous other sweets are available, many of which are made with condensed milk and raw sugar. *Cajetas* are popular handmade candies, made from sugar and various mixes of evaporated, condensed, and powdered milk. They are sold in differing-size bits and chunks at most *pulperías* (general stores) and street-side food stands.

BEVERAGES

Frescos, refrescos, and *jugos naturales* are my favorite drinks in Costa Rica. They are usually made with fresh fruit and milk or water. Among the more common fruits used are mangoes, papayas, blackberries *(mora),* and pineapples *(piña).* You'll also come across passion fruit *(maracuyá)* and carambola. Some of the more unusual frescos are *horchata* (made with rice flour and a lot of cinnamon) and *chan* (made with the seed of a plant found mostly in Guanacaste—definitely an acquired taste). The former is wonderful; the latter requires an open mind (it's reputed to be good for the digestive system). Order *un fresco con leche sin hielo* (a *fresco* with milk but without ice) if you're avoiding untreated water.

If you're a coffee drinker, you might be disappointed here. Most of the best coffee has traditionally been targeted for export, and Ticos tend to prefer theirs weak and sugary. Better hotels and restaurants are

starting to cater to gringo and European tastes and are serving up better blends. If you want black coffee, ask for *café negro;* if you want it with milk, order *café con leche.*

If you want to try something different for your morning beverage, ask for *agua dulce,* a warm drink made from melted sugar cane and served either with milk or lemon, or straight.

WATER   Although water in most of Costa Rica is safe to drink, bottled water is readily available and is a good option if you're worried about an upset stomach. *Agua mineral,* or simply soda, is sparkling water in Costa Rica. If you like your water without bubbles, request *aqua mineral sin gas,* or *agua en botella.*

BEER, WINE & LIQUOR   The German presence in Costa Rica over the years has produced several fine beers, which are fairly inexpensive. Most Costa Rican beers are light pilsners. The most popular brands are Bavaria, Imperial, and Pilsen. I personally can't tell much of a difference between any of them. Licensed local versions of Heineken and Rock Ice are also available.

You can find imported wines at reasonable prices in the better restaurants throughout the country. You can usually save money by ordering a Chilean wine over a Californian or European one.

Costa Rica distills a wide variety of liquors, and you'll save money by ordering these over imported brands. The national liquor is *guaro,* a crude cane liquor that's often combined with a soft drink or tonic or mineral water. If you want to try *guaro,* stick to the Cacique brand. The Café Britt and Salicsa brands produce a couple of types of coffee-based liqueurs. Café Rica is similar to Kahlúa and quite good. You can also find delicious cream-style coffee liqueurs.

Appendix B:
Glossary of Spanish
Terms & Phrases

Costa Rican Spanish is neither the easiest nor the most difficult dialect to understand. Ticos speak at a relatively relaxed speed and enunciate clearly, without dropping too many final consonants. The *y* and *ll* sounds are subtly, almost inaudibly, pronounced. Perhaps the most defining idiosyncrasy of Costa Rican Spanish is the way Ticos overemphasize, and almost chew, their *r*'s.

1 Basic Words & Phrases

English	Spanish	Pronunciation
Hello	**Buenos días**	*bweh*-nohss *dee*-ahss
How are you?	**¿Cómo está usted?**	*koh*-moh ehss-*tah* oo-*stehd*
Very well	**Muy bien**	mwee byehn
Thank you	**Gracias**	*grah*-syahss
Good-bye	**Adiós**	ad-*dyohss*
Please	**Por favor**	pohr fah-*vohr*
Yes	**Sí**	see
No	**No**	noh
Excuse me (to get by someone)	**Perdóneme**	pehr-*doh*-neh-meh
Excuse me (to begin a question)	**Disculpe**	dees-*kool*-peh
Give me	**Deme**	*deh*-meh
Where is . . . ?	**¿Dónde está . . . ?**	*dohn*-deh ehss-*tah*
the station	**la estación**	la ehss-*tah*-syohn
the bus stop	**la parada**	la pah-*rah*-dah
a hotel	**un hotel**	oon oh-*tehl*
a restaurant	**un restaurante**	oon res-tow-*rahn*-teh
the toilet	**el servicio**	el ser-*vee*-syoh
To the right	**A la derecha**	ah lah deh-*reh*-chah
To the left	**A la izquierda**	ah lah ees-*kyehr*-dah
Straight ahead	**Adelante**	ah-deh-*lahn*-teh
I would like . . .	**Quiero . . .**	*kyeh*-roh
to eat	**comer**	ko-*mehr*
a room	**una habitación**	oo-nah ah-bee-tah-*syohn*

English	Spanish	Pronunciation
How much is it?	¿Cuánto?	*kwahn*-toh
The check	La cuenta	la *kwen*-tah
When?	¿Cuándo?	*kwan*-doh
What?	¿Qué?	keh
Yesterday	Ayer	ah-*yehr*
Today	Hoy	oy
Tomorrow	Mañana	mah-*nyah*-nah
Breakfast	Desayuno	deh-sah-*yoo*-noh
Lunch	Almuerzo	ahl-*mwehr*-soh
Dinner	Cena	*seh*-nah
Do you speak English?	¿Habla usted inglés?	*ah*-blah oo-*stehd* een-*glehss*
I don't understand Spanish very well.	No (lo) entiendo muy bien el español.	noh (loh) ehn-*tyehn*-do mwee byehn el ehss-pah-*nyohl*

NUMBERS

1 uno (*ooh*-noh)
2 dos (dohs)
3 tres (trayss)
4 cuatro (*kwah*-troh)
5 cinco (*seen*-koh)
6 seis (sayss)
7 siete (*syeh*-tay)
8 ocho (*oh*-choh)
9 nueve (*nway*-bay)
10 diez (dee-ess)
11 once (*ohn*-say)
12 doce (*doh*-say)
13 trece (*tray*-say)
14 catorce (kah-*tor*-say)
15 quince (*keen*-say)
16 dieciseis (de-*ess*-ee-sayss)

17 diecisiete (de-*ess*-ee-*syeh*-tay)
18 dieciocho (dee-*ess*-ee-*oh*-choh)
19 diecinueve (dee-*ess*-ee-*nway*-bay)
20 veinte (*bayn*-tay)
30 treinta (*trayn*-tah)
40 cuarenta (kwah-*ren*-tah)
50 cincuenta (seen-*kwen*-tah)
60 sesenta (say-*sen*-tah)
70 setenta (say-*ten*-tah)
80 ochenta (oh-*chen*-tah)
90 noventa (noh-*ben*-tah)
100 cien (see-*en*)
200 doscientos (*dos*-se-en-tos)
500 quinientos (keen-ee-*ehn*-tos)
1,000 mil (meal)

DAYS OF THE WEEK

English	Spanish	Pronunciation
Monday	lunes	(*loo*-nehss)
Tuesday	martes	(*mahr*-tehss)
Wednesday	miércoles	(*myehr*-koh-lehs)
Thursday	jueves	(*wheh*-behss)
Friday	viernes	(*byehr*-nehss)
Saturday	sábado	(*sah*-bah-doh)
Sunday	domingo	(doh-*meen*-goh)

2 Some Typical Tico Words & Phrases

Birra Slang for beer.

Boca Literally means "mouth," but also a term to describe a small appetizer served alongside a drink at many bars.

Bomba Translates literally as "pump" but is used in Costa Rica for "gas station."

Brete Work, or job.

Casado Literally means "married," but is the local term for a popular restaurant offering that features a main dish and various side dishes.

Chapa Derogatory way to call someone stupid or clumsy.

Chepe Slang term for the capital city, San José.

Choza Slang for house or home.

Chunche Knickknack; thing, as in "whatchamacallit."

Con mucho gusto With pleasure.

De hoy en ocho In 1 week's time.

Diay An untranslatable but common linguistic punctuation, often used to begin a sentence.

Goma Hangover.

La sele Short for *la selección,* the Costa Rican national soccer team.

Macha or **machita** A blond woman.

Mae Translates like "man"; used by many Costa Ricans, particularly teenagers, as frequent verbal punctuation.

Maje A lot like *mae,* above, but with a slightly derogatory connotation.

Mala pata Bad luck.

Mejenga An informal, or pickup, soccer game.

Pachanga or **pelón** Both terms are used to signify a big party or gathering.

Ponga la maría, por favor This is how you ask taxi drivers to turn on the meter.

Pulpería The Costa Rican version of the "corner store" or small market.

Pura vida Literally, "pure life"; translates as "everything's great."

Qué torta What a mess; what a screw-up.

Si Dios quiere God willing; you'll hear Ticos say this all the time.

Soda A casual diner-style restaurant serving cheap Tico meals.

Tico Costa Rican.

Tiquicia Costa Rica.

Tuanis Means the same as *pura vida,* above, but is used by a younger crowd.

Una teja 100 colones.

Un rojo 1,000 colones.

Un tucán 5,000 colones.

Upe! Common shout to find out if anyone is home; used frequently since doorbells are so scarce.

Zarpe Last drink of the night, or "one more for the road."

3 Menu Terms

FISH

Almejas Clams
Atún Tuna
Bacalao Cod
Calamares Squid
Camarones Shrimp
Cangrejo Crab
Ceviche Marinated seafood salad
Dorado Dolphin or mahimahi

Langosta Lobster
Lenguado Sole
Mejillones Mussels
Ostras Oysters
Pargo Snapper
Pulpo Octopus
Trucha Trout

MEATS

Albóndigas Meatballs
Bistec Beefsteak
Cerdo Pork
Chicharrones Fried pork rinds
Cordero Lamb
Costillas Ribs

Jamón Ham
Lengua Tongue
Pato Duck
Pavo Turkey
Pollo Chicken
Salchichas Sausages

VEGETABLES

Aceitunas Olives
Alcachofa Artichoke
Berenjena Eggplant
Cebolla Onion
Elote Corn on the cob
Ensalada Salad
Espinacas Spinach
Frijoles Beans

Lechuga Lettuce
Maíz Corn
Palmito Heart of palm
Papa Potato
Pepino Cucumber
Tomate Tomato
Yuca Yucca, cassava, or manioc
Zanahoria Carrot

FRUITS

Aguacate Avocado
Banano Banana
Carambola Star fruit
Cereza Cherry
Ciruela Plum
Durazno Peach
Frambuesa Raspberry
Fresa Strawberry
Granadilla Sweet passion fruit
Limón Lemon or lime
Manzana Apple

Mango Mango
Maracuya Tart passion fruit
Melón Melon
Mora Blackberry
Naranja Orange
Papaya Papaya
Piña Pineapple
Plátano Plantain
Sandía Watermelon
Toronja Grapefruit

BASICS

Aceite Oil
Ajo Garlic
Arreglado Small meat sandwich
Azúcar Sugar
Casado Plate of the day
Frito Fried
Gallo Corn tortilla topped with meat or chicken
Gallo pinto Rice and beans
Hielo Ice
Mantequilla Butter
Miel Honey

Mostaza Mustard
Natilla Sour cream
Olla de carne Meat and vegetable soup
Pan Bread
Patacones Fried plantain chips
Picadillo Chopped vegetable side dish
Pimienta Pepper
Queso Cheese
Sal Salt
Tamal Filled cornmeal pastry
Tortilla Flat corn pancake

DRINKS

Agua purificada Purified water
Agua con gas Sparkling water
Agua sin gas Plain water
Bebida Drink
Café Coffee
Café con leche Coffee with milk
Cerveza Beer
Chocolate caliente Hot chocolate

Jugo Juice
Leche Milk
Natural Fruit juice
Natural con leche Milkshake
Refresco Soft drink
Ron Rum
Té Tea
Trago Alcoholic drink

OTHER RESTAURANT TERMS

Al grill Grilled
Al horno Oven-baked
Al vapor Steamed
Asado Roasted
Caliente Hot
Cambio Change
Cocido Boiled
Comida Food
Congelado Frozen
El baño Toilet

Frío Cold
Frito Fried
Grande Big
La cuenta The check
Medio Medium
Muy cocido Well-done
Pequeño Small
Poco cocido Rare
Tres cuartos Medium-well-done

Appendix C:
Costa Rican Wildlife

with assistance from E. Z. Weaver

For such a small country, Costa Rica is incredibly rich in biodiversity. With just .01% of the earth's landmass, Costa Rica is home to some 5% of its biodiversity. Whether you come to Costa Rica to check 100 or so species off your lifetime list, or just to check out of the rat race for a week or so, you'll be surrounded by a rich and varied collection of flora and fauna. The information below is meant to be a selective introduction to some of what you might see.

In many instances, the prime viewing recommendations should be taken with a firm dose of reality. Most casual visitors and even many dedicated naturalists will never see a wildcat or kinkajou. However, anyone working with a good guide should be able to see a broad selection of Costa Rica's impressive flora and fauna.

See "The Natural Environment" in appendix A for more information, as well as "Tips on Health, Safety & Etiquette in the Wilderness" in chapter 4.

1 Fauna

MAMMALS

Costa Rica has more than 225 species of mammals. Roughly half of these are bats. While it is very unlikely that you will spot a wildcat, you have good odds of catching a glimpse of a monkey, coatimundi, peccary, or sloth, or more likely any number of bats.

SCIENTIFIC NAME *Panthera onca*

WORTH NOTING This cat measures from 1 to 1.8m (3½–6 ft.) plus tail and is distinguished by its tan/yellowish fur with black spots. Often called simply *tigre* (tiger) in Costa Rica.

PRIME VIEWING Jaguars exist in all major tracts of primary and secondary forest in Costa Rica, as well as some open savannahs. However, jaguars are endangered and extremely hard to see in the wild. The largest concentrations of jaguars can be found in Corcovado National Park on the Osa Peninsula.

Jaguar

Ocelot

SCIENTIFIC NAME *Leopardus pardalis*

WORTH NOTING Known as *manigordo*, or "fat paws," in Costa Rica, the tail of this small cat is longer than its rear leg, which makes for easy identification. **Ocelots** are mostly nocturnal, and they sleep in trees.

PRIME VIEWING   Forests in all regions of Costa Rica, with the greatest concentration found on the Osa Peninsula.

SCIENTIFIC NAME   *Agouti paca*

WORTH NOTING   The **paca,** a nocturnal rodent, inhabits the forest floor, feeding on fallen fruit, leaves, and some tubers dug from the ground.

PRIME VIEWING   Known as *tepezquintle* in Costa Rica, these are most often found near water throughout many habitats of Costa Rica, from river valleys to swamps to dense tropical forest. However, since they're nocturnal, you're much more likely to see their smaller cousin, the diurnal agouti or *guatusa.*

Paca

Baird's Tapir

SCIENTIFIC NAME   *Tapirus bairdii*

WORTH NOTING   Known as the *danta* or *macho de monte,* **Baird's tapir** is the largest land mammal in Costa Rica. Tapirs are active both day and night, foraging along riverbanks, streams, and forest clearings.

PRIME VIEWING   An endangered species, tapirs can be found in wet forested areas, particularly on the Caribbean and south Pacific slopes.

SCIENTIFIC NAME   *Nasua narica*

WORTH NOTING   Known as *pizote* in Costa Rica, the raccoonlike **coatimundi** can adapt to habitat disturbances and is often spotted near hotels and nature lodges. Active both day and night, it is equally comfortable on the ground and in trees.

PRIME VIEWING   Found in a variety of habitats across Costa Rica, from dry scrub to dense forests, on the mainland as well as the coastal islands. Social animals, they are often found in groups of 10 to 20.

Coatimundi

Collared Peccary

SCIENTIFIC NAME   *Tayassu tajacu*

WORTH NOTING   Called *saino* or *chancho de monte* in Costa Rica, the **collared peccary** is a black or brown piglike animal that travels in small groups (larger where populations are still numerous) and has a strong musk odor.

PRIME VIEWING   Low- and middle-elevation forests in most of Costa Rica.

SCIENTIFIC NAME   *Tamandua mexicana*

WORTH NOTING   Also known as the collared anteater (*oso hormiguero* in Spanish), the **northern Tamandua** grows up to 77 centimeters (30 in.) long, not counting its thick tail, which can be as long its body. It is active diurnally and nocturnally.

PRIME VIEWING   Low- and middle-elevation forests in most of Costa Rica.

*Northern
Tamandua*

Three-Toed Sloth

SCIENTIFIC NAME   *Bradypus variegatus*

WORTH NOTING   The larger and more commonly sighted of Costa Rica's two sloth species, the **three-toed sloth** has long, coarse brown-to-gray fur and a distinctive eye band. They have three long and sharp claws on each foreleg. Except for brief periods used for defecation, these slow-moving creatures are entirely arboreal.

PRIME VIEWING   Low- and middle-elevation forests in most of Costa Rica. While sloths can be found in a wide variety of trees, they are most commonly spotted in the relatively sparsely leaved Cecropia (see later in this appendix).

SCIENTIFIC NAME   *Alouatta palliata*

WORTH NOTING   Known locally as *mono congo,* the highly social **mantled howler monkey** grows to 56 centimeters (22 in.) in size and often travels in groups of 10 to 30. The loud roar of the male can be heard as far as 1.6km (1 mile) away.

PRIME VIEWING   Wet and dry forests across Costa Rica. Almost entirely arboreal, they tend to favor the higher reaches of the canopy.

Mantled
Howler Monkey

Red-Backed
Squirrel
Monkey

SCIENTIFIC NAME   *Saimiri oerstedii*

WORTH NOTING   The smallest and friskiest of Costa Rica's monkeys, the **red-backed squirrel monkey,** or *mono titi,* is also its most endangered. Active in the daytime, these monkeys travel in small to midsize groups. Squirrel monkeys do not have a prehensile tail.

PRIME VIEWING   Manuel Antonio National Park and Corcovado National Park.

BIRDS

Costa Rica has more than 850 identified species of resident and migrant birds. The variety of habitats and compact nature of the country make it a major bird-watching destination.

SCIENTIFIC NAME   *Jabiru mycteria*

WORTH NOTING   One of the largest birds in the world, the **jabiru stork** stands 1.5m (5 ft.) tall, with a wingspan of 2.4m (8 ft.) and a .3m (1 ft.) bill. An endangered species, the jabiru is very rare, with only a dozen or so nesting pairs in Costa Rica.

PRIME VIEWING   The wetlands of Palo Verde National Park and Caño Negro Wildlife Reserve are the best places to try to spot the jabiru stork. The birds arrive in Costa Rica from Mexico in November and fly north with the rains in May or June.

Jabiru Stork

Keel-Billed Toucan

SCIENTIFIC NAME   *Ramphastos sulfuratus*

WORTH NOTING   The rainbow-colored canoe-shape bill and brightly colored feathers make the **keel-billed toucan** a favorite of bird-watching tours. The toucan can grow to about 51 centimeters (20 in.) in length. It's similar in size and shape to the chestnut mandibled toucan. Costa Rica also is home to several smaller toucanet and aracari species.

PRIME VIEWING   Lowland forests on the Caribbean and north Pacific slopes.

SCIENTIFIC NAME   *Ara macao*

WORTH NOTING   Known as *guacamaya* or *lapa* in Costa Rica, the **scarlet macaw** is a long-tailed member of the parrot family. It can reach 89 centimeters (35 in.) in length. The bird is endangered over most of its range, particularly because it is so coveted as a pet. Its loud squawk and rainbow-colored feathers are quite distinctive.

PRIME VIEWING   Carara National Park, Corcovado National Park, and Piedras Blancas National Park.

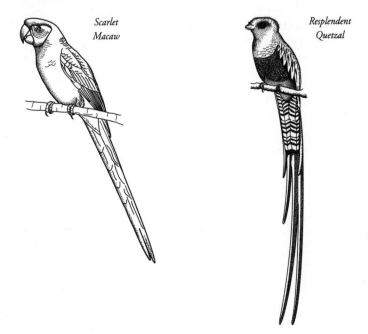

Scarlet
Macaw

Resplendent
Quetzal

SCIENTIFIC NAME   *Pharomchrus mocinno*

WORTH NOTING   Perhaps the most distinctive and spectacular bird in Central America, the **resplendent quetzal,** of the trogon family, can grow to 37 centimeters (14½ in.). The males are distinctive, with bright red chests, iridescent blue-green coats, yellow bill, and tail feathers that can reach another 76 centimeters (30 in.) in length. The females lack the long tail feathers and have a duller beak and less pronounced red chest.

PRIME VIEWING   High-elevation wet and cloud forests, particularly in the Monteverde Cloud Forest Preserve and along the Cerro de la Muerte.

SCIENTIFIC NAME   *Fregata magnificens*

WORTH NOTING   The **magnificent frigate bird** is a naturally agile flier and it swoops (unlike other sea birds, it doesn't dive or swim) to pluck food from the water's surface—or more commonly, it steals catch from the mouths of other birds.

PRIME VIEWING   Along the shores and coastal islands of both coasts. Often seen soaring high overhead.

Magnificent
Frigate Bird

Montezuma's
Oropendola

SCIENTIFIC NAME   *Psarocolius montezuma*

WORTH NOTING   **Montezuma's oropendola** has a black head, brown body, a yellow-edged tail, a large black bill with an orange tip, and a blue patch under the eye. These birds build long, teardrop-shape hanging nests, often found in large groups. They have several distinct loud calls, including one that they make while briefly hanging upside down.

PRIME VIEWING   Low and middle elevations along the Caribbean slope, and some sections of eastern Guanacaste.

SCIENTIFIC NAME   *Ajaia ajaja*

WORTH NOTING   The **roseate spoonbill** is a large water bird, pink or light red in color and with a large spoon-shape bill. Also known as *garza rosada* (pink heron). They were almost made extinct in the United States because their pink wings were sought for feather fans.

PRIME VIEWING   Low-lying wetlands, both fresh and salt water, along both coasts.

Roseate
Spoonbill

Cattle
Egret

SCIENTIFIC NAME   *Bubulcus ibis*

WORTH NOTING   The **cattle egret** changes color during breeding: A yellowish buff color appears on the head, chest, and back, and a reddish hue emerges on the bill and legs. They are usually seen anywhere there are cattle, hence the name, but can also often be found following behind tractors.

PRIME VIEWING   Throughout the country.

SCIENTIFIC NAME   *Cochlearius cochlearius*

WORTH NOTING   The midsize **boat-billed heron** (about 51cm/20 in.) has a large black head, a large broad bill, and a rusty brown color.

PRIME VIEWING   Throughout the country, near marshes, swamps, rivers, and mangroves.

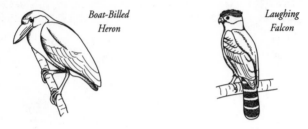

Boat-Billed
Heron

Laughing
Falcon

SCIENTIFIC NAME   *Herpetotheres cachinnans*

WORTH NOTING   The **laughing falcon** is also known as the *guaco* in Costa Rica. It gets its name from its loud, piercing call. This largish (56cm/22 in.) bird of prey's wingspan reaches an impressive 94 centimeters (37 in.). It specializes in eating both venomous and nonvenomous snakes but will also hunt lizards and small rodents.

PRIME VIEWING   Throughout the country, most commonly in lowland areas, near forest edges, grasslands, and farmlands.

AMPHIBIANS

Frogs, toads, and salamanders are actually some of the most beguiling, beautiful, and easy-to-spot residents of tropical forests.

SCIENTIFIC NAME   *Bufo marinus*

WORTH NOTING   The largest toad in the Americas, the 20-centimeter (8-in.) wart-covered **marine toad** is also known as *sapo grande* (giant toad). The females are mottled in color, while the males are uniformly brown. These voracious toads have been known to eat small mammals, along with other toads, lizards, and just about any insect within range. They also have a very strong toxic chemical defense mechanism.

PRIME VIEWING   In forests and open areas throughout Costa Rica.

Marine
Toad

Mexican
Burrowing
Toad

SCIENTIFIC NAME   *Rhinophrynus dorsalis*

WORTH NOTING   The bloblike, 7.6-centimeter (3-in.) Mexican **burrowing toad** will inflate like a blowfish when frightened. It often has a single red, orange, or yellow line down the center of its brown or black back.

PRIME VIEWING   Pacific lower-elevation forests and moist grasslands and farmlands.

SCIENTIFIC NAME *Agalychnis callidryas*

WORTH NOTING The colorful 7.6-centimeter (3-in.) **red-eyed tree frog** usually has a pale or dark green back, sometimes with white or yellow spots, with blue-purple patches and vertical bars on the body, orange hands and feet, and deep red eyes. This nocturnal amphibian is also known as the gaudy leaf frog or red-eyed tree frog.

PRIME VIEWING Low- and middle-elevation wet forests throughout Costa Rica. This is a very beautiful and distinctive-looking frog that you will certainly see on T-shirts and postcards if not in the wild.

Red-Eyed Tree Frog

Green and Black Poison Arrow Frog

SCIENTIFIC NAME *Dendrobates auratus*

WORTH NOTING Also called the harlequin poison-arrow frog, the small **green and black poison arrow frog** ranges between 2.5 and 4 centimeters (1–1½ in.) in length. It has distinctive markings of iridescent green mixed with deep black.

PRIME VIEWING On the ground, around tree roots, and under fallen logs, in low- and middle-elevation wet forests on the Caribbean and southern Pacific slopes.

REPTILES

Costa Rica's reptile species range from the frightening and justly feared fer-de-lance pit viper and massive American crocodile to a wide variety of turtles and lizards. ***Note:*** Sea turtles are included in the "Sea Life" section below.

SCIENTIFIC NAME *Boa constrictor*

WORTH NOTING Adult **boa constrictors** (*bécquer* in Costa Rica) average about 1.8 to 3m (6–10 ft.) in length and weigh over 27 kilograms (60 lb.). Their coloration camouflages them, but look for patterns of cream, brown, gray, and black ovals and diamonds.

PRIME VIEWING Low- and middle-elevation wet and dry forests, countrywide. They often live in rafters and eaves of homes in rural areas.

Boa Constrictor

Fer-de-Lance

SCIENTIFIC NAME   *Bothrops atrox*

WORTH NOTING   Known as *terciopelo* in Costa Rica, the aggressive **fer-de-lance** can grow to 2.4m (8 ft.) in length. Beige, brown, or black triangles flank either side of the head, while the area under the head is a vivid yellow. These snakes begin life as arboreal but become increasingly terrestrial as they grow older and larger.

PRIME VIEWING   All regions.

SCIENTIFIC NAME   *Phyllodactylus xanti*

WORTH NOTING   Spotting the 6.8-centimeter (2½-in.) **leaf-toed gecko** is easy—it loves to be around buildings and other areas of human activity.

PRIME VIEWING   Common on the ground and in the leaf litter of low- and middle-elevation forests throughout the country.

Smooth Gecko

Leaf-Toed Gecko

SCIENTIFIC NAME   *Thecadactylus rapicauda*

WORTH NOTING   The **smooth gecko**'s autonomous tail detaches from its body and acts as a diversion to a potential predator; it grows back later in a lighter shade.

PRIME VIEWING   Low-elevation wet forests on the Caribbean and southern Pacific slopes, as well as in urban and rural residential environments.

SCIENTIFIC NAME   *Iguana iguana*

WORTH NOTING   **Green iguanas** can vary in shades ranging from bright green to a dull grayish-green, with quite a bit of orange mixed in. The iguana will often perch on a branch overhanging a river and plunge into the water when threatened.

PRIME VIEWING   All lowland regions of the country, living near rivers and streams, along both coasts.

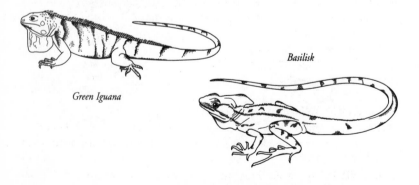

Basilisk

Green Iguana

SCIENTIFIC NAME   *Basiliscus vittatus*

WORTH NOTING   The **basilisk** can run across the surface of water for short distances by using its hind legs and holding its body almost upright; thus, the reptile is also known as "the Jesus Christ lizard."

PRIME VIEWING   In trees and on rocks located near water in wet forests throughout the country.

SCIENTIFIC NAME   *Crocodylus acutus*

WORTH NOTING   Although an endangered species, environmental awareness and protection policies have allowed the massive **American crocodile** to mount an impressive comeback in recent years. While these reptiles can reach lengths of 6.4m (21 ft.), most are much smaller, usually less than 4m (13 ft.).

PRIME VIEWING   Near swamps, mangrove swamps, estuaries, large rivers, and coastal lowlands, countrywide. Guaranteed viewing from the bridge over the Tarcoles River, on the coastal highway to Jacó and Manuel Antonio.

American Crocodile

SEA LIFE

Boasting over 1,290km (780 miles) of shoreline on both the Pacific and Caribbean coasts, Costa Rica has a rich diversity of underwater flora and fauna.

SCIENTIFIC NAME   *Rhincodon typus*

WORTH NOTING   Although the **whale shark** grows to lengths of 14m (45 ft.) or more, its gentle nature makes swimming with them a special treat for divers and snorkelers.

PRIME VIEWING   Can occasionally be spotted off Isla del Caño, and more frequently off Isla del Coco.

Whale Shark

Leatherback Sea Turtle

SCIENTIFIC NAME   *Dermochelys coriacea*

WORTH NOTING   The world's largest sea turtle (reaching nearly 2.4m/8 ft. in length and weighing more than 544kg/1,200 lb.), the **leatherback sea turtle** is now an endangered species.

PRIME VIEWING   While these large reptiles do nest off Tortuguero, their prime nesting site in Costa Rica is Playa Grande, near Tamarindo.

SCIENTIFIC NAME   *Lepidochelys olivacea*

WORTH NOTING   Also known as *tortuga lora,* the **olive ridley sea turtle** is the most common and popular of Costa Rica's sea turtles, famous for its massive group nestings, or *arribadas.*

PRIME VIEWING   Large *arribadas* occur from July through December, and to a lesser extent from January through June. Playa Nancite in Santa Rosa National Park and Playa Ostional are the prime nesting sites.

*Olive Ridley
Sea Turtle*

Moray Eel

SCIENTIFIC NAME   *Gymnothorax mordax*

WORTH NOTING   Distinguished by a swaying serpent-head and teeth-filled jaw that continually opens and closes, the **moray eel** is most commonly seen with only its head appearing from behind rocks. At night, however, it leaves its home along the reef to hunt for small fish, crustaceans, shrimp, and octopus.

PRIME VIEWING   Rocky areas and reefs off both coasts.

SCIENTIFIC NAME   *Megaptera novaeangliae*

WORTH NOTING   The migratory **humpbacked whale** spends the winters in warm southern waters and has been increasingly spotted close to the shores of Costa Rica's southern Pacific coast. These mammals have black backs and whitish throat and chest areas. Females have been known to calve here.

PRIME VIEWING   Most common in the waters off of Drake Bay and Isla del Caño, from December through April.

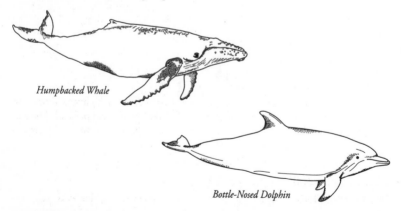

Humpbacked Whale

Bottle-Nosed Dolphin

SCIENTIFIC NAME   *Tursiops truncates*

WORTH NOTING   Their wide tail fin, dark gray back, and light gray sides identify **bottle-nosed dolphins.** Dolphins grow to lengths of 3.7m (12 ft.) and weigh up to 635 kilograms (1,400 lb.).

PRIME VIEWING   Along both coasts and inside the Golfo Dulce.

SCIENTIFIC NAME   *Diploria strigosa*

WORTH NOTING   The distinctive **brain coral** is named for its striking physical similarity to a human brain.

PRIME VIEWING   Reefs off both coasts.

Brain Coral

INVERTEBRATES

Creepy crawlies, biting bugs, spiders, and the like give most folks chills. But this group, which includes moths, butterflies, ants, beetles, and even crabs, includes some of the most fascinating and easily viewed fauna in Costa Rica.

SCIENTIFIC NAME   *Morpho peleides*

WORTH NOTING   The large **blue morpho** butterfly, with a wingspan of up to 15 centimeters (6 in.), has brilliantly iridescent blue wings when opened. Fast and erratic fliers, they are often glimpsed flitting across your peripheral vision in dense forest.

PRIME VIEWING   Countrywide, particularly in moist environments.

Blue Morpho   *Leafcutter Ants*

SCIENTIFIC NAME   *Atta cephalotes*

WORTH NOTING   You can't miss the miniature rainforest highways formed by these industrious little red **leafcutter ants** carrying their freshly cut payload. The ants do not actually eat the leaves, but instead feed off a fungus that grows on the decomposing leaves in their massive underground nests.

PRIME VIEWING   Can be found in most forests countrywide.

SCIENTIFIC NAME   *Nephila clavipes*

WORTH NOTING   The common Neotropical **golden silk spider** weaves meticulous webs that can be as much as .5m (2 ft.) across. The adult female of this species can reach 7.6 centimeters (3 in.) in length, including the legs, although the males are tiny. The silk of this spider is extremely strong and is being studied for industrial purposes.

PRIME VIEWING   Lowland forests on both coasts.

Golden Silk Spider

Mouthless Crab

SCIENTIFIC NAME   *Gecarcinus quadratus*

WORTH NOTING   The nocturnal **mouthless crab** is a distinctively colored land crab with bright orange legs, purple claws, and a deep black shell or carapace.

PRIME VIEWING   All along the Pacific coast.

2 Flora

TREES

Despite the cliché to the contrary, it's often a good thing to be able to identify specific trees within a forest. We've included illustrations of the leaves, flowers, seeds, and fruit to get you started.

SCIENTIFIC NAME   *Ceiba pentandra*

WORTH NOTING   Also known as the kapok tree, **ceiba** trees are typically emergent (their large umbrella-shape canopies emerge above the forest canopy), making the species among the tallest trees in the tropical forest. Reaching as high as 60m (197 ft.), their thick columnar trunks often have large buttresses. Ceiba trees may flower as little as once every 5 years, especially in wetter forests.

PRIME VIEWING   Countrywide.

Ceiba

SCIENTIFIC NAME   *Enterolobium cyclocarpum*

WORTH NOTING   The **guanacaste** tree is one of the largest trees found in Central America, and gives its name to Costa Rica's northwestern-most province. It can reach a total elevation of over 39m (130 ft.); its straight trunk composes 9 to 12m (30–40 ft.) of the height (the trunk's diameter measures more than 1.8m/6 ft.).

PRIME VIEWING   Countrywide.

Guanacaste

SCIENTIFIC NAME *Ficus aurea*

WORTH NOTING This parasitic tree gets its name from the fact that it envelops and eventually strangles its host tree. The *matapalo* or **strangler fig** begins as an epiphyte, whose seeds are deposited high in a tree's canopy by bats, birds, or monkeys. The young strangler then sends long roots down to the earth. The sap is used to relieve burns.

PRIME VIEWING Primary and secondary forests countrywide.

Strangler Fig

Cecropia

SCIENTIFIC NAME *Cecropia obtusifolia*

WORTH NOTING Several **Cecropia** (trumpet tree) species are found in Costa Rica. Most are characterized by large, handlike clusters of broad leaves, and a hollow, bamboolike trunk. They are "gap specialists," fast-growing opportunists that can fill in a gap caused by a tree fall or landslide. Their trunks are usually home to Aztec ants.

PRIME VIEWING Primary and secondary forests, rivers, and roadsides, countrywide.

SCIENTIFIC NAME *Bursera simaruba*

WORTH NOTING The bark of the **gumbo limbo** is its most distinguishing feature: A paper-thin red outer layer, when peeled off the tree, reveals a bright green bark. In Costa Rica the tree is called *indio desnudo* (naked Indian). In other countries it is the "tourist tree." Both names refer to reddish skin. The bark is used as a remedy for gum disease; gumbo limbo–bark tea allegedly alleviates hypertension. Another remarkable property is the tree's ability to root from its cut branches, which when planted right end up, develop roots and leaves, forming a new tree within a few years.

PRIME VIEWING   Primary and secondary forests, countrywide.

Gumbo Limbo

FLOWERS & OTHER PLANTS

Costa Rica has an amazing wealth of tropical flora, including some 1,200 orchid species.

SCIENTIFIC NAME   *Cattleya skinneri*

WORTH NOTING   The **guaria morada** orchid is the national flower of Costa Rica. Sporting a purple and white flower, this plant is also called the "Easter orchid" as it tends to flower between March and April each year.

PRIME VIEWING   Countrywide from sea level to 1,220m (4,000 ft.).

Guaria Morada

Heliconia

SCIENTIFIC NAME   *Heliconia collinsiana*

WORTH NOTING   There are more than 250 species of tropical heliconia, of which more than 40 are found in Costa Rica. The flowers of this species are darkish pink in color, and the underside of the plant's large leaves are coated in white wax.

PRIME VIEWING   Low to middle elevations countrywide, particularly in moist environments.

SCIENTIFIC NAME   *Psychotria poeppigiana*

WORTH NOTING   Related to coffee, **hotlips** is a forest flower that boasts thick red "lips" that resemble the Rolling Stones logo. The small white flowers (found inside the red "lips") attract a variety of butterflies and hummingbirds.

PRIME VIEWING   In the undergrowth of dense forests countrywide.

Hotlips

Red Torch
Ginger

SCIENTIFIC NAME   *Nicolaia elatior*

WORTH NOTING   Called *bastón del emperador* (the Emperor's cane) in Costa Rica, the tall **red torch ginger** plant has an impressive bulbous red bract, often mistaken for the flower. The numerous, small white flowers actually emerge out of this bract. Originally a native to Indonesia, it is now quite common in Costa Rica.

PRIME VIEWING   Countrywide, particularly in moist environments and gardens.

SCIENTIFIC NAME   *Gunnera insignis*

WORTH NOTING   The **poor man's umbrella,** a broad-leaved rainforest ground plant, is a member of the rhubarb family. The massive leaves are often used, as the colloquial name suggests, for protection during rainstorms.

PRIME VIEWING   Low- to middle-elevation moist forests countrywide. Commonly seen in Poás National Park and Braulio Carrillo National Park.

Poor Man's Umbrella

Index